Empathy, Intersubjectivity, and the Social World

New Studies in the History and Historiography of Philosophy

Edited by
Gerald Hartung and Sebastian Luft

Volume 9

Empathy, Intersubjectivity, and the Social World

The Continued Relevance of Phenomenology.
Essays in Honour of Dermot Moran

Edited by
Anna Bortolan and Elisa Magrì

DE GRUYTER

ISBN 978-3-11-135554-2
e-ISBN (PDF) 978-3-11-069878-7
e-ISBN (EPUB) 978-3-11-069888-6
ISSN 2364-3161

Library of Congress Control Number: 2021944015

Bibliographic information published by the Deutsche Nationalbibliothek
The Deutsche Nationalbibliothek lists this publication in the Deutsche Nationalbibliografie;
detailed bibliographic data are available in the Internet at http://dnb.dnb.de.

© 2023 Walter de Gruyter GmbH, Berlin/Boston
This volume is text- and page-identical with the hardback published in 2022.
Printing and binding: CPI books GmbH, Leck

www.degruyter.com

Table of Contents

List of Contributors —— 1

Editors' Introduction —— 3

Dermot Moran
From Empathy to Intersubjectivity: The Phenomenological Approach —— 23

Methodological and metaphysical issues

Thomas Nenon
Philosophy as a Fallible Science —— 47

Burt C. Hopkins
Back to Husserl. Reclaiming the Traditional Philosophical Context of the Phenomenological 'Problem' of the Other: Leibniz's "Monadology" —— 63

Sophie Loidolt
Plural Absolutes? Husserl and Merleau-Ponty on Being-In-a-Shared-World and its Metaphysical Implications —— 83

Nam-In Lee
Egological Reduction and Intersubjective Reduction —— 109

Kwok-ying LAU
Pathological Reduction and Hermeneutics of the Normal and the Pathological: the Convergence between Merleau-Ponty and Canguilhem —— 137

The experience of self and other

Niall Keane
Empathy, Intersubjectivity, and the World-Orienting Other —— 165

Sara Heinämaa
Self: Temporality, Finitude and Intersubjectivity —— 187

Liu Zhe
Towards Self-divided Subjectivity. Merleau-Ponty's Phenomenological-Ontological Theory of Intersubjectivity —— 201

Hernán G. Inverso
Phenomenology of the Inapparent and Michel Henry's Criticism of the Noematic Presentation of Alterity —— 225

Perception, emotion, and trust

Felix Ó Murchadha
Listening to Others: Music and the Phenomenology of Hearing —— 243

Elisa Magrì
(Un)learning to see others. Perception, Types, and Position-Taking in Husserl's Phenomenology —— 261

Íngrid Vendrell Ferran
Envy, Powerlessness, and the Feeling of Self-Worth —— 279

Anna Bortolan
Social Anxiety, Self-Consciousness, and Interpersonal Experience —— 303

Matthew Ratcliffe
Trauma, Language, and Trust —— 323

The social world: empathy, morality, and metapolitics

John J. Drummond
Empathy, Sympathetic Respect, and the Foundations of Morality —— 345

Andrea Staiti
Tolerance: A Phenomenological Approach —— 363

Alessandra Fussi
Anger, Hatred, Prejudice. An Aristotelian Perspective —— 389

Danielle Petherbridge
Habit, Attention and Affection: Husserlian Inflections —— 413

Nicolas de Warren
***Die äusserste Feindschaft:* Heidegger, Anti-Judaism, and the War to End All Wars —— 435**

Steven Crowell
Heidegger's Metapolitics: Phenomenology, Metaphysics, and the *Volk* —— 461

Index —— 485

Erratum —— 495

List of Contributors

Anna Bortolan. Lecturer in Philosophy, Swansea University.

Steven Crowell. Joseph and Joanna Nazro Mullen Professor of Humanities and Professor of Philosophy, Rice University.

Nicolas de Warren. Associate Professor of Philosophy and Jewish Studies, Penn State University.

John J. Drummond. Robert Southwell, S.J. Distinguished Professor of Philosophy and the Humanities, Fordham University.

Alessandra Fussi. Associate Professor of Moral Philosophy, University of Pisa.

Sara Heinämaa. Academy Professor (2017–2021 Academy of Finland) and Professor of Philosophy, University of Jyväskylä.

Burt C. Hopkins. Associate Member, Université de Lille/UMR-CNRS 8163 STL.

Hernán Inverso. Professor of Gnoseology, University of Buenos Aires (UBA); Researcher, National Scientific and Technological Research Council (CONICET).

Niall Keane. Visiting Researcher at the Department of Philosophy, Sociology, Education and Applied Psychology (FiSPPA), University of Padua.

Kwok-ying LAU. Professor in the Department of Philosophy and Director of the Edwin Cheng Foundation Asian Centre for Phenomenology, The Chinese University of Hong Kong (CUHK).

Nam-In Lee. Professor of Philosophy, Seoul National University.

Sophie Loidolt. Professor of Philosophy, Technical University of Darmstadt.

Elisa Magrì. Assistant Professor of Philosophy, Boston College.

Dermot Moran. Joseph Chair in Catholic Philosophy, Boston College.

Thomas Nenon. Professor of Philosophy and Provost, University of Memphis.

Felix Ó Murchadha. Professor of Philosophy, National University of Ireland, Galway.

Danielle Petherbridge. Assistant Professor in Philosophy and Director of the UCD Centre for Ethics in Public Life, University College Dublin.

Matthew Ratcliffe. Professor of Philosophy, University of York.

Andrea Staiti. Associate Professor of Moral Philosophy, University of Parma; Visiting Scholar, Boston College.

İngrid Vendrell Ferran. Heisenberg Fellow at the Institute of Philosophy, Goethe University Frankfurt.

Liu Zhe. Associate Professor at the Institute of Foreign Philosophy and the Department of Philosophy, Peking University.

Editors' Introduction

1 A *Festschrift* on the occasion of Dermot Moran's retirement from University College Dublin

In May 2017, a number of philosophers and scholars in phenomenology and phenomenological philosophy gathered in Dublin at the Royal Irish Academy (RIA) to celebrate Dermot Moran's retirement from the School of Philosophy at University College Dublin, where he taught for twenty-eight years (from 1989 to 2017), having also studied there from 1970 to 1973. The event was soon followed by a *Festschrift* in honour of Dermot Moran's sixty-fifth birthday (Burns et al., 2019). As Burns, Szanto, and Salice point out in their Introduction to the *Festschrift*, Dermot Moran's professional career is remarkable on many levels, including prestigious awards and distinctions of national and international significance (such as the RIA Golden Medal in Philosophy in 2012).

Of particular relevance is Moran's intellectual work and engagement with the phenomenological tradition, which have significantly shaped the way in which phenomenology is taught in Anglo-American contexts. This includes not only Moran's revision of the English translation of Husserl's *Logical Investigations* by J.N. Findlay, but also a number of thorough and accessible introductions to Husserl's phenomenology and the phenomenological tradition (Moran and Mooney 2002; Moran 2005; Moran 2012; Moran and Cohen 2012, among others). This volume honours Dermot Moran's retirement from University College Dublin as well as his contribution to the field by gathering papers presented at the 2017 conference *Phenomenology, Empathy, Intersubjectivity: New Approaches*[1], and other papers by experts in the field. In so doing, the volume seeks to also provide new insights on the nature of empathy, intersubjectivity and sociality within the phenomenological tradition.

The book spans discussions of methodological aspects concerning the emergence of empathy as a distinct experience in the realm of intersubjectivity, as well as new analyses of empathy in relation to morality, perception, lived experience, and the social world. The range of the contributions gathered in this volume, from scholars based in the USA, China, Korea, as well as across Europe, is a

---

[1] https://www.ucd.ie/philosophy/philosophy/phenomenology_newapproaches/aimoftheconference/, last accessed on 1 March 2021.

reflection of Moran's career and his efforts to connect Ireland to philosophy internationally.

Moran's interest in the topics of empathy and intersubjectivity has a longstanding history. Over the last two decades, Moran has consistently revisited and discussed the origins of empathy in the phenomenological tradition, focusing not only on Husserl's contribution but also on the role played by less well-known phenomenologists, such as Edith Stein, Max Scheler, and Alfred Schütz, and their relevance for contemporary debates on embodiment and social cognition. As his opening contribution *From Empathy to Intersubjectivity: The Phenomenological Approach* explains, empathy is often viewed as the basis for morality, and it lies at the core of various forms interpersonal experience. And yet it goes without saying that the vocabulary of empathy and the range of discussions in which empathy is currently employed is in constant expansion. Moran clarifies that the phenomenological roots of empathy help to shed light on the scope of empathy as a bedrock mental capacity that aims to apprehend the "*subjectivity* of the other". This means that, in empathy, one is primarily oriented to the first-personal egoity of another self. In empathy, we have a "non-originary" experience of others, namely an experience that is different from the one we have of our conscious states, but which still has an immediate or direct nature. This is an apprehension that has primarily a perceptual character, and it amounts to neither a form of imitation nor of inference.

Moran differentiates such a way of conceiving of empathy from contemporary approaches in analytic philosophy of mind and the cognitive sciences, where empathic understanding is often characterised as a form of "mindreading" dependent upon inferential or simulative processes. In contrast to the latter idea in particular, various phenomenological accounts – for example Scheler's and Stein's – emphasise the difference between *empathising* and *identifying* with someone, suggesting that empathy is a form of understanding of the other *qua other*, and not a fusion with the other or a projection on her of one's own experiences.

Drawing on Stein, Moran argues that, from a phenomenological point of view, the "primordial experience" of the other is given in empathy as an immediate, intuitive form of recognition, but it requires a gap between two subjects, for each experience is governed by one's own perspective (Stein 1989, p. 14; Stein 1917, p. 14). In his contribution, Moran also illustrates the claims that Husserl makes in works as different as the *Cartesian Meditations*, *Ideas II*, and the *Crisis* among others, showing to what extent empathy discloses both the meaning intention of another's bodily and affective state as well as the experience of a shared world. The latter is also emphasized by phenomenologists like Schütz and Heidegger, who—in different ways—bring to light the necessity of the world against which interpersonal experience takes shape.

The analysis carried out by Husserl in the *Cartesian Meditations* shows that alterity is already present within the sphere of ownness, in that the body of the other is given through a form of apperceptive transfer from one's own body. For Husserl, we encounter others as living subjects, and moreover, as illustrated in *Ideas II*, as persons, with distinct points of views on the things that are given as part of one and the same objective world. We share a world with others, but these are also apprehended "in the 'horizons' of their world", as having a perspective that overlaps, but does not coincide, with our own. Moran draws attention to the discussion of the structure of our "being-with-one-another" (*Miteinandersein*) in Husserl's late work, and concludes by illustrating how the Husserlian approach to empathy is overturned by Heidegger, for whom intersubjectivity grounds the capacity to empathise and not vice versa. Moran's analysis highlights how these two dimensions are "equiprimordial", while illustrating how for Husserl subjectivity remains in a key sense the foundation of intersubjectivity.

By and large, investigations of empathy in the phenomenological tradition tend to revolve around three main axes, namely intersubjectivity as the general experience of "being with others", empathy as a more direct form of interpersonal experience, that brings to the fore the affective salience of another's situated horizon, and the social world as the general background that informs both the metaphysics of being with others as well as the normativity of social encounters. The continued relevance of phenomenology lies in the ways such axes intersect with one another, generating questions and issues that are not exclusive to phenomenological research, but rather involve, among others, medical humanities, social sciences, and the arts.

In both classical and contemporary phenomenology, research on empathy, intersubjective experience, and the social world has indeed often been developed and nurtured through interdisciplinary dialogue, producing insights of theoretical, clinical, and practical relevance. For example, the investigation of the bases and modalities of interpersonal understanding has informed and has been informed by research in psychopathology (cf. Broome *et al.* 2012; Daly *et al.* 2020; Stanghellini *et al.* 2019), for instance concerning the disturbances characteristic of autism spectrum disorder, schizophrenia, and depression.

Phenomenological explorations of sociality also bear upon and have implications for the way in which the nature and behaviour of groups are accounted for (cf. Szanto and Moran 2016; Zahavi 2014, 2019), an area of interest for researchers working across disciplines such as psychology, sociology, and political science. In addition, a phenomenological investigation of empathy can contribute to debates concerning the way in which we relate to artefacts and works of art, as well as being increasingly relevant to the understanding of our interactions through the media that permeate life in the digital age (cf. Osler 2021).

2 The continued relevance of phenomenology: an overview of the volume

The first section of the volume is dedicated to methodological issues surrounding the phenomenological approach with a particular focus on Husserl's method, his use of the reduction and its appraisal by Merleau-Ponty, including an analysis of the metaphysical and ontological implications of Husserl's account of intersubjectivity. Related to such areas of investigation are also the essays of the second section, which is more specifically concerned with empathy as a form of self- and other relation rooted in finitude, ontological interdependency, and alterity.

The status of phenomenology as a philosophical and scientific discipline is at the core of **Thomas Nenon**'s chapter, *Philosophy as a Fallible Science*. Through a close examination of the critique of naturalism developed in *Philosophy as a Rigorous Science*, Nenon re-appraises Husserl's proposal and its relationship with his view of phenomenology expressed in later works.

Due to its inability to draw information from the immanent sphere, the investigation of consciousness propounded by empirical psychology is taken by Husserl to rely on an inadequate understanding of mental states or events, which are argued to be given directly to the subject and only indirectly to others. Phenomenology, as the investigation of pure consciousness, offers insights which are given "evidently and completely", but this, Nenon highlights, prompts a question concerning whether access to one's mental states, and the philosophical discipline that this grounds, are infallible.

Nenon rejects this interpretation by drawing attention to how in *Philosophy as a Rigorous Science* phenomenology is not conceived "in terms of a purported infallibility of access to one's mental states and the description of them as such". Rather, at the core of phenomenology as a scientific discipline is the development of "eidetic insights", which are not apodictic, but can be "confirmed or refuted" through "eidetic intuitions". Within this framework, Nenon highlights, phenomenology is required, if an adequate philosophical investigation of the objects of empirical psychology – and, in so far as they are intentional objects, of the objects of other sciences – is to be carried out, as well as being necessary to ground the normative criteria against which the sciences are assessed. The rigorous, scientific character of phenomenology, however, does not have to do with its being infallible, but rather depends on the fact that "phenomenology recognizes the appropriate method for adjudicating philosophical claims in a manner analogical to the methods for adjudicating claims in other areas of scientific inquiry".

On this basis, Nenon concludes that the emphasis, in Husserl's later writings, on the need for eidetic intuitions to be verified over time is not in tension with the idea that phenomenology can achieve the aims of philosophy 'as a rigorous science', but is rather a continuation of the phenomenological endeavour illustrated in this early essay.

Burt Hopkins, in *Back to Husserl. Reclaiming the Traditional Philosophical Context of the Phenomenological 'Problem' of the Other: Leibniz's "Monadology"*, focuses on Husserl's primordial reduction in the *Cartesian Meditations*. Hopkins proceeds by pointing out the difficulties that are intrinsic to the notion of the pure ego. Focusing in particular on the relation of immanence and transcendence between the ego and its stream of lived experiences, Hopkins argues that the constituting modality of the transcendental ego is distinct, but not separate, from the constituted modes of the mundane ego. However, such a distinction can only be made within the phenomenological attitude (not in the natural attitude), namely once the focus is on the ego as the generative source of meaning of the objects that belong to the world, of which the mundane ego is also a member. On this basis, Hopkins shows that the threat of solipsism is not consistent with Husserl's approach, which is further investigated in light of Husserl's Leibnizian background.

As Hopkins explains, the Leibnizian terminology employed by Husserl brings to light the fact that the objectivity and unity of the world are made manifest in the face of a plurality of points of view, and this is radically different from the Cartesian problem of establishing the existence of other minds. By illuminating the role of Leibnizian monadology in the *Cartesian Meditations*, Hopkins explains in what sense the relation between the field of ownness and that of the alien in Husserl is consistent with respect to three main objectives: the constitution of the other ego, as experienced in the sphere of immanence of the transcendental ego; the constitution of the objective transcendency of the world; and finally the monadic constitution of intersubjectivity, which is responsible for the meaning of the objective world.

The question of "transcendental subjectivity" plays a key role in **Sophie Loidolt**'s contribution, *Plural Absolutes? Husserl and Merleau-Ponty on Being-In-a-Shared-World and its Metaphysical Implications*, which pursues an interpretation of Husserl's monadology as compatible with the "outwardness of consciousness", and as not entailing more problematic ontological consequences than those engendered by Merleau-Ponty's phenomenological approach.

The chapter moves from a re-examination of Merleau-Ponty's criticism of the transcendental reduction, the *hyle*, the certainty of the *cogito*, and the immanence of consciousness. Loidolt argues that some of Merleau-Ponty's arguments are based on either a misconception of the Husserlian theses, or do not succeed in refuting their target. In doing so, she highlights how Merleau-Ponty's phenomenology leads to a blurring of the distinction between subjectivity and the world, promoting a conception of consciousness as "intentionality only", and conceiving of intersubjective life as emerging from a "collective anonymity". The singularity of subjectivity, on the other hand, is preserved in Husserl's account of the "monad", cardinal to which, Loidolt maintains, is also the co-existence with other subjectivities. Conceived as the "original unity of phenomenological experience" (HUA 14, p. 358) reached through the transcendental reduction, a monad is a unitary consciousness comprising all the experiences within it, or, in other terms, subjectivity *and* the world. Loidolt argues that alterity – the co-existence with other monads – is intrinsic to the monadic perspective, which is thus inherently "intermonadic"; monads, indeed, constitute the world and other monads.

Loidolt concurs with a reading of phenomenology as an exploration of experience with metaphysical implications and argue that the "Being-in-one-another" of the monads – the Husserlian 'metaphysical primal fact' – follows from the clarification of experience achieved through the transcendental, absolute attitude.

The nature and role of different forms of reduction in Husserl's phenomenology is the focus of **Nam-In Lee**'s chapter, *Egological Reduction and Intersubjective Reduction*. In particular, the contribution develops an original exploration of the egological reduction and the intersubjective reduction, and investigates how these concepts can illuminate our understanding of the phenomenological reduction. The egological reduction and the intersubjective reduction are characterised as the methods of the "two fundamental pillars" of Husserl's phenomenology: egology and the phenomenology of intersubjectivity. Lee identifies two kinds of egological and intersubjective reduction – one pertaining to phenomenological psychology and one to transcendental phenomenology – and it is with the latter that his analysis is concerned.

The transcendental egological reduction, or the primordial reduction, can take place after the shift from the natural to the transcendental attitude – the "universal transcendental reduction" – has been carried out, and its aim is the obtainment of the sphere of ownness or primordial sphere, which has both a noetic and a noematic side. The former can be given through "the act of reflection" and includes different temporal dimensions. Some of these can be given with apodictic evidence, while others require methods such as "interpretation". Lee illustrates how the transcendental intersubjective reduction, on the other hand, is carried out over the noema of the act of empathy performed in the natural attitude, and "it reveals the other subjectivity as another transcendental subjectivity". This reduction thus takes place through "transcendental empathy", of which there are three kinds and various sub-kinds. This reduction is carried out through the method of interpretation and other methods, but the experience it involves cannot have an apodictic character.

Lee argues that a "foundational relationship" exists between the egological and the intersubjective reduction, and shows how the two reductions can involve multiple lower levels, arguing that the universal transcendental reduction of which they are part is to be attributed a "stepwise character".

Lee then proceeds to show how such an account can contribute to solve some specific difficulties concerning Husserl's treatment of the phenomenological reduction, for example the ambiguity of the notion of primordial reduction, and the relation between the phenomenological, transcendental, epistemological, and apodictic reduction.

The nature of phenomenology as a philosophical method and discipline is central to **Kwok-ying LAU**'s contribution, *Pathological Reduction and Hermeneutics of the Normal and the Pathological: the Convergence between Merleau-Ponty and Canguilhem*. In particular, the chapter engages with Foucault's identification of two opposing strands in French philosophy: one the one hand, phenomenology as a philosophy of experience, and, on the other, a philosophy of the concept of living being propounded, among others, by Canguilhem. While the former is considered by Foucault to be still too positivistic, the latter is praised for having incorporated in the account of human subjectivity phenomena like error, illness, and disability.

Exploring the role played by investigations of pathological experience in the *Phenomenology of Perception*, the paper suggests that the phenomenological analysis of human capacity developed by Merleau-Ponty converges in various respects with Canguilhem's approach, suggesting, *contra Foucault*, that a dichotomy cannot be established between the philosophy of the subject and the philosophy of the concept they champion.

The relevance of the investigation of pathology in the *Phenomenology of Perception* is illustrated by Lau with regard to Merleau-Ponty's exploration of movement and language. More specifically, it is shown how the study of pathological behaviour caused by brain injuries grounds the distinction between "abstract" and "concrete movement". Similarly, the study of linguistic pathologies enables Merleau-Ponty to distinguish between the "concrete attitude" and the "categorial attitude", developing through the latter a conception of language as the accomplishment, and not mere expression, of thought. In so doing, and in contrast to the empiricist and intellectualist tradition, Merleau-Ponty treats pathological experience as containing meaning which needs to be interpreted, developing an "hermeneutics of the pathological". In his view, the phenomenological investigation of pathological behaviour involves a "pathological reduction", which "entails, at least in part, the function of an eidetic reduction" and allows for the identification of "structural invariants" of pathological behaviour, shedding light also on some of the experiential structures of transcendental subjectivity. Through a comparison with Canguilhem's understanding of the relation between normal and pathological, Lau highlights the existence of an affinity between Canguilhem's and Merleau-Ponty's approach, tracing this back to the work of Kurt Goldstein which exerted an influence on both.

The second section of the volume examines more closely the nature of selfhood and other-directed intentionality. Husserl's account of empathy and intersubjectivity is at the core of **Niall Keane**'s contribution, *Empathy, Intersubjectivity, and the World-Orienting Other*. Keane draws attention to the existence, in Husserl's account of "the self-other relation", of an "asymmetry", the exploration of which appears to have been comparatively marginal in the relevant literature. Encountered through the medium of perceptual experience as a subject of motivation and activity analogous to oneself, the other provides the perspective through which the objectivity and transcendence of the world can be constituted. At the same time, however, the other is central to the constitution of the self. It is indeed through the awareness of the other's perspective on the self that the latter can be fully constituted, in the first place as a material thing, but also, more importantly, as a "person".

Keane highlights how this process involves a transformation of the original "sphere of ownness", the first-personal conscious experience which is taken to be prior to the appearance of the other. Intrinsic to the encounter with the other within the Husserlian framework, Keane argues, is a frequently underplayed "self-differentiating experience", as the perspective of the other discloses new meanings of self and world which alter, expand, and enrich the original field of one's first-personal lived experience. Keane emphasises how the encounter with the other – by means of the "self-estrangement" and self-alienation it engenders and through which sociality and culture are grounded – is what enables the constitution of one's personality, and the transformation of what was originally, to a great extent, an anonymous "I".

Sara Heinämaa's contribution, *Self: Temporality, Finitude and Intersubjectivity*, focuses on Husserl's conception of selfhood, which is argued to exemplify a specific interpretation of the ambitions of Descartes, and one that is alternative to Kantianism. Heinämaa illustrates how, in the second volume of *Ideas* and in the fourth of the *Cartesian Meditations*, Husserl identifies two distinct, but inseparable, dimensions of selfhood: the self as an act-pole and the personal self. The former is the subject of intentional acts and non-intentional experiences, "that stand out from the streaming whole of consciousness". For Husserl, however, the self has also a temporal structure, and the notions of habit and habituality are central to its characterisation. These notions refer to the processes through which "egoic acts are established and new acts are layered on earlier ones, thus forming a kind of activity-form or activity gestalt", and it is thanks to these processes that the person emerges in internal time.

Heinämaa shows how such an account, involving two "parts or phases of the transcendental self", is further developed by Husserl in the manuscripts of the 1920s and 1930s. In particular, what emerges here is the "dimension of depth" associated with genuine experiences of love. According to Husserl, love, contrary to other emotions, has its grounds not in the object it is directed to, but rather in the subject who can, through it, "establish vocations and permanent personal relations of care" and thus acquire "inner profundity".

Heinämaa then proceeds to highlight how for Husserl the constitutive role of the self rests on the connection with other selves. From this perspective, "the full sense of the world" is rooted in the "communicative interaction" between embodied transcendental selves. The idea of generative intersubjectivity is then further unearthed by considering two special cases which, according to Husserl, are not part of such a community: the infant and the animal.

Liu Zhe, in *Towards Self-Divided Subjectivity. Merleau-Ponty's Phenomenological-Ontological Theory of Intersubjectivity*, further discusses the problem of the reduction in light of Merleau-Ponty's phenomenology. Drawing on Zahavi's critique of Merleau-Ponty, according to which Merleau-Ponty would not appropriately distinguish between intra- and intersubjective alterity, Liu Zhe argues that both forms of alterity can be accounted for by Merleau-Ponty's view of "self-divided subjectivity". On the basis of Merleau-Ponty's *Phenomenology of Perception* as well as of his 1950–1951 lectures notes on child psychology, Liu Zhe argues that, for Merleau-Ponty, pre-objective consciousness has a perceptual character. Perceptual consciousness is further regarded by Liu Zhe as a form of self-determination which must involve the transcendence of the other. The ultimate ground of such a condition is the inner distinction between reflected and un-reflected that is intrinsic to selfhood. From this perspective, Liu Zhe argues that the alterity in the self and that of intersubjectivity, which is illustrated in light of Merleau-Ponty's theory of child development, are both constitutive of subjectivity.

Hernán Inverso, in *Phenomenology of the Inapparent and Michel Henry's Criticism of the Noematic Presentation of Alterity*, examines Michel Henry's critique of Husserl, focusing in particular on Henry's view that genetic phenomenology is not adequate to capture and explain the experience of alterity and the inapparent. Inverso focuses on four main aspects of Henry's critique, including the problem of radical ipseity and the so-called degradation of the body, the imbalance between self- and other appresentation, the noematic unreality of the other, and the paradox of accessing another self as an object. On this basis, Inverso suggests the possibility of a more nuanced compatibility between Henry's and Husserl's phenomenology, based on the fact that Husserl's method provides a double way of grasping alterity. This implies a constitutive approach as well as an analysis of the dimension of the inapparent that exceeds static intentionality. More specifically, Inverso maintains that intersubjectivity can be explored as empathy, as generative plexus, and even, as in Henry's project, as an exceedance oriented to the self-affective dimension of life. In any case, Inverso argues that there are complementary levels that should not provoke collisions with Husserl's approach. From this point of view, Inverso's argument is that generativity and the inapparent are not dissociated phases nor have any aspiration to independence. Both derive from a genetic phenomenological approach, as they are both rooted in egological modality.

The third section of the volume is concerned with the phenomenological exploration of various dimensions of interpersonal experience, including perception, emotion, and trust. More specifically, the chapters included in this section explore how empathy is enacted as a form of perceptual understanding, involving the dimensions of seeing and hearing other selves, as well as the ways in which self-experience is involved in affects like envy and anxiety, and the experience of trust and trauma.

Felix Ó Murchadha's chapter, *Listening to Others: Music and the Phenomenology of Hearing*, outlines a phenomenology of hearing that centres on the structures of music, particularly on tone and rhythm, as well as on the relationship between music and empathy. As Ó Murchadha argues, music allows the materiality of sound to come to appearance. Taking Husserl's insights to the next level, Ó Murchadha conducts a phenomenological reduction of music that is inspired not only by Husserl's methodology but also by contemporary musicology. In particular, Ó Murchadha investigates the relations of motivation that hold in the realm of sound. On this view, to hear musical meaning means to follow "the directionality of sense", which is guided by an aural understanding that conveys a particular sense of incompleteness. In developing the relation between music and temporality, Ó Murchadha argues that music not only expresses emotions independently from the reference to a particular object, but it also enables the thematization of moods and atmospheres. In this sense, besides the reduction that brings to light the dimension of tone and temporality, a further reduction enables the thematization of what lies below the threshold of listening consciousness. Ó Murchadha further applies these insights to the encounter with another person, namely in the experience of listening to another. In so doing, Ó Murchadha shows that, in hearing another's voice, the qualities of tone of another's voice become the qualities of the sound itself. Alongside tone, rhythm is the other main structure that phenomenological analysis brings to light. Contrasting rhythm with sheer repetition, Ó Murchadha explains how the tendencies of liveliness and mechanicity co-exist in rhythm, producing adaptation to regularity and spontaneity. Together with tone, rhythm thus establishes the possibility of encountering another in hearing, an experience that is both dynamic and affectively situated.

Elisa Magrì, in *(Un)learning to see others. Perception, Types, and Position-Taking in Husserl's Phenomenology*, draws attention to the dynamic of perceptual learning that underpins Husserl's phenomenology. Magrì proceeds by explaining in what ways social perception is tied to the constitution of an intersubjective sense of reality that has social and moral significance, particularly when it comes to experiences of social alienation. With regard to this, Magrì explores the dynamic that is at stake in unlearning patterns of social perception that are involved in social indifference and white ignorance. On the individual level, this type of ignorance is brought about by doxastic dispositions that inform perceptual styles of seeing. In this regard, Magrì argues that the interruption of ingrained styles of perception crucially requires the clash between affectivity and the modality of belief that is sedimented in typification, prior to reflection and judgment. By further examining Husserl's account of typification, Magrì argues that modalities of perceptual unlearning depend on the alteration of the positionality of the self that is latent in perceptual acts informed by doxastic dispositions. On this view, the alteration of latent position-taking is brought about by phenomena of affective and cognitive dissonance, which Husserl arguably regards as critical moments of everyday experience. Taking up such critical and affective solicitations in the course of one's experience is essential to revise ingrained styles of perception, as well as to motivate social sensitivity. This concept is introduced by Magrì to define the subjective stance that seeks to further explicate the clues of a social context that suddenly become relevant because of the dissonance experienced. In so doing, social sensitivity transforms the typicality of perception, avoiding stereotypification while striving to better situate the experiential worldview or sense of reality of other selves.

Phenomenological investigations of affectivity are a key reference point for **Ingrid Vendrell Ferran**'s chapter, *Envy, Powerlessness, and the Feeling of Self-Worth*, which investigates the emotion of envy, focusing in particular on how the self is implicated in this experience. Vendrell Ferran conceives of envy as an emotion of self-assessment which depends on a comparison with another person who is considered to be similar to us and with whom we are familiar or close, and who has something that we desire. This comparison triggers a feeling of inferiority which is necessary to the experience of envy, but not sufficient for it. In order for envy to be experienced, Vendrell Ferran argues, also a feeling of powerlessness, and a related judgment concerning one's capacity to rectify the "situation of comparative inferiority", should be present. In addition, the desired good should be seen as something that one should be able to achieve.

Drawing on Voigtländer's work, Vendrell Ferran then proceeds to characterise the feeling of powerlessness integral to envy as a particular type of "feeling of self-worth", and, in particular, as an unpleasant feeling through which we become aware of our own value as being diminished. She argues that the features of envy highlighted by her account are clearly exemplified by cases of "existential envy". These are cases of envy in which the "coveted good" and the rival coincide, in so far as what is envied is the existence of the other person, thus involving both the presence of an unattainable good and a feeling of complete devaluation or lack of self-worth. Existential envy, however, is not a homogeneous experience, and Vendrell Ferran further explores the differences between envying the "existence of the other itself", and envying "some attributes of the existence of the other", arguing that they differ with regard to their scope, the emotions of the envious self, and the relation between the envious self and the rival.

Anna Bortolan's chapter, *Social Anxiety, Self-Consciousness, and Interpersonal Experience*, explores the distinction between different forms of self-consciousness, and investigates how alterations of these dimensions may be connected to the way in which social anxiety sufferers experience others and relate to them.

Bortolan starts by reconstructing how the notion of pre-reflective self-consciousness has been used to designate "non-observational" and "non-objectifying" forms of self-experience (Gallagher and Zahavi 2012, p. 52), while reflective self-consciousness refers to forms of experience in which one's body or self (or aspects of them) are given as objects of attention or observation. Bortolan then proceeds to discuss some of the applications of the distinction between pre-reflective and reflective self-consciousness in the phenomenological exploration of schizophrenia spectrum disorders.

The following sections of the chapter elaborate upon this body of research to suggest that alterations of self-consciousness are central also to the phenomenology of social anxiety disorder. Bortolan argues that the disorder is marked by a heightening of reflective self-consciousness, and, in particular, that socially anxious subjects tend to be aware of themselves as objects of other people's consciousness. She then claims, that, similar to what is the case in schizophrenia, disruptions of reflectivity in social anxiety are rooted in disturbances of pre-reflective self-experience, but these have a distinct character. More specifically, Bortolan argues that those who suffer from social phobia experience a low sense of self-esteem, which she conceives of as an "existential feeling" (Ratcliffe 2008), namely a background affective orientation that she characterises as conveying a pre-reflective, evaluative awareness of the self. Existential feelings are taken to have the capacity to shape and constrain one's intentional states, and Bortolan illustrates how, because of this feature, pathologically low self-esteem can engender specific alterations of reflective self-consciousness and interpersonal experience.

In **Matthew Ratcliffe**'s chapter, *Trauma, Language, and Trust*, a phenomenological approach is applied to the investigation of the experience of language failure in the context of trauma. When exceptional, disruptive, and distressing experiences are undergone, words may fail us, and the paper develops an account of what such an experience amounts to.

Ratcliffe starts by highlighting how the phenomenology of trauma may entail that one's experiential perspective is radically different from the one of her interlocutors, and words that are effective in describing the latter are experienced as inadequate in portraying one's present predicament. In his opinion, there are two main reasons why this may be the case.

First, Ratcliffe argues that the upheavals associated with trauma entail disturbances of a pre-reflective sense of belonging to the world, in which also the experienced meaning of words is anchored. Ratcliffe indeed highlights how words have a "self-referential" character, as they point towards "patterns of significant activities" and thus a specific set of possibilities that are open to one. Through a discussion in particular of the experience of bereavement associated with the loss of a partner, Ratcliffe argues that the alterations of one's lived world and possibility space may lead to a disruption of the "habitual patterns of experience, thought, and activity" in which the meaning of words is anchored, leading to the perceived erosion or loss of such meaning. He then moves to illustrate how this dynamic can be made more severe by the "pervasive loss of trust" that may accompany traumatic experiences. Ratcliffe suggests that an integral aspect of our pre-reflective experience of the world consists in expectations concerning the general benevolence and dependability of other people, a form of "confidence" or "certainty" on which the meaningfulness of our life projects depends. It is because of this that, by engendering a loss of trust in others, trauma may exacerbate the experience of linguistic failure, potentially leading also to the feeling, and anticipation, of not being understood, as others are (or are perceived to be) unable to offer uptake for one's illocutionary acts.

The fourth section of the volume explores the concept of intersubjectivity in its relation to morality and is more directly concerned with the phenomenology of the social world. It includes the exploration of the experiential dimension of tolerance, the nature of anger, and the normative and affective aspects of social recognition, as well as the ambiguity of Heidegger's late metapolitical thought.

John Drummond, in *Empathy, Sympathetic Respect, and the Foundations of Morality,* provides a unified account of empathy as a form of interpersonal experience that is rooted in the perceptual recognition of another's bodily state, change, and activity, while also underlying the moral dimension of respect and sympathy. Drummond proceeds by elucidating the phenomenological dimension of empathy in terms of perceptive and apperceptive recognition, which crucially differ from the perception of objects. As Drummond puts it, empathy is a "unique kind of perceptual recognition" which involves the disclosure of a common world. In recognizing another as a conscious agent, however, we move beyond the recognition of another bodily consciousness to the recognition of a person worthy of respect. Drawing on Darwall's distinction between appraisal respect and recognition respect, Drummond argues that the former is phenomenologically prior, whilst the latter has moral priority in the encounter with another agent. The two forms of respect presuppose and are affective complements of empathy. From this perspective, Drummond points out that sympathy builds on empathy, but distinguishes itself in that sympathy involves care for the well-being of another whereas empathy does not. Yet sympathy preserves the difference between myself as sympathizing with another's feeling and the other as experiencing that feeling. In so far as respect and sympathy are two affective responses to the empathically perceived other, they complement our understanding of others as well as of the world by introducing to the realm of values. In this regard, Drummond articulates the implications for morality of the respect-sympathy structure, focusing on the axiological centrality of virtues like intellectual humility and intellectual generosity.

Andrea Staiti's chapter, *Tolerance: A Phenomenological Approach*, explores the experiential dimension of tolerance. More specifically, having criticized the dominant "Two-Component View (TCV)" of tolerance, Staiti develops an alternative "One-Component View (OCV)" rooted in Husserlian phenomenology. Central to the TCV is the idea that tolerance consists of a positive and a negative component, and in the chapter Staiti examines four versions of this approach, namely the ones put forward by Preston King, Rainer Forst, Achim Lohmar, and Lester Embree. Staiti argues that neither of these accounts meets all the criteria for a persuasive theory of tolerance, identifying a paradox at the core of the TCV.

Staiti's original proposal of a OCV draws on Husserl's account of modalizations concerning positing acts. Through such acts, objects can be posited "as being and being such and such", and this positing can receive confirmation when fulfilled by a relevant intuition. For Husserl, however, positing acts can also undergo a "neutrality modification" through which we suspend the commitment to the "being or non-being" of the objects or states of affairs that are posited. This can be the case not only for positing acts such as perceptions and judgements, but also in the domain of valuing (and willing), where what becomes neutralized is one's commitment to the being of values (and goals) posited through the relevant acts. For Staiti, tolerance is to be understood as such a form of "neutralized valuing", and, in particular, as one which takes place in the context of empathy. More specifically, tolerance occurs when one neutralizes their position-taking towards the values that are posited by the person one empathizes with, suspending one's commitment to their being or not being.

Staiti maintains that this occurs when we come to see "the other's positing of value" as "illegitimate", namely when we realize that those valuings are not confirmed through intuitive fulfilment. In these cases, we choose to neutralize valuings so as to avoid conflicts which we think would be damaging to the other's "moral development", a feature which underscores the moral character of the attitude of tolerance.

In *Anger, Hatred, Prejudice. An Aristotelian Perspective*, **Alessandra Fussi** examines the intersubjective nature of anger from an Aristotelian angle, which allows for a fine-grained distinction between anger, contempt, and hatred. Drawing on Allport's definition of prejudice as having both an affective and a cognitive component, Fussi outlines the different ways in which individuals can jump to the wrong conclusion due to what Aristotle would call the incontinence of spirit, namely the failed communication between reason and passion. The Aristotelian metaphor of the servant and the dog in the *Nicomachean Ethics* is used by Fussi to illustrate the difference between anger and unjustified hatred. While prejudice based on anger is driven by spiritedness and reflects a misunderstanding of someone's deeds, unjustified hatred is caused by the wrong application of generalities to particulars. On this basis, Fussi examines the different manifestations of anger in Aristotle's *Rhetoric*, focusing on the experience of being slighted and its three main forms (contempt, spite, and insult). Fussi argues that, whether the slight reveals a lack of regard for someone's judgment (contempt), for his intentions (spite), or for the person as a whole (insult), the consequence is that being slighted provokes shame: one feels diminished, unimportant. In this respect, contempt points to moral feelings and issues of responsibility that have an intrinsic intersubjective relevance. Such communicative and intersubjective aspects are notably missing in hatred, which is rather oriented to the other not *qua* other but *qua* representative of a negative property. In this regard, Fussi suggests that hatred might be best interpreted as a disposition rather than an emotion properly. The chapter concludes with a discussion of the depersonalizing nature of hatred and its relation to a feeling of powerlessness.

Danielle Petherbridge, in *Habit, Attention and Affection: Husserlian Inflections*, examines the dimension of affective intentionality underlying Axel Honneth's account of social recognition, bringing it into dialogue with Husserl's genetic phenomenology. Drawing on the work of Charles Johnson, Petherbridge illustrates the way in which acts of recognition are affirmed through expressive and embodied gestures that indicate the perception of another human being. In this sense, Petherbridge argues that intentionality is not to be understood as a cold, detached process but is attentive or affective, for it presents objects through solicitations that are expressive of an evaluative perception. In Honneth's work, this account of affectivity and expressivity in perception depend on the reconceptualization of the relation between perception, cognition, and recognition. Honneth's view points to the reversal of the status of cognitive and recognitive acts: affective recognition is understood to be prior to cognition and forms the basis of our perception of others. Petherbridge suggests that the kinds of claims Honneth makes can be understood more fully if we bring them into view through a phenomenological analysis of attention. Thus, in the second part of her chapter, Petherbridge examines Husserl's approach, focusing in particular on the relation between attention, habit, and affectivity. Drawing on the work of Maren Wehrle, Petherbridge points out that attention is awakened by interest and affective solicitations that shape how the subject is affected by the outer world. On this basis, Petherbridge argues that affective intentionality is central in both Husserl's and Honneth's accounts, and it can be fruitfully employed to modifying habits of perception. More specifically, Petherbridge holds that affective intentionality in Husserl points to a particular type of reflexive attention and to the forgetfulness of the self, while in Honneth it represents the basis of a primary account of intersubjectivity from which a secondary normative account emanates and against which critique is then articulated.

Nicolas de Warren, in Die äusserste Feindschaft. *Heidegger, Anti-Judaism, and the War to End All Wars*, explores the opposition between philosophy and prejudice, taking into account the challenges posited to Heidegger's philosophy by the publication of the *Schwarze Hefte*. As de Warren puts it, "at issue is not the unthought of philosophical thought", but "the unthought of philosophical non-thinking". More specifically, de Warren reconstructs the role of prejudice in Heidegger's confrontation with history, drawing attention to the specific horizon within which Heidegger elaborated on his experience of the Great War. According to de Warren, it is the experience of the First World War that primarily informs Heidegger's philosophical search for another beginning for thinking during the 1930s. In so doing, de Warren sheds light on the "mobilization of philosophical discourse" in the years that preceded the First World War, as well as on the popularization of the figure of the enemy in the form of caricatures, clichés, and stereotypes. On this basis, de Warren interprets Heidegger's reference to the enemy in the *Schwarze Hefte* as "a metaphysical form of cliché." Heidegger's search for a new beginning in the 1930s is the symptom of the struggle for a "genuine metaphysical experience of thinking" that was not achieved by German Idealism. Drawing on the debate between Bruno Bauch and Ernst Cassirer on the role of Judaism in the constitution of the German nation, de Warren notices the constitutive function of prejudice as "non-thought" that "cements the flatlands of banality." In the case of Heidegger, the necessity of a confrontation between philosophy and prejudice becomes the struggle for another beginning "without genuine encounter," a non-dialectical purification "that is neither 'propaganda' nor 'apologetic'".

Steven Crowell, in *Heidegger's Metapolitics: Phenomenology, Metaphysics, and the* Volk, reconstructs Heidegger's metaphysical turn between 1927 and 1935, which is inspired by the ambition to lay out a "metontology," namely a metaphysics of finite, worldly entities (in Heidegger's words, this amounts to an *ontic* metaphysics). Crowell discusses the parallels between Heidegger's project of a "metontology" and the "metapolitics" of the *Black Notebooks*, in which the former aspiration to metaphysics turns into the first-plural person of the *Volk*. Crowell proceeds by first outlining Heidegger's departure from Husserl's transcendental method on the basis of Heidegger's concern with the finitude of reason. Such a concern guides the phenomenological exploration of the world from the point of view of the pre-reflective awareness, which is, however, not only descriptive but also normative. In this respect, Crowell argues that, in his metaphysical decade, Heidegger sought to determine the normative horizon that is disclosed in the experience of having a world. In so doing, Crowell sheds new light on Heidegger's appropriation of Leibniz's monadology, which informs his phenomenology of the life of worldly creatures, including animals. Crowell shows that, unlike Husserl, who appeals to Leibniz's metaphysics to illustrate his genetic understanding of intersubjectivity, Heidegger offers a "metontological pedagogy" that does not centre on empathy but rather on the liberation of the existence that is given in the human being. On this basis, Crowell argues that the transformation of "metontology" into "metapolitics" is realized in the *Black Notebooks* in order to reveal "the ontic ground of ontology" in the form of the "we", namely the socio-historical reality in which the "I" is always already dispersed. At the same time, Crowell shows that, while the concept of *Volk* does not amount to an organism but rather is voluntary, Heidegger's metaphysical foundation culminates in "an abject failure", for it is unable to justify its implications as well as to keep together the empirical and the transcendental without disempowering human freedom.

Acknowledgments

The editors wish to thank the International Centre for Newman Studies, the UCD School Philosophy (especially Jim O'Shea, Maria Baghramian, Helen Kenny, and Margaret Brady), and the Royal Irish Academy for their support and assistance in organizing the 2017 conference. Special thanks to Cinzia Ruggeri, Genevieve Hayman, Le Dong, and Junguo Zhang for their help in making that event possible. We are also grateful to David Abergel for his editorial assistance. Last but not least, we wish to thank all the authors in this volume for their insightful contributions and collaboration.

References

Broome, Matthew R./Harland, Robert/Owen, Gareth S./Stringaris, Argyris (Eds.) (2012): *The Maudsley Reader in Phenomenological Psychiatry*. Cambridge: Cambridge University Press.
Burns, Timothy/Szanto, Thomas/Salice, Alessandro (Eds.) (2019): "Phenomenology, Idealism, Intersubjectivity: A *Festschrift* in Celebration of Dermot Moran's Sixty-Fifth Birthday". In: *The New Yearbook for Phenomenology and Phenomenological Philosophy* 17.
Daly, Anya/Cummins, Fred/Jardine, James/Moran, Dermot (Eds.) (2020): *Perception and the Inhuman Gaze: Perspectives from Philosophy, Phenomenology, and the Sciences*. London, New York: Routledge.
Gallagher, Shaun/Zahavi, Dan (2012): *The Phenomenological Mind*. 2nd ed. London, New York: Routledge.
Husserl, Edmund (1973): *Zur Phänomenologie der Intersubjektivität. Texte aus dem Nachlass. Zweiter Teil: 1921–1928*. Iso Kern (Ed.). Husserliana XIV. The Hague: Martinus Nijhoff. [Hua 14]
Moran, Dermot/Mooney, Timothy (2002): *The Phenomenology Reader*. London, New York: Routledge.
Moran, Dermot (2005): *Edmund Husserl Founder of Phenomenology*. Cambridge: Polity Press.
Moran, Dermot (2012): *Husserl's Crisis of the European Sciences and Transcendental Phenomenology: An Introduction*. Cambridge: Cambridge University Press.
Moran, Dermot/Cohen, Joseph (2012): *The Husserl Dictionary*. London: Continuum.
Osler, Lucy (2021) Taking Empathy Online, Inquiry, DOI: 10.1080/0020174X.2021.1899045, last accessed on 12 September 2021.
Ratcliffe, Matthew (2008): *Feelings of Being: Phenomenology, Psychiatry and the Sense of Reality*. Oxford: Oxford University Press.
Stanghellini, Giovanni/Broome, Matthew, R./Fernandez, Anthony Vincent/Fusar-Poli, Paolo/Raballo, Andrea/Rosfort, René (Eds.) (2019): *The Oxford Handbook of Phenomenological Psychopathology*. Oxford: Oxford University Press.
Stein, Edith (1917): *Zum Problem der Einfühlung*. Edith Stein Gesamtausgabe 5. Freiburg, Basel, Wien: Herder 2008.

Stein, Edith (1989): *On the Problem of Empathy*. In: *The Collected Works of Edith Stein*. Vol. 3. Trans. Waltraut Stein. Washington, D.C.: ICS Publications.

Szanto, Thomas/Moran, Dermot (Eds.) (2016): *Phenomenology of Sociality: Discovering the 'We'*. London, New York: Routledge.

Zahavi, Dan (2014): *Self and Other: Exploring Subjectivity, Empathy, and Shame*. Oxford: Oxford University Press.

Zahavi, Dan (2019): *Phenomenology: The Basics*. London, New York: Routledge.

Dermot Moran
From Empathy to Intersubjectivity: The Phenomenological Approach

Abstract: In this paper I explicate the classical *phenomenological* approach to empathy (an umbrella term for a number of distinct interpersonal experiences of understanding others) to highlight some original and significant aspects of this approach that still have relevance for contemporary debates in the cognitive sciences and in analytical philosophy of mind and action. The focus is on Edmund Husserl, with some discussion of Max Scheler, Edith Stein, and Martin Heidegger. I briefly sketch the history of empathy and then focus on the classical phenomenological treatment of empathy as a direct quasi-perception and not an imaginative projection of simulation. Empathy, for Husserl and Stein, names this experiential sense of grasping *another subject* and immersing oneself in the other's subjectivity, leading to an 'intertwining' (*Verflechtung, Ineinandersein*) of subjects (intersubjectivity) and to the constitution of the world as objective 'world-for-all'. Empathy functions only within an entire social, historical and cultural world.

Introduction: The Nature and Importance of Empathy

The complex set of phenomena included under the umbrella term 'empathy' (*Einfühlung*) was originally discussed in eighteenth-century British sentimentalist philosophy as 'sympathy' (Hume, Adam Smith); in nineteenth-century German psychology (Lipps, Volkert, Münsterberg); in hermeneutics (Dilthey); and in twentieth-century phenomenology (Husserl, Scheler, Stein). More recently, empathy has been revived as a topic in empirical psychology (Baron-Cohen 2011, 2012; Coplan and Goldie 2011) and in contemporary analytic philosophy of mind (Goldman 1992, 2006). Empathy construed as a sensitive attunement to the *feelings* of others has been seen as the basis of morality.[1] In this chapter, I briefly sketch the history of empathy and then focus on the classical phenomenological treatment of empathy.

---

[1] Bazalgette (2017) claims empathy is needed for a caring society; Paul Bloom (2016) argues against empathy as it restricts sensitivity to those close to us. See also Prinz 2011.

https://doi.org/10.1515/9783110698787-003

Husserl and the phenomenological tradition (Scheler, Stein) employ the term 'empathy' as a catch-all term for all kinds of 'experience of the other [person]' (*Fremderfahrung*), but primarily the direct (quasi-) *'perception* of the other' (*Fremdwahrnehmung)*. Phenomenology treats empathy as direct, intuitive, quasi-perceptual grasp of the other subject's mental or emotional state, rather than as a simulation of or theorization about the other's behaviour. Empathy is a fundamental and distinctive form of *intentionality,* a *sui generis* mental capacity, and not just an emotional response, an imaginative envisaging, simulation, or inference (Stein 1989/1917).

For Husserl, empathy is not, first and foremost, any kind of imaginative projection (introjection) or imagining oneself in the other's shoes (although we are certainly capable of this kind of imaginative projection). Imaginative projection or *introjection* (Husserl uses *Introjektion*, Husserl 1989, § 49) is not yet empathy. The school boy excited by the passion of Shakespeare's Romeo is not having a *genuine* experience of Romeo's passion, since, Scheler suggests, the original ground for the valuing is not there. The school boy is, as it were, deceived into thinking Romeo's passion is his. It is at best a borrowed passion, according to Edith Stein's analysis (Stein 1989, p. 32; Stein 1917, p. 35).

Mental states are complex, stratified unities and experienced as seamless unities (perhaps best expressed adverbially; 'she *angrily* rebuffed his entreaties'). Empathy involves the recognition of other subjects as *intentional* beings—as *agents*, sense-makers, persons attentive to values. Empathy, moreover, for phenomenology, is not specifically a conscious 'mental' or metacognitive activity; rather it is an intuitive, embodied, flesh-to-flesh relation, constituted in and through our embodied subjectivities (Szanto and Moran 2015a; 2015b). I *see* someone's hand *pressing* on the desk, and have a transferred sense of what that experience feels like for them but at the same time distinguish the other's experience from mine.

In the phenomenological tradition, empathy is related to *intersubjectivity*, sociality, and our very 'being-in-the-world' or enworldedness or 'embeddedness' (*Einbettung*, to use Gerda Walther's term). Empathy involves a co-being or 'being-with' the other subject within an interpersonal world. Intersubjectivity, for phenomenology, founds objectivity. It is because I grasp different perspectives precisely as different perspectives on the one world, that I have a sense of *the* world in itself (*Welt an sich*, Husserl 1954, p. 62), a common world that transcends perspectives and is indeed our ultimate context that makes us understand that my immediate world-awareness actually is a perspective. *Empathy*, for Husserl and Stein leads to an intertwining (*Verflechtung, Ineinandersein*) of subjects (intersubjectivity) and to the constitution of the objective world as a 'world-for-all' (*Welt für alle*, Husserl 1954, p. 257).

Significant questions arise about the nature and scope of empathy. How does empathy differ from emotional identification, sympathy, compassion? Is it restricted to inter-human contact? Can humans genuinely empathize with animals, plants,[2] or even non-living nature (a 'brooding' sky) or works of art? Indeed, in nineteenth-century discussions of *Einfühlung* (by Stephan Witasek, Robert Vischer, and Johannes Volkert), the paradigmatic objects of empathy were 'expressive' works of art (Depew 2005).

What are the *limits* of empathy? Can one empathize only with people *similar* to oneself? Are there temporal limits to the reach of empathic connection? Can someone today really understand the historical Socrates' *motivation?* Besides historical figures, can I empathize with *fictional* characters, such as Hamlet (Harold 2000)?

In the contemporary analytic tradition, empathy is largely considered to be akin to what has been termed 'mindreading' (Goldman 2006). Thus, Alvin Goldman writes:

> *Having* a mental state and *representing* another as having such a state are entirely different matters. The latter activity, *mentalizing* or *mindreading* is a second order activity. It is a mind thinking about minds. It is the activity of conceptualizing other creatures (and oneself) as loci of mental life. (Goldman 2006, p. 3)

On this construal, mind-reading is an explicit second-order, meta-act of mentalization. Husserlian phenomenology rejects this characterization. Empathy is direct, intuitive, quasi-perceptual, needing no conceptualization or explicit mentalization. I simply *see* your face and *recognize* you are happy.

Husserl always says that empathy is not an 'inference' (*Schluss*) or reasoning process.[3] He calls it an 'apperception' (*Apperzeption, Vergegenwärtigung*, Husserl 1950, p. 139), a higher-order, more complex 'mediate' intuition (Husserl 1950, p. 138) that is *founded* on something given in immediate perception, in this case, the vibrant living body of the person being grasped empathically, e.g., a smiling face; a threatening tone of voice. Husserl also calls it a 'quasi-perception' (*Quasi-Wahrnehmung*, Husserl 1952, p. 263), because of its directness and the sense of immediate presence of the object (e.g., the other's gaiety), although this perception-like intuition lacks the full contours of external perception and is founded explicitly on direct perception of bodily expressions (and an accompanying 'apperceptive transfer'). Empathy is an act whereby one subject appre-

---

[2] Edith Stein maintains we can have an empathic relation with plants (Stein 1989, p. 67) as living things, even if not egoic consciousnesses (but see Marder 2012).
[3] Husserl writes: "*Also ist der Schluss ein* Sophisma" (Husserl 1973a, p. 38).

hends not just the other's mental state (as the intended 'content' of an act) but one's focus is drawn to the foreign *subjectivity* of the other (although, as Husserl makes clear, I cannot *live* through the other's *first-personness* as the other does directly).

In *Ideas* I (1913) § 1 (Husserl 2014, p. 8), Husserl introduced in print his distinction between 'originary' (*originär*) and non-originary experiences. Originary experiences are 'first-personal', e.g., my own flow of conscious states. Husserl says, however, that we do *not* have 'originary' experience of others in empathy (Husserl 2014, p. 10; 1913, p. 8); our experiences of others are 'non-originary' (*nicht originär*).

Husserl introduces a second distinction between the actual moments that are originally given or present themselves in a 'presentation' or 'exhibit' (*Darstellung*), in what he calls 'primary originarity' (*primäre Originarität*), and what he calls the 'secondary originarity' of the emptily co-presented other sides of the object that do not actually appear (from the side of the other subject). The other subject is also present in a kind of empty manner since I cannot experience her experience from the inside. I apprehend the other as the dark side of the moon. Empathy is non-original in that I never grasp your side of the experience but I grasp the experience (partly or wholly) as *yours*.

It is important to stress that empathy, then, for phenomenology, does not require both persons to be in the *same* mental or emotional state (as in emotional identification or fusion). We do not *share* a state with the other, or need to have previously experienced it in order to recognize it. Nor does empathy require me to *activate* the same emotion in myself in a rehearsal or simulation. Thus, attending a movie, I can apprehend and, in a sense, 'live through' the murderous rage of the killer on screen, although I may never have experienced previously such a consuming rage (and don't want to murder anyone).[4] Perhaps I can imaginatively amplify or 'dial-up' a current annoyance into a total rage (such 'amplification' David Hume assumed as one of the innate capacities of the mind), but it surely seems possible to apprehend novel experiences one has never personally had. Otherwise, as Husserl points out, I could never apprehend the other *as other* but only as a modification of myself (*alter ego*). My current mental state can even be the opposite of that which I apprehend in the other. I can actually be sad but apprehend you as happy. Indeed, your joy may itself infect me (through

---

[4] Much of the debate concerning empathic experiencing in art (literature, theatre, painting) in traditional German aesthetics, focused on the question of whether fiction-induced feelings or emotions (e.g., in his *Confessions* I.13 Augustine recalls weeping for the slain Dido in Virgil's *Aeneid*) are real feelings or aesthetic 'virtual' or fantasy feelings. Husserl and Stein maintain that motivations experienced in art are not genuine motivations founded in real experiences.

what Scheler called *Ansteckung*, 'emotional contagion', Scheler 1973a, p. 240) to also be happy, or at least to be able to calibrate my sadness against your joy. I can join in your happiness in a way that may *modify* my sadness. Or I may have reasons that *motivate* me to share in your joy and put aside my sadness; I start to feel joyful from this motivation. In that case, my sadness is shot through with rationalization. Or your joy may *irritate* me in my sadness, or make me *jealous* for your good fortune (and I do not have to be conscious that it is doing so— I can simply change mood in some kind of response to your emotional state).

Empathy, phenomenologists insist, is neither a simulation nor a form of inferential reasoning. Of course, empathy may well be accompanied by reasoning. One may apprehend an ambiguous or unclear aspect in the other's communicated self-presentation that requires further exploration. But here one is mining the richness of the given experience. Similarly, it may be the case that there are pathological conditions, e.g., severe autistic spectrum disorder (Baron-Cohen 1995), where the immediate intuitive apprehension that founds the reasoned inquiry is missing and, therefore, persons suffering this condition need to be educated to interpret, read signals, rationally comprehend how others respond to one's behavior, and so on.[5]

As Max Scheler and others have recognized, empathy is a grasp of the other subject, a kind of 'mind-sightedness', but it is not necessarily a morally good experience (although, in the English language, empathy has only positive connotations). There is empathy among thieves (as both Adam Smith and Scheler acknowledge). Empathy may not be benign or caring of others, e.g., pretending, lying, deceiving, spin-doctoring, acting, emotionally manipulating or influencing, love-bombing, may employ empathy. A torturer can use empathy to get inside their victim's head.

Let us briefly review the evolution of the concept of empathy (and its sister concept 'sympathy', see Moran 2004).

---

5 A total inability to comprehend or acknowledge another perspective would seem to also rule out the possibility of using language to attribute mental stances to others. Personal testimony from persons putatively on the autistic spectrum suggest they can rationally understand the implications of a particular social situation without personally undergoing the appropriate feeling.

A Short History of 'Empathy': From Greek to German

Both 'empathy' (English) and '*Einfühlung*' (German) are relatively modern lexical innovations to name an immemorial human capacity (Ewert 1995). The Greek '*empatheia*' (ἐμπάθεια) means intense physical feeling or passion (Liddell, Scott and Jones 1996). Plotinus, for instance, contrasts ἐμπάθεια (to be intensely involved in the feeling) with ἀπάθεια, *apathy*, absence of feeling. Of course, *sympatheia* (σὔμπάθεια) has a longer presence in Greek thought, especially in the Stoics and Plotinus, who saw sympathy as running through the whole cosmos (Schliesser 2015; Laurand 2005).

Scheler idiosyncratically uses the German term *Sympathie* ('sympathy', 'liking') in his *Zur Phänomenologie und Theorie der Sympathiegefühle und von Liebe und Haß* (Scheler 1913), and *Wesen und Formen der Sympathie* (Scheler 1973b, 2008), but also uses another term *Nachfühlen* ('feeling for'), for what he considers to be genuine empathy, as opposed to *Einsfühlung* ('feeling one with', 'identification') or *Mitgefühl* ('fellow feeling'). There are adjacent German terms: *Mitleid* (pity, compassion, sympathy).[6] Husserl, Scheler, and Stein all use *sich hineinversetzen*, 'to put oneself in the other person's position'. This imaginative transposition is just one very specific mode of empathy; not all empathy involves such transposition.

The reflexive verb *sich einfühlen* emerged in German Romanticism (e. g., Herder), but the noun *Einfühlung* ('feeling into') was coined by Hermann Lotze (1817–1871) (Lotze 1868), and, more or less at the same time, by Robert Vischer (1847–1933) (Vischer 1873, p. vii). Vischer understood *Einfühlung* as the 'self-objectification of the human spirit' in animals or entities in the natural world (e. g., a landscape can look 'somber' or 'melancholic'). Further discussions of *Einfühlung* emerged in late nineteenth-century German aesthetics, where *Einfühlung* is required to grasp emotions in painting, music, literature and the arts generally (Robert Vischer, Witasek, Lipps). Subsequently, Theodor Lipps also sees empathy as the *apprehension of the human spirit* in inanimate things, e. g., art-works.

Friedrich Schleiermacher and Wilhelm Dilthey sought to ground the human sciences on 'empathy' (*Einfühlung*, although Dilthey seldom uses this word) or *Mitgefühl* ('sympathy', 'commiseration'). For Dilthey, understanding (*Verstehen*) involves a 'projection of oneself' (*sich hineinversetzen*) and one's life-context

---

6 Indeed, '*compassio*' is an excellent translation of *sympatheia*.

into the life-context of the other in order to understand the other's motivations.[7] Dilthey distinguished this projection from 'sympathy' (*Mitfühlen*) and 'empathy' (*Einfühlen*, Dilthey 1977, p. 113; see Makkreel 1996). Husserl followed Dilthey explicitly in this regard in his *Phenomenological Psychology* lectures of 1925 (Husserl 1977, p. 13).

In his influential *Leitfaden der Psychologie* (Lipps 1909, p. 222), Lipps discusses one's knowledge of other 'I's through empathy. Lipps understands empathy largely as unconscious 'inner imitation' (*innere Anahmung*). He postulates an inherent imitation impulse (*Nachahmungsimpulse*, Lipps 1905; Lipps 2018). The perception of others' behaviour activates a response in us whereby we unconsciously and imaginatively run through the other's behaviour using our own internal movements as we apprehend them. There is spontaneous 'imitation of the movements' (*Bewegungsanahmen*) of the other subject. Husserl regarded Lipps' appeal to unconscious imitation as theoretically unsatisfactory. Stein also criticized Lipps' account of inner imitation as actually more focused *on oneself* (Fidalgo 1993). She writes: "I do not arrive at the phenomenon of foreign experience but at an experience of my own that arouses in me the foreign gestures witnessed" (Stein 1989, p. 23; Stein 1917, p. 24). *Copying* someone is not the same as empathically understanding them.

Edward Bradford Titchener (1867–1927) rendered Lipps' term *Einfühlung* (Titchener 1909) as 'empathy', defined as "the process of humanizing objects, of feeling ourselves or reading ourselves into them." Titchener writes:

> Not only do I see gravity and modesty and pride and courtesy and stateliness, but I feel or act them in the mind's muscles. This is, I suppose, a simple case of empathy, if we may coin that term as a rendering of *Einfühlung*. (Titchener 1909, pp. 21–22)

Titchener, following Lipps, understands empathy as an unconscious muscular reaction (he meant our internally felt muscles, e.g., when I feel myself smile, or feel myself tensing up) that he calls 'motor empathy' (Titchener 1909, p. 185). Unconscious motor empathy is a genuine phenomenon. I may, while talking with you, unconsciously start to *imitate* your accent, or posture, or mannerism. I may nod when you nod. But it is not empathy.

The terms '*Einfühlung*' and 'empathy', then, emerged as neologisms at the end of the nineteenth century, but the rag-bag or cluster of ideas that the

---

[7] Hans-Georg Gadamer's 'fusion of horizons' (*Horizontverschmelzung*) is a development of Dilthey's, Husserl's, and Heidegger's concept of 'understanding' (*Verstehen*) through contextualization with one's world.

terms capture has an older history, most notably with Adam Smith and David Hume. Hume writes in his 1739–1740 *Treatise on Human Nature*:

> No quality of human nature is more remarkable, both in itself and in its consequences, than that propensity we have to sympathize with others, and to receive by communication their inclinations and sentiments, however, different from, or even contrary to our own. [...] So remarkable a phaenomenon merits our attention, and must be trac'd back to its first principles [...] (Hume 1978, pp. 316–17)

Hume, however, tended to understand sympathy as a kind of emotional contagion: I 'catch' your feelings from your expressions.

In his 1759 *The Theory of Moral Sentiments* (Smith 2002), Adam Smith presents empathy as a basic human passion, possessed even by ruffians. Smith, in particular, invokes the image of the circus audience imitating the tight-rope walker in an almost unconscious bodily imitation. Smith interprets sympathy as imaginative *identification*, becoming *one* with the other. Scheler invokes both Hume and Smith in his two groundbreaking analyses (Scheler 1913; revised and expanded 1923; trans. Scheler 2008). Scheler correctly recognizes that there are many different levels of sympathy and offers a fourfold classification in his *The Nature of Sympathy* (Scheler 2008, p. 12; Scheler 1973b, p. 22):[8]

(1) Immediate community of feeling [*das unmittelbare Mitfühlen*], e. g. of one and the same sorrow, 'with someone' [*mit jemand*].
(2) Fellow-feeling [*das Mitgefühl*] 'about something' [*an etwas*]; rejoicing in his joy and commiseration with his sorrow.
(3) Mere emotional infection or contagion [*die blosse Gefühlsansteckung*].
(4) True emotional identification [*die echte Einsfühlung*]

In Scheler's emotional contagion (*Gefühlsansteckung*), an emotional state literally infects the other person, e. g., panic spreading involuntarily through a crowd (Scheler 2008, p. 15; Scheler 1973, p. 26). His *Mitfühlen* ('community of feeling') is genuine emotional sharing, where two persons share an emotion. Scheler's example, also discussed by Edith Stein, is about two parents grieving over their dead child (Scheler 2008, pp. 12–13; Scheler 1973, p. 23; cf. Stein 2000, pp. 134–36). Both have the *same* grief, their individual griefs have the same act-quality and the same identical object (the dead child) but, more than that, the two parents *know* that each shares their grief with the other (and that is dis-

---

8 Scheler's vocabulary, moreover, is fluid (see Zahavi 2010, p. 289): he fluctuates between *Nachfühlen* (reproduction of feeling), *Nachleben* ('reliving') or *Nacherleben* ('re-experiencing'), and *Mitgefühl* ('fellow feeling').

tinct from the grief of a fellow bystander attending the funeral). Scheler's analysis is illuminating. He writes that the parents literally share the same grief:

> ... they feel it together, in the sense that they feel and experience in common, not only the self-same value-situation, but also the same keenness of emotion in regard to it. The sorrow, as value-content, and the grief, as characterizing the functional relation thereto, are here *one and identical*. (Scheler 2008, p. 13; Scheler 1973, pp. 23–24)

They can each have the identical emotion, the *same grief*. Scheler perceptively comments that only *psychic* feelings and not *physical* suffering can be shared in that way.

Unfortunately, as Stein makes clear, Scheler's account is somewhat sketchy. His main contribution is to distinguish genuine empathy (his 'fellow feeling', where I can apprehend your experience without actually reproducing it or experiencing it directly myself) from various forms of emotional contagion or identification. He seems to reserve *Einfühlung* for Lipps' imaginative identification. Scheler and Stein both insist on the distinction between genuine empathy (*Einfühlung*) which maintains the distance or gap between self and other, and 'identification' (*Einsfühlung*), where there is no such gap. In true sympathy, on the phenomenological view, I respect the other's individuality and recognise her experience without substituting my feeling for hers (Vendrell Ferran 2015).

Is it really true that two people can have the same emotion (e.g., grief) felt in exactly the same way and with the same intensity, as Scheler claims? Two parents grieving over the loss of their child could with time start to separate their griefs and even calibrate one against the other. One might feel that the other has become *too attached* to her grief and perhaps has let it envelop her too long and that perhaps her emotion is now cloying or stultifying or has left her stagnant. The two 'token' griefs could initially be type identical, but then their trajectories might evolve in different directions. For one, it might be 'time to move on'; whereas the other may resent the first for being too easily able to bottle up or shut in their grief and for not letting it out. Furthermore, an individually experienced grief can always become the intentional object of further intentional and emotional states (impatience, resentment, irritation, and so on). The intentional analysis of any feeling state (and its trajectory) can be very complicated and Husserl speaks specifically about the ways these feelings may interlace, modify each other and 'sediment'. Stein speaks of the emotion being 'saturated by my individual life' (Stein 2000, p. 135). She writes:

> The same content (according to its sense-composition) can be felt more or less vehemently; more or less deeply; purely, or adulterated with something else. (Stein 2000, p. 138)

Genuine phenomenological description must be capable of disentangling the interwoven complexity of our emotional lives, apprehending its essential scaffolding and temporal trajectories as well as the capacities to absorb, combine with or mutate into other states. Emotions are extraordinarily shape-shifting; pity can morph into contempt, and so on. To date, the analytic philosophical literature on the emotions does not generally address this dynamic complexity, articulated so much better in fiction and in the classical phenomenology of Husserl, Scheler, and Stein.

Edmund Husserl: Other-Experience (Empathy) and Self-Experience

Husserl, inspired by Dilthey, understood lived experiences (*Erlebnisse*) as integrated into the wider 'nexus of life' (*Lebenszusammenhang*) with its web of intentional implications and motivations. We apprehend the other's conscious states as nested in and motivated by *situations* that belong within wider social contexts, and, ultimately, embedded in the historical, cultural life-world (*Lebenswelt*) that provides overall significance. Thus, being-in-the-situation is a necessary component for empathy. I understand others in the context of the network of motivations that frame the experience. Empathy involves casting this net of significance over the other.

Husserl's central phenomenological question about empathy is: how is it possible—the necessary a priori conditions of possibility—for me to recognize another living being precisely *as another individual conscious subject* that has its own concurrent, temporal stream of lived experiences in an overall world of significance? This other subject is 'governed' (*waltend*) by a 'foreign ego' (*ein fremdes Ich*) that I somehow apprehend, and whose experiences I can register, even if I cannot *live through* them myself first-personally. In the 'personalistic attitude' (*die personalistische Einstellung*), as Husserl clarifies in *Ideas* II (Husserl 1989, § 49), we simply accept that other human subjects are immediately apprehensible and intelligible in terms of their subjective lives, feelings, moods, cognitive attitudes, and so on (note that Stein does not employ the phrase 'the personalistic attitude' but it underlies her own work).

Husserl begins from a fundamental contrast between the first-person, 'originary' (*originär*), 'primordial' manner of self-givenness of one's experiences to oneself, in contrast to non-originary' (*nicht originär*) 'other experience' that is experienced in a representation or 'presentation' or 'presentification' (*Vergegenwärtigung*). All experience is primordially first-personal or, Husserl says, 'egoic' (*ichlich*). We experience the other in *second-person* experience. Husserl speaks of 'I-you relation' (*Ich-Du-Beziehung*). I grasp what 'you' are intending, and I can also join with *you* in various forms of shared 'we-intentionality' (*Wir-Intentionalität*), in an overall 'we-community' (*Wirgemeinschaft*). Forming a 'we' involves a complicated co-intending of a shared world.

Phenomenological empathy requires that there continues to be a *gap* between the subjects, even in higher states of empathy, such as love, discussed by Scheler (1954, p. 26). There has to be in one sense a permanent unbridgeable gulf between the first-person perspectives even when they are intentionally conjoined. Even in love, I do not want to merge entirely with the other, so that the other is completely smothered or stifled. I love *the otherness of the other*, and I apprehend the other's 'value' and seek to preserve it. There must be recognition of that permanent otherness even in the most unifying states of mutual love (Scheler 1954, p. 71). As Scheler and Stein put it, playing on the words, empathy (*Einfühlung*) is not *identification* or 'feeling-one-with' (*Einsfühlung*, Stein 1989, p. 17), i.e., fusion.[9]

In empathy, I experience the other as a "subject of his surrounding world ... a center of intentionality" (*Zentrum der Intentionalität*, Husserl 1989, p. 383; Husserl 1952, p. 373), i.e., as a personal agent. My experience has a 'you-directedness' in it. This capacity to pass through the experience of the other runs in two directions: towards the intentional object and towards the intending subject. According to Stein, when I experience empathy with another, the empathized experience *is located in* another subject and not in myself:

> The subject of the empathized experience, however, is not the subject empathizing, but another. And this is what is fundamentally new in contrast with memory, expectation, or the fantasy of our own experiences. (Stein 1989, p. 10; Stein 1917, p. 10)

For Stein, empathy, then, is a non-primordial experience "which announces a primordial one" (Stein 1989, p. 14; Stein 1917, p. 14). When I feel the other's joy, I do not experience it primordially as *my* joy. Let us examine Husserl's account in more depth.

---

[9] Scheler has an interesting discussion of identification in the case of a hypnotist and the hypnotized subject (see Scheler 1954, pp. 25–26).

Edmund Husserl: "The Nexus of Empathy"

Husserl's *Cartesian Meditations*, the main *published* discussion of empathy in his lifetime,[10] is a condensed but, by his own admission, deeply unsatisfactory and one-sided account.[11] Here Husserl elaborates on 'apperceptive transference'. I have to apprehend the other's body with a 'transfer of sense' from my own body (*Sinn von einer apperzeptiven Übertragung von meinem Leib*, Husserl 1950, p. 140). I see your hand grasping the pen and I apprehend in a certain sense what your grip is like. Indeed, I can see that your grip is tight or loose or awkward. I *see* your 'grip'. This is empathy at the level of bodily motricity involving a transfer of sense because of bodily similarity.

This perceptive apperception, furthermore, is not an inference in the sense of an explicit act of reasoning. Every apperception is based on a 'primal instituting' (*Urstiftung*), where the sense is initially acquired. In Husserl's example, a child sees a scissors and learns to use it and, then, through apperceptive transfer, can manipulate a different shaped scissors, not by explicit inference and comparison, but because of an inner universality and transcendence built into the experience itself. Husserl speaks of this 'transference' (*Übergträgung*) as experientially driven – it is an analogical widening of experience. Husserl insists on the universality of this component of experience; experience already includes an openness. It includes a set of possibilities. I never grasp just this-here-now particular (this was the error of classical empiricism, Husserl already claimed in his Second *Logical Investigation*). Rather, I am always *carried forward* into some futural possibility that Husserl will call 'transcendence'. Seeing a pair of scissors (Husserl 1950, § 50) and understanding its 'purposive sense' (*Zwecksinn*) is an act that contains a certain expansiveness or *freedom*—the freedom to transfer the sense in other situations and to other objects. Husserl insists that the grasp of the universal is already implicated in the particular. Sensory experience is already open to an *horizonal* enlargement of sense. This leads Husserl, more and more, to situate empathy and the grasp of the other within the overall holistic context of a 'world'. Every act of grasping the other has to also expand to consider the horizon of the other.

---

[10] Husserl published just a handful of books in his lifetime, but his *Nachlass* in the Husserliana edition extends to more than 42 volumes of research notes and lectures.

[11] Husserl's *Cartesian Meditations* was originally published only in French in a translation by Emmanuel Levinas and Gabrielle Pfeiffer; Husserl withheld the German version for reworking and his draft appeared posthumously as Husserliana Volume One (Husserl 1950).

The Personalistic Attitude and the Life-World

In the *Cartesian Meditations*, Husserl insists that what one experiences first and foremost (*zunächst und zumeist*, as Heidegger puts it) is another "living subject" ('*das lebendige Subjekt*') and, moreover, a subject encountered *within his or her world:*

> This living subject is the subject of actual life [...] standing towards his congeners [*mit seinesgleichen*] in a nexus of empathy [*Einfühlungszusammenhang*]. (Husserl 1989, p. 382; Husserl 1952, p. 372)

Husserl gradually saw empathy as involving an overall stance or attitude that he called, in *Ideas* II, the "personalistic attitude". The personalistic is the primary attitude – more basic than even the natural attitude. Husserl writes that the personalistic attitude is

> [...] the attitude we are always in when we live with one another, talk to one another, shake hands with another in greeting, or are related to another in love and aversion, in disposition and action, in discourse and discussion.
> (Husserl 1989, p. 192; Husserl 1952, p. 183)

Empathy is then something inside the personalistic attitude, a component of it. We are in the attitude of going with the flow (*Dahinleben*), living immersed in the present. Husserl connects empathic recognition with the recognition of persons as persons (Husserl 1952, p. 377). Thus, he writes in *Ideas* II:

> When I, in the act of empathy, experience others, I do not take them only as the experienced of my experiences, as my possession [*nur als Erfahrenes meiner Erfahrungen, als meine Habe*], but as subjects like myself, hence as subjects for their surrounding world, valid for them [*als Subjekte für ihre Umwelt*], and at the same time as subjects for one and the same world [...]. (Husserl 1989, p. 365; Husserl 1952, p. 354)

In his *Natur und Geist* lectures (Husserl 2002), that Stein attended, Husserl maintained that the objective world was the outcome of intersubjective agreement between communicating minds linked by 'empathy'.

The Shared Experience of One and the Same World

I live in a world of others in what Husserl calls a "nexus of empathy" (*Einfühlungszusammenhang*, Husserl 1952, p. 369). We are aware of each other as occupying perspectives on that world. One experiences immediately that the other occupies a point of view other than one's own. There is always an experienced *gap* between the two subjects' experiences, *overlapping* horizons that never coincide. To help overcome the inevitable 'gap' between subjects, Husserl strongly emphasizes the primacy of the *co-presence* of the other living subject in the "living present" (*lebendige Gegenwart*)—also emphasized by Scheler and by Alfred Schutz (1967; 1932). Schutz writes:

> Once the existence of the Thou is assumed, we have already entered the realm of intersubjectivity. The world is now experienced by the individual as shared by his fellow creatures, in short, as a *social* world. (Schutz 1967, p. 139)

Schutz continues a little later, emphasizing the 'we-relation' (*Wirbeziehung*):

> The living social relationship can occur in several different forms. In its purity and fullness, as we shall show later in detail, it is tied to the bodily givenness of the Thou in the face-to-face situation. As such, it is a living face-to-face relationship or a pure We-relationship [*Wirbeziehung*]. From it derive their validity all intentional Acts of Other-orientation not belonging to the domain of directly experienced social reality, all ways of interpreting subjective meaning, and all possibilities of attending to the worlds of mere contemporaries and of predecessors. (Schutz 1967, p. 157; Schutz 1932, p. 174)

The fullest form of empathic experience (for Husserl, Stein, Schutz, and Levinas) is the face-to-face confrontation in temporal co-presence. The full intuition of the other interconnects with the intuition of the world (*Weltanschauung* or *Weltapperzeption*). As Husserl writes (employing the term *Mitsein* usually associated with Heidegger):

> Being with others [*Mitsein von Anderen*] is inseparable from me in my living self-presencing [*in meinem lebendigen Sich-selbst-gegenwartigen*], and this co-presence of others is foundational for the worldly present, which is in turn the presupposition for the sense of all world-temporality with worldly-co-existence (space) and temporal succession. (Husserl 1973b, p. xlix)

This *Mitsein*, for Husserl, means we are embedded in a social and historical *Lebenswelt*. We are always 'coming from somewhere' in our interpretations of others (as Ricoeur emphasizes). This 'somewhere' includes our formative experiences personal, familial, educational, social-economic, class, gendered. The historical world of others permeates our individual styles (my dress, accent). Human subjectivity is always a 'co-subjectivity' (*Mitsubjektivität*) with others in the shared, evolving, historical world.

Husserl on the Belonging to the 'Interhuman Present' (die mitmenschliche Gegenwart)

Human beings possess an overall 'consciousness of world' (*Weltbewusstsein*). We apprehend others in the 'horizons' of their world. The primary experience of the objective world is of the *one shared world* "for all" (*für Jedermann*, Husserl 1974; Husserl 1969, p. 244). Husserl's late work interrogates the intersection between self-experiencing subjectivity, empathy with others, and the *Mitwelt* (a term, associated with Heidegger or Schutz, that does appear in his mature work). He writes in the *Crisis:*

> Factually I am within an interhuman present [*in einer mitmenschlichen Gegenwart*] and within an open horizon of humankind; I know myself to be factually within a generative framework [*generative Zusammenhang*], in the unitary flow of a historical development in which this present is mankind's present and the world of which it is conscious is a historical present with a historical past and a historical future. (Husserl 1970, p. 253; Husserl 1954, p. 256)

Husserl recognizes the complexity of this mutual shared co-consciousness that he calls *Ineinandersein*, being-with-one another: "That is egoic being-with-one-another [*Miteinandersein*], operating experientially with one another, valuing, acting, theorizing" (Husserl 1973b, p. 485, my translation). We intersect experientially with one another in mutual stance-taking. I co-validate what the other wishes, or inwardly negate it, while seeming to affirm it, but either way our wishes are intertwined. I stamp a value on the other's wish and calibrate it with my own. I intuitively grasp the *sense* of what you are wishing, and I weave my attitude and wishing around it. Husserl writes in a late text:

> Here, then, we have a wholly new concept of relying-on-each-other, being-dependent-on-one-another, being-interconnected-with-each-other [*Aufeinander-angewiesen, Voneinander-abhängig-sein, Miteinanderverbunden-sein*] and, of a more general kind, of being-with-one-another, coexisting [*Miteinander-sein, Koexistieren*], being-unified in being temporal, just as real being, being an ultimate substrate has a completely new, i.e, absolute sense [...]. (Husserl 1973b, pp. 193–4, my translation)

Empathy and Intersubjectivity: The Chicken and the Egg

A discussion of empathy in the phenomenological tradition would not be complete without reference to Martin Heidegger, for whom empathy is subsidiary to the existential dimension of Dasein that he terms 'being-with' (*Mitsein*). Heidegger inverts the Husserlian account that gives primacy of empathy. Heidegger rejects any account of empathy that casts it in the form of one isolated 'monadic' subjectivity reaching out to another subjectivity that is hermetically sealed. For Heidegger, Dasein as 'being-in-the-world' (*In-der-Welt-sein*) is always already 'being-with' (*Mitsein*) or 'being with one another' (*Miteinandersein*) and already has the character of 'disposition' (*Befindlichkeit*) or being in a shared mood. Human beings are already intrinsically social, collective and sharing this disposition with others ("*Teilung*" *der Mitbefindlichkeit*, Heidegger 1977, p. 215; Heidegger 1962, p. 205). Heidegger writes in *Being and Time* that one can only empathize with others because we already are in the world with others:

> But just as opening oneself up [*Sichoffenbaren*] or closing oneself off is grounded in one's having Being-with-one-another as one's kind of Being [*Seinsart des Miteinanderseins*] at the time, and indeed is nothing else but this, even the explicit disclosure of the Other in solicitude grows only out of one's primarily Being with him [*primären Mitsein*] in each case. [...] In this phenomenally 'proximal' manner it thus presents a way of Being with one another understandingly [*eine Weise des verstehenden Miteinanderseins*]; but at the same time it gets taken as that which, primordially and 'in the beginning', constitutes Being towards Others [*Sein zu Anderen*] and makes it possible at all. This phenomenon, which is none too happily designated as 'empathy' [*Einfühlung*], is then supposed, as it were, to provide the first ontological bridge from one's own subject, which is given proximally as alone, to the other subject, which is proximally quite closed off. (Heidegger 1962; pp. 124–125; Heidegger 1977, pp. 165–66)

For Heidegger our intersubjective social presence is shared existence (*Mitdasein*), even when specific others are absent (Heidegger 1992, p. 239; Heidegger 1994, p. 329), a point he inherited from Scheler (even Robinson Crusoe never leaves the human world). In fact, although Heidegger is emphasizing his departure from Husserl, his discussion is very reminiscent of the mature Husserl's discussion of the social world as disclosed practically in the natural attitude, especially as found in *Ideas* II (which Heidegger had read in manuscript, as he acknowledges in *Being and Time*, Heidegger 1962, p. 489). Our world is never just a 'thing world' (*Dingwelt*) but is socially (and historically) configured.

Does the capacity for empathy rest on a more primordial being together (*Mitsein*) as Heidegger asserts? There are places where Scheler––who influenced Heidegger in this regard—agrees. He regularly invokes emotional fusion with others as prior to separateness (e. g., Scheler invokes Freud's account of the early bond between mother and infant – where there are not yet two separate identities, Scheler 1954, p. 26).[12] There is not yet individuation. However, Freud's claims have been contested. Early neonate – and even child in the womb – experiments show the individuality of the infant in the womb – moving separately, sleeping at different times from the mother and so on (Trevarthen 2008; Gratier & Trevarthen 2008). Indeed, Scheler himself acknowledges that the pregnant mother already differentiates herself from the child in her womb (Scheler 1954, p. 26).

For Heidegger '*das Man*' expresses this collective, undifferentiated manner of living alongside others. But Husserl's position (and, in fact, Stein's and Merleau-Ponty's) remains that our experience begins from and is anchored around my first-personal experience. There must be a pure 'I' that is the center and unifying source of my rays of consciousness. In an absorbed encounter, the self may not be prominent, but I can quickly take a position, e. g., 'this crowd is too excited', 'I don't belong here'. Husserl's position can be summarized accurately with a quotation from the linguist Émile Benveniste – 'only an "I" can say "we"'. For Husserl, personal egoic subjectivity has primacy and *founds* intersubjectivity, since all conscious life is necessarily egoic-life, but subjectivity itself opens itself up to and can only function within intersubjectivity. They are equiprimordial.

The subject on its own could never progress without intersubjective communication through language. The community, likewise, cannot survive without being constantly re-instituted (Husserl speaks of *Nachstiftung*), and re-activated by individual intentionality. There is no ultimate priority of either intentional subjectivity or *Mitsein*; rather, there is, for Husserl, the fact that all intentional subjectivity, by virtue of its intrinsic intentionality, already transcends itself towards the communal world (the life-world) and is in turn supported by that world. Indeed, subjectivity, empathy and intersubjectivity all need the cocooning of the life-world (*Lebenswelt*), one of Husserl's late discoveries.

---

12 Indeed Merleau-Ponty, especially in his late notes collected in *The Visible and the Invisible* also follows Scheler and Heidegger in postulating a kind of anonymous collective 'flesh' in which human subjects originally find themselves – a kind of prior intersubjectivity or 'wild being' (Merleau-Ponty 1968, pp. 182–83) that he frequently invokes, sometimes using the Husserlian German term *Ineinander* (Merleau-Ponty 1968, p. 116, p. 172, p. 174, p. 180, p. 204).

Conclusion

Empathy is a central human capacity, a *sui generis* form of other-apprehension that preserves the difference between self and other (*Einfühlung* is not *Einsfühlung*, identification). For phenomenology, empathy is not primarily unconscious mimicry, or the identification of oneself completely with the other, nor is it identical with rational mind-reading, applying hypotheses, Sherlock Holmes inference, and so on. In his research manuscripts, Husserl's never-ending exploration uncovered many different layers to the self-other relation, and its being-with-one-another. Indeed, self-experience at its very heart is already a kind of other-experience. Self-awareness is in a sense an immediate encounter, but it always encounters the self or ego in a specific way, which suggests a difference or distantiation. I never grasp myself wholly even if there is no immediate objectivation of the self (which is another specific intentional act with its own structure). There are many layers to Husserl's account both of self-experience and 'other-experience' (experience of other persons). There is always the experience of the lived body, the fleshly 'co-presence' (*Kompräsenz*) of the other, which is apprehended through my lived body. But there is also – as Husserl came more and more to realize – the need for what he called "horizon-intentionality". We encounter one another in an already humanized and socialized world, against the background of the *Lebenswelt*. I experience the other person in an already given interpersonal context, one revealed by the antecedent 'personalistic attitude'.

References

Baron-Cohen, Simon (1995): *Mindblindness. An Essay on Autism and Theory of Mind.* Foreword by Leda Cosmides and John Tooby. Cambridge, MA: The MIT Press. Bradford Book.

Baron-Cohen, Simon (2011): *The Science of Evil. On Empathy and the Origins of Cruelty.* New York: Basic Books.

Baron-Cohen, Simon (2012): *Zero Degrees of Empathy: A New Theory of Human Cruelty and Kindness.* New York: Penguin Books.

Bazalgette, Peter (2017): *The Empathy Instinct. How to Create a More Civil Society.* London: John Murray.

Bloom, Paul (2016): *Against Empathy: The Case for Rational Compassion.* London: Bodley Head.

Coplan, Amy/Goldie, Peter (Eds.) (2011): *Empathy: Philosophical and Psychological Perspectives.* Oxford: Oxford University Press.

Depew, David (2005): "Empathy, Psychology, and Aesthetics: Reflections on a Repair Concept". In: *Poroi. An Interdisciplinary Journal of Rhetorical Analysis and Invention* 4(1), pp. 99–107.
Dilthey, Wilhelm (1977): "Ideas Concerning a Descriptive and Analytical Psychology". In: Zaner, Richard M./Heiges, Kenneth L. (Eds. and Trans.): *Dilthey's Descriptive Psychology and Historical Understanding*. The Hague: Martinus Nijhoff, pp. 23–120.
Ewert, Otto (1995): "Einfühlung". In: *Historisches Wörterbuch der Philosophie*. Vol. II. Darmstadt: Wissenschaftliche Buchgesellschaft [1972, corrected 1995], cols. 396–397.
Fidalgo, António (1993): "Edith Stein, Theodor Lipps und Einfühlungsproblematik". In: *Phänomenologische Forschungen* 26/27, pp. 90–106.
Goldman, Alvin I. (1992): "Empathy, Mind, and Morals". In: *Proceedings and Addresses of the American Philosophical Association* 66(3), pp. 17–41.
Goldman, Alvin I. (2006): *Simulating Minds: The Philosophy, Psychology, and Neuroscience of Mindreading*. Oxford: Oxford University Press.
Gratier, Maya/Trevarthen, Colwyn (2008): "Musical Narrative and Motives for Culture in Mother-Infant Vocal Interaction". In: *The Journal of Consciousness Studies*, 15(10–11), pp. 122–158.
Harold, James (2000): "Empathy with Fictions". In: *British Journal of Aesthetics* 40(3), pp. 340–355.
Heidegger, Martin (1962): *Being and Time*. Trans. John Macquarrie/Edward Robinson. New York: Harper & Row.
Heidegger, Martin (1977): *Sein und Zeit*. Gesamtausgabe 2. Frankfurt: Vittorio Klostermann.
Heidegger, Martin (1992): *History of the Concept of Time. Prolegomena*. Trans. Theodore Kisiel. Bloomington: Indiana University Press.
Heidegger, Martin (1994): *Prolegomena zur Geschichte des Zeitbegriffs*. Petra Jaeger (Ed.). Gesamtausgabe 20. Frankfurt: Vittorio Klostermann.
Hume, David (1978): *Treatise on Human Nature*. L. A. Selby-Bigge (Ed.). 2nd ed. rev. P.H. Nidditch. Oxford: Clarendon Press.
Husserl, Edmund (1913): *Ideen zu einer reinen Phänomenologie und phänomenologischen Philosophie. Erstes Buch: Allgemeine Einführung in die reine Phänomenologie*. Karl Schuhmann (Ed.). Husserliana III/1. The Hague: Martinus Nijhoff, 1977.
Husserl, Edmund (1950): *Cartesianische Meditationen und Pariser Vorträge*. Stephan Strasser (Ed.). Husserliana I. The Hague: Martinus Nijhoff, 1950. Dordrecht: Springer, 1991.
Husserl, Edmund (1952): *Ideen zu einer reinen Phänomenologie und phänomenologischen Philosophie. Buch II: Phänomenologische Untersuchungen zur Konstitution*. Marly Biemel (Ed.). Husserliana IV. The Hague: Martinus Nijhoff.
Husserl, Edmund (1954): *Die Krisis der europäischen Wissenschaften und die transzendentale Phänomenologie.Eine Einleitung in die phänomenologische Philosophie*. Walter Biemel (Ed.). Husserliana VI. The Hague: Martinus Nijhoff.
Husserl, Edmund (1969): *Formal and Transcendental Logic*. Trans. Dorion Cairns. The Hague: Martinus Nijhoff.
Husserl, Edmund (1970): *The Crisis of European Sciences and Transcendental Phenomenology. An Introduction to Phenomenological Philosophy*. Trans. David Carr. Evanston: Northwestern University Press.
Husserl, Edmund (1973a): *Zur Phänomenologie der Intersubjektivität. Texte aus dem Nachlaß. Erster Teil: 1905–1920*. Iso Kern (Ed.). Husserliana XIII. The Hague: Martinus Nijhoff.

Husserl, Edmund (1973b): *Zur Phänomenologie der Intersubjektivität. Texte aus dem Nachlaß. Dritter Teil. 1929–1935.* Iso Kern (Ed.) Husserliana XV. The Hague: Martinus Nijhoff.

Husserl, Edmund (1974): *Formale und transzendentale Logik. Versuch einer Kritik der logischen Vernunft. Mit ergänzenden Texten.* Paul Janssen (Ed.). Husserliana XVII. The Hague: Martinus Nijhoff.

Husserl, Edmund (1989): *Ideas Pertaining to a Pure Phenomenology and to a Phenomenological Philosophy. Second Book. Studies in the Phenomenology of Constitution.* Trans. Richard Rojcewicz/André Schuwer. Dordrecht: Kluwer.

Husserl, Edmund (2002): *Natur und Geist. Vorlesungen Sommersemester 1919.* Michael Weiler (Ed.). Husserl Materialien IV. Dordrecht: Kluwer.

Husserl, Edmund (2014): *Ideas for a Pure Phenomenology and for a Phenomenological Philosophy.* Trans. Daniel O. Dahlstrom. Indianapolis: Hackett.

Laurand, Valéry (2005): "La sympathie universelle : union et séparation". In: *Revue de Métaphysique et de Morale* 4, pp. 517–535.

Liddell, Henry George/Scott, Robert/Jones, Henry Stuart (1996): *A Greek-English Lexicon.* Oxford: Oxford University Press.

Lipps, Theodor (1905): "Weiteres zur 'Einfühlung'". In: *Archiv für die gesamte Psychologie* 4(4). Leipzig: Wilhelm Engelmann, pp. 465–519.

Lipps, Theodor (1909): *Leitfaden der Psychologie.* Leipzig: Verlag von Wilhelm Engelmann.

Lipps, Theodor (2018): "The Knowledge of Other Egos". Timothy A. Burns (Ed.). Marco Cavallaro (Trans.). In: *The New Yearbook for Phenomenology and Phenomenological Philosophy* 16, pp. 261–282.

Lotze, Rudolf Hermann (1868): *Geschichte der Aesthetik in Deutschland.* München: J.G. Cotta [reprinted Leipzig: F. Meiner, 1913].

Makkreel Rudolf A. (1996): "How is Empathy Related to Understanding?". In: Nenon, Thomas/Embree, Lester (Eds.): *Issues in Husserl's Ideas II. Contributions to Phenomenology.* Dordrecht: Springer.

Marder, Michael (2012): "The Life of Plants and the Limits of Empathy". In: *Dialogue*, 51(2), pp. 259–273.

Merleau-Ponty, Maurice (1968): *The Visible and the Invisible.* Trans. Alfonso Lingis. Evanston: Northwestern University Press.

Moran, Dermot (2004): "The Problem of Empathy: Lipps, Scheler, Husserl and Stein". In: Kelly, Thomas A./Rosemann, Phillip W. (Eds.): *Amor Amicitiae: On the Love that is Friendship. Essays in Medieval Thought and Beyond in Honor of the Rev. Professor James McEvoy.* Leuven, Paris, Dudley: Peeters, pp. 269–312.

Prinz, Jesse (2011): "Against Empathy". In: *Southern Journal of Philosophy* 49(1), pp. 214–233.

Scheler, Max (1913): *Zur Phänomenologie und Theorie der Sympathiegefühle und von Liebe und Hass. Mit einem Anhang Über den Grund zur Annahme der Existenz des fremden Ich.* Halle: Niemeyer [reprinted Fromm Verlag, 2011].

Scheler, Max (1913/1916): *Der Formalismus in der Ethik und die materiale Wertethik. Neuer Versuch der Grundlegung eines ethischen Personalismus.* In: *Jahrbuch für Philosophie und phänomenologische Forschung* 1(1913); 2(1916). Now in: Scheler, Max (1954): *Gesammelte Werke* 2. Maria Scheler (Ed.). Bern, München: Francke Verlag.

Scheler, Max (1973a): *Formalism in Ethics and Non-Formal Ethics of Values. A New Attempt Toward a Foundation of An Ethical Personalism*. Trans. Manfred S. Frings/Roger L. Funk. Evanston: Northwestern University Press.
Scheler, Max (1973b): *Wesen und Formen der Sympathie*. Bern, München: Francke.
Scheler, Max (2008): *The Nature of Sympathy*. Trans. Peter Heath. London, New York: Routledge.
Schliesser, Eric (Ed.) (2015): *Sympathy: The History of a Concept*. Oxford: Oxford University Press.
Schütz, Alfred (1932): *Der Sinnhafte Aufbau Der Sozialen Welt. Eine Einleitung in Die Verstehende Soziologie*. Wien: Springer.
Schütz, Alfred (1967): *The Phenomenology of the Social World*. Trans. George Walsh/Frederick Lehnert. Evanston: Northwestern University Press.
Smith, Adam (2002): *The Theory of Moral Sentiments*. Knud Haakonssen (Ed.). Cambridge: Cambridge University Press.
Stein, Edith (1917): *Zum Problem der Einfühlung*. Edith Stein Gesamtausgabe 5. Freiburg, Basel, Wien: Herder 2008.
Stein, Edith (1989): *On the Problem of Empathy*. In: *The Collected Works of Edith Stein*. Vol. 3. Trans. Waltraut Stein. Washington D.C.: ICS Publications.
Stein, Edith (2000): *Philosophy of Psychology and the Humanities*. In: *The Collected Works of Edith Stein*. Vol. 7. Trans. Mary Catharine Baseheart/Marianne Sawicki. Washington D.C.: ICS Publications.
Szanto, Thomas/Moran, Dermot (Eds.) (2015a): "Special Issue on Empathy and Collective Intentionality. The Social Philosophy of Edith Stein". In: *Human Studies* 38(4), pp. 445–600.
Szanto, Thomas/Moran, Dermot (Eds.) (2015b): *The Phenomenology of Sociality: Discovering the "We."* London, New York: Routledge.
Titchener, Edward Bradford (1909): *Lectures on the Experimental Psychology of the Thought-Processes*. New York: The MacMillan Company.
Trevarthen, Colwyn (2008): "The Musical Art of Infant Conversation: Narrating in the Time of Sympathetic Experience, without Rational Interpretation, before Words". In: *Musicae Scientiae* Special Issue 2008, pp. 11–37.
Vendrell Ferran, Ingrid (2015): "Empathy, Emotional Sharing and Feelings in Stein's Early Work". In: *Human Studies* 38(4), pp. 481–502.
Vischer, Robert (1873): *Über das Optische Formgefühl: Ein Beitrag zur Aesthetik*. Leipzig: Hermann Credner.
Zahavi, Dan (2010): "Empathy, Embodiment and Interpersonal Understanding: From Lipps to Schutz". In: *Inquiry* 53(3), pp. 285–306.

Methodological and metaphysical issues

Thomas Nenon
Philosophy as a Fallible Science

Abstract: This chapter revisits Husserl's famous essay "Philosophy as a Rigorous Science" to examine what Husserl says there about mental states and how his views about the differences between mental states and physical objects are related to his idea of philosophy as a possible science. I argue that phenomenological philosophy as a science does depend on a different mode of access to the phenomena than third-person observation, namely through an analysis of intentionality as the mode of access to one's mental states, i.e. through a first-person approach. However, as an analysis of the structures of intentional experience and the objects that present themselves in experience, phenomenology does not depend on the indubitable reliability of one's own direct awareness of (at least some) one's individual mental states.

Husserl's own critique of naturalism was first and most notably introduced just over one hundred years ago with the publication of the essay "Philosophy as a Rigorous Science" (Husserl 1987).[1] However, his proposal about the alternative to a naturalistic approach to mental states and our access to them, and the relationship between his views about our access to our own mental states and his conception of the status of philosophy as a rigorous science that would be an alternative to naturalistic approaches, in this essay is still not completely clear. In order to clarify the phenomenological method and its continued relevance as a method for philosophy in general, and to answer the question about whether and to what extent Husserl remained committed to the project of phenomenology as described in this early essay, as the key to realizing philosophy's aspirations to be a science at all, the first step would be to address these questions in that order. In a second, much briefer step, then, I will address the question about whether Husserl's views on these issues later changed and how these affect his views about the viability of phenomenology as a means to achieve the traditional goals of philosophy as he describes them in the essay.

The overall goal, Husserl states, is to establish philosophy as a "rigorous science ... that fulfills the loftiest theoretical needs and makes possible a life that is

---

[1] The page numbers listed in the citations will be taken from the original publication in 1911 in the journal *Logos*. The page numbers are listed in the margins of the Husserliana edition as most other scholarly editions of the essay. The translations into English are my own, but the page number from the Quentin Lauer's English translation (Husserl 1965) will be also provided.

ruled by purely rational norms in an ethical and religious regard" (Husserl 1987, p. 289; Husserl 1965, p. 71). However, the primary aims of the essay are much more modest. Its primary purpose is the refutation of what Husserl perceives as a two-fold threat to the very possibility of philosophy as a scientific enterprise, namely reductionism in the guise of naturalism on the one hand, and historicism on the other. The former he sees as a threat because it recognizes only empirical truths about externally observable events as valid forms of knowledge. The latter denies the very possibility of philosophical truth at all by reducing philosophical claims to expressions of the mentalities of the cultures and societies that formulate them, while denying the possibility of some means of adjudicating their validity. At stake, then, is the question whether and how philosophical claims can be reasonably confirmed or denied so that philosophy could join the rank of disciplines that, though "imperfect" (Husserl 1987, pp. 290–91; Husserl 1965, p. 73), either because they are incomplete or perhaps even flawed because they include content that will subsequently be refuted, have established means for deciding between competing claims about the content appropriate to their fields. In this sense, to be a "rigorous science" is to be a "discipline" in the sense that it limits itself to claims that can be verified by means of an established method.

However, instead of addressing the question of how philosophy can be established as a science in a straightforward way, Husserl instead addresses naturalism primarily in terms of the difference between the nature of external objects and our knowledge about them and the nature of mental events, what he calls "*das Psychische*," and how we know about them. He notes that naturalism includes both the tendency to reduce consciousness, including "all of the things given to consciousness as intentional and immanent" ("*aller intentional-immanenten Bewußtseinsgegebenheiten*") (Husserl 1987, p. 295; Husserl 1965, p. 80) and the tendency to reduce all "absolute ideas and norms" to natural phenomena as well. By "nature" he means a nexus of spatio-temporally located, causally determined phenomena.

Before turning to the primary object of his critique, namely the naturalization of consciousness, Husserl does note that the naturalistic approach to ideas is in a sense self-contradictory because even the naturalistic enterprise itself relies on norms like truth and falsehood as well as on the value of scientific thinking and rationality, which are non-natural entities and cannot themselves be empirically grounded. His argument for this observation is quite brief, but the reference to similar arguments from the *Prolegomena* to the *Logical Investigations* indicates the direction those arguments would take.

Along these same lines, the topic of consciousness is then explicitly broached as Husserl addresses the foundational relationship between philosophy and the natural sciences, along with all other "*Tatsachenwissenschaften*" ("factual" or "empirical sciences"), maintaining that the basic premises on which the empirical sciences are based are mere assumptions about the nature of reality and of knowledge that cannot be empirically justified for the very same reasons that Husserl had shown in the *Prolegomena* to the *Logical Investigations*. There, we recall, Husserl had focused on the foundational role that basic logical principles play for the idea of science, showing that it is impossible to ground them empirically without undermining their status as logical principles. Hence, Husserl's primary target in his refutation of naturalism here is the newly emerging field of experimental psychology that proposes to address questions about the nature of consciousness and the laws that govern it using methods adopted from mechanistic models that have been so successful in explaining and predicting natural phenomena in the externally observable world. Along the way, however, he again refers back to the refutations of psychologism from the *Logical Investigations*, when he notes that adherents of naturalist psychology not only claim to be able to unlock the mysteries of consciousness by means of experimental psychology, and thereby to render all other approaches to the study of psychic phenomena superfluous, but also to provide a solution to basic problems in the theory of knowledge, since knowledge is after all also a mental event.

Husserl's response to this challenge in the 1911 essay indicates, however, that he not only still endorses all of the arguments against this kind of approach that were presented in the *Logical Investigations*, but that he has in the meantime formulated a positive program of phenomenology that he sees as an appropriate alternative to psychologism and other naturalistic programs. If the fundamental problem for the "theory of knowledge (*Erkenntnistheorie*)" is the question of the relationship between "consciousness and being" (Husserl 1987, p. 301; Husserl 1965, p. 89), then being must be conceived as "the correlate of consciousness, ... as something 'meant' (or 'intended') by consciousness (*als bewußtseinsmäßig 'Gemeintes'*)." Instead of the study of consciousness as something factual (i.e. observable and measurable) and factual objects, he contends that a theory of knowledge must try to identify essential structures of consciousness, one of which had been identified in the *Logical Investigations*, following Brentano, as intentionality, i.e. directedness to an object of some kind or another. Hence in this kind of investigation, a study of the objects of consciousness is an essential part of the project, but explicitly as "intentional objects," since the objects may or may not be as they are intended and in some cases might not exist at all. However, part of what makes an intention 'this one' instead of 'that one' is the object towards which it is directed, even if it does not actually exist. Thinking about Santa Claus and thinking about Sherlock Holmes are different intentions, just as thinking about Dermot Moran is different from either of them, even though only one of these three objects actually exists. Moreover, such an investigation can also consider how we come not only to intend objects. It can also examine what kinds of experiences count as confirming (or disconfirming and thereby forcing us to revise) those intentions, i.e. which experiences legitimately "fulfill" those intentions and "exhibit (*erweisen*)" its object as "'actual' (or real) ('*wirkliches' Seiendes*') being" (Husserl 1987, p. 301; Husserl 1965, p. 90). Instead of attempting to establish empirically measurable correlations between consciousness and beings, he proposes an investigation into "what it means that objectivity *is* and that it showed itself as existing and existing in this way, must be made evidently and thereby completely comprehensible purely in terms of consciousness itself" (Husserl 1987, p. 302; Husserl 1965, p. 92). This investigation would study a different kind of correlation than the empirical correlations between observable and measurable events. It would focus on the kinds of objectivities intended in different intentional acts and what kinds of experiences would appropriately count as confirmation of the correctness of different kinds of intentions. Instead of being based on external empirical observations, they would be based on reflection about what he calls "essential structures" of consciousness and objectivity as such that, in his view, are presupposed by any empirical study. This kind of investigation is what he calls here "phenomenological" studies.

He thereby sets up an opposition between a "phenomenology of consciousness" versus a "natural science of consciousness" or psychology, each with its own "attitude" ("*Einstellung*") (Husserl 1987, p. 301; Husserl 1965, p. 90) and adds, "... that psychology concerns itself with 'empirical consciousness,' with consciousness in the attitude of experience, as something existing within the nexus of nature; by contrast, phenomenology concerns itself with 'pure' consciousness, i.e. consciousness in the phenomenological attitude" (*ibid.*).

This is not new, and I do not think very controversial up to this point. However, there are a few issues that still need to be addressed. First of all, what does he mean by "pure" consciousness? Does he just mean what we now commonly call "first-person awareness" or something else? If the two are not the same, then is "pure consciousness" simply a sub-species of first-person self-awareness or something different entirely? How do we get from one to the other? We also need to clarify what is entailed by his claim that the results obtained through phenomenology are given "evidently and completely" (*ibid.*). Does this mean that phenomenology can attain results that are not only true, but certain? Does it imply that phenomenology is therefore infallible? Can it really overcome the limitations of all of the other genuine, and yet "incomplete" sciences described at the beginning of the essay?

In order to address these questions, we first need to see what he says about our access to our own mental states. One of the primary failings of experimental psychology, he says, is its refusal to employ information derived from what Husserl calls "the immanent sphere": "The consistent fundamental direction of this psychology is the rejection of any direct and pure analysis of consciousness – namely of the 'analysis' and 'description' of the what is given in the various possible directions of immanent seeing – in favor of indirect fixations of psychological and psychologically relevant facts ..." (Husserl 1987, p. 302; Husserl 1965, p. 92). Husserl grants that this kind of psychology, just like similarly oriented sociology, can discover interesting, in some cases valuable regularities, but it presupposes a genuine familiarity with the phenomena it investigates, in his view, because without it "a systematic science of consciousness that conducts immanent research into the psychic lacks any possibility of a deeper comprehension and final scientific assessment" (Husserl 1987, p. 303; Husserl 1965, p. 93). In other words, empirical psychology might be able to register interesting regularities about, for instance, correlations between students' ability to memorize specific information and the order and frequency of the way that material is presented, but what it cannot do is clarify what we mean by memory itself.

Husserl, for instance, in his lectures on the "Phenomenology of Inner Time-Consciousness" famously distinguishes what one might call "primary memory" or "retention" from "secondary memory" or what we normally and more commonly call "memory," identifying very important differences between them. Or to use a more problematic example perhaps, at a phenomenology conference a few years ago, we heard about an experiment in which Australian researchers were trying to identify the part of the brain in which prejudices arise. Part of the experimental design involved presenting the research subjects with some examples of statements that the researchers considered "prejudices," such as certain behavioral characteristics associated with different ethnic groups, and then trying to find an area of the brain that exhibited increased activity when the subjects were responding to statements that exhibited such prejudices. Of course, the problem would be to distinguish "prejudices" from other, perhaps well-founded beliefs the subjects might hold. One person's prejudice might be something another person considers a politically incorrect, but nonetheless well-founded belief. So the researchers' first task would be to define exactly what one means by a "prejudice" and to come up with a way of deciding which beliefs are prejudices, which ones are accurate but perhaps over-hasty generalizations, and which ones are well-founded beliefs that are normally processed almost automatically. Husserl's comments about the limits of empirical psychology amount to saying that without a solid basis for such preliminary distinctions, the scientific value of any experiments that purport to tell us something about memory or prejudice is subject to doubt. One needs to merely recall the contentious discussions of Herrnstein and Murray's book *The Bell Curve* (Herrnstein and Murray 1994) for an illustration of how fundamental assumptions about the nature of intelligence and how it is measured are crucial in assessing the validity of any studies that purport to tell us something significant about how intelligence is distributed differently across various racial groups or not.[2]

Husserl's claim is that what he calls "immanent seeing," in English usually called "introspection," is crucial to addressing these kinds of issues adequately. The reason for this is that what are commonly referred to as "mental events" or "mental states" are by their very nature different and differently given than external objects are. He agrees with the view, common since Locke at the latest, that the ultimate justification for concepts must be based, directly or indirectly on an "experience" of the objects they name. Where he parts ways with many of the adherents of modern naturalistic psychology and philosophical approaches related to it is the question of how narrowly this notion is to be understood. The experience of externally perceptible objects, *"Dinge"* (translated sometimes as "things," but perhaps better simply as "physical objects") is always mediated by external perceptions. We know about them through the properties that we experience in external perception – their shapes, odors, and textures as given to us in visual, olfactory, and tactile perceptions of them. Moreover, these "things" essentially and always have multiple kinds of properties and perhaps even changing properties as they persist throughout time: "They are, *what* they are only in this unity, only in the causal relationship to or conjunction with each other do they obtain their individual identity (substance) and obtain it as the bearer of 'real properties'" (Husserl 1987, p. 310; Husserl 1965, p. 104).

He contrasts this with the world of the psychic, mental events that he refers to as "phenomena." They are different from physical objects, he observes. It is worthwhile to list the differences Husserl identifies:

1. "Mental events are distributed across monads (analogically and not metaphysically speaking) that do not have windows and stand in commerce with each other only through empathy." I take this to be equivalent to the insight guiding the distinction between things presented in the third-person and the first-person perspective. The first-person perspective is precisely that which is only accessible to me alone and to which I have access in other people based on things that they say or do, which I take as indications or expressions that communicate them to me (when that does happen) (Husserl 1987, p. 311; Husserl 1965, p. 106). They have them and know about them without

---

[2] From a non-phenomenological standpoint, Stephan Jay Gould makes a similar point on this debate in his essay "Mismeasure by Any Measure." See Gould 1996.

necessarily having to see what their bodies say or do. I know about them in other people, by contrast, because of what I see them say or do.
2. "Psychic being, being as a 'phenomenon,' is as a matter of principle not a unity that could be experienced as individually identical across several particular perceptions, not even in perceptions of the same subject" (*ibid.*). We can perhaps call different events of desiring or believing the same in light of what it is that we desire or believe across them as the same, but as *mental events*, phenomena, they are not the same when entertained by different people or even one person at different times. This is different from a chair that is the same chair when perceived by different persons or by the same person at different times.
3. For this reason: "In the psychic sphere, there is in other words no difference between appearance and being" (Husserl 1987, p. 312; Husserl 1965, p. 106), which is why he uses the Greek word for appearance, i.e. phenomenon, as another name for them.
4. "Hence a phenomenon is not a 'substantial' unity, it has no 'real properties,' it does not have real parts, no real (*realen*) changes and no causality, all of these words understood in the sense of natural science" (Husserl 1987, p. 312, Husserl 1965, p. 106).
5. In contrast to "things," mental events do not last across time (*ibid.*). It is therefore impossible to go back and confirm or disconfirm their properties by means of another look at them.
6. It is not experienced as "something that appears" (*ibid.*) in the sense of something that lies behind the appearing.
    a. It is the appearing of the event itself, which is why Husserl also describes it as an *Erlebnis*, an experience in the sense of thing that occurs in one's mental life. It does not have an existence apart from this occurring.
    b. Moreover, and this is *extremely* significant, it is "experience that is seen (*erschautes*) in reflection, appears as itself through itself ..."
    c. "... as now ..."
    d. "... and as continuously sinking back into a having-been (*Gewesenheit*) in a way that we can observe" (*ibid.*).

    Mental life is then populated by events that are events in mental life precisely because I am aware of them. Otherwise, they would not occur *as experiences*, they would not be phenomena or appearances at all. Moreover, each of them as an event occurs at a particular time, which is always a now that is constantly receding back into a having-just-been. This makes clear that what Husserl means by consciousness here is at the same time always also *self-consciousness*, mental events or states

that I am immediately aware of as my own, as appearing now, and as continuously appearing right afterwards as no-longer now.
7. Together, these events make up a "flux of phenomena" that constitute the mental life of the subject whose mental life it is (Husserl 1987, pp. 313–14; Husserl 1965, p. 108), "a 'monadic' unity of consciousness" (Husserl 1987, p. 313; Husserl 1965, p. 108) that is not a substance behind these appearances, but rather the unitary flow of these very events.
8. As mentioned earlier with regard to the status of the objects of consciousness, the mental events are all "intentional," they are ways of relating to things that they themselves are not: "All of them have the title 'consciousness of,' and 'have' a 'meaning,'" and 'intend' something 'objective,' that – even if there is a standpoint from which it is called a 'fiction' or 'reality' – can be described as an 'immanent objectivity,' as 'intended as such' and intends it in this or that mode of intending it." (Husserl 1987, p. 313; Husserl 1965, p. 109)
9. Each of them has some "essence" ("*Wesen*") that can be seen, described and captured in language, and it is these essences that are presupposed by psychology whenever it speaks of mental events of different kinds such as perceptions, memories, desires, or beliefs.

These observations are not the whole story Husserl tells about mental life, but they do include some very important points. First of all, mental events are directly given to the person whose mental life they compose, but they are given to others only indirectly by means of expressions and indications that are available to others from the third-person perspective. This means not only that mental events are things that are directly available only in the first-person perspective, but also that the first-person perspective involves not just that these mental events take place, but that the I who has them is aware of them as such. Hence mental life as described here involves not just first-order mental states (beliefs, desires, etc.) but at least some second-order mental states, namely the awareness of these mental states. Otherwise, they would not be phenomena at all because they would not be an appearing. They might be happenings, but not appearing. Or to use language from the Continental instead of the analytic tradition, the kind of consciousness Husserl is describing here also involves subjectivity as self-consciousness.

Another important point is that, if their appearing and their being are one and the same, then it would seem that it makes no sense to ask if they are actually occurring when they occur since their appearance is their occurring and vice-versa. In this regard, then, Husserl's description seems consistent with Descartes' basic insight that it makes no sense for the subject to doubt the existence of *cogitationes* as existing, i.e. as taking place as thoughts whenever I am thinking in the broadest sense. However, Husserl's statements by themselves do not imply, in fact they seem to deny, Descartes' interpretation of what is going on when Husserl describes these mental events as things that have a kind of being in themselves as events without necessarily pointing back to some substrate of which they are the properties or predicates (point 4 mentioned above). Together they constitute a "flux" a mental life as a series of mental events taking place in ever new now-moments and receding back while retaining a sense of temporal order within that flux of mental life, but this is not the same thing as seeing them as "properties" of a subject that somehow underlies them as a substance.

I should note, parenthetically, that Husserl has a more robust notion of personhood than mere subjectivity as self-awareness according to which a person's beliefs, values, and actions both constitute and point back to a personal character that one acquires of the course of a life; and that this "character" shares some features of traditional notions of substance such as continuity over time and across changes, but there are also very important differences even here from the way we conceive of external objects as substances with properties conceived of in causal terms.

An important question, especially for the question of the relationship between the nature of our access to mental states and the reliability of phenomenology of a science is whether Husserl here is assenting to Descartes' (and Brentano's) view that the subject not only has direct access to its mental states, but that the directness assures that the subject has complete and infallible access to all of his or her own mental states as long as one withholds assent to the further assumption that the things that they represent are indeed truly consistent with the way we represent them, i.e. if we concentrate on them simply as representations and withhold judgment about the states of affairs and objects of which they are representations. Certainly, Husserl's statements about the identity of appearing and being that we just recounted seem to suggest that he endorses this view. And many commentators (and critics) of Husserl also take this to be his view.[3] They read his comments here and in his descriptions of phenomenological reduction in the *Ideas I* and the lectures from 1907 later published under the title *The Idea of Phenomenology* as resting on this very assumption, namely that the first step towards phenomenology as a science is to bracket out assumptions

---

[3] Dan Zahavi, in his discussion of the relationship between phenomenology and introspection (Zahavi 2017, pp. 6–29), names Dennett as a prime example of this false equation. See Dennett 1997 and 1991. However, one can also read Jacques Derrida's critique of the notion of a "pure voice" as assuming that Husserl's "pure consciousness" is a form of "pure presence," i.e. immediate and infallible givenness (Derrida 1967).

about the validity of our position-takings, our intentions, by refraining from assent to any judgments about the existence and nature of the objects of our intentions and concentrating on our mental states, our intentions as such, about which we cannot be mistaken if we focus on them *as such*, namely as actual occurrences in our mental life.

However, this is not the path that Husserl actually takes in this essay (or in either of the other two programmatic works). In "Philosophy as a Rigorous Science," he introduces the project of phenomenology not in terms of a purported infallibility of access to one's mental states and the description of them as such, but rather in terms of what he calls "essential relationships" ("*Wesensbeziehungen*") or "essential connections" ("*Wesenszusammenhänge*") that obtain within the realm of pure reflection. Instead of making a claim about the completeness or infallibility of our access to mental life as such, he instead asserts that "Even if the phenomena as such are not [a part of] *nature*, they still have an *essence* that can be grasped and grasped adequately in immediate insight (*Schauen*)" (Husserl 1987, p. 314; Husserl 1965, p. 110).

The principle upon which phenomenology rests is then a sub-species of the principle of reason and knowledge in general.[4] The general principle, the so-called principle of all principles as stated in the *Ideas I* is "... that every originary presentive intuition is a legitimizing source of cognition, that everything originarily (so to speak, in its 'in-person' actuality) offered to us in 'intuition' is to be accepted simply as what it is presented as being, but also only within the limits in which it is presented there" (Husserl 1988, p. 44). Examples of such "originary presentive intuition" for natural events would be sense perceptions; in natural science, it would involve conducting the right kinds of experiments; for mathematical claims, it would be "doing the math"; for claims about essences, it would be eidetic intuitions in general, be they eidetic intuitions about spatial relationships in geometry or quantities in arithmetic, logical relationships in pure logic, or insights into the eidetic structures of what he is calling "consciousness" in this essay: "All statements that describe phenomena through direct concepts, do so, in as far as they are valid, based on eidetic concepts, hence through conceptual linguistic meaning that must be able to be cashed out in essential intuitions" (Husserl 1987, p. 314; Husserl 1965, p. 110). This, and not a purported complete and infallible access to one's mental states as such, is the basis for phenomenology as a science. Just like every other science, it must have its basis in some sort of intuition, and since it is making claims about what he calls "essences," its method must involve recourse to eidetic intuition.

---

4 For a fuller discussion of Husserl's notion of "reason," see Nenon 2004.

As I just suggested, phenomenological insights are not the only kind of eidetic insights based on eidetic intuition, since they are also the basis of other eidetic disciplines such as mathematics and formal logic. What distinguishes phenomenology from these other eidetic sciences is that phenomenology investigates eidetic structures not of space, quantities, or formal logic, but rather of what he is calls "consciousness" here. But what exactly does that mean if these are not descriptions of our mental states as events that we actually experience at various time points in our individual mental lives?

Husserl makes very clear that phenomenological claims are not empirical observations about individual mental events. Nor are they apodictic in the sense of supposedly infallible claims about mental events based on direct and privileged access to them. In fact, Husserl never claims in this essay that phenomenological claims are infallible. However, he does claim that eidetic claims in general are different from empirical claims and that they can be confirmed or refuted, namely through the method he calls "eidetic intuitions." His arguments in support of this assertion are derived not from an explanation of *how* this is possible, but rather from examples that to his mind demonstrate *that* it is possible. For instance, he says, it is clear to anyone who has experienced them that colors are different kinds of things than tones. This is not an empirical generalization, he believes, because if it were, then we would have to be able to imagine that we might encounter a color that were not different from a tone sometime in the future. But, he believes, that is not actually imaginable. Other examples would be the difference between "intuition" and "empty intending" or between "empty intending" and "fulfillment" or between "willing" and "perceiving." These are fundamentally different kinds of things and, when we think through the examples, we can ourselves "see" the differences – at first perhaps vaguely and imprecisely, but through further reflection and closer inspection much more clearly and distinctly. He also believes that these are not merely linguistic differences, but rather that the linguistic differentiations map more or less accurately the distinctions that one can verify for oneself in actual or imaginative variations on the reflective experience of the phenomena that the concepts refer to.

If phenomenology is then not a species of "introspection," if it does not rest primarily on the accuracy and reliability of our access to our own mental states, then why does Husserl insist that phenomenology has such an intimate connection with non-naturalistic conceptions of "consciousness"? And if many of the eidetic structures that are the topics of phenomenology have to do with differences between different kinds of objects, for instance between "natural objects" conceived of along the lines of modern natural science and "mathematical objects" such as numbers, or between either of them and "use-objects" or "persons," then why is it that Husserl claims that it is by reference to the eidetic structures of "consciousness" that phenomenology gains its insights? I do not think that Husserl provides a direct and clear answer to this question, but I believe that we can nonetheless discern what the answer should be based on things he does say in this essay and elsewhere.

First of all, with regard to the objects of psychology, mental states, I think the answer is clearest. The nine points summarized above make clear that Husserl believes that the very notion of mental life and mental events would not make any sense if we did not have access to them directly, if we did not already possess something like an at least implicit self-awareness of some of some of the mental events that make up our mental lives. As I have formulated it elsewhere with regards to subjects, "it takes one to know one" and even more strongly, "it takes one that knows it is one (namely the bearer of mental states) to know one," i.e. the very idea of "mental states" as such is based not on external observations of ourselves and others, but on the direct experience we have of at least some of them (Nenon 2002). To put it another way, only entities that have second-order mental states, an awareness of some first-order mental states, or self-consciousness, would ever come up with the category "mental states" or "consciousness" at all. That does not mean that only subjects, beings with second-order mental states or consciousness, have consciousness, but just that they are the only entities that are aware of them as such. I do believe, for instance, that there are some entities, for instance simpler non-human animals, that have beliefs and desires, i.e. consciousness or first-order mental states, without possessing self-consciousness, i.e. second-order mental states. Which entities these are is an empirical question. But I also believe that only beings with second-order mental states attribute any kind of mental states to other entities. I do not believe that most animals do that, even though we do know that they react to other animals' behaviors. We ourselves as humans often do more than that, we often rightly think we understand what animals or other persons are thinking and what they want because we understand what mental states are, based on our own awareness of having them ourselves. Husserl's claim about the necessary role that phenomenology plays for empirical psychology is that the latter presupposes mental life and uses distinctions drawn from our own everyday experience of our mental life as such in its own work, some of which are adequate, but some of which are vague and unclear. Phenomenological reflection on these phenomena can help draw those distinctions much more clearly and avoid problems and confusions resulting from a failure to reflect closely and carefully enough on the nature of these phenomena.

But what about other kinds of objects that are not mental events? Here the key insight guiding Husserl's assertions that a phenomenological approach to "consciousness" is essential for a proper philosophical approach to them as well, is the fact that these objects are, whether we recognize it or not, intentional objects. In spite of our everyday notion of objects as objective in the sense of just being "out there" with specific inherent properties that have nothing to do with us and how we know about and think of them, Husserl maintains that these non-mental objects are also, in an important sense, *phenomena*, that is, things that do or do not appear to us and are conceived of in relation to how they appear to us (including not just how they are present, but also how they are absent). Moreover, the way they appear to us is always mediated through *meanings*. "Objectivity" itself, in the sense of modern natural science, is a specific way of looking at things that involves complicated abstractions from our everyday experience and is in this sense also only conceivable in terms of a specific intentional framework that Husserl calls "nature" in this essay. In fact, the term "intentions" is actually shorthand for the full term as introduced in the First Logical Investigation, namely "meaning-intentions (*Bedeutungsintentionen*)." "Fulfillment" as the direct experience of the things as intended is the fulfillment of a "meaning-intention." So phenomenological investigations into the essential structures of different kinds of objectivities is possible only because they are also constituted in terms of some meanings, and meanings are present only for entities that possess consciousness. In *Ideas I*, Husserl expresses this essential co-relationship in terms of the necessary correlation between *noesis* and *noema*, whereby for any intended object there is a corresponding intending of that object and vice-versa. This also explains why, before Husserl turns to the phenomenological analysis of mental states as such, he first addresses consciousness as intentional, maintaining that the proper understanding of the structures of intentionality is the key to the solution of traditional problems in the theory of knowledge (Husserl 1989). Such a view can overcome what Husserl calls the naiveté not only of experimental psychology as a science, but of empirical sciences as a whole, which make certain assumptions about the nature of knowledge and objectivity that may or may not be correct and certainly are not themselves empirically verifiable.

Finally, as we mentioned above, Husserl also maintains that empirical sciences, including experimental psychology, presuppose norms that they themselves cannot ground. The fact that the very idea of norms only makes sense with regard to entities that possess consciousness seems almost obvious. Normative thinking involves a certain kind of awareness of things, an awareness not just of how things are, but also of how they are *not* in terms of some other desired or imagined way that they could or should be. Therefore, any analysis of the essential structure of norms will also at least implicitly involve an analysis of consciousness. Moreover, the most important normative questions are questions about the appropriateness of our own beliefs, values, and volitions. All of these things are mental events and our normative evaluations of them are forms of second-order mental states, beliefs about the appropriateness of those beliefs, valuings, and volitions. Self-assessments necessarily involve self-awareness, but also positive or negative valuing of those first-order mental states of believing, valuing, and willing that can also give rise to a resolve about how to believe, value, or will differently in the future. Husserl is very clear in the *Kaizo* articles and in his ethics lectures (Husserl 2004) that this ability that persons have based on their possession of second-order mental states and the ability of second-order mental states such as feelings of pride or shame to affect our own behavior in the future is the condition for the possibility of freedom. Similarly, normative evaluations of other persons can pertain to "objective" properties of them, such as their height or complexion, but more often concern about what they think, say, or do. Moral or legal evaluations of ourselves and others then implicitly involve imputations of freedom, i.e. second-order mental states and the role they can play in our lives so that any analysis of moral and legal norms also implicitly involves reference not just to structures of consciousness as such, but of self-consciousness as well.

In fact, as Husserl notes at the very beginning of the essay "Philosophy as a Rigorous Science," the traditional goal of philosophy is the normative assessment of the adequacy of our most basic theoretical beliefs and of the practical norms that guide our actions. Phenomenology, in Husserl's view, is the philosophical approach that is suited to make this possible in a systematic way by means of a thoroughgoing analysis of the intentional life of the subject, not just in terms of its theoretical claims, but also its valuing and willings, and above all through an eidetic analysis of what kinds of experiences would appropriately count as the fulfillment of different kinds of beliefs, values, and volitions. In each case, these fulfillments will have the general structure of some kind of intuitions. Moreover, the basis for the phenomenological claims about essential relationships between intentions and fulfillments will itself have the form of intuitions, namely eidetic intuitions into the structure of those essential relationships. This is Husserl's answer to the question of how to make philosophy a rigorous science.

Does this make it an infallible science? According to the common interpretation that bases phenomenology on the direct and complete access to one's own mental states, one could perhaps read Husserl's claims about philosophy as a rigorous science as also implying that it is or could be an infallible science if one just focuses carefully enough on those mental events as such. Many critics of Husserl attack this view, taking it to be Husserl's. And indeed, Husserl's own analyses, for instance in the Third Part of the *Ideas II*, show that there are many cases in which a person is not completely and directly aware of what he or she wants or values, but only discovers those things by interpreting his or her actions in a way that is similar to the way I discover what other people value or want based on the actions I see them perform. What I have tried to argue in this chapter is that this is not the way Husserl's argument proceeds, even in this relatively early lecture. Rather, his claim about the ability of phenomenology to fulfill the aspirations of philosophy to become a science are based on claims about the possibility of confirming (or refuting) philosophical assumptions and positions through eidetic intuitions.

Are eidetic intuitions then apodictic, and does this make them infallible? They are indeed, when they turn out to be genuine insights, not subject to empirical refutation and thus provide a different kind of certainty than empirical verification offers. This holds for all eidetic truths, not just philosophical ones as discovered through phenomenology. As Husserl points out in the *Logical Investigations* and many other places, statements about logical principles and mathematical states of affairs are either true or false, they are not probable. However, that is not to say that people who make claims about logical principles or mathematical matters are ever infallible. If you want to show that they are not, all you need to do is to give a test in a class on formal logic or mathematics; and even the expert teacher of those areas will start to have some problems, if they ingest enough alcohol for instance. So Husserl's claim that phenomenology can set philosophy on the path to becoming a rigorous science does not mean that phenomenological philosophy is a perfect science, but only that phenomenology recognizes the appropriate method for adjudicating philosophical claims in a manner analogous to the methods for adjudicating claims in other areas of scientific inquiry. When he says that phenomenological claims can be verified "evidently and completely," the claim is analogous to claims in logic and mathematics. In principle, we can all do the math and see that a given answer to a math problem is the correct one "evidently and completely." In practice, it is a good idea to check the math and look over a logical proof to make sure one has not made a mistake because the practitioners of logic, mathematics, and phenomenology are always still fallible human beings.

Against this background, one can read the famous passages from some of Husserl's final writings not as abandonments of the phenomenological project but as recognitions that it is an ongoing process and never a completed task. The famous passage from the *Formal and Transcendental Logic* in which he admits that even purported eidetic insights require verification across time (and, what he does not say but could: across various subjects) is not inconsistent with the claims from the *Logos* essay on my reading. When he says in the *Crisis* that the "dream of phenomenology is dreamt out (*ausgeträumt*)" (Husserl 1969,

p. 508), he is referring not to the possibility and necessity of philosophy as a science, but his hopes about phenomenology as an intellectual movement that would come to dominate philosophy. In fact, one can see the emphasis on self-responsibility and self-critical reflection in his final work as a continuation of precisely the phenomenological project that was articulated in print for the first time just a little over a century ago in his essay on "Philosophy as a Rigorous Science."

References

Dennet, Daniel (1991): *Consciousness Explained*. Boston: Little, Brown.
Dennett, Daniel (1997): *The Intentional State*. Cambridge, MA: The MIT Press.
Derrida, Jacques (1967): *La voix et le phénomène*. Paris: Presses Universitaires de France.
Herrnstein, Richard/Murray, Charles (1994): *The Bell Curve: Intelligence and Class Structure in the American Life*. New York: Simon and Schuster.
Husserl, Edmund (1965): "Philosophy as a Rigorous Science". Trans. Quentin Lauer. In:
Husserl, Edmund: *Phenomenology and the Crisis of Philosophy*. New York: Torchbook, pp. 71–147.
Husserl, Edmund (1969): *Die Krisis der europäischen Wissenschaften und die transzendentale Phänomenologie*. Reinhold N. Smid (Ed.). Husserliana VI. The Hague: Martinus Nijhoff.
Husserl, Edmund (1987): "Philosophie als strenge Wissenschaft". In: Husserl, Edmund: *Aufsätze und Vorträge (1911–21)*. Thomas Nenon/Hans Reiner Sepp (Eds.). Husserliana XXV. Dordrecht: Kluwer, pp. 3–62
Husserl, Edmund (1988): *Ideen zu einer reinen Phänomenologie und phänomenologischen Philosophie. Erstes Buch: Allgemeine Einfuhrung in die reine Phänomenologie*. Karl Schuhmann (Ed.). Husserliana III. The Hague: Martinus Nijhoff.
Husserl, Edmund (1989): "Fünf Aufsätze über Erneuerung". In: Husserl, Edmund: *Vorträge und Aufsätze 1911–1921*. Nenon, Thomas/Sepp, Hans Reiner (Eds.). Husserliana XXVII. Dordrecht: Kluwer, pp. 3–124.
Husserl, Edmund (2004): *Einleitung in die Ethik, Vorlesungen Sommersemester 1920/1924*. Henning Peucker (Ed.). Husserliana XXXVII. Dordrecht: Kluwer.
Gould, Stephan Jay (1996): *The Mismeasure of Man* (revised and expanded edition). New York: Norton.
Nenon, Thomas (2002): "Freedom, Responsibility, and Self-Awareness". In: *The New Yearbook for Phenomenology and Phenomenological Philosophy* 2, pp. 1–22.
Nenon, Thomas (2004): "Husserl's Conception of Reason as Authenticity". In: *Philosophy Today* 47, pp. 65–72.
Zahavi, Dan (2017): *Husserl's Legacy*. Oxford: Oxford University Press.

Burt C. Hopkins
Back to Husserl. Reclaiming the Traditional Philosophical Context of the Phenomenological 'Problem' of the Other: Leibniz's "Monadology"

Abstract: On the basis of an analysis of Husserl's account of the phenomenological problem of the Other in the *Cartesian Meditations*, I highlight its Leibnizian philosophical context. This context permits the non-Cartesian problem underlying Husserl's account to come into relief, namely, that of the constitution of not just "the Other" but the multiplicity of Others and the corresponding problem of the constitution of the unity behind their community. I argue that both the "first person" approach to subjectivity and the "one ego, two attitudes" account of the distinction between empirical and transcendental egos elide Husserl's non-Cartesian account of the constitutive source of the community of others.

Introduction

Husserl initially viewed the pure Ego as lacking essential content. This view was based on his account of the scope and limits of the evidence through which the pure Ego becomes manifest. This evidence is manifest to reflection and exhibits the pure Ego as the identical source of each essentially transient ray of regard that animates a given, and equally transient, lived-experience whose consciousness is *actionally* modified and thus exhibits the modality of the *cogito*. The peculiar status of such animation is characterized by Husserl as a transcendency in immanence, in the recognition that while the regard's conscious intention belongs to the immanent contents of the *cogito*, it nevertheless exceeds them in its function to render thematic its (the *cogito*'s) object (*cogitatum*). Despite its transcendency, however, the evidence in which the ray of regard is manifest perishes according to Husserl with the expiration of the transient stream of the lived-experience to which it belongs. Husserl drew two conclusions from this state of affairs. One, each ray of regard must have a source in something other than the manifold of transient streams of lived-experience, namely, in the pure Ego that shoots forth anew an essentially different ray of regard in each lived-experience animated by it. Two, that this pure Ego, other than its status as the source of the essentially different rays of regard animating the manifold of actionally modified consciousnesses that belong to it, is empty of essential content.

The question before us is what considerations led Husserl in the *Cartesian Meditations* not only to come to view the pure Ego as the possessor of essential content, but also to reformulate phenomenology as a whole in terms of the self-explication of the monadically concrete Ego. The answer is recollection—or, rather, a deepened understanding of its scope and capacity as a re-presentation to make present again (*vergegenwärtigt*) the objects of past experiences and these experiences themselves. Husserl's deepened understanding of recollection goes beyond previously perceived objects or one of the Ego's past lived-experiences to include its capacity to make present the essential connection between the structure and content of the Ego's present lived-experience and that of contents belonging to its horizonal lived-experience. In Husserl's account of the pure Ego as a pure identity and nothing more, the non-actional lived-experiences that composed the essential horizon of its actionally modified lived-experiences were described as belonging to the Ego. By this Husserl meant that the pure Ego, in accord with eidetic lawfulness, could always turn to any one of the non-actional lived-experiences and convert it into an actional *cogito* or incorporate it into such a *cogito* as its immanent content. But it also implied that, prior to the Ego's advertence and actional modification of the lived-experiences that compose its horizon, these lived-experiences do *not* belong to it. This is implied because other than the transient—and therefore non-essential—ray of regard (that issues from the pure Ego) whose transcendency in immanence animates (qua its actional modification of consciousness) each lived-experience in the mode of *cogito*, Husserl could find is no evidence for the pure Ego's existence, other than its empty identity as the source of these rays of regard.

All of this changes with Husserl's discovery that the non-actional lived-experiences that compose the horizon of actionally modified consciousness belong to the essential content of the Ego, and do so prior to either their actional modification or their inclusion in a consciousness that has been so modified. They belong to the Ego as "a *realm of the innate 'apriori'* (Husserl 1960, p. 81), without which an ego as such is unthinkable." Husserl characterizes this innate *apriori* as a realm of *passive* syntheses that generates both the objects that are already there (and therefore function as pregiven material) for the *active* synthesis accomplished by the Ego in the mode of the *cogito* and as a realm that generates the Ego *itself*. The passive syntheses that generate the Ego "produce a unity of *universal genesis of the ego*" (Husserl 1960, p. 109), a unity that according to Husserl is responsible for both the succession and simultaneity of the lived-experiences that constitute the single multiformity of the Ego's concrete intentional life. Thus, Husserl now can write that "[o]nly through the phenomenology of genesis does the ego become understandable" (Husserl 1960, p. 109).

Husserl's evidence for these remarkable claims is rooted in the Ego's capacity to, at any time, interrogate a given horizon and ask "*what 'lies in it'*" (Husserl 1960, p. 82), and thus "*explicate* or unfold it, and '*uncover*' the potentialities of conscious life at a particular time." This explication is accomplished in "awakenable recollections," to which there belongs "as horizon, the continuously intervening intentionality of possible recollections (to be actualized on my initiative, actively), up to the actual Now of perception." The horizons are thus "'predelineated' potentialities," the form of which "has its 'history'" (Husserl 1960, p. 112), insofar as these potentialities are the accomplishments of passive syntheses. Husserl therefore maintains that, "without putting ourselves back in the realm of passivity ... the meditating ego can penetrate into the intentional constituents of experiential phenomena themselves ... and thus find references leading back to a 'history' and accordingly making these phenomena knowable as formations subsequent to other, essentially antecedent formations" (Husserl 1960, p. 113). Husserl holds that by following the chain of intentional references in which are awakened historically ordered recollections, "we soon encounter eidetic laws governing a passive forming of perpetually new syntheses (a forming that, in part, lies prior to all activity and, in part, takes in all activity itself)." And he also maintains that this forming is itself something that "points back to the 'primal instituting' of this form" (Husserl 1960, p. 113).

The Universal Principle Responsible for Passive Syntheses

The universal principle of passive synthesis is association, by which Husserl understands not what he considers to be the naturalistic distortions of the genuine intentional concepts of association but "the conformity to eidetic laws on the part of the constitution of the pure Ego" (Husserl 1960, p. 114). The pure Ego here is the concrete monadic Ego, to which belongs not only the objects meant and constituted as existent (or non-existent) by its transcendental subjectivity but also the substrate of the habitualities that are constituted by its positing of these objects. At issue in the pure Ego's genesis are what Husserl refers to as the "eidetic laws of compossibility" (Husserl 1960, p. 109) that govern "the existence and possible existence together" of manifold streams of lived-experiences whose simultaneity and succession "constitute the intrinsic [*reellen*] contents of the transcendental Ego's being" (Husserl 1960, p. 109). The universal form of the Ego's genesis is time, understood as the unity form of both the streams of lived-experience that begin and end and of the one stream of lived-experiences that constitutes the singularity of the Ego's intentional life. Because the transcendental Ego's genesis not only occurs in time but also occurs in time now understood as the formal regularity pertaining to a universal genesis, Husserl draws the conclusion that "the ego constitutes himself in, so to speak, the unity of a 'history'" (Husserl 1960, p. 109). All the particular phases of the multiplicities belonging to each single lived-experience, as well as the multiplicity of lived-experiences themselves, have their respective places in the successively and simultaneously ordered unity of the universal genesis of the Ego.

Under the heading of "compossibility" Husserl is addressing the problem, so far unresolved in his phenomenology, of precisely how the temporal syntheses accomplish the unification for which they are responsible; namely, the unification of the manifold of transient lived-experiences into one streaming lived-experience belonging to the pure Ego. His answer, association, does not—on his view —signal a relapse into the empirical theory of association, the Humean concept of which he criticized in the *Logical Investigations* on the grounds that it is unable to provide a satisfactory account of the origin of the non-particular meanings presupposed by logic and by cognition generally. Rather, the phenomenological treatment of association is distinguished from the empirical theories by its focus on the eidetic lawfulness that governs the givenness of a similarity from a multitude of distinct phenomena. Specifically, Husserl maintains that similarity is constituted from a multitude composed of a minimum of two intuitive data presented to a consciousness, whose intentionality 1) encompasses them in their mutual distinctness, and 2) intends the similarity that exceeds this distinctness. The similarity here is purely passive, in the precise sense that it appears to consciousness whether or not it is noticed; what is presented as similar in the appearance of similarity is what Husserl calls "an overlaying of each [intuitively prominent datum] with the objective sense of the other" (Husserl 1960, p. 142). With this overlaying of sense "there takes place an association at a higher level" (Husserl 1960, p. 147), namely, a *"fusion,"* whereby the appearance of the one intuitively prominent datum is "supplemented" by the appearance of the other. This supplementation accommodates the sense of the one datum to the other, such that each appears as the analogue of the other, with the result that these analogous senses *"found phenomenologically a unity of similarity"* (Husserl 1960, p. 142). Because minimally two distinct (intuitively prominent) data are eidetically requisite for an association, Husserl refers to this primal associative form as "pairing."

Husserl's writings published during his lifetime do not provide phenomenological details in support of his claims about the passive character of the syntheses constitutive of time, especially (as one would expect from his remarks here) about the relation of these syntheses' universal principle of association to the constitution of the streaming succession and simultaneity of temporality and to the multiple modes of the internal time-consciousness of these temporalities. He does, however, work out in detail precisely how the basic structure of association, pairing, functions in the constitution—"in my monad" (Husserl 1960, p. 154)—of the meaning and being of, first, the other Ego, and then, other Egos. In order to understand precisely how Husserl thinks the Ego "can experience what is constituted in me as nevertheless other than me" (Husserl 1960, p. 154) and how, related to this, "I can identify a Nature constituted in me with a Nature constituted by someone else (or, with the necessary precision, how I can identify a Nature constituted in me with one constituted in me *as* a Nature constituted by someone else" (Husserl 1960, p. 155), the account of the distinction he makes between the psycho-physical human ego, the factical transcendental Ego, and the *eidos* transcendental Ego needs first to be addressed.

Eidetic Analysis of the Self-Constitution of Transcendental Ego

Prior to the *Cartesian Meditations*, Husserl's articulation of the phenomenological Ego draws on the distinction between the empirical Ego and pure Ego. To the being of the former the index of existence that characterizes all the objects given in the natural attitude remains inseparable, while to the being of the latter this index has been annulled subsequent to the phenomenological reduction. The result of this reduction is the merely intentional being of the essentially empty pure Ego. In the *Cartesian Meditations*, Husserl's account of the pure Ego's concreteness complicates considerably the phenomenological status of the Ego. Husserl speaks, first of all, of the Ego as "himself *existent for himself* in continuous evidence; thus, in himself, he is *continuously constituting himself as existing*" (Husserl 1960, p. 100). By the "Ego" here he evidently means the transcendental Ego, as his marginal note to this passage reads "Transcendental Self-Constitution" (Husserl 1960). He also speaks of "I, the reduced 'human Ego' ('psychophysical' Ego)" (Husserl 1960, p. 129), who is constituted, "accordingly, as a member of the 'world' with a multiplicity of 'objects outside of me'" (Husserl 1960, p. 129). And, again, he refers to "the transcendental Ego, who constitutes in his constitutive life everything that is ever objective for me—the Ego of all constitutions, who exists in his actual and potential life-processes and Ego-habitualities and who constitutes in them not only everything objective but also himself as identical Ego" (Husserl 1960, p. 130). Finally, there is the "eidos Ego," which Husserl characterizes as follows:

> After transcendental reduction, my true interest is directed to my pure Ego, to the uncovering of this factical Ego. But the uncovering can become genuinely scientific, only if I go back to the apodictic principles that pertain to this Ego as exemplifying the eidos Ego; the essential universalities and necessities by means of which the fact is to be related to its rational grounds (those of its pure possibility) and thus made scientific (logical). (Husserl 1960, p. 106)[1]

The appearance evident here of seemingly multiple Egos has given rise to two basic interpretative tendencies among phenomenologists. One maintains that the appearance of more than one Ego, for example, of a human or psychological Ego and the Transcendental Ego, is the result of the one and only identical Ego being apprehended in two different attitudes, the natural and the phenomenological. The other basically elides Husserl's talk of an Ego or Egos altogether in connection with phenomenological constitution and replaces such talk with the contrast between the "first person perspective" in which the subject is given and the "third person" perspective in which objects are given. Both of these tendencies, however, make it difficult (albeit for different reasons) to address a key aspect in Husserl's account of the transcendental Ego's self-constitution in evidence according to the distinctions noted directly above. Specifically, this aspect concerns the essential distinction at work in his account of the transcendental Ego as the constitutive source of all objects, as well as the source of the multiplicity that unites these objects themselves as unities of meaning and existence that belong together. The latter multiplicity, according to Husserl, includes the Ego itself as an empirical or worldly object among other objects, and all of these objects are characterized by Husserl as belonging to the concrete essence of the constituting Ego as an inseparable internal determination—but *not* as an identity. Husserl characterizes the transcendental Ego as a self-constitution involving two essentially distinct aspects that are nevertheless united in determining it as a whole. Thus, on the one hand, there is the constituting dimension of the Ego, which is responsible for the constitution of its own meaning

---

[1] Husserl's discussion of the "eidos Ego" reinforces the importance of 'eidetic intuition' (and, presumably, the 'eidetic reduction') for his conception of phenomenology. He writes in this connection: "'In itself', then, the science of pure possibilities precedes the science of actualities and alone makes it possible, as a science. With this we attain the methodological insight that, *along with phenomenological reduction, eidetic intuition is the fundamental form of all particular transcendental methods* (that both of them determine, through and through, the legitimate sense of a transcendental phenomenology)." (Husserl 1960, p. 106)

and being as an object among other constituted objects, and, on the other hand, there is the constituted meaning and being of the Ego itself so constituted, which is phenomenologically accessed as the *reduced* human Ego. Husserl therefore asks, "how I, the human Ego reduced to what is purely my own and, as thus reduced, included in the similarly reduced world-phenomenon and, on the other hand, I as transcendental Ego are related to one another?" (Husserl 1960, p. 131).

The first interpretative tendency's claim that there is one and only Ego, and that this Ego is the *identity* that constitutes itself as the unity underlying different manifolds of lived-experiences—one psychological the other transcendental—is therefore unable to account for the essential difference that Husserl maintains characterizes the transcendental Ego as *both* a constitutive *accomplishing* and as a constitutive *accomplishment*. While both modes of the transcendental Ego are unities, the unity of the former, according to Husserl, is a generative unity, in the exact sense that its unity functions to constitute both the units that compose the multitude of objects 'external' to the transcendental Ego that generates them and the unity of the multiplicity itself that encompasses this multitude as precisely a multitude of constituted objects. In other words, the constituting modality of the transcendental Ego responsible for the constituted meaning of objects, and, in so far as they possess being, their constituted being, is distinct from the constituted meaning and being of the mode of the Ego constituted by it. Husserl characterizes the unity of the constituted mode of the transcendental Ego— as a constituted unit among a multitude of other constituted units—as mundane. By this he does not mean the empirical or human Ego per se, but this Ego as a reduced phenomenon, which is constituted by the transcendental Ego through "a *mundanizing self-apperception*" (Husserl 1960, p. 130). Husserl characterizes the "mundanization" involved here by saying that "everything included in the ownness belonging to me transcendentally (as this ultimate Ego) enters, as something *psychic*, into 'my psyche'" (Husserl 1960, p. 130). Whatever phenomenological and philosophical difficulties Husserl's account here may involve, it is clear that for him *both* of these modes of the Ego presuppose the phenomenological attitude, as is evident by his characterization of the 'mundane' Ego as the *reduced* human Ego. The Ego that is the focus of the natural attitude is therefore the Ego *prior* to the reduction at issue in Husserl's account here, namely, the human (psychophysical) Ego. Talk of an identity of the Ego across the natural and phenomenological attitudes therefore makes sense with respect to the human Ego and the reduced mundane Ego. The distinction, however, between the mundane Ego, accessed as the constitutive accomplishment of the transcendental Ego, and the latter as the constituting source of this accomplishment, is a distinction that is made *within* the phenomenological attitude. It is therefore not properly a distinction that has its basis in the difference between the natural and phenomenological attitudes.

To interpret as identical the aspect of the Ego's self-constitution that is constituting and that aspect that is constituted, and to ascribe the difference between them as only an apparent one, determined by the character of two different apprehending attitudes, leaves out of account the difference in the descriptive character of the unity belonging to each of these egological dimensions that informs Husserl's account. The transcendental Ego, as the generative source of the meaning and being (or non being) of the manifold objects that belong to the world and are therefore outside of 'me' as the mundane Ego that is constituted as a member of this world, is 'one' in the sense of the unity that encompasses a multitude. Such a unity, as the unity of a multiplicity, is essentially different from the unity of the items that make up the multiplicity, which, in this case, are the constituted objects belonging to the world. Each of these worldly items—*including the reduced human Ego* (or the terminologically equivalent mundane Ego)—are 'one' among the other objects belonging to this world, each of which, as a member of this multiplicity, is likewise itself 'one'. In precisely this sense, as members of a multiplicity, the constituted units are comparable in a way that the Ego responsible for their constitution is not, for the constituting Ego's unity is precisely such as to not admit its comparison with other units; neither those it constitutes nor those of other putative constituting Egos. The constituting Ego's unity is incomparable with the unity of the objects it constitutes, because the being one of each of these objects is a one among a multitude of other objects, each of which is likewise one, while the constituting Ego's unity is precisely such as to not be a one among a multitude of objects. Likewise, incomparable is the constituting Ego's unity in relation to other constituting Egos, any one of which, as we will see, is necessary given to the constituting Ego in a mode other than that of the constituting Ego's own self-givenness as the unmediated source of all constitution.

To elide all reference to an Ego as either a constituting or constituted phenomenon in Husserl's account of transcendental subjectivity and to refer, instead, to the "first person" perspective of his account of subjectivity, is to leave out of account the role Husserl assigns to the Ego as a constitutive source of meaning and being (or non-being) and to fail to confront the fundamental phenomenological problem of egological unity. Husserl's engagement with subjectivity, being fundamentally reflective, therefore cannot be first personal. While the first person singular—"I"—and first person plural—"we"—figure in Husserl's investigation of the being and structure of subjectivity, each as a unit of meaning is not only maintained by him to be constituted by a dimension of subjectivity that is not unequivocally first personal, but also each is characterized as being uncovered as a reflected phenomenon by a phenomenological reflection whose proper subject can only be said to be "I" by equivocation.

From the shortcomings of these interpretations it does not, of course, follow that Husserl's account of the status of the transcendental Ego in phenomenology is consistent, let alone phenomenologically and philosophically compelling. However, the problem that neither interpretation can capture adequately is precisely the problem that Husserl endeavors to solve in the *Cartesian Meditations*, namely, how the transcendental Ego can constitute a meaning and being (and non-being) that, qua this meaning and being, transcends the meaning and being of the subjectivity that is its constitutive source—*while nevertheless being inseparable from this source's subjectivity.* Husserl's term for the transcendence in question here is 'immanent transcendency', which is similar to the term 'transcendency in immanence' that he used prior to the *Cartesian Meditations* to characterize the pure Ego's structural relation to the transient stream of lived-experience that has been actionally modified by it. The phenomenon indicated by 'immanent transcendency', however, is radically different, as it concerns not the pure Ego's relation to manifold lived-experiences that come and go but rather the relation of the object constituted in such experiences to this Ego now characterized as its constitutive source. Specifically, it concerns that object's meaning and potentially its existence as an ideality whose synthetic unity, on the one hand, is "'*external*' *to my own concrete Ego* (but not at all in the natural spatial sense)" (Husserl 1960, p. 136) while, on the other hand, "it is *still a determining part of my own concrete being*, the being that belongs to me as concrete Ego" (Husserl 1960, p. 136).

Husserl's account of the constitution of the meaning of the intentional object as an identity describes it as the correlate of multiplicities of modes of consciousness that belong together synthetically. Among these multiplicities Husserl maintains that there are syntheses that are verifying, in the precise sense that their intention is directed toward making evident and having as evident the meant object. When such syntheses take place, the meant object has the evident characteristic 'existing', and when they fail to take place it has the evident characteristic 'non-existing'. As such, these synthetic occurrences are characterized by Husserl as higher level intentionalities than those in which the intentional object's meaning is constituted, and are described by him "as acts and correlates of 'reason', essentially producible by the transcendental Ego, which pertain (in exclusive disjunction) to all objective senses" (Husserl 1960, p. 92). Thus, for Husserl, "*reason and unreason*, as correlative titles for being and non-being" (Husserl 1960, p. 91), become "an all-embracing theme for phenomenology" (Husserl 1960, p. 91). And, with the development of his notion of the pure Ego to include the concretion of the transcendental Ego as monad, this theme is seemingly threatened by his claim that transcendental phenomenology is transcendental philosophy and that, as such, it has the ability to solve the problems connected with the possibility of objective knowledge.

Transcendental Phenomenology's Appearance as Solipsism

The basis of this threat is transcendental phenomenology's appearance as solipsism, insofar as the very notion of 'immanent transcendency' seems to be a contradiction in terms. 'Transcendent' and 'immanent,' as *conceptual* opposites, are incapable of being combined, as the former refers to the status of something that is independent of the being of the subject and the latter to something that is included in the subject's mode of being. Husserl's response to this threat and the seeming contradiction that composes it is twofold. On the one hand, he explicates the very meaning of 'objectivity' to show that it *includes* a reference to subjectivity, albeit subjectivity in the plural, insofar as the very meaning of the objectivity of anything is inseparable from the conviction that it is the same for *all* subjects. On the other hand, he makes a distinction between the 'immanent transcendency' of the meanings constituted by and therefore belonging to the concrete transcendental Ego whose transcendental experience has been reduced by a phenomenological abstraction to what intrinsically belongs to it, and the 'immanent transcendency' of the meanings constituted by this Ego but that nevertheless do not intrinsically belong to it.

To the first 'immanent transcendency' there belongs what Husserl characterizes as the "*'primordial*' *transcendency*" (Husserl 1960, p. 136) of the world, namely, the world as a constituted unity that "*is inseparable from the original constitution itself*, with the inseparableness that characterizes an immediate *concrete* oneness" (Husserl 1960, p. 134). Where and insofar as this concrete oneness obtains, Husserl maintains "not only the constitutive perceiving but also the perceived existent belongs to my concrete very-ownness" (Husserl 1960, p. 134). Included in the primordial transcendency of the transcendental Ego's concrete ownness are sensuous data constituted as the Ego's immanent temporalities, the Ego as mere Ego pole and as its habitualities, transcendent objects as unities belonging to multiplicities of sensuous modes of appearance, and the body as it is lived (*Leib*)—in contrast to the body as one object among the other objects that belong to the objective world—that belongs to this Ego. To the second 'immanent transcendency' there belongs the intrinsically first non-Ego, namely, the other Ego, which makes possible the constitution of an objective nature and the whole objective world, as a nature and world identically there for an Ego-community that "includes me" (Husserl 1960, p. 137). This other Ego, together with others like it, become "constituted (in my sphere of ownness, naturally) as a community of Egos existing with and for each other—*ultimately, a community of monads*, which, moreover (in its communalized intentionality), constitutes the *one identical world*" (Husserl 1960, p. 137).

By means of what Husserl characterizes as the 'communalization' of constitutive intentionality, the multiplicity of transcendental Egos that make possible the objectivity of nature and the world, a multiplicity that he terms 'transcendental intersubjectivity', comes itself to have 'an *intersubjective* sphere of ownness'. And because of this, Husserl maintains that "the objective world does not, in the proper sense, *transcend* that sphere or that sphere's intersubjective essence, but rather inheres in it as an 'immanent' transcendency" (Husserl 1960, p. 137). Husserl explicitly connects *this* sense of immanent transcendency with the transcendental idealism of phenomenology, and therefore maintains that the "objective world as an *idea*" (Husserl 1960, p. 138) is essentially related to intersubjectivity, as its "ideal correlate" (Husserl 1960, p. 138). Thus, the idealism of phenomenology concerns precisely the constitution of the world's objective status in the intersubjectively communalized experience of a multitude of transcendental Egos, a multitude that, in the "ideality of endless openness" (Husserl 1960, p. 108) is itself constituted on Husserl's view, as we have seen, in the transcendental Ego's sphere of ownness.

The Non-Cartesian Problem of the Other for Transcendental Phenomenology

Before turning to Husserl's accounts of the intentional explications that "actually execute the transcendental idealism of phenomenology" (Husserl 1960, p. 108) two things need to be pointed out. One, that the transcendental Ego described in Husserl's account of the inseparability of its self-constitution and the objective world's constitution, is the "*all embracing eidos, transcendental Ego as such*, which comprises all pure possibility-variants of my factical Ego and this Ego itself qua possibility" (Husserl 1960, pp. 105–106). Two, the Leibnizian metaphysical context deliberately invoked by Husserl's account of the communalized experience of a multitude of transcendental Egos, as essentially involving "*a 'harmony' of the monads*" (Husserl 1960, p. 138), each one of which is a particular subject "equipped with mutually corresponding and harmonious constitutive systems" (Husserl 1960, p. 138) calls attention to a non-Cartesian metaphysical problem that Husserl thinks his phenomenology can solve. Specifically, the Leibnizian problem invoked by Husserl's terminology is that of establishing the objectivity and unity of the world in the face of the manifest plurality of other minds with uniquely subjective 'points of view', which is radically distinct from the Cartesian problem of establishing the existence of other minds, since for Leibniz the existence of not just one other mind but of a plurality of them is assumed from the outset.

Because Husserl's descriptions of the transcendental Ego are eidetic, they do not have 'empirical' significance, as signifying "factical occurrences in the factical transcendental Ego" (Husserl 1960, p. 104). Rather, they have the significance of essentially determined and therefore essentially necessary descriptions of "a *purely possible Ego*, a pure possibility-variant of my *factical Ego*" (Husserl 1960, p. 105); or, as in the case of the eidetic description of perception, they are descriptions of "free variations" (Husserl 1960, p. 105) that start out "by imagining this Ego to be freely varied" (Husserl 1960, p. 105), such that "the problem of exploring eidetically the explicit constitution of any transcendental Ego whatever" (Husserl 1960, p. 105) is set. Because in either case "the variation being meant is an evident one, accordingly as presenting in pure intuition the possibilities themselves as possibilities, its correlate is an *intuitive and apodictic consciousness of something universal*" (Husserl 1960, p. 105). This means for Husserl that "the eidos itself is a beheld or beholdable universal, one that is pure, 'unconditioned'—that is to say: according to its own intuitional sense, a universal not conditioned by any fact" (Husserl 1960, p. 105). Moreover, it means that the eidos "is *prior to all 'concepts'*, in the sense of verbal significations; indeed, as pure concepts, these must be made to fit the eidos" (Husserl 1960, p. 105).

Husserl makes it clear that "in the transition from my Ego to an Ego as such [i.e., an eidos Ego], neither the actuality nor the possibility of other Egos is presupposed" (Husserl 1960, p. 106). He also makes it clear why this is the case: "I phantasy only myself as if I were otherwise; I do not phantasy others" (Husserl 1960, p. 106). How, then, does Husserl think that the constitution of the other Ego, which is necessary for phenomenology to overcome the semblance of solipsism, can be accounted for in an eidetic analysis founded in "my" transcendental Ego? The answer is that Husserl does not think that the other Ego, in either the guise of the other pure Ego (the other Ego who does not yet have a worldly sense) or the other Ego as monad (the other Ego as a world constituting concrete transcendental Ego), is constituted as a variation of the perception of my own Ego, which is what the other Ego would have to be in order to be constituted in a phantasy of *my* Ego. Rather, for Husserl the very meaning of the other Ego as *other* precludes precisely the mode of access to its constitution that takes it departure from the experience of my Ego. The mode of access is rather, as it always is for Husserl's phenomenology, the 'transcendental clue' ultimately traceable back to the straightforward consciousness of something and the examination of its noetic-noematic structure. In the case at hand, the transcendental clue is "the experienced other, given to me in straightforward consciousness and as I immerse myself in examining the noematic-ontic content belonging to him (purely as correlate of my cogito)" (Husserl 1960, p. 123). The problem of the other Ego for Husserl is therefore clearly not that of establishing that the other Ego exists; Descartes' worry that his cogito may be all alone is not Husserl's. Husserl's problem is the subtler one of accounting for how the very meaning of the other Ego, as *other*, that is given in my experience, can nevertheless arise in a constitution that essentially and necessarily is constituted in *my* transcendental Ego, as the constitutionally 'primal' monad.

Leibniz's importance for Husserl's account of phenomenology as a transcendental idealism, which is signaled by Husserl's invocation of Leibniz's notion of the 'monad', can be established by a brief consideration of the three aspects of Leibniz's "Monadology" that are at stake in all of Husserl's "deliberate suggestions of Leibniz's metaphysics" (Husserl 1960, pp. 176–7). The first aspect is the multiplicity and diversity of Leibniz's monad, the second is the reason why, despite the many different universes that correspond—one to one—to this multiplicity and diversity, for Leibniz they are only perspectives of one single universe, and the third and last is the pre-established harmony that Leibniz maintains is responsible for the apriori rather than contingent status of this reason.

Leibniz's monads, as the very term monad suggests, are irreducible unities, which nevertheless enter into composites. Each monad possesses the minimal quality of involving a multitude in its unity, which he calls perception. Among monads, only some possess "apperception, or consciousness" (Leibniz 1997, p. 2), which should be distinguished from perception, otherwise all monads will be thought to be minds, which Leibniz thinks is Descartes' mistake. And even fewer possess the maximal quality of "*reflective acts*, which enable us to think of that which is called 'I' and enable us to consider this or that in us" (Leibniz 1997, p. 4). No two monads are identical, each possessing "a different point of view" (Leibniz 1997, p. 7), but all are nevertheless related to each of the others in an interconnection or accommodation "that express all others" (Leibniz 1997, p. 7). Each monad is therefore "a perpetual, living mirror of the universe" (Leibniz 1997, p. 7), which, despite their being as many universes as monads, is viewed as the *same*. That is, even though each monad's point of view, when "multiplied in perspective" (Leibniz 1997, p. 8), yields an infinite multitude of universes as a function of the different perspectives expressed by each, these perspectives are but the perspectives of a "single universe" (Leibniz 1997, p. 8). The harmony that unites the infinite multitude of diverse monads into a regulated whole has its basis in "a priori reasons" (Leibniz 1997, p. 8), and is therefore "pre-established" (Leibniz 1997, p. 10) between all monads, "since they are all representations of a single universe" (Leibniz 1997, p. 10). Finally, the source of a priori reasons is God, because it must be recognized by reflective acts that no contingent ratiocination is capable of accounting for the original unity of the truths of these ultimate reasons, and because each truth rules out, in principle, its opposite, thereby establishing its necessity. As the source of these truths, God must be a "unique" (Leibniz 1997, p. 5) (incomparable) being whose existence is both possible, because it is conceivable without contradiction, and necessary, because otherwise the ultimate reasons would have to be thought without an origin, which *is* a contradiction.

The Leibnizian context of Husserl's monadology is especially evident in Husserl's account of the following: the 'unity in multitude' that structures egological perception; the distinction between perception and apperception in the transcendental Ego's self-constitution (and, as we will see, in the transcendental Ego's constitution of the Other Ego); the status of the objective world as a single unity, despite the intersubjective multitude of the concrete and therefore factically diverse transcendental Egos that constitute it; and, finally, the harmonious course of transcendental experience that characterizes the intersubjective community of Egos' constitution of the one and only objective world. Indeed, Husserl holds that "Leibniz is right when he says that the infinitely many monads and groups of monads are conceivable but that it does not follow that all these possibilities are *compossible*; and, again, when he says that infinitely many worlds might have been 'created', but not two or more at once, since they are incompossible" (Husserl 1960, p. 167). Compossibility is Leibniz's term for the actual coexistence of two or more realties whose existence is possible, that is, conceivable without contradiction. Husserl initially employs this term to refer to the existence and possible existence together of the transcendental Ego's successive and simultaneous streams of lived-experiences. Husserl's agreement here with Leibniz does not extend, of course, to what Husserl considers Leibniz's "metaphysical construction" (Husserl 1960, p. 177), which grounds both the selection of compossible monads and the incompossibility of more than one world in theoretical "presuppositions or helpful thoughts drawn from the historical metaphysical tradition" (Husserl 1960, p. 177). Rather, Husserl's phenomenological transcendental idealism, despite being presented as a monadology, "draws its content purely from phenomenological explication of the transcendental experience laid open by transcendental reduction" (Husserl 1960, p. 177).

With the Leibnizian context in view, we can see that the other Ego is of importance for Husserl, above all, to establish the community of Egos necessary for the intersubjectivity presupposed by the objectivity proper to the world's meaning. And, by keeping this context in view, we will also see Husserl's account of the phenomenological basis for metaphysical implications of phenomenology as a transcendental idealism. Specifically, he holds that the foundation in ultimate cognitions provided by phenomenology establishes the impossibility of even the conceivability of the coexistence of two or more separate pluralities of monads, "i.e., pluralities *not in communion*" (Husserl 1960, p. 166) and, correspondingly, the "pure absurdity" (Husserl 1960, p. 166) of separate groups of monads constituting *two* spatio-temporal worlds that are "separate ad infinitum" (Husserl 1960, p. 166).

The Constitution of the Meaning and Being of the Other Ego as Pure Ego and Concrete Transcendental Ego (Monad) in 'My' Transcendental Ego

The key to Husserl's account of 'my' transcendental Ego as the source of the plurality of monads and the a priori harmony that governs both the meaning and existence of their interrelations is the peculiar phenomenological abstraction that separates off from the immanence of the Ego everything given to it by transcendental constitution as "'alien' and 'other'" (Husserl 1960, p. 127), including other ego-subjects and "everything '*other-spiritual*'" (Husserl 1960, p. 127). By the latter Husserl understands both the world as it is there for others at a given time, what he calls the 'surrounding world', as well as the world that is given for everyone at any time, the objective natural world. Subsequent to this abstraction the Ego's transcendental experience is reduced to what, taken concretely, is inseparable from its experience. As mentioned, this primordial experience includes the transcendencies in immanence of the Ego's sensuously constituted immanent temporalities, the Ego as the pole that acquires enduring habitualities, unities of sensuous modes of appearance, and the lived-body "'in' which I '*rule and govern*' *immediately*" (Husserl 1960, p. 128). Despite the meaning-exclusion of everything alien Husserl maintains that the reduction to the transcendental Ego's ownness "leaves us a *kind of* 'world' still, a nature reduced to what is included in our ownness and, thanks to the lived-body, a nature that includes a psychophysical Ego with 'body and soul' and personal Ego as utterly *unique* members of this reduced 'world'" (Husserl 1960, p. 129). Husserl refers to this world as "primordial nature" (Husserl 1960, p. 149), and stresses that "[b]ringing to light my lived-body, reduced to what is included in my ownness, is itself a part of bringing to light the *ownness-essence* of the objective phenomenon: '*I, as this man*'" (Husserl 1960, p. 128).

The lived-body is the key to how Husserl thinks that "every *consciousness of* what is other, every mode of appearance *of* it, belongs" (Husserl, 1960, p. 131) to the transcendental Ego's ownness. The physical body of the other Ego appears in the sensuousness that is inseparable from the experience of the concrete transcendental Ego's lived-body, which is to say, in the sensuousness of this Ego's self-apperception as a mundane Ego to which a lived-body essentially belongs as 'my' lived-body. Husserl describes what appears in the transcendental Ego's concrete experience *as* the body of the other Ego, and not as a body that is "merely an indication of someone else" (Husserl 1960, p. 151). His description is based on the fact that "we are not dealing here with a temporal genesis of such experience, on the basis of a temporally antecedent self-experience" (Husserl 1960, p. 151) but rather with "only a precise explication of the intentionality actually observable in our experience of someone else" (Husserl 1960, p. 151). The results of this explication uncover three basic dimensions at work in the constitution of the alien: one, the constitution of the other Ego as the pure Ego belonging to the other's body experienced in the immanence of the transcendental Ego's sphere of ownness; two, the constitution of the *objective* transcendency of the world, as the one and the same world there for the Ego community that includes 'me' as a pure Ego; and, three, the constitution of the monad community as the transcendental intersubjectivity whose collective constitutive intentionality is responsible for the objective world's meaning and being as an objective transcendency.

The crucial aspect belonging to the initial constitution of the other Ego as the pure Ego belonging to the experience of someone else's body is the passive associative 'pairing' of my lived-body with the experience of another physical body. Based on the *perception* of the similarity between my lived-body, "which is always there and sensuously prominent" (Husserl 1960, p. 143) and my perception of a different body, an overlaying of the meaning of my lived-body as a psychophysical unity with the meaning of the body appearing in my perceptual field occurs. As already mentioned, the resulting passive association yields a 'fusion' of meaning, which presents a unity of similarity at a higher level than the perceptual similarity of the two distinct intuitive data involved (my lived-body and the physical body in my lived-body's perceptual field). Husserl characterizes the associative unity as 'apperception' or more precisely 'appresentation'. He does so because the meaning content in question, although co-given with perception, is strictly speaking not constituted perceptually but in an "*intentional modification*" (Husserl 1960, p. 144). Whatever can become *originally* presented and evidently verified "is something *I* am; or else it belongs to me as peculiarly my own" (Husserl 1960, p. 144), whereas whatever "is experienced in that founded manner that characterizes a primordially unfulfillable experience—an experience that does not give something itself originally but that consistently verifies something indicated—is 'other'" (Husserl 1960, p. 144). The other Ego, qua its very meaning and being as other, is something that cannot be originally given in *my* experience. Its meaning constitution therefore necessarily involves the modification—rather than the variation or extension—of my experience. This modification concerns both my transcendental Ego, "which is the first to be objectivated" (Husserl 1960, p. 144) as an (mundane) Ego and my primordial 'world', each of which are "appresented, in an analogizing modification" (Husserl 1960, p. 144) with the other Ego.

The appresentation of the other Ego—in an analogizing modification—as an analogue of myself as a mundane Ego, constitutes both 'my' self as *mine*, "by virtue of the contrastive pairing that necessarily takes place" (Husserl 1960, p. 144), and brings about the constitutionally secondary transcendency of the objective world. Moreover, the analogizing modification of my primordial 'world' appresents "*his* primordial world, and then his fully concrete Ego" (Husserl 1960, p. 144), which is to say, "'in other words, *another monad* becomes constituted appresentatively in mine" (Husserl 1960, p. 144). The analogizing appresentation responsible for these three interrelated and interdependent aspects of the constitution of the objective transcendency of the world takes place in what Husserl refers to as a "*combination* (Verbindung) accomplished through the medium of representation" (Husserl 1960, p. 155).

Combination (*Verbindung*) founded in Recollections as the Source of the Objectivity of the Meaning and Being of the Other Ego

Combination in general brings about the constitution of an identity whose unity as "'the Same'" (Husserl 1960, p. 155) is accomplished by an identifying synthesis that unites a multitude of repeated representations, each of which is "separate from the others," into the evident consciousness of an identical intentional object. Because each of the lived-experiences is a "*separate conscious lived-experience*" (Husserl 1960, p. 155), the "object immanent in them" (Husserl 1960, p. 155) is so "only as something non-intrinsically (*irreelles*) inherent" (Husserl 1960, p. 155) in any one of them. According to Husserl, the 'combination' proper is accomplished through repeated representations of an absent original presentation, with each repetition accompanied by the consciousness that the original can be gone back to "with the evidence: 'I can always do so again'" (Husserl 1960, p. 155). Each repeated representation, therefore, synthetically combines the representation occurring in the present stream of lived-experiences with the relevant separate past representations of 'the Same' original presentation. Husserl terms this synthesis "recollection" and maintains that "through the medium of recollective representations, the synthesis extends—within my stream of lived-experiences (which is always already constituted)—from my living present into my currently relevant separate pasts and therewith brings into relief their *combination*" (Husserl 1960, p. 155). Because each of these repeated representations is evident as a separate temporal sequence, each represents the original presentation as an object that is 'ideal', namely, as an object that is constituted as 'the Same' across a multitude of temporally separate streams of lived-experiences.

Husserl maintains that the combination constituted through a multitude of representations is responsible for "my own lived-experiences" (Husserl 1960, p. 155) coming to "acquire for me the meaning and validity of something existent, something existing with its identical temporal form and identical temporal content" (Husserl 1960, p. 155), as well as for "the constitution of objects that are ideal in the precise sense—for example: all logically ideal objects" (Husserl 1960, p. 155) and, finally, for the "experience of the alien (*Fremderfahrung*)" (Husserl 1960, p. 156). In the latter case, a combination comes about between the concrete Ego, together with his primordial sphere, and "the *alien sphere* represented therein" (Husserl 1960, p. 155). This combination first accomplishes the indentifying synthesis of the primordially given lived-body of someone else and the same body, "but *appresented* in other modes of appearance" (Husserl 1960, p. 155). That is, combined into the unity of the consciousness of 'the Same' are separate lived-experiences of the other's lived-body, each one linked through a chain of recollections to its initial apperception. From this unity, the experience of the alien accomplishes "identifying synthesis of the same nature, given and verified primordially" (Husserl 1960, p. 155), which is to say, the nature given "with pure sensuous originality" in 'my' uninterrupted, "purely passive original self-appearance" (Husserl 1960, p. 155) is combined "appresentationally" (Husserl 1960, p. 155) with the primordial nature constituted by the other Ego's concrete intentional life. Thus, for Husserl, the combination constitutes the "*coexistence of my Ego and the other Ego*" (Husserl 1960, p. 155) and therewith primordially institutes "a *common time-form*" (Husserl 1960, p. 155) such that "every primordial temporality automatically acquires the significance of being merely an original mode of appearance of objective temporality to a particular subject" (Husserl 1960, p. 155).

The combination mediated by representations described here is the source of Husserl's confidence that Leibniz was right—though for the wrong reasons—about the impossibilities of both the separate existence of two or more pluralities of monads and of the existence of more than one objective world. Phenomenology, as transcendental idealism, is able to show—on the basis of reflectively uncovered and verifiable evidence—that both the meaning and being of any possible other Ego and any possible world is inseparable from the constitution of each as an ideal unity in 'my' transcendental Ego or monad. More exactly, the combination brought about by the multiplicity of recollective representations yields the primordial transcendence of nature that appears in each monad—originally in 'my' monad and appresentatively in the other monad—as the one and only source of the meaning. Moreover, when this meaning is verified with evidence, the being of the *plurality* of monads whose community is constitutive of the objectivity of the one spatio-temporal nature and world, becomes an identical world for everyone.

References

Husserl, Edmund (1960): *Cartesian Meditations. An Introduction to Phenomenology*. Trans. Dorion Cairns. The Hague: Martinus Nijhoff.
Leibniz, Gottfried Wilhelm (1997): "The Principles of Philosophy, or, the Monadology" (1714). Trans. Robert Latta; rev. Donald Rutherford. http://philosophyfaculty.ucsd.edu/faculty/rutherford/Leibniz/translations/Monadology.pdf, last accessed on 25 September 2020.

Sophie Loidolt
Plural Absolutes? Husserl and Merleau-Ponty on Being-In-a-Shared-World and its Metaphysical Implications

Abstract: Phenomenology has largely agreed on conceiving consciousness as an openness and an "outwardness." Only Husserl's "monadology," which alone by its name suggests a certain enclosedness, does not seem to fit into the picture and is consequently neglected or attacked in the literature. In order to gain a fresh view on this difficult piece of Husserl's phenomenology, I read it in terms of what he calls "absolute world-interpretation": an intentional interpretation all the way down. I claim that this is a consequent attitude following from his conception of transcendental intersubjectivity and that it faces no more severe ontological consequences than Merleau-Ponty's version of phenomenology, whose arguments against the transcendental reduction, the hyle, the certainty of the cogito, and the immanence of consciousness I re-examine. Furthermore, I promote an understanding of monadology that does not contradict the outwardness of consciousness but rather views it from the angle of the being-in-one-another of plural consciousnesses.

Phenomenology after Heidegger has largely agreed on conceiving consciousness as an openness and an "outwardness." To a significant extent, this conception is targeted against a Cartesian (mis-) understanding of consciousness as an "enclosed mind," which has repeatedly and wrongly been associated with Husserl's phenomenology. As we know from many valuable studies of the last twenty-five years (cf. Zahavi 1999; Zahavi 2001; Steinbock 1995; Crowell 2001; Moran 2005; etc.), these accusations of a Cartesian internalism against Husserl are not only misguided; they essentially ignore the central importance of intersubjectivity for Husserl's phenomenology, on the transcendental, mundane, genetic, and generative levels.

The main topics of investigations demonstrating this importance have been transcendental intersubjectivity, historicity, generativity, normality, empathy and social cognition, as well as collective intentionality, sociality and emotions. What has been discussed a lot less, however, is Husserl's "big picture," which is closely interrelated with his detailed investigations. In fact, he claims that it is demonstrated, "*erwiesen*" by them (Hua 1, p. 119).[1] His claim is that transcendental intersubjectivity qua "the universe of monads" is "the intrinsically first being" (Husserl 1960, p. 156; Hua 1, p. 182) and that the "intentional Being-in-another of the absolute" is plainly "*the 'metaphysical' primal fact*" (Hua 15, p. 366).[2]

What are we to make of this? Doesn't the concept of the "monad" alone suggest a certain enclosedness and immanence? And are we therefore to reject these parts of Husserl's phenomenology and replace them with more moderate, less "idealistic" versions of a worldly Being-with? Is there a certain point where should we draw a line? I would like to suggest that we should reconsider some questions before we do so. This is why I will engage with passages of Husserl's work that are usually discreetly bypassed. My thesis will be that Husserl's terminology ("metaphysical fact," "universe of monads," "the absolute") might be unsettling for those who worry about enclosed worldless minds, but that, in fact, everything he says is perfectly compatible with his well-received analyses of intersubjectivity that might sound "worldlier" and more interrelated. This is also the reason why I will argue that "drawing a line" is a rather tricky business that risks giving up some of Husserl's core convictions and arguments—and therefore, some central phenomenological views about the interrelation of subjectivity, intersubjectivity, and world. This also makes this issue more important than just being a mere immanent problem of Husserl-interpretation.

Regarding the present phenomenological discourse, one could sometimes get the impression that the "outwardness of consciousness" has become an attractive slogan for authors to flag out that they reject a Cartesian or internalist misconception of phenomenology, while their ontological or metaphysical consequences remain somewhat unclear. Instead, we often read that phenomenologists are beyond these questions anyway (of realism/idealism, and metaphysics in general). Although Husserl would happily subscribe to the claim that his philosophy couldn't be framed in the classic setup of an idealism-realism debate, he was, by contrast, very clear sighted about the respective implications of his tran-

---

[1] Husserl uses the noun "*Erweis*" in that passage (the English version translates "proof," cf. Husserl 1960, p. 86). Cf. Julia Jansen's (2017, p. 32) paper, whose exposition of the problem of transcendental idealism in Husserl I completely agree with.

[2] This is not a statement from the period of Husserl's "proofs of idealism" (Hua 36), but a rather late research manuscript from 1931 that incorporates his phenomenology of transcendental intersubjectivity and the primal facticity of the lifeworld. As László Tengelyi (2014, pp. 171–228) has pointed out, Husserl's later phenomenological metaphysics is based on the idea of the primal fact (*Urfaktum*), a contingent necessity which precedes all eidetic variation. Of these *Urfakta*, the central one is the "intentional Being-in-another of the absolute" ("*intentionales Ineinander des Absoluten*").

scendental phenomenology. I see it as a virtue that he boldly confronted questions, especially metaphysical and transcendental questions, that after him were often not asked anymore—or were declared senseless.[3]

In his recent book, *Husserl's Legacy. Phenomenology, Metaphysics, and Transcendental Philosophy*, Dan Zahavi (2017) argues that Husserl's aim was indeed to demonstrate that reality is nothing apart from its givenness—which is far from remaining "metaphysically neutral." I agree with his interpretation that being and potential givenness coincide for Husserl, in contrast to Steven Crowell's and David Carr's softer semantic interpretation that suggests that Husserl only talks about *meaning* and remains silent about the question of the mind-dependency of *being*. But I even want to take this thesis one step further, in order to make its metaphysical implications clear, which lead Husserl to talking of a "plurality of monads" as "the primal metaphysical fact." Zahavi avoids this explicit conclusion. Instead, he divides up Husserl's use of the term "metaphysics" into (1) "a philosophical engagement with questions of facticity, birth, death, fate, immortality" and (2) "a fundamental reflection on and concern with the status and being of reality. Is reality mind-dependent or not, and if yes, in what manner?" (Zahavi 2017, p. 205). It seems to me that this distinction deflates the latter meaning of metaphysics too much by making it indistinguishable from transcendental philosophy.[4] At the same time, it associates the former version of metaphysics only with speculative and existential questions.

I would like to suggest a slightly different distinction between metaphysical elements in Husserl's philosophy that both deserve the name. One strand of Husserl's metaphysical investigations (all left unpublished by him) indeed deals with "border problems" and therefore has to leave the phenomenological meth-

---

[3] This, of course, largely goes back to Heidegger's reading of Husserl. But Heidegger himself is not utterly clear about the relation of *"Seiendes"* before or without *"Sein"* (cf. Heidegger 1967, pp. 211f.) and leaves us confused about what kind of "realism" we are actually dealing with – after not asking the "wrong questions" (of realism and idealism) anymore. For an elucidating analysis of the reception of Husserl's transcendental idealism cf. Bernet (2010; a reworked version in English: 2015).

[4] I agree that "transcendental philosophy" in Husserl means something different than in Kant (where metaphysical questions are shown to be undecidable in principle), and that it would therefore be closer to metaphysics. But it seems of importance to me that Husserl himself speaks only of "metaphysical results" (Hua 1, § 60) of his transcendental phenomenology and thus indeed does seem to make a difference. One could try to differentiate it this way, following Husserl's hints: While transcendental philosophy confronts problems of constitution, metaphysics is about "being": the "ultimate" or "first" being (cf. Hua 1, pp. 166, 182).

odology of justification through demonstration (*Ausweisung*).⁵ If there is a line to be drawn, also concerning how far to go with Husserl, I would do it here, for methodical rather than thematic reasons. As for the other use of the term metaphysics, however, it seems to me that Husserl very clearly says that metaphysics is about "*letzte Seinserkenntnisse*" (Hua 1, § 60, p. 166): ultimate insights into being. This goes beyond a mere reflection on the mind-dependency of reality in the sense that it *spells out its ontological consequences*.⁶ And this is exactly what Husserl does in the last paragraphs of the Cartesian Meditations, clearly calling this "metaphysical results" which are "not speculative" (Hua 1, § 60).⁷

I take it that Husserl's monadic transcendental idealism is a radical and very consequent attempt of *thinking intentionally all the way through*; he sometimes calls this the "absolute attitude" or "absolute world-interpretation" (Hua 14, pp. 244, 366).⁸ We know Husserl as a thinker of "attitudes" and I want to claim that this is crucial also for understanding his metaphysical (non-speculative) reflections. In the absolute attitude, which I regard to be the most consequent articulation of the transcendental attitude, the naiveté of the natural attitude together with its forms of causality is "transcendentally elucidated" (*aufgeklärt*). This means that our natural way of thinking causation on consciousness from "outside" is replaced by terms of intentional relations. While we often relapse into the natural attitude even in phenomenological descriptions, for example, by tacitly equating the objective space between us with the difference between our bodily consciousnesses, the absolute attitude aims at forms of expression that prevent that we can even start thinking in these terms. The monad is such a form of expression, forcing us to radically think in intentional relations by leaving inside-outside-distinctions behind us. Since monads are, as we will see, not at all encapsulated substances for Husserl but are intrinsically inter-

---

5 This also includes theoretical problems, like teleology, sleeping monads, the problem of ancestrality, etc.

6 In Husserl's case, these consequences are ontological, and if we understand the term ontology in a classic Wolffian context (which I assume Husserl did), it is "metaphysica generalis." This is also the reason why I would not like to equate metaphysics with transcendental philosophy, as the latter in its Kantian form precludes any ontological consequences (and, in a certain sense, Crowell's and Carr's semantic interpretations hold on to this Kantian tradition of the "transcendental").

7 "Actually, therefore, *there can exist only a single community of monads*, the community of *all* co-existing monads. Hence there can exist *only one Objective world*, only one Objective time, only one Objective space, only one Objective Nature." (Husserl 1960, p. 140)

8 Text no. 13 in Husserliana 14 is called by Husserl himself: "The transcendence of the alter ego as opposed to the transcendence of the thing. Absolute monadology as expansion (*Erweiterung*) of transcendental egology. Absolute world-interpretation" (Hua 14, p. 244)

twined, he describes what *sharing a world and interacting means from this radical perspective*.

What I would like to do in the following is to present some of the main features and problems of this "absolute perspective" so that we can better assess if or why we should take its side at all. As Husserl sees it, ultimate transcendental clarification and understandability are *only* achieved if we engage in this viewpoint (Hua 15, p. 370). As a contrast foil, I will start out with portraying a position that seems to make much more sense for many phenomenologists: Merleau-Ponty's approach to the interrelation of subjectivity, intersubjectivity, and world. In this paper, I cannot go into details of Merleau-Ponty's philosophy; I just want to point out where also his conception might have some difficulties that could be avoided with Husserl. Both philosophers, I think, push their ontologies very consequently to their logical ends, whereas Husserl ends up with a transcendental idealism and Merleau-Ponty drifts in the direction of Schelling's philosophy of identity. Or, one could also put it this way: Merleau-Ponty's (1968) "ontology of the flesh of the world," if taken seriously, is certainly no less metaphysically bold than Husserl's ultimate conclusion concerning the plurality of monads. Often, however, Merleau-Ponty's metaphysical speculations are ignored in favor of presenting him as a soft and acceptable link to a discourse with the sciences.[9] This might be due to some central arguments concerning the limitations of Husserl's transcendental attitude that were happily welcomed as a relief from the burden of transcendental idealism without scrutinizing their consequences (with the exception of Levinas [1987]). Let us reexamine some of these arguments from the *Phenomenology of Perception* (PP).

---

9 In a forthcoming article, Petra Gehring (2021) shows that many central transcendental features of Merleau-Ponty's philosophy are simply ignored when he is presented as the appropriate reference for the project of naturalizing phenomenology. I would like to add that Merleau-Ponty's reflections on art and ontology also do not seem to fit into that picture.

1 Merleau-Ponty's arguments against the transcendental reduction, the hyle, the certainty of the cogito, and the immanence of consciousness in the *Phenomenology of Perception*

Most phenomenologists are familiar with Merleau-Ponty's famous, meanwhile canonic claims that "there is no inner man" (PP, p. xi) and that "the most important lesson which the reduction teaches us is the impossibility of a complete reduction" (PP, p. xv). I think that the first claim uses Husserl as a strawman (invoking his Augustin quote at the very end of the *Cartesian Meditations*),[10] and that the second claim misconceives Husserl's transcendental subjectivity as a sort of hyper-self-transparent spectator.[11] As happens once and again in the

---

[10] "'*Noli foras ire,*' says Augustine, '*in te redi, in interiore homine habitat veritas*'." (Husserl 1960, p. 157; Hua 1, p.183)

[11] I admit that it is often hard to say what exactly Merleau-Ponty's reading of Husserl is. In the famous passage on the reduction in the preface (which is followed only by very few comments on the issue throughout the book) it seems as if he is granting Husserl the philosophical instinct/ insight that his intellectualist inclinations are inhibited by the phenomena themselves: "The most important lesson which the reduction teaches us is the impossibility of a complete reduction. This is why Husserl is constantly re-examining the possibility of the reduction. If we were absolute mind, the reduction would present no problem. But since, on the contrary, we are in the world, since indeed our reflections are carried out in the temporal flux on the which we are trying to seize (since they *sich einströmen*, as Husserl says), there is no thought which embraces all our thought." (PP, p. xv) The argument seems to shift from world to time within the sentence here. That time-consciousness cannot be "looked upon" is something that Husserl would agree on. Still, I think, he would not consider this to be a reason to declare the phenomenological reduction impossible, as it is not about getting a complete grip on everything from a distance. Another passage I would like to quote at length here shows better in which way Merleau-Ponty separates the "good Husserl" of world-reflection from the "bad Husserl" of transcendental philosophy. And here I think Merleau-Ponty misreads Husserl in the sense that "all world's obscurities are elucidated": "Husserl in his last period concedes that all reflection should in the first place return to the description of the world of living experience (*Lebenswelt*). But he adds that, by means of a second 'reduction', the structures of the world of experience must be reinstated in the transcendental flow of a universal constitution in which all the world's obscurities are elucidated. It is clear, however, that we are faced with a dilemma: either the constitution makes the world transparent, in which case it is not obvious why reflection needs to pass through the world of experience, or else it retains something of that world, and never rids it of its opacity. Husserl's thought moves increasingly in this second direction, despite many throwbacks to the logicist period [...]." (PP, p. 425, footnote 8) What I would like to

great *Phenomenology of Perception*, Husserl gets mixed up or identified with "intellectualism," one of Merleau-Ponty's main opponents (along with empiricism), only to present him later as having come up with the solution to the dilemma as well (cf. PP, p. 425, footnote 8). Be that as it may, and not denying the merits of Merleau-Ponty's seminal work, I would like to point to one movement in his theory-building where he modifies some essential Husserlian claims, taking them into the direction of his very own view of ontology.

Through his famous analyses of the lived body, Merleau-Ponty pushes subjectivity into an enactive communion with the world. He puts this "being-in-the world" or, as he coins it, "*être au monde*" in contrast to a conception of "consciousness *of* the world." The latter he associates with a spectatorial subject or with a subject that encompasses and pervades everything in thought—that "thinks" everything and thereby puts it in a distance. In doing so, Merleau-Ponty narrows down transcendental idealism to a certain type. At the same time, he presents a very attractive counter-conception to this sovereign subject who seems to have everything under its transcendental control. But there is a price to be paid for this solution with limited alternatives. And that price is that subjectivity diffuses into the world at its fringes. This blurs the ontological difference between subjectivity and world, as well as the correlational difference between experiencing and the experienced. Merleau-Ponty deliberately seems to argue in favor of both theses: he denies, e.g., that there is something like a lived experience of red qua sensation or hyletic datum. Instead, the only thing there is, is the perceived red object (cf. PP, p. 5). Hence, there is no adumbration but only adumbrated objects with their properties and embodied consciousness dynamically relating to it. We know this thesis directed against any "hyletic" moments of consciousness also as the "transparency thesis." In Merleau-Ponty's version of this thesis, the quality of conscious givenness is somehow identical with the world, but not in the sense of a Husserlian correlational correspondence, but in the sense of an indistinguishable ontological interwovenness. Given our bodily immersedness into the world, Merleau-Ponty similarly argues with respect to pain, and so-called "inner feelings" (cf. PP, pp. 437 f.):

> [I]t is no less difficult for me to know whether or not I have felt something than it is to know whether there is really something there [...]. When, on the other hand, I am sure of having felt, the certainty of some external thing is involved in the very way in which the sensation

---

argue for in this article is that (1) absoluteness in Husserl is something else than Merleau-Ponty suggests with his "absolute mind," and that (2) the world-relatedness of consciousness is the wrong reason to declare the reduction incomplete; rather, this eventually leads to Merleau-Ponty's own ontology where the difference between consciousness and world is blurred.

is articulated and unfolded before me: it is a pain *in the leg*, or it is *red*, and this may be an opaque red on one plane, or a reddish three-dimensional atmosphere. The 'interpretation' of my sensations which I give must necessarily be motivated, and be so only in terms of the structure of those sensations, so that it can be said with equal validity either that there is no transcendent interpretation and no judgement which does not spring from the very configuration of the phenomena—or that there is no sphere of immanence, no realm in which my consciousness is fully at home and secure against all risk of error. (PP, pp. 437 f.)

Two lines of argumentation can be differentiated here. Let us first look at the more straightforward one: It often seems in these passages directed against the certainty of the Cartesian *cogito* (PP, pp. 429–476), that Merleau-Ponty equates the correctness of my judgment concerning the (worldly) state of affairs with the Cartesian certainty concerning the pure "thatness" of my sensations. But these two versions of certainty are not the same, and the latter does not even need to be a judgment.[12] Of course, consciousness, when producing judgments of the form "S is p," is not "secure against all risk of error," and whenever we start articulating judgments, this involves some sort of "interpretation." But how and in which sense could I be wrong about feeling pain? I might be wrong about where to locate it (not in the leg but somewhere else) or even what kind of object caused it (very hot or very cold).[13] But how does the fact that I can be wrong or fuzzy about something in that interpretation refute the fact that I feel that pain in this very moment, *unclearly located, unclearly identified*?[14] Even if all sensations are intrinsically and indistinguishably bound up with transcendent world-interpretations, all of it is "there" in a way for me I cannot deny, no matter how unclear it presents itself to my judging grasp. The absoluteness in conscious givenness does not necessarily have to be a *clara et dis-*

---

[12] I can see that if one pursues an epistemic foundational project like Descartes the question of producing valid judgments becomes more pressing. In Husserl's case, however, I take the ontological distinction between "consciousness" and "reality" to be the decisive argument for the absoluteness of givenness (cf. Hua 3/1, §§ 54–55).

[13] One could think of examples of hypnosis or torture here, where I am brought into a state of absolute panic and fear and therefore feel something that might not be the case: pain from a burning stick which was, in fact, an ice cube. Although I might indeed be wrong about *what* I feel here, I find it hard to claim that the pain was just an illusion I didn't really feel, because I lack certainty of exactly where I feel it and what caused it. To turn Merleau-Ponty's claim around: There would be no transcendent interpretation if there was no immanent feeling. Even if the transcendent interpretation is necessarily bound up with a given feeling, it does not abolish the special nature of its givenness.

[14] Merleau-Ponty sometimes switches to the problem of memory here which I think is illegitimate. Even if it were true that the fuzziness of a felt pain makes me insecure in hindsight if I felt it at all, this is no argument against Descartes or Husserl.

tincta perceptio, and not being able to doubt it does not equal being able to produce a clear and distinct judgment about it.

This brings us to the second line of argumentation: Even if it is true that I always have to "apperceive" the sensation of pain in a "transcendent interpretation" (and I am not sure if this adequately describes overwhelming pain), we should worry about how to conceive this "interpretation." Equating it with a predicative form would eventually lead us to the claim that beings who are not able to produce worldly judgments would not feel anything. I am convinced that Merleau-Ponty would not want to head in that direction, even if the argument in the passage cited above builds on locating the certainty of feelings in the context of a certainty of judgments. A more generous reading, however, will grant that Merleau-Ponty in fact further develops Husserl's concept of *intentionale Auffassung* ("interpretation") from the *Logical Investigations* which becomes *"intentionale morphé"* in *Ideas I*. By dropping the hyletic component which, for Husserl, intrinsically belongs together with its *Auffassung*, Merleau-Ponty heads towards a conception of consciousness that views it as "intentionality only." This leads to the crucial shift that instead of being intrinsically bound up with hyle (and thereby constituting what the very dimension of the flow of consciousness is "made of"), intentionality is now bound up with "world." Merleau-Ponty is definitely not the only one making this move. Both Jan Patočka (1970) and Jean-Paul Sartre (2003), just to name two, pursue a similar shift, thereby denying the "immanence" of consciousness. But one has to be very precise about what "bound up with 'world'" actually means in each and every theoretical proposal. The given differences reveal ontological conceptions of such a different nature (from asubjective anonymity to Sartre's prereflective cogito) that it will be hard to speak of a unified move away from Husserl. In Merleau-Ponty's case, it seems that this move ultimately serves as a vehicle to collapse the correlation and meld the special dimension of givenness qua embodied consciousness/operative intentionality with the world it constitutes—not only as a noema which would allow for adumbration, but indeed with the adumbrated itself. Embodied consciousness must therefore be as uncertain about its self-givenness as it is or can be about the givenness of worldly objects.

But hyletic data and its intentional *Auffassung* can, in a different interpretation, also simply mean that something is "there" for someone (also in a primitive bodily/*leiblich* sense that comprises no objectification at all). This involves the claim that the hyle is nevertheless never raw "data" and that its intrinsic interwovenness with intentional *Auffassung* precisely describes the nature of consciousness: that something "is" in the sense being "given" to me. Although, most of the time, a "world" is given to us, I find it hard to rule out, especially when thinking of less developed forms of conscious life or severe states of pain, that there couldn't be a very minimal form of this givenness that is *just a "thereness" of pain* and precisely a closing down of worldliness. But even if Merleau-Ponty would insist that there is still always a worldly structure in the givenness of sensations—and I think this is his most refined argument in this passage—, it is hardly a proof against an own sphere of givenness (which is nothing else but the alleged "immanence" of consciousness). This would only be the case if this worldly structure would be conceived as a quasi-causal imprint of the transcendent world on bodily consciousness. And this would eventually result in a "myth of the given" in a structural variant. Instead, I would argue with Husserl that the worldly structure of sensations rather *is itself a givenness* that manifests and continues to manifest itself correlatively to the transcendent world[15] (and this not only holds for pain but one could similarly argue with respect to the sensation of red).

Yet, Merleau-Ponty is determined to exteriorize the whole dimension of lived experience and aims at destroying all claims about the certainty of "inner life." Shortly after the above cited claims on the transparence of "pain" and "red," he moves on to refute the Cartesian thesis that "a feeling, considered in itself, is always true once it is felt" (PP, p. 439). Like the early Sartre, Merleau-Ponty rather compares the givenness of such feelings to the inadequacy we encounter when constituting an object. What follows, is a rather long discussion of the example of authentic love (PP, pp. 439–445), which might be considered interesting from an existential perspective. But one cannot help thinking that these considerations concerning the question if my feeling of love was "authentic" or not, at some point simply touches upon a wholly different problem. I repeat myself: Not knowing *what* my feeling is (in terms of the difficult socio-cultural connotations of "love," all the more "true love") or doubting *that* it is are really two very different things. All in all, I think it is fair to conclude that this line of argumentation does not touch the claim of the certainty of the cogito at all. And as far as I can see, Merleau-Ponty does not come up with any other arguments. So it seems to me that neither the thesis of a hyletic component of consciousness nor the thesis of the certainty, i.e. the absoluteness of its givenness in contrast to transcendent objects are successfully refuted—that is, to a point where one could not take them up again.

But it might be that the attractiveness of Merleau-Ponty's approach rather lies in the whole setup of the consciousness-world-relation anyway. The dimension of *"Erlebnis"* for Merleau-Ponty *is* the bodily and perceptual encounter with

---

[15] This claim should be compatible with both Husserl's earlier interpretation of hyle as "reell" part of consciousness and his latter one as a noematic component.

the world. This gets us out of the stuffy interiority of consciousness and throws us *into* the world. But what is the world actually? Merleau-Ponty very nicely develops and enriches Heidegger's being-in-the-world, where the intentional correlation already gets dynamized into a movement of "transcending." In addition to this, subjectivity for Merleau-Ponty is conceived as bodily embeddedness in the world, a world that transcends subjectivity in all matters. I am holistically situated "in" something that eludes me, instead of looking "on" to something (consciousness of...). To use a metaphor, it's like being a fish in the water, only that there are no more boundaries between the fish and the water. Rather, subjectivity is the pure movement of swimming. As a totally exteriorized movement, I move "in" something. My inside is my outside. I am the pure movement of my projection: "The world is inseparable from the subject, but from a subject which is nothing but a project of the world [...]. The subject is a being-in-the-world and the world remains 'subjective'. (PP, pp. 499 f.)

I have to admit that I find it easier to conceptualize the physical world and nature with Husserl's constitutional theory (starting from the lifeworld, but opening up to different levels of abstraction)[16] than with a conception that is and remains so tightly tied to the subject's perception. Merleau-Ponty ontologizes the world as it is given in perception, and for those reasons holds on to fundamental ambivalences. Since the world *is* the movement of the subject, Merleau-Ponty also denies that subjectivity could ever have itself in an indubitable way (another argument against Cartesian certainty): "I know myself only in my inherence in time and in the world, that is, I know myself only in ambiguity." (PP, p. 402) Experiencing can never mean getting a fully transparent view on everything, not even everything that concerns myself. But did Husserl ever claim that? Of course not. Its intentional life, its past, its spatial surroundings also elude into a dark horizon for the Husserlian subject. I sometimes have the impression that Merleau-Ponty intentionally confuses the absolute givenness of consciousness (in contrast to spatio-temporal objects) with a total grip and total sovereignty over the experienced. But Husserl never defended the latter thesis. He also never claimed that sense-bestowal only comes from a sovereign subjective side. What he defends is rather an irreducible ontological dimension of an experiential mineness that is not to be conflated or dissolved into anything else.

---

16 Just to make sure that I am not misunderstood: I do not mean to substrue those abstract levels as a sort of "real nature," but rather see them, with Husserl, as intentional accomplishments on the basis of the lifeworld. These accomplishments and their correlates, however, indeed do intend more abstract and therefore objective features of givenness in a justifiable intentional "*Aufgestuftheit*," as it happens e.g. in the scientific practices of physics and mathematics.

Even if I elude myself, this eluding is *my* experiential dimension and not diffusing into yours.

> The others have a say in the matter of the existence of my world. My world, i.e. the world with all its content of reality [...]. Of course, I occasionally have to correct my opinions about worldly things and even experiences of the world through the others' [opinions]. This can also concern myself, I can be wrong about myself concerning soul and body, and they can instruct me. What they cannot instruct me about, however, is my being in the ultimate sense, my transcendental being. This precedes the being of the world that is for me and it also precedes the being or non-being of others, who I experience. (Hua 15, pp. 112f.)

Certainly, Merleau-Ponty also sees and emphasizes the undeniable features of the *cogito* (as he calls this dimension). However, his aim of establishing a "situated cogito" often leaves us wondering if the darkness and opacity of retention, myself, birth, and death etc. are not somewhat blurred paths into an anonymity that dissolves the cogito into something else. In fact, Merleau-Ponty makes this elusiveness and intransparency a condition of the possibility to be involved in the world at all and to encounter others at all. Although I think we are factically opaque to ourselves, I really do not see why this should be a *condition* for experiencing otherness or an alter ego. It has to be noted that Merleau-Ponty does not only mean the opacity that time-consciousness brings with itself. Sometimes he sounds as if consciousness would have to be brittle in order to be able to experience others, in order to be able to "let something in." This again, is a reason why he argues that plural absolutes are impossible,[17] and that a subjectivity conceived as absolute can only be solipsist (cf. PP, p. 434). But is this not a misunderstanding of the absolute as we find it in Husserl—or, rather, a different conception of the absolute which Merleau-Ponty attacks, one which Husserl does not defend? The absoluteness of consciousness, the *nulla re indiget ad existendum*, refers first to its manner of givenness which coincides with its being, and ultimately to the self-phenomenalization of the flow of consciousness.[18] In all its absoluteness, it allows for passiveness, involvedness, elusiveness—because absoluteness is to be understood as a form of givenness and not as the

---

[17] "The plurality of consciousness is impossible if I have an absolute consciousness of myself." (PP, p. 434)

[18] That this self-temporalization or phenomenalization of consciousness always involves a "non-I," as Husserl says, does not stand against this, because this non-I is also *reell* and absolutely given (definitely not *"real"* and transcendent). I can just point to the argument here that absolute givenness is not to be equated with I-ness; for a more detailed discussion cf. Loidolt 2017, pp. 100–110.

metaphysical property of a substance that closes it off.[19] For Husserl, au contraire, the absolute *must* be plural (Hua 15, pp. 366–371), because he never conceptualized consciousness as an absolute *"reell"* incorporation of everything, but rather as an *absolute dimension of manifestation*, where a *real transcendence of otherness becomes manifest*. In Merleau-Ponty, however, the boundaries between me and the other diffuse into a collective anonymity:

> The solitude from which we emerge to intersubjective life is not that of the monad. It is only the haze of an anonymous life that separates us from being; and the barrier between us and others is impalpable. If there is a break, it is not between me and the other person; it is between a primordial generality we are intermingled in and the precise system, myself–the others. What 'precedes' intersubjective life cannot be numerically distinguished from it, precisely because at this level there is neither individuation nor numerical distinction. (Merleau-Ponty 1964, p. 174)

Although I cannot go deeper into this, I do have my problems with passages like these in Merleau-Ponty's overall approach. At its fringes, Merleau-Ponty's subjectivity frazzles into an anonymity and, ultimately, into a "flesh of the world," which differs essentially from Husserls two clear and abyssal distinctions: that between lived experience and reality. And that between me and the other. These two distinctions are central for finding his monadology at least plausible. And only these distinctions allow to understand what an "intentional Being-in-another" means that is maybe not so far from Merleau-Ponty's "common system" of I and Thou in its description; but quite different with respect to its ultimate ontological claims, since it refuses to diffuse everything in an "anonymous life."

2 Husserl's Monadology

2.1 On monads

Many deep and difficult questions come up with the concept of the "monad" in Husserl: the teleology and evolution of monads, the constitution of nature, the question of "sleeping monads," the problem of birth and death. I will not treat any of these problems here. As I have pointed out above, I think that these problems go beyond stating metaphysical consequences that follow from

---

[19] Still, if we want to remain phenomenologists, there will be no way of "jumping out" of this realm of absolute givenness and relativizing it from some "view from nowhere." This, in Husserl's sense, would indeed be bad metaphysics.

transcendental phenomenology. Therefore, I think it is essential to start with what Husserl calls the *"Urfaktum,"* the primal fact that we find ourselves intertwined with others, sharing an objective world—in order to have a chance to understand this conception at all. By staying with this primal fact, I also aim to stay within the phenomenologically demonstrable, instead of confronting bold metaphysical questions that might be rightfully motivated by phenomenology, but cannot be answered within the realm of its methods.

So: What is a monad?

> To each monad belongs the unity of an I, the identity of the I with all that belongs to the I (*mit allem Ichlichen*) extended over the whole duration of time; furthermore: that which is alien to the I but still something 'subjective,' a necessary non-egoic (*ichfremder*) part of the monad. Hence, a sphere of hyletic elements (*hyletische Gegenstände*) extended through immanent time, and possibly a sphere of posited transcendent objects which present themselves as appearances through the immanent elements. (Hua 14, p. 14)
>
> This unity of universal life in lived experience (*im Erleben*), with participation of the I or not, in any case containing the possibility of participation, we call the monadic life [...]. (Hua 14, p. 46)

In its "full concreteness" (as Husserl likes to say) this not only involves the I as the subject of its capacities and habitualities, but also its full *"Umwelt,"* its *"Gegenüber"*—i.e. *all* that manifests itself in the monad in the unity of its immanent time consciousness (Hua 14, pp. 14 ff., 46 f.). The monad is its world, or, to be more precise, it is the givenness of its world, including this world that is given to it. Another quote defines the monad as the "original unity of phenomenological experience (as unity of phenomenological self-experience)" (Hua 14, p. 358). So, basically, there is nothing "outside" the monad considered as an experiential unit, since the monad is the (self-)experiencing unity and all that it correlatively experiences. This brings me to two theses concerning Husserl's conception of monads:

> T1: What Husserl understands by monad is only accessible via the transcendental reduction.
>
> T2: One central claim about monads is that they are a "self-sufficient coherence of being" (*"in sich geschlossener Seinszusammenhang"*) whose relation to everything else is strictly intentional.

Before I move to T1 and the transcendental reduction, let me very shortly call to mind what Husserl's transcendental idealism is *not* about:
- Monism. Claim: "Only consciousness is real." Husserl, by contrast: "[...] as if one wanted to say, every other kind of Being would be merely apparent, an

unreal appearance, a fiction. This, of course, would be *dead wrong*." (Hua 36, p. 70)
- Reductionism. Claim: "Nature is to be conceived phenomenalistically." Husserl, by contrast: "[...] to say, science does not deal with nature, the true objects it is concerned with would be sensations, and what we call things, atoms etc., would be mere symbols, economic cognitive abbreviations for sensations and clusters of sensations, this is the height of perversity." (Hua 36, p. 71)
- Creationism. Claim: "Consciousness creates its/the world, there is no room for passivity. Equals: Everything is deducible from the transcendental ego." Husserl, by contrast: "The primal phenomenon with respect to world-experience, world-cognition [...] is the Heraclitean flow of subjective world-givenness *(Welthabe)*, of the world that is subjectively pregiven." (HuaMat, pp. 8, 1)

As these quotes demonstrate, the challenge to understand Husserl lies in being able to hold on to a full-blown, anti-reductionist realism while, at the same time, claiming that consciousness is "the root" or "the source of everything else that is called or can be called 'Being'" (Hua 36, p. 70)—simply because Being coincides with possible givenness in an actual consciousness. Husserl's central claim is that "to be" does not have any meaning and is nothing beyond possible manifestation. This is why he does not see a contradiction in his claims. In intentional experience, the thing gives itself and not a representation. Its physical properties are not to be reduced to mental ones or to sensations. Nature is what it is. Nevertheless it "is" only, insofar as it manifests itself in consciousness. Yet: That something is "dependent" on consciousness (not only in its appearance but in its being) importantly does not equate the claim that it is not, or that it is nothing. It does not become somewhat translucent, or a dream. It also does not imply that it is made of the fabric or substance of consciousness. And, finally, it does not mean that consciousness has created it. These are the challenges that Husserl leaves us with, and even if I cannot go into a closer discussion of these complicated claims, I find it important to take Husserl seriously in what seems to be an unusual and radical conception of transcendental idealism that very much looks like a direct realism at the very same time. In order to get these two ties together, one has to remember that philosophical reflection for Husserl is an elucidation of the natural attitude that does not abolish it but that truly makes us *understand* it.

Now, if we go back to thesis T1, the transcendental reduction is the crucial operation in order to be able to develop this understanding by thematizing it. What is "naturally there" for us is traced back *(re-ducere)* to its givenness in appearance; at the same time, the reduction in fact doesn't "reduce" but rather enlarges psychologically conceived consciousness, normally perceived as locked up in our heads, to "transcendental consciousness," by which it can be conceived as being the place of the appearance of world and the very dimension of givenness. However, this happens not by construing a spectatorial subject, but by suspending the inner/outer boundaries which locate consciousness "in my head" and reality "out there." The "bearer" instead also appears as given, in the form of a constantly constituted bodily location of perspective.

The reduction hence does not install a distanced look but reveals a dimension of manifestation in which reality shows itself. Furthermore, when it inhibits locating consciousness "in" a spatio-temporal bearer, it does this without suspending its intrinsic first-personal character. This means that the field of appearance that emerges now does not become anonymous or third-personal through this move. Instead, what is recognized and held onto is that givenness is and remains always givenness for. It can never be turned just into a brute (or rather mysterious) fact of "appearance" from which later egos emerge like from a sort of "primeval soup." Instead, the transcendental reduction unfolds the first-person perspective as a constituted bodily orientedness in the world and thus as an irreducible first-personal givenness *of* the world and others. What happens additionally through this operation is that also the "mundane ego" becomes conceivable as a coherence of real, orientated, bodily, intersubjective experiences, and thus as *constituted* in a fundamental first-personal dimension of manifestation.

And now the second thesis (T2) becomes important: As such, transcendental subjectivity coincides intentionally with the world, it *is* the world in this sense. But only in intentional terms and not in the sense of an identity of matter or substance. This implies that what manifests itself is not of the same "stuff" as the dimension of manifestation, it does not coincide with the world in that sense: My perception of this furry carpet does not in any way consist of its material nor is it in any way "interwoven" with it in terms of real physical relations. Certainly, constituting and constituted dimensions are mostly experienced *as one*, but that does not ontologically mix them up or collapse them into each other. My hearing *is* the sounding of the tone in an "identity of actualization," but not in the sense that it would be the tone out there.

Furthermore, the dimension of manifestation is not "in" something. Nothing gets out of it and nothing into it. It is not "next to" any other being and it does not mix up with it (Hua 3/1, p. 105). There is not a lived experience next to a table or beneath it as its ground of appearance. Everything that is, is *"for"* it. *There is no other relation to consciousness than this "for."* Hence, "immanence" in Husserl is not something enclosed again "in" something, but a constantly self-reproducing coherence (*"ein in sich geschlossener Seinszusammenhang"*) that is the open field of appearance. It may sound paradoxical, but *immanence is openness*, it's the self-weaving fabric through which things can manifest themselves without becoming this fabric. And this field is first-personal not in the sense of an active or spectatorial I, but in the sense of the "mineness" of experiences. This mineness neither dissolves at its fringes nor is it causally affected by anything—except *intentional* causation.

If Merleau-Ponty claims that the complete reduction is impossible, he has in mind that we cannot totally distance ourselves from ourselves and that the dimension of appearance cannot be fully made transparent. But both claims are *not* necessary for the reduction to be fully carried out. *The only thing we need for the full reduction is that we consider everything in the relationship of "for"*. And I do not see why this should not be possible. As Husserl is happy to admit, there is always an "open, undetermined, dark horizon" and "what the soul is actually conscious of is paltry (*armselig*)" (Hua 15, p. 377). But that does not touch the fact that the dimension of givenness is necessary for anything to be "there" at all, since there is no "thereness" without consciousness. And this always implies a *"for"*: In other words: An intentional relation is neither real in the sense of *"real"*, natural causality; nor real in the sense of *reell* (the tone is not a part of the stream of consciousness).

2.2 The Being-in-one-another of monads

Let me now proceed to the *"Ineinander"* (Being-in-one-another) of the monads. The facticity of sharing an objective world with others is transcendentally elucidated through the phenomenological reduction; and that means it is neither thought in a naturalistic-causal nor in a representationalist way. If this attitude is consequently taken to its end, any talk about being affected from "outside" must be suspended. As Husserl notes himself, this might get in the way with how we speak about persons and how we perceive ourselves in the natural attitude. Still, he does not see a contradiction here. Rather, one has to spell out the very same thing with a depth-dimension (Hua 6, p. 122) and hence in a different language in order to understand that consciousness "has" everything in relation of the "for." Let me quote a longer passage to make this non-contradictory coexistence of attitudes clearer:

> Don't we have to say: We have to distinguish the monadic subjectivity and the person; i.e. the personal intersubjective and the intermonadic context? Isn't every monad an absolutely cohesive coherence, only of the wonderful kind, that each one can reach every other one

through appresentation (*Vergegenwärtigung*), through empathy (*Einfühlung*), and that it can recognize effects of others on itself despite the coherence (*Geschlossenheit*) of its motivations? Yet, as a person, everybody is possibly causally dependent on everybody. As a person, everybody is a person of her *Umwelt*. Each monad, through constitution, encompasses in itself its person and the *Umwelt* as that of its person. And each one, through constitution, encompasses in itself other subjects as other human beings, other bodies, other souls, [...] other persons related to their *Umwelt*. This takes place in the way that they all, with "myself," encompass the identical objective world [...] in their subjectively intended *Umwelten*.

[...] Each person has her life in the world, and each one can reduce herself to her pure subjectivity—to her monadic being, which then again has her place in the world. This is the one realm of truth, that of the natural attitude, within which the phenomenological reduction reveals the pure monadic unities as psychological (*seelische*) unities. On the other hand, in the absolute phenomenological attitude, in the transcendental one, we have the absolute monads and the absolute coherence of monads, not of monads in the world, but of monads that constitute the world within themselves and that constitute themselves for themselves in a certain way and are also able to reveal themselves to themselves phenomenologically. (Hua 14, p. 366)

While as persons we encounter a "you" in an *Umwelt* and are causally affected within that system, the monad constitutes this whole system and, within it, herself as a person and other persons, other alterities, and thus, monads. Within the monad, alterity is hence differently, perhaps more "immanently" implied than in the person who "encounters" her "you" as a *Gegenüber*.[20] But this immanent implication does not absorb alterity; it neither lessens it nor makes it transparent. It remains, to paraphrase Sartre (2003, p. 256), a "hole" in the monad itself and one should view the monad as constituted by a myriad of these holes. Hence, alterities constitute the monad as much as they are constituted by it. Coexistence is therefore implied already in its very being, and vice versa for every other monad.[21]

The radicalization and consequent follow-up of transcendental clarification hence is, for Husserl, the monadic and intermonadic perspective. It reconstructs *sharing an objective, real world* not from "outside" objects and persons causally affecting me, but indeed from a whole first-personally given "world" in which *other* whole first-personally given "worlds" are implicated as "holes." How does this work? First of all, embodiment is a necessary requirement. As we know from Husserl's reflections on transcendental intersubjectivity, there is

---

[20] This might also make conceivable in which sense Husserl denies that the *Urich* does not have a "you" and is indeclinable, while at the same time holding on to the necessary plurality of monads.

[21] Cf. for this thesis closely connected to the constitution of transcendental intersubjectivity also Iso Kern's commentary in the introduction to Hua 15, pp. xxxii f.

no objectivity without intersubjectivity (cf. Zahavi 2001). And there is no intersubjectivity without embodiment. Consequently, there is no common world without embodiment. A monad needs to "mundanize," i.e. self-objectify itself in the world which is only possible by being bodily located. This means: This "unity of experience" must have experiences that locate it in the world. Furthermore, others can manifest themselves in my experience only if they appear and are experienced as psychophysical unities and, in a further step, as transcendental egos. My world-experiences obtain the validity-character of reality only through the appresentation of others. Hence: monads need to mundanize, self-objectify, *and self-alienate* themselves to have a common world—while always remaining strictly indivisible and while everything that appears *appears for me, in the character of mineness, while it is shared*. In this whole operation of "understanding," the transcendental reduction methodically aims to guarantee that I can never "jump out" of my experience. Instead, it enables me to trace my self-constitution as an embodied subject and person, as well as see the radical transcendences that manifest themselves "(with)in" my transcendentally reduced experience. The deeper we then go into it—and that is what Husserl means by the *"in te reddere"* of Augustin—, the more pluralized and interrelated this "immanence" of experience becomes; it is, as it were, pierced through by transcendences that manifest themselves for it, as a fundamental and inescapable form of coexistence, while remaining *"ein in sich geschlossener Seinszusammenhang."*

To spell out this intermonadic sharing, a set of issues would need to be discussed in detail, which I cannot do here. Let me just point out the main stages and challenges:
a) Intermonadic time
b) Identity of appearances
c) Mirroring
d) Monadic causality
e) Primal facticity of "coordination"

Ad a) At the very basis of it all, there is the question of the constitution of intermonadic time: In which sense do two streams of consciousness share a "now"? This cannot be a pregiven, but must be constituted in each and every monad as a sharing of appearances, where the other subject is "present" as empathically (*eingefühlt*) given *presence within my presence* (inner time-consciousness).

> This fundamental relation of Being as Being-for-another must be made evident as a relation of coexistence in an intersubjective time. This is not objective, but immanently-intersubjective time of coexisting according to all modes of subjective time, and then according to identifiable stretches and positions of time. (Hua 14, p. 360)

This implication of multiple presences within my presence is, according to Husserl, the foundation for all intersubjective relations. He calls them "spiritual" (*geistige*) and "personal (*personale*) causalities" (Hua 14, p. 360), in order to mark that they are intentional causalities. And he explicitly notes among those causalities: "passive imitation, passive determination through others, [...] affectedness through others, but also active personal causalities, all I-Thou acts, we-acts, social acts of every kind" (Hua 14, p. 360). To be an absolute coherence qua stream of time-consciousness hence does not mean at all for Husserl that one cannot be influenced, even determined by others, and that one cannot act with others.

Ad b) But what is sharing appearances exactly? It is obviously not sharing the world like sharing a blanket. We rather have to ask what it means that we have "the same" appearances, that the same thing appears to us, in different streams of consciousness. Husserl slightly changed his position on this matter: Until around 1915 (Hua 14, pp. 250 f., footnote 2), he conceived the sameness of shared objects appearing in different streams of consciousness (and thus through *different* appearances) as "unities of a higher level that constitute themselves in '*Eindeutung*' [unifying interpretation]" (Hua 14, p. 250). As of 1915, he prefers to speak of "intersubjective appearances." The tricky question to be answered here is: Do the appearances "belong" to the monad or are they intersubjective? (Hua 14, p. 250) Of course, they cannot be numerically the same. But this is not a "new" problem, rather a basic question of constitution, as also in a single stream of consciousness the appearances of the same object through time are not numerically the same, while the appearing object of course is numerically the same. What Husserl hence means here by "intersubjective" is rather: the same "sight for everybody" (*Anblick für jedermann*), meaning that this view is exchangeable:

> Every human being has his own consciousness, his subjectivity, his coherences of cogitationes. [...] [S]o every human being has his groups of appearances [*Erscheinungsgruppen*], but they are 'exchangeable' with respect to the fact that every human being has 'the same' appearances of every object at every place [*Raumstelle*]. Insofar, the appearances are one's own only relatively and transiently and in a certain sense common to all normal human beings. This is how the 'sight' [*Anblick*] of a thing objectifies itself. Each of us has the same sight/view of a landscape standing at the same place with the same lighting conditions. (Hua 14, p. 251, footnote 2)

Ad c) To repeat: the difficulty is that we are not allowed to think the sameness of the object by starting out from the sameness of the object that affects us, as we would do in the natural attitude. The sharedness is thus a sharedness that only appears in a depth dimension of my own stream of consciousness through which the world and others are given to me—and vice versa for every other monad. Spelling this out would amount to the Husserlian version of Leibniz' "mirroring." But to arrive at a full picture of the "Being-in-each-other" in "mirroring" we have to consider more closely what has shortly been addressed above as monadic interaction.

Ad d) Here the question is: Do monads have "doors" and/or "windows"? Husserl's answer is that they do not have "doors" in the sense of *"reell"* points of entrance into their streams of consciousness, since everything is *for* them.[22] But they *do have windows* in the sense of being able to determine one another intentionally (Hua 14, p. 260). In order to modify this rather misfortunate metaphor that suggests monads are houses inhabited by transcendental egos (who look out of their windows and lock their doors), I would suggest to say: Monads do not "have" windows, they *are* in a sense windows, being this "openness" that is receptive of others. And that everything is *for* them *does not necessarily imply a spectatorial distance* but can also be *passive involvedness*. Now, monadic causality can be causality with respect to things or causality with respect to others. I think it is fair to argue that Husserl does not give us an explanation how psychophysical causality is possible, but rather simply describes the fact that I can move my body and change things in the world: I experience this *"Vermöglichkeit"* via the coordinated kinesthetic successions of experiences. But why doesn't Husserl need an explanation? The decisive point is that monadic causality is *experienced* causality, and thus something radically different from natural causality (which is a relation that is non-experiential). And in this view, it is plainly sufficient if the causality in question is constantly experienced and not "explained" otherwise. Husserl also makes clear that monadic causality is "not like throwing something in a pot" (Hua 14, p. 365) but essentially a relation of motivation. This holds all the more for intermonadic causation (Hua 14, pp. 260, 267; Hua 15, pp. 376 f.).

Ad e) Finally, there is the question of "coordination." Husserl says:

> The monads are not a mere heap of isolated unities with a regulation imposed on them from outside concerning which lived experiences occur in them. They are *"orientated"* by and through each other [*Sie "richten" sich nacheinander*]. In a monad, a nature is constituted and the monadic I intervenes in nature by action. Already the activity of perception is an intervention that changes nature, even if it does not change the order of nature itself. An I remodels things, the human being reshapes his earth. What each single person has actively created, is then pregiven for every other I. It is there, and that means that every action of

---

[22] "It is impossible to take a piece out of one monad *(abstücken)* and piece it together with another monad *(sicheinstücken)*. In this sense, no monad has windows into which monadic 'matter' could flow in or out." (Hua 15, p. 376)

> a monad that is directed at nature, at the world in general [...] is something that happens in the monad. It is not an action directed at another monad, but nevertheless it is a causality which affects every other monad, and which necessarily changes its content. Evenmore, as each monad in its whole 'interiority' is reachable for the other, there is nothing that happens in a monad which does not prescribe a rule for every other monad. (Hua 14, pp. 267 f.)

This means that monads "prescribe rules" (Hua 14, p. 268) for one another which is the most passive form of monadic Being-in-one-another. Even if they are totally passive, they are never *not* affected by another. Rather they regulate each other, like a holistic system: "The monads in their absolute being condition themselves." (Hua 14, p. 268) We have thus arrived at a holistically interrelated system that might indeed not be so far from what Merleau-Ponty is describing—only with different premises and consequences: While in Merleau-Ponty there seems to be one perceived world from or into whose "flesh" the single subjectivities emerge or dissolve, in Husserl there are many perceived worlds which are *implicated* in one another and thereby constitute the one objective world, while leaving the singularities intact. Nothing could be farther from an encapsulated, solipsist entity that is in no connection to others.

Furthermore, it should be clear by now that Husserl does not conceive monads as correlated "things" or clocks being spatially exteriorized—one monad "here" and another one "there," located in objective space. Of course, such kinds of monads would additionally need something or someone to bring them "in line." However, monads are "outside" of each other primarily in the sense of *"reelle Immanenz,"* which is *not spatial*. This is an imaginatively challenging thought, but a decisive one in order not to objectify consciousness into a spatially individuated thing (and to remain within the natural attitude). The spatial, *"real"* outside-relation is a constituted and thus a constitutionally consecutive one. At the same time, it is just as necessary as the embodiment of consciousness. One could say, it is the spatio-temporal equivalent of the "reell" separation: "The *reell* Being-outside of each other and having to appear outside of each other in a worldly form is a manner of self-separation of each own existence as being for-itself vis-à-vis others who are also for-themselves"[23] (Hua 15, p. 368).

Being *for another* is, intentionally explicated, being in another. Sharing a world is not sharing a hyle (the blanket-model); neither is it being affected by the same thing that then causes the hyle in each monad to be thus and so (the causal representational model). Instead, it is intentional reciprocal determination in the sense that someone is implicated in my experience as I am impli-

---

[23] We find a similar thought in Sartre's *Being and Nothingness* (cf. Sartre 2003, p. 339).

cated in his/her experience—through our bodily appearance and the actions we can take in the world. And this experience has no outside. So: It's not that we are dreaming the same dream, somewhere separated. Rather, it is in the "immanence" of my exteriorized world-experience where I discover the most radical transcendence, co-existence and reality. That *"relles Außereinander"* is at the same time *"intentionales Ineinander"* (Hua 15, p. 371) is thus no contradiction (Hua 15, p. 377) but two correlating sides of the same thing, says Husserl (Hua 15, p. 590). This also implies that *being for each other* is a relation that cannot be properly expressed in terms of spatio-temporal reality, which will always lead us to think in terms of causation from a "real outside" and thus miss or blur what the intentional "for" is about. Maybe this is why Husserl invokes, pace all impending misunderstandings, the *"in te reddere."*

2.3 The absolute attitude and the impossibility to elude coexistence

To conclude: Why should we even consider thinking like that?

As I have mentioned at the very beginning: Husserl's proposal is the most consequent way of *thinking intentionally all the way through* I know of. And Husserl's intention is to carry this out without distancing himself from experience, i.e. without becoming "metaphysical" in a detached sense. According to his own standards, the "absolute attitude" is a transcendental elucidation of experience, including its metaphysical consequences. Now: I do not see an argument why thinking intentionally (in the mode of the "for") would be wrong. And I also do not see an argument why it should stop here or there. What I wanted to make clear in this paper is that there is a direct line that leads from Husserl's analyses of intersubjectivity to their metaphysical articulation in terms of a monadology. One does not have to go there, of course, but wanting to have it half way with Husserl (by, for example, wanting to preserve radical alterity) and half way with Merleau-Ponty (by simply buying all his arguments against Husserl), seems inconsequent or at least washy to me. I agree with Husserl and, for that matter, also with Merleau-Ponty, that it does make sense to try to go all the way with one's theory and to try to spell out its metaphysical/ontological implications—or, for a quietist or Kantian version, to demonstrate why this cannot be done.

Still, the question is allowed for the sake of common sense: Even if Husserl's conception is philosophically consequent, does it make sense to think like that? Astonishingly, Husserl claims it is the only way to think that really makes sense (Hua 15, p. 370; Hua 6, p. 171). Because it makes us understand the "riddle of all riddles": that *something is (real) for me.* In a certain sense, Husserl never seeks to further explain this facticity; to go behind it is "nonsense" for him (Hua 15, p. 370). But to understand it—that is the great task of transcendental phenomenology, as Husserl also makes clear in the very last paragraph of the *Cartesian Meditations* as well as in § 49 of the *Crisis* (Hua 6, p. 171). So, to move from the naïve *"Außenbetrachtung"* of the natural attitude to the phenomenological *"Innenbetrachtung"* of the absolute attitude doesn't actually overthrow the realism of the natural attitude. Rather it is, as it were, an "idealist" clarification of "realism"—implying the claim that clarification can only be intentional and thus thinking through the "for."

Be that as it may, I think the most astonishing insight of Husserl's phenomenological metaphysics is that the absolute cannot be one. It must be plural (Hua 15, pp. 370, 341). Hence, the clarification that something is real *for me* leads me to the insight that something can only be real *for us* and that this *"being real for" is necessarily a being real for many.* Transcendental existence is "transcendental coexistence" (Hua 15, p. 370: *"transzendentales Mit-Ich"*).

> To be absolute with one another, to coexist is to coexist in and through reciprocal cognition (*Wechselerkenntnis*) [...]. There is no absolute that could elude universal coexistence, it is *nonsense*, that something is and is not connected to any other Being, that it is alone. Not only am I not *solus ipse, no* thinkable absolute is *solus ipse,* this is straightforward nonsense. (Hua 15, p. 371)

So why talk about monads? The more you go inside, the more transcendent, exteriorized and pluralized everything becomes. We are not only factically many, the claim is that it cannot be other than that, if the realism of experience is to make any sense. And in this sense, being *in* each other as being *for* each other is the metaphysical absolute (Hua 15, pp. 366, 373).[24]

References

Bernet, Rudolf (2010): "Was kann Phänomenologie heute bedeuten?" In: *Information Philosophie* 4, pp. 7–21.
Bernet, Rudolf (2015): "Transcendental Phenomenology?" In: de Warren, Nicolas/Bloechl, Jeffrey (Eds.): *Phenomenology in a New Key: Between Analysis and History.* Dordrecht: Springer, pp. 115–133.
Crowell, Steven G. (2001): *Husserl, Heidegger, and the Space of Meaning.* Evanston: Northwestern University Press.

---

[24] I would like to thank Dan Zahavi for very helpful comments on an earlier version of this text.

Gehring, Petra (2021): "Vivisektion des Naturproblems: Maurice Merleau-Ponty". Forthcoming in: Sturma, Dieter (Ed.): *Natur, Ethik und Ästhetik*. Münster: Brill/Mentis.
Heidegger, Martin (1967): *Sein und Zeit*. Tübingen: Max Niemeyer. In English: Heidegger, Martin (1962): *Being and Time*. Trans. John Macquarrie/Edward Robinson. Oxford: Basil Blackwell.
Husserl, Edmund (1950): *Cartesianische Meditationen und Pariser Vorträge*. Stephan Strasser (Ed). Husserliana I. The Hague: Martinus Nijhoff. [Hua 1]
Husserl, Edmund (1960): *Cartesian Meditations*. Trans. Dorion Cairns. Dordrecht: Springer.
Husserl, Edmund (1976): *Ideen zu einer reinen Phänomenologie und phänomenologischen Philosophie*. Karl Schuhmann (Ed.). Husserliana III/1. The Hague: Martinus Nijhoff. [Hua 3/1]
Husserl, Edmund (1954): *Die Krisis der europäischen Wissenschaften und die transzendentale Phänomenologie. Eine Einleitung in die phänomenologische Philosophie*. Walter Biemel (Ed.). Husserliana VI. The Hague: Martinus Nijhoff. [Hua 6]
Husserl, Edmund (1973a): *Zur Phänomenologie der Intersubjektivität. Texte aus dem Nachlass. Zweiter Teil: 1921–1928*. Iso Kern (Ed.). Husserliana XIV. The Hague: Martinus Nijhoff. [Hua 14]
Husserl, Edmund (1973b): *Zur Phänomenologie der Intersubjektivität. Texte aus dem Nachlass. Dritter Teil: 1929–1935*. Iso Kern (Ed.). Husserliana XV. The Hague: Martinus Nijhoff. [Hua 15]
Husserl, Edmund (2003): *Transzendentaler Idealismus. Texte aus dem Nachlass (1908–1921)*. Robin Rollinger/Rochus Sowa (Eds.). Husserliana XXXVI. Dordrecht: Kluwer. [Hua 36]
Husserl, Edmund (2006): *Späte Texte über Zeitkonstitution (1929–1934). Die C-Manuskripte*. Dieter Lohmar (Ed.). Husserliana Materialien VIII. Dordrecht: Kluwer. [Hua Mat 8]
Jansen, Julia (2017): "On Transcendental and Non-Transcendental Idealism in Husserl: A Response to De Palma and Loidolt". In: *Metodo. International Studies in Phenomenology and Philosophy* 1(2), pp. 27–39.
Loidolt, Sophie (2015): "Transzendentalphilosophie und Idealismus in der Phänomenologie". In: *Metodo. International Studies in Phenomenology and Philosophy* 1(1), pp. 103–135.
Loidolt, Sophie (2017): "Ein Kippbild? Realismus, Idealismus und Husserls transzendentale Phänomenologie". In: *Metodo. International Studies in Phenomenology and Philosophy* 1(2), pp. 83–121.
Levinas, Emmanuel (1987). "De l'intersubjectivité. Notes sur Merleau-Ponty." In: *Hors Sujet*. Paris: Fata Morgana, pp. 131–140.
Merleau-Ponty, Maurice (1964): *Signs*. Trans. Richard C. McCleary. Evanston: Northwestern University Press.
Merleau-Ponty, Maurice (1968): *The Visible and the Invisible*. Claude Lefort (Ed.). Alphonso Lingis (Trans). Evanston: Northwestern University Press.
Merleau-Ponty, Maurice (2005): *Phenomenology of Perception*. Trans. Colin Smith. London, New York: Routledge. [PP]
Moran, Dermot (2005): *Edmund Husserl: Founder of Phenomenology*. Cambridge: Polity Press.
Patočka, Jan (1970): "Der Subjektivismus der Husserlschen und die Möglichkeit einer 'asubjektiven' Phänomenologie". In: *Philosophische Perspektiven* 2, pp. 317–334.
Sartre, Jean-Paul (2003): *Being and Nothingness: An Essay in Phenomenological Ontology*. Trans. Hazel E. Barnes. London, New York: Routledge.

Steinbock, Anthony (1995): *Home and Beyond. Generative Phenomenology after Husserl.* Evanston: Northwestern University Press.
Tengelyi, László (2014): *Welt und Unendlichkeit. Zum Problem phänomenologischer Metaphysik.* Freiburg, München: Alber.
Zahavi, Dan (1999): *Self-awareness and Alterity: A Phenomenological Investigation.* Evanston: Northwestern University Press.
Zahavi, Dan (2001): *Husserl and Transcendental Intersubjectivity: A Response to the Linguistic-pragmatic Critique.* Athens: Ohio University Press.
Zahavi, Dan (2017): *Husserl's Legacy. Phenomenology, Metaphysics, and Transcendental Philosophy.* Oxford: Oxford University Press.

Nam-In Lee
Egological Reduction and Intersubjective Reduction

Abstract: Husserl conceives of his phenomenology as a systematic whole that consists of egology and the phenomenology of intersubjectivity; he accordingly addresses the egological reduction as the method of egology and the intersubjective reduction as the method of the phenomenology of intersubjectivity. Yet even though these methods are of crucial importance for the development of his phenomenology and he practices them implicitly throughout, their basic structures still remain unclear. This paper aims to clarify these structures as well as to resolve some difficulties concerning the phenomenological reduction. In section 1, I introduce three such difficulties. Then in section 2, I will specify exactly which reductions are the topic of this paper: namely, the transcendental egological reduction and the transcendental intersubjective reduction. Thereafter, in sections 3–4, I will clarify the basic structures of these reductions, and in section 5, I will show that they are two partial reductions within the universal transcendental reduction. Next, in section 6, I will show that each of these reductions must be carried out step by step, revealing different layers of each reduction. In section 7, I will use the results of section 6 to address the difficulties raised in section 1. Finally, in section 8, I will identify some future tasks related to these issues.

The egological reduction and the intersubjective reduction play a central role in the development of Husserl's phenomenology.[1] As I will show, Husserl conceives of his phenomenology as a systematic whole that consists of egology and the phenomenology of intersubjectivity; he accordingly addresses the egological reduction as the method of egology and the intersubjective reduction as the meth-

---

[1] There are many places in Husserl's works where one can come across expressions like "egological reduction" and "intersubjective reduction", as well as such other related expressions as "reduction to the sphere of ownness", "reduction to my transcendental sphere of peculiar ownness", and "primordial reduction". See. e.g., Hua 1, pp. 124, 125, 135, 136 (Husserl 1960, pp. 92, 104, 106); Hua 8, pp. 173, 316 (Husserl 2019, pp. 374, 512); Hua 9, pp. 246, 260, 262, 275, 276, 283, 324, 448, 505, 510, 511, 515, 529 (Husserl 1997, pp. 93, 112, 114, 132, 164, 232); Hua 13, pp. 77, 439 (Husserl 2006, p. 91); Hua 14, pp. 360, 419, 444 ff.; Hua 15, pp. 50, 69, 117 ff., 527 ff.

od of the phenomenology of intersubjectivity, putting them into practice for the development of the various fields of phenomenology.

Even though these methods are of crucial importance for the development of Husserl's phenomenology and he practices them implicitly throughout, he does not discuss them extensively in any of the works published during his lifetime. To the best of my knowledge, he discussed the issue of the egological reduction only on one occasion (see Hua 1, pp. 124ff.; Husserl 1960, pp. 92ff.) and never attempted to deal with the issue of the intersubjective reduction in works published during his lifetime. This is the main reason why these issues have not been discussed extensively in the literature on Husserl's phenomenology. There are some studies on the egological reduction (see, e.g., Kersten 1989; Overgaard 2002; Cairns 2013), but there are only a few studies on the intersubjective reduction (Zahavi 1996, p. 23; Schnell 2010; Park 2016), and no studies on the relationship between the egological reduction and the intersubjective reduction have been published. Their basic structures still remain unclear. And this is the reason why we need to study them systematically.

Moreover, such systematic study could provide us with a clue toward solving some difficulties concerning the phenomenological reduction in general. Even though Husserl has dealt with the phenomenological reduction over and over again and has left many texts dealing with this issue, there are still many difficulties concerning the phenomenological reduction (I will introduce three of them below in section 1). But a systematic study of the egological reduction and the intersubjective reduction can reveal an essential trait of the phenomenological reduction—namely, that it can be carried out step by step—and this essential trait can provide us with a clue to solve some of the difficulties concerning the phenomenological reduction.

This paper therefore aims to clarify the basic structures of the egological reduction and the intersubjective reduction as well as to show how some difficulties concerning the phenomenological reduction could be solved with recourse to this essential trait of the phenomenological reduction. As mentioned, in section 1, I will introduce three difficulties related to the issue of the phenomenological reduction. Then in section 2, I will specify that among four possible reductions—the transcendental egological reduction, the transcendental intersubjective reduction, the psychological egological reduction, and the psychological intersubjective reduction—the first two are the topic of this paper. Thereafter, in sections 3–4, I will clarify the basic structure of the transcendental egological reduction and the transcendental intersubjective reduction. In section 5, I will show that the transcendental egological reduction and the transcendental intersubjective reduction are two partial reductions within the universal transcendental reduction. Next, in section 6, I will show that the transcendental egological reduction and the transcendental intersubjective reduction should be carried out step by step and that each of them has different layers. In section 7, I will try to solve the difficulties introduced in section 1 by turning to the stepwise character of the transcendental egological reduction and the transcendental intersubjective reduction as discussed in section 6. Finally, in section 8, I will close with two remarks concerning some future tasks related to the issue of the egological reduction and the intersubjective reduction.

Before I start, however, I would like to make a terminological point concerning the phenomenological reduction. Husserl employs the concept of the phenomenological reduction ambiguously. For example, he sometimes uses it to designate the phenomenological-psychological reduction, sometimes to designate the transcendental-phenomenological reduction. Moreover, as will be discussed below, he employs it to designate different types of transcendental-phenomenological reduction. Yet he himself was conscious of the ambiguity of the concept of the phenomenological reduction. For example, in the lecture course on *Einleitung in die Philosophie* from 1922/23 (Hua 35, 98, p. 100), having used "phenomenological reduction" and "transcendental reduction" as two interchangeable concepts, he then makes a proposal to use the term "transcendental reduction" rather than the term "phenomenological reduction".[2] And in his *Nachwort* from 1930, when he uses the term "phenomenological reduction" to designate the transcendental reduction, he adds that in order to name it more clearly, we should employ the term "transcendental-phenomenological reduction" (Hua 5, p. 144) to designate it. Considering the ambiguity of the concept of the phenomenological reduction, I will use the term "phenomenological reduction" as a general concept that can include all of the different types of such reductions; I will use the term "transcendental reduction" to designate the transcendental-phenomenological reduction; and I will use the term "psychological reduction" to designate the phenomenological-psychological reduction.

---

[2] Thus he writes, "[...] phänomenologische oder besser transzendentale Reduktionen" (Hua 35, p. 100).

1 Some difficulties concerning the phenomenological reduction

Even though Husserl discusses the issue of the phenomenological reduction extensively, there are still many difficulties related to it. Let me introduce three of them.

1) There are certain difficulties directly related to the issue of the egological reduction, and I will mention one of them here. Husserl identifies the egological reduction with the primordial reduction.[3] After he has dealt with the issue of the primordial reduction in the Fifth Cartesian Meditation, he repeatedly attempts to clarify the concept in his manuscripts from the 1930s. In these manuscripts, when dealing with the egological reduction, Husserl addresses manifold concepts of the reduction such as "reduction to the sensuously perceivable world" (*Reduktion auf sinnlich wahrnehmbare Welt*) (Hua 15, p. 507); "the ultimate reduction that directs the seeing glance to the absolute primal life" (*die letzte Reduktion, die den schauenden Blick richtet auf das absolute urtümliche Leben*) (Hua 15, p. 585); "radical reduction to the streaming-living present" (*radikale Reduktion auf die strömend-lebendige Gegenwart*) (Hua 34, p. 185); and "the reduction to streaming primal 'immanence'" (*die Reduktion auf die strömende Ur-'Immanenz'*) (Hua 34, p. 385), as well as the "primordial reduction to the streaming now" (*primordial Reduktion auf das strömende Jetzt*) (see Hua Mat 8, pp. 204 ff.) and the "reduction to ultimate perceptions in the sense of hyletic data" (*Reduktion auf letzte Perzeptionen im Sinne hyletischer Daten*) (Hua Mat 8, pp. 133 ff.), etc. Are the primordial reduction and these other reductions having different names the same or not? If not, how do they belong together?

2) It is in *Ideen I* (1913) that Husserl first published his theory of the phenomenological reduction. The so-called Cartesian way to the transcendental reduction developed there has some difficulties that he explicitly addresses in his later phenomenology (see, e.g., Hua 6, p. 157; Husserl 1970, p. 155). But there is also another difficulty for readers of *Ideen I*. A careful reader of this text cannot overlook the fact that Husserl sometimes refers to the phenomenological reduction in the singular (e.g., Hua 3/1, pp. 131, 137, 158, 181, 188; Husserl 1982, pp. 140,

---

[3] Husserl defines both the egological reduction and the intersubjective reduction as a kind of thematic abstraction within the sphere of the universal transcendental sphere and contrasts both the "primordial" and the "egological" reduction to the intersubjective reduction. See Hua 1, p. 124 (Husserl 1960, p. 93); Hua 9, pp. 263, 276 (Husserl 1997, pp. 115, 132); Hua 14, pp. 360, 419, 444 ff. I will discuss why the egological reduction and the primordial reduction are the same in section 3 below.

149, 171, 192, 199) and sometimes refers to "reductions", in the plural (e.g., Hua 3/1, pp. 5, 6, 122, 130, 164, 182; Husserl 1982, pp. xix, xx, 131, 139, 176, 193). What is the reason for this? Are the phenomenological reduction in the singular and the plural phenomenological reductions the same or not? If they are different, how do they belong together?

3) If we take a look at Husserl's works as a whole, including *Ideen I* and his unpublished manuscripts, we encounter many difficulties concerning the phenomenological reduction. For example, while developing his transcendental phenomenology in *Die Idee* (1907), he uses the concept of the phenomenological reduction as a synonym for the transcendental reduction. Sometimes he even calls it "the epistemological reduction" (*die erkenntnistheoretische Reduktion*) (Hua 2, pp. 39, 43; Husserl 1999, pp. 30, 33). In some other later works developing transcendental phenomenology, including the 1922/23 lecture course *Einleitung in die Philosophie*, he mentions the apodictic reduction as one type of transcendental reduction (Hua 35, p. 98). How do the epistemological reduction and the apodictic reduction belong together? Are they the same or not? If not, what is the difference between them concretely?

Later I will try to solve these difficulties in section 7, after I deal with the transcendental egological reduction and the transcendental intersubjective reduction. At this point, however, let me first take into account the reason why it is necessary to develop the egological reduction and the intersubjective reduction.

2 Egological reduction and intersubjective reduction as two different types of psychological reduction as well as of transcendental reduction

It is the discovery of the possibility of developing phenomenology as a systematic whole consisting of egology (Hua 8, pp. 173, 176; Husserl 2019, pp. 374, 377) and the phenomenology of intersubjectivity as its two fundamental pillars that motivated Husserl to develop the egological reduction and the intersubjective reduction. It is the task of egology to clarify the structure of the egological subjectivity that is accessible to the phenomenological onlooker[4] through the act of re-

---

[4] In this paper, the phenomenological onlooker or the transcendental onlooker means what

flection, while it is the task of intersubjective phenomenology to clarify the structure of the other subjectivity that is accessible to the phenomenological onlooker through the act of empathy. From the perspective of the phenomenological onlooker, the essential structure of egological subjectivity as the matter of egology is totally different from the essential structure of the totality of the other subjectivities as the matter of the phenomenology of intersubjectivity.

Since the essential structure of the matters of egology and those of the phenomenology of intersubjectivity are different, they have to adopt different methods, namely, the egological reduction and the intersubjective reduction. The difference between the methods pertaining to these two kinds of phenomenology is based on the basic principle of phenomenology. According to this principle, there is an essential correspondence between the matter of a discipline and the method that this discipline has to employ in order to clarify the matter appropriately, as expressed in a passage from *Ideen I:*

> A method, after all, is nothing which is, or which can be, brought in from outside. [...] a *determinate* method [...] is a norm which arises from the fundamental regional specificity and the universal structures of the province in question, so that a cognitive seizing upon such a method depends essentially on knowledge of these structures. (Husserl 1982, p. 173)
> Methode ist ja nichts von aussen an ein Gebiet Herangebrachtes und Heranzubringendes. [...] *bestimmte* Methode [...] ist eine Norm, die aus der regionalen Grundartung des Gebietes und seiner allgemeinen Strukturen entspringt, also in ihrer erkenntnismässigen Erfassung von der Erkenntnis dieser Strukturen wesentlich abhängig ist. (Hua 3/1, p. 161)

Husserl has developed his phenomenology as an egology in two major works published during his lifetime—*Logische Untersuchungen* (1900/01) and *Ideen I* (1913). In these works, he confines his discussion to egological subjectivity by abstractively setting aside any intersubjective relations with other subjectivities. In this context, analyzing the relationship between expression and meaning in *Logische Untersuchungen*, he excludes "expressions as they function in communication" (*die Ausdrücke in kommunikativer Funktion*) (Hua 19/1, p. 39; Husserl 2001, p. 189) from the discussion and takes into account only "expressions in solitary life" (*die Ausdrücke im einsamen Seelenleben*) (Hua 19/1, p. 41; Husserl 2001, p. 190). In this way the phenomenology developed there takes the form of an egology. This is also the case in *Ideen I*. For instance, in one of its closing sections, we find the following passage that clearly indicates that the phenomenology developed in this work is an egology:

Husserl calls "the phenomenologizing ego" (das phänomenologisierende Ich) (Hua 8, p. 440; cf. Hua 34, pp. 176, 184, 477).

> The *next higher level* is then the *intersubjectively identical physical thing*—a constitutive unity of a higher order. Its constitution is related to an open plurality of subjects standing in a relation of "understanding one another". The intersubjective world is the correlate of intersubjective experience, i.e., experience mediated by *"empathy"*. (Husserl 1982, p. 363, trans. altered)
>
> Die *nächsthöhere Stufe* ist dann das *intersubjektiv identische Ding*, eine konstitutive Einheit höherer Ordnung. Ihre Konstitution ist bezogen auf eine offene Mehrheit im Verhältnis des "Einverständnisses" stehender Subjekte. Die intersubjektive Welt ist das Korrelat der intersubjektiven, d.i. der durch *"Einfühlung"* vermittelten Erfahrung. (Hua 3/1, p. 352)

But the undeniable fact that Husserl developed his phenomenology in *Logische Untersuchungen* and *Ideen I* as an egology should not motivate one to believe that he first tried to develop the phenomenology of intersubjectivity only in his later philosophy. Contrary to what one might think, Husserl was engaged in the phenomenology of intersubjectivity as early as 1905 (see Hua 13, pp. 1 ff.).

From the very beginning, then, Husserl tried to develop his phenomenology as a systematic whole consisting of egology and the phenomenology of intersubjectivity as its two pillars. Correspondingly, he tried to develop the egological reduction as the method of egology and the intersubjective reduction as the method of the phenomenology of intersubjectivity.

Both the egological reduction and the intersubjective reduction are each divided into two main kinds. In this context, it should be noted that Husserl has developed two dimensions of phenomenology, namely, phenomenological psychology as the phenomenology of the natural attitude and transcendental phenomenology as the phenomenology of the transcendental attitude. There are accordingly two kinds of egological reduction—(1) the psychological egological reduction and (2) the transcendental egological reduction—as well as two kinds of intersubjective reduction, (3) the psychological intersubjective reduction and (4) the transcendental intersubjective reduction.

The psychological reduction is a pre-stage of the transcendental reduction and the latter is the deepened form of the former. For this reason, I will deal only with the transcendental reduction, namely, the transcendental egological reduction and the transcendental intersubjective reduction. Let me first clarify the basic structure of the transcendental egological reduction.

3 The transcendental egological reduction

The transcendental egological reduction can first be carried out only after the universal transcendental reduction, as a total and radical change from the natural attitude to the transcendental attitude, has been carried out in advance.

If the transcendental onlooker carries out the universal transcendental reduction, she/he obtains a universal research field comprising her/his own transcendental subjectivity along with the other transcendental subjectivities, together with the different kinds and layers of the world and the worldly objects that these subjectivities have constituted. Husserl calls this universal research field "the universal transcendental sphere" (*der transzendentalen Universalsphäre*) (Hua 1, p. 124; Husserl 1950, p. 93). From the perspective of the transcendental onlooker, the transcendental universal sphere consists of 1) the primordial sphere as the sphere of her/his own transcendental subjectivity and 2) the sphere of the other transcendental subjectivities.

It is the aim of the transcendental egological reduction to obtain "the sphere of ownness" (*die Eigenheitssphäre*) (Hua 1, p. 124; Husserl 1960, p. 92), or primordial sphere, of the transcendental onlooker as the sphere of her/his own transcendental subjectivity, which is different from the other transcendental subjectivities. In other words, it is a "reduction of transcendental experience to the sphere of ownness" (*Reduktion der transzendentalen Erfahrung auf die Eigenheitssphäre*) (Hua 1, p. 124; Husserl 1960, p. 92). This is why Husserl calls it the primordial reduction. In order to carry out the transcendental egological reduction or the primordial reduction, the transcendental onlooker has to take worldly experience "purely as immanent, and thereby disregard, or explicitly abstractively exclude, the co-acceptance of the experiences of others" (*rein als immanente [...] und dabei die Mitgeltung der Erfahrungen Anderer übersehe oder ausdrücklich abstraktiv ausschalte*) (Hua 14, p. 419). Husserl describes the process of transcendental egological reduction as follows:

> As regards method, a prime requirement for proceeding correctly here is that first of all we carry out, within the universal transcendental sphere, a peculiar kind of epoché with respect to our theme. For the present, we exclude from the thematic field everything now in question: we *disregard all constitutive effects of intentionality relating immediately or mediately to foreign subjectivity* and delimit first of all the total nexus of that actual and potential intentionality in which the ego constitutes itself in its peculiar ownness and in the synthetic unities inseparable from its peculiar ownness, unities that are themselves therefore to be ascribed to this ownness. (Husserl 1960, p. 93, trans. altered)
>
> Um hier richtig vorzugehen, ist es ein erstes methodisches Erfordernis, dass wir zunächst innerhalb der transzendentalen Universalsphäre eine eigentümliche Art thematischer Epoché durchführen. Wir schalten alles jetzt Fragliche vorerst aus dem thematischen Felde aus, das ist, wir *sehen von allen konstitutiven Leistungen der auf fremde Subjektivität unmittelbar oder mittelbar bezogenen Intentionalität ab* und umgrenzen zunächst den Gesamtzusammenhang derjenigen Intentionalität, der aktuellen und potentiellen, in der sich das ego in seiner Eigenheit konstituiert und in der es von ihr unabtrennbare, also selbst ihrer Eigenheit zuzurechnende synthetische Einheiten konstituiert. (Hua 1, pp. 124–125)

As this passage shows, in order to obtain the primordial sphere, the transcendental onlooker has to exclude the transcendental sphere of the other subjectivities from the transcendental universal sphere and pay attention solely to its own transcendental subjectivity. Thus, the transcendental egological reduction turns out to be a kind of thematic abstraction,[5] which Husserl describes as follows:

> It is possible in any case to perform a phenomenological *abstraction,* or to delimit phenomenological experience—and the research based on it—in such a way that one moves only within the concrete unitary nexus of one's own transcendental subjectivity, and—refraining from any empathy—takes no foreign subjectivity into account. (Husserl 2019, pp. 376–377, trans. altered)
>
> Es ist jedenfalls möglich, eine phänomenologische *Abstraktion* zu vollziehen oder die phänomenologische Erfahrung und auf Erfahrung beruhende Forschung so zu beschränken, dass man nur in dem konkreten Einheitszusammenhang der eigenen transzendentalen Subjektivität sich bewegt und, von jeder Einfühlung absehend, keine fremde Subjektivität in Rechnung zieht. (Hua 8, p. 176)

The primordial sphere has two sides, namely, the noetic side as the totality of the constituting acts of the transcendental onlooker and the noematic side as the world and worldly objects constituted by the noetic side. The noetic side of the primordial sphere is an immanent sphere that can be grasped by the transcendental onlooker through the act of reflection. It is called an immanent sphere since the reflecting act and the act reflected upon belong together to the same stream of consciousness, namely, that of the transcendental onlooker (see Hua 3/1, p. 78; Husserl 1982, p. 79). The act of reflection is normally considered to be an act in which the reflecting act grasps the reflected-upon act in the mode of apodictic evidence. In Husserl's phenomenology, however, the noetic side of the primordial sphere as an immanent sphere is conceived as a sphere that cannot be grasped without residue in the mode of apodictic evidence, since it is a stream of consciousness and has temporal dimensions such as the transcendental present, the transcendental past, and the transcendental future (see Hua 8, pp. 82 ff.; Husserl 2019, pp. 286 ff.), as well as transcendental retention, transcendental protention, etc.

---

5 Here one might refer to the interconnectedness of the subjectivities and to the impossibility of divorcing one subjectivity from the other subjectivities, and therefore claim that it is impossible to carry out the egological reduction. It should be noted, however, that the egological reduction as a thematic abstraction is different from divorcing one subjectivity from the other subjectivities. Even though one subjectivity cannot be divorced from the other subjectivities, the egological reduction could still be carried out as a *thematic* abstraction. I have discussed issues related to this topic in Lee 2002, Lee 2010.

It is in "transcendental experience" (*transzendentale Erfahrung*) (Hua 34, p. 164; Hua 6, p. 156; Husserl 1970, p. 153, and see also Hua 8, pp. 69 ff., 75 ff., 146 ff., 169 ff., 360; Husserl 2019, pp. 274 ff., 279 ff., 347 ff., 370 ff.; for "transzendentale Empirie", see Hua 35, pp. 112 ff.) that the different temporal dimensions of the noetic side of the primordial sphere can be experienced. It should be noted, however, that each of the different temporal dimensions is experienced in a specific transcendental experience corresponding to it. For example, the transcendental present is experienced in "phenomenological [transcendental] *perception*" (Hua 13, pp. 159 ff.; Husserl 2006, pp. 53 ff.); the transcendental past is experienced in "transcendental recollection" (Hua 35, p. 133; cf. Hua 13, pp. 162 ff.; Husserl 2006, pp. 56 ff.); and the transcendental future is experienced in "phenomenological [transcendental] expectation" (Hua 13, p. 165; Husserl 2006, p. 59).

Of course, some of the temporal dimensions of the noetic side of the primordial sphere can indeed be experienced in the mode of apodictic evidence. A typical example is the transcendental present. Moreover, Husserl admits that even though the transcendental retention is a "*'transcendence' within the phenomenological attitude*" (Hua 13, p. 161; Husserl 2006, p. 56), it too could be experienced in the mode of apodictic evidence (see also Hua 3/1, p. 168.; Husserl 1982, p. 180 f; Hua 35, pp. 133 ff.). In this context, he even maintains "that to mistrust such a givenness is tantamount to surrendering to the forces of absolute skepticism" (*dass solcher Gegebenheit misstrauen so viel hiesse wie sich dem absoluten Skeptizismus in die Arme werfen*) (Hua 13, p. 162; Husserl 2006, p. 56).

Nevertheless, in contrast to the transcendental present and transcendental retention, the transcendental past or the transcendental future cannot be experienced in the mode of apodictic evidence. Transcendental recollection as the experience of the transcendental past and transcendental expectation as the experience of the transcendental future are not justified "as absolutely indubitable" (*als absolute Zweifellosigkeiten*) (Hua 13, p. 163; Husserl 2006, p. 57). It is possible for the transcendental onlooker to doubt their validity.

As the examples of transcendental reflection show, some of them, such as the transcendental experience of the transcendental present or of transcendental retention, can be carried out immediately without the help of any other method such as the method of interpretation. However, some of them cannot be carried out immediately and do need the method of interpretation. A typical example would be a transcendental memory directed to the remote past of the noetic side of the primordial sphere, a past that the transcendental onlooker might not remember clearly. In this case, in order to carry out the transcendental memory of the remote past, the phenomenological onlooker would have to interpret it with the help, for example, of others who know something about it. In this way, some transcendental reflections have to be combined with the method of interpretation.

Moreover, there are some forms of transcendental reflection that need the method of dismantling or deconstruction (*Abbau*) as well as that of construction (*Aufbau*) and reconstruction (*Rekonstruktion*).[6] It should be noted that the noetic side of the primordial sphere has a depth dimension filled with habits, drives, instincts, and other possible unconscious elements that cannot be grasped immediately by the reflecting ego. In order to clarify the structure of the depth dimension of the noetic side of the primordial sphere systematically, the transcendental onlooker has to dismantle, construct, and reconstruct the various layers of consciousness.

4 The transcendental intersubjective reduction

To the best of my knowledge, Husserl develops the method of intersubjective reduction for the first time in a manuscript from 1910 (Hua 13, pp. 77 ff.; Husserl 2006, pp. 91 ff.) that was written as a preparation for the lecture course on *Grundprobleme der Phänomenologie* (1910/11). There he defines "the intersubjective reduction as reduction to the psychologically pure intersubjectivity" (*Die intersubjektive Reduktion als Reduktion auf die psychologisch reine Intersubjektivität*) (Hua 13, p. 76; Husserl 2006, p. 91), that is, as a type of psychological reduction. Thus, the intersubjective reduction is initially introduced as a psychological intersubjective reduction, not as a transcendental intersubjective reduction. However, this undeniable circumstance should not motivate one to believe that Husserl never developed a transcendental intersubjective reduction.

In fact, Husserl already conceives of the intersubjective reduction as a transcendental intersubjective reduction in these 1910/11 lectures. In this context, he deals with the question whether the phenomenological reduction, i.e., the transcendental-phenomenological reduction, means a "restriction" (*Einschränkung*) (Hua 13, p. 184; Husserl 2006, p. 79) to individual consciousness. What matters here is the question whether the transcendental reduction is an egological reduction or not. To this question, he replies in the negative, since transcendental subjectivity is not merely an egological subjectivity, but an intersubjectivity as a multiplicity of monads (see Hua 13, pp. 183, 188 ff.; Husserl 2006, pp. 79, 84 ff.). In order to clarify the other transcendental subjectivities as a multiplicity or plu-

---

[6] The method of reconstruction is discussed in Bower 2014; I have dealt with the methods of dismantling, constructing, and reconstructing in Lee 1993.

rality of monads, the transcendental onlooker has to adopt the transcendental intersubjective reduction.

The transcendental intersubjective reduction is carried out in the transcendental empathy that Husserl calls "phenomenological empathy" (*phänomenologische [...] Einfühlung*) (Hua 13, p. 172; Husserl 2006, p. 67). In order to understand what the transcendental intersubjective reduction means, one has to grasp what transcendental empathy means. The transcendental reduction that is performed upon empathy as it has already been carried out in the natural attitude provides us with a clue to grasp what the transcendental intersubjective reduction is. The empathy that is carried out in the natural attitude has a noetic-noematic structure: it has the act of empathy as the noesis, on the one hand, and on the other hand, it has the object to which the act of empathy is directed as its noema. The noema to which the act of empathy is directed is the other subjectivity.

Corresponding to the noetic-noematic structure of empathy, the transcendental onlooker can then carry out phenomenological (transcendental) reduction in a *"twofold manner"* (*die doppelte Art der phänomenologischen Reduktion*) (Hua 13, p. 189; Husserl 1982, p. 84) on the empathy that is already carried out in the natural attitude. On the one hand, she/he could carry out the transcendental reduction on her/his own act of empathy as the noesis. This reduction reveals the act of empathy as a constituting act. On the other hand, she/he could carry out the transcendental reduction on the other subjectivity as the noema of the act of empathy. This reduction reveals the other subjectivity as a transcendental subjectivity that constitutes the world and worldly objects.

Among these two kinds of transcendental reduction, the second transcendental reduction that reveals the other subjectivity as another transcendental subjectivity is the intersubjective transcendental reduction. It should be noted that the other transcendental subjectivity that reveals itself through the second reduction does not belong to the primordial sphere of the transcendental onlooker. In the 1910/11 lectures on *Grundprobleme der Phänomenologie*, Husserl does attempt to clarify the structure of the transcendental intersubjective reduction, although he does not use the expression "transcendental intersubjective reduction" or expressions equivalent to it. However, in his later manuscripts, he does deal with the transcendental reduction to intersubjectivity (see Hua 13, pp. 438f.), speaking of the "reduction to the ultimately constituting intersubjective life" (*Reduktion auf das intersubjektiv letztkonstituierende Leben*) (Hua 15, p. 69) or of "the reduction to the universe of the intersubjective [...] that encompasses everything individual-subjective" (*die Reduktion auf das Universum des Intersubjektiven [...], das alles Einzelsubjektive in sich fast*) (Hua 15, p. 69).

So far, we have seen that the transcendental intersubjective reduction is carried out through transcendental empathy. As an experience of the other transcendental subjectivity, transcendental empathy is itself a kind of transcendental experience. It should be noted, however, that it is not a type of transcendental reflection. As already indicated, it is one of the essential traits of transcendental reflection that the reflecting act and the reflected-upon act belong to the same stream of consciousness. But transcendental empathy displays a different structure, since the reflecting act of the phenomenological onlooker does not belong to the same stream of consciousness to which the reflected-upon act of the other transcendental subjectivity belongs. For this reason, it cannot be called a type of transcendental reflection.

The other transcendental subjectivity is experienced in transcendental empathy in different ways, and correspondingly, there are different kinds of transcendental intersubjective reduction. In order to understand the different kinds of transcendental intersubjective reduction, we have to analyze the different ways in which the other transcendental subjectivity can be experienced in transcendental empathy. There are many perspectives from which the other transcendental subjectivity could be experienced. If we take the historical perspective, the other transcendental subjectivity could be experienced as a transcendental ancestor, a transcendental contemporary, or a transcendental descendent. There are accordingly three different kinds of transcendental empathy, such as transcendental empathy of a transcendental contemporary, that of a transcendental ancestor, and that of a transcendental descendent.

These three kinds of transcendental empathy could in turn be divided into different sub-kinds, since there are different ways in which the transcendental contemporary, ancestor, and descendent could be more concretely experienced. For example, the transcendental contemporary could be concretely experienced in different ways, i.e., it could be experienced by the transcendental onlooker differently from different perspectives. From the spatial perspective, for instance, it could be experienced as a transcendental subjectivity that is in the present field of the transcendental onlooker or in the field that goes beyond the scope of the latter. From the communicative perspective, it could be experienced as a transcendental subjectivity with whom the transcendental onlooker could communicate or not. There are, of course, further perspectives beyond these two, and the combination of different perspectives could yield manifold ways of experiencing the other transcendental subjectivity. Thus, it turns out that there are manifold kinds of transcendental empathy that correspond to the manifold ways of experiencing the other transcendental subjectivity.

It is an essential structure of the transcendental intersubjective reduction that it is carried out by means of the method of interpretation, since the transcendental empathy through which the transcendental intersubjective reduction is carried out is nothing other than the act of interpreting the other transcendental subjectivity. It is totally different from the transcendental egological reduction, since there are some kinds of transcendental egological reduction, such as the reduction to the transcendental present or to transcendental retention, that do not need the method of interpretation at all.

Corresponding to the different kinds of transcendental empathy, there are different kinds of transcendental intersubjective reduction. It should be noted, however, that the transcendental intersubjective reduction needs different kinds of interpretation that have their origin in different kinds of transcendental empathy as an act of interpretation. For example, the transcendental empathy into a transcendental contemporary whom the transcendental onlooker experiences in the present field is a different kind of interpretation than the transcendental empathy into a transcendental ancestor, since the former does not need to rely upon the method of linguistic interpretation that may well be necessary for the latter.

Since the transcendental intersubjective reduction employs the method of interpretation, it is different from the transcendental egological reduction in yet another respect. Carrying out the transcendental intersubjective reduction, the transcendental onlooker cannot have the transcendental experience in the mode of apodictic evidence. This makes it essentially different from the transcendental egological reduction, since in carrying out the transcendental egological reduction, the transcendental onlooker can indeed have the transcendental experience in the mode of apodictic evidence. A typical example of this would be the transcendental present or the transcendental retention already mentioned.

Finally, interpretation is not the only method that transcendental empathy employs. The method of dismantling or deconstruction (*Abbau*), that of construction (*Aufbau*), and that of reconstruction that were mentioned above are needed for some types of transcendental empathy, since—like the transcendental subjectivity of the transcendental onlooker—the other transcendental subjectivity also has its depth dimension that could only be grasped by these methods.

5 The relationship between the egological reduction and the intersubjective reduction

What is then the relationship between the transcendental egological reduction and the transcendental intersubjective reduction? We may take empathy, as the act through which the intersubjective reduction is carried out, as a clue toward understanding this relationship. A person cannot carry out the act of empathy as an act of experiencing a certain kind of consciousness pertaining to the other subjectivity if she/he has not experienced the same kind of consciousness in her/his own stream of consciousness. For example, if a person has not experienced a certain kind of pain, she/he cannot carry out an act of empathy regarding the same kind of pain as experienced by the other subjectivity. This implies that the egological reduction is the condition of the possibility of the intersubjective reduction. The phenomenological onlooker cannot carry out the intersubjective reduction of a certain kind of consciousness pertaining to the other subjectivity if she/he has not carried out the egological reduction of the same kind of consciousness in herself/himself. Husserl himself also considers the egological reduction to be the condition of the possibility of the intersubjective reduction. In this context, he describes the relationship between the egological reduction and the intersubjective reduction as follows:

> The carrying out of the phenomenological reduction in my actual and possible acceptance of a "foreign" subjectivity in the evidential form of concordant empathy is the intersubjective reduction. On the basis of the egological reduction the intersubjective reduction renders accessible the foreign psychic life originally confirmed in it, along with this life's pure psychic nexuses. (Husserl 1997, p. 115, trans. altered)
>
> Die Durchführung der phänomenologischen Reduktion in meinem wirklichen und möglichen in Geltung Setzen "fremden" Seelenlebens in der Evidenzform einstimmiger Einfühlung ist die intersubjektive Reduktion. Auf dem Grunde der egologischen Reduktion macht sie das in ihr ursprünglich sich bewährende fremde Seelenleben in seinen rein psychischen Zusammenhängen zugänglich. (Hua 9, p. 263)

It should be noted that the egological reduction and the intersubjective reduction mentioned in this passage mean, respectively, the psychological egological reduction and the psychological intersubjective reduction. Thus, it turns out that Husserl claims that the psychological egological reduction is the condition of the possibility of the psychological intersubjective reduction. However, the foundational relationship between the egological reduction and the intersubjective reduction is valid not only for the psychological reduction, but also for the transcendental reduction: the transcendental onlooker could not carry out the transcendental intersubjective reduction on the other subjectivity if she/he were not able to carry out the transcendental egological reduction on her/his own subjectivity.

Considering the foundational relationship between the transcendental egological reduction and the transcendental intersubjective reduction, Husserl describes the latter as a "broadened intersubjective reduction" (<die> erweiterte intersubjektive Reduktion) (Hua 35, p. 103). This phrase might give the impression that as a widened form of reduction, the intersubjective reduction is the whole of the transcendental egological reduction, while the latter, as the less broad form of reduction, is a part of the former. In other words, it might give us the impression that the relationship between the transcendental egological reduction and the transcendental intersubjective reduction might be a relationship between part and whole.

It should be noted, however, that the relationship between the transcendental egological reduction and the transcendental intersubjective reduction is not that of part and whole. Rather, they are two different parts of the universal transcendental reduction. In other words, they are two different partial reductions that could be carried out after the universal transcendental reduction has been carried out in advance. This is the reason why Husserl describes the transcendental egological reduction as a reduction that is carried out through "a peculiar kind of thematic epoché" (*eine eigentümliche Art thematischer Epoché*) performed first of all "within the universal transcendental sphere" (*innerhalb der transzendentalen Universalsphäre*) (Hua 1, p. 124; Husserl 1960, p. 93, trans. altered). It should be noted, however, that not only the transcendental egological reduction, but also the transcendental intersubjective reduction is a reduction that is carried out by means of such a thematic epoché performed within the universal transcendental sphere. In this respect, there is no basic difference between the transcendental egological reduction and the transcendental intersubjective reduction: they are two different partial reductions within the universal transcendental reduction.

6 The stepwise character of the transcendental reduction

The transcendental egological reduction and the transcendental intersubjective reduction as two partial reductions of the universal transcendental reduction could once again be divided into partial reductions at a lower level. In other words, after the transcendental onlooker has carried out the transcendental egological reduction or the transcendental intersubjective reduction, she/he could further carry out lower levels of the transcendental egological reduction or the transcendental intersubjective reduction. Again, after the transcendental onlooker has carried out any of these lower levels of either the transcendental egological reduction or the transcendental intersubjective reduction, she/he could carry out even lower levels of the transcendental egological or the transcendental intersubjective reduction. Thus the transcendental reduction can be carried out step by step. The stepwise character of the transcendental reduction is one of the essential traits of the transcendental reduction.

It is precisely the stepwise character of the transcendental reduction that motivates Husserl to recognize that "we must in fact develop various different concepts of reduction" (*wir werden in der Tat den Begriff der Reduktion vervielfältigen müssen*) (Hua 35, p. 98). It is the stepwise character of the transcendental reduction that engenders the different "layers of [transcendental] reduction" (*Reduktionsstufen*) (Hua Mat 8, p. 68). The transcendental reduction has to pass through these different layers so that it can become concrete and fulfill its task. In this context, clarifying the structure of the transcendental reduction, Husserl points out that: "In the alteration of these partial attitudes [...] the universal task of inquiry, that of the transcendental reduction, is brought to realization" (*Im Wechsel dieser ineinander fundierten partialen Einstellungen [...] verwirklicht sich die universale Forschungsaufgabe der transzendentalen Reduktion*) (Hua 6, p. 177; Husserl 1970, p. 174).[7]

Not only the transcendental egological reduction, but also the transcendental intersubjective reduction could be carried out step by step and become concrete. I will now show how the transcendental intersubjective reduction can be carried out step by step.[8]

After the transcendental onlooker has carried out the transcendental intersubjective reduction, she/he could carry out the transcendental intersubjective reduction to the other transcendental intersubjectivity as a transcendental contemporary, ancestor, or descendent. Moreover, after she/he has carried out any of these kinds of transcendental intersubjective reduction, she/he could carry out different kinds of transcendental intersubjective reduction at a lower level. For example, after she/he has carried out the transcendental intersubjective reduction to the other transcendental subjectivity as a transcendental contemporary, she/he could carry out the transcendental intersubjective reduction to the other transcendental subjectivity in the present field or in the non-present field.

Husserl seems to denounce the stepwise character of the phenomenological reduction in § 40 of the *Crisis*. There he refers to "the temptation to misconstrue it [i.e., the "total epoché" pertaining to the transcendental-phenomenological reduction] as a withholding of all individual validities, carried out step by step"

---

[7] One could get "the partial attitudes" mentioned in this passage only through a phenomenological reduction that is carried out step by step. In this respect, it should be noted that the phenomenological reduction is characterized in terms of a "change of attitude" (*Einstellungsänderung*) (Hua 15, pp. 25, 506; Hua 34, p. 225), namely, the change from one attitude to another.
[8] In section 7 below I will show in detail how the transcendental egological reduction can be carried out step by step.

(*die Verführung, sie als eine schrittweise zu leistende Enthaltung von allen einzelnen Geltungen misszuverstehen*) (Hua 6, p. 151; Husserl 1970, p. 148). Here Husserl explicitly warns against the temptation to believe that the transcendental reduction is carried out in stepwise fashion. For this reason, one might get the impression that what I have described above with respect to the stepwise character of the transcendental reduction is not valid.

It should be noted, however, that the stepwise character Husserl mentions in § 40 of the *Crisis* is not the same as the stepwise character that I have clarified. When he is warning us against the stepwise character of the transcendental reduction in § 40 of the *Crisis,* what he has in mind is the first step of the transcendental reduction, that is, the universal transcendental reduction that should be carried out before carrying out the transcendental egological reduction and the transcendental intersubjective reduction as its partial reductions. The universal transcendental reduction as a radical change from the natural attitude to the transcendental attitude is to be carried out totally and all of a sudden, not step by step. However, after the transcendental onlooker has carried out the universal transcendental reduction, she/he can only carry out different layers of the transcendental reduction step by step, as discussed above.

With respect to the stepwise character of the transcendental reduction, I would like to mention the following three points.

First, I have dealt only with the stepwise character of the transcendental reduction. However, not only the transcendental reduction, but also the psychological reduction could be carried out step by step.

Second, the pluralistic concept of the phenomenological reduction advocated by some scholars (see, e.g., Orth 2002; Lohmar 2002) has its origin in the stepwise character of the phenomenological reduction. Since the phenomenological reduction that is to be carried out concretely must be carried out step by step, it has to take different forms, and thus the concept of the phenomenological reduction turns out to be pluralistic.

Third, with respect to the stepwise character of the phenomenological reduction, it should be noted that the phenomenological reduction is "a method that leads to a field of experience" (*eine Methode, die auf ein Erfahrungsfeld zurückführt*) (Lohmar 2002, p. 753), a field that can be disclosed only by such a method. Not only the universal transcendental reduction, but also each of the different forms of the transcendental reduction as the partial reductions of the universal transcendental reduction—as well as each of the different forms of the psychological reduction—is a method leading to a field of experience that is only accessible in this way.

7 Solutions to some difficulties concerning the phenomenological reduction

The stepwise character of the transcendental reduction can give us a clue toward solving the three difficulties mentioned above in section 1. Let me clarify how these could be resolved with recourse to the stepwise character of the transcendental reduction.

7.1 The difficulty concerning the different concepts of reduction related to the primordial reduction

I will first deal with the difficulty concerning the different concepts of reduction related to the primordial reduction. While dealing with the primordial reduction in his later manuscripts from the 1930s, Husserl addresses multiple concepts of reduction. The concept of the reduction in these manuscripts is really ambiguous in many respects. I will show that many of them are different types of primordial reduction.

As discussed above, the primordial sphere that the transcendental onlooker obtains through the primordial reduction has two sides, namely, the noetic side and the noematic side. Thus, it is necessary to make a distinction between two types of primordial reduction, namely, the reduction to the noetic side and the reduction to the noematic side of the primordial sphere (see Hua 14, p. 446). Moreover, there are different kinds of primordial reduction to the noetic side of the primordial sphere as well as to the noematic side. Let me first clarify the different kinds of primordial reduction to the noetic side of the primordial sphere.

After the transcendental onlooker has carried out the transcendental egological reduction, she/he could further carry out different kinds of transcendental reduction. For instance, she/he could carry out a reduction to the noetic side or to the noematic side of the primordial sphere. Here the reduction to the noetic side of the primordial sphere could be called a reduction to the stream of consciousness of her/his own transcendental subjectivity. In a manuscript from the 1930s, Husserl makes a distinction between the world on the one hand and the I as the transcendental subjectivity that constitutes the world on the other, and he deals with the possibility of carrying out the reduction to "I as the identical I of present, recalled, [and] possible perceptions—having and confirming experiential unity" (*Ich als identisches Ich jetziger, wiedererinnerter, vermöglicher Wahrnehmungen—Erfahrungseinheit habend und bewährend*) (Hua 15,

p. 557). Husserl calls this reduction the "first reduction" (*erste Reduktion*) (Hua 15, p. 557) and claims that "in this reduction I find the I-pole, the stream of lived experience or of life as a temporal stream, I-acts, capability, appearances-of, etc" (*In dieser Reduktion finde ich vor Ichpol, Erlebnis- oder Lebensstrom als Zeitstrom, Ichakte, Vermöglichkeit, Erscheinungen von etc.*) (Hua 15, p. 557).

After the transcendental onlooker has carried out the reduction to the noetic side of the primordial sphere as the stream of consciousness, she/he could carry out further reductions. For example, she/he could carry out the reduction to the transcendental past, the transcendental present, or the transcendental future of her/his stream of consciousness. In this way, she/he could then also carry out different kinds of primordial reduction at a lower level, such as the reduction to the transcendental past, the transcendental present, or the transcendental future. Among these, the reduction to the transcendental present[9] could be called the reduction to the "streaming of the present" (*Strömen der Gegenwart*) (Hua 15, p. 585). Here the "streaming of the present" is a part of the stream of consciousness that has "temporal modalities" (*Zeitmodalitäten*) (Hua 15, p. 585) such as the past, the present, and the future.

Furthermore, after the transcendental onlooker has carried out the reduction to the transcendental present of her/his own stream of consciousness, she/he could further carry out "the ultimate reduction that directs the seeing regard to the absolute primal life, to the primal I-am, to the streaming, to the primally passive streaming" (*die letzte Reduktion, die den schauenden Blick richtet auf das urtümliche Leben, auf das urtümlich Ich-bin, auf das Strömen, auf das urpassive Strömen*) (Hua 15, p. 585). What matters here is the reduction to "the absolutely primal pre-being of the streaming" (*das absolute urtümliche Vorsein des Strömens*) (Hua 15, p. 585) that does not initially have the temporal modality of the past, the present, and the future, but then immediately becomes a "temporal stream with temporal modalities" (*Zeitstrom mit Zeitmodalitäten*) (Hua 15, p. 585). Husserl uses different expressions to designate this reduction, such as "radical reduction to the streaming-living present" (*radikale Reduktion auf die strömend-lebendige Gegenwart*) (Hua 34, p. 185) and "the reduction to *streaming primal 'immanence'*" (*die Reduktion auf die strömende Ur-'Immanenz'*) (Hua 34, p. 385), as well as employing a "primordial reduction to the streaming now in which the temporal modalities are constituted" (*primordiale Reduktion auf das strömende Jetzt, in dem sich die Zeitmodalitaten konstituieren*) (see Hua Mat 8,

---

[9] Held calls this "the transcendental-phenomenological reduction to the streaming perceptual present" (die transzendentalphänomenologische Reduktion auf strömende Wahrnehmungsgegenwart) (Held 1966, p. 17).

pp. 204 ff.) or a "reduction to the primally original in the sense of that which is no longer appearance: absolute perception" (*Reduktion auf das Uroriginale im Sinne desjenigen, das nicht mehr Erscheinung ist: die absolute Perzeption*) (see Hua 15, p. 560).[10]

Now I will take into account the primordial reduction to the noematic side of the primordial sphere. After the transcendental onlooker has carried out the primordial reduction to the primordial sphere, she/he can carry out the reduction to the noematic side of the primordial sphere. What matters here is the reduction to the transcendental onlooker's experiential world, a world that consists of the world of perception, the world of memory, and the world of expectation, which can also be expressed as a "primordial reduction (abstraction) to my world of experience, first of all to my perceptual world—presentation and appresentation" (*Primordiale Reduktion (Abstraktion) auf meine Erfahrungswelt, zunächst auf meine Wahrnehmungswelt. Präsentation und Appräsentation*) (see Hua 15, p. 117).

After the transcendental onlooker has carried out the primordial reduction to her/his experiential world consisting of the world of perception, the world of memory, and the world of expectation, she/he could carry out a further reduction to each of these three kinds of world. One of them is the reduction to the world of perception as the world of presentation. This can be termed "the reduction to the core sphere of the perceptual present under the exclusion of memory and of the future" (*die Reduktion auf die Kernsphäre der Wahrnehmungsgegenwart unter Ausschluss von Erinnerung und Zukunft*) (Hua Mat 8, p. 115).

The reduction to "the core sphere of the perceptual present" is not yet the final primordial reduction. It should be noted that this core sphere is the unity of transcendental subjectivity's original impression, retention, and protention, and the transcendental onlooker can carry out the primordial reduction upon each of these. Among them, the reduction to the original impression is the "reduction to the sensuously perceivable world" (*Reduktion auf sinnlich wahrnehmbare Welt*) (Hua 15, p. 507).

I have clarified that there are different kinds of primordial reduction. And it is precisely the step-by-step character of the primordial reduction that makes it possible for us to grasp the existence of the different kinds and layers of the primordial reduction. It is the stepwise character of the primordial reduction, together with the distinction between the primordial reduction to the noetic and to the noematic side of the primordial sphere, that makes the concept of the primordial reduction highly ambiguous. However, it should also be noted that it is

---

10 Held calls this "the radicalized reduction to the living present" (die radikalisierte Reduktion auf die lebendige Gegenwart) (Held 1966, p. 17).

ambiguous in another respect that I have not yet discussed. Even though I have dealt with the primordial reduction as a type of transcendental reduction, it is possible to conceive it as a type of psychological reduction. Here we might consider the distinction between "the reduction to primordiality in the natural attitude and in the transcendental attitude" (*die Reduktion auf die Primordialität in natürlicher Einstellung und in transzendentaler Einstellung*) (see Hua 15, p. 530). The distinction between them makes the concept of the primordial reduction even more ambiguous than I have already indicated.

7.2 The concept of the transcendental reduction in the singular and in the plural

Next, I will deal with the difficulty that in *Ideen I*, Husserl adopts the concept of the transcendental reduction both in the singular and in the plural. Now I will give an explanation of the reason why Husserl does so.[11] When he talks about the transcendental reduction in the singular, he has in mind the universal transcendental reduction as the radical change from the natural attitude to the transcendental attitude, as is the case in the following passage: "Instead, then, of living naively in experience and theoretically investigating what is experienced—transcendent nature—we effect the 'phenomenological reduction'" (*Anstatt also in der Erfahrung naiv zu leben und das Erfahrene, die transzendente Natur, theoretisch zu erforschen, vollziehen wir die 'phänomenologische Reduktion'*) (Hua 3/1, p. 106; Husserl 1982, p. 113, trans. altered).

With respect to the possibility of speaking about transcendental reductions, in the plural, we have to pay attention to the fact that in *Ideen I*, Husserl develops transcendental phenomenology as an egology. As already mentioned, in order to develop transcendental phenomenology as an egology systematically and concretely, we have to carry out not only the universal transcendental egological reduction, but the other partial transcendental egological reductions that follow it. There are different kinds of partial transcendental egological reduction that follow the universal transcendental reduction, as the following passage from *Ideen I* indicates: "This first reduction is, after all, what makes it at all possible in the first place to turn one's regard to the phenomenological field and seize upon its givens. The other reductions, because they presuppose the first, are secondary;

---

[11] I do not claim that my explanation can cover all cases of Husserl's use of the concept of the phenomenological reduction in the singular and in the plural in *Ideen I*. There might be cases that cannot be clarified in this way.

but this by no means implies that they have less significance" (*Durch diese erste Reduktion wird ja die Blickwendung auf das phänomenologische Feld und die Erfassung seiner Gegebenheiten überhaupt erst möglich. Die übrigen Reduktionen, als die erste voraussetzend, sind also sekundär, aber darum keineswegs von geringer Bedeutung*) (Hua 3/1, p. 130; Husserl 1982, p. 139, trans. altered). This is the reason why he talks about transcendental reductions in the plural.

Husserl was clearly aware that in *Ideen I*, he was developing transcendental phenomenology as a transcendental egology. Moreover, he was also aware that in order to develop transcendental egology systematically, he had to adopt a transcendental egological reduction that has a stepwise character. In this context, clarifying the structure of the transcendental reduction, he indicates the stepwise character of the transcendental reduction as follows:

> As a method this operation will be divided into different steps of "excluding", "bracketing", and thus our method will assume the characteristic of a stepwise reduction. For this reason, we shall, on most occasions, speak of *phenomenological reductions* (but also, with reference to their collective unity, we shall speak of *the* phenomenological reduction) [...]. (Husserl 1982, p. 66, trans. altered.)
>
> Methodisch wird diese Operation sich in verschiedene Schritte der "Ausschaltung", "Einklammerung" zerlegen und so wird unsere Methode den Charakter einer schrittweisen Reduktion annehmen. Um dessentwillen werden wir und sogar vorwiegend von *phänomenologischen Reduktionen* (bzw. auch einheitlich hinsichtlich ihrer Gesamtheit von *der* phänomenologischen Reduktion) sprechen [...]. (Hua 3/1, p. 69)

7.3 The relationship between the phenomenological reduction, the transcendental reduction, the epistemological reduction, and the apodictic reduction

Finally, I will clarify the difficulty concerning the relationship between the phenomenological reduction, the transcendental reduction, the "epistemological reduction" (Hua 2, pp. 39, 43; Husserl 1999, pp. 30, 33), and the "apodictic reduction" (Hua 35, p. 98). Let me first clarify the relationship between the phenomenological reduction and the transcendental reduction in *Die Idee*.

In *Die Idee*, Husserl uses the concept of the phenomenological reduction (Hua 2, pp. 7 ff., 44, 55, 60; Husserl 1999, pp. 64 ff., 34, 41, 45) as a synonym for the transcendental reduction. However, the concept of the transcendental reduction in *Die Idee* is ambiguous. First, it means the universal transcendental reduction that opens up the universal transcendental sphere for the transcendental onlooker. This is clear when he says: "If I place the ego and the world and the experience of the ego as such in question [...]" (*Stelle ich Ich und Welt und Icher-*

lebnis als solches in Frage [...]) (Hua 2, p. 44; Husserl 1999, p. 34)—a passage that clearly shows that the transcendental onlooker has carried out the transcendental epoché concerning the general thesis of the natural attitude so that she/he can experience the universal transcendental sphere as the research field of transcendental phenomenology.

Second, the phenomenological reduction as the transcendental reduction in *Die Idee* means a sub-type of the universal transcendental reduction, one that Husserl calls the epistemological reduction. What does this mean? In order to grasp what the epistemological reduction is, one has to understand its aim. According to Husserl, it is the aim of the epistemological reduction to obtain the sphere of the *"absolutely itself-given"* (*absolute Selbstgegebenheit*) (Hua 2, p. 56; Husserl 1999, p. 42, trans. altered) that is free from any doubt. This implies that the epistemological reduction in *Die Idee* is similar to the primordial reduction to the transcendental present of the transcendental onlooker's stream of consciousness discussed above, since the primordial sphere secured by this reduction is the sphere of the absolutely itself-given, free from any doubt.

However, in developing phenomenology as a transcendental phenomenology, Husserl himself does not make an explicit distinction between the universal transcendental reduction and the primordial reduction in the way just mentioned above. This is the reason why the concept of the phenomenological reduction in *Die Idee* is ambiguous. In order to eliminate this ambiguity, Husserl should have developed the theory of the egological reduction systematically and clarified "the relationship between the primordial reduction and the transcendental reduction" (*das Verhältnis von primordialer und transzendentaler Reduktion*) (Hua 15, p. 526) more concretely.

Now let me clarify the relationship between the transcendental reduction and the apodictic reduction. Since Husserl defines the apodictic reduction as "the reduction to transcendental subjectivity, but under the restriction to established apodicticity" (*die Reduktion auf die tranzendentale Subjektivität, aber unter Einschränkung auf festgestellte Apodiktizität*) (Hua 35, p. 98), it is a type of transcendental reduction. In order to understand what the apodictic reduction really is, here too we have to pay attention to its aim. For Husserl, its aim is "to delimit the scope of the *ego cogito* with its apodictic contents" (*den Umfang des ego cogito mit seinen apodiktischen Gehalten zu umgrenzen*) (Hua 35, p. 146). It should be noted that it is once again the primordial reduction to the transcendental present of the transcendental onlooker's stream of consciousness that enables the transcendental onlooker to delimit and secure this realm along with its apodictic contents. Thus, it turns out that the apodictic reduction is identical to the primordial reduction to the transcendental present of the transcendental onlooker's stream of consciousness.

We can accordingly see that the epistemological reduction in *Die Idee* is the same as the apodictic reduction, since both of them are the same as the primordial reduction to the transcendental present of the transcendental onlooker's stream of consciousness. It is precisely because they are the same that Husserl speaks of "the *apodictic, specifically critical-epistemological reduction*" (*die apodiktische, spezifisch erkenntniskritische Reduktion*) (Hua 35, p. 406).

8 Concluding remarks

In this paper, I have clarified the basic structure of the transcendental egological reduction and the transcendental intersubjective reduction; I have demonstrated their stepwise character; and with recourse to the latter, I have tried to solve some difficulties concerning the phenomenological reduction. I will close by pointing out two future tasks related to the issue of the egological reduction and the intersubjective reduction.

(1) There are some issues dealt with in this paper that need a more extensive discussion than has been possible here. Let me give two examples. First, with respect to the concrete methods of the transcendental egological reduction and those of the transcendental intersubjective reduction, I have mentioned the method of dismantling or deconstruction, that of construction, and that of reconstruction. However, I have yet to clarify what these methods really are and how they could be employed to carry out the egological reduction and the intersubjective reduction systematically and concretely. Second, in this paper, I have mainly discussed the transcendental reduction and have only touched upon the issue of the psychological reduction on occasion. It is one of my future tasks to discuss in a more detailed manner the psychological egological reduction/the psychological intersubjective reduction and the relationship between these reductions and the transcendental egological reduction/the transcendental intersubjective reduction discussed in this paper.

(2) There are some further issues related to the issue of the egological reduction and the intersubjective reduction that I could not address in this paper. Let me once again give two examples. First, there are different paths to the transcendental reduction (see Kern 1962). It is one of my future tasks to clarify the relationship between the transcendental egological reduction/the transcendental intersubjective reduction and each of the different paths to the transcendental reduction. The clarification of these relationships could contribute to a more precise understanding of them. Second, Husserl makes a distinction between static phenomenology and genetic phenomenology. It is one of my future tasks to clar-

ify how the egological reduction and the intersubjective reduction could be used as methods of static phenomenology as well as of genetic phenomenology.

Acknowledgments

A German version of this paper was presented at a colloquium that was held on July 17th, 2017, at the Husserl Archives at the University of Cologne in Germany. I thank Professor Dieter Lohmar for his kind invitation to the colloquium as well as all the participants.

References

Bower, Matt (2014): "Husserl's Motivation and Method for Phenomenological Reconstruction". In: *Continental Philosophy Review* 47, pp. 135–152.
Cairns, Dorion (2013): *The Philosophy of Edmund Husserl*. Dordrecht: Springer.
Held, Klaus (1966): *Lebendige Gegenwart*. The Hague: Martinus Nijhoff.
Husserl, Edmund (1950): *Cartesianische Meditationen und Pariser Vorträge*. Stephan Strasser (Ed.). Husserliana I. The Hague: Martinus Nijhoff. [Hua 1]
Husserl, Edmund (1960): *Cartesian Meditations: An Introduction to Phenomenology*. Trans. Dorion Cairns. The Hague: Martinus Nijhoff.
Husserl, Edmund (1950): *Die Idee der Phänomenologie. Fünf Vorlesungen*. Walter Biemel (Ed.). Husserliana II. The Hague: Martinus Nijhoff. [Hua 2].
Husserl, Edmund (1999): *The Idea of Phenomenology*. Trans. Lee Hardy. Dordrecht: Kluwer.
Husserl, Edmund (1976): *Ideen zu einer reinen Phänomenologie und phänomenologischen Philosophie. Erstes Buch: Allgemeine Einführung in die reine Phänomenologie*. Karl Schuhmann (Ed.). Husserliana III/1. The Hague: Martinus Nijhoff. [Hua 3/1].
Husserl, Edmund (1982): *Ideas Pertaining to a Pure Phenomenology and to a Phenomenological Philosophy. First Book: General Introduction to a Pure Phenomenology*. Trans. Fred Kersten. The Hague: Martinus Nijhoff.
Husserl, Edmund (1952): *Ideen zu einer reinen Phänomenologie und phänomenologischen Philosophie. Drittes Buch: Die Phänomenologie und die Fundamente der Wissenschaften*. Marly Biemel (Ed.). Husserliana V. The Hague: Martinus Nijhoff. [Hua 5]
Husserl, Edmund (1954): *Die Krisis der europäischen Wissenschaften und die transzendentale Phänomenologie. Eine Einleitung in die phänomenologische Philosophie*. Walter Biemel (Ed.). Husserliana VI. The Hague: Martinus Nijhoff. [Hua 6].
Husserl, Edmund (1970): *The Crisis of European Sciences and Transcendental Phenomenology: An Introduction to Phenomenological Philosophy*. Trans. David Carr. Evanston: Northwestern University Press.
Husserl, Edmund (1959): *Erste Philosophie (1923/24). Zweiter Teil: Theorie der phänomenologischen Reduktion*. Rudolf Boehm (Ed.). Husserliana VIII. The Hague: Martinus Nijhoff. [Hua 8]

Husserl, Edmund (2019): *First Philosophy: Lectures 1923/24 and Related Texts from the Manuscripts (1920–1925)*. Trans. Sebastian Luft/Thane M. Naberhaus. Dordrecht: Springer.

Husserl, Edmund (1962): *Phänomenologische Psychologie. Vorlesungen Sommersemester 1925*. Walter Biemel (Ed.). Husserliana IX. The Hague: Martinus Nijhoff. [Hua 9]

Husserl, Edmund (1997): *Psychological and Transcendental Phenomenology and the Confrontation with Heidegger (1927–1931)*. Thomas Sheehan/Richard E. Palmer (Eds. and Trans.). Dordrecht: Kluwer.

Husserl, Edmund (1973): *Zur Phänomenologie der Intersubjektivität. Texte aus dem Nachlaß. Erster Teil: 1905–1920*. Iso Kern (Ed.). Husserliana XIII. The Hague: Martinus Nijhoff. [Hua 13].

Husserl, Edmund (2006): *The Basic Problems of Phenomenology: From the Lectures, Winter Semester, 1910–1911*. Trans. Ingo Farin/James G. Hart. Dordrecht: Springer.

Husserl, Edmund (1973a): *Zur Phänomenologie der Intersubjektivität. Texte aus dem Nachlaß. Zweiter Teil: 1921–1928*. Iso Kern (Ed.). Husserliana XIV. The Hague: Martinus Nijhoff. [Hua 14]

Husserl, Edmund (1973b): *Zur Phänomenologie der Intersubjektivität. Texte aus dem Nachlaß. Dritter Teil: 1929–1935*. Iso Kern (Ed.). Husserliana XV. The Hague: Martinus Nijhoff. [Hua 15]

Husserl, Edmund (1984): *Logische Untersuchungen. Zweiter Band: Untersuchungen zur Phänomenologie und Theorie der Erkenntnis, Erster Teil*. Ursula Panzer (Ed.). Husserliana XIX/1. The Hague: Martinus Nijhoff. [Hua 19/1]

Husserl, Edmund (2001): *Logical Investigations*. Vol. 1. Trans. J.N. Findlay. Rev. Dermot Moran. London, New York: Routledge.

Husserl, Edmund (2002): *Zur phänomenologischen Reduktion. Texte aus dem Nachlass (1926–1935)*. Sebastian Luft (Ed.). Husserliana XXXIV. Dordrecht: Kluwer. [Hua 34]

Husserl, Edmund (2002): *Einleitung in die Philosophie. Vorlesungen 1922/23*. Berndt Goossens (Ed.). Husserliana XXXV. Dordrecht: Kluwer. [Hua 35]

Husserl, Edmund (2006): *Späte Texte über Zeitkonstitution (1929–1934). Die C-Manuskripte*. Dieter Lohmar (Ed.). Husserliana Materialien VIII. Dordrecht: Springer. [Hua Mat 8].

Kern, Iso (1962): "Die drei Wege zur transzendental-phänomenologischen Reduktion in der Philosophie Edmund Husserls". In: *Tijdschrift voor Filosofie* 24, pp. 303–349.

Kern, Iso (1977): "The Three Ways to the Transcendental Phenomenological Reduction in the Philosophy of Edmund Husserl". Trans. Frederick A. Elliston/Peter McCormick. In: Elliston, Frederick A./McCormick, Peter (Eds.): *Husserl: Expositions and Appraisals*. Notre Dame: University of Notre Dame Press, pp. 126–149.

Kersten, Fred (1989): *Phenomenological Method: Theory and Practice*. Dordrecht: Kluwer.

Lee, Nam-In (1993): *Edmund Husserls Phänomenologie der Instinkte*. Dordrecht: Kluwer.

Lee, Nam-In (2002): "Static-Phenomenological and Genetic-Phenomenological Concept of Primordiality in Husserl's *Fifth Cartesian Meditation*". In: *Husserl Studies* 18, pp. 165–183.

Lee, Nam-In (2010): "Phenomenology of Language beyond the Deconstructive Philosophy of Language". In: *Continental Philosophy Review* 42, pp. 465–481.

Lohmar, Dieter (2002): "Die Idee der Reduktion". In: Hüni, Heinrich/Trawny, Peter (Eds.): *Die erscheinende Welt. Festschrift für Klaus Held*. Berlin: Duncker & Humblot, pp. 751–771.

Orth, Ernst Wolfgang (2002): "Die Pluralität der transzendentalphänomenologischen Reduktion und das Problem des Reduktionismus". In: Hüni, Heinrich/Trawny, Peter (Eds.): *Die erscheinende Welt. Festschrift für Klaus Held*. Berlin: Duncker & Humblot, pp. 737–749.

Overgaard, Søren (2002): "Epoché and Solipsistic Reduction". In: *Husserl Studies* 18, pp. 209–222.

Park, Ji-Young (2016): "The Idea of Husserl's Phenomenology and Intersubjective Evidence" (in Korean). In: *Cheolhaksasang* 61, pp. 307–338.

Schnell, Alexander (2010): "Intersubjectivity in Husserl's Work". In: *META: Research in Hermeneutics, Phenomenology, and Practical Philosophy* 2(1), pp. 9–32.

Zahavi, Dan (1996): *Husserl und die transzendentale Intersubjektivität. Eine Antwort auf die sprachpragmatische Kritik*. Dordrecht: Kluwer.

Zahavi, Dan (2001): *Husserl and Transcendental Intersubjectivity: A Response to the Linguistic-Pragmatic Critique*. Trans. Elizabeth A. Behnke. Athens: Ohio University Press.

Kwok-ying LAU

Pathological Reduction and Hermeneutics of the Normal and the Pathological: the Convergence between Merleau-Ponty and Canguilhem

Abstract: This paper attempts to show first of all that Merleau-Ponty's phenomenology of the body-subject, constructed around the pivotal concept of body schema in *Phenomenology of Perception*, is a very original hermeneutics of the normal and the pathological. In his *magnum opus*, Merleau-Ponty unveils the meaning of pathological behaviors by practicing a specific mode of phenomenological reduction which I propose to call "pathological reduction". Thanks to this specific mode of reduction, Merleau-Ponty can thematize pathological behaviors of the body subject and carry out the hermeneutical reading of pathological phenomena in order to establish a theory of the basic capacity of the human subject. In the second part of the paper, Canguilhem's non-positivistic conception of pathology will be introduced to show that Merleau-Ponty shares a conception of the normal and the pathological in close affinity with Canguilhem. By drawing our attention to the proximity of these two philosophers on this issue we hope to show that Merleau-Ponty, though a phenomenologist through and through, is exempted from the criticism of positivist naivety as is presented by Foucault. In addition, we want to argue that Foucault's dichotomy of the two separate lines of development of contemporary French philosophy, phenomenology as philosophy of subject, sense and experience on one side, and philosophy of science, concept and rationality on the other side, are not as oppositional as he has presented.

1 Introduction: the constitutive role of moments of negativity

A philosophical discussion of the problem of human capacity is based on the conviction that human being is capable of truth in general and capable of truth about the human being in particular. But this conviction is inseparable from the recognition that human being is a being of finitude. To such a being of finitude truth is a matter of overcoming error; thus truth is a function of error in the reversed way. Or even: truth is rooted in error in one way or another.

Understood in this manner, the conceptualization of truth must include the thematization of error as one of its constitutive elements. Likewise, a phenomenological approach to the study of human capacity must thematize as its constitutive moments the phenomena of disability, of illness and of the pathological. These phenomena should not be taken as evidence leading to the denial of human capacity; they should rather be understood as moments of constitutive negativity of the human being as a being of capacity. For those who understand phenomenological philosophy not as a naturalism nor a positivism, the recognition of the positive role played by moments of constitutive negativity such as nothingness, absence, difference, *écart* and the invisible in the manifestation of phenomena should not be a subject of great dispute.

Yet sometimes it needs thinkers at the peripheral or even outside the phenomenological movement proper to remind us of the above state of affairs. Among such thinkers Michel Foucault is one of those who always raise embarrassing questions to phenomenology. For example, in his "Introduction" to the English Translation of the French philosopher of biology and life-science Georges Canguilhem's *The Normal and the Pathological*, Foucault interrogates phenomenology in relation to the role of error in the search for truth in the following manner:

> Phenomenology asked of 'actual experience' the original meaning of every act of knowledge. But can we not, or must we not look for it in the living being himself?... a living being who is never at home, a living being dedicated to 'error' and destined, in the end, to 'error.' And if we admit that the concept is the answer that life itself gives to this chance, it must be that error is at the root of what makes human thought and its history.... If the history of science is discontinuous, that is, if it can be analyzed only as a series of 'corrections', as a new distribution of true and false which never finally, once and for all, liberates the truth, it is because there, too, 'error' constitutes not overlooking or delaying a truth but the dimension proper to the life of men and to the time of the species. (Foucault 1994, pp. 773–775; Foucault 1989, pp. 20–22)

Indeed if a science as a system of knowledge is rooted in error, a philosophy of the human subject will have the same fate. It will not be enough to merely attest to the positive manifestation of truth by recording experiential evidence in order to "collect" knowledge on the human subject. We must, according to Foucault, also incorporate the moment of error in the constitution of our knowledge of the subject such that "the entire theory of the subject must ... be reformulated" (Foucault 1994, p. 776; Foucault 1989, p. 23).

To Foucault, phenomenology, at least as it was practiced in France from the years 1930s to 1960s, has not proceeded to reformulate the theory of the subject as it should be. French phenomenology is still too positivistic:

Phenomenology could indeed introduce the body, sexuality, death, the perceived world into the field of analysis; the *Cogito* remained central; neither the rationality of science nor the specificity of the life sciences could compromise its founding role. It is to this philosophy of meaning, subject and the experienced thing that Canguilhem has opposed a philosophy of error, concept and the living being. (Foucault 1994, p. 776; Foucault 1989, pp. 23–24)

By praising Canguilhem for introducing the study of error in a philosophy of the concept of the living being and of life in opposition to the theory of the subject practiced by phenomenologists, Foucault thinks that Canguilhem is able to overcome the positivist naivety of phenomenology. With this demarcation Foucault proposes a dichotomy of the development of French philosophy since the 1930s to his time. This dichotomy is situated on the two sides of a line

that separates a philosophy of experience, of sense and of subject and a philosophy of knowledge, of rationality and of concept. On the one hand, one network is that of Sartre and Merleau-Ponty; and then another is that of Cavaillès, Bachelard and Canguilhem.(Foucault 1994, p. 764; Foucault 1989, pp. 8–9)

To Foucault these two trends of development, namely the philosophy of experience, sense and subject represented by phenomenology on the one hand, and the philosophy of knowledge, rationality and concept represented by the history and epistemology of sciences on the other, form the two completely different and separated modalities of philosophical thought in contemporary France in the decades immediately before and after the Second World War. By the time Foucault wrote these lines, he was already well-known as the author of *History of Madness* (1961), *The Birth of the Clinic* (1963) and *Discipline and Punish* (1975), works which aim at showing that madness is constitutive of reason in Modern Western rationalist culture, that illness is constitutive of the healthy body in Modern Western medicine, and that criminal behavior is constitutive of normativity in the legal order of Modern Western liberal society. In short, Foucault is a philosopher who has incorporated the study of constitutive negativity into the archaeological and genealogical study of rationalities. He considers himself being part of the second line, the French school of epistemology and history of sciences, and separated from the first, namely French phenomenology. To Foucault, French phenomenology remains some sort of remnant of a positivist conception of philosophy in its study of experience, sense and the subject.

While we think that Foucault is entirely right to raise from the viewpoint of theory construction the question of the constitutive role played by moments of negativity in the formation of the concepts of life, rationality and world, his historical line of demarcation should be subjected to a more nuanced revision. The young Sartre's phenomenological studies of the imaginary as consciousness of irreality and absence, as well as the thematization of nothingness as the ontological basis of the entire field of phenomenality in his 1943 systematic treatise *Being and Nothingness* are precisely pioneering works in the study of negativity as constitutive elements of reason and world. As for Merleau-Ponty, he is well-known for working on the ultimately unfinished ontology of the intertwined relation of the visible and the invisible with the notions of flesh and *écart* in his later years. Arrived at his stage of philosophical maturity, Merleau-Ponty's awareness of the constitutive role of negativity was entire. But even in his earlier works, especially in *Phenomenology of Perception*, the constitutive role of negative elements is already well thematized. This is shown in his hermeneutics of the normal and the pathological in the well-known phenomenology of the body-subject as the basis of the formulation of a phenomenology of human capacity.

Merleau-Ponty's phenomenology of the body-subject is constructed around the pivotal concept of body schema, a concept which enables him to demonstrate the priority of the "I can" on the "I think". The very concept of body schema is precisely introduced through detailed descriptions of pathological behaviors of patients suffering from physiological, psychological and psychiatric illness. On the basis of these phenomenological descriptions, Merleau-Ponty goes on to decipher the meaning of these pathological behaviors for human existence. Merleau-Ponty himself calls this analysis existential analysis. But we think that this meaning deciphering work is a very original hermeneutics of the normal and the pathological, as Merleau-Ponty has established a phenomenological theory of the basic capacity of a normal bodily human subject by unveiling the meaning of pathological behaviors. Merleau-Ponty proceeds to this hermeneutical work by first of all practicing a specific mode of phenomenological reduction which I propose to call "pathological reduction". Thanks to the practice of this specific mode of reduction, Merleau-Ponty is able to thematize pathological behaviors of the body subject and carry out the hermeneutical reading of pathological phenomena in order to establish a theory of the basic capacity of the human subject.

In the following parts of this paper, essential elements of Merleau-Ponty's hermeneutics of the normal and the pathological as the basic elements of his phenomenological theory of human capacity in *Phenomenology of Perception* will be presented in the first place. Then Canguilhem's non-positivistic conception of pathology will be explained in order to show that Merleau-Ponty shares a conception of the normal and the pathological in close affinity with Canguilhem. The proximity of these two philosophers on this issue can be further traced back to the clinical and theoretical works of the originally German non-positivistic neurologist and psychiatrist Kurt Goldstein (1878–1965), works which have influenced both Merleau-Ponty and Canguilhem. By this detour this paper attempts to show first of all that Merleau-Ponty, though a phenomenologist through and through, is exempted from the criticism of positivist naivety as is presented by Foucault. In addition, we want to argue that Foucault's dichotomy of the two separate lines of development of contemporary French philosophy, phenomenology as philosophy of subject, sense and experience on one side, and philosophy of science, concept and rationality on the other side, are not as oppositional as he has presented. There are intertwining moments between these two lines of thought in both Merleau-Ponty and Canguilhem.

2 Merleau-Ponty's hermeneutics of the normal and the pathological as phenomenology of human capacity

It is well-known that the basis of a phenomenology of the human capacity has already been laid down by Husserl in the phenomenology of the living-body in *Ideas II* by means of the conceptualization of the body-subject as "I can". In § 38 of *Ideas II* devoted to the study of "the Body as organ of the will and as seat of free movement", Husserl points out the essential bodily character of the human subject in the following terms:

> The subject, constituted as counter-member of material nature, is ... an Ego, to which a Body belongs as field of localization of its sensations. The Ego has the 'faculty' (the 'I can') to freely move this Body—i.e. the organ in which it is articulated—and to perceive an external world by means of it. (Husserl 1952, p. 152; Husserl 1989, pp. 159–160)

As a body-subject, the Ego not only can perceive and move at will, she can also imagine, remember, desire and wish, etc. Merleau-Ponty's phenomenology of human capacity has followed Husserl's indication in *Ideas II* in which the subject is a living-body, rather than that in the *Ideas I* in which the subject is pure consciousness.

Heidegger has also contributed to a phenomenology of the human capacity in the thematization of the Dasein's potentiality for Being (*Seinkönnen*) in *Being and Time:* the Dasein is a being of possibilities. Yet his emphasis of death as Dasein's "ownmost potentiality for Being" and as "the possibility of the absolute impossibility of Dasein" (Heidegger 1927, p. 250; Heidegger 1962, p. 294) is not shared by Merleau-Ponty.

The author of *Phenomenology of Perception* retains the formal concept of the body-subject as a being of possibility on the backdrop of her facticity. But this being of possibility is shown through the descriptions that the body-subject is a center of kinesthetic intentionality at the pre-reflective level. In other words, Merleau-Ponty has transferred the *topos* of intentionality from Husserl's pure consciousness to an incarnate consciousness: in our pre-reflective experience corporeal intentionality is a privileged form of intentionality. Merleau-Ponty shows this by means of the concept of body schema. The body schema is a kind of know-how and a form of latent knowledge which enables the body-subject to execute bodily movements in view of accomplishing tasks and activities motivated by the great varieties of interests in human life. Merleau-Ponty finds that at the basis of all kinds of such activities is the basic capacity of the body-subject to execute concrete movements and abstract movements.

What is of particular interest in Merleau-Ponty's enterprise is his use of clinical studies of psychiatry and psychopathology of his time to demonstrate concretely what a normal person can do in terms of basic bodily movements by contrast with what patients suffering from cortical brain injuries can do and cannot do.

a) The distinction between concrete movement and abstract movement using clinical studies of pathological behavior as example

By abstract movement Merleau-Ponty means that kind of bodily actions which a body-subject can do without reference to the actual situation in which she finds herself. This is the kind of imaginary actions which reveal the potentiality of the body-subject, showing that the latter is a being of possibility. By concrete movement Merleau-Ponty refers to the kind of vital actions which a body-subject executes in response to the actual situation in which she finds herself. Concrete movements reveal the facticity of the body-subject. With reference to the clinical studies of Gelb and Goldstein, Merleau-Ponty gives a vivid description of the pathological phenomena of patients suffering from cortical brain injuries.

> One patient, whom traditional psychiatry would class among those suffering from psychic blindness, is incapable of performing 'abstract' movements with his eyes closed, namely, movements that are not directed at any actual situation, such as moving his arms or legs upon command, or extending and flexing a finger... He only accomplishes abstract movements if he is allowed to see the limb in question, or to execute preparatory movements involving his whole body. The localization of stimuli and the recognition of tactile

objects also become possible with the aid of preparatory movements. Even with his eyes closed, the patient executes the movements that are necessary for life with extraordinary speed and confidence, provided that they are habitual movements... He can even, without any preparatory movements, execute these 'concrete' movements on command. (Merleau-Ponty 1945, pp. 119–120; Merleau-Ponty 2012, p. 105)

The distinction between concrete movement and abstract movement reveals a profound philosophical significance: they represent two types of bodily movements which are operated in two different kinds of spatiality. While concrete movement is operated in actual space, abstract movement is executed in imaginary space. Merleau-Ponty explains this by showing the difference between the action of grasping (*saisir*) as concrete movement and that of indicating (*montrer*) as abstract movement: the former is immediate and non-representational in nature, while the latter is a representational action. A patient with cortical brain injuries cannot indicate her nose at will, but can only grasp it, especially when she receives a mosquito bite which makes her uncomfortable. Merleau-Ponty explains:

> The patient is conscious of bodily space as the envelope of his habitual action, but not as an objective milieu. His body is available as a means of insertion into his familiar surroundings, but not as a means of expression of a spontaneous and free spatial thought. When ordered to perform a concrete movement, he first repeats the order in an interrogative tone of voice, then his body settles into the overall position required by the task, and finally he executes the movement. The whole body can be seen collaborating here, and the patient never reduces it to the strictly indispensable traits as does the normal subject.(Merleau-Ponty 1945, p. 121; Merleau-Ponty 2012, pp. 106–107)

Concrete movements as actions in response to the situation in actual space show that the body-subject is situated in the world of localized space and time. They are executed without passing through representation by the acting body-subject. This state of affairs is incomprehensible for the representational model of Kantian intellectualism:

> I can thus—by means of my body as a power for a certain number of familiar actions—settle into my surroundings as an ensemble of *manipulanda* without intending my body or my surroundings as objects in the Kantian sense, that is, as systems of qualities linked by some intelligible law, as entities that are transparent, free of all local or temporal adherence.(Merleau-Ponty 1945, p. 122; Merleau-Ponty 2012, pp. 107–108)

The patient, while she executes a concrete movement, is not in an unconscious state. Her consciousness is rather a pre-reflective consciousness, as the consciousness of a concrete movement is non-thetic.

> In concrete movement, the patient has neither a thetic consciousness of the stimulus nor a thetic consciousness of the reaction: quite simply, he is his body and his body is the power for a certain world.(Merleau-Ponty 1945, p. 124; Merleau-Ponty 2012, p. 109)

By contrast, an abstract movement practiced by the normal subject is a movement deprived of any practical motivation and executed in fictional situations and in an imaginary space without necessary reference to actuality. Merleau-Ponty explains this in admirably clear terms:

> The normal subject immediately has several 'holds' on his body. He does not have his body available merely as implicated in a concrete milieu, he is not merely situated in relation to the tasks set by his trade, nor is he merely open to real situations. Rather, in addition he possesses his body as the correlate of pure stimuli stripped of all practical signification; he is open to verbal and fictional situations that he can choose for himself or that a researcher might suggest. (Merleau-Ponty 1945, p. 126; Merleau-Ponty 2012, p. 111)

Thus the abstract movements of a normal subject inaugurate the spatiality of the virtual, a capacity which the pathological bodily actions of a patient has lost by virtue of its enclosure within the space of actuality.

> The normal subject's body is not merely ready to be mobilized by real situations that draw it toward themselves, it can also turn away from the world, apply its activity to the stimuli that are inscribed upon its sensory surfaces, lend itself to experiments and, more generally, be situated in the virtual.(Merleau-Ponty 1945, p. 126; Merleau-Ponty 2012, p. 111)

In contrast to the pathological subject, the normal subject can execute both concrete movements and abstract movements. Abstract movements as movements of reflection and projection into the possible are executed on the basis of a physical space in which the body-subject actually finds herself. Upon the actual physical space an abstract movement is projected onto an imaginary space which is a space of virtuality and non-being.

> Within the busy world in which concrete movement unfolds, abstract movement hollows out a zone of reflection and of subjectivity, it super-imposes a virtual or human space over physical space. Concrete movement is thus centripetal, whereas abstract movement is centrifugal; the first takes place within being or within the actual, the second takes place within the possible or within non-being; the first adheres to a given background, the second itself sets up its own background. The normal function that makes abstract movement possible is a function of 'projection' by which things that do not exist naturally can take on a semblance of existence. (Merleau-Ponty 1945, p. 129; Merleau-Ponty 2012, p. 114)

With these patient descriptions and detailed explanations, Merleau-Ponty arrives at the crucial difference between the normal and the pathological subject: while the normal subject retains her capacity of opening a space of possibility and the imaginary upon the space of actuality and of presence, the pathological subject has no access to the possible and the imaginary and is limited to the space of actuality and the field of presence.

> The normal person *reckons* with the possible, which thus acquires a sort of actuality without leaving behind its place as a possibility; for the patient, however, the field of the actual is limited to what is encountered in real contact or linked to these givens through an explicit deduction.(Merleau-Ponty 1945, p. 127; Merleau-Ponty 2012, p. 112)

While the pathological subject is limited to the space of actuality, this does not entail that she is incapable of any action; rather, her actions are more or less repetitive and follow mostly the routine. By contrast, since the normal subject can open a space of possibility, she is capable of creating a quasi-existing world by the projection of an imaginary space upon the actual space. Merleau-Ponty succeeds in drawing the line of difference between the normal subject and the pathological subject in terms of their basic capacity by studying closely the pathological behaviors of patients suffering from cortical brain injuries. The pathological subject is limited to actions which are more or less responses to actuality. However, the normal subject can, by projection of a virtual space which is the spatiality of the imaginary, open the spatiality of creativity and cultural creation. While the mode of consciousness of the imaginary is reflective and representational, the pre-reflective consciousness of the concrete movements of the body-subject is non-representational.

Thus Merleau-Ponty arrives at the similar conclusion with Husserl that "consciousness is originally not an 'I think that', but rather an 'I can'"(Merleau-Ponty 1945, p. 160; Merleau-Ponty 2012, p. 139). If the 'I can" is the essential character of consciousness, the knowledge of this essence is not acquired through the self-reflection or self-objectification of the transcendental meditative subject, but by careful observation of her pathological otherness. That is to say, the normal reflective epistemological subject has to recognize the basic fact that there exist pathological subjects and pathological behaviors. It is only through the study of the pathological that the cognitive reflective subject can arrive at the knowledge of the essential capacity of a normal body-subject. We can call this specific approach to the study of pathological phenomena the pathological approach, and the phenomenological reduction, which leads to the thematization of pathological phenomena, the pathological reduction (we will return to this later).

b) The distinction of linguistic capacities between normal and pathological speaking-subjects

In *Phenomenology of Perception*, Merleau-Ponty demonstrates further the strength of the pathological way of the phenomenological reduction by studying the pathological phenomena of the speaking subject. By doing so, he is able to explain the concrete difference in linguistic capacities between the normal and the pathological body-subject, a state of affairs which the intellectualist conception of linguistic phenomena fails to come to terms with.

To intellectualism language is merely a pure instrument of thought. The thinking subject is always sovereign and occupies a purely commanding position with regard to the speaking subject. But Merleau-Ponty proposes some counter demonstrations through the pathological studies of aphasia. He makes a first distinction relative to pathological behaviors of the speaking subject: the distinction between anarthria (disorder in articulation such that there is difficulty to pronounce a word) and true aphasia which is connected to intellectual disorder (disorder in the capacity of thinking). In true aphasia "what the patient had lost, and what the normal person possessed, was not a certain stock of words, but rather a certain manner of using them"(Merleau-Ponty 1945, p. 204; Merleau-Ponty 2012, p. 180).

Upon this first distinction Merleau-Ponty makes a second distinction with respect to two types of language use: automatic language or concrete language, on the one hand, and spontaneous language or intentional language on the other hand. Automatic language or concrete language is a motor phenomenon in the pre-personal manner; it is language use in vital situations in which the word serves as an instrument of action with practical purposes. Spontaneous language or intentional language is language use in the first person in which the word is a means of disinterested denomination and serves to articulate a thought.

From the distinction of these two types of language use Merleau-Ponty digs out a further layer of hidden significance: "Thus behind the word we discover an attitude or a function of speech that conditions it"(Merleau-Ponty 1945, p. 204; Merleau-Ponty 2012, p. 180). With this discovery Merleau-Ponty can advance a third distinction, the one between "concrete attitude" and "categorial attitude".

The concrete attitude is shown in the pathological case of amnesia of colour names, for example inability to tell the paleness of colour tons of a same object or the blueness of different blue objects: "The same patients who fail to name the colors presented to them are equally incapable of classifying them according to a given rule"(Merleau-Ponty 1945, p. 204; Merleau-Ponty 2012, p. 181).

By contrast, the categorial attitude is the aptitude to classify a given object under a category:

> For to name an object is to tear oneself away from what its individual and unique properties are in order to see it as the representative of an essence or of a category. And if the patient cannot name the samples, this is not because he has lost the verbal image of the word 'red' or the word 'blue', it is because he has lost the general power of subsuming a sensory given under a category, it is because he has fallen back from the categorial attitude into the concrete attitude.(Merleau-Ponty 1945, p. 205; Merleau-Ponty 2012, p. 181)

Thus from the study of pathological behaviors of the speaking subject, Merleau-Ponty is able to distinguish between two basic linguistic capacities of the body-subject: the concrete attitude which is the use of words to denominate and identify a thing, and the categorial attitude which is at the basis of the linguistic capacity to articulate thought. The concrete attitude is at the basis of the categorial attitude which underlies the intellectualist conception of thinking. Yet without the basic concrete attitude to designate objects by words, there is no recognition of objects by thought.

> The word bears the sense, and, by imposing it upon the object, I am conscious of reaching the object. As often been said, the object is only known by the child once it has been named; the name is the essence of the object and resides in it, just like its color or its form. (Merleau-Ponty 1945, p. 207; Merleau-Ponty 2012, p. 183)

Thus language does not presuppose thought, but accomplishes thought: "For the speaker, speech does not translate a ready-made thought; rather, speech accomplishes thought."(Merleau-Ponty 1945, p. 207; Merleau-Ponty 2012, p. 183)

Through pathological studies Merleau-Ponty is able to clarify the interwoven relationship between language and thought, as well as the founding role of language with regard to thought. Upon this, Merleau-Ponty goes on to propose the distinction between language as living speech from language as culture and institution. Language use in the form of living speech is non-representational: "For the speaking subject, thought is not a representation; that is, thought does not explicitly posit objects or relations"(Merleau-Ponty 1945, p. 209; Merleau-Ponty 2012, p. 185).

The articulation of living speech functions in the manner of the body schema, i.e. it is the manifestation of pre-reflective intentionality:

> I have no need of representing to myself the word in order to know it and to pronounce it. It is enough that I possess its articulatory and sonorous essence as one of the modulations or one of the possible uses of my body. I relate to the word just as my hand reaches for the place on my body being stung. (Merleau-Ponty 1945, p. 210; Merleau-Ponty 2012, p. 186)

Thinking shows the transcendence of the body-subject, but it must be exercised on the basis of language acquisition which one receives necessarily from his cultural environment as a given order, i.e., of the order of facticity. Language as expression of thought is not merely an instrument of thought, as language has its constitutive function with regard to thought. Thus speech is not the external "sign" of thought, if by this we mean a phenomenon that announces another phenomenon such as smoke announces fire. Rather, speech is the body of thought: "Speech and thought ... are enveloped in each other; sense is caught in speech, and speech is the external existence of sense" (Merleau-Ponty 1945, pp. 211–212; Merleau-Ponty 2012, p. 187).

In other words, the operation of reflective consciousness, considered by phenomenological idealism as the constitutive origin of the meaning of thought, has to depend on the constituted—basic language acquisition in a given cultural setting. This state of affairs—the distinction between different capacities of the speaking subject as well as the interwoven character between language and thought which lead to a non-idealist and non-intellectualist conception of language use—receives its phenomenological elucidation thanks to pathological studies.

c) The pathological reduction

The distinction between concrete movement and abstract movement with respect to motricity of the body-subject and the distinction between concrete attitude and categorial attitude in regard to the speaking subject by the study of pathological behaviors join hands to reveal the dual ontological structure of the human subject: concrete movements of the body-subject and the concrete attitude of the speaking subject manifest the facticity of the subject with her motor movements and language use limited to the space of actuality and presence, while abstract movements and the categorial attitude manifest the transcendence of the human subject who can open a space of possibility and projects a future through the faculty of imagination. The common feature of pathological behaviors is their loss of the categorial function of the human subject which enables the creative projection of a virtual space into the temporal horizon of the future. To the patient, "the future and the past are nothing but the 'shrivelled up' continuations of the present. He has lost 'our power of seeing according to the temporal vector"(Merleau-Ponty 1945, p. 157; Merleau-Ponty 2012, p. 137). Thus the normal subject is one whose capacity of access to the temporal horizons of past, present and future remains intact. But this also means that in her natural existence the human subject is a temporal existence which accounts for her character of transcendence.

Merleau-Ponty succeeds in obtaining the stunning result of penetrating into the secret of the ontological basis of the subject as "I can": understanding what renders possible the basic capacity of the human subject by unveiling the meanings of pathological behaviors, traditionally denied by both empiricism and intellectualism. Merleau-Ponty obtains this by a new mode of analysis which goes beyond the traditional dichotomy between the empiricist and the intellectualist approaches. These two apparently different approaches share in fact in common the basic positivistic mode of thinking: the separation of essence from fact and the separation of the normal from the pathological, on the one hand, and the denial of meaning to pathological behaviors on the other. Merleau-Ponty inaugurates this new mode of analysis which reads the essential from the factual and which deciphers the normal from the pathological. He calls this new mode of analysis "existential analysis"(Merleau-Ponty 1945, p. 158; Merleau-Ponty 2012, p. 137). But we can also understand it as a hermeneutics of the normal and the pathological, for it does not consider the pathological as the degree zero of meaning. Rather, pathological behaviors are modes of conduct in which the human subject with diminished capacity caused by injuries modifies her milieu in order to pursue activities motivated by life-interests. Merleau-Ponty uses the term "intentional-arc" to describe the structure of intentional life of the normal human subject. Thanks to the intentional-arc, the normal human subject projects around her perceptual, practical, moral and desiring life a human milieu and a physical milieu. To Merleau-Ponty the intentional-arc still prevails to a pathological subject. This is because the intentional arc provides the different senses of the body with a unity such that sensorimotor activities always exhibit unitary meaning. Being bearer of meanings, these conducts are comprehensible. The difference between a normal subject and a pathological subject is that the intentional-arc in the patient "becomes loose" (*se détend*) (Merleau-Ponty 1945, p. 158; Merleau-Ponty 2012, p. 137).

Though the intentional-arc of a patient is loosened, in so far as the intentional structural essence inherent to her bodily behaviors remains intact, the latter, though pathological, still carry meaning in the form of bodily expressions. They are thus intelligible.

Merleau-Ponty's phenomenological studies of pathological behaviors resulting in the unveiling of their otherwise hidden meanings are thus a hermeneutics of the pathological. It is a hermeneutics because it is not a passive recording of evidence of a state of affairs given to the naked eye. It goes deep down into the hidden existential dimension of human pathological behaviors. It can overcome the positivist naivety of understanding the essence as that which exhibits the regularity of a natural law and considers the factual as the merely accidental deviation from the pre-existing rationality and normality. Merleau-Ponty is attentive to "error, illness, madness" as pathological phenomena rooted in the phenomenon of embodiment(Merleau-Ponty 1945, p. 145; Merleau-Ponty 2012, p. 126). He does not reduce them "to the status of mere appearance" posed in front of "the pure consciousness of the object"(Merleau-Ponty 1945, p. 145; Merleau-Ponty 2012, p. 126). The latter is a naturalistic reductionism which just "retreats into causal thought and naturalism" (Merleau-Ponty 1945, p. 147; Merleau-Ponty 2012, p. 128).

On the contrary, Merleau-Ponty practices an epoché with regard to both the positivist mode of explication in terms of naturalistic causality, as well as to the intellectualist mode of understanding which attributes the capacities of the human person to some intellectual functions of the human mind. Merleau-Ponty operates a reduction via the pathological phenomena in order to gain insight into the essential capacities of the body-subject. I propose the term "pathological reduction" to name this specific mode of reduction. With this Merleau-Ponty inaugurates a mode of phenomenological reduction by way of a detour via pathological phenomena. The pathological reduction is a reduction which, paradoxically, leads us to a *topos* where we are able to see the convergence of sense and existence as well as a partial coincidence of generality and individuality without complete coincidence. This is because the existence and the sense of pathological phenomena, in order to be comprehensible, have to be read with an eye of difference and *écart* in contrast to those of the normal subject.

The term pathological reduction I risk to propose here refers to the specific mode of phenomenological reduction practiced by Merleau-Ponty in the study of pathological behaviors of patients who suffer from brain injuries. This pathological reduction has its eidetic moments. This is because it entails, at least in part, the function of an eidetic reduction which is the methodological procedure to read and to grasp the structural invariants of the phenomena under investigation from the observation of a variety of empirical factual cases. Its mode of operation is something like the reflective judgment in the Kantian sense: it proceeds from the bottom-up way in diametrical difference from the top-down manner of the determining judgment.

The theoretical motivation to undertake pathological studies is to understand the basic capacities of a carnal human subject. Through these studies Merleau-Ponty is able to make the crucial distinction between human behaviors which are conducted in two different kinds of spatiality: the concrete space of actuality and the virtual space of possibility and imagination. Yet these two spatialities of qualitative difference are intermingled in the life-interests drifted and modulated activities or actions of the carnal human subject in the ordinary life-world. They could be distinguished only when patients with brain injuries have lost the capacity to construct a space of virtuality by projecting into a future, while retaining the more basic and underlying capacity to navigate within the space of actuality and of the present.

What constitutes the eidetic moments of this pathological reduction is then the distinction between the capacity to live in two qualitatively different spatialities—the actual and the possible—by a normal bodily subject on the one hand, and on the other the general capacity of the pathological subject to navigate in a space reduced to actuality and the present. The space of actuality, though a qualitatively reduced space, is however a more rudimentary form of spatiality which still exhibits the structural invariants of the basic capacity of a pathological human subject. Without the recognition of the basic capacity of the pathological subject to live in an existential spatiality of actuality and of the present, it is impossible for a phenomenologist to come to the knowledge that a normal human subject lives in two different modes of existential spatiality intertwined with one another.

Thus the pathological reduction is a specific mode of phenomenological reduction conducted first of all through the suspension of both the scientific positivist attitude and the intellectualist attitude. Both of these attitudes share the common prejudice, which holds either that pathological cases are meaningless or irrational, or that the meaning of pathological behaviors can only be read with reference to some distinctive normative standards of behaviors of a normal human subject which are supposed to be established *a priori*. However, there is precisely no knowledge of normal behaviors of a bodily human subject prior to the acquisition of knowledge of her pathological behaviors. It is only by suspending and neutralizing the prejudices toward pathological phenomena that a phenomenologist can go back to the pathological cases and thematize them in order to unveil the structural invariants inherent to pathological behaviors. The deciphering of the structural invariants of pathological behaviors enables the phenomenological gaze to penetrate into the essential characteristics of the basic capacity of the human subject: the capacity to interact and even modify her immediate ambient world in order to accomplish actions and tasks motivated by life-interests.

But the identification of the structural invariants of pathological behaviors leads also to the identification of the two aforementioned qualitatively different spatialities a normal human subject used to live through in a pre-reflective manner in natural life. Yet the natural life is precisely so natural that the naturalistic attitude which underlies it is unable to distinguish between these two structurally-invariant levels of existential spatialities lived through by a normal bodily subject. Thus, the recognition of the normal through pathological studies, which result in the distinction between two existential spatialities inherent to the normal human subject, acquires a transcendental status with regard to the being of the bodily subject. Then, we are even tempted to say that the thematization of the pathological behaviors of the body subject through the pathological reduction paves the way to the characterization of some of the moments constitutive of the transcendental status of the bodily human subject.

Thus, it can be said that the pathological reduction is not merely a specific employment of the Husserlian phenomenological reduction understood in its general terms; it also contributes to the recognition of moments which confer to the bodily human subject her transcendental status. In this connection, we can also say that by the introduction of pathological studies and the practice of pathological reduction Merleau-Ponty is able to establish an existential phenomenology of the incarnate human subject in the *Phenomenology of Perception*. Since this existential phenomenology contributes to the elucidation of the constitutive moments of the transcendental status of the bodily human subject, Merleau-Ponty's existential phenomenology acquires a certain transcendental character too.

d) The pathological as a moment of constitutive negativity

Our preceding discussions aim at showing that Merleau-Ponty's hermeneutics of the normal and the pathological in his phenomenology of the human capacity is a demonstration of the constitutive role played by negative moments in the structure of phenomenalization. Nothingness, absence, difference, *écart* and the invisible need to be thematized in view of obtaining a proper understanding of the structure of phenomenal appearance. We have shown with Merleau-Ponty that the condition of possibility of a human subject as a being of possibilities lies in the basic fact that the human subject is a temporal being. The consciousness of a human subject remains intact in so far as she gets hold of a holistic consciousness of time, namely she has a sense of future and past which accompany her sense of present. The loss of the holistic consciousness of time by a patient results in the disruption of her sense of existence and gives rise to pathological behaviors, which limit the patient to the present and to actuality. But the holistic consciousness of time is precisely a consciousness in which there is the essential interplay of presence and absence as well as that of present, past and future. In Husserl, the understanding of the consciousness of time is modelled by the intertwinement of the consciousness of absence (retention and protention) more than by the consciousness of simple presence. Husserl emphasizes that there is no consciousness of now which is not intermingled with the consciousness of the just-past, such that if there is no retention which is hanged on a consciousness of now provoked by a primordial impression, it will be impossible for us to have the consciousness of this very moment of now (Husserl 1966, p. 119; Husserl 1991, p. 123). Thus, Husserl's phenomenology of internal time consciousness is already a conception in which moments of absence (retention and protention) play the role of constitutive negativity. Merleau-Ponty has never lost sight of the moments of constitutive negativity in the phenomenological heritage left behind by Husserl.

3 Canguilhem's non-positivistic conception of pathology

The French philosopher of medicine and life-science Georges Canguilhem (1904–1995), a contemporary of Merleau-Ponty, shows a strong convergence in the understanding of the phenomena of the normal and the pathological with the author of *Phenomenology of Perception*. In his seminal work *The Normal and the Pathological* (Canguilhem 1966; Canguilhem 1989),[1] Canguilhem succeeds in showing in what way the positivistic natural scientific approach fails to understand the complex and paradoxical relation between the normal and the pathological and norms and normativity on the one hand, and between the diseased and the healthy on the other. Below are some summary points of Canguilhem's conceptual clarification of the complex relation between normal, normativity and the norm on the one hand, and between health and illness on the other hand in *The Normal and the Pathological*. The latter is a work which shows that Canguilhem conceptualizes the pathological and the disease as constitutive negativity.

---

[1] The first edition (1943) of Georges Canguilhem's work is entitled *Essai sur quelques problèmes concernant le normal et le pathologique* ("Essay on some problems concerning the normal and the pathological"). The second edition (1966) is supplemented by "Nouvelles réflexions concernant le normal et le pathologique (1963–1966)" ("New reflections on the normal and the pathological") and receives the present title *Le normal et le pathologique* (Paris: Presses Universitaires de France, 1966).

a) A dynamic approach to the study of norms: norms are derived from abnormal cases

From the viewpoint of pure logical reasoning, the pathological is commonly understood as the abnormal which is the negation of the normal. According to this mode of reasoning, the abnormal, conceived as deviation from normality, is thus posterior to the normal. On the other hand, the normal draws its legitimate status from some kind of norms which is seen to have an *a priori* status, exhibiting some essential characteristics of necessity like those of a natural law. To Canguilhem, a closer examination of the genesis of norms, in particular with reference to contemporary anthropological studies, will find that norms are not *a priori*; they are rather originated from facts. Prior to the appearance of norms there are only facts; thus norms are posterior to facts. At the same time, the term "normal" as the adjective of "norm" is not a static and peaceful concept, but rather a "dynamic and polemic concept" (Canguilhem 1966, p. 176; Canguilhem 1989, p. 239). The setting up of a norm is an act of valorization against other values or counter-values:

> To set a norm (*normer*), to normalize, is to impose a requirement on an existence, a given whose variety, disparity, with regard to the requirement, present themselves as a hostile, even more than an unknown, indeterminant. (Canguilhem 1966, p. 176; Canguilhem 1989, p. 239)

The motivation of setting up a norm comes from the awareness of the impossibility of unitary understanding in the face of the great variety of empirical cases of existence. The setting up of a norm expresses the will to settle the large variety of deviant cases, which otherwise will remain indeterminate. Compared to the norm, the slightly deviant cases are considered as more or less normal, while the extremely deviant cases are considered as abnormal. Thus the act of setting up a norm is an act of inversion of values into counter-values and an act of polarization: it involves the designation of the abnormal and depreciation of all those cases which deviate from the norm itself. Thus to set a norm is an act of normalization in view of settlement of differences and disputes. But the normative function played by such a norm is only suggestive; it cannot exert a necessity like that of a natural law. Rather, it expresses the preference of a certain possibility over other possibilities. Yet a preference is never purely natural, but always relative to anthropological or cultural situations. Canguilhem explains this in very clear terms:

> A norm offers itself as a possible mode of unifying diversity, resolving a difference, settling a disagreement. But to offer oneself is not to impose oneself. Unlike a law of nature, a norm does not necessitate its effect... A norm is in effect the possibility of a reference only when it has been established or chosen as the expression of a preference and as the instrument of a will to substitute a satisfying state of affairs for a disappointing one. (Canguilhem 1966, p. 177; Canguilhem 1989, p. 240)

Thus, from the point of view of purely formal reasoning, the abnormal is the negation of the normal, which has the status of the originary. Yet from the existential and anthropological standpoint, a norm is never originary; on the contrary, it is a result of infraction:

> Rule begins to be rule only in making rules and this function of correction arises from infraction itself... It is not just the exception which proves the rule as rule, it is the infraction which provides it with the occasion to be rule by making rules. In this sense the infraction is not the origin of the rule but the origin of regulation. (Canguilhem 1966, pp. 178–179; Canguilhem 1989, pp. 241–242)

In other words, a rule obtains its status of rule in so far as there is contestation of its normative status: the exceptions to this rule and infraction of this rule constitute its status as rule. Thus the normative status of a norm is derivative from the varieties of existence of abnormalities. In brief, a norm is never originary.

b) A non-quantitative approach to the distinction between the normal and the pathological

Since the setting up of a norm is an act of valorization, of inversion of values and of polarization as expression of preference of a certain possibility over other possibilities relative to anthropological and cultural situations, there is no precise line of demarcation or definite boundary between the normal and the pathological. This does not mean that there is simple continuity between the normal and the pathological in the sense that they are identical in essence. This means rather that the difference between the normal and the pathological is not merely a question of quantitative variations. Since a norm does not have the effect of necessity comparable to natural laws and expresses a preference, this means that a norm always allows flexibility:

> The normal does not have the rigidity of a fact of collective constraint but rather the flexibility of a norm which is transformed in its relation to individual conditions. (Canguilhem 1966, p. 119; Canguilhem 1989, p. 182)

To Canguilhem the flexibility of a norm can go so far as to allow for reversibility in the sense that the normal can become the pathological in a different situation and vice versa:

> In order to be normative in given conditions, what is normal can become pathological in another situation if it continues [to be] identical to itself. It is the individual who is the judge of this transformation because it is he who suffers from it from the very moment he feels inferior to the tasks which the new situation imposes on him. (Canguilhem 1966, p. 119; Canguilhem 1989, p. 182)

If the normative function of a norm is defined with reference to the accomplishment of a task in definite anthropological and cultural situations, the distinction between the normal and the pathological is never a question of simple quantitative variations, but of qualitative difference.

c) The positive role played by disease in lived experience

The understanding of the pathological is closely linked to the understanding of illness and disease, which refers back to health. To Canguilhem, being in good health does not mean that one never falls sick; rather "to be in good health means being able to fall sick and recover" (Canguilhem 1966, p. 132; Canguilhem 1989, pp. 198–199). Canguilhem adds further that such a capacity "is a biological luxury", meaning that a person with good health can afford to contract disease in so far as she can recover.

In other words, it is perfectly normal that a healthy person contracts disease as long as she can recover from it. To Canguilhem, a human person is sometimes well aware that in trying to accomplish certain difficult tasks she will run the risk of sacrificing her health by contracting some diseases. Yet she still takes this risk: a healthy person "measures his health in terms of his capacity to overcome organic crises in order to establish a new order" (Canguilhem 1966, p. 132; Canguilhem 1989, p. 200). Thus the concept of health includes in itself its opposite: disease. Disease does not play a purely negative role in human life. It is not a question of purely quantitative variation of functional indices of bodily organs. Disease is another dimension of life qualitatively different from that of the healthy state.

> Disease is a positive, innovative experience in the living being and not just a fact of decrease or increase. The content of the pathological state cannot be deduced, save for a difference in format, from the content of health; disease is not a variation on the dimension of health; it is a new dimension of life. (Canguilhem 1966, p. 122; Canguilhem 1989, p. 186)

If disease is a new dimension of life and not the total negation of life, and if it is normal that a health body falls sick, disease as the pathological state of the human body acquires a certain normative status: it can no more be understood as abnormal in the absolute sense, but only in a relative sense.

> If we acknowledge the fact that disease remains a kind of biological norm, this means that the pathological state cannot be called abnormal in an absolute sense, but abnormal in relation to a well-defined situation. (Canguilhem 1966, p. 130; Canguilhem 1989, p. 196)

Thus not only health enjoys a normative status, disease has a normative status too. This implies that the pathological is not inferior or subordinate to the normative; it rather joins hand with the normal to define the normative. Thus the pathological is constitutive of the normative too.

d) The constitutive role of the *pathos* and the abnormal with regard to the *logos* and the normal

In a summary statement stunningly close to Merleau-Ponty's demonstration of the constitutive role of pathological behaviors of the body-subject and the speaking subject, Canguilhem also declares that the *pathos* is constitutive of the *logos* and that the abnormal is constitutive of the normal:

> Summarizing the hypotheses we proposed in the course of examining Leriche's ideas, we can say that in biology it is the *pathos* which conditions the *logos* because it gives it its name. It is the abnormal which arouses theoretical interest in the normal. Norms are recognized as such only when they are broken. Functions are revealed only when they fail. Life rises to the consciousness and science of itself only through maladaptation, failure and pain. (Canguilhem 1966, p. 139; Canguilhem 1989, pp. 208–209)

Here the recognition of the constitutive role of the pathological by both Merleau-Ponty and Canguilhem recalls Heidegger's famous analyses of the relation between the pragmatic attitude and the theoretical attitude of the *Dasein* in her involvement with the objects of the ambient world in *Being and Time*. It is at the discovery of the malfunction of the objects as tools that the *Dasein* changes her hitherto pragmatic attitude into the scientific-theoretical attitude with regard to these objects-tools in question in view of reparation and restoration of their normal functions.

e) The study of the pathological is not a science based uniquely on physiology

If the distinction between the normal and the pathological is not based merely on quantitative variations of indices of organs, pathological phenomena cannot be reduced to purely physiological explanations. If the normal and the pathological are relative to life situations and life interests, they cannot be determined by physiology as a pure positive science.

> If it has not seemed possible to maintain the definition of physiology as the science of the normal, it seems difficult to admit that there can be a science of disease, that there can be a purely scientific pathology. (Canguilhem 1966, p. 143; Canguilhem 1989, p. 213)

Canguilhem has given the following stunning example in support of his non positive scientific approach to the study of pathology:

> Certainly a living being's excrement can be food for another living being but not for him. What distinguishes food from excrement is not a physicochemical reality but a biological value. (Canguilhem 1966, p. 148; Canguilhem 1989, p. 220)

In the text Canguilhem does not give any example. But such examples can be easily drawn from our knowledge of the structural operation of an eco-system. Canguilhem's position is at times so radical that he even quotes the declaration of Goldstein with the apparent effect of assimilating the latter's position as his own: "Disease and health would not be biological concepts!" (*Maladie et santé ne seraient pas des notions biologiques!*) (Canguilhem 1966, p. 148; Canguilhem 1989, p. 220).

Canguilhem's use of the conditional implies at least that disease and health as different dimensions of life are irreducible to biology as a pure positive science.

f) Pathology, as study of the patient who is a subjectivity and of the disease, has an axiological dimension

In the course of his detailed analyses of pathological phenomena and the interwoven character between the normal and the pathological, Canguilhem often uses the terms of life, existence, experience and value, terms referring to the patient as a subjectivity.

> Thus it is first and foremost because men feel sick that a medicine exists. It is only secondarily that men know, because medicine exists, in what way they are sick. Every empirical concept of disease preserves a relation to the axiological concept of disease. Consequently it is not an objective method which qualifies a considered biological phenomenon as pathological. It is always the relation to the individual patient through the intermediary of clinical practice, which justifies the qualification of pathological. While admitting the importance of objective methods of observation and analysis in pathology, it does not seem possible that we can speak with any correct logic of 'objective pathology.' Certainly a pathology can be methodical, critical and fortified experimentally. It can be called objective with reference to the physician who practices it. But the pathologist's intention is not that his object be a matter without subjectivity. One can carry out objectively, that is impartially, research whose object cannot be conceived and constructed without being related to a positive and negative qualification, whose object is not so much a fact as a value. (Canguilhem 1966, pp. 156–157; Canguilhem 1989, p. 229)

Not only Canguilhem privileges the terms of life, existence and experience to the terms of science and concept, he himself asserts the primacy of experience over science:

> We maintain that the life of the living being, were it that of an amoeba, recognizes the categories of health and disease only on the level of experience, which is primarily a test in the affective sense of the word, and not on the level of science. Science explains experience but it does not for all that annul it. (Canguilhem 1966, p. 131; Canguilhem 1989, p. 198)

Thus, contrary to the strict demarcation drawn by Foucault between French phenomenologists as philosophers of experience, sense and subject on the first line and philosophers of science, rationality and concept on the second line, Canguilhem, classified as belonging to the second line by Foucault, uses often the terms and categories of the first line to articulate his conception of the normal and the pathological. Don't we have reason to soften or revise Foucault's too strict line of demarcation?

Conclusion

If our analyses conducted above are correct, Merleau-Ponty and Canguilhem not only share the non-positivistic conception of the pathological, but also see the pathological as constitutive negativity of human existence. Yet their conceptions of the pathological are not entirely identical. Being a phenomenologist, Merleau-Ponty proceeds to study the pathological via the practice of a specific mode of phenomenological reduction, namely the pathological reduction. The pathological reduction paves the way to the establishment of a certain eidetic study of pathological phenomena. Canguilhem does not proceed from the position of phenomenology but from that of philosophy of science. But his conception of science is not positivistic. His concept of norm is a dynamic and polemic concept. This raises the question of whether such a dynamic and polemic concept of norm can be compatible with Merleau-Ponty's concept of the normal and the pathological, which is based on a certain eidetic of the pathological. Our answer to this question is: though Merleau-Ponty's pathological reduction which leads to an eidetic study of pathological behaviors sound paradoxical, it is impossible to rule out the possibility of eidetic study of pathological phenomena in order to establish modern medicine as a scientific study of illness and abnormal life phenomena. Though Canguilhem claims that the concept of norm is dynamic and polemic, this does not rule out the possibility of establishing an eidetic study of illness and the abnormal in so far as he has to conceptualize these very phenomena. In order to proceed to the work of conceptualization, a minimum level of eidetic description is required, upon which concept formation is possible. Seen from this perspective, the concepts of normal and pathological in Merleau-Ponty and in Canguilhem are not incompatible with one another.

The proximity of the interwoven conceptions of normal and pathological in Merleau-Ponty and Canguilhem presented above allows us to revisit Foucault's dichotomy of contemporary French philosophy. Foucault's dividing line which separates phenomenology as a philosophy of subject, sense and experience and French philosophy of science as a philosophy of concept and life is to be reconsidered, because this line of demarcation is valid neither for Merleau-Ponty nor for Canguilhem. In the case of Merleau-Ponty, his philosophy of experience is mediated by a philosophy of concept, namely the concepts of the pre-reflective experience and of body schema. Thus Merleau-Ponty's phenomenology, though a philosophy of subject and experience, is not against the concept. Phenomenology is a philosophy which operates on concepts to clarify experience. In the case of Canguilhem, his concept of life is precisely life as existence and experience, and not life against existence and experience. This is because Canguilhem's epistemology of the science of life is not that of a purely formal science; rather, the formation of concepts pertaining to the disciplines of life science must pass by the concrete experience of life intermingled with motivation, life-interest, and value. A philosophy of life science constructs its concepts on the basis of experience and with constant reference to experience, but never against experience. On the one hand, there is no philosophy without concept. Phenomenological philosophy works toward concept formation on the basis of faithful description and elucidation of experience. On the other hand, there is no science without experience, and concept formation in life science necessitates the assistance of experience. Thus, concept formation and experience are the two constitutive and indispensable moments of any form of philosophy. Merleau-Ponty and Canguilhem share a convergent view on this important issue though their philosophical practices are apparently different.

The convergence between Merleau-Ponty and Canguilhem in their understanding of the phenomena of the normal and the pathological is not a pure coincidence. In fact they share a common source of inspiration, namely that of the clinical studies and theoretical elucidations of the originally German non-positivistic neurologist and psychiatrist Kurt Goldstein (1878–1965). The studies collected in Goldstein's 1934 ground-breaking work *Der Aufbau des Organismus* (English Translation *The Organism*, 1939) are particularly inspiring to both. It can be shown that through Goldstein's own explanation of his holistic method in opposition to the analytic or dissecting method used by positivistic neurologists, there is a close proximity between Goldstein's approach and the phenomenological approach. However, the demonstration of this linkage exceeds the objective of the present essay and can only be done in another work.

References

Canguilhem, Georges (1966): *Le normal et le pathologique*. Paris: Presses Universitaires de France.
Canguilhem, Georges (1989): *The Normal and the Pathological*, with an introduction by Michel Foucault. Trans. Carolyn R. Rawcett/Robert S. Cohen. New York: Zone Books.
Foucault, Michel (1989): "Introduction by Michel Foucault". In: Canguilhem, Georges: *The Normal and the Pathological*. Trans. Carolyn R. Fawcett/Robert S. Cohen. New York: Zone Books, pp. 7–24.
Foucault, Michel (1994): "La vie: l'expérience et la science". In: *Dits et écrits*. Vol IV. Daniel Defert/François Ewald (Eds.). Paris: Éditions Gallimard, pp. 763–776.
Heidegger, Martin (1927/1979): *Sein und Zeit*. Tübingen: Max Niemeyer.
Heidegger, Martin (1962): *Being and Time*. Trans. John Macquarrie/Edward Robinson. London, New York: SCM Press.
Husserl, Edmund (1952): *Ideen zur einer reinen Phänomenologie und phänomenologischen Philosophie. Zweites Buch: Phänomenologische Untersuchungen zur Konstitution*. Marly Biemel (Ed.). Husserliana IV. The Hague: Martinus Nijhoff.
Husserl, Edmund (1966): *Zur Phänomenologie des inneren Zeitbewusstseins (1893–1917)*. Rudolf Boehm (Ed.). Husserliana X. The Hague: Martinus Nijhoff.
Husserl, Edmund (1989): *Ideas Pertaining to a Pure Phenomenology and to a Phenomenological Philosophy. Second Book: Studies in the Phenomenology of Constitution*. Trans. Richard Rojcewicz/André Schuwer. Dordrecht: Kluwer.
Husserl, Edmund (1991): *On the Phenomenology of the Consciousness of Internal Time (1893–1917)*. Trans. John Barnett Brough. Dordrecht: Kluwer.
Merleau-Ponty, Maurice (1945): *Phénoménologie de la perception*. Paris: Éditions Gallimard.

Merleau-Ponty, Maurice (2012): *The Phenomenology of Perception*. Trans. Donald A. Landes. London, New York: Routledge.

The experience of self and other

Niall Keane
Empathy, Intersubjectivity, and the World-Orienting Other

Abstract: This chapter addresses the self-other relation through Husserl's account of empathy and phenomenological encounter. While respecting the centrality and importance of the first-person character of subjective consciousness in Husserl's phenomenology, this contribution takes a slightly different approach. By emphasising the often-marginalized self-differentiating experience of the subject's encounter with the other, it will be shown that there is a particular form of asymmetry in Husserl's analysis of the encounter with the other and what it brings about. The chapter demonstrates how the experience of the other both frees the subject from the confinement of original and quasi-anonymous self-belonging and opens the subject to a sense of the world in which it is necessarily situated. It also shows how the encounter with the other opens it to a form of worldly objectivity, self-differentiation and de-centering that would be absent without such an interruptive experience or encounter.

Introduction

When it comes to the self-other relation, phenomenologists drawing on Husserl, have argued that one of the most important aspects of his multi-layered account of intersubjectivity is the reciprocal and symmetrical nature of the embodied subject's experience of other embodied subjects. Even if phenomenologists point to an asymmetrical aspect in Husserl's analysis of the self-other relation, they tend to focus more on the original nature of my relation to myself in *prima persona* in contrast to my experience of the givenness of another in a non-original manner. My claim is that the asymmetry, borne out in Husserl's analyses of empathy and intersubjectivity, is in effect more constitutive of the self-other relation than is usually recognised.

Without downplaying the commitment to the first-person character of consciousness or the original self-belonging that defines Husserlian phenomenology and its desire to safeguard a necessary principle of individuation, I will take a slightly different approach, one contained latently in Husserl's writings, by emphasizing the oft-marginalized self-differentiating or de-centring experience involved in the encounter with the other. In doing so, I will show how the experience of the other both frees the subject from the confinement of original and quasi-anonymous self-belonging and opens it to a form of worldly objectivity and actualized self-differentiation which would be absent without the altering and augmenting appearance of the other. This is what Rudolf Bernet has referred to, albeit in reference to Levinas, as the way "the other liberates the subject from its captivity within the immanence of its own self-belonging" (Bernet 2002, p. 93).

Husserl's intersubjective analyses stop short of articulating a theory of radical alterity, preferring to give an account of relative alterity starting in abstraction from what he terms the original "sphere of ownness" (*Eigenheitsphäre*) (Husserl 1988, p. 92), before building towards the social and cultural objectivities found at the level of transcendental intersubjectivity. Yet in the rich phenomenological analyses that Husserl carries out there is still to be found a theory of 'self-alteration', often neglected in the reciprocal and more epistemologically motivated co-constituting picture found in the secondary literature. My claim is that with the experience of the other's givenness there occurs something in and to the life of the subject which is promised by and yet exceeds the standard Husserlian co-constituting account. What I am interested in is how the encounter with the other shatters the illusion of perfect self-belonging, indicating a world always in excess of our intersubjective perceiving and epistemic verification. In so doing, the other grants the subject access to the world and to itself as worldly in a way that would be otherwise impossible, opening up a world that will be there long after this or that group of verifiers and co-constitutors have perished.

The analysis will move from the more traditional phenomenological approach, which addresses how the other is given to me in perceptual experience to the precise nature of the self-transforming encounter with the other. Consequently, I am not so much concerned with how the other is intuitively given to me, nor with how the other is given to me *qua* other, but with the altering effect this encounter has on the life of the subject, giving life to the subject, and in what is indicated beyond the encounter. Here the point becomes not simply one of the co-constituted meaningfulness of the world as it is established in the reciprocal opening of the self towards the other but, more saliently, the self-differentiating effect the other has on the life of the subject in alerting me to the world as always more than our perceiving, thematizing or conceptual circumscription of it.

Thus, while Bernhard Waldenfels has built a phenomenologically significant system out of Husserl's analysis of the self-other relation by emphasising a "responsive form of phenomenology" over an "intentionally constitutive" one (Waldenfels 1994, pp. 195–210), my primary focus will not be on the self's inability to fully respond to the demands of the other, although this is also indirectly relevant to my claims. Rather, I will explore how the other does not cause me to take leave of my senses, but alters my senses to such an extent as to render the subject self-differentiated, causing the subject to become genuinely worldly, to become a subject that did not simply reside within itself prior to the encounter, and to become cognizant of the world's independence. And while Husserl primarily focused on co-constitution and reciprocal interdependence, on the self-other relation as an iterative one, I will instead focus on the encounter with the other and how the altering effect of the other on my original sphere causes the emergence of a worldly self in unprecedented ways.

Admittedly, Husserl would have seen these two foci as continuous and consistent with one another. However, for the sake of redressing what I take to be an interpretative imbalance, I will draw on what Michael Theunissen termed "*Veränderung*" (Theunissen 1965, pp. 141,143) and examine the alteration undergone by the subject in the encounter with the embodied alter-ego. I will claim that this is not simply an encounter that leads to a modification of the original sphere, or a "transformation of sense" (*Sinnverwandlung*) (Husserl 1976a, pp. 214–210), but rather one which gives me the sphere from which I always already start my phenomenological analysis. My claim is the following: what is peculiarly my own stems from an encounter that precedes and exceeds me. Husserl clearly struggled to reconcile the uniqueness and primacy of the subject with a notion of the subject as always already containing the sense of the other within it, which is evinced in Volume 15 of the Husserliana (Husserl 1973c, p. 586). What we have here then is not simply an original subject, a myself, which is cognitively and dispositionally open to others, but rather a subject which is opened by others, drawn out by others, and open to the mind-independent reality of the world because of others.

1 The Self-Other Relation

When it comes to providing an account of the self-other relation, one must recognise at least three distinct but interrelated moments: (1) The original experience of being a psycho-physical unity that takes place within my sphere of ownness. (2) The appearance of a body in my perceptual field that is similar to my own. (3) Interpretable activity on the part of another, which is the expression of embodied intentions, motivations and interests. Building on this, one has the basis for what Husserl terms the "apperceptive transfer" (*apperzeptive Übertragung*) (Husserl 1988, p. 110) or transposition of my experiences as a psycho-physical unity, one that moves within a shared system of meaning and motivation to the other, and in so doing of "explicating" or better "interpreting" (*aus-*

legen)¹ the other's psycho-physical unity as analogous to my own (Husserl 1988, p. 110). As Husserl has it, the other is thus explicated or even better interpreted as an "intentional modification of myself" (Husserl 1988, p. 115) and it is at this moment that Husserl's phenomenology of intersubjectivity becomes what Paul Ricoeur terms a "hermeneutics of alterity" (Ricoeur 1986, pp. 67–72).

At the risk of serious understatement, one could say that for Husserl the other whom I encounter is similar to me and yet also distinct from me. From this perspective, the explication of the phenomenon under discussion leads Husserl to the conclusion that when the other appears to me and for me, there occurs a doubling of the present. More simply put, my present comes to be constituted not only starting from the self-experience of myself as a centre of activity, motivation, and interest, but also from the fact that I encounter another who has a centre of activity, motivation, and interest all of its own. Thus, when I perceive another subject, I always perceive it in the mode of its being similar to me and yet being over *there*.

The appearance of the other's body gives rise to what Husserl terms a "pairing association" (Husserl 1988, p. 119), i.e., the passive and reciprocal association of my embodied capacities with those of another subject. This is an association between two similar centres of activity given simultaneously in which one is given in an immediate and originary manner, while the other is given as an animate body that expresses psychic life, yet not experienced for me as lived from within.

I see the other's body from without and can thus never experience the other's manner of governing its own embodied movements or mental episodes as volitional. I cannot experience the other as a unique or individual "organ of perception" as it does in its mastery of its surrounding world. Therefore, when Husserl speaks in *Cartesian Meditations* of "the way my body would look 'if I were there'" (Husserl 1988, p. 119), he does not mean that one infers one's own mental states from another subject, or that one draws on something like the memory of having been there or somewhere similar previously. Husserl is addressing a rather different act, one of "presentification" (*Vergegenwärtigung*), which is a directly paired associative perceiving. What Husserl means by this is an intuited apprehension of the simultaneity and similarity of two intentionally related and embodied centres, but given with the knowledge that one is *here* and the other *there*. Or in Husserl's own words:

> I do not apperceive the other ego simply as a duplicate of myself and accordingly as having my original sphere or one completely like mine. I do not apperceive him as having, more

---

1 See László Tengelyi (2012), pp. 429–443.

particularly, the spatial modes of appearance that are mine from here; rather, as we find on closer examination, I apperceive him as having spatial modes of appearance like those I should have if I should go over there and be where he is. (Husserl 1988, p. 117)

2 Analogising Empathy

It is important to state from the outset that Husserl's account of empathy (*Einfühlung*) is not an analysis based on conjecture or hypothetical inference. When we encounter another living subject, what we experience is "the body of someone else and not as merely an indication of someone else" (Husserl 1988, p. 121). It is a verifiable and mediated perceptual experience of the other (Husserl 1982, p. 363) emerging from what Husserl terms a "unity of similarity" (Husserl 1988, p. 112). Empathy is thus an awareness of something both seen and unseen in perceptually lived experience. Importantly, however, the 'appresentation' (*Appräsentation*), the act of presentified co-intending of the other, is still a mode of original givenness, which is of course distinct from the original self-givenness of first-person presentation, or the original act of 'presentation' (*Gegenwärtigung*). In one's experience of the other something is necessarily withheld from me which opens me to an encounter with the other *qua* other.² What is productively withheld in the alerting and altering encounter with the other is the essence of the 'presentification' that constitutes the motivation to know more of this transformative other. What is withheld therefore enables the impactful perception of the other to be what it is, namely, "*perception through originary interpretation*" of the other's life, of their "distinctive essence" (Husserl 2019, p. 267) as constitutively emergent in the embodied subject's analogous and shared perceptual field (Husserl 1959, p. 63).

However, it must be stressed that this approach does not imply some kind of existential solipsism, but rather a methodological solipsism, i.e., a necessary "constitutional abstraction" (Husserl 1988, p. 93) or "thought experiment" (Merleau-Ponty 1964, p. 173) designed to show the insufficiencies of all forms of solipsism. By inquiring into the modes in which I experience my lived body and my bodily activity from the first-person perspective, these analyses shed light not on the inconsistency, or better "absurdity" (Husserl 1988, p. 83) of solipsism and Husserl's attempts to dissolve "the illusion of solipsism" (Husserl 1988, p. 150) from within. His analyses show clearly, for instance, that through such an experience I cannot in principle completely objectify my own body, nor can I consti-

---

2 See Nicolas de Warren (2009), p. 239.

tute it as a material thing. The body is, as Husserl puts it, a "remarkably imperfectly constituted thing" that "obstructs me in the perception of it itself" (Husserl 1989, p. 167). Only thanks to intersubjective experience, to the comprehending interiorization of other's perspectives on me and on the world at large, can the latter be constituted as a properly psycho-physical thing, and yet never perfectly so. In experiencing the other's lived body as an alluringly distinct but analogous centre of activity and interest, one discovers the co-significance of the other's experience as another way of presenting the world and its objectivities.

This is the basis of the 'analogising' that Husserl speaks of, which is not inference, simulation or imitation,[3] or a way of thinking about the other, but rather a distinction that takes place *in* consciousness itself. For example, in my 'original sphere' I have the experience of being conscious and hence experience what it means to have a perspective on the world and to be a centre of activity and orientation. But when the other appears to me, another's perspective on the world and another's orientation in the world is made manifest to me. The other is perceived henceforth as a distinctly living mode through which the world is given and comprehended as objective and transcendent. This not only allows the subject to consider another perspective on the world, which does not amount to inhabiting or having the perspective of the other, but of understanding another mode of the world's appearance or the world becoming objective as one and the same world. Hence, with the interruptive and impacting appearance of the other, it is the otherness of the world that is brought into view insofar as others are experienced, like myself, as "*subjects for this world*" and the world is given "as there for everyone, accessible in respect of its Objects to everyone" (Husserl 1988, p. 91).

That the other is similar to me does not mean, therefore, that the other lives as I do, but rather that the other is analogous to me, that I can transpose the term 'embodied ego' from myself to that other 'over there'. The point here is that the other, like me, encounters a common horizon of sense starting from an understanding of the world and of ourselves as subjects in and for this world. That the other is analogous to me means simply that one acts on the basis of understandable and shareable motivations and intentions and understands that the world, while experienced diversely, is not simply my world but a shared intersubjective world. The concept of 'analogy' is thus reclaimed as a philosophical term of art in the sense of the analogising apprehension 'like me,' understood as an

---

[3] Examples of such approaches are Leslie (1987), pp. 139–142; Goldman (2006); Gallese (2009), pp. 519–536; Gallese and Goldman (1998), pp. 493–501; Gopnik and Wellman (1994), pp. 257–293; and Heal (1998), pp. 44–67 and (2000), pp. 83–99.

embodied consciousness similar to my own with interests and motivations of which I can make sense and come to understand more clearly. Consequently, each and every human subject is endowed with an intentional attitude that carries it along and pre-delineates its movements, which amounts to an irreducibly unique perspective on the world. However, it would be a mistake to conclude that one's perspective is private or merely self-referential, mainly because one's perspective is necessarily exposed to and shaped by the analogous perspectives of others as guarantors of the unity of the world's givenness as objective.

3 The Other

As mentioned previously, the other is clearly a here and now for itself, just as I am for myself, but without being understood (by me) as the here and now which I am for myself. We are of the same form, but we differ in terms of content, in the manner of our distinct self-givenness to ourselves in perceptual experience, which necessarily differs from our givenness to others. We are distinct centres of activity and motivation around which the world is given, and yet my encounter with the other's distinct centre, motivation, and horizon causes my ego, my here and now as a unique or singular subject, to be de-centred and altered, pulled into and engaged with a world which while experienced differently is one and the same world. The other side of this is that neither the self nor the other is simply a pole of its own unique activity and interest, but also and simultaneously an object of affinity for another's activity and interest, another source of meaning to which I must respond, outside the here and now of first-person intentional life.

If at first my 'here' were identical to my lived body, in the encounter with the other, which is disruptive and world-guaranteeing, my 'here' would be modified and assume the sense of a 'here' which is inclined towards objective space, in the midst of many other 'heres', which are always and necessarily impacting and altering 'theres' for me, soliciting a response. In this way, the very original "sphere of ownness" is transformed due to what Husserl terms the "self-estrangement of the original I and of its original sphere" (Husserl 1973c, p. 634). It is at this point that the subject can understand itself as other, i.e., as any other 'here' and as amongst a plurality of other 'heres' in objective space and as one of a plurality of perspectives on one and the same world. Thus with the appearance of the other, a discrete volitional centre makes itself felt, one which refers to diverse and distinct horizons of appearance. These are horizons whose givenness cannot be reduced to those that are originally present (*urpräsent*) to me. The horizons are constitutive of what appears to me objectively, since they are experienced as manifestations of one world, common to all, in which we actually live, and yet they are given from the other's point of orientation.

It is important to note here that it is not only my given reality that can be grasped thanks to the kinetic powers of my lived body, but the actual reality experienced by another subject that I co-experience. For experiencing the other means precisely co-experiencing the distinct manner in which the world reveals itself in and to the orientation of another. In this sense, one's relation to the other signifies a relation to what the other subject sees as a different manifestation of a shared world.

The term 'subjective' does not, however, indicate an inside that stands over against an objective outside, but refers to the moved and motivated subject in as much as it relates to its world and to those others that enable the world to appear *as* an objective world. Thus when one moves within what offers itself to experience, one soon realizes that one's experiences are not simply private mental episodes, but ways in which one and the same world is given plurally. My lived experiences thus yield further modes of the intersubjective manifestation of a common world that other centres see and experience from different points of view. In other words, one could say that our experience of others does not only consist of experiencing how they encounter one and the same world, but how their interruptive appearance gives me a world in the first place by alerting me to the otherness of the world – the world as being continually there for anyone – as distinct from how it is merely given to me. This is precisely how the other introduces me to the world as objectively there and my standpoint as only one among many.

On foot of this, the other is a distinct embodied 'I can' and is thus understandable as another possibility which is nonetheless constitutive of my possibilities, unique and individual and yet intimately and necessarily bound up with my life and lives of others. It is the other that affectively draws the subject out of itself, insofar as various possibilities get actualised in this encounter and the encounter is one that points to the possibility of further world-enlarging encounters with other subjects thanks to their affective impact. Our respective possibilities are hence intertwined and come to depend on the manner in which they are recognised by the other as *my* possibilities and vice versa. Therefore, the appearance and appeal of the other's discrete motivational nexus, the apperception of the other's animated life, modifies and augments the subject's own motivational nexus. The subject's thoughts and actions are thus drawn into the other's horizon of sense, which shapes the contours of my own possibilities as shared objective worldly possibilities, allowing the subject to see that its 'I can' is ultimately framed by and transformable into a 'we can.'[4]

The living present (*die lebendige Gegenwart*) is thus diversely parsed out in the doubling of the extended present: my time and the time of the other as a shared and yet uniquely experienced time.[5] In this encounter I discover that I am no longer the sole source of the present, and a manifold stratification and broadening of the living present is established. The impact of the other on the life of the subject signifies nothing other than a presence that is simultaneously there for me and for all others, with the other nonetheless given as an embodied other with a free and discrete living present all of its own. In reality, this multiplication or pluralisation of the living present gives rise to the full-fledged individuality of the subject as coming to the fore because of the encounter with what is other as worldly.

The appearance of this other that sees things from 'over there' cannot be reduced to my intentional state, mainly because I cannot be both 'here' and 'there' simultaneously. Therefore, the relation between two subjects is a relation between two temporalities, between two distinct temporal streams, experiencing one another directly, touching one another without ever merging. That the other, constituted as it is by the subject, eludes my sphere of ownness means that the temporality of the other is not strictly speaking my temporality. The other's lived body manifests itself in my temporal stream as a similar system of spatiotemporal orientation, reminding me that I can never constitute myself perfectly and hence need the other to be who I am in the most enlarged and world-orienting sense. The other is conceived in as much as this other lived body is a concrete expression of another worldly system of spatiotemporal orientation and only genuinely after I have returned to myself as self-differentiated, more thoroughly constituted due to the encounter.

Accordingly, as I experience it, to my stream of consciousness there belongs the intentional *act* of experiencing another who is similar to me, and yet I do not and cannot apprehend the lived experience of the other *as* the other experiences it. This experience belongs to the other's stream of consciousness, and yet it is accessible to me 'directly', although not 'originally': we do not have the same kind of first-person acquaintance with the other's stream of consciousness that we have with our own, and to argue that we do is tantamount to claiming that we are capable of inhabiting the conscious life of another or of fusing with it. More than that, however, it is also to claim that the difference or produc-

---

4 See Joona Taipale (2014), p. 156.
5 See Rudolf Bernet (1998), pp. 137–149.

tive gap that exists between self and other, which is constitutive of world-objectivity, can be closed or eliminated altogether, which would lead for Husserl to undermining the world's transcendence and objectivity.

The experience of the other is given directly, "in flesh and blood" (*leibhaft*) (Husserl 1973c, p. 332), as the lived experience of another given in and through my acts of embodied consciousness. Importantly, this is not the limitation of phenomenological analysis that it may appear to be, but rather the description of the conditions of the possibility of the appearance of the other and the world. Put otherwise, if the other did not manifest itself as both similar to me and different from me, as another point of view on the world, as another temporal stream, one could not even experience the other, or even know what the terms 'relation' and 'other' might mean. It is the distinct 'mineness' of the psycho-physical unity, the distinctness of the two discrete temporal streams, which makes the interaction and the understanding of the interaction possible. Or as Dan Zahavi articulates it:

> The fact that my experiential access to and acquaintance with the minds of others differs from my first-person acquaintance with my own mind is precisely not an imperfection or shortcoming. On the contrary, it is a difference that is constitutional. It is precisely because of this difference, precisely because of this asymmetry, that we can claim that the minds we experience are other minds. Indeed, a more precise way of capturing what is at stake is by saying that we experience bodily and behavioural expressions as expressive of an experiential life that transcends the expressions. There is, so to speak, necessarily more to the mind of the other than what we are grasping, but this doesn't make our understanding non-experiential. We must respect the difference between self-access and self-ascription and our access to the other's mental life and other-ascription. (Zahavi 2014, p. 166)

For the Husserlian phenomenologist it is vital to avoid two particular pitfalls: (1) that our access to other subjects amounts to turning the subjective and intentional life of the other into a derivative and modified form of my own self-awareness; and (2) that the psycho-physical life of another is inaccessible or alien to me in its originality, giving rise to a sense of subjective isolation. Consequently, when it comes to experiencing the other, the other is most certainly not an open book, insofar as I am precluded from having an inner perception or internal apprehension of the other's psycho-physical experiences. That said, it is patent that the other's feelings and thoughts are evidentially present in the world by way of their words and deeds. They strike me directly, and are not given by mere inference or deduction, as would be the case if the conscious life of another were altogether inaccessible to me. Because of this, the asymmetry between my self-experience, what presents itself originally to me, and the other's self-experience or self-perception is as original for them as mine is for me, is something that Husserlian phenomenology not only wants to uphold, but something the phenomenologist needs to thematise as a constitutive component of the self-other relation that demands both respect and recognition. Again Dan Zahavi provides a highly instructive reading of this, writing:

> As Husserl points out, had I had the same access to the consciousness of the other as I have to my own, the other would cease being an other and would instead become a part of me (Hua 1, p. 139). In addition, although I do not have access to the first-personal character of the other's experience, the fact that the other's experience has this elusive surplus is indeed accessible to me, as Husserl repeatedly emphasizes (Hua I. p. 144, Hua XV, p. 631). To demand more, to claim that I would only have a real experience of the other if I experienced her feelings or thoughts in the same way as she herself does, is nonsensical, and fails to respect what is distinct and unique about the givenness of the other. It would imply that I would only experience an other if I experienced her in the same way that I experience myself, i.e., it would lead to an abolition of the difference between self and other, to a negation of that which makes the other other. (Zahavi 2012, p. 233)

4 Embodiment and Relationality

It is only from the perspective of embodied self-differentiation that it makes sense to talk about a relation. And it is only on this basis that there can emerge a unique form of inter-action which we call the self-other or I-thou relation. In fact, interpreting the experiential life of the other, the other as an expression of its conscious life, also means that the other is an embodied consciousness. It is on this basis that one can claim that collective-intentionality is founded on a type of interaction in which each and every subject is determined reciprocally by the other because we are first and foremost acting and experiencing subjects who live embodied meaning-constituting lives with others. Thus, if that lived body 'over there' is experienced as an animate body, one that is looking directly at me, I also experience the fact that I am blushing as an expression of a socially accessible and meaningful aspect of my life as experienced by the other; and the other might subsequently appear embarrassed when it experiences my blushing within its perceptual field. In this way, there is established the iterative and always to be further determined structure that constitutes higher order forms of social interdependence as a field of open-ended interaction, concretised in the reciprocity of perspectives within a common or shared world.

Now thematising the body signifies that the other's body is experienced by me as an expression of a uniquely intelligible way of being. Husserl, for example, insists on the fact that the mediating character of empathy, made possible by our embodiment, is the condition of the possibility of the appearance of the other *qua* other. The decisive point is this: the other does not exist in my consciousness, but is nevertheless given *in* my conscious experience as an embodied, world-referring and independent point of view on the world.

As it stands, the other is outside of my conscious life and yet is also part of it in a certain manner, but only insofar as embodied consciousness experiences this other in the manner of a given embodied alter-ego to which I do not have first-person access or control. This means that the embodied other is a unity given within my intentional life, a unity constituted in me, and yet one that contains within itself a free for-itself that is other than mine, capable of frustrating me, antagonizing me, or loving me. Nonetheless, the other is manifest in virtue of a concordant or harmonious experience, while the experience of a mannequin or a doll, neither of which expresses a reciprocal and interested rapport with the surrounding world, would not be considered 'other' in terms of having an embodied and uniquely intentional point of view on the world or as world-altering. Or as Merleau-Ponty captures perfectly:

> Other persons are there too...To begin with they are not there as minds, or even as 'psychisms,' but such for example as we face them in anger or love – faces, gestures, spoken words to which our own respond without thoughts intervening, to the point that we sometimes turn their words back upon them even before they have reached us, as surely as, more surely than, if we had understood – each one of us pregnant with the others and confirmed by them in his body. (Merleau-Ponty 1964, p. 181)

Hence, from a theoretical perspective one could say that the other 'over there' is merely a machine, but when it comes to phenomenological experience, one cannot relate to the encountered other as if it were a machine. One does not try to persuade a machine of something; one does not try to understand or elicit affection or love from a machine; one does not try to dissimulate or project an image of oneself when faced with a machine, at least not in genuine or normal social interaction, which the example of blushing and causing embarrassment brings out nicely. Here one is dealing with conscious subjects whose appearance and behaviour manifest an intentional and motivational relation to the world. Hence, when it comes to the self-other relation, Husserl's analysis revolves around the direct access we have to the lives of others, which is not the same as saying the access is straightforward or original. Quoting Zahavi again:

> One can concede that our typical understanding of others is contextual without endorsing the view that our engagement with others as minded creatures is primarily and fundamentally a question of attributing hidden mental states to them. Likewise, it is a mistake to consider directness as necessarily opposed to complexity. Saying that we can be directly acquainted with certain mental states of others is consequently not to argue that the process that allows for this direct apprehension must necessarily be simple. The crucial

point, and this is what the term 'direct' is supposed to capture, is that the object of my apprehension, the mental state of the other, is my primary intentional object. It is the state itself that I am facing, there is nothing that gets in the way, and the state is experienced as actually present to me. (Zahavi 2014, p. 180)

Accordingly, phenomenological analysis is structured around an encounter with the other as an intentional object with a life of its own and around the general structure of intentionality. Hence, for Husserl at least, interpersonal and intersubjective understanding and interaction are founded upon the structure of intentionality itself, on the harmony and stability of a co-existence founded on reciprocal self-givenness and multiple layer of co-intending, and on the animated, interested, and inherently expressive nature of intentional life.

5 Intersubjective Constitution

To the extent that the other is constituted by me, and I am constituted by the other, it follows that our respective self-consciousness is modified or transformed jointly in the act of constitution. My 'here' ceases to be a privileged spatial location. In fact, my here and now are constituted starting from and together with another 'there'. The identification of a temporal space which belongs uniquely to my sphere of ownness is modified, disrupting my self-enclosedness, mainly because the living present is given simultaneously as this moment *here* and that moment *there*. The other is co-present, a present other than mine, which cannot be "given in consciousness as originary" (Husserl 1982, p. 6) but which nonetheless accompanies, transforms and amplifies my self-awareness and personal individuality. The other's life is thus intimately connected to my life, and we are inextricably bound to one another in the ever broadening intentionality of empathetic experience. Through the altering and self-differentiating experience of the other's appearance to me *qua* other, consciousness is opened up by and to the experience of something other-than-itself and towards wholly new horizons of objective sense and richer forms of personal self-awareness and self-responsibility. As Husserl puts it in *Erste Philosophie:*

> I experience the person sitting opposite me as one who is directed at myself in his experience. Hence, on the basis of this most originary form of being-*for-one-another*-reciprocally the manifold *I-you-acts* and *we-acts* become possible, acts which in turn can be empathized by others and by communicative pluralities as unities. Hence the most multi-layered communal life becomes possible whose strange peculiarity is that not only many subjects as such live, but they live in a way that each and every one of them has, through the intentionality of empathizing experience, all others as his others; as co-existing, partly in the

form of originary experience, partly in that of a determinate or open indeterminate knowing, they are in his existential field. But not enough yet: immediately or mediately, partly in reality, partly in practical possibility to be achieved, he is with all others in a *social nexus*, and this is owed to the communicative, the specific social acts, I-you-acts, we-acts, and so on, "trafficking" with them, actually or possibly, experiencing from them personal effects and exercising effects on them; but all that in the context of one's—and everybody's—intentionality, such that "everybody" knows himself as somebody, as a member of a *personal effective community* extending itself into indeterminate endless expanses, and ultimately [into the community] of a humanity. (Husserl 1959, pp. 136–37/338–39)

Because of the embodied other, one encounters another lived temporality, another source of the world's appearance, and even of shared humanity's appearance to itself, which entails the simultaneous confirmation of the world as both constituted and as a transcendent reality. The other, even if also constituted by me, does not belong to my temporal life, but transforms the sense of my temporal life, altering both the sense of the ego as *solus ipse* and the sense of the world as given initially in the singularity of my intentional life as there *for me*. The bodiliness (*Leiblichkeit*) of another appears in my temporal stream, or better it is associatively apperceived, but only insofar as it manifests itself *as* another temporality whose words, deeds and gestures pull me up short, frustrate me, surprise me, and yet make sense to me. The other's expressions are expressions of a unique lived temporality, interpreted on the basis of past and future experiences, and only as such do they become worldly intentions that can be shared.

Again, this is Husserl's way of ensuring a balance between the inexhaustible plurality of constituting standpoints and the unity of the world, by insisting on an insurmountable limit when it comes to self-other relation, which as indicated earlier is in fact not a limit in the sense of an impediment or obstacle to be overcome, but rather the productive source of my being-for and being-together-with others. Even if the experiences of another are necessarily and productively distinct from my own and from my temporal stream, I am not separable from the other, nor is the other separable from me. Each and every subject exists *for* itself and yet also and simultaneously exists *for* others and necessarily so in the continually present co-validity of the other's intentional life as world-alerting and world-alluring. This is the basis of the continually enriching interplay between self-experience and other-experience that defines the phenomenological primacy or absoluteness of the intersubjective sphere.[6]

My givenness to myself is thus traceable to a mutually apperceptive system of co-existence and meaning transfer with other motivated and motivating sub-

---

[6] See Dermot Moran (2016), p. 114.

jects. This is a system of expectations and counter-expectations, of reciprocal obligations, embedded in a complex web of interactions which are first thematised with the appearance of the other, understood as another system of possibilities and expectations which are discrete and unpredictable, and yet understandable and shareable. For Husserl, this is a system of open-ended and co-existent act-interactions, which amounts to experiencing the altering alter-ego as one who, in turn, experiences another as other to itself, further constituting and ensuring the continued objectivity of the world and the inexhaustible plurality of perspectives on that world. Consequently, the nature of objectivity should be seen as the outcome of the continual interaction and ongoing process of transcendental intersubjectivity and its achievements and not as a fabrication of the life of the mind. This system of manifold act-interaction, which is in principle ideally infinite, is the basis of social systems and social interaction and without this productive interaction we would not have a common world, or at least a common world that is meaningfully shared.

While it is true that Husserl's *Cartesian Mediations*, specifically the Fifth Meditation, does not contain an extensive elucidation of *Fremderfahrung* in the broadest sense of the term,[7] i.e., culturally, politically and socially, it nonetheless contains the seeds of a move from an order of static act-interaction analysis, which is singularly face to face, to a higher order of more broadly encompassing socially and historically interdependent interactions with those who are absent and yet nonetheless impactfully motivating for the subject in their absence.

Thanks to the direct embodied experiences of another's life, I can encounter other intentional spheres or centres of experience, other motivations and other immanent streams of experience without reducing them to a derivative or mere variant of my intentional life. Moreover, and to stress this again, the fact that I cannot experience other intentional lives and other immanent streams of experience from the first-person perspective, or as my own, means that the awareness of these unique lives and these singular streams constitutes the sense that the world in its enduring thereness for everyone and anyone is infinitely more than its there-ness for me and my intentional awareness. This fact also reminds me that this world will exist long after I and you are gone. The other who de-centres me, drawing me out of my simple self-belonging or self-attachment, is experienced as a source of the world's appearance that exceeds and supplements my own perceptual experience of the world as a world for me. What I am saying here is perhaps putting it a bit stronger than Zahavi does

---

7 See Anthony Steinbock (1995), p. 66.

when he writes, "The other is consequently not given in isolation or purity for me; rather, the other is given as intentional, as directed at the same world as I, and the other's world, and the objects that are there for him, are given along with the other" (Zahavi 2014, p. 139).

My claim is that the subject entering into a relation with the other signifies that the time of the other transforms my time and my time transforms their time, bringing about a broadening of perspectives on and understandings of the world that is always more than this or that perspective on it. In this sense, the altering and augmenting appearance of the other on my horizon brings about a de-centring transformation of the subject, a transformative expansion of the pure or original ego, illustrating the fact that the jarring or impactful experience of the other is accompanied by the unfolding transformation of the self as worldly, which is a jolt into full self-apprehension, into animate and worldly life, making us a personal and responsible (as responding) self in the fullest sense of the term (see Husserl 1973b, p. 175).

With the presence of another being, over whom I have no control and no originary access, there emerges a being that looks me in the face, frustrates me, hurts me, betrays me, listens to me or fails to listen, and in so doing makes a claim on me in a myriad of ways, both tacit and explicit. If the other is manifest to me insofar as I transpose my originary experience of being a self to the other, the appearance of the other also signifies the appearance of another embodied self that ascribes an intentional life to me and whose appearance pulls me up short, causing me to question myself and understand myself differently. The upshot is that I become someone who is experienced genuinely as other by the other in a world that is given to me as objective because of this de-centering encounter. This gives rise to a self-altering differentiation within myself, a newly self-understood distinction between the other's experience of me and the experience of me that I can never have, namely, the other's experience of me as an altering alter-ego for them.

This raises a problem as to how these two experiences, these two points of view, are aligned with one another, since the continuity of my identity is underwritten somewhere between my experience of myself, my experience of the other, and the other's experience of me. Hence my self-continuity is bound up essentially, though not exclusively, with the continuity of a community founded on a shared tradition or on experiences, values and norms that are in principle shareable. This in turn opens up the issue of sociality and human community, understood as a form of generative and diachronic other-directed interaction in which each and every subject is influenced by others, who are in turn influenced by others. Or as Husserl has it:

> Sociality is constituted by *specifically social, communicative acts,* acts in which the Ego turns to others and in which the Ego is conscious of these others as ones toward which it is turning, and ones which, furthermore, understand this turning, perhaps adjust their behaviour to it and reciprocate by turning toward that Ego in acts of agreement or disagreement, etc. It is these acts, between persons who already 'know' each other, which foster a higher unity of consciousness and which include in this unity the surrounding world of things as the surrounding world common to the persons who take a position in regard to it. (Husserl 1989, p. 204)

When this takes place, when the field of interaction takes on a life and a history of its own, the sphere of sociality, culture and collective responsibility emerge, and with that an experience of others as temporally finite and hence in possession of a tradition and culture which is necessarily intersubjectively communal and historically ancestral in nature (see Husserl 1973b, p. 223). At this juncture the move is made from the more restricted examination of the intentional and plural structure of empathy which I have examined thus far to the broader question of social ontology; the latter being analyses of the structures of collective intentionality, interpersonal experience and the modes of givenness which define our interdependency in a more historically multifaceted, collective, and communal sense (Husserl 1973a, pp. 98–104). It is this move that brings Husserl from his analysis of individual acts, which are necessarily conjoined, to an analysis of the higher order life of consciousness which is the essence of the collective spirit of human community (Husserl 1973c, p. 199). Accordingly, it is fair to say that the fullest or most concrete sense of the person is to be found in empathy and in the higher social acts that are grounded on it. To have personality or to be a person, then, it is not enough that the subject simply becomes self-aware or that it understands itself as the centre of its acts and rational position-takings, although this is of fundamental importance when it comes to understanding what it means to be rationally free. More than this, far from being the self-achievement of active and autonomous position-taking, personality is also constituted expansively as the subject enters into social relations with others, takes positions with and against others, and is persistently transformed in its encounter with others who continually confirm the objective existence of the world as more than the sum of our perspectives on it. As Patočka puts it, "The other is the most powerful component of our experience, revealing to us what we ourselves are and can do" (Patočka 1998, p. 66).

6 Conclusion

While Husserl would never depart from his insistence on the centrality of the rudimentary self-affection and self-perception of the operating ego, which is pre-reflexive and quasi-anonymous, i.e., unthematic and unobjectified self-awareness, what his phenomenology promises, but does not always deliver, is an analysis of higher order self-emergence and identity constitution, which are triggered by the altering, de-centering hetero-affection of the other. What we have is an interdependent intersubjectivity, an "inseparable being for one another" (*untrennbares Füreinandersein*) (Husserl 1973c, pp. 191, 194) which is not an inter-monadic fusion, which would destroy the intersubjectively discrete plurality of streams. In explicating and amplifying me by drawing me out, the other is hence not only a necessary condition for my experience of the objectively valid world that precedes and exceeds me, but the very *alter*-source of my self-alteration, freeing me up by making me other and more than my egoic self. This is precisely what Michael Theunissen called "*die immanente Veränderung*," understood as "self-alienation" or "self-estrangement" (Theunissen 1965, pp. 141, 143).

To reiterate, just as Husserl talks in the *Crisis* of the emergence of a "primal division between 'I' and 'other'" in the "reducing epoché" (Husserl 1970, p. 185), one also needs to take into account the originary process of self-differentiation, self-alienation, and self-division that takes place in the encounter with the other by way of empathy and intersubjective life. Thus, it is both the 'primal division between 'I' and 'other'' and the self-differentiation and self-division brought about by the impact of the other, the other who awakens me to my drives and interests as essentially understandable and meaningful to others, which constitutes the intentional complexity and interdependence of the common personal life and world apperception. That said, throughout all the self-modifications, self-differentiations, and self-amplifications that take place thanks to the altering impact of the other, it is important to note that Husserl will always insist on the unmodified and indeclinable 'primal 'I'' or "'unmodalized' primal form" (Husserl 1982, p. 251) of first-person experience as the necessary, though not sufficient, condition of individuation and self-conscious life.[8] It is this 'primal form' of temporal self-affection which is "peculiarly my own," (Husserl 1988, p. 114) it is that to which all self-differentiation, self-alienation, dis-appropriation, and self-amplification must refer back as its incipient and pre-personal source. However, there is still a tendency in Husserl's work to oscillate between prioritising the above 'primal I' while making statements such as, "The other is the first

---

8 See Dan Zahavi (2015), p. 11.

human being, not I" (Husserl 1973b, p. 418). Is it thus the case that the 'primal I' is not a human being in the fullest sense of the word and only becomes such in and through the encounter with others as world-orienting? How should one understand the ontological, or metaphysical, status of the 'primal I' prior to the encounter with the other? Or, as Merleau-Ponty has it, does even such a formal, 'primal I' already contain within it the seeds of an "*Urgemeinschaftung* of our intentional life, the *Ineinander* of others in us"? (Merleau-Ponty 1968, p. 180).

These concerns notwithstanding, it is nonetheless accurate to say that the dislocating or de-centering experience brought about by my encounter with the embodied and expressive other is one of temporal and historical influence, co-constitution and dynamic interaction. Characteristic of this interdependent interaction and historical influence is that the other transcends what I 'know' of her or him: I know that the other is like me, I know that the other has a life history of their own, and I understand the words and concepts that this other uses when it comes to expressing their unique experience and life history. And yet I cannot *possess* or *have* that life history, those essentially embodied thoughts or feelings, from the other's point of view. However, I can attempt to *adopt* their perspective, insofar as I can make sense of it; I can share or contradict it. I can even form part of a group that shares or contradicts it, all the while aware that I can never *have* it as my own.

Nonetheless, what Husserl brings to the fore is that my ineluctable and worldly 'mineness' (*Meinheit*), my who, stems from the altering and augmenting encounters I have with other embodied alter-egos and without such encounters one would not have a sense of the oneself as a person or of the shared objective world as before and beyond me which is constitutive of my person. Therefore, the appearance of the other, the self-differentiating and self-displacing impact of the other on my originary sphere, is the appearance of another to whom I must ascribe a mental and intentional life all of their own, one which is directly experienceable and understandable without being something I can possess or inhabit. Hence, what we can learn from Husserl's analyses is that even though our first-person lived experiences are necessarily individuated and indexed back to a 'primal I', we must recognize that it is a formal, largely anonymous and hollow kind of individuating principle, one that characterizes every other possible subject and yet one that does not make me *who* I am, i.e., the person I am in my frustrating, joyful, unpredictable and broadening encounters with the world. It is only by entering into social relations, being open for and opened by the personal encounter with the altering and enlarging other, making promises and embracing the promises that issue from the other, that the subject can become rich in content and increasingly concrete, purged of the abovementioned anonymity and hollowness.[9]

In sum, the subject, the ego, "cannot be thought without the non-ego to which it is intentionally related" (Husserl 1973b, p. 244). More than this, however, the other is not just an alter-ego with an intentional life of its own, the other is a liberating path towards the truth of one and the same world, and as such the other constitutes "the broadening of the contextual horizon of evidence" (Soffer 1998, p. 165), propelling us towards higher forms of self-consciousness that are fundamentally social, objective and interpersonal in nature.

References

Bernet, Rudolf (1998): "My Time and the Time of the Other". In: Zahavi, Dan (Ed.): *Self-awareness, Temporality and Alterity*. Dordrecht: Kluwer, pp. 137–149.
Bernet, Rudolf (2002): "Levinas's Critique of Husserl". In: Critchley, Simon/Bernasconi, Robert (Eds.): *The Cambridge Companion to Levinas*. Cambridge: Cambridge University Press, pp. 82–99.
de Warren, Nicolas (2009): *Husserl and the Promise of Time: Subjectivity in Transcendental Phenomenology*. Cambridge: Cambridge University Press.
Gallese, Vittorio/Goldman, Alvin (1998): "Mirror Neurons and the Simulation Theory of Mind-Reading". In: *Trends in Cognitive Sciences* 2(12), pp. 493–501.
Gallese, Vittorio (2009): "Mirror Neurons, Embodied Simulation, and the Neural Basis of Social Identification". In: *Psychoanalytic Dialogues* 19(5), pp. 519–536.
Goldman, Alvin (2006): *Simulating Minds*. Oxford: Oxford University Press.
Gopnik, Alison/Wellman, Henry M. (1994): "The Theory Theory." In: *Mapping the Mind: Domain Specificity in Cognition and Culture*. Cambridge: Cambridge University Press, pp. 257–293.
Heal, Jane (1998): "Simulation and Cognitive Penetrability". In: *Mind and Language*, 11(1), pp. 44–67.
Husserl, Edmund (1959): *Erste Philosophie (1923/24). Zweiter Teil. Theorie der phänomenologischen Reduktion*. Rudolf Boehm (Ed.). Husserliana VIII. The Hague: Martinus Nijhoff.

---

[9] As Merleau-Ponty puts it: "The solitude from which we emerge to intersubjective life is not that of the monad. It is only the haze of an anonymous life that separates us from being; and the barrier between us and others is impalpable. If there is a break, it is not between me and the other person; it is between a primordial generality we are intermingled in and the precise system, myself-the others. What 'precedes' intersubjective life cannot be numerically distinguished from it, precisely because at this level there is neither individuation nor numerical distinction." (Merleau-Ponty 1964, p. 174).

Husserl, Edmund (1970): *The Crisis of the European Sciences and Transcendental Phenomenology: An Introduction to Phenomenological Philosophy.* Trans. David Carr. Evanston: Northwestern University Press.

Husserl, Edmund (1973a): *Zur Phänomenologie der Intersubjektivität: Texte aus dem Nachlass. Erster Teil: 1905–1920.* Iso Kern (Ed.). Husserliana XIII. The Hague: Martinus Nijhoff.

Husserl, Edmund (1973b): *Zur Phänomenologie der Intersubjektivität: Texte aus dem Nachlass. Zweiter Teil: 1921–1928.* Iso Kern (Ed.). Husserliana XIV. The Hague: Martinus Nijhoff.

Husserl, Edmund (1973c): *Zur Phänomenologie der Intersubjektivität: Texte aus dem Nachlass. Dritter Teil: 1929–1935.* Iso Kern (Ed.). Husserliana XV. The Hague: Martinus Nijhoff.

Husserl, Edmund (1976a): *Die Krisis der europäischen Wissenschaften und die transzendentale Phänomenologie: eine Einleitung in die phänomenologische Philosophie.* Walter Biemel (Ed.). Husserliana VI. The Hague: Martinus Nijhoff.

Husserl, Edmund (1982): *Ideas Pertaining to a Pure Phenomenology and to a Phenomenological Philosophy. First Book: General Introduction to a Pure Phenomenology.* Trans. F. Kersten. The Hague: Martinus Nijhoff.

Husserl, Edmund (1988): *Cartesian Meditations.* Trans. Dorion Cairns. Dordrecht: Kluwer.

Husserl, Edmund (1989): *Ideas Pertaining to a Pure Phenomenology and to a Phenomenological Philosophy. Second Book: Studies in the Phenomenology of Constitution.* Trans. Richard Rojcewicz/André Schuwer. Dordrecht: Kluwer.

Leslie, Alan (1987): "Children's Understanding of the Mental World". In: Gregory, Richard L. (Ed.): *The Oxford Companion to the Mind.* Oxford: Oxford University Press, pp. 139–142.

Merleau-Ponty, Maurice (1964): "The Philosopher and His Shadow". In: *Signs.* Trans. Richard C. McCleary. Evanston: Northwestern University Press, pp. 159–181.

Merleau-Ponty, Maurice (1968): *Visible and Invisible.* Claude Lefort (Ed.). Alphonso Lingis (Trans). Evanston: Northwestern University Press.

Moran, Dermot (2016): *"Ineinandersein* and *l'interlacs:* The Constitution of the Social World or 'We-World' (*Wir-Welt*) in Edmund Husserl and Maurice Merleau-Ponty". In: Szanto, Thomas/Moran, Dermot (Eds.): *Discovering the We: The Phenomenology of Sociality.* London, New York: Routledge, pp. 107–126.

Patočka, Jan (1998): *Body, Community, Language, World.* James Dodd (Ed.). Erazim Kohák (Trans.). Chicago: Open Court.

Ricœur, Paul (1986): "Phénoménologie et herméneutique: en venant de Husserl". In: *Du texte à l'action.* Paris: Seuil, pp. 43–81.

Soffer, Gail (1998): "The Other as Alter Ego: A Genetic Approach". In: *Husserl Studies* 15, pp. 151–166.

Steinbock, Anthony (1995): *Home and Beyond, Generative Phenomenology after Husserl.* Evanston: Northwestern University Press.

Taipale, Joona (2014): *Phenomenology and Embodiment: Husserl and the Constitution of Subjectivity.* Evanston: Northwestern University Press.

Tengelyi, László (2012): "The Role of Interpretation in the Phenomenological Approach to the Other". In: *Life, Subjectivity and Art.* Dordrecht: Springer, pp. 429–443.

Theunissen, Michael (1965): *Der Andere: Studien zur Sozialontologie der Gegenwart.* Berlin: De Gruyter.

Waldenfels, Bernhard (1994): *Antwortregister.* Frankfurt: Suhrkamp.

Zahavi, Dan (2012): "Empathy and Mirroring: Husserl and Gallese". In: Breeur, Roland/Melle, Ullrich (Eds.): *Life, Subjectivity, and Art: Essays in Honor of Rudolf Bernet*. Dordrecht: Springer, pp. 217–254.

Zahavi, Dan (2014): *Self and Other: Exploring Subjectivity, Empathy, and Shame*. Oxford: Oxford University Press.

Zahavi, Dan (2015): "Vindicating Husserl's Primal I". In: de Warren, Nicolas/Bloechl, Jeffrey (Eds.): *Phenomenology in a New Key: Between Analysis and History*. Dordrecht: Springer, pp. 1–14.

Sara Heinämaa
Self: Temporality, Finitude and Intersubjectivity

Abstract: European philosophy is often criticized as an outdated form of thinking and characterized as individualistic, anthropocentric and Euro-centric. What is common to many such critical approaches is the notion that the main source of problems lies in an inherited Cartesian understanding of selfhood. In this paper, I confront this anti-Cartesian critique of European philosophy by arguing that Husserlian phenomenology offers a robust and viable reinterpretation of the Cartesian self, and a reinterpretation that avoids the Kantian impasses of formalism and intellectualism. I follow Husserl's and Merleau-Ponty's analyses and show that the self that constitutes the sense of the world is not a mere form of representations nor a *solus ipse*. Rather than being a static form or a solitary agent, the sense-constituting self is a dynamic formation with an internal structure and generative relations to other similar selves.

European philosophy is often criticized and attacked as an outdated form of thinking, unable to address the problems of today's world. It is characterized as individualistic, anthropocentric and Euro-centric and contrasted to supposedly more pluralistic, communitarian and ecological approaches, put forward and elaborated most vigorously in today's political philosophy, philosophy of nature and ontology.

Posthuman(istic), new realistic, new materialistic and neovitalistic movements of thought aim at taking on this challenge by creating alternative conceptualizations for the service of the global politics of equality and justice – not just for all human beings and cultures, but also for the animal kingdom and ultimately for the earth itself.

One of the most prevalent arguments put forward in these discussions is the claim that the philosophical landscape of Europe can be remodeled by fresh conceptual tools offered by pre-modern forms of thinking. Many contributors also contend that European philosophy should be impregnated by non-European traditions of wisdom and learning. A third, growingly popular set of concepts is found in mathematical and mathematized natural sciences, most importantly in system theory, quantum physics and set theory (e.g. Badiou [1969] 2007; Barad 2007).

What is common to many of these approaches is the notion that the main source of the problems of contemporary European philosophy lies in its inherited Cartesianism (e.g. Meillassoux 2006; Bennett 2010; Braidotti 2013; Braidotti 2016; Harman 2018). If this holds, then all Cartesian principles would have to be uprooted from European thinking if it is to be reinvigorated and re-energized. The dualistic framework that Descartes left for us as a philosophical heritage – the framework in which thinking is opposed to extension, mind to body, and the self to whatever remains alien to it – has to be replaced by monistic conceptualizations, be they of unprecedented events or of dynamic forces and processes.

The Cartesian *ego cogito*, the thinking self, is usually taken to be adequately captured by Kant in his contention that the ego is a form that accompanies all our representations. In this Kantian reinterpretation, the ego is nothing but a formal factor of thinking and experiencing and thus universally the same for all human subjects, independently of historical, cultural and lived bodily factors.

However, this Kantian version of Cartesianism is not the only possible way of interpreting and developing Descartes' arguments about the unavoidability of the ego. In this paper, I want to question the dominant Kantian understanding of Cartesianism by arguing that the basic aspirations of Descartes' philosophy were taken over by 20th century phenomenologists and reinterpreted in a manner that differs from Kantianism. The two phenomenologists who have developed Descartes' philosophical insights most innovatively, in my mind, are the founder of the movement Edmund Husserl and his French critic Maurice Merleau-Ponty. In the introduction to his collection of essays titled *Signes*, Merleau-Ponty even contends that the debate on Cartesianism "does not make much sense, since those who reject this or that in Descartes do so only in terms of reasons which owe much to Descartes" (Merleau-Ponty [1960] 1998, p. 17/11).

I will here follow Husserl's and Merleau-Ponty's analyses of experience and argue that the self or ego that constitutes the sense of the world is not a *solus ipse* nor a mere form of representations. Rather than being a solitary agent or a static form, the sense-constituting self is a dynamic formation with temporal thickness and an internal structure. Moreover, in the phenomenological account, the transcendental self does not just operate in intellectual acts but also in affectivity and motility, expression and communication (cf. Schutz [1957] 2005, pp. 114–115). Thus, the self is not just bound to declare "I judge" and "I reflect" but also "I feel", "I suffer", "I move", "I smile" and "I am addressed and called."

1 Structures of Selfhood

In the fourth of his *Cartesian Meditations*, Husserl clarifies his understanding of selfhood by distinguishing between two different dimensions: on the one hand the self as an act-pole and on the other hand the personal self (*personales Ich, Person*).[1] These two dimensions of selfhood are already discussed and clarified in the second volume of *Ideas* from the 1910s and 1920s, but Husserl does not explicate them fully until *Cartesian Meditations*, first published in French in 1930.

In Husserl's explication, the self as an act-pole is the subject of intentional acts, that is, the self, conceived and studied as a mere performer of acts. Husserl argues that every act discernible from the stream of intentional experiencing "radiates" or "emanates" from one identical center; every intentional act is given to us as such an emanating ray (Hua 1, p. 100/66, 129/98; Hua 4, pp. 97–98/103–104, 104–106/110–112; Hua 4/5, pp. 305–306, 313, 528–239; Ms F III 1 240b; cf. Hua 3, pp. 63–66/72–76, 85–86/100–103, 109–110/132–133, 150/180, 159–161/190–191; Hua 4, pp. 265/277–278).

The stream of experiencing consists of egoic acts of intending and also nonintentional sensations, feelings and drives. For Husserl, egoic acts include not only the theoretical acts of thinking, judging, knowing and believing but also the axiological acts of intentional feeling and valuing and the practical acts of desiring, willing and deciding – all in their various modalities and modifications. Moreover, the self also operates in the receiving mode of experiencing and, so to speak, in the dative rather than the nominative case. "I judge" and "I know" thus alternate with "I love", "I hate", "I regret", "I hope", "I want" and "I decide", but also with "I am touched", "I am moved" and "I am affected" (e.g., Hua 4, pp. 98–99/104–105; Steinbock 1995, p. 34).

So, to begin with, the self, as disclosed by phenomenological analyses, is the pole of all the multiple acts – actual and possible – that stand out from the streaming whole of consciousness. It is as if the acts were centered round the self in a similar manner as they are centered round the object-poles. However, having made this basic point, Husserl argues that the self is not merely an act-pole or an identical center of transient acts. It also has a temporal structure, and always refers back to its own past. Acts are not isolated atom-like units but have internal references to one another and thus form an integrated continuum (e.g., Hua 3, pp. 165/195–196; Hua 4, pp. 106/112, 135/143; Husserl 1994, p. 114).

---

[1] For the self in its full concreteness, temporal as well as intentional, Husserl uses the Leibnizian term "monad" (e.g., Hua 1, pp. 102–103/67–68, 125–126/94; Hua 14, pp. 34–35).

Husserl uses the terminology of "habit" and "habituality" (*Habitus, Habitualität*) to describe the temporal constitution of the self as distinct from the self as the performer of isolated acts (Hua 1, p. 100ff./66ff.; Hua 4, pp. 111–114/118–121; Hua 4/5, pp. 349–353; 585–586; Hua 14, p. 36; cf. Bernet, Kern and Marbach [1989] 1995, p. 199ff.; Moran 2014a; Steinbock 1995, pp. 33–36; Cavallaro 2016; Sakakibara 1997). He warns that we should not take this terminology in the everyday sense of routines and social customs (Hua 4, p. 111/118; Hua 4/5, p. 351; Hua 29, p. 365). The reference is to certain processes in internal time in which egoic acts are established and new acts are layered on earlier ones, thus forming a kind of activity-form or activity-gestalt. This temporal gestalt is unique to the individual, and we can thus say that the self has a specific rhythm and style of acting and relating (Hua 4, pp. 276–278/289–290, 349/360; Hua 4/5, p. 585; Hua 14, pp. 14–15, 46–47; cf. Merleau-Ponty [1945] 1993, pp. 100/73–75; 214/164–165; 519/406; Steinbock 1995, pp. 34–36).

Husserl calls "transcendental person" (or "personality" of the transcendental self) (*Person, Pesönlichkeit*) the gestalt that is formed in the establishment and habituation of egoic acts in internal time (Hua 1, p. 101/67, cf. p. 67/28, 129/98).[2] For him, the concrete self is not a momentary agent that wills, enjoys and posits being but always comes with a past of willing, enjoying and/or positing being. The self is not merely the totality of simultaneous acts but has an immanent "history" of intentional acting, formed in internal time. In other words, the self has a *genesis*:

> [T]his centring ego is not an empty pole of identity, any more than any object is such. Rather, according to a law of 'transcendental generation', with every act emanating from her and having a *new* objective sense, she acquires *a new abiding property*. (Hua 1, p. 100/66, cf. Hua 4, pp. 310–311/324; Hua 14, pp. 195–196)

Husserl illuminates the process of the habituation of acts by studying the case of judgment formation.[3] He explains that always when we make a judgment, the judgment becomes our own in a specific way: it becomes part of our transcendental habitus. The judgment remains our own in this way, until we refute it

---

[2] Husserl distinguishes this transcendental sense of personhood from several other senses: person as subject of manners of relating, person as motivational agent, and person as empirical subject and human being.

[3] Husserl argues that all habituation of intentional activity entails the time-span characteristic of volitional intending (Hua 29, p. 368). A volitional thesis, in distinction from simple doxic and axiological theses, is able to overcome the limits of the present; it "awards being" to the future, as Husserl formulates (Hua 28, p. 107). Rather than positing being, a volitional thesis posits what ought to be (*Seinssollen*).

by another act, and after this it still remains ours as a judgment once held and acted on, and then refuted (Hua 1, pp. 100–101/66–67; Hua 4, p. 113 ff./120 ff.; cf. Jacobs 2010; Moran 2011; Jacobs 2014; Moran 2014b). This does not mean that we repeat the judgment in every moment until we refute it, but that we are, from the very moment of making the judgement, the ones who thus judge and believe.

In a similar manner, when my friendship ends, I do not in any miraculous way get rid of or liberate myself from the emotions of appreciating and loving, but continue carrying them in myself, now in the mode of the past. It is not that I think that I was mistaken about my feelings, that I had confused friendship with comradeship, for example, or with confidence, acquaintance or mutual benefit. I am aware that I really have loved my friend, but at the same time I am aware that I have lived through this emotion and moved on, and that the feeling now belongs to my past. I do not live anymore as loving – I live as having loved.

Husserl emphasizes that we should not confuse the permanence of decision, belief or emotion with the experience of remembering or imagining such states (Hua 1, p. 101/66; cf. Hua 4, p. 114 ff./120 ff.). It is of course possible for me to remember my experience of a recent encounter with my friend, really and genuinely recall it as past, but only after I have abandoned my belief that she is present here and now. As long as I hold the belief in her presence, or carry the emotion and the accompanying valuing, as long as I have not refuted them, I can always return to them and I find them unchanged and as my own, as part of me. According to Husserl, the permanence of the conviction holds even through sleep. He argues:

> Likewise [as in the case of judgments] in the case of all kinds of decisions, value-decisions and volitional decisions. I decide: the act-process vanishes but the decision persists; whether I become passive and sink into heavy sleep or live through other acts, the decision is continuously in validity and, correlatively, I am so decided from then on, as long as I do not give the decision up. (Hua 1, p. 101/67)

So as a summary, we can say that with the concept of transcendental person as elaborated in the second volume of *Ideas* and defined in the fourth *Cartesian Meditation*, Husserl starts a new discussion about the temporality of the transcendental self: the act-pole is an identical center of acts, but the temporally concrete self, the transcendental person, is a structure formed in internal time by the habituation of experiences, transient as acts but permanent as egoic accomplishments and layered on one another. The act-pole and the person are not two separate parts or phases of the transcendental self but essentially bound together, and only distinguishable by analysis.

In his research manuscripts from the 1920s and 1930s, Husserl specifies further this analysis of the self. But now his focus is in the axiological acts of valuing and feeling, and a new dimension of selfhood comes to the fore. This is the dimension of depth.[4]

When analyzing diverse forms of valuing emotion, Husserl realizes that a certain variant of love differs from all other types of emotions in drawing its force and intensity not from the experienced object but from the experiencing subject herself. He then argues that this particular emotion has a regulative function in our lives, since it allows us to establish vocations and permanent personal relations of care and thus organize our lives into unified meaningful wholes.[5] In the introductory lectures to philosophy from 1919, *Einleitung in die Philosophie*, we read: "The *daimon* that leads to true calling or vocation speaks through love. So, it arrives, not only to objective goods and the objectively greatest good, but each has her sphere of love and her 'duties of love'" (Hua Mat 9, p. 146 n.1; cf. Melle 2002; Loidolt 2012).

In Husserl's analysis, genuine loving originates from the opposite pole of intentional experiencing than other emotions and other types of experiences, which all have their affective grounds "out there" (e.g. Husserl [1939] 1985). In other words, the affective source of this emotion is different from those of other acts; it is in the experiencing ego herself, in her most inner and deepest living core.[6]

In the reflections included in the *Grenzprobleme* volume, Husserl first explains: "[L]ove-inspired valuation flows from the subject toward the individual object and imparts or bestows a value to the latter that does not derive from the object itself but, ultimately, from her [the ego]" (Hua 42, p. 352). A few pages further, he then explicates what this analysis of love implies about the structure of the self:

> The ego is a pole, but is not an empty point. It is not an empty and dead substrate for qualities, but is an ego-center of actions, that has its own egoic depths (...) A distinctive feature, however, is that the ego is not only a polar centering inwardness, thereby accomplishing sense and value and deed out of itself, but that it is also an individual ego, who, in all its presenting, feeling, valuing, deciding, has a deepest center, the center of love in the distinguished personal sense; the ego who in this love follows a 'call', a 'calling', an innermost

---

4 These late reflections can be found in the Husserliana volumes, *Grenzprobleme der Phänomenologie* (Hua 42) and *Einleitung in die Philosophie* (Hua Mat 9).
5 For a full explication and discussion, see Heinämaa 2020.
6 Husserl emphasizes this fact by writing that "not all [acts] are similarly ego-centered" (Hua 42, p. 358).

call, that strikes the innermost center of the ego itself, and that becomes determined for new kinds of decisions. (Hua 42, pp. 358–359)

This specification entails that the constituting self has a three-dimensional structure. As we already saw above, *Cartesian Meditations* explicates two necessary dimensions of the self: the ego as the centering pole of intentional activity and the ego as a gestalt of such activity formatted in inner time. But now we come to notice that Husserl's reflections on emotions and vocations illuminate a third dimension of selfhood, that of an inner profundity. We are not mere "plane-beings," as he argues in *The Crisis*, but are vertical beings with depths (Hua 6, pp. 120–123/118–121).

These explications help us see that the Husserlian self is very different from that of Kant: it is not just cognitive but also affective, emotive, valuing and striving; it is not fixed or stable but developing; it is not beyond time but trans-temporal, not universal but individual.

With this account of the self, it also becomes easier to see why and how Husserl would argue that the constitutive basis of the full sense of world is not in the transcendental self or ego but is in the community of such selves, that is, in transcendental intersubjectivity.

Husserl argues for this position in many contexts and by means of different concepts, systematic as well as historical. The topic binds the epistemological and methodological reflections of *Cartesian Meditations* to the late cultural-philosophical and ethical works, *The Crisis of European Sciences and Transcendental Phenomenology* and the *Kaizo* essays (Hua 27). To prepare ground for the explications provided in the next section, I start by quoting one of Husserl's most explicit statements, formulated in the manuscripts that supplement *The Crisis*. Here we read:

> Certainly, when one interprets transcendental subjectivity as an isolated ego and, following the Kantian tradition, overlooks the whole task of explicating the transcendental community of subjects, all prospects of a transcendental understanding of the self and the world are lost. (Hua 29, p. 120)

2 Intersubjectivity and Generativity

Starting in the 1920s, Husserl consistently argues that the full sense of the world is a constitutive achievement of an open community of transcendental selves. The experiencing ego does not establish the sense of the world by itself or in solitary activities but constitutes this sense in community and communication with other selves. "Subjectivity is what it is – an ego functioning constitutively – only within intersubjectivity", Husserl famously states in *The Crisis of European Sciences and Transcendental Philosophy* (Hua 6, p. 175/172). In a manuscript written for the fifth Cartesian Meditation in 1929, he contends:

> Thus subjectivity expands into intersubjectivity, or rather, more precisely, it does not expand, but transcendental subjectivity understands itself better. It understands itself as a primordial monad that intentionally carries within itself other monads. (Hua 15, p. 17)

Focusing on such arguments and reflections, contemporary Husserl scholarship has rectified the surprisingly persistent and tenacious misconception that classical transcendental phenomenology is a simple reformulation of Kantianism. It demonstrates that for Husserl the constitutive source of worldliness is not in an ego that isolates itself from everything alien nor in a universal principle or form shared by all selves equally and without distinctions (e. g. Zahavi 1996; Sakakibara 1997; Carr 1999; Zahavi 2014; 2015; cf. Cavallaro 2020).

If one wants to find a proper philosophical predecessor of transcendental phenomenology one must take seriously Husserl's references to Leibniz' monadology (e. g., Hua 8, p. 190; cf. Mertens 2014; Strasser 1975). The Leibnizian concepts of monads and monadological harmony converge and help with interpreting Husserl's argument that the constitutive ground of the objective world is in an endless plurality of selves which communicatively interact with one another.

For Husserl, however, the intersubjective harmony is not a pre-established state but is also a historical task.[7] This fundamentally historical reformulation of the idea of "the monadic community" becomes possible for Husserl when he conceives transcendental subjectivity as essentially factic and deeply temporal (Hua 1, pp. 103–107/69–72, 167–168/140–141d). What we have is not a stable fraternity of pure spirits but a communicative generation of embodied selves or egos with unique styles of acting and relating. The constituting self is intentionally tied to other constituting selves – present, past and future –, and together, in communicative interaction these selves establish the full sense of the world. In one of his manuscripts from 1930/1931, Husserl explicitly states:

---

[7] The concepts of monadology and transcendental intersubjectivity are mutually informing but distinct. Monadology is a pure possibility concept whereas transcendental intersubjectivity is delimited by the facticity of the transcendental ego (Hua 1, pp. 166–168/139–141, cf. pp. 140/110–111). This entails that monadology is atemporal whereas transcendental intersubjectivity has a generative form (cf. Steinbock 1995).

> The transcendence in which the world is constituted consists of it being constituted by means of others and the generatively constituted co-subjectivity, and thereby acquiring its ontic sense as an endless or infinite world. (Hua Mat 8, p. 393)

We find this idea of generativity paraphrased in several different ways by Husserl himself as well as by his early interpreters. Merleau-Ponty, for example, underscores the operative expressive bodiliness of transcendental subjects and uses the metaphors of crossroads to illuminate their constitutive connection:

> Transcendental subjectivity is a revealed subjectivity, revealed to itself and to others, and is for that reason an intersubjectivity. (Merleau-Ponty [1945] 1993, p. 415/323; cf. Moran 2013)
> The phenomenological world is not pure being, but the sense which is revealed where the paths of my various experiences intersect, and also where my own and other peoples' intersect and engage each other like gears. It is thus inseparable from subjectivity and intersubjectivity, which find their unity when I either take up my past experiences in those of the present, or other people's in my own. (Merleau-Ponty [1945] 1993, p. xv/xviii)

The idea of generative intersubjectivity involves a crucial insight about the role of the consciousness of finitude and mortality in world-constitution. In order to consciously relate to one another in multiple generations, the world-constituting selves have to be conscious of their own finitude, that is, natality and mortality (e. g., Hua 15, pp. 140, 168–169, 177–181, 280; cf. Steinbock 1995, p. 36). This is because the sense of future others, successors and descendants, remains merely verbal unless we are able to conceive our own lives as finite formations, threatened and delimited by the interruptive event of death. In other words, a self who lacks the sense of her own temporal limits is unable to conceive any past or future others separated from herself by the borders of death and birth.

In order to see the main implications of Husserl's and Merleau-Ponty's argument that the full sense of the world is constituted by a generative community of selves or egos, it is instructive to study two special cases that Husserl excludes from the intersubjective community of co-constituters: the infant and the animal. Both are excluded by Husserl on the same grounds: neither experiences itself as a member of a generation that is connected to other generations and to an open totality of generations.[8]

Husserl contends that both the infant and the animal consciously participate and intentionally live in many different types of communities of contemporaries, and even in communities that use signs for multiple practical purposes. However, what he considers crucial is that neither the infant nor the animal experiences itself as a being who is born and who will die, a being who shares a communal

---

8 For a fuller explication, see Heinämaa 2013.

past and future with other similar beings who are not present, and cannot become present in flesh and blood.

The others who in our mature human experience are separated from us by our birth and death are not just contingently absent for us but absent in their very essence: some lived before our birth, and others will live after our death. Neither type of other can be intended by infant and animal subjects in so far as these subjects lack the sense of themselves as natal and mortal beings (Hua 15, pp. 140, 171, 184–185; cf. Merleau-Ponty [1945] 1993, pp. 415–416/361–362).

We mature adults can reach both types of absent other by means of language, and this can be realized in several different ways (Hua 15, pp. 224–225, 169, 180–181; Hua 6, p. 307/328). We may hear and read stories about our ancestors and address such others in prayer or orison, for example, and we can also capture their words as repeated by our older contemporaries and read their writings without any mediation of any third parties (or any mediation other than language). Similarly, we can address our successors by our own writing, and we can rehearse our younger contemporaries to repeat our words for others. This is all senseless for the prelinguistic infant and the animal in so far as they do not understand themselves as mortal and natal beings who have generations of others behind and ahead of them in time. Husserl explains:

> An animal (…) does not have a unity of time which spans over generations as historical time nor a unity of the world which continues through time, it does not 'have' this consciously. We, we human beings, are the ones who have the chains, the successions and branching of [animal] generations etc. in our world as valid for us. The animal itself has no generative world in which it would live consciously, no conscious existence in an open endlessness of generations and correlatively no existence in a genuine environing world, which we humans, anthropomorphizing, attribute to it. (Hua 15, p. 181)

Several deprivations or lacks are implied by the fundamental lack of generative time and trans-generational communication: in so far as the infant and the animal have no conscious membership in chains of generations, they cannot participate in transgenerational practices and cannot share the accomplishments of such practices. This deprives them of culture and cultural objectivities in a crucial sense: cultural-historical goals that are shared with multiple generations in an endless openness; cultural-historical tools and utensils that are retained, maintained and repaired in the view of coming generations; and ultimately the cultural-historical world which contains all this openness.

Thus, Husserl argues that the senses of culture, tradition and history go hand in hand, and that all these senses depend on the senses of death and birth (Husserl Hua 15, pp. 140–141, 168–169, 177–181, 280; Hua 1, p. 169/142;

Hua 6, pp. 191/188, 262–263/258–259). For him, no subject who lacks these fundamental senses can intend cultural objectivities as such or the cultural-historical world that includes these objectivities in an infinite openness.

> Each tool, each utensil, a house, a garden, a statue, a sacrificial altar, a religious symbol is an example of [this]. The goal of such cultural object is to fulfill an infinite endlessness of goals, which refers to an endlessness of persons and real possible circumstances. And this holds for each cultural object in general. (Hua 27, p. 98)

Conclusion

I have argued in this paper that Husserlian phenomenology offers a robust and viable reinterpretation of the Cartesian concept of the self, and one that avoids the Kantian impasses of formalism and intellectualism. In Husserl's and Merleau-Ponty's expositions, the self is not a mere form of representation nor a solitary agent of constitutive activities of sense making. Rather, the self has an inner structure with three dimensions: (i) the ego-pole as the center of conscious life and intentional activity, (ii) the personal ego as the habituated gestalt of egoic activities, and (iii) the egoic depths of axiological intending. These three dimensions are crucial for our understanding of the constitutive role of transcendental intersubjectivity: The constitutive source of the full sense of the world is not in an isolated ego nor in the community of contemporaneous monads. Rather, the world receives its horizontal structure and infinite openness as the correlate of the generative community of transcendental persons.

References

Badiou, Alain ([1969] 2007): *The Concept of Model: An Introduction to the Materialist Epistemology of Mathematics.* Melbourne: re.press.
Barad, Karen (2007): *Meeting the Universe Halfway: Quantum Physics and the Entanglement of Matter and Meaning.* Durham, London: Duke University Press.
Bennett, Jane (2010): *Vibrant Matter: A Political Ecology of Things.* Durham, London: Duke University Press.
Bernet, Rudolf/Kern, Iso/Marbach, Eduard ([1989] 1995): *An Introduction to Phenomenology.* Evanston: Northwestern University Press.
Braidotti, Rosi (2013): *The Posthuman.* Cambridge: Polity Press.
Braidotti, Rosi (2016): "Anthropos redux: A defence of monism in the anthropocene epoch". In: *Frame* 29(2), pp. 29–46.
Carr, David (1999): *The Paradox of Subjectivity: The Self in the Transcendental Tradition.* Oxford: Oxford University Press.

Cavallaro, Marco (2020): "Ego-splitting and the transcendental subject: Kant's original insight and Husserl's reappraisal". In: Apostolescu, Iulian (Ed.): *The Subject(s) of Phenomenology: Rereading Husserl*. Dordrecht: Springer, pp. 107–133.

Cavallaro, Marco (2016): "Das 'Problem' der Habituskonstitution und die Spätlehre des Ich in der genetischen Phänomenologie E. Husserls". In: *Husserl Studies* 32(3), pp. 237–261.

Harman, Graham (2018): *Object-Oriented Ontology: A New Theory of Everything*. St. Ives: Pelican Books.

Heinämaa, Sara (2013): "Transcendental intersubjectivity and normality: Constitution by mortals". In: Moran, Dermot/Thybo Jensen, Rasmus (Eds.): *The Phenomenology of Embodied Subjectivity*. Dordrecht: Springer, pp. 83–103.

Heinämaa, Sara (2020): "Values of love: Two forms of infinity characteristic of human persons". In: *Phenomenology and the Cognitive Sciences* 19, pp. 431–450.

Husserl, Edmund (1950): *Cartesianische Meditationen und Pariser Vorträge*. Stephan Strasser (Ed.). Husserliana I. The Hague: Martinus Nijhoff. In English: Husserl, Edmund (1960): *Cartesian Meditations*. Trans. Dorion Cairns. The Hague: Martinus Nijhoff. [Hua 1]

Husserl, Edmund (1952): *Ideen zu einer reinen Phänomenologie und phänomenologischen Philosophie. Zweites Buch: Phänomenologische Untersuchungen zur Konstitution*. Marly Biemel (Ed.). Husserliana IV. The Hague: Martinus Nijhoff. In English: Husserl, Edmund (1993): *Ideas Pertaining to a Pure Phenomenology and to a Phenomenological Philosophy, Second Book: Studies in the Phenomenological Constitution*. Trans. Richard Rojcewicz/André Schuwer. Dordrecht: Kluwer. [Hua 4]

Husserl, Edmund (1954): *Die Krisis der europäischen Wissenschaften und die transzendentale Phänomenologie: Eine Einleitung in die phänomenologische Philosophie*. Walter Biemel (Ed.). Husserliana VI. The Hague: Martinus Nijhoff. In English: Husserl, Edmund (1988): *The Crisis of European Sciences and Transcendental Phenomenology: An Introduction to Phenomenological Philosophy*. Trans. David Carr. Evanston: Northwestern University Press. [Hua 6]

Husserl, Edmund (1959): *Erste Philosophie. Zweiter Band: Theorie der phänomenologischen Reduktion*. Rudolf Boehm (Ed.). Husserliana VIII. The Hague: Martinus Nijhoff. [Hua 8]

Husserl, Edmund (1973a): *Zur Phänomenologie der Intersubjektivität, Texte aus dem Nachlass. Zweiter Teil: 1921–1928*. Iso Kern (Ed.). Husserliana XIV. The Hague: Martinus Nijhoff. [Hua 14]

Husserl, Edmund (1973b): *Zur Phänomenologie der Intersubjektivität, Texte aus dem Nachlass. Dritter Teil: 1929–1935*. Iso Kern (Ed.). Husserliana XV. The Hague: Martinus Nijhoff. [Hua 15]

Husserl, Edmund (1989): *Aufsätze und Vorträge (1922–1937)*. Hans Rainer Sepp/Thomas Nenon (Eds). Husserliana XXVII. Dordrecht: Kluwer. [Hua 27]

Husserl, Edmund (1988): *Vorlesungen über Ethik und Wertlehre (1908–1914)*. Ulrich Melle (Ed.). Husserlina XXVIII. Dordrecht: Kluwer. [Hua 28]

Husserl, Edmund (1993): *Die Krisis der europäischen Wissenschaften und die transzendentale Phänomenologie. Ergänzungsband: Texte aus dem Nachlass 1934–1937*. Reinhold Smid (Ed.). Husserliana XXIX. Dordrecht: Kluwer. [Hua 29]

Husserl, Edmund (2013): *Grenzprobleme der Phänomenologie: Analysen des Unbewusstseins und der Instinkte, Metaphysik, Späte Ethik, Texte aus dem Nachlass (1908–1937)*. Rochus Sowa/Thomas Vongehr (Eds.). Husserliana XLII. Dordrecht: Springer. [Hua 42]

Husserl, Edmund (2006): *Späte Texte über Zeitkonstitution (1929–1934). Die C-Manuskripte*. Dieter Lohmar (Ed.). Husserliana Materialien VIII. Dordrecht: Springer. [Hua Mat 8]

Husserl, Edmund (2012): *Einleitung in die Philosophie, Vorlesungen 1916–1919*. Hanne Jacobs (Ed.). Husserliana Materialien IX. Dordrecht: Springer. [Hua Mat 9]

Husserl, Edmund (1994): "'Phenomenology,' Edmund Husserl's article for the Encyclopaedia Britannica 1927–1931". In: Joseph J. Kockelmans: *Edmund Husserl's Phenomenology*. West Lafayette: Purdue University Press.

Jacobs, Hanne (2010): "Towards a phenomenological account of personal identity". In: Ierna, Carlo/Jacobs, Hanne/Mattens, Filip (Eds.): *Philosophy, Phenomenology, Sciences: Essays in Commemoration of Edmund Husserl*. Dordrecht: Springer, pp. 333–361.

Jacobs, Hanne (2014): "Transcendental subjectivity and the human being". In: Heinämaa, Sara/Hartimo, Mirja/Miettinen, Timo (Eds.): *Phenomenology and the Transcendental*. London, New York: Routledge.

Loidolt, Sophie (2012): "The 'daimon' that speaks through love: A phenomenological ethics of the absolute ought – Investigating Husserl's unpublished texts". In: Sanders, Mark/Wisnewski, J. Jeremy (Eds.): *Ethics and Phenomenology*. Lanham, Boulder, New York: Lexington, pp. 9–38.

Meillassoux, Quentin (2006): *After Finitude: An Essay on the Necessity of Contingency*. London: Bloomsbury.

Melle, Ulrich (2002): "Edmund Husserl: From reason to love". In: Drummond, John/Embree, Lester (Eds.): *The Phenomenological Approaches to Moral Philosophy*. Dordrecht: Kluwer, pp. 229–248.

Mertens, Karl (2014): "Husserl's phenomenology of the monad: Remarks on Husserl's confrontation with Leibniz". In: *Husserl Studies* 17(1), pp. 1–20. Reprinted in: Drummond, John J./Höffe, Otfried (Eds.): *Husserl: German Perspectives*. New York: Fordham University Press.

Merleau-Ponty, Maurice ([1945] 1993): *Phénoménologie de la perception*. Paris: Gallimard. In English: *Phenomenology of Perception*. Trans. Colin Smith. London, New York: Routledge.

Merleau-Ponty, Maurice ([1960] 1998): *Signes*. Paris: Gallimard. In English: *Signs*. Trans. Richard C. McCleary. Evanston: Northwestern University Press.

Moran, Dermot (2011): "Edmund Husserl's phenomenology of habituality and habitus". *Journal of the British Society for Phenomenology* 42(3), pp. 53–77.

Moran, Dermot (2013): "'There is no brute world, only an elaborated world': Merleau-Ponty on the intersubjective constitution of the world". In: *South African Journal of Philosophy* 32(4), pp. 355–371.

Moran, Dermot (2014a): "Defending the transcendental attitude: Husserl's concept of the person and the challenges of naturalism". In: *Phenomenology and Mind* 7, pp. 37–55.

Moran, Dermot (2014b): "The ego as substrate of habitualities: Edmund Husserl's phenomenology of the habitual self". In: Bower, Matt/Carminada, Emanuele (Eds.): *Mind, Habits, and Social Reality, Phenomenology and Mind, The Online Journal of the Research Center in Phenomenology and Sciences of the Person* 6, pp. 26–47.

Sakakibara, Tetsuya (1997): "Das Problem des Ich und der Ursprung der genetischen Phänomenoogie bei Husserl". In: *Husserl Studies* 14(1), pp. 21–39.

Schutz, Alfred ([1957] 2005): "The problem of transcendental intersubjectivity in Husserl". In: Bernet, Rudolf /Welton, Donn/Zavolta, Gina (Eds.): *Edmund Husserl: Critical*

Assessments of Leading Philosophers, Volume I: Circumscriptions: Essays on Husserl's Phenomenology. London, New York: Routledge, pp. 90–116. Original paper presented at the *Husserl-Colloquium* in Royaumont on 28 April 1957.

Steinbock, Anthony J. (1995): *Home and Beyond: Generative Phenomenology After Husserl.* Evanston: Northwestern University Press.

Strasser, Stephen (1975): "Grundgedanken der Sozialontologie Edmund Husserls". In: *Zeitschrift für philosophische Forschung* 29(1), pp. 3–33.

Zahavi, Dan (1996): *Husserl und die transzendentale Intersubjektivität: Eine Antwort auf die sprachpragmatische Kritik.* Dordrecht: Springer. In English: Zahavi, Dan (2001): *Husserl and Transcendental Intersubjectivity.* Trans. Elisabeth A. Behnke. Athens: Ohio University Press.

Zahavi, Dan (2014): "Husserl's intersubjective transformation of transcendental phenomenology". In: *Journal of the British Society for Phenomenology* 27(3), pp. 228–245.

Zahavi, Dan (2015): "Husserl and the transcendental". In: Gardner, Sebastian/Grist, Matthew (Eds.): *The Transcendental Turn.* Oxford: Oxford University Press, pp. 228–243.

Liu Zhe
Towards Self-divided Subjectivity. Merleau-Ponty's Phenomenological-Ontological Theory of Intersubjectivity

Abstract: Merleau-Ponty articulates the problem of intersubjectivity in terms of "the transcendence in the immanence" that involves a sort of unification of presence and de-presentation of the self, taking place at once. In the *Phenomenology of Perception*, the early Merleau-Ponty insists on a peculiar form of "lived solipsism" which regards the embodied selfhood of transcendental subjectivity as the ultimate condition for the existence of the other and the intersubjective experience. His later turn to the primary fusion of self and other may well be interpreted as an *implicit* self-criticism with respect to the non-compromised alterity of the other. In this paper, I will draw on both his *Phenomenology of Perception* and his Sorbonne lecture "The Child's Relations with Others" to argue that Merleau-Ponty's radicalized form of the alterity of the other results in an innovative notion of *self-divided subjectivity*.

In the phenomenological movement for more than a century, the recurrent problem of intersubjectivity was never separately dealt with in opposition to that of subjectivity (Zahavi 2001a; 2001b; 2004).[1] While renewing our fundamental conception of rationality, Merleau-Ponty follows and develops a Husserlian idea to thematize the system of "the self-others-world" as the "transcendental field." For both Husserl and Merleau-Ponty, the three equally primordial components cannot be reduced to one another. While rejecting what he understands as the Husserlian intellectualist theory of transcendental constitution, Merleau-Ponty emphasizes another Husserlian idea of transcendence he found in Husserl's later manuscripts to account for such a transcendental field. At the end of the second part on the "Perceived World" in *Phenomenology of Perception* (*PhP* in the following), Merleau-Ponty argues:

> The problem of the existential modality of the social world here meets up with all of the problems of transcendence. Whether it is a question of my body, the natural world, the past, birth or death, the question is always to know how I can be open to phenomena that transcend me and that, nevertheless, only exist to the extent that I take them up

---

[1] I thank Professor Dan Zahavi for making his article (Zahavi 2001a) available to me.

https://doi.org/10.1515/9783110698787-011

and live them, *how the presence to myself (Urpräsenz) that defines me and that conditions every external presence is simultaneously a depresentation (Entgegenwärtigung) and throws me outside of myself.* (Merleau-Ponty 1945 [2012], p. 417 [381])

Like Husserl, Merleau-Ponty also supposes that my perception of the object already implicitly involves others who are not necessarily present but implicated in invisible aspects of the perceived object for my perceptual experience. In the quotation above, he specifically concentrates on the problem of intersubjectivity which concerns both the other and the social world. For him, the social world should not be understood as an independent object for empirical observation but rather as "modes of coexistence" soliciting individual comportment to live with one another. According to Merleau-Ponty, an adequate understanding of our social existence as the coexistence of an indefinite number of subjects presupposes the existence of the other as another subject. Although he never reduces the "constitution of society" to mere gathering of several individuals, his inchoate description of the social and cultural world in the chapter on "Others and the Human World" of *PhP* begins with his primary phenomenological theory of the subject-subject encounter. Both the "existential modality" of the social world and the other are then accounted for as a sort of "transcendence." It is the transcendence of the other that most concerns Merleau-Ponty's phenomenological theory of intersubjectivity in *PhP*. Yet he does not interpret such transcendence of the other as foreignness but rather as "depresentation" grounded in the immanent unity of subjective life. For him, the unity of subjective life constitutes not only the selfhood but also the transcendental condition of "every external presence." Because of Merleau-Ponty's thorough rejection of contemporary French Neo-Kantian transcendental idealism, the immanent unity of subjective life in question can no longer be equated to the absolute self-enclosure of the transcendental subject but always involves a moment of otherness which drives the development of the subjective life into the next phase. Due to such unavoidable self-displacement of the subjective life, Merleau-Ponty in the quotation above characterizes such otherness inherent in the subjective unity as "depresentation" (*Entgegenwärtigung*) in contrast to the other moment of the fundamental self-presence (*Urpräsenz*). He is thus able to account for the problem of the transcendence of the other in connection with the unity of the subjective life.

As one of the most prominent contemporary phenomenologists, Dan Zahavi argues that intersubjectivity is only introduced to account for self-apprehension as "mundane self-awareness" and hence concrete contents of self-awareness (Zahavi 1999, p. 164). He maintains that intersubjectivity consists above all of a "subject-subject relation" in which each subject is "somebody with a first-person perspective of her own" (Zahavi 2014, p. 193). As such, he proposes to solve the seeming contradiction between the self-presence of subjectivity and the transcendence of the other on the basis of the inspiring Husserlian account of the living body. According to Zahavi's interpretation, Merleau-Ponty *continues and radicalizes* the Husserlian conception of embodied subjectivity so that "it per definition comprises an exteriority" (Zahavi 2001a, p. 163). The exteriority of my own body which is implicated in my bodily self-experience anticipates the intersubjective experience. Although he approves the approach to the transcendence of the other through the embodied self-awareness, Zahavi criticizes the later Merleau-Ponty's more radical proposal that the intersubjective relation, or again a differentiation between self and other is grounded in a common anonymity. For Zahavi, Merleau-Ponty is mistaken "to exaggerate the moment of alterity, and to overlook the difference between intra-and intersubjective alterity" (Zahavi 1999, p. 173).[2] He argues that Merleau-Ponty's neglect of the difference between intrasubjective and intersubjective alterity may result in the loss of the indispensable differentiation between the first-person and the third-person perspectives. He thus concludes that the later Merleau-Ponty not only denies the possibility to self-awareness but also to intersubjectivity. It turns out that Zahavi's ambivalent interpretation of Merleau-Ponty's theory of intersubjectivity deals with the notion of subjectivity concerning what he calls "the minimal or core self," namely, the mode of the first-person givenness of one's own experience. For Zahavi, Merleau-Ponty's final denial of the distinction between the self and the other in their common anonymity cancels the minimal condition of subjectivity and thereby of intersubjectivity.

Zahavi follows Husserl to make a crucial distinction between the "pure ego" and the "personal ego." Whereas the "pure ego" as the "first-person mode of givenness of the stream of consciousness" constitutes "a kind of pure, formal, and empty individuality," the "personal ego" as the mundane self-awareness only "manifests itself on the personal level, in its individual history, in its moral and intellectual convictions and decisions" (Zahavi 1999, pp. 165–166). For Zahavi, the "pure ego" is such a form of self-awareness that is directly accessible to the Husserlian pure reflection. By contrary, the "personal ego" as the mundane self-awareness takes shape in the relation to the other. On the basis of such a *methodological* restriction, Zahavi characterizes the "personal ego" as "founded objectifying self-interpretation" (Zahavi 1999, p. 166). He then concludes that "the problem of self-awareness is not primarily a question of a specific 'what', but of a unique 'how'" (Zahavi 1999, p. 180). In contrast to Zahavi's

---

[2] The same criticism of Merleau-Ponty is repeated in Zahavi's later publications (Zahavi 2005, p. 162, 170; 2014, pp. 78–87).

focus on the constitution of different levels of self-awareness, Merleau-Ponty's interpretation of the primordial self-awareness and its relation to the other is elaborated for the epistemic purpose of "recovering the consciousness of rationality" to begin with (Merleau-Ponty 1996, p. 67). Merleau-Ponty thus thematizes the problem of intersubjectivity in connection with the unity of subjective life which he regards as the *transcendental condition* of our primordial experience of the world. From such an epistemological perspective, Zahavi's fundamental concept of the "pure ego" or the "minimal self" turns out to be *insufficient* for establishing the transcendental condition of our primordial experience of the world. In other words, it is not the "pure, formal and empty individuality" but rather the *concrete identity of the transcendental subjectivity* that is presupposed all throughout our multiple contents of experiences.³

Admittedly, Merleau-Ponty's theory of intersubjectivity must be interpreted in connection with the epistemological role that the transcendental unity of the subjective life plays in his endless return to our primordial experience and original source of human rationality. Zahavi correctly points out that the early Merleau-Ponty insists on a peculiar form of solipsism in *PhP* by virtue of which the transcendence of the other is accounted for. Yet Merleau-Ponty's later turn to the primary fusion of the self and the other may well be interpreted as an *implicit* self-criticism with respect to his own early notion of transcendental subjectivity.⁴ The early Merleau-Ponty's theory of intersubjectivity rejects the Cartesian cogito and its associated objectivism, which only distorts the other into an observable object. Because Cartesianism merely allows one's direct access to one's own mind, my experience of the other as another subject is explained according to the defective theory of analogy which associates the behaviour of other bodies with experiences similar to those I have myself (Zahavi 2014, p. 121). In substituting Cartesian self-certainty with his concept of pre-reflective self-consciousness, Merleau-Ponty can argue for a direct access to the other subject. Insofar as pre-reflective self-consciousness is supposed as the *transcenden-*

---

3 Zahavi does acknowledge the Husserlian differentiation between "the act-transcendence of the ego" and "the pure and formal ego" in his early work (Zahavi 1999, pp. 148–151). However he neither explicates the transcendental role of "the ego as an act-transcendent identity-pole" nor the structure of self-consciousness involved in the notion of this ego because of his focus on the "minimal self" through and through. Yet Zahavi never equates the Husserlian ego in the sense of "the act-transcendent identity-pole" to the mundane personal self-awareness.

4 Merleau-Ponty's implicit self-criticism becomes explicit in his later notes collected in his posthumous manuscript *The Visible and the Invisible*. In a working note dated January 1959, he explicitly makes the self-criticism that "what I call the tacit cogito is impossible" (Merleau-Ponty 1964, p. 224; Merleau-Ponty 1968, p. 171).

tal ground of "my subjectivity and my transcendence toward the other" both at once, we will argue that for the early Merleau-Ponty the other merely plays the role of a necessary condition for the fundamental form of self-consciousness (Merleau-Ponty 1945 [2012], p. 413 [377]). In other words, the existence of the other is transcendentally grounded in the possible construal of transcendental subjectivity. Such loss of originality cannot but compromise the otherness of the other. From this perspective, one may wonder whether the late Merleau-Ponty's return to the primary fusion between the self and the other in childhood should *not* be interpreted as what Zahavi criticizes as "panpsychism," but rather as an effort towards uncovering the uncompromised *alterity* of the other in a phenomenological way.

This paper will mainly concentrate on two of Merleau-Ponty's texts. His early theory of intersubjectivity is worked out in the chapter on "Others and the Human World" in *PhP*. Despite what most of his commentators may believe, his very early self-criticism has already emerged in the middle period of his philosophical development when he was teaching psychology at the Sorbonne from 1949 to 1952.[5] Apart from this chapter in *PhP*, we will draw on one of his most famous Sorbonne lectures notes titled "The Child's Relations with Others" (*CRO* in the following) to which Zahavi's criticism refers. We will then take the following four steps to explicate the extent to which the otherness of the other can be understood in an uncompromised way without a cancellation of the self. First, we will show what Merleau-Ponty's primordial form of consciousness amounts to. Second, we will demonstrate that his conception of perceptual consciousness allows room for the possible experience of the other. Third, we will explain the extent to which the otherness of the other is compromised in the early Merleau-Ponty. Finally, we will explicate his implicit self-criticism in order to expose the uncompromised alterity of other inserted within the selfhood of embodied subjectivity. One can only do justice to the alterity of the other through such a conception of intersubjectivity by virtue of which the self paradoxically originates in the experience of self-loss. As a result, we will finally be able to argue against Zahavi that the later Merleau-Ponty's radical approach neither cancels the possibility of subjectivity nor intersubjectivity, but rather inserts the other into the constitution of selfhood as such, thereby exposing the innermost self-division within the unity of the subjective life.

---

5 Saint Aubert makes a meticulous analysis of Merleau-Ponty's conceptual development at the Sorbonne (Saint Aubert 2013).

1 Merleau-Ponty's Primordial Form of Consciousness

The early Merleau-Ponty's phenomenological reflection on the *concept* of consciousness is sketched in the chapter on "The Cogito" in the final section of *PhP*. He understands this chapter as a "phenomenology of phenomenology" that intends to recapitulate all previous results derived from direct phenomenological description in the book (Merleau-Ponty 1945 [2012], p. 419 [382]). In this chapter, he apparently opposes his primordial form of consciousness simultaneously both to modern empiricism and intellectualism. His renewed conception of consciousness is grounded, on the one hand, on a pre-objectivist notion of intentionality which may allow the transcendence of things while avoiding any retreat into modern empiricism. On the other hand, his pre-objectivist consciousness involves a non-Cartesian form of transcendental subjectivity which does not objectify but rather "lives" in the world to begin with. In this way, Merleau-Ponty intends to deprive the Cartesian cogito of its supposed absolute self-sufficiency and self-transparency.

Insofar as it presupposes metaphysical realism, Merleau-Ponty objects that modern empiricism, in his view, cannot but postulate the existence of the external object as independent of the subject. Hence, it results in scepticism about our possible knowledge of the external world. On the contrary, Merleau-Ponty's transcendental phenomenology only acknowledges the unavoidable transcendence of things in *correlation* to transcendental subjectivity without any reduction of such transcendence into metaphysical independence. The transcendence of things can be demonstrated at a certain point through aspects hidden from my current experience. As the *noema* of the intentional correlation, things themselves appear to transcendental subjectivity without losing their transcendence. Merleau-Ponty thus articulates an intentional appearance of the transcendent object as *phenomenon*. His transcendental phenomenology then differentiates the conception of the phenomenon from the subjective representation in modern empiricism.

In the meanwhile, Merleau-Ponty never understands the notion of the transcendental in the same sense as the Kantian and neo-Kantian forms of transcendental idealism. His transcendental phenomenology rather uses the term "transcendental" in a *homonymous* way. Although he emphasizes the appearance of things in person, it is impossible to interpret the intentional appearance in terms of the intellectualist form of transcendental constitution which makes all things into objects of intellectual knowledge. For Merleau-Ponty, Kantian transcendental idealism deals with the *a priori* epistemic norms of the possibility of objective knowledge. Yet Merleau-Ponty's transcendental phenomenology can no longer take for granted such a possibility. The objective reality which underlies the Kantian tradition must be grounded in the phenomenon of the world. In this sense, both natural and scientific objects must appear intentionally to the factual life of transcendental subjectivity where objective reality originates. To the extent that intentional appearance is non-objective, or more precisely, pre-objective, Merleau-Ponty's concept of transcendental subjective life as the fundamental ground of the pre-objective phenomenon entirely differs from the Cartesian ego, which consists of absolute self-certainty and self-sufficiency. In opposition to modern intellectualism, which unites both the Cartesian and the Kantian traditions, Merleau-Ponty's renewed transcendental subjectivity should not separate from, but always remains immersed in, the pre-objective world.

As a consequence, Merleau-Ponty replaces the Cartesian ego with his idiosyncratic concept of the "tacit cogito" in *PhP*. The concept of the "tacit cogito" that grounds the existence of our pre-objective experiences opposes a sort of immediate self-consciousness to the Cartesian cogito which involves self-reflection in the sense of self-objectification and self-knowledge. Like Zahavi's concept of the "minimal self," Merleau-Ponty's immediate self-consciousness equally involves the moment of the first-person givenness of lived experiences that he characterizes as "experience (*épreuve*) of myself by myself" (Merleau-Ponty 1945 [2012], p. 460 [426]). Although the first-person mode of givenness is an indispensable component of self-consciousness, immediate self-consciousness cannot be merely formal and empty, but always contains determinate *contents* through which I am conscious of my self-identity. Only in this way can transcendental subjectivity play the epistemological role of the transcendental condition for our pre-objective experiences of the world. It can be argued that Merleau-Ponty's *concretization* of the immediate self-consciousness in question is of a practical nature on the basis of his notion of comportment (Liu 2009; Barbaras 2009, pp. 173–175). It is such practical self-consciousness that differentiates our embodied experiences in the pre-objective world from physical events on the one hand. On the other hand, such practical concretization of immediate self-consciousness requires my primary *exposure* to the transcendence of things, others and the world.

Admittedly, Merleau-Ponty characterizes the pre-objective form of consciousness as *perceptual* consciousness. Insofar as perception for him involves both my primary exposure toward and reciprocal constitution with the world, he is justified to privilege sensorial experiences in order to account for both the pre-objective character of primordial consciousness and the finitude of transcendental subjectivity. Merleau-Ponty thus explicitly argues that "the *fundamental truth* is certainly that 'I think', but only on condition of understanding by this that

'I belong to myself in being in the world" (emphasis added, Merleau-Ponty 1945 [2012], p. 466 [430]). It is through the practical form of immediate self-consciousness that the early Merleau-Ponty is able to make sense of the seemingly contradictory synthesis of "transcendence in the immanence" in *PhP*. In contrast to Zahavi's single emphasis on the "minimal self" inherent in each of our subjective experiences, it is not the "first-person mode of givenness" but *concrete identity of the transcendental subjectivity* that for Merleau-Ponty must fundamentally ground my experiences of the world (Zahavi 2005, pp. 124–132). As we will see, the transcendence of others is then introduced as a condition for the concretization of the fundamental self-consciousness of transcendental subjectivity.

2 The Phenomenon of the Other

Merleau-Ponty develops his transcendental phenomenological account of intersubjectivity in the chapter on "Others and the Human World" in *PhP*. Here, he does not yet work out a complete theory of intersubjectivity (Merleau-Ponty 2005, pp. 22–23). For him, it is far more important to make room for the possibility of the other as the other *subject* before a later elaboration of any systematic theory of intersubjectivity. The major goal in this chapter is then to uncover the phenomenon of the other and thereby to integrate the intersubjective experience into the overall project of his early transcendental phenomenology of perception. To begin with, we have seen that the overall phenomenological problem of perception for Merleau-Ponty concerns the openness of transcendental subjectivity to the phenomena which both grounds in and transcends subjectivity. On the basis of the primordial form of consciousness above, the nature of such openness in question must be pre-objective. One may wonder to what extent I can make a pre-objective access to the transcendence of the other in intersubjective experience. For this purpose, Merleau-Ponty, on the one hand, develops an ontological argument to reject the modern objectivism which results in the Cartesian dualism between mind and body. On the other, he makes an epistemological criticism of the prevalent analogy theory, which fails to explain our experience of the other and cannot be verified by our experience either. In this way, he finally can make room for my direct experience of the other as the other subject.

Merleau-Ponty primarily works out an *ontological* criticism of Cartesian objectivism in order to make sense of the existence of the other as the *embodied* subject. He then tends to demonstrate the transcendence of the other subject in the pre-objective sense. According to Merleau-Ponty, it is the presupposed objectification of human body that thoroughly blocks my access to the other subject. For him, modern Cartesianism results in the notorious substance dualism between mind and body. The being of consciousness is characterized as "being-for-itself" whereas the objective being and thereby the human body are understood as "being-in-itself". The other thus can only be reduced to a physical differentiation from me as a single knowing subject and hence distorted as an object in the physical world. In the meanwhile, the other *subject* as a "being-for-itself" can never become accessible to me unless she is the same as me. As a consequence, the objectivism in modern Cartesianism only creates an unavoidable contradiction in my experience of the other as both physically different from and mentally identical to me. Whereas the other is only experienced as the object different from me, she, as another subject, also cannot differ from me at the same time. The Cartesian form of objectivism denies to me the possibility of experiencing the other as another subject. Merleau-Ponty thus concludes that "there is no room, then, for others and for a plurality of consciousnesses within objective thought" (Merleau-Ponty 1945 [2012], p. 402 [365]).

Nevertheless, Merleau-Ponty's ontological criticism of Cartesian objectivism does not cancel the mediating role which the human body may play in my experience of the other. He rather means to appeal to the non-objective conception of the *living body* which he develops as the alternative to Cartesian substance dualism in the first section of *PhP*. Merleau-Ponty's renewed concept of the living body is grounded in his phenomenological conception of perception as our pre-objective experience of the world. Due to such pre-objective characteristics, our primordial correlation to the world can neither be explained in terms of the accumulation of causal chains, nor regarded as the intellectual constitution of the transcendental subject, but rather regarded as "the suturing of my phenomenal body onto the primordial world" (Merleau-Ponty 1945 [2012], p. 402 [366]). In the primordial experience of the world, it is my living body that opens toward and takes up the unity of the world in the form of a sketch of the world. My pre-objective experience of things likewise involves a reciprocal relation between the solicitation of things and my inter-sensorial response. For Merleau-Ponty, our perception as the primordial experience of the world *by nature* consists of the comportment of the perceiving subject. On the basis of the pre-objective nature of perceptual experience, Merleau-Ponty emphasizes the living body as the primordial unity of the subject-object which opposes the Cartesian dualism. For him, the living body, then, is no longer an anatomical, physiological or biological object but a meaningful whole of actual and virtual comportment. Further, the concept of subjectivity is no longer equated to the self-enclosed Cartesian ego but rather to the perspective inherent in the experience of the world. Insofar as the invisible aspects of things and the world for my current perception implicates other perceivers, the existence of the other can be established as that of embodied subjectivity.

Admittedly, the anti-Cartesian unity of the living body is the "body-for-us" or the "body of human experience" in opposition to the physical and physiological body. The living body, then, cannot be objectively represented through the physiological observation. It rather only becomes accessible to us as the "visible body" in the pre-objective way. The "visible body" is equally the "perceived body" because Merleau-Ponty's concept of perception means to characterize our primordial and pre-objective form of experience. For him, human comportment articulates and manifests the "visible body." To make sense of the visibility of the living body, one may draw on the concept of "body schema" (*schema corporel*) to which Merleau-Ponty in *PhP* was only able to gain limited access on the basis of his reading of Jean Lhermitte.[6] Despite such an early reference, Merleau-Ponty primarily follows his contemporary neurologists to differentiate the concept of the "body schema" from the association of various sensations in the human body. The "body schema" for him amounts to a *global structure* of the *ensemble* of the human body which involves "the spatial and temporal unity, the inter-sensorial unity, or the sensorimotor unity of the body" (Merleau-Ponty 1945 [2012], pp. 115–116 [101–102]). The association of various sensations must be grounded on the global structure of the "body schema." Further the "body schema" is never a blind rule which the human body unconsciously follows to form an organic unity. Merleau-Ponty rather understands the concept of the "body schema" as one's global *awareness* of her own posture in the inter-sensorial world. As the self-manifestation of the global bodily structure, the "body schema" then constitutes the self-awareness of embodied subjectivity. Finally, for Merleau-Ponty, the "body schema" does not consist of a fixed and permanent scheme but *dynamically* takes shape in our actual or virtual comportment. As such, the "body schema" only manifests itself in and through our bodily movement. It becomes clear that the living body only becomes visible on the basis of the formation and self-manifestation of "body schema" in and through human comportment.

Clearly, the subjective dimension of the phenomenal body is rooted in the self-manifestation of the "body schema." On the basis of the notion of embodied subjectivity, Merleau-Ponty works out an *epistemological* argument to clarify the mode of my possible access to the other as another subject. Although the exis-

---

6 In the early phase, Merleau-Ponty only had a very limited access to the innovative concept of "body schema" in his contemporary neurological and psychological theories. In the later development, he continuously returned to the rich concept of "body schema" which proves to be one of the major inspirations for his phenomenological ontology. Moreover, only in his later phase did Paul Schilder play an even more important role in Merleau-Ponty's understanding of the concept of "body schema" (Saint Aubert 2013, pp. 70–72).

tence of embodied subjectivity as the primordial unity of subject-object constitutes a pre-objective transcendence in opposition to modern Cartesianism, the early Merleau-Ponty maintains the crucial distinction between the self and the other in the intersubjective experience. By all means, I am not identical to the other as one and the same embodied subject. One can thus expect to gain access to the other subject through the perception of the other's comportment. To clarify such a mediated access to the other subject, Merleau-Ponty argues:

> When I turn toward my perception itself and when I pass from direct perception to the thought about this perception, I reenact (*ré-effectue*) it, I uncover a thought older than I am at work in my perceptual organs and of which these organs are merely the trace. I understand others in the same way. Here again I have but the trace of a consciousness that escapes me in its actuality and, when my gaze crosses another, I reenact the foreign existence in a sort of reflection. (Merleau-Ponty 1945 [2012], p. 404 [367])

Surprisingly Merleau-Ponty here compares intersubjective experience with one's self-reflection. In this quotation, he characterizes my perception of the other as "a sort of reflection." For him, one can neither directly gain access to one's own self nor to the other. For him, this always involves an experience of "reenaction" which, for Merleau-Ponty, maintains the indispensable distance between the reflecting and the reflected as well as that between the self and the other. Nevertheless, it may seem *as if* his conception of intersubjective experience through the moment of "reenaction" were a qualified return to the analogy theory once prevalent in the modern world. Analogy theory begins with my objective observation of the other's bodily behaviours. Through a reflection on the correlation between my similar behaviours and my own mind, I am supposedly able to infer that if the other's behaviours are similar to mine then her mind is also similar to mine. However analogy theory can at most infer a correlation between the other's bodily behaviours and my mind. I am neither aware of the correlation between the other's mind and her bodily behaviours nor even certain of that between my own bodily behaviours and my own mind. Merleau-Ponty thus only acknowledges Scheler's criticism in passing that the analogy theory failed to derive the other's mind or even its existence from mine without begging the question. For Merleau-Ponty, the mediated access to the other in question can never be explained through the fallacy of the analogy theory.

The analogy theory can neither avoid the fallacy of *petitio principii* nor be verified by human experiences. To disprove the analogy theory, Merleau-Ponty further introduces the interesting experience that a child can imitate another person's biting act at the age of fifteen months. He argues that the child "perceives his intentions in his body, perceives my body with his own, and thereby perceives my intentions in his body" (Merleau-Ponty 1945 [2012], p. 404 [368]). In contrast to the intellectual inference which analogy theory presupposes, the child's imitation seems *as if* were demonstrating an *immediate* comprehension of the act of another person's "biting." Yet when in taking a closer look at his argument, one will soon find that Merleau-Ponty does not suppose an immediate access to the other but rather a non-intellectual and *embodied mediation* for the child's perception of the other. For him, the child's imitation of the other depends on her appropriation of the other's comportment as the embodied intention. He further argues that such a bodily appropriation of the other is not confined to human experiences in childhood. It is generally at stake in our perception of the other as another viewpoint toward one and the same world, in our learning to manipulate tools from the other as well in our dialogue with each other. To explicate the bodily appropriation of the other, Merleau-Ponty argues:

> Now, it is precisely my body that perceives the other's body and finds there something of a miraculous extension of its own intentions, a familiar manner of handling the world. Henceforth, *just as the parts of my body together form a system*, the other's body and my own are a single whole, two sides of a single phenomenon, and the anonymous existence, of which my body is continuously the trace, henceforth inhabits these two bodies simultaneously. (Emphasis added, Merleau-Ponty 1945 [2012], p. 406 [370])

For Merleau-Ponty, our perception of the other concerns our bodily comprehension of the other's "body schema." Earlier on, we have shown that the living body only forms and manifests its own "body schema" in and through our comportment. My perception of the other is then based on the possibility of my appropriation and hence imitation of the other's bodily movement as a response to the task in the world. When I imitate the other's comportment, both the other's and my own bodies are oriented by things common to us. In the quotation above, Merleau-Ponty explicitly interprets the relation between the other's body and mine in the same way as that of the inter-sensorial communication within the single unity of the living body. In *PhP*, he characterizes the inter-sensorial connection as "system of equivalence" which allows a direct transfer between different modes of sensorial experiences. As such, I imitate the other's comportment in the same way that an experienced organist is able to make a direct connection between a musical piece, her performance and the instrument. For Merleau-Ponty, our mutual appropriation of bodily gestures reveals the *generality* of the "body schema" that undergrounds the transfer of my perspective to the other and *vice versa*.

Now it is clear that in our perception of the other the "reenaction" of the other subject in question is grounded in the possibility of one's appropriation of the other's comportment. For Merleau-Ponty, the living body establishes and manifests the subjective dimension in the "body schema" which constitutes the self-awareness of the embodied subject. Because the "body schema" only takes shape in and through comportment, the possibility of imitating the other's comportment then means no more than the appropriation of the other's "body schema" which makes possible one's access to the other. It is on the basis of the innovative notion of the living body as the phenomenal body that Merleau-Ponty finally is able to make room both for the existence of the other subject and our intersubjective experience.

3 The Compromised Otherness of the Other

Merleau-Ponty's demonstration of the intersubjective experience of the other both relies on his idiosyncratic notion of embodied subjectivity and perceptual consciousness as comportment oriented by things and the world. Insofar as the subjective dimension of the living body only emerges in the "body schema", the other subject for Merleau-Ponty is directly expressed in and through her bodily gestures. The other is then made accessible to me when her comportment is appropriable to the "body schema" of my living body. Here one may wonder whether Merleau-Ponty's conception of bodily appropriation could still maintain the otherness of the other. The otherness of the other can mean nothing other than the *transcendence beyond* and the difference from what constitutes the self in the "body schema." It thus seems *as if* Merleau-Ponty could only solve the problem of intersubjective experience at the big price of a "general confusion" between the self and the other. He is aware of the difficulty concerning the otherness of the other that arises in his conception of the living body and its associated theory of intersubjectivity. In the second half of the same chapter on "Others and the Human World," he turns to a peculiar form of "solipsism" in our primordial relation to the world without returning to the Cartesian ego that he has thoroughly rejected. In this section, we will show the extent to which Merleau-Ponty can make sense of the otherness of the other on the basis of the non-Cartesian self-consciousness.

Merleau-Ponty's argument begins with a clarification of the *fundamental* self-consciousness which we have demonstrated as the transcendental condition of our primordial experiences in the above. For him, transcendental subjectivity consists of such fundamental self-consciousness. He thus argues:

> The given background of existence is what the *cogito* confirms: every affirmation, every engagement, and every negation and every doubt takes place in a previously opened field, and attests to a self in touch with itself prior to the particular acts in which it loses contact with itself. This self, who is the witness of every actual communication, ... seems to prevent

any resolution of the problem of others. Here we see a lived solipsism that cannot be transcended. (Merleau-Ponty 1945 [2012], p. 411 [374])

Here Merleau-Ponty characterizes transcendental subjectivity as "a self in touch with itself." His concept of the primordial self does not presuppose the absolute self-certainty of the Cartesian ego on the one hand. On the other hand, such primordial subjectivity as the transcendental condition of our experiences does not ground the Kantian categories of understanding but rather grounds "a previously opened field." In *PhP*, Merleau-Ponty understands the world as "the horizon of all horizons" or "the style of all styles" which, as the ultimate field, constitutes the pre-objective unity of "compatibility and compossibility" in contrast to the intellectual unity of categories. As such, the unity of "compatibility and compossibility" must presuppose the *identity* of transcendental subjectivity all throughout my various experiences which I attribute to myself. Because of such a clear distinction from the Kantian transcendental subject, Merleau-Ponty emphasizes his theory of transcendental subjectivity as a "lived solipsism." Further, the selfhood in Merleau-Ponty's transcendental subjectivity does not merely consist of an empty self-relation inherent in each of our experiences but involves *what* I am conscious of as my own self. Because he primarily regards the problem of self-awareness as a "question of a unique 'how', Zahavi's fundamental concept of the "minimal self" means nothing other than the first-person mode of givenness (Zahavi 1999, p. 180). Although he appraises Merleau-Ponty's solipsism in the intersubjective experience, it turns out that Zahavi conflates his "minimal self" with Merleau-Ponty's self-identity of transcendental subjectivity (Zahavi 2014, p. 86). Due to such a conflation, Zahavi does not interpret Merleau-Ponty's theory of intersubjectivity in connection to the problem of transcendental subjectivity but merely to that of "mundane self-awareness" or the "personal I." In contrast to Zahavi's (mis)interpretation, Merleau-Ponty's "lived solipsism" transcendentally grounds all our primordial experiences in the non-Cartesian self-identity of transcendental subjectivity.

Admittedly, my perception of the other as a sort of pre-objective experience must equally be grounded in Merleau-Ponty's transcendental subjectivity. The other subject only becomes accessible to me to the extent that her comportment can be appropriated into my "body schema" and integrated into the unity of the world. Although the unity of the world as "compatibility and compossibility" for Merleau-Ponty differs from the conceptual homogeneity, the "lived solipsism" in question seems *as if* only allowing room for the other as another *self*. One may wonder to what extent Merleau-Ponty's non-Cartesian conception of transcendental subjectivity is able to maintain the *otherness* of the other. Clearly the otherness of the other concerns not merely the distinction of different subjects but also a sort of *asymmetry* between the self and the other. For the purpose of explaining such an asymmetry, Merleau-Ponty turns to the inner structure of transcendental subjectivity which involves the non-Cartesian self-consciousness. For him, the self-consciousness of transcendental subjectivity should not be characterized as self-transparency and self-certainty. The fundamental self-consciousness in question rather contains an ineluctable *inner differentiation* between the reflecting and the reflected self which he articulates as "open reflection upon the unreflected" or "reflective taking up of the unreflected" (Merleau-Ponty 1945 [2012], p. 413 [376]). According to Merleau-Ponty, it is such inner differentiation within transcendental subjectivity that finally conditions the asymmetry and makes room for the otherness of the other. He thus argues:

> The central phenomenon, which simultaneously grounds my subjectivity and my transcendence toward the other, consists in the fact that I am given to myself. *I am given*, which is to say I find myself already situated and engaged in the physical and social world; *I am given to myself*, which is to say that this situation is never concealed from me, it is never around me like some foreign necessity, and I am never actually enclosed in my situation like an object in a box. My freedom, that fundamental power I have of being the subject of all of my experiences, is not distinct from my insertion in the world. (Merleau-Ponty 1945 [2012], p. 413 [377])

Clearly, the inner differentiation between reflecting and the reflected self in question allows my primordial exposure to the other. In the meanwhile, Merleau-Ponty makes a crucial distinction between such primordial openness and the causal necessitation. For him, the transcendence of the other does not causally necessitate my acts but demands or rather invites my response. On the one hand, my perceptual consciousness as my comportment does not result from the causal effect of the other but depends on my *own* decision to take up the other's invitation and make a response. Yet the constitution of my response does not completely originate in me but depend on my appropriation of the demand from the other. As such, my comportment is equally oriented and hence determined by the other. In contrast to the unilateral causation in the necessitation, there exists a *reciprocal* relation between the self and the other in the intersubjective experience. Merleau-Ponty thus maintains in the quotation above that "my freedom is not distinct from my insertion in the world." For him, the self-consciousness of transcendental subjectivity consists of her *self-appropriation* in the demand from the other.

Merleau-Ponty's phenomenological reflection is intended to uncover the original source of our rationality through and through. Due to such methodological restriction, one cannot stop with the above description of the reciprocal relation between the self and the other in the intersubjective experience. One may ask what constitutes *the ultimate condition* of our perception of the other, that is either self-consciousness or the demand of the other. We have shown above that Merleau-Ponty exclusively regards the "I think" as *the* fundamental truth in *PhP*. It is thus the non-Cartesian self-consciousness that fundamentally conditions my perception of the other. Fundamental self-consciousness is a unity that involves the "reflective taking up of the unreflected." For Merleau-Ponty, it is through the relation to the other that transcendental subjectivity obtains concrete contents for her self-identity. His concept of fundamental self-consciousness, which constitutes the self-identity of transcendental subjectivity, then means no more than *self-determination*. In other words, the self determines herself to be the one that accepts and responds to the demand of the other.

Let us take a look at the nature of the otherness of the other that Merleau-Ponty attempts to explicate through the non-Cartesian self-consciousness. For this purpose, we must examine the *systematic* status of the self and the other in the argument for the possibility of one's perception of the other. As we have acknowledged above, the otherness of the other concerns the asymmetrical relation between the self and the other. It is thus in the *transcendental conditional relation* between the self and the other that one should find their asymmetry. For the early Merleau-Ponty, it certainly is the existence of transcendental subjectivity as an incessant self-determination that opens the self toward the other as an indispensable condition. The fundamental self of transcendental subjectivity is established as the transcendental condition for the existence of the other. In spite of the reciprocal relation between the self and the other in intersubjective experience, the otherness of the other is only recognized in the sense of a *necessary condition* for the endless self-determination of transcendental subjectivity. Insofar as the existence of the other is transcendentally conditioned by the fundamental self of transcendental subjectivity, the otherness of the other is then deprived of her original alterity and *compromised* as a necessary condition for the existence of transcendental subjectivity in the early Merleau-Ponty's transcendental system.

Admittedly, Merleau-Ponty's "lived solipsism" is only presupposed at the price of compromising the original alterity of the other for the existence of transcendental subjectivity. According to Merleau-Ponty's methodological principle, one can only expect to recover the uncompromised alterity of the other through uncovering the original or originary existence of the other. His philosophical development in the Sorbonne's lectures mostly concentrates on children's experiences in which fundamental self-consciousness cannot be taken for granted but gradually takes shape in the development of their early lives. As we will see shortly, Merleau-Ponty's return to the anonymity of child in the Sorbonne lecture *CRO* is not intended to cancel the distinction between the self and the other, but rather to uncover the uncompromised other by splitting the innermost selfhood as presupposed in his early conception of transcendental subjectivity.

4 The Uncompromised Alterity of the Other

In *PhP*, Merleau-Ponty works out his primary conception of intersubjectivity in line with his transcendental phenomenology of perception. For him, the possibility of my perception of the other is both grounded on the innovative notion of the embodied subject as well as my bodily appropriation of the comportment of the other. Yet Merleau-Ponty's transcendental phenomenology argues that the existence of the other subject is transcendentally grounded in the ultimate condition of the self-consciousness of transcendental subjectivity. For this reason, the otherness of the other is deprived of the original alterity and distorted as a necessary condition for the possibility of the self-identity of transcendental subjectivity. Merleau-Ponty's development of an alternative theory of intersubjective experience must wait until his later turn to phenomenological ontology in the period of *Collège de France*. In this section, it is not the system of his alternative theory itself but rather the fundamental *motivation* of his turn that concerns us. It is thus necessary to explicate the major problem implicated in the compromise of the other in his early transcendental phenomenology.

Merleau-Ponty's renewed understanding of intersubjectivity can be traced back to his Sorbonne period. Among a number of his lectures at the time, the lecture on "The Child's Relations with Others" is of particular importance for us, not only because this lecture specifically focuses on the development of intersubjective experience at the childhood but also because the significance of the intersubjective relation for the fundamental conception of the selfhood is renewed.[7] It is worth acknowledging in passing that in the lecture Merleau-Ponty begins with a crucial reconsideration of the theoretical relation between our perceptual and intersubjective experience. For him, my perception of the other should *not* be subordinated to the perception of the world in general and merely

---

[7] One may find two versions of the lecture notes on "The Child's Relations with Others" both in French and English. Whereas one version includes the complete résumé of the lecture, the other only contains a revised and expanded text of the first part of the same lecture (Merleau-Ponty 1997 [1964], pp. 147–229 [96–155]; 2001 [2010], pp. 303–396 [241–315].). Yet the major points of Merleau-Ponty's argument in the first part of the lecture do not vary across the two versions. Since we are here concerned with the first part of this lecture, we will exclusively concentrate on the revised edition which was published for the first time by the Centre de Documentation Universitaire in 1951.

understood as one particular sort of our cognition. On the one hand, his pre-objective notion of perceptual experiences does not allow us to interpret our intersubjective experiences as a sort of intellectual cognition. On the other hand, Merleau-Ponty draws on his contemporary psychological research concerning the role of personality in the development of outer perception and linguistic acquisition. His intention is to show "a correlation between the manner of perceiving and the manner of structuring the social world" as well as "unity and solidarity of the two phenomena (i.e. "the linguistic process and the affective process") (Merleau-Ponty 1997 [1964], p. 163 [107]; 170 [113]). In this sense, Merleau-Ponty implicitly criticises his early theory of intersubjectivity in *PhP* and changes his way of dealing with the problem of intersubjectivity. For him, the relation with others is not only regarded "as one of the contents of our experience but as an actual *structure in its own right*" (emphasis added, Merleau-Ponty 1997 [1964], p. 208 [140]).

Here one may wonder what kind of novel structure the intersubjective experience involves. To make sense of the peculiar nature of intersubjectivity, Merleau-Ponty once again repeats his early criticism of the analogy theory. As in *PhP*, so here as well both the conception of the other as another subject and the possibility of intersubjective experience must be grounded on the renewed concept of the living body in the sense of the "body schema," which we have seen above. Apart from a succinct repetition of the "body schema," in the lecture Merleau-Ponty particularly emphasizes the importance of Henri Wallon's developmental psychological *framework* in order to demonstrate that the distinction between the self and the other should not be taken for granted, but it gradually takes shape. His further reference to Lacan tends to complement and renew Wallon's analysis of this theme. It is not our purpose here to provide a detailed commentary on the rich lecture notes. It is sufficient for us to show that Merleau-Ponty's reference to the child's intersubjective experience is not only intended to describe a chronological development. It further aims at an alternative theory of the intersubjective structure and its associated notion of subjectivity. According to him, the child's form of the relation to the other does not completely disappear but continues to a certain extent in adulthood (Merleau-Ponty 1997 [1964], p. 227 [154]).

Due to his emphasis on *reciprocity* in the mutual bodily appropriation between the self and the other, Merleau-Ponty supposes it necessary to return to the "state of pre-communication" where the child is not yet aware of her distinction from the other. Clearly, such reciprocity cannot be justified in his early transcendental phenomenology, which regards the fundamental self-consciousness of transcendental subjectivity as the ultimate transcendental condition for the existence of the other. It is thus not surprising that Merleau-Ponty in the lecture attempts to return to the *origin* of selfhood and to reveal the insertion of the other into the formation of self-identity. Merleau-Ponty follows Wallon in dividing the child's psychological development into two stages. The first stage of "precommunication" is characterized by the non-distinction of self and other and hence their anonymous confusion before the third year of age. At the second stage from around 3, the child gradually halts the previous confusion and develops the awareness of her distinction from the other. According to Wallon, the child's psychological development begins through prior perception of the living body which is simultaneously accompanied with the development of perception of the other. From birth to the age of 6 months, the infantile experience of the living body is supposed to be too fragmentary to achieve the awareness of the *ensemble* of the entire body. In the meanwhile, the infantile experience of the other is likewise retarded and fragmentary. Only after 6 months does the period of what Wallon calls "incontinent sociability" occur. In the phase extending from 6 months to the third year of age, it is extremely important to observe the occurrence of the phenomenon of the "mirror image." According to Merleau-Ponty, Wallon supposes that the child primarily regards her mirror image as a relatively independent existence in the quasi-space inside the mirror. Wallon explains the stage of the mirror image as one moment in the development of child's intellection which eventually identifies her mirror image with her interoceptively perceived body. Furthermore, he explains the child's continued interests in her mirror image after her successful recognition of the image, as efforts at understanding the natural causality of the phenomenon of reflection in the mirror. According to Merleau-Ponty, Wallon's *intellectualist* explanation of the mirror image presupposes, on the one hand, the quasi-reality of image-space which for Wallon must be reduced to an "ideal space" of the child's one and same body. On the other hand, Wallon's explanation presupposes the notion of the child's development as the growth of intellection and thereby characterizes the mirror image as the negative moment to be reduced in the developmental process. For this reason, Merleau-Ponty objects that Wallon cannot explain the positive significance underlying the phenomenon of the child's continuous interests in the mirror image.

Despite such criticism, Merleau-Ponty agrees with Wallon that, from the point of view of child development, the mirror image plays a very crucial role in making accessible to the child, for the first time, the global image of her body in contrast to her former fragmented interoceptive experiences. Insofar as the child does not differentiate between interoception and exteroception, Wallon argues that the mirror image as the visual experience of the child's entire body participates in the existence of the same body. Furthermore, the mirror image is what the child's body manifests to the other. Merleau-Ponty then acknowledges that for Wallon "the child himself feels he is in the other's body just as he feels himself to be in his visual image" (Merleau-Ponty 1997 [1964], p. 199 [134]). In short, Merleau-Ponty approves of Wallon's psychological framework that the mirror image *both* constitutes the child's "body image" and implies her primordial relation to the other *simultaneously*.

Because Wallon's intellectualism means to finally do away with the mirror image in the development of human intellection, Merleau-Ponty turns to Lacan to reveal the tremendous significance of the mirror image for the formation of the selfhood. According to Merleau-Ponty, Lacan understands the acquisition of the mirror image in the sense of the passage from one state of personality to another in contrast to Wallon. For Lacan, the personality prior to the appearance of the mirror image only consists of the "collection of confusedly felt impulses." It is the mirror image that brings forth a "contemplation of self" or an "ideal image of oneself." Merleau-Ponty thus emphasizes in line with Lacan that the mirror image constitutes the primordial form of the child's self-consciousness of her identity.

According to Merleau-Ponty's interpretation, the mirror image for Lacan not only concerns the new content which contributes to the formation of the child's self-consciousness but also the new *function*, namely, what is called "the narcissistic function." Lacan characterizes "the narcissistic function" as the "de-realization" by virtue of which "I leave the reality of my lived me in order to refer myself constantly to the ideal, fictitious, or imaginary me, of which the mirror image is the first outline" (Merleau-Ponty 1997 [1964], p. 203 [136]). In this sense, for Lacan the mirror image as the child's primordial self-consciousness simultaneously creates a *distance* and even a conflict "between the *me* as I feel myself and the *me* as I see myself or as others see me" (Merleau-Ponty 1997 [1964], p. 204 [137]). In other words, the mirror image both constitutes the *self-manifestation* and self-alienation or *self-concealment* of the child through the "de-realizing" function *at the same time.* To the extent that the mirror image is equally what others see me, Lacan regards the self-alienation in the mirror image as a precondition for my future alienation by others. For Merleau-Ponty, the problem that concerns the development of the child through the phase of the mirror image then deals with a "synthesis of co-existence with others." It is such a reciprocity between the self-manifestation and the self-alienation of embodied subjectivity that motivates Merleau-Ponty to abandon the transcendental asymmetry between the self and the other in the early transcendental phenomenology of perception in *PhP.*

Admittedly, Merleau-Ponty follows Wallon and Lacan to renew the conception of intersubjectivity. He draws on their psychological explanations of the mirror image to demonstrate that the relation to the other is not merely a particular form of perception but also plays a crucial role in forming the primordial self-consciousness of embodied subjectivity. It is worth emphasizing that the inchoate relation to the other in the mirror image inevitably alienates the self while simultaneously constituting her self-consciousness. It is such function of alienation that manifests the alterity of the other within the innermost region of the selfhood. In contrast to Merleau-Ponty's transcendental phenomenology in *PhP*, the relation to the other in *CRO* is no longer transcendentally grounded in the ultimate condition of transcendental subjectivity. In the Sorbonne lecture, the relation to the other is understood as one of the originary sources for the emergence of selfhood. As such, the alterity of the other is no longer compromised but rather inserted in the innermost core of selfhood.

5 Conclusion

Before coming to my conclusion, let us take look at Merleau-Ponty's concept of embodied subjectivity. To begin with, we have acknowledged that the problem of intersubjectivity is never separate from that of subjectivity in Merleau-Ponty's phenomenological thinking. Unlike Zahavi's "minimal self," Merleau-Ponty's theory of subjectivity is developed for the epistemological purpose of renewing our conception of rationality. At the end of the long introduction to *PhP*, Merleau-Ponty replaces the intellectualist concept of the absolute subject with his own conception of the "perpetual beginning of reflection" (Merleau-Ponty 1945 [2012], p. 75 [63]). The latter view articulates his alternative concept of transcendental subjectivity. As we have shown, Merleau-Ponty grounds the endless process of reflection in the inner differentiation between reflection and the un-reflected. He also articulates the inner differentiation in terms of the paradoxical unity between the "self-presence" and the "depresentation" of transcendental subjectivity.

In *PhP*, the inner distinction in question that brings forth the endless process of reflection amounts to the self-determination of transcendental subjectivity in its openness to the world. For the early Merleau-Ponty, such self-determination does not amount to Cartesian self-sufficiency and self-transparency, but rather to the self-appropriation in the practical response to the demand of the other and the world. Insofar as the early Merleau-Ponty presupposes transcendental subjectivity as the ultimate source of all our primordial experiences, the relation to the other can only be transcendentally grounded in the fundamental self-consciousness of transcendental subjectivity. As a consequence of such transcendental asymmetry, the otherness of the other is inevitably distorted to be a necessary condition for the existence of fundamental selfhood. In contrast, the *non*-compromised otherness of the other can only be uncovered through an alternative conception of intersubjective experience that must substitute the asymmetry between the self and the other with reciprocity. As we have demonstrated, Merleau-Ponty in his Sorbonne lecture reconsiders the intersubjective relation with respect to the innermost self-division of embodied subjectivity.[8] Drawing on Wallon's and Lacan's explanation of the mirror image in childhood, Merleau-Ponty shows that the "body image" as one's own embodied self-manifestation simultaneously constitutes her alienation or self-loss. The other as a constitutive condition has already been inserted into the innermost selfhood of embodied subjectivity to begin with. Based on the peculiar reciprocity of self-awareness and the self-loss, one may conclude that the later Merleau-Ponty understands *the uncompromised alterity of the other as an originary constituent of the self-division within embodied subjectivity.* Enveloping the innermost self-division, embodied subjectivity then can only come into being as a gift of self-seeking in the ineluctable self-loss.

Acknowledgments

This paper is a modified version of my presentation in the conference on "Phenomenology, Empathy, Intersubjectivity" convened by Professor Dermot Moran in Dublin in 2017. I owe him my deep gratitude for his invitation. I am extremely grateful to all the participants for their very helpful comments and remarks.

References

Barbaras, Renaud (2009): *Le Tournant de L'Expérience*. Paris: Vrin.
Bernet, Rudolf (1996): "The Other in Myself". In: Critchley, Simon/Dews, Peter (Eds.): *Deconstructive Subjectivities*. Albany: SUNY Press, pp. 169–184.
Bernet, Rudolf (2004): "Le Sujet Traumatisé". In: Bernet, Rudolf (Ed.): *Conscience et existence*. Paris: Presses Universitaires de France, pp. 269–93.
Merleau-Ponty, Maurice (1945): *Phénoménologie de la Perception*. Paris: Editions Gallimard.
Merleau-Ponty, Maurice (1964): *Le Visible et L'Invisible*. Paris: Editions Gallimard.
Merleau-Ponty, Maurice (1964): *The Primacy of Perception and Other Essays*. James M. Edie (Ed. and Trans.). Evanston: Northwestern University Press.
Merleau-Ponty, Maurice (1968): *The Visible and the Invisible*. Trans. Alphonso Lingis. Evanston: Northwestern University Press.
Merleau-Ponty, Maurice (1996): *Le Primat de la Perception*. Lagrasse: Editions Verdier.

---

8 For the overall theme of self-divided subjectivity in the Kantian, phenomenological and psychoanalytic tradition, see Bernet 1996 and 2004.

Merleau-Ponty, Maurice (1997): *Parcours 1935–1951*. Lagrasse: Editions Verdier.
Merleau-Ponty, Maurice (2001): *Psychologie et Pédagogie de L'Enfant*. Lagrasse: Editions Verdier.
Merleau-Ponty, Maurice (2005): *Parcours Deux 1951–1961*. Lagrasse: Editions Verdier.
Merleau-Ponty, Maurice (2010): *Child Psychology and Pedagogy*. Trans. Talia Welsh. Evanston: Northwestern University Press.
Merleau-Ponty, Maurice (2012): *Phenomenology of Perception*. Trans. Donald A. Landes. London, New York: Routledge.
Saint Aubert, Emmanuel De (2013): *Être et Chair*. Paris: Vrin.
Zahavi, Dan (1999): *Self-awareness and Alterity*. Evanston: Northwestern University Press.
Zahavi, Dan (2001a): "Beyond Empathy". In: *Journal of Consciousness Study* 8(5–7), pp. 151–167.
Zahavi, Dan (2001b): *Husserl and Transcendental Intersubjectivity*. Trans. Elizabeth A. Behnke. Athens: Ohio University Press.
Zahavi, Dan (2005): *Subjectivity and Selfhood*. Cambridge, MA: The MIT Press.
Zahavi, Dan (2014): *Self and Other*. Oxford: Oxford University Press.
Liu, Zhe (2009): "A Fundamental Limit of Merleau-Ponty's Transcendental Phenomenology". In: *Chiasmi International* 11, pp. 133–143.

Hernán G. Inverso
Phenomenology of the Inapparent and Michel Henry's Criticism of the Noematic Presentation of Alterity

Abstract: Husserl's explorations on intersubjectivity inspired many turns in contemporary philosophy. Among them, Michel Henry tries to show in what sense intentionality and constitution are not good phenomenological ways to explain the universal *a priori* of the experience of alterity. Indeed, his approach not only queries the noematic presentations of alterity but requires the adoption of a self-affective perspective. However, we will suggest in this work that this theoretical option is compatible with Husserl's phenomenological views. We will examine Henry's criticism of the Husserlian approach in order to provide an interpretation that indicates the relevance of the phenomenology of the inapparent as a legitimate phenomenological field consistent with the original programme.

Husserl's theory of empathy was often revisited by other phenomenologists. Many positions that moved away from the original phenomenological views justify their claim of inversion or overcoming on this ground, as it happens in the case of recent French trends. We will explore Michel Henry's criticism of Husserl's alleged silence on our life's particular modalities and the consequent failure of the noematic approach. In this light, the association between subject and representation, as well as between alterity, intentionality, and constitution, cannot explain the nature of intersubjectivity. This aspect is accessible only from a self-affective perspective, i.e., leaving aside intentionality to stress Life's immanence. In what follows, we will examine the field of the phenomenology of the inapparent as an instrument to evaluate Michel Henry's criticism of Husserl. We will suggest that there is not a fundamental incompatibility between these positions. Furthermore, Henry is not able to propose an overcoming of the Husserlian view. On the contrary, these explorations on exceedance, i.e., the inexhaustible aspects behind every phenomenon, have encouraged the study of the whole range of phenomena with different and consistent tools.

1 The context of generativity

In *Material Phenomenology*, Henry analyses the experience of alterity presented by Husserl in the *Cartesian Meditations* as appealing to three assumptions that will be analysed in point 2 but are worth mentioning here as a synthesis of Henry's objections: the other is given to my experience; the other is a noematic item, i.e. an intentional correlate, and therefore, the other is given to me as something transcendent. Furthermore, for Henry, alterity, as we experience it, implies a whole plexus of emotions provoked by the presence or absence of the other. This occurrence is alluded to in the notion of "pathos-with". A non-affective condition could not account for the affection of the inter-pathetic life (*Phénoménologie materiel*, henceforth *PhM*, p. 141). Therefore, at first glance, this perspective seems incompatible with Husserlian phenomenology. However, these issues belong to a legitimate phenomenological field. This field accounts for relevant aspects oriented to inapparent phenomena, whose exceedance can be better comprehended if we pay attention to immanence.

Moreover, it allows for understanding the criticisms from French phenomenology and the new realisms. To what extent Henry's complaints challenge Husserl's approach? As we will suggest, they provide a helpful way to reinforce it.[1] Let us begin by introducing a new level of phenomenological analysis beyond generativity. This addition strengthens phenomenology as an approach oriented to account for different types of phenomena with distinct methodological features (Inverso, 2016 and 2018). It is well-known that beyond the basic version associated with static and genetic stages the idea of a generative dimension has gained traction in recent years. It aims at providing insights into cultural, geo-historical and intersubjective phenomena. Indeed, Husserl conceived the method as a flexible approach that promotes a comprehensive analysis of phenomenality. If so, it can include exceedance in a network of interconnected layers of research.

Husserl introduced the static and generative approaches noting their complementarity in texts of the 1920s. He claimed that the distinction between static and genetic methods is not thematic—it is not a detachment of the study about temporality—but methodological.[2] Husserl claims in *On Phenomenology of Intersubjectivity* that "every such [static] analysis is in itself already to a certain extent genetic analysis" (Hua 14, p. 480). He means that static analysis points in the direction of genetic analysis. It is also possible to reverse the view and switch from

---

[1] See a broader approach to this proposal in Inverso (2018, *passim*).
[2] On this topic, see Geniusas (2012, p. 90) and Inverso (2016, pp. 93–116).

the genesis to investigate the static constitution and its structure. This shift allows reviewing the results of static analysis from the perspective of the genesis to strengthen both approaches.

At the same time, the 'history' of the monad enables a dimension that in the context of the genetic approach is not fully thematised. On the contrary, an additional approach is required to account for this aspect. The generative approach takes history as its primary phenomenon on the horizon of the world of life, its rituals, traditions, language and inter-generational relationships.[3] This approach points to a process of generation that lasts generations, in the manner of a new absolute that becomes a crucial issue of phenomenology, according to Anthony Steinbock's characterisation (Steinbock 2003, p. 292).

Generativity does not imply a different stratum beyond static and genetic phenomenology. In fact, genetic phenomenology unfolds towards generativity by its deepening in the manner of self-improvement (Walton 2012, p. 328). This precision is useful to avoid the idea of isolated sections or topics that are externally overcome or abandoned. Indeed, it is possible to describe phenomena in their horizons, and each layer emphasises certain aspects with various devices that fit better in each dimension.

However, if the generative approach is oriented mainly to history, the sphere of exceedance is beyond this realm. The latter was considered as a meta-historical dimension since it points to what underlies the world and subjectivity. But these are not isolated spheres either (Walton 2012, p. 337). Generativity and the inapparent are not dissociated phases nor have any pretension of independence. Both come out from geneticity since they are rooted in the egological modes. This perspective leads us to the idea of phenomenology as an exhaustive work of investigation of unexplored horizons.

Why should we divide these two realms? Anthony Steinbock compresses these two spheres into a single one. He distinguishes between 'generativity' (lower case) and 'Generativity' (with an initial capital letter) (2003, p. 290). This latter category belongs to limit-phenomena such as unconsciousness, sleep, birth and death, the other, animal and vegetal life, God, etc. (Steinbock 2003, pp. 315–6). However, in so doing, the internal boundary of the stratum is not wholly clear because it deals with both the finite and the transfinite.[4] The growing attention to exceedance reveals that it is not just a segment in the shadows of historicity.

By contrast, we can change Generativity into phenomenology of the inapparent. Its central topic is what is not shown or what escapes the horizon, beyond

---

3 See Steinbock (1995, pp. 3–4), and Seebohm (2015, pp. 23–24).
4 About this methodological point, see Inverso (2018, pp. 242–257).

intentional activity. If we want to grasp this dimension, a subjective disposition that allows us to deal with the excess is needed. At the same time, it is not an oddity since exceedance underlies all appearance. For this reason, the method requires specific mechanisms that emphasise radicality and point to the very fact of givenness. Notwithstanding, it also implies a different perspective on intentionality. As a result, phenomena and their correlation become affected in their functioning. In this sense, it involves an evaluation of the limits of correlation carried out within phenomenology.

The phenomenology of the inapparent is connected with the previous phenomenological levels. It has all its developments and achievements at its disposal since it deals with the exceedance present in all phenomena. In some sense, the phenomenology of the inapparent is the most concrete dimension because it deals with that whose excess is at the base of all appearance. Viewed from the inapparent, generativity is an instantiation of its contents on the level of history. In turn, it can go back into individual historicity—that is to say, the genetic dimension—and again towards the constitutive structures of the static phenomenology. It is still possible to advance to the empirical sciences and from there to the natural attitude. In this vein, Thomas Seebohm highlights the importance of considering the connection between levels (Seebohm 2015, pp. 56–60 and pp. 390–6). The inapparent would be, in our proposal, the level that needs to be made explicit.

In this context, ontological questions linked to the being of the things in the natural attitude lead to constitutive questions, both in the static and genetic realms. The static issues result in problems of genesis, generativity and the inapparent. We can change the direction or act locally in two or more dimensions.

This point is related to progression and regression referred to by Fink in his *Sixth Cartesian Meditation* (Fink 1995, p. 11).[5] The analysis is progressive when it starts from the absolute donation and exercises an immanent intuitive reflection through which the thing itself is given as being of the consciousness (Steinbock 1995, p. 25). Critical or ontological approaches, on the other hand, apply the regressive approach. They begin from the world and the pre-given character of mundane disciplines until they reach transcendental analysis.

These different levels draw upon a primarily intentional view. However, this is passed over in the stage of the inapparent. In this context, the direction evolves into concretion, against a regressive destratification oriented to the abstract core underpinning concrete life-worldly being, as Husserl characterises nature in the texts about the *Lebenswelt* (Hua 39, pp. 326–327, Hua 15, p. 138, Hua

---

5 See also Welton (2002, pp. 227–8) and Gomes de Castro and Barbosa Gomes (2015, pp. 90–9).

Mat 8, p. 87; Walton 2012, p. 346). Thus, the progression from consciousness to meta-history and the regression from the world to the pre-intentional self-affection experience are different processes that combine themselves in the plexus of presence and absence that permeates everything, including ecstatic and non-ecstatic variants. Let us take an example dear to contemporary philosophy: Hegel's description of Napoleon's entry in Jena in 1806, where he declares: "I have seen the World Spirit on horseback". The same phenomenon can be addressed from the natural attitude or can be the object of a static phenomenological description in which acts and contents, as they are given to consciousness, prevail. Or it can be seen in its genetic dimension focusing on constitutive elements. Or it can be understood from its historical, generative dimension. Or it can be seen from the point of view of exceedance, as Hegel does, which brings us to the level of inapparency, that is, that which occurs without open manifestation.

In sum, the phenomenological analysis allows us to go from the world of life to the appearance of appearing in both directions, appealing to progressive or regressive procedures. This movement is related to the idea of a methodology supported by what Husserl calls 'zig-zag' in two striking passages, at the beginning and the end of his works. In the *Logical Investigations* and *The Crisis of European Sciences*, he uses this notion to point out the interconnection of theoretical developments that provides reciprocal light (Hua 19/2, p. 22 and Hua 6, p. 54).[6]

This view allows us to think of a broad methodological conception that fits the study of all types of phenomena. In a sort of zig-zag, directionality is clarified: the most basic and pre-reflexive *intentio* embodies the most basic model oriented to the world. It is followed by the *reflectio*, which operates the reduction and advances with reverse directionality. Thirdly, constitutive intentionality goes towards the object in a reduction regime. All this procedure is completed with a fourth movement dominated by *affectio*. It accounts for the non-primarily rational way in which things are experienced in this field.

In connection with the latter, the various dimensions of phenomenological research and their intrinsic links with method lead us to the second question regarding access to the transcendental realm, where the discussion goes back to the abandonment—or absence—of Cartesianism in Husserl's thought.[7] This

---

[6] See Gasché (1994, pp. 1–18), Sandmayer (2009, pp. 19–27). On zig-zag method as an inspiration of Heidegger discussion on the hermeneutic circle, see the mention in *Sein und Zeit* (GA 2, p. 8), and Moran (1989, pp. 21–25).
[7] On this issue, see Landgrebe (1970/2004, p. 261) and Geniusas (2012, pp. 128–134).

topic becomes a third problem associated with the ways to reduction.[8] As in the case of phenomenological levels, it should be noted that there is not an evolutionary movement or abandonment but mechanisms of access to the transcendental realm. In this manner, they are better suited to different local devices. Thus, the Cartesian way best fits the extreme levels of staticity or the inapparent. The others best fit the pursuits of geneticity and generativity precisely because they start from psychology and the world of life (Inverso 2016, pp. 93–116).

This review of the general design allows us to review the method, the phenomenon and the subject of phenomenology. The introduction of the phenomenology of the inapparent provides consistency to the overall scheme. If so, it is unnecessary to suggest to overcome or break away from the developments that deal with excess. In fact, the notion of inapparent refers to the program suggested by Heidegger at the *Zähringen Seminar* in 1973. Concerning tautological thinking, he speaks about Parmenides and invites the audience to build a phenomenology that "lets that before which it is led show itself" and states that "this phenomenology is a phenomenology of the inapparent" (GA 15, p. 399).[9] This is an exploration beyond intentional correlation – precisely what represents this fourth layer.

2 The experience of alterity

Let's go back to Michel Henry. His contributions are an indication of the relevance of the phenomenology of the inapparent. To identify its most compelling arguments, we must detach the objections and interpret them as a complement for the Husserlian developments, which emerge from the investigation of the inapparent. Let us quickly review some arguments that support this idea. As we mentioned in the previous section, Henry identifies three assumptions in Husserl's thought that deserve criticism. First, "there is other for me only if I have experience of him, if under any form or aspect, the other is given to me so that I find him in my own Life, and, in a sense, he/she is in me" (*n'y a un autre pour moi que si j'en ai une expérience, que si, sous quelque forme ou sous aspect que ce soit, l'autre m' est donné, en sorte que je le trouve daris ma propre vie et que, d 'une certaine façon, il est en moi)*" (*PhM*, p. 137). This idea echoes the

---

[8] About this topic, see Hua 1, p. 16, Hua 9, p. 294 and Hua 6, p. 212 and the discussion about the ways to the transcendental phenomenological reduction in Kern (1966), Luft (2004, pp. 198–234), and Staiti (2012).
[9] See Courtine (1993, pp. 241–257), Scheier (1993, pp. 60–74), Bassler (2001, pp. 117–133), Roesner (2006, pp. 63–88).

Epicurean argument about death as "nothing for us". It implies an impossible contact incapable of producing even the concept of death (Diogenes Laertius, X.124).[10] This is also the main tenet of Husserl's statement which claims: "these experiences [i.e. the experiences of alterity] and their results are transcendental facts of my phenomenological sphere" (*Diese Erfahrungen und ihre Leistungen sind ja transzendentale Tatsachen meiner phänomenologischen Sphäre*)" (Hua 1, p. 121).

The second assumption is not openly present in the fifth *Cartesian Meditation*, but it traverses all Husserl's works. It indicates how the other is given to me according to the intentional structure. Henry says: "to enter in my experience means: in that primordial Outside where intentionality throws itself, in that place of light where attains and sees everything which it sees (*Qu'il entre dans mon expérience, cela veut dire: dans ce Dehors primordial où se jette l'intentionalité, dans ce lieu 'de lumière où elle atteint et voit tout ce qu'elle voit*)" (*PhM*, p. 138).[11]

Lastly, the third assumption of Husserl's analysis joins the previous statements: the other is given to my experience—first assumption—as a noematic appearance in the form of intentional correlate—second assumption. In sum, according to Henry, the fifth *Cartesian Meditation* points out that the other is given to me as something transcendent. In this approach, the experience of alterity and the range of emotions arising from the presence or absence of the other—represented by the notion of pathos-with—fails to be considered. A non-affective condition cannot account for the affective aspects of the inter-pathetic Life (*PhM*, p. 141).

These assumptions reveal the weaknesses of the concrete modalities of our experience of alterity. On this basis, Henry queries how the intentional view could be a condition of something necessarily affective – i.e. the experience with the other –. In this manner, to demonstrate the limitations of the intentional approach, Henry criticises the problems of the Husserlian presentation: the determination of the ownness of the ego, the circularity in the analogising transference, and the degradations of the original ego, the body and alterity.

Henry reminds us that in the Fifth *Cartesian Meditation*, Husserl applies a "second thematic reduction" after the transcendental reduction, which brackets all the senses of my experience that refer to or were originated in "other egos".

---

[10] This allusion is connected with the discussion about the phenomenological principles in *Incarnation*, 44. On the Epicurean formula, see Warren (2004).
[11] See *Cartesian Meditations*, § 42, where Husserl claims that "we should see how, with which intentionalities, synthesis, with which motivations the sense 'other ego' emerges in me, and as 'single experience of alterity' (*einstimmiger Fremderfahrung*), appears as existent" (Hua 1, p. 121).

My body is within this sphere of property. It is the organ of my movement and the centre of my orientation. Indeed, Husserl says that intentional mediation apprehends the other through the presentation of a material or physical body in a primordial sphere as something analogous to my own body (Hua 1, p. 139 and p. 141).

The resemblance of my own body and the body of the other gives rise to a "pairing", that is, a synthesis of association of pairs. There is no knowledge of the other but an original institution of the meaning "own body" and an analogising transference that results in apprehension. Thus, the other is not a duplication of the ego but an intentional modification of myself. According to Henry, "the model which guides the self-explanation of the transcendental Ego (*l' auto-explicitacion de l'Ego*) in the reflection over itself that established the transcendental reduction is the perceptive experience of the object (*l' expérience perceptive de l'objet*) [...] towards which the gaze is directed" (*PhM*, p. 144). That is, the self-explanation of the ego is carried out in the mode of perception. Then, how can this intentional object that belongs to me be other than me, something transcendent?

Concerning the ego's ownness, Henry remarks that the grasp of self-donation within the intentional approach goes beyond the idea of a mere point of intersection of the constitutive syntheses. Hence, only the nature of the ego can say and define what is its own. However, Husserl avoids this line of research where the ego determines ownness because he associates this path with the risk of solipsism and the ego's dissociation from what is its own (*PhM*, p. 142).

Together with the paradoxical presentation of the other separated from the ego, Michel Henry indicates a second problem. To clear up the ownness of the ego, Husserl does not begin from the world. The procedure requires to discard, by abstraction from the horizon of experience, all which is alien, all which is referred to others, all which confers the character of living beings to the animals, the character of the personal beings to the human beings, and the set of features to the objects (*PhM*, p. 143). As a result, within this nature reduced to the ownness, the others are constituted realities, and I am an ego alone in front of constituted elements. Then, the ownness is reduced to the structure of the world (*PhM*, p. 143). This is clear because the model to analyse alterity is not different from the model to examine objects. From Henry's view, Husserl applies the structure of the perception to "the immediate self-revelation of the absolute subjectivity, within the inner essence of Life (*l' auto-révélation immédiate de la subjectivité absolue, à l'essence intèrieure de la vie*)" (*PhM*, p. 144).

Four points are worth noting. First, Henry asserts that Husserl correctly begins having as a common thread for his analysis the notion of *alter*. If the other is another self, I am the original ego. This view leads to the expression of a radical ipseity. Still, Henry claims that then the ego that operates the constitution is already a constituted ego that inhabits the body and makes it an organism. Strictly speaking, there is no contradiction. Instead, this raises a double way to grasp alterity, which implies a constitutive approach and enables an analysis of the dimension of the inapparent that underlies all other approaches.

By analogy, Husserl's device recognises the body of the other and connects that other body with mine within my primordial sphere (*PhM*, p. 148). In this description, Henry detects circularity since analogy presupposes the other as an organism. At the same time, the pairing present in apperceptive transference obscures the experience of alterity, given that pairing occurs amongst objects. Therefore, its use implies considering the other as an object, and putting myself also as an object (*PhM*, p. 147). Hence, it applies objective categories, degrading the original transcendental ego to a psycho-physical ego.

Moreover, there are two more levels of degradation: the degradation of the body, which is a constituted body and loses the traits of immanence and ipseity, and the degradation of the alterity, produced by the displacement of the radicality of the ego and the body (*PhM*, p. 149). This diagnosis of generalised degradation could be an indication of the need for another perspective. Indeed, Henry says that Husserl does not perform his study on the ultimate level, and therefore his research is not exhaustive. In a positive way, we can say that Husserl adopts the static and genetic views, which may be supplemented by the analysis at the level of the inapparent. Hence, the description of alterity in terms of pairing can coexist with more radical studies based on moderate intentionality. From Henry's point of view, the exploration of alterity in terms of pairing requires additional developments. These developments belong to a different dimension, but they do not compromise the validity of the outcomes from other layers of phenomenological description. The intentional analysis is not cancelled but becomes part of a broader approach that includes more radical perspectives.

Second, Henry detects in the fifth *Cartesian Meditation* an imbalance in the understanding of alterity. Unlike perception, the object that supports the transferred sense is my body and is always present, but the object to which the sense is transferred is never given but only appresented. While the perceptive experience makes the objects' pairing reversible, this does not happen in the experience of alterity. The other's appresentation gives me as co-represented his psyche along with his body, in a set of appresentations based on his nexus with presentations of my own (*PhM*, p. 150). If this is the case, the degraded body does not give an original and immanent presence. Without that persistence, Henry says, "Husserl's argument falls apart (*l'argument de Husserl se défait*)" (*PhM*, p. 151).

In fact, this step is not evident. Henry offers an internal criticism and enters into Husserl's argument, but halfway. The argument requires absolute unconstituted evidence to work. Indeed, as we saw, Henry claims that pairing occurs amongst objects. This kind of radicality, which is alien to constitutive analysis, impedes this process in the case of alterity. Hence, it would be impossible to connect absolute patency and the appresentation of the other. However, adopting a self-affective revelation model within the model of analogical transference is contradictory. We could say that what falls apart is Henry's attempt. If the goal is to cancel the analysis, the strategy is understandable. Still, it introduces an inappropriate assumption and ensuing confusion. As we have said, it would require an alternative approach to alterity in the realm of the inapparent.

Third, Henry points out that the impossibility of accessing the other's lived experience has two meanings. I cannot reach his subjectivity directly so that I appresent it. But there is also a primordial impossibility of perceiving the other's absolute subjectivity through intentionality. In fact, subjectivity always exceeds intentionality. The other is not his/her body constituted through intentionality by me. Therefore, he/she is a "noematic unreality". His/her life is not given to me either in the immanence of my life or in representation. The other is absolute transcendence. As another side of the previous objection, Henry points out that transcendental Life does not admit internal distance. Therefore, we need not an intentional approach but a view based on impression. That is, impression should substitute intention as the main phenomenological start point.

This path aims to solve the problem of transcendence and the risks of solipsism at once. However, this entails absolutising self-affective levels of phenomenological research. It compromises the legitimacy of perceptual-oriented examination, where the distance between subjectivity and phenomenon is a primary trait and should not be omitted. So, alterity shows the limitations of certain approaches and points to other levels of research, but at the same time indicates that the simple inversion that substitutes an intentional structure for impression reduces the methodological effectiveness in the case of common phenomena. Henry's explorations outside the particular domain of Life, the flesh, and its essential traits, subsist in a framework of intentionality, in the model of a conscience concerned with what appears to it.

Fourth, Henry argues that Husserl appeals to the other's appresentation from his nexus with perceptual presentations of the body perceived as an object. It would imply the paradox that instead of accessing subjectivity, the ego accesses an object. If so, this operation precludes the grasp of living and pathetic intersubjectivity. It is tied to the perceptual presentation laws and not to the "pathos of subjectivities in their internal co-belonging at the basis of Life (*les lois du 'pathos de ces subjectivités dans leur co-appartenance interne au Fond de la vie)*"

(*PhM*, p. 153). Let us insist that nothing in the phenomenological device suggests that this investigation exhausts the other's traits (*PhM*, p. 153). This point is evident in the studies of generativity, where intersubjectivity is in the foreground. As we suggest, investigations of the latent can still be added to the static, genetic and generative approaches.

This development brings us to the level of the community. Henry maintains that the community is prior to the constitution of the ipseities and monadic subjectivities so that there is strictly no intersubjectivity but a transcendental community. Henry states two cases of communities showing that the community happens at a level prior to them. Strictly speaking, there is no intersubjectivity but a transcendental community. First, he mentions the case of the admirers of Kandinsky, who never met but are united by the contemplation of an artist. This relation is not objective since it belongs to the invisible, radically subjective and immanent dimension. What prevails is "the pathos of the work (*le pathos de l'oeuvre*)" where Kandinsky as a creator, and all the members of this pathetic community, are gathered together (*PhM*, p. 154).

As a second case, he offers the example of the community with the dead. There are memory traces provoked by those we met, but there is even something that exceeds this realm. These traces are not only memories but "that pathos in us which withdraws from our acts of thinking and covertly determines them (*ce pathos en nous soustrait à nos actes de pensé et les déterminant secrètement*)" (*PhM*, p. 154). That is, there is a community with the dead that is not reducible to the logic of perception. At the same time, the rest of the dead whom we did not meet make up this community of humanity in us (*PhM*, p. 154).

The very category of "dead" blurs because the dead are not only those who have left this world but also other living members of our community "many of whom we could meet again and, in this manner, perceive again, although this new meeting would not alter their death in us, making it only more noticeable (*la rendant seulement plus sensible*)" (*PhM*, p. 154). Then, death is not merely the absence of life. It is a more complex state that coexists with it in pathetic immanence and tends to be omitted in a techno-scientific age that interprets everything in objectual terms. However, the case of the community with the dead is not a good example. Husserl himself pointed out that empathy cannot be applied to the case of the dead or the unborn, who play a fundamental role in the projection of political communities, according to the basic model. Still, it is possible to do so through intentional modifications (Walton 2012, p. 327).

Through these intentional modifications, the dead and the unborn can become familiar. The generative approach to intersubjectivity explores the constitution of historical sense focusing on tradition as the narrative dimension of the chain of generations (Hua 15, pp. 145 and 472–475).[12] Thus, the diversity of dimensions implies the inconvenience of absolutising any of them. Following Husserl's path, we could say that Henry detects the multiple dimensions of analysis. The overall Husserlian view coincides with this diagnosis. Intersubjectivity can be seen as empathy, as generative plexus, and even, as in Henry's project, as a phenomenon with exceedance oriented to the self-affective dimension of Life. In any case, there are complementary levels that should not provoke collisions with Husserl's approach. It is worth noting that some critical lines that seek to demolish it end up reinforcing its basis. In this sense, the scope of material phenomenology regarding foundation justifies the intentional analysis in other levels and never denies their validity. On the contrary, this approach invites us to think about the link between these levels.

Henry claims that perception should be substituted by affection, not based on a noetic or noematic presentation. It is not associated with intentionality and constitution but it refers to "the donation that consist of the transcendental affectivity and thus in Life itself (*une donation consistant dans l'affectivité transcendantale et ainsi dans la vie elle-même*)", which is the way to grasp "the real being of the other in me (*l' être réel de l'autre en moi*)" (*PhM*, p. 155). In this view, the community is an experience incompatible with representation. It is related to the hypnotic trance where intentionality becomes suspended so that community is the blind pathos of Life where the elements of self, other and background occur together.

With these arguments, Henry declares the failure of the noetic-noematic presentation of otherness associated with intentionality and constitution. Strikingly, he claims that Husserl acknowledged this failure. On the one hand, Husserl would have recognised the problem of reducing the real being to unreality, a mere "correlate of an intentional mention (*le corrélat d'une visée intentionnelle*)" (*PhM*, p. 157). For that reason, he would have insisted that the original community is nothing, but "being with another in an intentional community" (*PhM*, p. 157). This view would imply an admitted failure or at least a perceived and silenced inconvenience. If we change the angle, Husserl's assertion could be a legitimation of generative studies.

Moreover, Henry detects a second example of Husserl's recognition of his failure in his suggestion of a hidden enigma in the inter-monadic distance. If there is such distance, we should stop all analysis of the other's experience or deny it because it is affected by an enigma. Therefore, we would only have the experience of excess. However, this is not a sign of a failure of the noematic pre-

---

[12] On the notions of community and pathos-with, see Fainstein Lamuedra (2011, pp. 186–190).

sentation of alterity but, again, another indication of an additional field of inquiry. Husserl detects an enigma whose examination is fulfilled in another dimension of analysis. Indeed, "the enigma only emerges when both original spheres have been distinguished, and this is a distinction that entails that the experience of the other has accomplished its task" (*PhM*, p. 207).[13]

Indeed, Henry claims that intentional phenomenology fails to understand the tie amongst living beings, because Life—and not intentionality—links its products in its radical immanence. However, it could be said that intentionality is amongst those products, and the intentional analysis should be considered a mode of its self-donation. In this sense, it is as valid to focus on the ultimate source, the background, as on the local movements through intentional analysis. Henry highlights the irreducible heterogeneity of immanence regarding the transcendent manifestation. On the contrary, we could underline a primal coexistence within the phenomenological method. This method includes mechanisms to describe different realms of phenomena, from staticity, geneticity and generativity until their immanent, inapparent basis.

3 Conclusions

Phenomenology describes phenomena and even considers the way of looking at what is not shown. Thus, it is possible to diffuse Henry's condemnation against the noematic presentation by accepting its terms to explore alterity in the constitutive intentional framework. This frame contains marks of the "enigmatic" traits that must be solved in other levels, deepening their radicality. In sum, Henry's ideas are an example of a broader turn towards exceedance. He condemns all genetic and generative developments on intersubjectivity because intentional parameters would trap them. In the latter case, generativity is not radical enough to be the soil of the genetic dimension. Faced with this, in the line of the distinction between generativity and Generativity, with a capital letter suggested by Steinbock, it is possible to solve this ambiguity by establishing a dimension of the study of the inapparent (1995, pp. 315 ff.). This field is an approach on its own, but at the same time, it cooperates with the other approaches. Any friction typical of the early stages of a theoretical field can be left behind.

Early stages usually involve taking distance from the previous ideas to stress the novelties. This resource is valuable because it takes advantage of what is already known. Still, if this stage of negativity continues, it begins to mark a break,

---

[13] This is a reference to Hua 1, p. 150.

as is the case of the so-called "theological" or "onto-theological" turn.[14] The phenomenological explorations on the limits of intentionality and exceedance should not be considered any more deviations that turn against the previous ground. Defined positively, these are phenomenological studies on the inapparent, understood as a legitimate level in a four-dimensional Phenomenology.

This analysis shows the accuracy of Henry's opinion: "phenomenology distrusts of ultimate explanations and is devoted mainly to description issues. But a description that misses the essence of the 'thing itself', in this case the concrete intersubjectivity, cannot be legitimate not even on the level of facticity" (*PhM*, p. 158).

The way out of this situation requires redefining the basic terms of the discipline to include the new elements. If so, the ideas associated with "turns", the attempts of non-intentional phenomenologies, as well as all the explorations on exceedance, are not deviations that attack the common bases. They are positive explorations on the phenomenology of the inapparent, which have a legitimate space and enhance the power of phenomenology as a whole.

References

Bassler, O. Bradley (2001): "The Birthplace of Thinking: Heidegger's Late Thoughts on Tautology". In: *Heidegger Studies* 17, pp. 117–133.
Courtine, Jean (1993): "Phenomenology and/or tautology". In: Sallis, John (Ed.): *Reading Heidegger: Commemorations*. Bloomington: Indiana University Press, pp. 241–277.
Fainstein Lamuedra, Graciela (2011): "Alteridad, intersubjetividad y comunidad en la vida en el pensamiento de Michel Henry". In: *Investigaciones fenomenológicas* 3, pp. 186–190.
Fink, Eugen (1995): *Sixth Cartesian Meditation*. Ronald Bruzina (Ed.). Bloomington: Indiana University Press.
Gasché, Rodolphe (1994): "On Re-presentation, or Zigzagging with Husserl and Derrida". In: *The Southern Journal of Philosophy* 32, pp. 1–18
Geniusas, Saulius (2012): *The Origins of the Horizon in Husserl's Phenomenology*. Dordrecht: Springer.
Gomes de Castro, Thiago/Gomes Barbosa, William (2015): "Da intencionalidade da consciencia ao método progressivo regressivo em Husserl". In: *Psicologia USP* 26(1), pp. 90–99.
Heidegger, Martin (1977): *Sein und Zeit*. Friedrich-Wilhelm von Herrmann (Ed.). *Gesaumtausgabe* 2. Frankfurt: Vittorio Klostermann. [GA 2]
Heidegger, Martin (1986): *Seminare* (1951–1973). Curd Ochwadt (Ed.). Gesamtausgabe 15. Frankfurt: Vittorio Klostermann. [GA 15]

---

[14] On this topic, see Janicaud (1991), Schrijvers (2011), Restrepo (2010, pp. 115–26), and Inverso (2018, pp. 217–25).

Henry, M. (1990) *Phénoménologie matérielle*. Paris: Presses Universitaires de France. [*PhM*]
Husserl, Edmund (1950): *Cartesianische Meditationen und Pariser Vorträge*. Stephan Strasser (Ed.). Husserliana I. The Hague: Martinus Nijhoff. [Hua 1]
Husserl, Edmund (1954): *Die Krisis der europäischen Wissenschaften und die transzendentale Phänomenologie: Eine Einleitung in die phänomenologische Philosophie*. Walter Biemel (Ed.). Husserliana VI. The Hague: Martinus Nijhoff. [Hua 6]
Husserl, Edmund (1962): *Phänomenologische Psychologie*. Walter Biemel (Ed.). Husserliana IX. The Hague: Martinus Nijhoff. [Hua 9]
Husserl, Edmund (1973a): *Zur Phänomenologie der Intersubjektivität. Texte aus dem Nachlass. Zweiter Teil: 1921–28*. Iso Kern (Ed.). Husserliana XIV. The Hague: Martinus Nijhoff. [Hua 14]
Husserl, Edmund (1973b): *Zur Phänomenologie der Intersubjektivität. Texte aus dem Nachlass. Dritter Teil: 1929–35*. Iso Kern (Ed.). Husserliana XV. The Hague: Martinus Nijhoff. [Hua 15]
Husserl, Edmund (1984): *Logische Untersuchungen*. Vol. 2. Ursula Panzer (Ed.). Husserliana XIX/2. The Hague: Martinus Nijhoff. [Hua 19/2]
Husserl, Edmund (2008): *Die Lebenswelt*. Rochus Sowa (Ed.). Husserliana XXXIX. Dordrecht: Springer. [Hua 39]
Inverso, Hernán (2016): "La fenomenología de lo inaparente y el problema de las vías hacia el plano trascendental". In: *Eidos* 26, pp. 93–116.
Inverso, Hernán (2018): *Fenomenología de lo inaparente*. Buenos Aires: Prometeo.
Janicaud, Dominique (1991): *Le Tournant théologique de la phénoménologie française*. Combas: Éd. de l'Éclat.
Kern, Iso (1966): "The Three Ways to the Transcendental Phenomenological Reduction in the Philosophy of Edmund Husserl". In: Elliston, Frederick/McCormick, Peter. (Eds.): *Husserl: Exposition and Appraisals*. Notre Dame: University of Notre Dame Press, pp. 126–149.
Landgrebe, Ludwig (1970/2004), "Husserl's departure from Cartesianism". In: Moran, Dermot/Embree, Lester (Eds.): *Phenomenology: Critical concepts in philosophy* 5: *Heritage of phenomenology*. London, New York: Routledge.
Luft, Sebastian (2004): "Husserl's Theory of the Phenomenological Reduction: Between life-world and Cartesianism". In: *Research in Phenomenology* 34(1), pp. 198–234.
Marion, Jean-Luc (1989): *Reduction et donation*. Paris: Presses Universitaires de France.
Moran, Dermot (2005): *Edmund Husserl: Founder of Phenomenology*. Cambridge: Polity Press.
Restrepo, Carlos (2010): "El giro teológico de la fenomenología". In: *Pensamiento y cultura* 13(2), pp. 115–126.
Roesner, Martina (2006): "De la tautologie: Heidegger et la question de l'esprit". In: *Les Études Philosophiques* 76(1), pp. 66–88.
Sandmayer, Bob (2009): *Husserl's Constitutive Phenomenology: Its Problem and Promise*. London, New York: Routledge.
Scheier, Claus (1993): "Die Sprache spricht. Heideggers Tautologien". In: *Zeitschrift für philosophische Forschung* 47, pp. 60–74.
Schrijvers, Joeri (2011): *Ontotheological Turnings? The Decentering of the Modern Subject in Recent French Phenomenology*. New York: Author House.
Seebohm, Thomas (2015): *History as a Science and the System of the Sciences: Phenomenological Investigations*. Dordrecht: Springer.

Staiti, Andrea (2012): "The Pedagogic Impulse of Husserl's Ways into Transcendental Phenomenology". In: *Graduate Faculty Philosophy Journal* 33(1), pp 39–56.

Steinbock, Anthony (1995): *Home and Beyond: Generative Phenomenology After Husserl*. Evanston: Northwestern University Press.

Steinbock, Anthony (2003): "Generativity and the Scope of Generative Phenomenology". In: Welton, Donn (Ed.): *The New Husserl: A Critical Reader*. Bloomington: Indiana University Press, pp. 289–325.

Walton, Roberto (2012): "Teleología y teología en Edmund Husserl". In: *Estudios de filosofía* 45, pp. 81–103.

Warren, James (2004): *Facing Death. Epicurus and his Critics*. Oxford: Oxford University Press.

Welton, Donn (2002): *The Other Husserl: The Horizons of Transcendental Phenomenology*. Bloomington: Indiana University Press.

Perception, emotion, and trust

Felix Ó Murchadha
Listening to Others: Music and the Phenomenology of Hearing

Abstract: This chapter explores listening through a phenomenological account of sound and rhythm, showing a musical structure in experience. This structure follows the rhythm of a sequence, leading the listener through an event of meaning that allows an other to appear as a self within a temporally constituted sequence of sense. While subject to such relations, listening is constitutively directed towards re-sensing, because we hear in terms of virtualities, whereby sense contains the power of new and unheard of meaning in each moment of its appearance. Such sense appears acoustically in an affective register between joy and despair, forming affective atmospheres, in which emotions are expressed in a manner irreducible to narrative context. The situation described here is characterized by a certain rhythm in which awareness is directed not so much to the corporeal boundaries of self and other but to the event of movement in which each person finds themselves.

Being in the world is to be immersed in sound. Even the most silent moments have aural rhythms. We hear the world around us before we listen to a particular voice, a rustle of something light, the thud of a heavy object or the organic movement of inhaling and exhaling. Prior to any particular content of the sound to which we listen, be it the coming of a storm, the flight of a flock of swans, the request of a friend, we hear things in the materiality of their sound. But the relation to this materiality differs from that which we experience in vision and in touch. In the latter, boundaries of inner and outer, self and other, are maintained even in the act of transgressing them. While both sight and touch in different ways tend toward keeping their objects at a distance, beyond the embodied being of the self; through hearing phenomena penetrate into me, as I diffuse myself aurally in the world through voice and movement. The world of sound is dynamic, lacking clear boundaries.

The world of sound is not simply that which we hear through our aural sense organs, it is a world which we feel, around us and within us, but one which is characterized not by the solidity of things but by relations of temporal implication and change. This is possible because in sound the spatial relation is infused with temporality. In hearing, I am aware of a coming to be (beginning) of sound, the duration of a particular series of sounds (enduring), the fragility of this sounding (decaying) and of the manner in which sound impacts on me and on others (encountering). Sound comes to me spatially, i.e. as that which arises elsewhere or from within, as when I feel the sound of my own breathing, but precisely in its diffuseness over space, in hearing I am subjected to the temporal rhythms of sound and their becoming expressive as tone.

In this paper, I wish to look to music to help us reflect phenomenologically on such worlds of sound. Music is being understood here as that human creation which allows us to discover the world of tone and rhythm, music understood as that artistic form which opens us to the musicality of nature and everyday life. What is at issue here is the structure and logic of tone and rhythm that forms the manner in which we hear the world, in which the world is audible to us. In the context of such a world, then, the question will be how others are manifest to a self for whom from the beginning tone overflows any barriers between it and the world, such that it exists in a world tonally constitutive of it.

This chapter is divided into four parts. The first part will discuss in broad terms the appeal to art in phenomenologically reflecting on phenomena, on the phenomenological reduction as related to music and the relevance of this to questions concerning empathy (1). The second part will then turn to sound (2). The third part will deal with rhythm (3), followed by a short conclusion (4).

1 Art, Phenomenology and a Musical Reduction

It is striking that phenomenologists after Husserl have repeatedly had recourse to art within their phenomenological reflections. It is not simply that they have 'done' a phenomenology of art; rather for each art in some way made possible the bringing to appearance of the event of appearing more generally. Whether with Heidegger's discussion of van Gogh's shoes or Merleau-Ponty's analysis of Cézanne's paintings of Mont St. Victoire or Henry's reflections on Kandinsky's move to abstraction – to name just the most prominent examples – art revealed what remains hidden in normal experience.

Interestingly, in the cases of Heidegger, Merleau-Ponty and Henry, the recourse to art comes after their early major works, which have relatively little to say about art (*Being and Time*, *Phenomenology of Perception* and the *Essence of Manifestation* respectively). In the case of each, art is a way of returning to the themes of these major works, to find a way of either deepening or transforming their insights. The reason art can function like this is not hard to find. If phenomenology begins with appearance, if its goal is to clarify the appearing of appearance, then the philosopher is coming late to territory already populated by the artist. The artist works with the material of appearing, whether color, figure, space, movement, time, sound, to produce a work or to perform an event in which those very materials are brought thematically to appearance. Above all, art breaks with the everyday, but does so in such a way as to allow the viewer, the audience, the participant to reflect back onto the everyday, allowing the everyday to be de-constructed (*Abbau*) and rebuilt again. In phenomenological terms, what it achieves is a phenomenological reduction. Art allows for both a break with the everyday and a reflection on the constitution of appearance. We see this being affirmed by Heidegger when he states that in the proximity of the artwork we are suddenly somewhere unaccustomed (Heidegger 2002, p. 15), by Merleau-Ponty who speaks of Cezanne's paintings as reducing the world to the totality of frozen appearances (Merleau-Ponty 1964, p. 20) and by Henry when he says of painting that it allows us to see "what is not seen and cannot be seen" (Henry 2009, p. 11).

The artist works on certain material in order to produce the relationality of, and to, the world in such a manner that we can perceive it. In so doing, the artist performs a reduction in the very act of production. The history of art seems to have involved – in the West at least – a separating out of the senses, such that music has become the art of the sense of listening, while dance is that of movement, and poetry of listening within the practice of reading. Painting has become the art of sight, the reconstitution of the world on the basis of color and figures.

Music produces a world of sound and in so doing brings the event of sound to appearance. In music we enter a world primarily constituted by sound and rhythm. Music works on sound, sound is its material. Art has the capacity to work material sometimes against the grain, so as to produce on its basis that which appears foreign to the material. Color and lines on canvas can produce the representation of three dimensional figures in a two dimensional medium. Sound is one dimensional – fundamentally temporal – yet it can represent (spatially defined) entities, events, abstract ideas and emotions (Kivy 1991, p. 100). Following Adam Smith, the musicologist Peter Kivy argues that part of the aesthetic quality of music is precisely the recalcitrance of its medium (Kivy 1991, pp. 97–98). This has an interesting consequence: if art works with but also against its material, it functions at once to reveal and to hide that material. In a manner related to language, music employs sound to articulate the happening of aural experience. What allows it to do this is in part what separates it from language: while linguistic sounds have general meanings in the form of conceptual sense, music has emotional sense, awakens a primarily emotional response (see Cooke 1962, p. 26). This is not to say that music has no intelligible sense, but this sense does not relate directly to conceptual meaning defining an object. Abstract ideas in music are ideas without objects, ideas expressed as feeling.

The question then is what characterizes a world sensed, understood and lived in, with a primary orientation to sound? Francis Wolff imagines a cave as that of Plato's, except a cave of sound not vision. The prisoners in an aural cave could only make their world comprehensible by an act of production: making sound (Wolff 2015, p. 44). To understand the world of sound is not to see through the eyes of the intellect, reflecting on the paradoxes of sense experience, but rather it is to engage in the activity of making sound and rhythm, to engage in a rudimentary fashion in the art of music making. In the absence of such activity, there are sounds but these are indistinct, the relations of inner and outer remain inarticulate, there is no distinction between the real and the imaginary. As Wolff puts it: "[I]n the temporal sequence there is no point of reference which would permit the individualization of events [of sound]" (Wolff 2015, p. 36) and while color and form are immediate qualities of things, sounds are aural qualities of events. It is only through an act of making sounds that these events can be reproduced in an ordered manner, individuating the sounds and their relations to each other. In this sense, music performs a reduction of the multiplicity of aural impressions – the noise all around us – to the sounds which make them up and orders them in tonal relations. This appears as a peculiar reduction, because it operates not actively, not by reflection, but rather by the production of sound as tone (see Ó Murchadha 2018, pp. 185–7).

This reduction seems peculiar, however, only if we fail to take seriously Husserl's repeated declaration that the reduction is something that needs to be performed. The philosopher for Husserl performs it reflectively, in the sense that she unnaturally reverses her view; the musician, on the other hand, is concerned with moving forward. The phenomenological reduction in Husserl's terms is concerned not with the production of sense as rather, so to speak, with the retracing of that production, backwards to its origins. In this sense the reduction, is, as Merleau-Ponty puts it, a stepping back "in order to see transcendences spring forth" (Merleau-Ponty 2013, p. lxxvii), which needs first to be lived. And what music tells us in this living performance is that the object of aural perception is not a thing but an event, not an entity but the (audible) expression of that entity or a plurality of entities. For Plato's cave to account for sound, it is not enough for images to be projected on a screen, there needs first to be music. We think of the cave as a realm of illusion, and yet that which produces the illusion is real. The illusion is not the image, but the taking of the image as real. But in the case of aural perception, there is no place behind the backs of the prisoners which can count as real: nothing which happens behind the prisoners can be less real than that which occurs before them. While the visual scene is a production on the screen before them but is perceived as not being such a production, the audible phenomenon is of necessity a production and can only be perceived as such.

Music places sound beyond the level of the actual in the sense of physical causation and brings it to a level of the imaginary or the virtual, where the relations of sounds to one another are no longer relations of simple physical contiguity, but are relations of sense in which the one sound 'motivates' the other.[1] In listening to a piece of music, I am not attending to the manner in which each individual sound is caused by the instrument playing it, but rather am focused on the way in which one sound causes or leads to another, that dynamic relation of tones through which melody is formed. In Roger Scruton's words, we listen to music by "attending to sounds without focusing on their material causes" (Scruton, 2007, p. 229). In doing this, material causality is replaced with virtual causality, the objects in the world are displaced in favor of the melody, harmony and rhythm of their coming to be as sounds. Both with respect to production and reception there is here an intertwining of actual and virtual, perceptual and imaginary, which makes the object of aural perception neither simply the physical object nor an idea, but the physical object as idea or the object as expression.

We will return in more detail to questions of sound, tone and rhythm below, but first it is important to show how such a musical reduction can be employed. The crucial claim being made here is that music allows the materiality of sound to come to appearance. When an other is heard, the sounds she makes are not simply experienced as disturbances of the aural sphere, but rather as expressive of herself as a being in relation to the perceiver. This is the case whether the sounds are immediately voluntary or not. Clearly when someone speaks she is willingly making sounds, when she walks or gestures with her hand she may also make sounds which, though not immediately voluntary – she did not directly intend to make that particular sound –, are expressions of her willed bodily movement. But the sounds she makes are expressions of her being that are beyond or rather below the level of volition: from accent to timbre to rhythm and affective color, the sound of someone expresses her being in ways that are often more apparent to others than to the person herself. They are habituated embodied modes of being, which express a concrete orientation toward the world, beyond the specific content of particular spoken words or discrete gestures toward. It is precisely this expressive world of the other to which empathetic sense at-

---

[1] The relation of cause here is that which Husserl describes as the "lawfulness of the life of the spirit", namely, 'motivation'. Understood as such, perception receives expression or rather "expression and expressed as a totality" in "concordant experience" (Husserl 1990, p. 245).

tends. As Elisa Magrì puts it, "from a phenomenological point of view, empathy implies that we attend not just to features of perception but also to ... the affective world of the other subject" (Magrì 2019, p. 335). Music by bringing to bear a reduction allows the elements that give aural expression to such an affective world, to be reflectively brought to appearance.

It is the case that music, like any other art form, has a history and looking to music for relations of appearance we are looking at a phenomenon embedded contingently in certain sedimented practices. Within the Western tradition the domain of music is generally restricted and compartmentalized, excluding poetry and dance, distinguishing with varying degrees of sharpness between song and instrumental music. This development broke with the original sense of *musiké* in Greek culture. The musicologist, Thrasyboulos Georgiades, shows how the original Greek sense of *musiké* included not alone dance but language also, so that the distinction of poetry and prose is already indicative of a breakdown in its original sense (see Georgiades 1982, pp. 5–7). While I cannot go into these issues in this paper, this insight is important for us in indicating the wider sense of rhythm beyond what we would consider to be music, particularly as it is manifest in speech, and also that music has a bodily sense manifest in dance. With respect to language, Georgiades states that "the Greek verse line was a linguistic and simultaneously a musical reality. The connecting element, common to language and music, was rhythm." As he goes on to explain, in Ancient Greek the "individual syllables could neither be extended nor abbreviated. They were by nature long or short ... The substantive concrete aspect of the ancient Greek language was its musically concreted rhythm" (Georgiades 1982, p. 4). If there is a language of music, it is one which has separated from everyday language and indeed through the employment of language in Christian ritual it has been employed to mark that difference. While speech becomes more subjective in the sense of more liberated from musical rhythm, the performance of speech in proclaiming the "word of god" needed to be fixed musically in order to at once distance it from everyday speech and give sacred speech a sense of inviolability (c.f. Georgiades 1982, pp. 7, 10, 16).

Music and language are two sides of the Greek *musiké*, the inner unity of which remains foreign to Western modernity. This manifests itself in respect to language which for the Ancient Greek, Georgiades concludes, must have felt more powerful than the speaker, each word having its own rhythmic sense, such that it spoke things through the speaker (Georgiades 1958, p. 43).[2] In speak-

---

[2] Not accidently here, of course, we are reminded of Heidegger's dictum: "*Die Sprache spricht* (language speaks)" (Heidegger 2001, p. 198).

ing about music, specifically about music as a phenomenological reduction, we are speaking also about the power of language primordial to our sense of control over our speech. That power of language, manifest in its inner musicality, is that which resists us both in our speaking and our listening, is the materiality of rhythm and sound, traced in the linguistic utterances of the other and in that which remains other to me in my own speech. This materiality is made manifest musically in a way that shows the pre-propositional address primordial to articulated sense. Therein lies a level of expressivity, which cannot be captured conceptually.

2 Sound

Before introducing his famous keyhole example, Sartre in discussing the gaze of the other describes the other's appearance first in aural terms: "I apprehend immediately when I *hear the branches crackling* behind me ... that I am vulnerable ... that I am seen" (Sartre 1992, p. 347 [my emphasis]). When he comes to the case of the man disturbed in the act of spying through the keyhole, he states: "all of a sudden I *hear footsteps* in the hall. Someone is looking at me" (Sartre 1992, p. 349 [my emphasis]). I hear myself being seen, because it is through sound that I am aware of a world as the limit of my perceptual consciousness, but a world that already penetrates me. In hearing, I know myself as vulnerable to a world in which I am always already exposed. Before being seen, I am summoned by a sound which is coming from elsewhere, yet against which I can offer no protection.

Music produces sound and tone. Tone, as the musicologist, Victor Zukerkandl points out, is the only experience of our senses which belongs exclusively to life, is peculiarly expressive of living beings. Non-living things have light, color, sound, odor and taste, but "living beings, out of themselves, add tone to the physical world that confronts them" (Zukerkandl 1969, p. 1). Tone is not mere sound nor is it sound utilized to signify something else such as the tapping of a Morse code on metal pipes. Rather, tone is the making expressive of sound through its being produced as meaningful. What music produces through such a productive reduction is not alone sound and tone, but the relation of tone to tone, the relations which make an aural sense, in order to reduce the aural to its constituent elements and show the inner relations of those elements. The production of sound in actual things is transferred to those things created for no other reason than to create musical sound. The violin or the piano or the oboe are made in terms of a range of tones, high and low, which they create. The human body itself can be molded for the same purpose, specifically in the case of the voice trained to sing.

As we have seen, music places sound beyond the level of the actual in the sense of physical causation and brings it to a level of the imaginary or the virtual, where the relations of sound to one another are no longer relations of simple physical causation, but are relations of sense in which the one sound motivates the other. In listening to a piece of music I am not attending to the manner in which each individual sound is caused by the instrument playing it, but rather to the way in which one sound leads to another, that dynamic relation of tones through which melody is formed. It is this totality of expression and expressed toward which consciousness turns; it is that spiritual unity which draws consciousness attentively to it. In the realm of sound this relation of motivation is ontologically constitutive of the object itself. While a visual object can motivate the perceiver in different ways – left or right, up or down, in or out, such that the temporal relation of the perceiver's impressions is independent from the reality of the thing – in the case of sound, to listen is to follow the irreversible motivational direction whereby one sound brings about the next, where the logic of the present and future sound is contained virtually in the melody and musical structure of the sounds just past. Listening in this way is an awareness – not necessarily attentive, it can be unconscious – of a meaningful pattern in sound that operates protentially by a relation of waiting on the future sound, on the coming climax of the piece, on the recurring theme of the sonata or movement (see Wiskus 2019, pp. 403 – 4). But the necessity of these relations depends not on the discrete physical causal actions whereby sounds are produced, but rather on an imaginary web of relations. These relations receive their sense from a dynamic whereby one tone appears as an occurrence virtually suggested by the previous one. Indeed, as Francis Wolff states, "to understand a piece of music is simply and wholly to hear that imaginary causality" (Wolff 2015, p. 162). Such a causality is imaginary in the sense that it is not explainable in physical terms. This causality is rather such that one note contains virtually within itself the notes that arise from it in the course of the melody, forming, as it were, an aural image which is temporal rather than spatial, musical rather than pictorial.

The nature of a melody is to give a promise of meaning, which introduces a tension that the melody resolves in its ending (see Zukerkandl 1969, p. 19). That promise of meaning calls me to wait, while the piece endures in sound, letting me anticipate the course toward an ending in which each note opens up possible futures (finite but plural), of which only one will be realized. In listening, therefore, I am subject, and must subject myself, to the sound itself as melody but also as harmony, cadence, meter, rhythm, tempo, beat, pitch, as an aural pattern of sense is set out. To hear a piece of music is to hear those imaginary relations and to follow them. In following the piece, I am following an order of sound that calls me to 'obedience' – obedience, i.e., submission to another, is a fundamentally aural relation. This is suggested not simply by etymology (*ob-audire*), but also by the fact that while seeing and touch immediately bring me into relations of things with qualities (this red ball, that tall man, this smooth desk), hearing does not relate me to things but rather to events of sound, in which the relations are between sounds. I can perceive this only if I follow their imaginary relations thereby giving myself over to the sense – the articulate intelligibility and above all the directionality – of the sound relation. Crucial here is the dynamic nature of musical meaning. Again to quote Zuckerkandl: "Musical tones are conveyors of forces. Hearing music means hearing an action of forces" (Zuckerkandl 1969, p. 37). To hear musical meaning is to follow the directionality of sense, anticipating the next tone guided by an aural understanding which hears meaning in the notes being played. This is to say that in hearing I am attending to a particular kind of incompleteness: while visually incompletion is overcome through addition – I walk around the desk so as to see it from every angle – aurally "what is lacking must appear *in place of* what is given ... the auditory-incomplete can become complete only by the fact that what is lacking *succeeds* to the datum." As such "to hear incompleteness is to hear time" (Zukerkandl 1969, p. 253). While temporal duration is necessary to perceive visibly and tangibly, in aural terms the objects themselves are temporal objects containing "temporal extension in themselves", as Husserl states (Husserl 2019, p. 43).

In 'obedience' to that meaning and directionality of sense, I am already drawn into the event of sound. Sound penetrates me, resonates through me, bathes and – in certain cases – tortures me. As Jean-Luc Nancy puts: "Sound ... is not first 'intentioned': on the contrary, sound is what places its subject, which has not preceded it with an aim, in tension or under tension" (Nancy 2007, p. 20). In listening, I am attentive to that which is outside of itself in that to which I am listening: "something (itself) that identifies itself by resonating from self to self, in itself and for itself, hence outside of itself, at once the same as an other than itself, one in the echo of the other" (Nancy 2007, p. 9).

In listening to music, I am listening to nothing which can be given precise conceptual form. Music is pre-conceptual: it is not possible to render a specific scene musically in terms of its descriptive content or make an argument or even describe feelings of love or hatred or sadness or joy directed at a particular object. Following those musicologists who affirm the representational capacity of music (and setting aside the issue of representing specific types of entities and events), it seems evident that music expresses emotion.[3] But it expresses emotion independently from the relation to particular objects. We can say of a particular piece of music that it expresses sadness or joy or happiness or rage or desire or anxiety or anguish, but it is difficult to find music which expresses jealousy or pity or resentment or embarrassment. The more the emotion indicates a general atmosphere or mood, the more clearly it can find musical expression; the more the emotion relates to specific objects, the less music can express it (except, of course, vocally through the words of song). It makes sense to speak of being sad or joyful or enraged or happy or desiring or anxious without the sense of these emotions being dependent on specific objects, while resentment or jealousy or pity or embarrassment are necessarily transitive, referring to an object or a plurality of objects. The emotions music expresses, on the other hand, form affective atmospheres, in which we can find emotions expressed in a manner which is irreducible to a narrative context, i.e., it expresses something essential about the emotion itself. It is in this sense that Felix Mendelssohn can say that "the thoughts expressed by the music that I love are not too imprecise to be put into words, but on the contrary too precise" (Mendelssohn 1867, p. 276; see also Cooke 1962, p. 12 and Wolff 2015, p. 249). It is clear from his further discussion in this letter that what Mendelssohn means by 'thoughts' are feelings, such as resignation, melancholy and praise of god. Such feelings are those that the composer wishes to express and in listening to the music we hear it well, when we apprehend that specific emotional expression. As the musicologist Deryck Cooke puts it, in listening to the funeral march in Beethoven's Eroica symphony, the particular manner in which he employed the C minor key will arouse "the listener's capacity for experiencing grief ...into feeling ... the person grief of Beethoven made incarnate in that music" (Cooke 1961, p. 19). Note the emphasis on the listener's capacity, which he parses as "sympathetic understanding" (Cooke 1961, p. 21, n. 1), i.e., the listener's empathetic capacity to grasp the music as expressive of a particular emotional experience or, as Cooke puts it, "the supreme expression of universal emotions, in an entirely personal way" (Cooke 1961, p. 32).

What happens in music is the particular expression of universal emotions, expressing the emotion not in its relation to this or that object, but rather in itself as pure feeling. In other words, in music there is the expression of emotion independent of both the actual feeling of the listener (who feels the grief of a fu-

---

[3] This is not of course a universally held position amongst musicologists, particularly for those of the formalist tradition for whom music is, in Eduard Hanslick's terms, "sounding form in motion [*tönend bewegte Formen*]" (Hanslick 1986, p. 74) For an account of the history of this debate see Kerman 1998.

neral march without actually herself grieving) and any relation to a specific object. In that sense in listening to a piece of music, we understand the world of the piece in which we find ourselves as colored by the emotions expressed. This is experienced independently of any emotional response the perceiver may have to it: I can hear joy expressed in Bach's Orchestral Suite No. 2 in B Minor, while feeling myself sad, or sadness expressed in Mozart's Sonata No. 8 in A Minor, while feeling myself happy. Wolff refers to this as the climate, the "tonality of the world" of the piece, *in which* I find myself while listening to it (Wolff 2015, p. 259). In listening to a piece of music a further reduction is achieved, a reduction from the engaged emotions of the everyday to the affective situation of a mood peculiar to the world of the singular piece of music, to which I am listening. My attention is focused not on my feelings but on the feeling being expressed by the music. This is achieved musically through the use of major and minor keys which supply the fundamental orientations of pleasure and pain on which the emotional syntax of music is based. The interplay of major and minor keys, the harmonizing effects of this interplay and the various expressive affects of the tones on both the major and minor scales allow for the remarkable emotional range of musical expression, which makes possible many variations of emotional expression along the continuum of pleasure and pain. As Cooke states, "a composer does not express pleasure or pain simply by using the major or minor system, but by bringing forward and emphasizing certain tensions in these systems" (Cooke 1964, p. 94).

In listening, I am hearing these resonating relations. I listen to sound structured meaningfully, musically, identifying the temporal flow of a particular imaginary relation of sounds, following its coming to be, awaiting its fulfilling meaning, reveling in its expression of joy, awed at the somber tones of despair or anguish. Such hearing is a following of imaginary causation, of hearing the series of sounds in their inner relation to one another, as individual series of sounds distinct from others around them, and as sense bearing or rather as sense traced in the sound, the mix of sound and sense (see Nancy 2007, pp. 6–7). What music thematizes here, is that which remains below my listening consciousness within the context of everyday interactions. In attending to the content of their words or the visible gestures of their bodies, I hear the melody of another's voice, and therein a direction of sense irreducible to the meaning of their words, I hear in short the materiality of their aural expression. In coming into a room, I hear the intersubjective symphony of these voices and immediately understand the mood as joyful or somber, peaceful or enraged, hopeful or despairing. On coming upon a conversation, I can hear the tone as friendly or hostile before being able to make sense of the words – indeed, at times the words themselves are at odds with the tone I hear. It is in this tone that I hear something which is distinct from the expressed conceptual sense, but without which the latter cannot be said.

In listening to an other, I am hearing her in the musicality of her being when I follow in her singular expression the directedness of sense by which her sound leads me. In doing so I follow the singular expression of love, of hate, of joy, of despair. The joy, the despair, the sadness, the hope expressed in her voice has sense for me because I can recognize and follow it. In that way, it is more or less foreseeable for me, but I have no option but to wait upon it or to give up on her expressive being. The direction of sense expressed by her being is one that I cannot enact from my position because constitutive of it is its temporal structure and hence its irreversibility. The other's sense is that which I cannot hear all at once, but which demands of me that I attend to it, that I pay attention to the event of its manifestation.

The affectivity which sounds in the other is not intentional in the sense of being directed toward an intentional object. Of course, in understanding her words I know that she is hopeful about her new job, she is despairing of her country, she is joyful about a new love, she is sad about her friend's death, but what I hear in her voice is the mood of hope, despair, joy or sadness. Such moods can transcend the intentional objects and become the atmosphere of her being. In hearing the other, as in hearing a piece of music, I am not perceiving any thing.[4] The qualities of tone, the melody of the voice of the other, the manner in which those tones relate to one another, are for me qualities of the sound itself. In following them, I hear the other in her gestural being. What motivates me in listening to her is not an aspect of her being drawing me toward further aspects, but rather that which has no reality except in the manner in which one tone gives way to another. While the meaning of her words can allow me to picture her or some object of the theme of her discourse, her tone is not the quality of anything other than a gesture of her being. Such a gesture as the product of her body, depends on her physical self but, as expression, it is the manifestation of her living body, which has reality for me not in its physical continuity, but rather as an expressive movement of tone or of rhythm.

---

4 This distinction mirrors Heidegger's discussion of fundamental moods, which disclose the world rather than particular entities in the world. On this question, see Held 1993.

3 Rhythm

Rhythms are everywhere around us, things both animate and inanimate move around me and toward me in their own distinctive rhythms. Indeed, we may go so far as saying that rhythm is a universal phenomenon, perceivable in the manner in which things are in their modes of expression. We feel and hear, indeed even see rhythm in speech, in movement, in nature. More specifically, rhythm seems to arise from life – musical rhythm is founded in imitations and sympathetic variations on rates of heartbeat and breathing. As in hearing sound I hear a directionality of sense, with rhythm I hear and feel a moving force, a force which binds me to it in a relation of kinetic sympathy. In sensing another in their expressive being, I can recognize the beat of their intonation, the accent of their inflections, the tempo of their movements. In each case I recognize general types – people who are heavy or light on their feet, melodious or flat in their speaking, hurried or leisurely in their movements. These rhythms can become national or regional stereotypes, can more concretely be incarnated in a characteristic way in a particular person and situationally can vary, demonstrating changes in mood as someone I know betrays excitement or despondency in their changes in rhythm. In all these ways we find time being embodied in an other. This embodiment occurs as repetition, but also as taking leave from the past and giving oneself over to a new rhythm. As Gadamer puts it, "the new comes to be precisely by way of the old being remembered in its dissolution" (Gadamer 1970, p. 351).

In rhythm we have a movement of to and fro, which in music becomes an experience of waves, moving forward and back, in a movement whereby the future is contained in the present and the present is only in relation to a still efficacious past. To quote Zukerkandl again, "the mere fact of temporal succession of tones and nothing else ... produce[s] the distinction between to and fro ... the wave is not an event *in* time but an event *of* time" (Zuckerkandl 1969, p. 184). In the experience of rhythm, I experience time itself in the very specific sense of a force of advance and recurrence, which produces its own effects in the tones themselves. The future is already contained in the present, but only through the action of time in the sense of rhythm, does that future emerge.

In living in a world of sound, I am in relation to a plurality of rhythms resonating with one another sometimes harmoniously, sometime as cross rhythms, but in each case appearing as virtualities, virtual movements through and in space enveloping and penetrating me. Listening to the rhythm in which others appear to me, is to listen musically. Rhythm unites time and space; indeed, musical time is not conceivable without spatialization, but as a temporal expression of bodily motion apprehended acoustically (Lefebvre 2013, p. 60). To attend to these rhythms requires a stepping outside of them; Lefebvre speaks in this context of the "marvelous inventions of balconies" (Lefebvre 2015, p. 28) in allowing him to observe the rhythms of a street. But that stepping outside is itself a kind of phenomenological reduction – not an observation from outside, but an observing *as if* from inside, "to grasp a rhythm it is necessary to have been grasped by it", as Lefebvre puts it (Lefebvre 2015, p. 27). Being grasped by rhythm – but to varying degrees and in differing ways – it is made possible for us to grasp it, by focusing our attention toward the acoustical constitution itself in music.

Rhythm is a matter of repetition that sets up a pattern. This occurs through accent, stress and tempo. Rhythm can only at a certain limit become homogenous; its repetitions are of strong and weak beats, long and short times, silences, intervals, resumptions, regularities of movement. As such, rhythm happens as differentiated time, qualified durations (see Nancy 2007, p. 78). At its limit, this reduces the other to the mechanical, as such predictable and manipulable. In this case the expressive being of the other approaches the null point for us. Yet, even where repetition occurs monotonously, we tend to hear the repetition rhythmically. In so doing we tend interpretatively to form the mechanical into the living, monotonous sound into the movement of dance or speech. What we find in the roots of rhythm are two elementary tendencies, those of liveliness and of mechanicity and alongside these two elementary forms of our being rhythmic, those of speech and of dance. Attending to rhythm happens through a sympathetic act of the body, a living of the rhythm in the body. Scruton refers to rhythm as the "virtual energy that flows through the music and which causes me to move with it in sympathy" (Scruton 2007, p. 231). Prior to music, pre-musically, this virtual energy guides and moves my attention, toward the world and toward others in their expressive being. As Andy Hamilton puts it: "The experience of musical rhythm does not only involve experiencing music as behaving like a human body; it also involves experiencing the human body as behaving musically" (Hamilton 2007, p. 144). In speech and in dance the body lives such rhythm: in these two primal modes of interacting, speaking to others and ourselves, and gesturing toward each other in attitudes of welcome and refusal, our meaning cannot be abstracted from a certain cadence, and step and a tone, which places us in time with the world around us or appears untimely, out of step, taking the wrong tone, making a false step.

The rhythm of such situations, in its twin modes of dance and speech, indicates a struggle between liveliness and spontaneity, on the one hand, and mechanicity and automaticity on the other. Rhythm through its repetitions gives way to measurement, meter, to the regular measure of a beat, but a mechanical performance would be judged unmusical. This is not simply an aesthetic judgement: it refers us to an underlying sense of rhythm and meter in our auto-affective and hetero-affective perceptions of movement. The mechanical is the adaption to a regularity which knows no deviation, relentless and stubborn (*ostinato*) – a single directedness which is characterized by a lack of responsiveness to the other, which is manifest as a failure to grasp the new and take leave of the past. But it is precisely that temporal capacity to begin which the musicologist Moritz Hauptmann, in speaking of the metrical accent, calls "the energy of beginnings (*Energie des Anfangs*)", in which a rhythm is projected onto the next note from the previous note(s). Indeed, it is not so much that rhythm requires energy, as that all energy seems to have a rhythmic structure (see Lefebvre 2015, p. 65).

In my relation with the other, there is a certain rhythmic economy of supply and demand, give and take, *do ut des*. This powerful rhythm is one which Gaston Bacherlard is referring to when he talks of the undulations of moral duality: "Personality lives according to the rhythm of conciliation and aggression .... I respect in order to be respected" (Bachelard 2016, p. 134). This moral economy is a kind of dance, where I freely move toward the other in the understanding and confidence that the other will move toward me. Schiller with reference to Eighteenth century English figure dancing described this as follows: "Everything has been arranged so that the first has made room for the second before he arrives" (quoted in Scruton 2007, p. 240). This rhythmic economy is vulnerable to disruption, however. In approaching the other I have to be receptive to her as a source of her own energy of beginnings, and the musicality of that experience calls upon me to be attentive to the rhythm, which may spontaneously emerge between us, but which is always liable to fall back into mechanicity through the lack of musical sense for the "musicality of the everyday" (see Russon 2009, pp. 16–22).

4 Conclusion

In listening to others, I hear the affectivity of their being and do so – to allude to Mendelssohn – more precisely than any words can express. In hearing others in their affective expression my focus is not so much on the propositional and conceptual content either of their own acts or of a third party description of them, but rather on the tone and rhythm immanent in their expression of themselves. In hearing this we recognize in the sound itself the peculiar intonation of affective response through which in hearing the other I hear the world of the other. The world of the other is that world which I share with her, but which in this moment is given unique articulation through her. I hear in her tone and the rhythm and melody of her lived body, sadness or joy or despair or rage as if for the first time: I recognize it in the imaginative relations of tone and rhythm that we share, but I also hear it as her unique affective expression. The movement from tone to tone, contained in the musicality of her expression, is one in which I sense the affective expression of her being.

The situation in which I find myself with others – with all others – is characterized by a certain rhythm and tone in which my awareness is directed not so much at the corporeal boundaries of self and other but to the event of to and fro, of advance and return, a wave of movement in which each finds themselves in accord or not. My relation to such movement is one of varying degrees of submission and self-forgetting. To be in a rhythm is to give oneself over to its action, to be subject to the action of time through which my future movements are already anticipated, but in which also new futures are opened up. Such a rhythm is neither in my power nor in any other's, rather the movement of respective bodies in terms of such rhythm is itself a response to a way of being bodily, which happens between us. In listening to others, I am hearing and feeling this tone and this rhythm and within them the expressive being of myself and others in our proto-musical life.

References

Bachelard, Gaston (2016): *The Dialectics of Duration*. Trans. Mary McAllester Jones. London: Rowman & Littlefield International.
Cooke, Deryck (1962): *The Language of Music*. Oxford: Oxford University Press.
Gadamer, Hans-Georg (1970): "Concerning Empty and Fulfilled Time". In: *Southern Journal of Philosophy* 8(4), pp. 341–353.
Georgiades, Thrasyboulos (1958): *Musik und Rhythmus bei den Griechen: Zum Ursprung der abendländischen Musik*. Hamburg: Rowohlt.
Georgiades, Thrasyboulos (1982): *Music and Language: The Rise of Western Music as Exemplified in the Settings of the Mass*. Trans. Marie Louise Göllner. Cambridge: Cambridge University Press.
Hamilton, Andy (2007): *Aesthetics and Music*. London: Continuum.
Hanslick, Eduard (1988): *On the Musically Beautiful*. Trans. Geoffrey Payzant. Indianapolis: Bobbs-Merril.
Heidegger, Martin (2001): "Language". In: *Poetry Language, Thought*. Trans. Albert Hofstadter. London: Harper Perennial, pp. 185–208.
Heidegger, Martin. (2002): "The Origins of the Work of Art". In: *Off the Beaten Track*. Julian Young/Kenneth Haynes (Eds.). Cambridge: Cambridge University Press, pp. 1–56.
Held, Klaus (1993): "Fundamental Moods and Heidegger's Critique of Contemporary Culture". Trans. Anthony Steinbock. In: Sallis, John (Ed.): *Commemorations: Reading Heidegger from the Start*. Bloomington: Indiana University Press.
Henry, Michel (2009): *Seeing the Invisible:* On *Kandinsky*. Trans. Scott Davidson. London: Continuum.

Husserl, Edmund (1990): *Ideas Pertaining to a Pure Phenomenology and to a Phenomenological Philosophy, Book II*. Trans. Richard Rojcewicz/André Schuwer. Dordrecht: Kluwer.
Husserl, Edmund (2019): *The Phenomenology of Internal Time-Consciousness*. Trans. James S. Churchill. Bloomington: Indiana University Press.
Kerman, Peter (1998): "How we got into Analysis and how to get out". In: *Write All These Down: Essays on Music*. Berkeley: University of California Press, pp. 12–32.
Kivy, Peter (1991): *Sound and Semblance*. Ithaca, London: Cornell University Press.
Lefebvre, Henri (2013): *Rhythmanalytics: Space, Time and Everyday Life*. Trans. Stuart Elden/Gerald Moore. London: Bloomsbury.
Magrì, Elisa (2019): "Empathy, Respect, and Vulnerability". In: *International Journal of Philosophical Studies* 27(2), pp. 327–346.
Mendelssohn, Felix (1867): *Letters of Felix Mendelssohn Bartholdy from 1833 to 1847*. Trans. Lady Wallace. London: Longmans, Green.
Merleau-Ponty, Maurice (1964): "Cézanne's Doubt". In *Sense and Non-Sense*. Hubert Dreyfus/Patricia Dreyfus (Eds.). Evanston: Northwestern University Press.
Merleau-Ponty, Maurice (2013): *Phenomenology of Perception*. Trans. Donald A. Landes. London, New York: Routledge.
Nancy, Jean-Luc. (2007): *Listening*. Trans. Charlotte Mandell. New York: Fordham University Press.
Russon, John (2009): *Bearing Witness to Epiphany: Persons, Things, and the Nature of Erotic Life*. Albany: SUNY Press.
Sartre, Jean Paul (1992): *Being and Nothingness*. Trans. Hazel E. Barnes. London: Simon and Schuster.
Scruton, Roger (1976): "Representation in Music". In: *Philosophy* 51, pp. 273–287
Scruton, Roger (2007): "Thoughts on Rhythm". In: Stock, Kathleen (Ed.): *Philosophers on Music*. Oxford: Oxford University Press.
Wiskus, Jessica (2019): "On memory, nostalgia, and the temporal expression of Josquin's *Ave Maria... virgo serena*". In: *Continental Philosophy Review* 52, pp. 397–413.
Wolff, Francis (2015): *Pourquoi la musique?* Paris: Fayard.
Zukerkandl, Victor (1976): *Sound and Symbol*. Princeton: Princeton University Press.

Elisa Magrì
(Un)learning to see others. Perception, Types, and Position-Taking in Husserl's Phenomenology

Abstract: From a phenomenological perspective, social perception allows degrees of flexibility and critical self-assessment that are not entirely conditioned by the social environment. My goal in this chapter is to take into closer consideration the processes that engender perceptual learning and unlearning in Husserl's phenomenology. I proceed by examining the relation between social perception and the intersubjective sense of reality, before identifying the doxastic positionality that characterizes perception, and its relation to typification and perceptual unlearning. By way of conclusion, I explain in what sense Husserl's approach lends itself to an account of social sensitivity.

Social perception and the sense of reality

Current epistemological and phenomenological research has extensively shown that perception has ethical significance in that it is through perceptual practices of seeing and listening to people that we let others realize whether we are ascribing them normative status and axiological qualities (Mills 2007; Al-Saji 2009; Fricker 2007; Waldenfels 2010; Beyer 2015; Jardine 2020). Ellison's novel *Invisible Man* is often cited as a paradigmatic illustration of this set of issues, which are closely related to the concept of recognition.[1] As is well-known, *Invisible Man* is the first-person narrative of a Black man, who undergoes racist abuses and mistreatments that culminate in racial trauma. While the beginning of the novel has been often cited before, let me here draw attention to the very ending of the novel, where the narrator, in the attempt to save himself from a riot, falls into a manhole. It is at this point that the narrator acknowledges that racial alienation entails not only deprivation of his normative status as a person, but also the denial of his own sense of reality. As the narrator puts it:

---

[1] For a discussion, see especially Honneth 2001. Honneth's approach to critical theory has been compared in the literature with phenomenological accounts of empathy. See Breyer (2015), Jardine (2015, 2017), and Petherbridge in this volume.

> Here I had thought they accepted me because they felt that colour made no difference, when in reality it made no difference because they didn't see either colour or men...[...] They were very much the same, *each attempting to force his picture of reality upon me*, and neither giving a hoot in hell for how things looked to me. (Ellison 2014, pp. 507–508, my emphasis)

Ellison gestures to the nexus between social perception and that common sense of reality that forms the fabric of one's orientation in the world. The sense of reality is the backdrop of all our experiences, providing a felt sense of coherence and validity to everyday life (Ratcliffe 2008). In this regard, the sense of reality corresponds, in Husserl's phenomenology, to the natural attitude, in which I find myself already practically disposed towards my environment (*Umwelt*) and the things included (*Ideas* I, §§ 27–29)[2]. The surrounding world or *Umwelt* is not a sheer physical reality but refers to the world experienced and posited by consciousness in representation, feeling, and judgment, thereby instituting a practical and moral dimension (Nenon 2012). As such, the *Umwelt* is in a constant process of becoming, transforming and evolving alongside new acquisitions of sense and knowledge.

While each sense of reality constituted in the natural attitude is individual and subject-dependent, its objective validity rests on the ties that link each individual worldview to that of everyone else in broader objective contexts, which represent "*our environment, existing for all, to which we ourselves nonetheless belong*" (*Ideas* I, § 29, p. 51). On Husserl's view, each individual sense of reality positions itself against the background of multiple worldviews that are inhabited by a wider community of selves. In the manuscripts on *Ideas* II (§ 50), Husserl makes it clear that the surrounding world of any person is a reality grasped and posited by the individual through her acts of apperception and cognition, "while at the same time a plurality of persons in communication with one another has a common surrounding world" (*Ideas* II, § 50, p. 195). Such intersubjective environment is instituted and held by a plurality of points of view with various degrees of awareness. For example, just because someone was raised in a certain cultural milieu does not make them cognizant of the values and principles of her tradition and culture. Using Husserl's example, the discoveries of physics or psychology may have little if no significance for a person who does not know or learn about them, even if that content belongs to her culture. Similarly, to per-

---

[2] For a discussion of the sense of reality in Husserl and its potential limits, see Ratcliffe 2008 (see also Ratcliffe in this volume for an analysis of trauma that parallels the shock described by Ellison, Fanon, and Baldwin). For an analysis of the natural attitude in Husserl, see also Moran 2013 and Weiss 2016.

ceive others as subjects of moral worth means to be able to acknowledge them as inhabiting the common surrounding world, namely to adopt a personalistic stance that regards other selves as centers of their own *Umwelt*.

Husserl emphasizes the necessity for individuals to act *in concert* with one another, namely to share a common sense of reality based on individual position-taking. To this end, he stresses that the relation between the individual and her surrounding world is a disposition that builds on practical and historicized formations of sense, yet it requires the individual stance of appropriation and position-taking in order to institute an actual reality based on acts of communication. In this respect, from a Husserlian perspective, social perception represents the capacity of attending to another's world-horizon as a meaningful, specific viewpoint that partakes in a common horizon. It follows that social alienation is initiated and reinforced by perceptual and cognitive styles that frame another's involvement in the common world in terms of non-belonging.

This is a crucial aspect that Ellison stresses throughout the novel, and particularly in the passage mentioned above. The sense of reality to which Ellison appeals is the sense of belonging to a community of equals, who partake in the social practices and traditions of their common world as actual participants of a shared reality[3]. In this regard, the sense of powerlessness experienced by the protagonist of *Invisible Man* reflects the impossibility of actualizing one's sense of reality as one of the possible and legitimate worldviews that are intrinsic to the constitution of a common world. From a subjective point of view, this phenomenon is epitomized by the "greater shock" that James Baldwin described in his talk to hundreds of Cambridge students in 1965:

> It comes as a great shock around the age of 5, 6, or 7 to discover that the flag to which you have pledged allegiance, along with everybody else, has not pledged allegiance to you. It comes as a great shock to see Gary Cooper killing off the Indians, and although you are rooting for Gary Cooper, that the Indians are you. [...] It comes as a great shock to discover that the country which is your birthplace and to which you owe your life and identity has not, in its whole system of reality, evolved any place for you. (Baldwin 1965)

The shock to which Baldwin refers in 1965 is reminiscent of the experience described by Frantz Fanon in *Black Skin, White Masks* (1952), where he compares attending the showing of a Tarzan movie while Black in Europe and in the An-

---

3 As Ellison states in an interview, "[...] In the United States, the values of my people are neither 'white' nor 'black', they are American. Nor can I see how they could be anything else since we are people who are involved in the texture of the American experience. [...] We [...] are not fighting for the separation from the 'whites', but for a fuller participation in the society which we share with the 'whites'" (Ellison 1964, p. 270).

tilles (Fanon 2008, p. 131). Fanon, Ellison, and Baldwin point to the ways in which identity builds on a common texture of reality that is normally taken for granted until one finds it shattered by the cognitive and affective shock of being denied the sense of belonging to that very reality. Racial trauma is also sustained by a form of epistemic injustice towards Black testimony, which Mills has called "white ignorance," a cognitive tendency or a doxastic disposition that, while not being insuperable or uniformly common among the white population, involves "not merely ignorance of facts with moral implications but moral non-knowings, incorrect judgments about the rights and wrongs of moral situations themselves" (Mills 2007, p. 22). Moral ignorance, for Mills, implies not simply that one does not know what is ethically required of them in a given situation, but also that one fails to realize that such non-knowing has in itself moral implications. Mills points out that such ignorance is rooted in perception, which relies on individual and social beliefs, as well as on individual and social memory, thereby constituting a doxastic environment in which particular varieties of racial ignorance flourish.

Mills' thesis that social perception is related to a doxastic environment whether or not one is cognizant of it is compatible with the phenomenological account of the sense of reality, which informs individual and collective styles of self- and other orientation. It is, however, worth noting that, from a phenomenological angle, social perception allows degrees of flexibility and critical self-assessment that are not entirely conditioned by the social environment. My goal in this chapter is to further examine this aspect, focusing on the processes that engender perceptual learning and unlearning.

As I have argued elsewhere (Magrì 2020), a Husserlian approach can be fruitfully explored to articulate an account of social sensitivity, broadly defined as a form of cultivated discernment that builds on dynamics of attitude change. Furthering this line of inquiry, in this chapter, I focus on the relation between typification and the modality of belief that is sedimented in perception prior to cognition and judgment, corresponding to a latent modality of position-taking. As I will argue, Husserl's phenomenology provides the conceptual framework to investigate patterns of perceptual (un)learning that point to the alteration and transformation of one's sense of reality. While my account in this chapter is necessarily limited, I hope to clarify the contribution of Husserl's phenomenology to a critical appraisal of perception, gesturing to a theory of social sensitivity. I will proceed as follows: I will first consider the positionality of the self at the level of perception, before considering the relation between typification and perceptual unlearning. By way of conclusion, I will explain in what sense Husserl's approach lends itself to an account of social sensitivity.

Latent intentionality in Husserl's phenomenology

As is well-known, from a phenomenological perspective, perception does not reach its object in a simple experience but through continuous acts of explication of the horizon, which are founded on the affective pre-givenness of the world. In this sense, acts of perceptual identification do not amount to individuation *tout court*. Perception is an achievement, namely a form of learning that is directed to objects and subjects within their horizon, the explication of which involves certain degrees of typification. In order to explain how typification informs a subjective stance or perceptual orientation, it is however essential to take into closer account the role of position-taking (*Stellungnahme*). Such a concept is normally associated to the active stances of the ego, such as judgments, convictions, and thoughts. However, position-taking plays a crucial role also at the level of receptivity as a form of doxastic disposition.

To begin with, position-taking translates in Husserl *Stellungnahme* or stance-taking, which is how the ego takes a position towards reality through acts of perception, valuing, and judging, where perception represents the founded act upon cognitive, axiological, or practical judgments are based (Drummond 2007, p. 165, Moran and Cohen 2012, p. 258). While position-taking can be expressed in a propositional form (e.g. 'take S as P'), it does not necessarily translate into an active judgment. It is best described as a form of abidance by the truth or value of a certain state of affairs that informs perception and affectivity, not just judgment. Indeed, it is by enduring and being exposed to the felt quality of a given situation that position-takings signals a disagreement between how things present themselves to us and how we take them to be (Jacobs 2016). As Husserl writes in *Philosophy as Rigorous Science* (PRS), "all life is position-taking, and all position-taking is subject to an ought, to a verdict concerning validity or invalidity according to claimed norms that have absolute validity" (PRS, p. 290).

Husserl's argument is that we do not perceive any intentional object from a neutral standpoint, and that experience does not take place in a vacuum, as if we contemplated propositions and then decided whether they are true or false. On the contrary, we form passive stances towards objects and situations on the basis of the felt quality of our certainty, and we then subject them to reflection and verification. Once experiential position-takings are solidified in the course of one's experience, they constitute active stances of approving or rejecting beliefs and presentations of states of affairs. Accordingly, in *Philosophy as Rigorous Science*, Husserl defines experience, in a broader sense, as a personal habitus, namely as "the precipitation of acts of natural, experiential position-taking that have occurred in the course of life" (PRS, p. 284).

Husserl's idea is that the stratification of position-takings in the course of one's life determines an individual habitual approach to events and situations. In this sense, position-taking lies at the core of attitudes and formed personalities (De Monticelli 2011). The personalistic attitude, for example, regards other selves as minded beings whose personhood is irreducible to physical reductionism. By contrast, in the naturalistic attitude, we abide by the laws and principles of natural sciences. In each attitude, a general form of position-taking prevails, informing our motivational stances. However, it is worth noting that position-takings are not only related to full-fledged attitudes, but they also emerge in the course of one's experiential learning. In this sense, position-taking informs perception as a passive or "latent intentionality" (Hua 38, p. 377).

Passive position-takings correspond to latent functions of positionality that are not fulfilled in a positive or negative judgment (Hua 38, p. 378). Husserl refers to the flux of perceiving which may alter the orientation we have towards the object (Hua 38, p. 379). Thus, for any alteration or fluctuation experienced in attention and perception, there is arguably an alteration of their underlying disposition. Such dispositions can be understood in terms of motivational states that inform an individual orientation in the experiential world prior to cognition and judgment. In *Experience and Judgment* (EJ), Husserl provides a more complex and nuanced account of such dispositions that centers on the relation between affect, interest, and certainty.

Husserl's argument is that for any element that we attend to in perception there is a striving or interest, which he describes as an affective tension that permeates perception (EJ, §§ 19–20, Steinbock 2004, Wehrle 2015, Magrì 2019). The notion of interest captures the way in which perception is animated by sensitivity and responsiveness to the intentional object within its horizon. It is in virtue of the striving to orient ourselves in the surrounding world that we continuously uncover, in perception, the various profiles of the intentional object, thereby instituting in perception shifting horizons of familiarity. When I wait for my friend at the train station, I expect to recognize him from afar, anticipating the way in which he will emerge from the crowd and stand out because of his height, stride, and familiar expression. Accordingly, interest represents an affective and subjective quality of perception that makes us sensitive to shifts and variations of the thematic field as well as of the background. Even though the horizon in which consciousness is situated is always in motion, the perceptual apprehension of the intentional object and its affective qualities are not ephemeral, but are retained in the form of a habitus. As such, a disposition arises to not only recognize the same intentional object in certain circumstances, but to also posit it as actual until something else will change or modify my originary certainty.

Perceptual learning thus consists in sedimentations of sense that predispose consciousness to give her assent or denial to the presentations of intentional objects and states of affairs. This corresponds to a passive modality of position-taking, which is characterized by various degrees of doxastic validity, including negation, possibility, and doubt (EJ, § 21). For example, in perception, one may doubt whether the object seen is actual or illusory, as well as oscillate between different interpretations of the same intentional object. In this respect, Husserl's argument is that our basic and habitual orientation in the world is originally instituted in perception on the basis of our subjective tendency to anticipate connections of events or meaning. Once beliefs and judgments enter the constitution of meaning and engender active stances and attitudes, consciousness is inclined to interpret events and situations following the route provided by the sedimentation of prior assumptions and beliefs.

At the same time, given that a basic modality of certainty is originally instituted in perception, it is noteworthy that, when a particular experience overrides or is in conflict with sedimented position-takings, reflection may not suffice. What needs to change is not just whether an individual believes or not in the truth of the proposition that reflects a state of affairs but their personal and affective abidance by that belief. While changing beliefs is a process that requires individuals to go through their set of beliefs and critically reconsider them, the ingrained certainty instituted in perception (or passive position-taking) may produce a strong resistance due to the consolidated habitus of taking something to be the case under those given circumstances.

However, as indicated before, perceptual learning is as an open-ended and fluctuating process that is sensitive to changes and shifts of the horizon as well as of the intentional objects that co-partake in it. Connections of sense formed on a perceptual level are not static and fixed orientations, but are driven by fluctuations of interest, hence they are open to change and verification. Thus, on Husserl's view, the existence of prior perceptual routes does not prevent the alteration and modification of certainty. This bears important consequences for typification, as I shall now discuss.

Type-orientation and dissonance

We know for a fact that every perception involves certain degrees of typification. To identify others means to see them as fitting more or less certain typicalities to which we are passively exposed in experience. Indeed, there can be as many typicalities as general classes of objects. Unlike pure and empirical concepts, however, types are plastic and subject-dependent. They do not provide any exhaustive anticipation of the object that concretely appears in experience, nor do they coincide with essences or universals. On the contrary, types enable acquaintance with the physiognomy of new objects on the basis of the sedimentation of specific characteristics that awaken subjective interest. In this sense, types are influenced by culture and reflect the manner in which meaning emerges in the pragmatic use of language[4].

The relevant traits that inform typification are neither necessary nor sufficient conditions of individuation. This means that types may anticipate the qualities and forms of the entities encountered in experience, yet actual individuals are irreducible to their corresponding types, as they possess a unique way of affecting attention. When we say that the apple is a type of fruit, we are not thereby using any prescriptive schema that dictates the exact shape or colour or smell of the apple, even though we may have in mind a specific type of apple (e.g. a red one rather than a green one). Types produce an indeterminate horizon that we can further enrich and articulate in the course of the experience in a process of indeterminate determinability. In this sense, types provide a plastic blueprint for the apprehension of objects, which helps classify and categorize various phenomena.

On Husserl's account, types are constituted at the pre-conceptual level of experience[5]. This is the field of investigation undertaken by genetic phenomenology, which analyses pre-predicative experience in order to identify the fundamental structures of receptivity without directly subsuming them to the rules of understanding[6]. In *Experience and Judgment*, Husserl describes at length how

---

[4] The notion of type has a longstanding tradition since the aftermath of Kant's first *Critique* with particular regard to the relationship between thinking and language, starting with Wilhelm von Humboldt's philosophy of language. According to Humboldt, concepts cannot be separated from words, which possess an individual physiognomy that is influenced by history and culture. Merleau-Ponty refers notably to Humboldt's *Sprachphilosophie* when discussing the relationship between thought, language, and style: cf. Merleau-Ponty 2010, p. 49. For the relevance of types in aesthetics, see Sibley 1959, 1965 (I am grateful to Dan Dahlstrom for pointing me to Sibley's work). For a discussion of types in social and legal philosophy, see Passerini Glazel 2005.

[5] An early theory of types can also be found in the *Logical Investigations*, particularly in the First Investigation, where typicalities of sensory experience (for example, types of sound and color) are associated with fluctuations of meaning, which allow for further differentiations depending on the circumstances and the context. See LI, I, § 27.

[6] Husserl's so-called transition from static to genetic phenomenology was probably motivated by his extensive research on the phenomenology of time consciousness as well as by his interest

typification allows the formation of empirical concepts that are used in natural sciences. On this view, typification establishes horizons of familiarity that allow the recognition of entities in the world. Unlike pure concepts, empirical concepts that are obtained through typification correspond to classes of entities that open up fields of perceptual anticipation and passive interpretation. On this view, the empirical concept of any object or living being is obtained on the basis of the similarities passively apprehended in the course of perceptual experiences. This means that my experience of an object is informed by the way in which I interact with it, orienting my future expectations. In this sense, types can be enriched and adjusted the more we are confronted with other specimens of the same object, engendering a passive disposition or habitus (EJ, § 83).[7]

Due to its plasticity and pervasive role in perception, the notion of types plays a pivotal role in sociological research. Alfred Schütz was particularly attracted by Husserl's theory of types, arguing that they provide interpretative schemes for understanding others in the context of social action. By drawing on general typicalities, which are based on personal experience and common knowledge, Schütz argues that the sociological observer can bring social agents into wider meaning-contexts that help figure out the agent's motives. For instance, according to Schütz's example, the observation of a factory worker on any ordinary day entails the formation of wider contexts of meaning in which the worker is placed in light of his movements, gestures, and behavior. In so doing, the observer seeks to reconstruct the social context of the worker, associating him with the ideal type of 'urban worker' or 'Berlin worker of the year 1931' (Schütz 1967, pp. 192–193).

Schütz argues that schemes of interpretation can be expanded or modified depending on the system of relevance that prevails in different circumstances. For example, if the sociological observer is interested in the religious beliefs of the worker, she would hardly be able to extract such information from the worker's job, and she would need to place him in different social contexts. For Schütz, every interpretation based on an ideal-typical construction is only probable, underpinning a form of we-relation that never attains the concrete immediacy of face-to-face encounters. In the latter, I am concerned with the particularity of the other person, and not with the characteristics that s/he has in com-

---

in the laws of association. For a thorough introduction and discussion of this topic, see Zahavi (2003, p. 94ff) and Vergani (2003).

7 As Lohmar (2003) has pointed out, "the application of a type is comparable to an action. [...] Our ability to see objects by means of a type is also a form of habituality. However, the 'I can' of a passively constituted typifying apperception is situated on a level of constitution and activity that is far deeper than that of a conscious action" (Lohmar 2003, p. 112).

mon with others in wider social contexts. This is why, on Schütz's view, there can be two forms of orientation to others, one in which we interpret their behaviour as "one of them", as a member of a group based on relevant typicalities, and another orientation in which we see others as "one of a kind", as individuals that cannot be reduced to any given type.

For instance, the philosopher I talk to at a conference and that originally strikes me for her brilliant insights could be easily associated with the type of the academic due to my familiarity with people working in academia. However, in the course of other chats and conversations, I learn that she originally trained as a legal consultant, and only later in her life she decided to pursue a Ph.D in philosophy. Besides, she is not only a philosopher, but also a musician with her own band. In this case, a previous type is expanded and modified thanks to the interaction with the subject that I situate in more complex horizons depending on my capacity to understand her motives and dispositions. Indeed, the recognition of types is not instantaneous, and it involves different forms of interaction, thereby contributing to the ramification of types themselves. As a result, in forming types, we produce open fields of interpretation that can be variously fulfilled in actual events and interactions.

Taipale speaks, in this regard, of a difference between "type-orientation" and "token-orientation", where the shift from the former to the latter corresponds to empathy, which proceeds from the apperception of the style or manner of a person towards the recognition of her unique and non-typical features. In particular, Taipale argues that "personal uniqueness is not gained by way of *stripping off* the supra-individual (cultural, historical, biological, etc.) typicalities, but by way of appropriating and thus *clothing oneself* with these typicalities in a unique and hence personal manner" (Taipale 2015, p. 149). Taipale's argument is that, in empathy, one seeks to understand how others really are in and through the types under which we see them. Failure to appreciate the unique way in which individuals are clothed in their typicalities causes the deterioration and invisibility of the other person, who is then strongly stereotypified. In this sense, for Taipale, "a token-oriented experience of others may accordingly be characterized as the perception of a 'freedom that shines through' the situational role" (Taipale 2015, p. 155).

While Taipale's insights touch on important aspects of typification, his analysis mainly rests on Merleau-Ponty's and Schütz's accounts, as he maintains that Husserl "discusses typification rather generally, and mainly in respect to the familiarity of sensuously perceived objects" (Taipale 2015, p. 151). To be sure, Husserl's account of typification was strongly criticized by Schütz, who remarked that Husserl did not sufficiently explain how types are formed and on the basis of what relevance they are constituted. For Schütz, the analysis of types cannot do without the point of view of the observer, hence Husserl's genetic phenomenology would hardly be able to explain the motives underlying the association at work in typification without compromising the very distinction between receptivity and activity laid out by EJ.

However, despite its generality, Husserl's theory of types has important implications for social perception. On his view, typification is a necessary moment in the process of seeing, but it also involves the modality of belief under which we recognize intentional objects as fitting more or less certain types. To begin with, Husserl is very clear that types are generated via association. That former experiences cohere together, informing our viewpoint, is not an idea that Husserl would take issue with[8]. For Husserl, typification is characterized by a teleological fulfilment to establish concordance and unity of experience. At the same time, a key aspect of Husserl's approach concerns the way in which former presentations are stratified and sedimented in experience. This is not the result of sheer exposure to similar experiences, but it is rather instituted by the passive modality of position-taking. Husserl's idea is that perception does not simply objectify something in the flesh, but also posits something as valid until something else will change or modify my originary certainty. For this reason, receptivity and activity are distinguished in EJ for the sake of explanation, but they are not to be taken as distinct or separate from each other ontogenetically.

The "I" that is operative at the level of receptivity represents the passive modality of position-taking, which informs presentations as having a certain degree of validity. In this sense, Husserl argues that perception does not only involve the presentation of the object, but also "a variable mode of being or validity" (EJ § 21, p. 93). As such, the constitution of a type is not so much a morphological anticipation of what the other person looks like, but the positing of a certain way of being, which is directly connected to my modality of belief (e.g. as certain, dubious, or uncertain).

The relevance of Husserl's approach lies in the fact that it makes perceptual contrast and dissonance compatible with and even constitutive of social perception. Perceptual dissonance refers to the myriad of occasions in which people find themselves at odds with what they see around them because it is contrary to their prior expectations. Husserl refers quite often in his writing to experiences of being mistaken and confused by ordinary experiences (among others, Husserl's famous example of the Panopticum waxwork in the fifth *Logical Investigation*, LI II, pp. [442–43] 137–38).

---

[8] For Husserl, Hume was indeed a precursor of genetic phenomenology particularly because of his theory of association. For a discussion, see Lohmar (1998).

The illusion in the Panopticum is due to the fact that the ego wanders from one perception to the other until the contradiction is – in Hegelian terms – sublated (*aufgehoben*). This means that an objective change has taken place at the level of the apprehension of the object, but such a change involves the modality of belief according to which the object is experienced. The shock or dissonance caused by the illusion in the Panopticum produces a stance of hesitation that informs my way of seeing as well as my overall orientation in the Panopticum. Hesitation, as described by Al Saji (2014), is not meant to produce any paralysis of action and thought. To the contrary, it corresponds to a sense-enabling function that facilitates the disclosure of a plurality of perspective in the now. For example, when facing opposite aspects of the same situation or object, we do not immediately take side with one interpretation or the other, but we experience a conflict between our apprehensions. This is a case that appears again in the *Analyses Concerning Passive Synthesis,* where Husserl offers yet another case of being led astray by a wax figure: "Instead of it being given to consciousness precisely as being there in a straightforward manner, like in normal, univocal perception, i.e., in perception running its course concordantly, it is now given to us as questionable, as dubious, as contentious: It is contested by another givenness, a givenness in the flesh, a givenness of another <apprehension> permeating it and in conflict with it" (Hua 11, pp. [36] 74)[9].

Husserl insists on several occasions on the conflicting situations experienced by perception in order to clarify that, when something conflicts with our previous experiences, the ego is "torn": it was inclined to endorse its original apprehension, that is to say to carry out the tendencies of its expectations, but it now finds itself inhibited, for it is drawn towards an opposite apprehension. When syntheses of concordance are disappointed or contrasted, as it happens when we fail to associate a person with a culturally established type, we strive to re-establish concordance because we need to restore the ordinary quality of our natural attitude. If the perception of a man suddenly changes in that of a mannequin, then the objective reality of the mannequin is not affected, and yet the modality of certainty of the perceiver has changed[10]. Conflicting experiences can be described in terms of affective and cognitive shocks, for they affect

---

[9] Page numbers in square brackets refer to the German edition and are followed by the page numbers of the English translation.

[10] According to Heinämaa, on the basis of perceptual typicalities, we also constitute sexual styles (see Heinämaa 2003 and 2011). The notion of style is employed by Heinämaa to identify manhood and womanhood as two different ways of relating to the world, which are not anchored on any positivistic or naturalistic set of bodily features or activities. On this issue, see also Tullmann 2017.

not only expectations but also the originary position-taking of the individual. As Husserl writes: "the mode of belief, and in consequence, the mode of being are essentially changed; the way in which what appears is present to consciousness has become other" (EJ, p. 93).

Situations that provoke dissonance produce a motivation to change and readjust one's attitude to reality. Such motivation results from the dissonance experienced, which extends backwards as to correct and revise past and sedimented apprehensions of the same object (EJ, § 21). Accordingly, experiences of dissonance determine a modification of the habitual certainty that informs future expectations of the same object or individual (Hua 11, p. [55] 95). This indicates that, out of conflict and hesitation, a style of learning may arise, which is based on sensitivity and active recognition of the contextual elements that inform beliefs and expectation. It follows that, on Husserl's view, the very possibility of shifting from types to tokens, which is crucial for interpersonal understanding, requires a fundamental alteration in the corresponding modality of position-taking that underlies typification.

In this regard, Husserl's phenomenology provides the basis for an account of social sensitivity, which challenges ingrained styles of perception in two main ways: first of all, by cultivating the disposition to be affected by dissonance and conflicts, and secondarily, by shifting, resisting, and critically altering the social norms underlying typification. As noted by Steinbock (1995), what is striking about Husserl's account is that he does not only account for the internal development and institution of norms, but also for the possibility of transcending those norms and instituting new ones despite the presence of a norm that already functions teleologically. As Husserl states: "To the extension of the pure concept 'human being' (*Mensch*) belong all men whom I can imagine, whether or not they are also to be found in the world, whether or not they are possible in the unity of this world, whether or not they are put in relation to it" (EJ § 91, p. 354). The power of symbolic norms is, for Husserl, constantly challenged by the irreducibility of first-personal experience to a given matrix. While social contexts and practices enter formations of sense and influence our apperception of others, the basic and primary form of assent or denial to perceptual presentations is intrinsically subject-dependent.

Most notably, Husserl's approach reveals that there cannot be any active change of attitude towards people and the social world unless our own subjective and affective stances to reality are affected (Magrì 2020). A socially sensitive stance builds on the tendency that is inherent in perceptual experience to further explicate the clues of a social context that suddenly become relevant because of the dissonance experienced. In so doing, social sensitivity produces an ethos of cultivated discernment, which constantly shifts the focus of attention within and against typification, striving to better situate the experiential worldview or sense of reality of other selves.

Conclusions

Husserl's approach is rooted in the idea that receptivity is a form of activity because it manifests responsiveness to individuals and events on an affective level. While attitude change is a complex process that cannot be here discussed here in full, I have argued that Husserl's phenomenology gestures to an account of social sensitivity, which builds on affective and cognitive dissonance. This means that the motivation to engage in the revision of one's attitude requires an affective change in the tonality of one's experience, that is, a shift in the overall disposition of the perceiver, including the affective tonality in which individuals inhabit their own worldview. In this light, it is possible to reconsider the relation between perception, types, and doxastic position or position-taking.

Husserl's strategy consists in recasting the relationality between seer and seen as the interlocking of two senses of reality, that of the perceiver and that of the perceived. For Husserl, the worker of Schütz's example is not simply the particular representative of the class of workers, but rather the center of an *Umwelt* that one can approach in continuous acts of perception, feeling, willing, and valuing. In this respect, Husserl's view of interest is not too generic or too broad. Husserl's account of typification actually indicates that all our encounters with other selves are permeated by a sense of co-participation in their sense of reality, to which we respond with different degrees of sensitivity. The challenge of social sensitivity consists in responding to the clashes engendered by individual biases in order to fully and deeply confront the doxastic positions sedimented in one's experience. In so doing, social sensitivity establishes the basis for unlearning ingrained styles of seeing and confronting moral ignorance at the very level of one's perceptual orientation.

Acknowledgments

This chapter builds on a series of conference papers I presented between 2016 and 2020 in Galway, Dublin, Lisbon, Copenhagen, and Boston. I am grateful to all participants for their feedback and questions. Special thanks to Anna Bortolan for her helpful comments as well as her thoughtful and supportive collaboration on this volume.

References

Al-Saji, Alia (2009): "A Phenomenology of Critical-Ethical Vision: Merleau-Ponty, Bergson, and the question of seeing differently". In: *Chiasmi International* 11, pp. 375–398.
Al-Saji, Alia (2014): "A Phenomenology of Hesitation: Interrupting Racializing Habits of Seeing". In: Lee, Emily S. (Ed.): *Living Alterities. Phenomenology, Embodiment, Race*. Albany: SUNY Press, pp. 133–172.
Baldwin, James (1965): "The American Dream and the American Negro". *The New York Times*, 7 March 1965.
Breyer, Thiemo (2015): "Social Visibility and Perceptual Normativity". In: Doyon, Maxime/Breyer, Thiemo (Eds.): *Normativity in Perception*. Basingstoke: Palgrave Macmillan, pp. 140–160.
De Monticelli, Roberta (2011): *"Alles Leben ist Stellungnehmen*–Die Person als praktisches Subjekt." In: Mayer, Verena/Erhard, Christopher/Scherini, Marisa (Eds.): *Die Aktualität Husserls*. Freiburg, München: Verlag Karl Alber, pp. 39–55.
Drummond, John (2007): *Historical Dictionary of Husserl's Philosophy*. Lanham: Scarecrow Press.
Ellison, Ralph (1964): *Shadow and the Act*. New York: Random House.
Ellison, Ralph (2014): *Invisible Man*. London: Penguin Books.
Fanon, Frantz (2008): *Black Skin, White Masks*. Trans. Richard Philcox. New York: Grove Press.
Fricker, Miranda (2007): *Epistemic Injustice. Power and the Ethics of Knowing*. Oxford: Oxford University Press.
Heinämaa, Sara (2003): *Towards a Phenomenology of Sexual Difference*. Lanham: Rowman & Littlefield.
Heinämaa, Sara (2011): "A Phenomenology of Sexual Difference: Types, Styles, and Persons". In: Witt, Charlotte (Ed.): *Feminist Metaphysics. Explorations in the Ontology of Sex, Gender, and the Self*. Dordrecht: Springer.
Honneth, Axel (2001): "Recognition: Invisibility: On the Epistemology of 'Recognition'". In: *Proceedings of the Aristotelian Society* 75, pp. 111–139.
Husserl, Edmund (1913): *Logische Untersuchungen. Zweiter Band. Untersuchungen zur Phänomenologie und Theorie der Erkenntnis*. Voll. I-II. Halle: Max Niemeyer. In English: Husserl, Edmund (2001a): *Logical Investigations*. Trans. J.N. Findlay, rev. Dermot Moran. London, New York: Routledge. [LI]
Husserl, Edmund (1952): *Ideen zur einer reinen Phänomenologie und phänomenologischen Philosophie. Zweites Buch: Phänomenologische Untersuchungen zur Konstitution*. Marly Biemel (Ed). Husserliana IV. The Hague: Martinus Nijhoff. In English: Husserl, Edmund (1989): *Ideas Pertaining to a Pure Phenomenology and to a Phenomenological Philosophy. Second Book: Studies in the Phenomenology of Constitution* Trans. Richard Rojcewicz/André Schuwer. Dordrecht: Kluwer. [*Ideas* II]
Husserl, Edmund (1966): *Analysen zur Passiven Synthesis*. Margot Fleischer (Ed.). Husserliana XI. The Hague: Martinus Nijhoff. In English: Husserl, Edmund (2001b): *Analyses Concerning Passive and Active Synthesis*. Trans. Anthony J. Steinbock. Dordrecht: Kluwer. [Hua 11]
Husserl, Edmund (1973): *Experience and Judgment. Investigations in a Genealogy of Logic*. Trans. James S. Churchill/Karl Ameriks. London: Routledge & Kegan Paul. [EJ]

Husserl, Edmund (1977): *Ideen zu einer reinen Phänomenologie und phänomenologischen Philosophie. Erstes Buch: Allgemeine Einführung in die reine Phänomenologie.* Karl Schuhmann (Ed.). Husserliana III. The Hague: Martinus Nijhoff. In English: Husserl (2004): *Ideas I.* Trans. Daniel O. Dahlstrom. Indianapolis, Cambridge: Hackett. [*Ideas* I]

Husserl, Edmund (2002): 'Philosophy as Rigorous Science'. Trans. Marcus Brainard. In: *The New Yearbook for Phenomenology and Phenomenological Philosophy* 2, pp. 249–95. [PRS]

Husserl, Edmund (2005): *Wahrnehmung und Aufmerksamkeit. Texte aus dem Nachlass (1893–1912).* Thomas Vongehr/Regula Giuliani (Eds.). Husserliana XXXVIII. Dordrecht: Springer. [Hua 38]

Jacobs, Hanne (2016): "Socialization, Reflection, and Personhood". In: Rinofner-Kreidl, Sonja/Wiltsche, Harald (Eds.): *Analytic and Continental Philosophy. Methods and Perspectives: Proceedings of the 37th International Wittgenstein Symposium.* Berlin: De Gruyter, pp. 323–336.

Jardine, James (2015): "Stein and Honneth on Empathy and Emotional Recognition". In: *Human Studies* 38, pp. 567–589.

Jardine, James (2017): "Elementary Recognition and Empathy. A Husserlian Account." In: Magrì, Elisa/Petherbridge, Danielle (Eds.): *Metodo. International Studies in Phenomenology and Philosophy.* Special issue on Intersubjectivity and Recognition 5(1), pp. 143–170.

Jardine, James (2020): "Social Invisibility and Emotional Blindness". In: Daly, Anya/Cummins, Fred/Jardine, James/Moran, Dermot (Eds.): *Perception and the Inhuman Gaze: Perspectives from Philosophy, Phenomenology, and the Sciences.* London, New York: Routledge.

Lohmar, Dieter (1998): *Erfahrung und kategoriales Denken.* Dordrecht: Springer.

Lohmar, Dieter (2003): "Husserl's Types and Kant's Schemata". In: Welton, Donn (Ed.): *The New Husserl: A Critical Reader.* Indiana: Indiana University Press.

Lohmar, Dieter (2008): *Phänomenologie der schwachen Phantasie. Untersuchungen der Psychologie, Cognitive Science, Neurologie und Phänomenologie zur Funktion der Phantasie in der Wahrnehmung.* Dordrecht: Springer.

Magrì, Elisa (2019): "Situating Attention and Habit in the Landscape of Affordances". In: *Rivista Internazionale di Filosofia e Psicologia* 10(2), pp. 120–136.

Magrì, Elisa (2020): "Towards a Phenomenological Account of Social Sensitivity". In: *Phenomenology and the Cognitive Sciences.* Dordrecht: Springer. https://doi.org/10.1007/s11097-020-09689-9, last accessed on 25 July 2020.

Mills, Charles (2007): "White Ignorance". In: Sullivan, Shannon/Tuana, Nancy (Eds.): *Race and Epistemologies of Ignorance.* Albany: SUNY Press, pp. 13–38.

Moran, Dermot and Cohen, Joseph (2012): *The Husserl Dictionary.* London: Continuum.

Moran, Dermot (2013): "From the Natural Attitude to the Life-World". In Embree, Lester/Nenon, Thomas (Eds.): *Husserl's Ideen.* Dordrecht: Springer, pp. 105–124.

Merleau-Ponty, Maurice (2010): *Child Psychology and Pedagogy. The Sorbonne Lectures 1949–1952.* Trans. Talia Welsh. Evanston: Northwestern University Press.

Nenon, Thomas (2012): "*Umwelt* in Husserl and Heidegger". In: *Proceedings of the 43rd Annual Meeting of Husserl Circle.* Boston College Philosophy Department, Boston, pp. 1–18.

Passerini Glazel, Lorenzo (2005): *La forza normative del tipo. Pragmatica dell'atto giuridico e teoria della categorizzazione*. Macerata: Quodlibet.

Ratcliffe, Matthew (2008): *Feelings of Being: Phenomenology, Psychiatry, and the Sense of Reality*. Oxford: Oxford University Press.

Schütz, Alfred (1967): *The Phenomenology of the Social World*. Trans. George Walsh/Fredrick Lehnert. Evanston: Northwestern University Press.

Schütz, Alfred (1970): *Collected Papers III. Studies in Phenomenological Philosophy*. Ilse Schütz (Ed.). The Hague: Martinus Nijhoff.

Sibley, Frank (1959): "Aesthetic concepts". In: *The Philosophical Review* 68(4), pp. 421–450.

Sibley, Frank (1965): "Aesthetic and non-aesthetic". In: *The Philosophical Review* 74(2), pp. 135–159.

Steibock, Anthony (1995): *Home and Beyond. Generative Phenomenology after Husserl*. Evanston: Northwestern University Press.

Steinbock, Anthony (2004): "Affection and Attention. On the Phenomenology of Becoming Aware". In: *Continental Philosophy Review* 37, pp. 21–43.

Taipale, Joona (2015): "From Types to Tokens: Empathy and Typification". In: Szanto, Thomas/Moran, Dermot (Eds.): *Phenomenology of Sociality. Discovering the 'We'*. London, New York: Routledge, pp. 143–158.

Tullmann, Katherine (2017): "Gendered seeing". In: *The Southern Journal of Philosophy* 55(4), pp. 475–499.

Vergani, Mario (2003): "Saggio introduttivo". In: Vergani, Mario (Ed.): *Metodo fenomenologico statico e genetico*. Milano: Il Saggiatore.

Waldenfels, Bernhard (2010). "Attention suscitée et dirigée". In: *Alter* 18, pp. 33–44.

Wehrle, Maren (2015): "Normality and Normativity in Experience". In: Doyon, Maxim/Breyer, Thiemo (Eds.): *Normativity in Perception*. Basingstoke: Palgrave McMillan, pp. 128–140.

Weiss, Gail (2016): "De-Naturalizing the Natural Attitude: A Husserlian Legacy to Social Phenomenology". In: *Journal of Phenomenological Psychology* 47, pp. 1–16.

Zahavi, Dan (2003): *Husserl's Phenomenology*. Stanford: Stanford University Press.

Íngrid Vendrell Ferran
Envy, Powerlessness, and the Feeling of Self-Worth

Abstract: While standard definitions of envy tend to focus on the coveted good or the envied rival, this paper describes envy by reflecting on the envious self and its feelings. The paper begins by describing envy and establishing its key features and objects. It presents envy as an emotion of self-assessment which necessarily involves a sense of powerlessness and a feeling of one's own diminishing value as a person. The second section illustrates the link between envy and the feeling of self-worth by exploring one of its most radical manifestations: the phenomenon of existential envy.

Introduction

In general terms, envy can be described as the painful feeling we experience when another person with whom we might identify has something we covet. As an emotion, it involves three different elements: the desired object or "good"; the possessor of this object who functions as our "rival"; and the envying subject or "envious self". While envy has commonly been characterized in relation to the desired good and the feeling of inferiority towards the rival, few accounts consider envy in respect of how this emotion is relevant for the envious self. Against this background, this paper seeks to explore envy by focusing on the subject and its feelings. More specifically, I will argue that envy involves the painful experience of feeling powerless to change a situation of comparative inferiority and the consequent feeling of diminution in one's own value. I will take the phenomenon of existential envy to be illustrative of this claim.[1]

As indicated by Kristjánsson, emotions might be self-relevant in at least three respects: they might be self-constitutive, self-comparative, and self-conscious (Kristjánsson 2010, pp. 75–77). Drawing on this model, all three dimensions of self-relevance can be identified in the case of envy. Envy is a *self-constituting emotion* in the sense that it defines the person we are. The experience of envy reveals our commitments, ideals, and what we care about. It is constitutive

---

[1] In this paper, I describe envy as a hostile emotion. In my view, envy cannot be benign. Those authors who disagree with this view and argue that some instances of envy can be benign can nonetheless read this paper as a description of hostile envy.

https://doi.org/10.1515/9783110698787-015

for those who, when confronted with the fortune of others, are prompted to feel sadness rather than empathic joy. Envy is also an *emotion of self-comparison* in which the self compares itself with others regarding the coveted goods. Finally, envy is a *self-conscious emotion:* it is an emotional experience in which the self is not merely involved; it is also an experience – as Kristjánsson put it for the self-conscious emotions – *about* the self. From these three dimensions pertaining to the relevance of envy for the self, this paper will be concerned with the latter aspect, that is, its self-conscious character. Without denying that envy reveals the values we endorse and that it presupposes a comparison of one's own value with that of others, it is also central for envy that we experience a diminution of our own value. As I shall argue, envy has a self-disclosive dimension. It reveals the value of oneself as being at a disadvantage, as being inferior to the rival, as feeling powerless to rectify or alter this situation of comparative inferiority, and as diminished in worth.[2] The relation between envy and the feeling of one's own value will be at the center of this paper. To refer to this feeling I will use a concept coined by Else Voigtländer (an early phenomenologist of the Munich circle) in her book *Vom Selbstgefühl* and speak of envy as involving a "feeling of self-worth" (Voigtländer 1910).[3]

The paper is organized in two main sections. The first section describes envy as an emotion of self-assessment which necessarily involves feeling powerless in the face of a situation of comparative inferiority and the consequent feeling of diminution of one's own worth. The second section provides an illustration of this by way of an extreme case of envy: the phenomenon of existential envy.

1 Envy and the Feeling of Self-worth

To develop my argument according to which envy is an emotion of self-assessment related to the feeling of diminution of one's own worth, I will proceed in four steps. I begin with a general description of the envious self and its feelings. In the next section, I argue that for envy to arise, we need not only to feel inferior, but also to feel powerless to change a situation of comparative inferiority. Next, I show that these feelings suggest that envy is a self-disclosive emotion. Finally, I argue that the specific aspect of our person revealed in envy is that of self-worth.

---

[2] For an analysis of the self-disclosive dimension of emotions, see Breyer 2018, pp. 76–86.
[3] Voigtländer's book elaborates a typology of the "feelings of self-worth" (*"Selbstwertgefühle"*, also called *"Selbstgefühle"*). Though she does not analyze envy in particular, I think that many of her thoughts can be applied to a set of feelings about one's self-worth involved in this emotion.

1.1 The Envious Self and Its Feelings

I begin my analysis of the envious self by examining the feelings involved in this emotion. To this end, I will focus on two pivotal features of this emotion: it is embodied; and it has a cognitive-intentional character. According to the first moment, envy is an experience in which the body is involved in multifarious ways. Envy is accompanied by concomitant sensations such as a tightening in the chest or an acceleration of the heart rate. It has a negative hedonic valence because it is unpleasant and even painful. It entails symbolic and real action tendencies aimed at the destruction of the envied rival (and, less often, of the envied object and/or of the envious self). Moreover, envy might motivate actions that strive to transform the situation of disadvantage (including damaging and/or eliminating the envied other, and less commonly the object, and/or the envious self). All these aspects of the embodied dimension of envy reveal a central feature of this emotion: the discomfort it causes to the subject, the pain linked to the incapacity of the subject to cope with a situation in which it is disfavored and which one perceives as difficult or impossible to change.

Though one could develop an analysis of envy and the feelings involved in this emotion by focusing on its embodied dimension, for the purposes of my analysis is more revelatory to pay attention to its cognitive-intentional structure. Envy has been characterized as involving three elements – the good, the rival, and the envious self – which interact in a complex set of evaluations and beliefs and which involve a multifaceted cluster of feelings. First, envy presupposes that we evaluate the envied object to be a good, that is to say, we find it desirable and valuable. Envy also involves the belief that we deserve this good and that it would be a good in itself to possess it. To not possess the coveted good triggers a *feeling of loss, nostalgia or grief* in the envious self. It also triggers a *feeling of injustice*, since the envious self considers that it deserves to own the coveted good.

In addition, envy presupposes a comparison with another person. To feel envy implies to identify first a significant other with whom we might compare ourselves. The envied other must be judged as similar (they must not be de facto similar) and they must be familiar to us and close enough to give us occasion for a comparison. Rather than comparing ourselves with those who are socially or culturally distant from us, we tend to establish comparisons with those who belong to the same group (Ben-ze'ev 1992, p. 554). Envy is directed towards another who is close enough to be member of an in-group, but distant enough for us not to share in their achievements as if they were our own. We tend to identify with this significant other and we compare ourselves with them because we have the conviction that this comparison has some relevance for us: as a result of the comparison, we expect to have a better knowledge of our place in the social world and to appreciate our value in relation to the value of others (this is the reason why it is necessary that we regard the person with whom we compare ourselves as being similar to us).

Envy also entails that, as a result of a comparison with another person, we *feel* ourselves and judge our position as *being at a disadvantage. Feeling disfavored* is central for envy, and as such many authors have interpreted this as triggering a *feeling of comparative inferiority.* In order to feel envy, we must become aware of our own value being lower than that of the rival, and this prompts a judgment about oneself as being less worthy than the envied one. Moreover, envy is accompanied also by the *feeling (and consequent judgment) of being powerless* to change the situation of comparative inferiority.

Summarizing, the feelings experienced in envy involve feelings of loss, nostalgia, and grief, feelings of injustice, of being at a disadvantage, and of being disfavored, as well as feelings of inferiority and powerlessness. Among the different feelings mentioned above, the literature on envy has focused mainly on the feelings of inferiority as sufficient for envy to arise. In fact, the feeling of inferiority has been regarded as encompassing many of the previous mentioned feelings such as the feeling of loss, of being at a disadvantage, and of feeling disfavored.[4] However, in what follows, I will argue that the feeling of inferiority, though necessary, is not the most characteristic feeling involved in envy. Much more definitory for envy than the feeling of inferiority is the feeling of powerlessness.

1.2 The Feeling of Inferiority and the Feeling of Powerlessness

The feeling (and consequent judgment) of inferiority alone cannot explain envy because this feeling might be constitutive of reactions other than envy. For a start, the feeling of inferiority might lead to a set of positive reactions: we might consider the other as a person to admire, to follow (as an exemplar), and therefore as someone worth emulating. This might motivate us to have the good and thus it might prompt positive rather than destructive actions, and in

---

[4] For instance, Protasi interprets the feeling of being at a disadvantage as "perceiving ourselves as inferior to a similar other with respect to a good in a domain that is relevant to our sense of identity" (Protasi 2016, p. 537).

my view the latter are essential for envy. In this regard, then, neither admiration (a) nor emulation (b) constitutes envy.

The feeling of inferiority might also be involved in negative reactions. (a) It might be constitutive of *resignation* and the acceptance that a person close to us has something we covet and that we (might) also deserve. (b) It might be part of the *sadness* we experience for not having the coveted good. (c) If we are very righteous, it might even be definitory of certain instances of *anger and/or indignation*. This happens when we consider it to be unfair that the other has something we desire and that we also see ourselves as deserving. It is not unusual for the envious self to present its envy disguised as a feeling of injustice (one might claim that one would also have obtained the good if the social, cultural, political, etc. conditions had been more favorable). In some cases, though, it might well be appropriate to feel angry or indignant: for instance, we might be angry that our colleague secured a promotion at work instead of us because we believe that we deserved it more than her, not because we are envious of her. (d) It is also possible that in discovering that we are at a disadvantage in some way, we enter into a situation of *competition and rivalry* with the other and even think that we should take some kind of *revenge*. (e) But if we are very ambitious, the felt inferiority might make us feel *anxious* and motivate us to undertake actions aimed at changing the disadvantageous situation. (f) The feeling of inferiority (and the corresponding judgment) might be part of self-recriminating reactions such as *shame, blame or embarrassment (and even self-reproach)*. When this happens, we think that we should have been able to obtain the good and that it is our fault (and not just the external conditions as in case (b)) that we have not achieved it (because of some failure in our action and thought or because of some flawed aspect of our character such as being too lazy, not industrious enough, lacking perspective, etc.). (g) Finally, the feeling of inferiority might be a constituent of *envy*. But for this – as I shall argue – a further ingredient is necessary.

This reflection on the feeling of inferiority demonstrates that while the feeling of inferiority is necessary, it is not the most characteristic of the constitutive feelings involved in envy because the feeling of inferiority might also be involved in other emotions which have nothing to do with envy. The feeling of inferiority is an important ingredient of envy, but it is not the only feeling necessarily involved in it.

What is the further ingredient needed for envy? A *feeling of impotence or of powerlessness* regarding our capacity to change the disadvantageous situation. This view was advanced by Scheler who, in his analysis of ressentiment, writes: "'Envy', as the term is understood in everyday usage, is due to a feeling of impotence which we experience when another person owns a good we covet"

(Scheler 2010, p. 29).[5] In order to feel envy, we have to feel impotent and powerless, we have to feel that we lack the necessary resources to change the situation in our favor. Powerlessness is necessary for envy.

If we do not experience powerless in respect of our situation of inferiority, then it is not envy but something different: resignation, sadness, anger and indignation, feeling of injustice, rivalry and revenge, shame, blame and embarrassment, or admiration and emulation. The feeling of powerlessness necessarily involved in envy prompts a judgment about our own person as being unable to change a situation of comparative inferiority.

There are two aspects of the feeling of powerlessness constitutive of envy that should be mentioned here. First, while we experience this feeling, we are simultaneously convinced that *we should be able to have the good*, given that others who are similar to us have already been able to achieve the coveted good. Thus, the feeling of powerlessness must be accompanied by the feeling that we should have been able to obtain that good.[6] Second, the feelings of powerlessness must involve hostility towards the rival (who in our view does not deserve the good). These feelings of powerlessness and the fact that we should have had the capacity to secure the good in question and that we react with hostility towards the rival are the most characteristic elements of envy's cognitive-intentional structure. In experiencing envy, we feel powerless and we also feel that we do not meet our own expectations.

1.3 Envy as an Emotion of Self-Assessment

Let's focus now on the feelings mentioned in the preceding sections and examine what these feelings reveal about the nature of envy. While the feelings of loss, nostalgia, grief, and injustice focus on the coveted good, and feelings of inferiority focus on the rival, the feelings of powerlessness are revelatory of the self-disclosive nature of envy, i.e., its ability to disclose central aspects of the self. The feelings of powerlessness show us more clearly than the other feelings

---

[5] Scheler's view on envy has not gone unnoticed by contemporary authors; see Fussi (2019) and more explicitly Salice and Montes Sánchez (2019) who speak about hostile envy as involving a sense of "disempowerment".

[6] This suggests that envy involves in fact a double comparison: one between our self and the envied other, and one between our real self and our ideal self. Envy arises when we discover that another person is closer to our ideal self than we are, such that the other reminds us of the unfulfilled possibilities inherent to our being.

that while envy can focus on the good or the rival, it can also have a focus on the self.

Definitions of envy which make central to this emotion the feeling of loss, nostalgia, or grief over another's good or even anger (in terms of a feeling of injustice) aim at describing envy in terms of the coveted good. Aquinas' view of envy is a good example of a definition which makes the feeling of sorrow explicative for this emotion (Perrine 2011, p. 433), while Melanie Klein's psychoanalytical account exemplifies the focus on anger. According to Klein: "Envy is the angry feeling that another person possesses and enjoys something desirable – the envious impulse being to take it away or to spoil it" (Klein 1997, p. 181).

Definitions which focus on the feeling of comparative inferiority tend to explain envy in terms of the relation between the envious self and the rival. For instance, Ben-ze'ev writes: "Unlike covetousness and discontent, which are merely concerned in gaining something or achieving a certain state, envy *is mainly concerned with someone else* who has something or is in a certain state" (Ben-ze'ev 2001, p. 285, my emphasis). More recently, Fussi brings this possible focus of envy to the fore, when she writes: "envy is *not* primarily concerned with the *good* possessed by the other, but with the fact that *the other* possesses the good" (Ben-ze'ev 2019, p. 125). However, Fussi focuses also on the agent's self-evaluation in relationship to having failed to acquire the good. It is precisely this self-evaluative dimension that is going to be my main focus of concern in this section.

The idea that envy might be explained by focusing on the good or the rival is so extensive that some taxonomies of this emotion are elaborated precisely from this point of view (this is not the only criterion, but it is a significant one). Take, for instance, Taylor's distinction between the "good possessed" and the "possessor of the good" according to which there is an "object-envy" and a "state-envy". She writes:

> In cases of object-envy the envy is of the good the other has; its possessor plays a relatively minor role as being merely the occasion for the envious person's realization of her deficiencies. [...] In state-envy, on the other hand, the envy is of the-other-having-that-good. Here the other is seen as not merely that which happens to prompt her disagreeable view of herself, but it is thought of as somehow crucially involved in her finding herself in an inferior possession. (Taylor 2006, p. 43)

Taylor's taxonomy is more complex since she distinguishes between emulative and destructive, between primitive and sophisticated envy, and so on. Yet, the idea that envy can in principle be concerned with the good or with the rival is central for her account. In a more recent account, Protasi has distinguished different foci of concern of envy (the "focus of concern" is only one of the two variables for envy in her account, the other one being "the perceived obtainability of the good"). She writes: "the envier is either focused on the good or focused on the envied" (Protasi 2016, p. 538). Again, these taxonomies do not take into account that a focus of concern of envy might be oneself. This is precisely the aspect of envy that I want to underscore in my account.

As is clear, the majority of definitions of envy have described this emotion by accentuating either the object or the rival, and sometimes both. These definitions are right in indicating two important concerns of the envious self, but they ignore the fact that the subject itself might also be an object of concern.[7]

In this context dominated by a concern on the good or the rival, a few insightful accounts have indicated the importance of the envious self for a description of this emotion. For instance, in his description of envy as an emotion of social comparison, Elster distinguishes between different thoughts that might be involved in this emotion: "it is not the case that it should not have been me" (the one to possess the good), which points to an undeserved inferiority; the stronger claim "it should have been me"; and this other thought that "it should not have been him" as an indicator of the other's underserved fortune. In Elster's view, however, many cases of envy involve this other thought: "*I could have had that*" (Elster 1999, p. 171). These subtle differences might be regarded as different foci of concern of the envious self. In particular, the last one suggests that one of the concerns of envy is the status of the envious self. In a different vein, Kristjánsson has described envy as a self-comparative emotion in which we compare with ourselves (Kristjánsson 2010, p. 76), and Fussi – as mentioned above – presents envy as having a self-evaluative dimension (Fussi 2019, p. 130).

The most notable contribution in this respect is a recent paper by Salice and Montes Sánchez who describe envy as a self-conscious emotion insofar as in envy, we have the feeling of being disempowered. They write: "'hostile envy' identifies a single kind of emotion, which can be characterized as a self-conscious emotion or an emotion of negative self-assessment, insofar as the emotion is intentionally directed to its very subject, who evaluates herself as disempowered or as a loser when compared to the rival" (Salice and Montes Sánchez 2019, p. 228). They highlight two phenomenological accents of this emotion: "When the accent is on hostility, the emotion is thematically directed at the

---

[7] The authors mentioned recognize the participation of the self. For instance, Ben-ze'ev even discusses the possibility of self-envy; Taylor notes that envy is experienced as a threat to self-esteem; Protasi mentions the relevance of the self for this emotion, etc. Yet, in their descriptions of envy, they do not emphasize the fact that envy is an emotion *about* the self, an emotion in which we become *conscious of an aspect of ourselves*.

rival and is non-thematically about the self. When the accent is on disempowerment, the converse is the case: the emotion is thematically directed at the self and is non-thematically about the other" (*ibid*). They add: "This shows that, in envy, the other impacts the sense of self, which is a feature that envy shares with other self-conscious emotions, like shame and pride, when these emotions are induced by others" (*ibid*). As they put it, in experiences of envy, "the subject is intentionally directed at the very envier, and not at the rival" (*ibid*). Though one could discuss the existence of some forms of envy primarily focused on the object (central for definitions of the first type),[8] the point to underscore here is that for Salice and Montes Sánchez, envy is always about the self who is assessed as being at a disadvantage; there is a sense of "disempowerment" grounded in a comparison with the rival. I completely agree with this description, but I prefer to describe the situation as "feeling powerless" for the following reason: "Disempowerment" suggests that we once had the power and subsequently lost it, but "powerlessness" is more neutral in this regard: perhaps we never had the power to change the disadvantageous situation (though maybe we thought we had the power). The virtue of this account is that it focusses on envy as a self-referential, self-reflective, and self-conscious emotion.

These considerations show that envy might have the self as a focus of concern. Reformulating Fussi's description of envy provided above: envy is not primarily concerned with the good, nor with the fact that the rival possesses the good, but rather with the fact that *I* am not the one who possesses the good. The self-disclosive character of envy is clearly present in the feelings of powerlessness: in them, the envious self is directed towards herself. However, to a lesser extent it can be present also in feelings of loss, nostalgia, grief, injustice as well as in the feelings of inferiority insofar as they involve an assessment of the self in relation to the good and the rival. The difference is that while in the feelings of powerlessness the self-evaluation is clearly given, in the other feelings, the self-evaluation is only secondary.

1.4 Envy and the Feeling of Diminution of Self-Worth

I argued above that envy has a self-disclosive nature, but I have not specified what exactly envy discloses to the envious self. Here I will argue that the self-disclosive capacity of envy consists in presenting to us our own value as a person. Envy indicates not merely that we do not have the ability to change a situation in

---

[8] In this case, the accent would be on covetousness.

which we feel inferior, but also that our value is diminished for lacking this ability.

To elaborate this claim, I will first discuss the account presented by Perrine in his paper "Envy and Self-Worth" (Perrine 2011). In his critique of Aquinas, Perrine underlines that envy is related to self-worth – a claim I also endorse; however, in contrast to my approach that stresses the importance of the feeling of powerlessness, Perrine explains the link between envy and self-worth by focusing exclusively on the "feeling of inferiority" as the perception of one's own good as inferior to that of another. Perrine defines envy "as sorrowing over another's good because of a perception of inferiority regarding that good" (Perrine 2011, sec. 3). As I have argued above, this claim is problematic. For envy to take place, a feeling of powerlessness also has to be involved.

Perrine is right in linking envy with self-worth and in claiming that the inferiority involved in envy must be felt, i.e., it must be a *feeling* of inferiority and not merely a judgment that one is inferior. Insightfully, he writes:

> Here we should distinguish two types of inferiority. One type is simply noticing that another person has surpassed one. This is not the type of inferiority in a perception of inferiority. Rather, the inferiority is an evaluative judgment. One does not simply notice that another person has surpassed one's self; one feels as if one's own self-worth is thereby diminished. The difference between these two types of inferiority can be indicated in another way. Other people may be able to see that you are inferior – in this first sense – to another. But only you can feel your own perceived inferiority to that other person. (Perrine 2011, sec. 3)

However, as I already argued above, in envy we do not only feel our value to be inferior, but we feel this inferiority to be irremediable, to be something we cannot change. It is precisely this felt powerlessness, together with the feeling and belief that we should have had the power to obtain the envied good and the hostility experienced towards the rival, that makes envy so painful.[9] We feel our self-worth to be damaged, diminished, lowered, not "only" because we feel inferior to the other, but because we feel incapable of changing this situation of comparative inferiority.

Having stated the need to include different feelings and, in particular, the feelings of powerlessness, to explain how in envy we feel the diminution of one's own worth, I turn now to the very notion of "feeling of self-worth" involved in envy. As mentioned at the outset, I employ this term by drawing on Voigtländer who coined it to refer to how some feelings are responsible for giving us an

---

9 Moreover, in contrast to Ressentiment which leads to deny the values of the good and the rival, the envious self remains aware of the values of the good and its possessors.

experience of our own value. According to Voigtländer, a feeling of self-worth is "an affective valuating consciousness of one's own Self which each of us has and which is subjected to fluctuations" (Voigtländer 1910, p. 19, my trans.). In this experience, our own sense of self-worth is given to us. Feelings of self-worth imply self-assessment, i.e., we are aware of our own value or disvalue. Thus, inherent in them is a cognitive moment in which the value of ourselves is given to us. Voigtländer speaks of an "apprehension of value" (*Wertauffassung*) (Voigtländer 1910, p. 11). This apprehension of value is not a judgment about our value, but a feeling in which we become affectively aware of our own value (Voigtländer 1910, p. 13).

There are three main features that characterize feelings of self-worth. (1) They have a qualitative dimension. Pleasure and pain belong to our experiences of feeling uplifted or depressed. When our feeling of self-worth is elevated, we have a pleasant experience, while a degradation in our feeling of self-worth is unpleasant. (2) There is a cognitive moment which involves an awareness of our own value. Such awareness is conceived as a non-conceptual grasping of one's own worth. Rather than an objective judgment about ourselves, the moment of self-assessment involved in the feelings of self-worth is of a different kind: it is a valuating awareness of the self. (3) Feelings of self-worth are also necessarily accompanied by an awareness of the Self, which might occupy a central or peripheral position (Voigtländer 1910, p. 54).

There are similar concepts in contemporary philosophy. For instance, Keshen speaks of "self-esteem feelings" as those feelings in which the agent experiences an enhancement or a diminution of the self (Keshen 1996, pp. 3–4). The idea is further elaborated by Kristjánsson who speaks of "self-conscious emotions" (Kristjánsson 2010, p. 83). Salice and Montes Sánchez refer to this kind of feelings and to envy in particular as a "self-conscious emotion" (Salice and Montes Sánchez 2019, p. 232). I prefer Voigtländer's terminology for two reasons. First of all, feelings of self-worth are not emotions. As Voigtländer observed, emotions and feelings of self-worth differ from each other in at least three respects: (1) emotions are mental episodes, feelings of self-worth are background feelings; (2) emotions are directed towards particular objects, feelings of self-worth are focused on the Self; and (3) emotions are responses to certain features of the objects towards which they are directed, while in feelings of self-worth it is one's own value that is affectively given (Voigtländer 1910, pp. 10 and 19). Drawing on this, it is clear that envy is an emotion, i.e., a mental state directed towards an object we consider valuable and a rival, while the feelings involved in envy are better understood as feelings of self-worth, i.e., states in which we experience the value of our self as diminished. Second, Voigtländer's term also makes clear the relation of this kind of feeling with the value of the self.

In my view, this conception is clearly superior in two respects. First, Kristjánsson and Salice and Montes Sánchez use the term "emotion" to refer to these feelings, but this use is misleading by virtue of the differences between emotions and feelings noted above. Envy is an emotion; the feeling of self-worth is a feeling. Moreover, my claim is that envy necessarily involves a feeling of self-worth, and not that envy itself is a feeling of self-worth as these authors seem to claim. Furthermore, in claiming that envy is a self-conscious emotion, they refer to the capacity of envy to be about the self, but they do not specify which aspect of the self we become aware of. In contrast, the use of Voigtländer's terminology allows us to emphasize that in these feelings we affectively assess our own value. Secondly, to speak about a feeling of self-esteem, as Keshen does, is problematic, since self-esteem might be itself an affective phenomenon.[10]

As a result, envy is not a feeling of self-worth, but involves feelings in which we feel our own worth diminished. Envy involves feelings of the diminution, diminishment, devaluation of one's own value. The feelings of loss, nostalgia, grief, the feelings of being at a disadvantage, of being disfavored, of being inferior and of being powerless involved in envy can all be characterized in terms of feelings of self-worth. These feelings are unpleasantly felt; they involve a consciousness or awareness of our own value as being devalued; and they are accompanied by a consciousness of the self and its values. In these feelings we become conscious of a diminution of our own value. It is this diminishment of our own worth that is painfully revealed to us in envy. Among all these feelings, the most crucial for envy is the feeling of powerlessness. Here we not only feel diminished in worth, but also feel the pain of being unable to change this situation of comparative inferiority.

2 The Worst and Most Terrible of All Envies: Existential Envy

2.1 Existential Envy: A Descriptive Analysis

If the considerations above are right, envy is intimately related to the feeling of one's own value being diminished by virtue of being powerless to change our situation of inferiority. And given that it is the feeling of powerlessness that makes the devaluation involved in envy so painful, we can expect that envy is

---

[10] For the idea that self-esteem might be a kind of feeling, see Bortolan (2020).

experienced most painfully when the feeling of powerlessness and of being worthless is at its strongest. This happens when the good is unobtainable and beyond the reach of our human possibilities. In this second part of the paper, I will analyze a case of envy which has been described as the "most terrible" (Scheler 2010, p. 30) and the "worst case of envy" (Taylor 2006, p. 52), namely the case of "existential envy". This kind of envy refers to cases in which the target is the existence of another person. That is, the coveted good is not an object or a status, but the sheer existence of another person. This good is unobtainable because we cannot become a person who is radically different from who we are. This is Cain's envy for Abel.

One could object that this form of envy is too strong and too rare to illuminate aspects which might be central for more mundane cases of envy. However, in my view, the contrary is the case. Precisely because of its radicality, existential envy might be used as a heuristic tool: in this phenomenon key features of envy are presented in a more salient and poignant way. Moreover, for my argumentation, I will employ a literary example which functions as a thought experiment in which the central aspects of envy have been selected as variables for research.

The phenomenon of existential envy has been masterfully depicted by Miguel de Unamuno in his novel *Abel Sanchez* (1917). The book narrates the lives of *Joaquín* (whose name resembles Cain) and Abel, two friends who have known each other since birth. Hidden behind this friendship, however, we find the story of a "sombre passion": Joaquín envies Abel, and his envy is directed to the very nature of Abel. Already as a child, he envied Abel's talent and popularity which seemed to emerge so effortlessly. The envy becomes even worse when Abel marries Helena, the woman with whom Joaquín is also in love, and they have a son. After his marriage with the devoted Antonia, Joaquín becomes a father to Joaquina, but feels envious of Abel because of his son. Later on, Abel's son will follow Joaquín's path and become a doctor, marry his daughter, and give Abel and Joaquín a common grandson. In the end, Joaquin's envy does not merely target Abel's talents, recognition or love relations, but his entire existence. Joaquín would like to exchange lives with Abel, believing that Abel has the life that he should have had. Interestingly, the novel is written as a confession for his daughter and Joaquín explicitly admits to be an envier (an exceptional case given that in real life we tend not to admit to being envious, and instead attribute better motives to ourselves and disguise our envy as a feeling of injustice).[11] The envy described by Unamuno can be called "existential". It has

---

[11] There are few examples of explicit confessions of envy and most of them can be found in

also been described as "ontological envy" because it targets another's person being (Olson 2003, p. 109). Joaquín asks himself "who am I?" and "who do I want to be?" and he painfully discovers that he wants to be Abel.[12]

The novel exemplifies all the features of envy described above, but in a more radical form. Joaquín's envy is accompanied by *strong feelings*. For instance, after discovering that Helena will marry Abel, Joaquín experiences an acute episode of envy which he describes in the following terms:

> [I]n the days following the one on which he told me that they were getting married [...] I felt as if my whole soul were freezing over. An icy coldness ate into my heart. I felt like flames made of ice. I had difficulty breathing. My hatred for Helena and above all for Abel, because it was really hatred, a cold hatred whose roots reached down into my soul, had become hard as rock. [...] It was as if my soul had become totally frozen within that hatred. (Unamuno 2009, p. 53)

Joaquín's envy is *painfully* experienced. It causes him discomfort and suffering and he is unable to cope with it.

Moreover, this envy is related to *destructive action tendencies* and it *motivates vicious actions* which are directed towards the destruction of the rival. In the novel, these destructive tendencies become worse as Joaquín ages and the envy progresses until they become a constitutive part of his character. Joaquín reveals that his first thought after seeing the ill Abel was not to cure him (as one might expect given that they are friends and that Joaquín is his doctor!), but to imagine his death: "And what if he were to die?" (Unamuno 2009, p. 59). Later, when Abel's son was due to be born, he refused to help at the birth because he feared that he might strangle the newborn. At the end of the novel, it is Joaquín's aggressive behavior towards Abel that mainly causes Abel's death. Joaquín's suspicion that Abelín – their common grandson – prefers Abel leads to a violent confrontation in which Joaquín grabs Abel who subsequently dies from a heart attack.

At the cognitive-intentional level, existential envy also displays all the features of envy established above, but it has an intriguing peculiarity. In existential envy, the good and the rival coincide. To put it another way, the rival *is* the envied good.[13] It is the rival himself who is regarded as *valuable*, as worthy, and as a good in himself. The envier thinks he also *deserves* this good and, thus, that he

---

fiction. In his analysis of envy, Elster mentions how Iago explicitly acknowledges envying Cassio (1999, p. 164).

12 For an analysis of envy in Unamuno, cf. Vendrell Ferran 2019, pp. 77–96.

13 Taylor describes this type of envy as the owner of the good and the good itself coinciding (2006, p. 51). I will return to this point in the next section.

should be (like) the rival (the use of "like" in parentheses will become clear in the next section). The sense of loss and grief is stronger than when we just envy an object possessed by the rival, since here what we envy is the existence of the rival, and this is unachievable.

Existential envy involves a *comparison* with the rival who is someone with whom the envier fully *identifies*, who is *similar, familiar,* and *close* to him. Joaquín has known Abel since their childhood; they come from similar backgrounds; their lives develop in parallel; they are similar in age and social condition; they belong to the same peer group and are familiar and close to one another. For Joaquín, it seems only natural to compare himself with Abel, because Abel functions like a mirror for him. In comparing himself with someone he considers similar to him, Joaquín can better get to know who he is. What the specific case of existential envy makes clear is that there is an implicit *affective ambivalence* with regard to the other with whom we compare and identify. Unlike hatred or contempt, which tend to break interpersonal bonds, in envy the envious self remains emotionally attached to his rival. The envier hates the envied person, but he cannot help but see him as so beautiful, valuable, and worthy of admiration. Moreover, the comparison implicit in envy always targets someone belonging to our life horizon (a sibling, friend, neighbor, etc.). Thus, envy cannot just avoid the envied rival because the envier and the envied shared a world.

As a result of this comparison, a *feeling of inferiority* arises. The envier desires to be (like) the envied but he – like Joaquín in the novel – feels the gap between the desired self (to be like Abel or to be Abel) and the real one (he is Joaquín). This feeling gives rise to *the belief that he is inferior* which in turn serves to reinforce his low self-esteem. Given that Joaquín cannot change who he is and become Abel, he experiences a strong and intense *feeling of powerlessness*. The fact that it is metaphysically impossible to become a different person from the one we are is experienced as being painful and revealing of our inability to evolve according to our own ideals. The linkage between envy and self-esteem becomes clear in the case of existential envy. This emotion is the expression of a very low sense of self-worth (if we want to become another person, we do not like ourselves), but it also has consequences for the feeling of self-worth: in being absolutely powerless to become the other, we experience a radical diminution of our own value. In this regard, existential envy is the expression of low self-esteem, while at the same time the envier actively seeks to confirm their own lack of value.[14] In envying an unobtainable good, the envier experiences a strong

---

14 For an analysis of envy and its relation to self-worth, see Vendrell Ferran (2006, pp. 43–68).

devaluation of their own person and ends up feeling completely *worthless*. Thus, in existential envy, we do not just experience a diminution of our own value, but a complete lack of self-worth.

2.2 Envying *Being* the Other and Envying *Being Like* the Other

In existential envy, all features of envy are found in a more salient way. What I am primarily interested in here is the *object* of this kind of envy. To this end, I will start by considering existential envy as a variety of envy. A rather uncontroversial way to establish a taxonomy of envy is to focus on the different types of envied goods.[15] Envy might target: (1) material possessions (e.g., a house, a car); (2) social status (e.g., belonging to a specific social class) and/or relations in the interpersonal world (e.g., being a friend of or acquainted with someone); (3) particular qualities, talents or abilities of the other person (e.g., being talented, well-educated); (4) and it might target the existence of the other person (e.g., being the other). In a strict sense, existential envy refers to the fourth kind of object, but as we will see, when envy targets features linked to the existence of the other – also the third kind of object – this might be considered a case of existential envy too. An important aspect that was noted in the first part of the paper was that, in existential envy, "the rival" is in fact what counts as the "coveted good".

However, this coincidence between the rival and the good is far from obvious and requires further clarification. The coincidence can be – and in fact, in the scarce literature on this phenomenon, has been – interpreted in two senses. It can be interpreted (1) in a strong sense as envying the existence of the other, i.e., envying *being* the other, or (2) in a less radical sense as envying *being*

---

[15] See Taylor (2006) and Protasi (2016) for other taxonomies which I take to be controversial because they do not sufficiently distinguish between envy and similar emotions. Fussi has argued that Taylor's object-envy is not significantly different from covetousness (2019, pp. 126 and 130 ff.). Thus, Taylor's object-envy lacks what many have considered essential for this emotion: namely the search for social recognition. For her part, Protasi distinguishes between emulative, inert, aggressive, and spiteful envy. However, emulative envy could be regarded as a case of ambivalent admiration and aggressive envy as a case of rivalry. In both cases, the envious self does not experience the feeling of impotence because the good is something that the self considers obtainable. According to Protasi, only inert and spiteful envy involve the belief that the good is unobtainable and thus they involve what I regard to be central for envy: the feeling of powerlessness (the phenomenon that I call existential envy would be close to her description of spiteful envy).

like the other, i.e., as envying some attributes of the existence of the other, so that we would like to be *like* the other in some respects. According to both definitions, existential envy targets the existence of the other, but they differ in their (a) scope, (b) the relation of the envier with himself and (c) the relation with the rival.

a) I begin with the *differences of scope*. The first interpretation corresponds to a definition provided by Max Scheler in his book on *Ressentiment* (1912) and it defines existential envy as a kind of envy that targets the entire existence of the other. According to Scheler:

> The most powerless envy is also the most terrible. Therefore *existential envy* which is directed against the other person's very nature, is the strongest source of Ressentiment. It is as if it whispers continually; "I can forgive everything, but not that you are – that you are what you are – that I am not what you are – indeed that I am not you". This form of envy strips the opponent of his very existence, for this existence as such is felt to be a "pressure", a "reproach", and an unbearable humiliation. (Scheler 2010, p. 30)

For Scheler, envy has its origins in the non-fulfillment of a desire and in the hatred that we experience towards the person who possesses the coveted good and who is considered to be the cause of our privation. Since, as already mentioned, for Scheler envy implies not only a feeling of inferiority but also the feeling of impotence or powerlessness (a point that I made central to my description of envy), envy must be most terrible when it targets the existence of another person because this is a good that we can never obtain. The other is then regarded as the usurper of our existence and as living the life that we deserve to live. We experience the pain that another person is what we would like to be (the existence of the other is painful for us) and we experience the pain that we are not the other (our existence is experienced as faulty, defective, as not living up to our own ideals). There is an absolute idealization of the existence of the other accompanied by an absolute devaluation of our own existence. The consciousness, awareness and the feeling of impotence in changing the situation of inferiority is extreme in this case. What the envier envies is in fact *being the other*.

The second interpretation was provided by Gonzalo Fernández de la Mora in his book *Egalitarian Envy: The Political Foundations of Social Justice* (1984). After distinguishing three varieties of envy regarding the targeted objects – (1) existential envy directed at qualities of the other, (2) social envy directed at the position of the other, and (3) patrimonial envy directed at the possessions of the other – he goes on to describe existential envy in the following terms:

> Existential envy is grounded on the conviction that the other is happier because he is more intelligent, energetic, capable, elegant, etc. The envy is almost existential, caused by qual-

> ities that are not congenital; but they are so intimately embodied within the nature of the envious person that they become a part of his own makeup, like a habit – thus sanctity and some other capacities. Existential envy is rather uncommon for it tends to explain unnatural inferiorities through destiny or chance and this favors a fatalistic attitude and therefore the resigned acceptance of the adverse imbalance. But if existential envy is not directed or deactivated through some form of reasoning it becomes exceedingly rigid and stubborn due to the strength and immobility of its object, and it is very damaging for it affects the very essence of the envious person. (Fernández de la Mora 2000, pp. 69–70)

Each variety of envy has a different source: the origin of existential envy is located in pride; social envy is nourished by the will to power; and patrimonial envy is founded in greed. For the specific case of existential envy, Fernández de la Mora writes: "Pride underlies personal inferiority and gives rise to existential envy. Egocentricity is less common among the excellent than among the mediocre and might appear as very radical among the lowest levels" (de la Mora 2000, p. 70). In existential envy, we envy a person not for what she *has*, but for what she *is*.

Note that in Fernández de la Mora's description, the existential envier is depicted as envying personal qualities, attributes, and talents such as being intelligent, strong, elegant, etc., characteristic of another person's existence. The envied qualities are qualities that refer to the way in which we are regarded by others. It is the gaze of others that makes us intelligent, strong or elegant, because one can have these qualities only in a shared world in which comparisons between different persons can be made (it is not easy to change how we are perceived by others and how we in turn perceive ourselves mirroring the gaze of others). We envy the other's attributes and qualities, we can even envy all the attributes and qualities that are characteristic of this person, but we still want to remain the person we are. We do not want to be the other. What we want is to become *like* the other in some respect because we think that having this or that feature of the other would lead to an improved version of ourselves. Therefore, we envy *being like* the other in some respects, i.e., we envy having some (perhaps many) of the other's attributes and qualities.

What I want to underline here is a relevant difference regarding the scope of both definitions. In Scheler's definition what is targeted is the entire existence of the other, while in Fernández de la Mora's definition what is targeted are properties (call them attributes or qualities) that characterize the other's existence and as such deserve the adjective "existential." It is one thing to envy the existence or identity of the other (envying *being* the other); it is another to envy features which are definitory of the other's existence (envying *being like* the other in some or many respects). The identity of a person cannot be reduced to a bundle of properties, though the identity of a person can be described by mentioning bundles of properties.

b) There is a second significant difference in terms of *the emotions of the envious self* about itself in each of these definitions. Both interpretations make clear that existential envy is related to a low or non-existent feeling of self-worth and to an absolute lack of self-esteem. We do not like who we are or some aspects of who we are, and we would like to become the other or like the other. However, wanting to become another person is one thing, but it is something else to want to remain the person we are while desiring to have certain attributes that are typical of another person. In the first case, we *hate* everything in ourselves and want to exchange existences with the other, but in the second case, we are merely *unsatisfied* with some aspects of ourselves and think that if we had some of the attributes that are typical of the other, we would be a better version of our self.

c) Furthermore, there are also differences regarding *the relation between the envious self and the rival*.[16] In Scheler's definition, existential envy targets the entire existence or identity of the other and not merely some of her traits. In this view, even if one day we discover that person B better exemplifies some definitory qualities of person A, even if one day we discover that person B is more talented, more intelligent, etc., than person A, our envy might remain focused on person A. The rival as such is irreplaceable and one could say that we have "fallen in hate" with the rival (this concept was coined by Ortega y Gasset 1988, p. 19). In the same sense that in falling in love there is a narrowing of our attention to a single person, a similar phenomenon is possible in the case of hate. In "falling in hate", no matter what happens to the other person, we remain focused on her. In the case of existential envy, we hate her for being the person we would like to be (in hating her for this, we also hate ourselves, we hate the person we are).

In contrast, in Fernández de la Mora's definition, envy is focused on a set of qualities (x, y, z), which are only contingently exemplified by person A, but which could have been also exemplified by person B. There is no narrowing of our attention to person A because if one day we were to discover that person B better instantiates the desired qualities (x, y, z) than person A, then the object of our envy might change from person A to person B. This kind of existential envier has not "fallen in hate" with the rival: he is focused on the desirable qualities rather than the person who instantiates them. Insofar as the focus is on the qual-

---

[16] These reflections draw inspiration from Jerome Neu's analysis of jealousy and love (Neu 1980, p. 445).

ities, the other is interchangeable with another person if this person better instantiates the desired properties. As noted, he wants to remain the person he is, but he wants to have some of the desired qualities which incidentally are typical of another's existence.

Though the definition of existential envy in terms of envying *being* the other (1) and the definition of existential envy in terms of envying *being like* the other (2) differ in these three significant respects (scope, the relation of the envier with himself, and the relation of the envier with the rival), both definitions do not represent incompatible views on existential envy. In fact, each of these definitions can be regarded as describing a distinct phase of an emotion which evolves over time. Ordinary envy might begin targeting the objects and status of the rival, but it might progress to existential envy by targeting some of the other's attributes until it culminates in a desire to be the other.

Consider again the case of Joaquín, the protagonist of Unamuno's novel. His envy at the beginning is focused on certain goods (his wife),[17] on the status (his popularity) and on the personal qualities of Abel (his talent as a painter). But as time progresses, his envy focuses gradually on Abel's identity. Abel's goods or status are not important for Joaquín: both come from similar backgrounds, and since Joaquín is a physician and Abel is a painter, one can imagine that he is even richer and enjoys more social recognition than the envied one. What counts for Joaquín are the qualities attributed to Abel: his creativity, his capacity to be liked by others, his powers of seduction, etc. This causes Joaquín to focus step by step on Abel as the person who exemplifies all that he wants to be. His attention is narrowed – he has "fallen in hate" with him – so that in the end nobody else counts as a possible object of comparison. Abel dominates Joaquín's entire life horizon. As he puts it:

> [...] for in his solitude he never managed to be alone, for the other was always there. The other! It got to the point where he suddenly found himself in dialogue with him, inventing what the other one said to him. And the other, in these solitary dialogues, in these dialogued monologues, said inconsequential and agreeable things to him, and never showed him any rancor. "My God, why does he not hate me!", he came to ask himself. (Unamuno 2009, p. 135)

This focus on a single person has the character of surveillance, zeal, and control. Abel is the only point of reference in Joaquín's life. Rather than living centered

---

[17] In this case, envy is intimately linked to jealousy. Sometimes Joaquín is envious of Abel for having married his cousin Helena (he envies Abel because he would also have married her), but sometimes he is jealous of him (when he is jealous, he feels pain because he has lost her potential affection).

on himself, he lives centered on the other. As a result, a situation of dependency arises. All that he undertakes is put into a relation with Abel. And given that Joaquín cannot free himself from this situation of dependency, the relation with the envied is a cause of anxiety: he feels prosecuted by the other who has become the center of all his thoughts. To compensate for this anxiety, Joaquín desires, wishes, and dreams that Abel at least thinks of him. Abel has become part of his self-definition; the envied is internalized and is omnipresent in his mind. Joaquín considers Abel guilty of his misfortune: because Abel exists, he is now condemned to fail. Abel is described as having misappropriated his life and he feels that he has had to develop his existence in the shadow of the envied rival. The feeling of powerlessness reaches a peak: he cannot become the other, though he would like to exchange places with him. And finally, an absolute devaluation of oneself takes place: he feels worthless because he is not the other.

There is a progression of feeling in existential envy so that the envier might start envying the goods and the status of others, progressing to envying *being like* the other (the second definition of existential envy mentioned above) and ending up envying *being* the other (the first definition of existential envy provided above). Though existential envy might begin by focusing on such qualities which are by chance exemplified by person A, it can progressively become focused on this person rather than on particular qualities. Because we compare ourselves again and again with person A as an example of someone who has the desired qualities, because others might have also been comparing us with person A and because person A belongs to our life horizon and we often interact with her, having multiple occasions to experience the painful feeling that she has what we also would like to have, it might happen that we progressively "fall in hate" with her, so that the desired qualities move to the background of our attention while the person who instantiates such qualities comes to the foreground. Little by little there is a progressive fixation of our attention on a particular individual who in the end becomes irreplaceable. Therefore, we can consider Fernández de la Mora's definition as describing existential envy in its initial state, while Scheler's view can be regarded as a depiction of existential envy in its full development.

Though existential envy presupposes that envy has undergone a temporal development which lasts in time, we are dealing here with an emotion and not just with a character trait. As an emotion, existential envy is based on cognitions; it targets the rival as good, and it is also felt. However, it is not acutely felt all the time that the envier is dominated by this emotion. Joaquín is able to live his life, to marry, to have a daughter, to practice as a physician, and he does constantly experience acute episodes of envy. Sometimes this envy is in the foreground of our consciousness, while at other times it is in the background. In this regard, envy can become a mode of existence and be constitutive of our character, determining how we perceive, attend, judge, believe, think, desire, and feel.[18]

3 Concluding Remarks

Standard definitions of envy tend to focus on the good and the rival, leaving aside the role played by the envious self. Against this background, this paper has provided a description of envy that considers the envious self and its feelings. I have demonstrated that envy involves feeling powerless to change a situation of comparative inferiority and leads to a feeling of diminishment of one's self-worth. This claim was illustrated through an analysis of existential envy as the worst and most terrible form of envy.

References

Ben-ze'ev, Aaron (1992): "Envy and Inequality". In: *Journal of Philosophy* 89(11), pp. 551–581.
Ben-ze'ev, Aaron (2001): *The Sublety of Emotions*. Cambridge, MA: The MIT Press.
Bortolan, Anna (2020): "Self-Esteem, Pride, Embarrassment and Shyness". In: Szanto, Thomas/Landweer, Hilge (Eds.), *The Routledge Handbook of Phenomenology of Emotion*. London, New York: Routledge, pp. 358–368.
Breyer, Thiemo (2018): "Self-conscious Emotions: Reflections on their Bipolarity, Normativity, and Perspectivity". In: Parker, Rodney K.B./Quepons, Ignacio (Eds.): *The New Yearbook for Phenomenology and Phenomenological Philosophy* 16, pp. 76–86.
Elster, Jon (1999): *Alchemies of the Mind. Rationality and the Emotions*. Cambridge: Cambridge University Press.
Fernández de la Mora, Gonzalo (2000): *Egalitarian Envy. The Political Foundations of Social Justice*. New York: ToExcel.
Fussi, Alessandra (2019): "Envy and Its Objects". In: *Humana.Mente: Journal of Philosophical Studies* 35, pp. 124–149.
Keshen, Richard (1996): *Reasonable Self-Esteem: A Life of Meaning*. Montreal: McGill University Press.
Klein, Melanie (1997): *Envy and Gratitude and Other Works 1946–1963*. London: Vintage Classics.
Kristjánsson, Kristján (2010): *The Self and Its Emotions*. Cambridge: Cambridge University Press.
Magrì, Elisa (2018): "Emotions, Motivation, and Character: A Phenomenological Perspective". In: *Husserl Studies* 34(3), pp. 229–245.
Neu, Jerome (1980): "Jealous Thoughts". In: Rorty, Amélie O. (Ed.), *Explaining Emotions*. Berkeley: University of California Press, pp. 425–464.

---

18 For an analysis of how emotions influence our character, see Magrì (2018, pp. 229–245).

Olson, Paul R. (2003): *The Great Chiasmus: Word and Flesh in the Novels of Unamuno*. West Lafayette: Purdue University Press.
Ortega y Gasset, José (1988): "Falling in Love". In: Norton, David L./Kille, Mary F. (Eds.): *Philosophies of Love*. Lanham: Rowman & Littlefield, pp. 14–20.
Perrine, Timothy (2011): "Envy and Self-Worth: Amending Aquinas' Definition of Envy". In: *American Catholic Philosophical Quarterly* 85(3), pp. 433–446.
Protasi, Sara (2016): "Varieties of Envy". In: *Philosophical Psychology* 29(4), pp. 535–549.
Salice, Alessandro/Montes Sánchez, Alba (2019): "Envy and Us". In: *European Journal of Philosophy* 27(1), pp. 227–242.
Scheler, Max (2010): *Ressentiment*. Trans. Lewis B. Coser/William W. Holdheim. Milwaukee: Marquette University Press.
Taylor, Gabriele (2006): *Deadly Vices*. Oxford: Oxford University Press.
Unamuno, Miguel de (2009): *Abel Sánchez*. Oxford: Aris & Phillips.
Vendrell Ferran, Íngrid (2006): "Über den Neid. Eine phänomenologische Untersuchung". In: *Deutsche Zeitschrift für Philosophie* 54(1), pp. 43–68.
Vendrell Ferran, Íngrid (2019): "Exploring Self and Emotion: Unamuno's Narrative Fiction as Thought Experiment". In: Hagberg, Garry (Ed.): *Narrative and Self-Understanding. Between Literature and Philosophy*. Cham: Palgrave, pp. 77–96.
Voigtländer, Else (1910): *Vom Selbstgefühl*. Leipzig: Voigtländer Verlag.

Anna Bortolan
Social Anxiety, Self-Consciousness, and Interpersonal Experience

Abstract: The chapter explores some aspects of the relationship between self-consciousness and consciousness of others, by looking in particular at the phenomenology of social anxiety disorder. More specifically, drawing on the phenomenological distinction between pre-reflective and reflective self-consciousness, and its application to the study of schizophrenia spectrum disorders, I suggest that the disturbances of social experience characteristic of social anxiety disorder are rooted in certain alterations of self-experience, and I endeavour to provide an account of the latter. More specifically, I claim that a) pathological social anxiety involves a heightening of the subject's reflective self-consciousness, and b) that this, at least partly, originates in the experience of a low sense of self-worth, which I refer to as low "self-esteem", and conceive of as a particular kind of background affective orientation.

1 Introduction

In both classical and contemporary phenomenological research investigations of self- and other-experience have often been intertwined. Phenomenologists have indeed explored not only the multiple ways in which we can be conscious of ourselves, and different forms of intersubjective and interpersonal understanding; they also have unearthed fundamental connections between these two experiential dimensions. They have done so, for example, by showing how empathy for another is rooted in an apprehension of the subject we are empathising with as an embodied being fundamentally similar to oneself (cf. Husserl 1989; Stein 1989), and by showing that self-consciousness itself can incorporate the perspective, or "gaze" of the other (e.g. Sartre 1989).

These insights have significantly contributed to our understanding of both ordinary and psychopathological experience, as they have been grounded in and further applied to the exploration of disturbances such as those characteristic of autism spectrum disorder and schizophrenia (e.g. Grünbaum and Zahavi 2013; Stanghellini 2004; Zahavi 2008).

This paper builds upon this body of research to develop a phenomenological analysis of some of the alterations of experience which characterise social anxiety disorder or social phobia (American Psychiatric Association [APA] 2013; WHO

1992, 2021).[1] Within existing psychiatric classifications, these are conceived as complex syndromes, central to which are various disturbances of interpersonal experience. In particular, a significant fear of being scrutinised or evaluated by others and a consequent tendency to avoid social situations are key aspects of these conditions (cf. APA 2013, pp. 202–203; WHO 1992, 2021).

In this paper I explore these predicaments by drawing on a series of distinctions which have been put forward by phenomenologists. In particular, I suggest that the disturbances of social experience characteristic of social anxiety disorder are rooted in particular alterations of self-experience, providing a phenomenological account of the latter. As highlighted by empirical research (e. g. Hackman *et al.* 1998; Moscovitch *et al.* 2009; Wilson and Rapee 2006), disturbances of one's self-conception are integral to social phobia, and the aim of this study is to offer a phenomenological clarification of the way in which disruptions of self- and other-experience are here intertwined.

2 Pre-Reflective and Reflective Self-Consciousness

The distinction between pre-reflective and reflective self-consciousness has roots in classical phenomenology, but has also been used extensively in the contemporary phenomenological literature. For example, Shaun Gallagher and Dan Zahavi, describe pre-reflective self-consciousness as a "non-observational" and "non-objectifying" awareness of the self (2012, p. 52), namely as a form of awareness that is not developed through introspection, and entails an experience of the self as a subject rather than an object.

In our ordinary dealings with the world we are often pre-reflectively aware of ourselves, and an example of this is provided by phenomenological analyses of bodily experience. Phenomenologists have indeed drawn attention to the fact that, typically, in perceptual experience the body is not given thematically – as the focus of perception – but rather it remains "in the background", constituting the perspective from which our perceptual field is structured. The body in these cases is given, according to Merleau-Ponty (2012: 94), not as an object among other objects, but rather as that in virtue of which there are objects.

---

[1] In the ICD-11 (WHO 2021), the term "social anxiety disorder" is used instead of "social phobias" (WHO 1992), and the former is also employed to refer to the disorder in the current version of the DSM (APA 2013). In this chapter, the terms "social phobia" and "social anxiety" are used interchangeably.

A key phenomenological distinction in this regard is indeed that between the subjective body (*Leib*) and the objective body (*Körper*) (Husserl 1989), or, in other terms, between the lived, unthematised body and the observed, thematised one (Zahavi 1999, p. 104). By drawing attention to the fact that originally the body is not given as one among other perceptual objects, but rather as that through which other objects can be perceived, Husserl (1989) and Merleau-Ponty (2012) provide an account of the body as it is subjectively lived. This kind of bodily experience has a non-objectifying and non-observational character and can thus be considered to be a form of pre-reflective self-consciousness.

Pre-reflectivity has been attributed also to other, more general forms of self-related experience, for example the "sense of ownership". Gallagher and Zahavi, for instance, have suggested that we do not need to explicitly direct attention to our experiences in order to be aware that we are the owners of these experiences (cf. Gallagher and Zahavi 2012, pp. 56–58; Gallagher 2000). Such an awareness has an implicit character and is indeed taken to be the cornerstone of pre-reflective self-consciousness.[2]

Intrinsic to the pre-reflective experience we have of our body is also a felt sense of our agentive capacities, and Gallagher and Zahavi (2012, p. 176 ff.; Gallagher 2000) emphasise how actions that are performed intentionally are normally accompanied by the sense of being the author of those actions, that is "the one who is causing or generating" them (Gallagher 2000, p. 15). Such a "sense of agency" is considered to be distinct from the sense of ownership, but it is maintained that they both operate at the pre-reflective level. This is not to deny that we can be reflectively aware of being an agent or the owner of our experiences and that we are able to express this awareness linguistically. However, as observed by Gallagher and Zahavi (2012, pp. 180–181), "attributions" of ownership and agency at the reflective level depend on a prior pre-reflective experience. In other terms, according to this position, it is because I already experience myself as an agent pre-reflectively that I can reflectively conceive of myself as the author of my own actions.

Reflective self-consciousness encompasses different forms of awareness of the self in which the self is given as an object – for instance perceptual forms

---

[2] For Gallagher and Zahavi (e.g. 2012), pre-reflective self-consciousness is ubiquitous – it is a constitutive aspect of every form of conscious experience, and can be identified with a basic form of selfhood, the "minimal self" (see also Bortolan 2020b for a critical reconstruction of this idea). Although I am sympathetic to this view, my analysis in this paper does not assume or defend the ubiquity of pre-reflective self-consciousness. Here, I only claim that we are *frequently* aware of ourselves pre-reflectively and that a heightened reflectivity can be associated with various forms of pathological experience.

(as is the case when I look at myself in the mirror) – or cognitive forms, such as thinking, imagining, or remembering myself in certain ways. Reflective self-consciousness can also be associated with certain forms of interpersonal experience, where we become aware of ourselves as the object of another person's attention. This is famously exemplified by the Sartrean account of "The Look" (Sartre 1989) and the experience of shame associated with it. Sartre considers the experience of being seen by someone while in the act of peeping through a keyhole. The voyeur, Sartre suggests, would feel ashamed (Sartre 1989, p. 259 ff.), and through this experience would become aware of himself in a distinct way, namely he would become aware of himself as the object of another's consciousness. Shame is not the only experience through which we can develop such an awareness, and indeed, within the Sartrean framework, it is a paradigmatic example of what is considered to be more broadly the structure of self- and other-consciousness in interpersonal relationships (cf. Danto 1975, pp. 103 – 106).

3 Self-Consciousness and Psychopathology: The Case of Schizophrenia

The distinction between pre-reflective and reflective self-consciousness has played an important role in the field of phenomenological psychopathology, for example in the exploration of the experiential disturbances associated with schizophrenia spectrum disorders. In particular, it has been argued that patients who suffer from schizophrenia experience an intensification of forms of experience associated with reflective self-consciousness, and that this is rooted in a disruption of processes which usually take place at the pre-reflective level. In other terms, both disturbances of reflectivity and pre-reflectivity have been identified as central to the phenomenology of schizophrenia, and the latter have been attributed a key role in the generation of the symptoms of the disorder (cf. Fuchs 2005; Parnas and Sass 2001; Sass and Parnas 2003; Stanghellini 2004).

It has been argued that these symptoms can be explained as dependent on a fundamental experiential alteration, a "trouble générateur" (Minkowski 1997) – a generative disturbance – that can be detected in the prodromal stages of the illness and underpins the formation of psychotic symptoms (Parnas and Sass 2001, p. 101). Such a disturbance involves a disruption of the "natural self-evidence of everyday existence" (Blankenburg 2001, p. 309), a loss of the *common sense* which allows us to take for granted many aspects of the world and ourselves, without having to constantly question them. Blankenburg enumerates various possible alterations of common sense observed in schizophrenic patients, which often begin with a reduced capacity to "take things in their right light", and manifest in "a withering away of a sense of tact, a feeling for the proper thing to do in situations, a loss of awareness of the current fashions or what is 'in,' and a general indifference toward what might be disturbing to others" (Blankenburg 2001, p. 305). Some of these phenomena become often evident in the difficulty or incapacity to carry out ordinary self-care activities and routines, which can then be maintained only by means of a conscious effort. As Elyn Saks explains in her memoir: "[t]aking care of myself meant doing more than reading a book or finishing a term paper; it meant strategizing, organizing, keeping track. And some days, there just wasn't enough room in my head to keep all that together" (Saks 2011, pp. 33–34).

Parnas and Sass agree with the idea that a disruption of common sense is central to various symptoms of schizophrenia, and have investigated the role played by disturbances of self-experience in this context. More precisely, they conceive of disorders of pre-reflective self-awareness as the "core" disturbance on the basis of which also a unitary explanation of positive, negative, and disorganisation symptoms can be given (Parnas and Sass 2001; Sass and Parnas 2003). In particular, they identify two main aspects as key to the disruption of self-experience in schizophrenia: "diminished self-affection" and "hyperreflexivity" (Sass and Parnas 2003). The former term indicates a diminution in the felt experience of oneself as a subject of awareness and action. Hyperreflexivity, on the other hand, indicates an unusual awareness of aspects of experience which normally go unnoticed, awareness which displays a reflective structure.

The notion of hyperreflexivity is further characterised by Sass with regard to the stage of the illness it appears in and the function it plays (Sass 2000; Zahavi 2008, p. 137). "Basal hyperreflexivity" is part of the primary schizophrenic disturbance itself: it happens automatically and disrupts the subject's experience by bringing into the foreground aspects of the experience that would normally be implicit. As a result of this phenomenon, "consequential hyperreflexivity" may develop, as further attention might be drawn to the experiential aspects that were previously unnoticed, and the subjects might increasingly engage in self-scrutinising and self-objectifying processes. Finally, as a reaction to diminished self-affection, patients might intentionally take a reflective attitude towards their own experiences, trying to compensate for their reduced pre-reflective sense of self through excessive self-monitoring, a process which is referred to as "compensatory hyperreflexivity".

These phenomena are exemplified by the tendency to become explicitly aware of aspects of one's bodily and cognitive processes which typically go undetected, and to objectivate and spatialise one's inner experience. Schizophrenic patients often feel detached or decentred from their body, actions, or stream of consciousness – as if they had taken a spectatorial stance, observing themselves from another's perspective (Fuchs 2005, p. 102). In other terms, they experience a shift from a first-personal to a third-personal point of view on their own experience (e.g. Parnas 2003).

As observed by Fuchs (2005, p. 105), the experience of schizophrenia may thus be marked by what can be referred to as a "disembodiment of the self", a particular form of depersonalisation in which embodied, pre-reflective self-consciousness is replaced by a form of intellectual awareness. It is in virtue of this dynamic that, according to Stanghellini (2004, Ch. 8), it becomes possible to liken some of the experiences undergone by those who suffer from schizophrenia to those of cyborgs or scanners, namely experiences in which bodies become somehow "deanimated" and "disembodied".

In the following, I will show that anomalies of pre-reflective and reflective self-consciousness are central also to the phenomenology of social anxiety or social phobia, suggesting, however, that these have a distinct character from the ones which have been identified as key to schizophrenia spectrum disorders.

4 Social Anxiety and Self-Experience: Heightened Reflective Self-Consciousness

Research on social anxiety has highlighted that those who suffer from this condition engage in detailed self-monitoring in social situations (Clark and Wells 1995; Rapee and Heimberg 1997). In these circumstances, social phobia sufferers tend to see themselves from the perspective of an observer (Wells *et al.* 1998), and this often involves the presence of negative self-imagery (Hackmann *et al.* 1998): the person imagines how she would appear to another, and such a depiction is fraught with negative attributes. For example, in a first-person testimony reported by Hackmann and colleagues, a patient describes her self-experience during episodes of social anxiety in the following terms:

> Picture of me looking guilty, nervous, anxious, embarrassed. It's my face—features distorted, intensified, big nose, weak chin, big ears, red face. Slightly awkward body posture, introverted body posture, turning in on myself. Accent more pronounced. I sound stupid, not articulate or communicating well. (Hackmann *et al.* 1998, p. 9)

Another report provided by Ford in her memoir of the illness highlights how socially anxious individuals tend to visualise themselves as they would be perceived by others:

> The imagined thoughts of my classmates bombarded me from all sides: "Her hair is so ugly." "Yeah, but did you see those yellow teeth?" "Look at what she's wearing." "She's covered in cat hair." "She's covered in her own hair. Did you see her arms?" "She better not be my lab partner." (Ford 2007, p. 28)

This excerpt describes an experience in which one's self-perception is saturated with the anticipation of how others might be thinking of or judging oneself, and such an anticipation is permeated with negativity. This predicament, is also often accompanied by the tendency to overestimate how much of one's experience is actually visible from the outside: one's alleged shortcomings are felt as being particularly prominent, so that it would be impossible for others not to notice them. As Ford explains:

> I believed that I wore my emotions on my sleeve for the whole world to see. So why didn't anyone notice? Didn't anyone care? It seemed impossible for people *not* to notice my torment, when everything from walking across a room to getting a drink of water was so excruciating for me. (Ford 2007, p. 38)

These reports point towards the existence, in social anxiety, of an increased level of reflective self-consciousness. The person is indeed frequently and intensely conscious of herself as the object of other people's attention and observation.[3] She sees herself as she imagines she would be seen by others, and thus is often taking a spectatorial or third-personal perspective on her own experience. This tendency is again highlighted by various first-personal reports. As explained by Grazia:

> Imagine walking through a mall with your head down in an effort to avoid eye contact thinking all eyes are on you and everyone is talking about you. Imagine feeling like you're always on the outside trying to get in. Imagine not knowing where to be. (Grazia 2010, p. 9)

The alterations of self- and other-experience highlighted so far are an integral part also of the cognitive-behavioural model of the disorder developed by Rapee and Heimberg (1997). According to this model, social anxiety involves a

---

[3] Tanaka (2021) has suggested that at the core of the phenomenology of social anxiety is an experience of the "body-as-object for others", which corroborates the idea that reflective self-consciousness is central to this predicament. However, Tanaka does not suggest that the pathological aspect of social anxiety depends on an exacerbation of reflective self-consciousness. Rather, he argues that the experience of the body-as-object for others in social anxiety disorder has specific features (e.g. it is marked by an increased tendency to perceive uncertainty as danger).

prediction of the likelihood of being negatively evaluated by others, and depends on a mental representation of how the self appears to an audience (Rapee and Heimberg 1997, p. 749).

As mentioned before, phenomenological research in psychopathology has evidenced how heightened reflective self-consciousness may be an integral aspect of the experiential alterations which mark certain forms of psychopathological experience. This research has also drawn attention to how increased reflectivity is linked to disruptions of the pre-reflective level of self-awareness. As we have seen previously in the case of schizophrenia, it is argued that "hyperreflexivity" goes hand in hand with an impoverishment of one's pre-reflective experience, and, often, of the implicit sense we usually have of being the owners and authors of our own mental states and actions.

Pathological forms of social anxiety are marked by a heightening of reflective self-consciousness too, but does this entail the presence of disruptions of pre-reflectivity? In other terms, is it the case that, similarly to what happens in schizophrenia spectrum disorders, disturbances of reflective and pre-reflective self-consciousness are both present in social phobia?

People who suffer from social anxiety do not appear to have a diminished sense of themselves as subjects of experience or authors of their own actions. However, there are multiple aspects to self-experience at the pre-reflective level, and I will argue in the following that it is indeed one of these other dimensions which is altered in social phobia, claiming that both reflectivity and pre-reflectivity are disrupted in the illness.

In particular, my suggestion will be that socially anxious subjects have a low pre-reflective sense of their own ability and achievements – what I will call "self-esteem" – and it is in this feature that a number of transformations characteristic of the disorder are rooted. More specifically, I will illustrate how, due to self-esteem being low, socially anxious subjects tend to see their worth as determined primarily by comparative and social assessments, and this is what leads to the increased self- and other-monitoring – and thus heightened reflective self-consciousness – that is typical of the disorder.

In order to illustrate and defend this view, I will first show how a felt sense of one's worth is a key component of one's pre-reflective self-experience. I will explain how this can be considered to be a particular background affective orientation, or "existential feeling", highlighting the way in which such forms of experience can impact on one's cognition and affectivity. In light of this, I will then move to explain how very low self-esteem may be at the origin of some of the transformations of self- and other-experience undergone by socially anxious subjects.

5 Self-Esteem

As highlighted above, in the contemporary phenomenological literature, pre-reflective self-consciousness tends to be associated with an experience of the self as an embodied perceiver and agent. However, these are not the only features of selfhood that emerge in pre-reflective awareness. As I have suggested elsewhere (Bortolan 2020a), pre-reflective self-consciousness can also have an evaluative character, and, more specifically, be a consciousness of the self as more or less worthy. This claim is rooted in the idea that self-worth is first and foremost a matter of affective experience (cf. Bortolan 2018, 2020b), and draws on classical and recent phenomenological accounts of affectivity.

Phenomenologists have significantly contributed to the understanding of the relationship between feeling and intentionality, supporting the idea that what we generally refer to through the concept of "emotion" can be both a felt state and a state that is directed at a particular object. From this perspective, affective phenomena include "intentional feelings", and it is thus possible to talk about a specific kind of "affective intentionality" (Slaby 2008).

In addition to this, however, a central contribution of phenomenological research on affects consists in the identification and exploration of specific non-intentional affective states, examples of which are Martin Heidegger's account of "moods" (Heidegger 1962) and Matthew Ratcliffe's account of "existential feelings" (e.g. Ratcliffe 2005, 2008).

The type of experience that is the focus of these investigations is not generally directed at any particular object – moods and existential feelings are not about anything in particular; however, lack of intentionality is not their only defining characteristic. What is key to these affects is indeed also the role they play in shaping other aspects of our experience and, in particular, the influence they have on our capacity to undergo other cognitive, affective, and volitional states. For Ratcliffe (2010, p. 604), for instance, existential feelings determine the range of intentional states that we can experience, a feature which is designated by the notion of "pre-intentionality". From this perspective, not only existential feelings typically lack an object, but they also constrain the possible ways in which we can relate to objects, modulating intentionality in a radical manner.

I have suggested elsewhere that Ratcliffe's notion of existential feeling is best suited to account for the nature of what we call "self-esteem" (Bortolan 2018, 2020b). I have argued that, while it may motivate a variety of self-focused beliefs and judgments, self-esteem is first and foremost a felt experience, integral to which is an evaluation of the self as more or less worthy. Self-esteem, in other terms, is a particular type of feeling, through which we appraise ourselves as being valuable to various degrees.

In addition, self-esteem appears to play a fundamental role in shaping the way in which one can think and feel about oneself, and, drawing also on a phenomenological analysis of experiences of low self-esteem, I have argued that it has the power to constrain our thoughts and emotions in ways that make it appropriate to attribute to this phenomenon a pre-intentional character (Bortolan 2018, 2020b). Self-esteem, from this perspective, is a self-evaluative affective experience which deeply moulds our cognitive, emotional, and practical life. However, as previously illustrated, there are different forms of self-consciousness, and it is now important to clarify whether the particular type of awareness of the self conveyed by self-esteem has a pre-reflective or reflective structure.

Experiences of self-esteem do not require us to turn our attention inward and to observe ourselves. Certainly, we do sometimes think about our worth, we ponder over how valuable we are or are taken to be, we wonder about how "good" or "bad" we are, or how well regarded we are by others. However, most of the time, in ordinary circumstances we are not reflectively engaged in such forms of self-assessment. On the contrary, our focus tends to be on the external world, other people, or the varieties of projects and activities we are involved in. This, however, does not mean that we are not having an experience of self-worth (or lack thereof).

When we are carrying out a particular task or talking to a person, we do not stop experiencing ourselves. As phenomenological research on the lived body suggests, for instance, we still have an implicit sense of the location of our limbs, and of our bodily conditions and potentialities. Even if we are not thinking about it, we feel that we are tired or full of energy, thirsty, ill, or sleepy, and we have a sense of what it might be possible for us to do in our current circumstances. For example, a person who is feeling exhausted or depleted will have an implicit sense that walking long distances might not be something she is able to do, and may as a result feel inclined to avoid this kind of activity.

Self-esteem, I believe, is generally felt in the same peripheral way: it is an experience of the self as more or less worthy which accompanies us through our daily activities and interactions, but which is, most of the time, not in the "foreground". We feel more or less valuable and this shapes the way in which we see others and the world, but this feeling is not generally at the forefront of our attention. This is another reason why the notion of existential feeling seems to be suited to account for the nature of self-esteem, as the former is characterised as a particular kind of background affective orientation (Ratcliffe 2008), namely something that structures our experiential field without, however, being at the centre of it.

Such an account is consonant with phenomenological explorations of experiences of ability and affectivity. Jan Slaby (2012), for instance, suggests that integral to all our affective states is a sense of our embodied capabilities and potentialities, which shapes the way in which we view ourselves, others, and the world. Because of its felt character, background structure, and experience-shaping role, this "sense of ability" is recognised by Slaby to be akin to an "existential feeling" (Slaby 2012, p. 153), and what appears to be an analogous type of experience has been called by Hans Bernhard Schmid "the most fundamental existential feeling" (Schmid 2011, p. 230).

As mentioned by Slaby himself, there is a close connection between the sense of ability and self-esteem (Slaby 2012, p. 153). We can indeed observe that the feelings of our own capabilities and potentialities are both causally and phenomenologically integral to the experience of self-esteem. Our sense of self-worth is influenced by what we take ourselves to be able to do or not, and feeling more or less worthy amounts to feeling more or less able to do certain things, undertake certain challenges, seize certain opportunities, etc.

However, I have recently argued (Bortolan 2020b) that, in addition to the sense of ability, part and parcel of self-esteem is also a felt sense of one's accomplishments, a feeling of one having been more or less effective in obtaining certain results. While the sense of ability is an experience of oneself as having certain capacities and possibilities, this other form of experience amounts to an implicit sense of oneself as having achieved more or less, as having had a more or less extensive impact, we can say, on oneself and the world.

Drawing on existing terminological distinctions in the philosophical and psychological literature, I have suggested that the sense of ability can also be referred to as "self-efficacy" while what I have described as a sense of achievement can be considered as a form of "self-respect" (Bortolan 2020b). I have argued that the two are key to the phenomenology of self-esteem, in so far as intrinsic to our sense of self-worth is not only a felt sense of being able (or unable) to do certain things, but also an experience of oneself as having achieved something, as having been effective to a certain extent in shaping one's and outer circumstances.

The claim that a sense of both ability and achievement are at the core of self-esteem may lead us to to wonder to what extent this experience can be identified with one type of existential feeling, or whether it would be more appropriate to think of it as a set or range of affects. In this regard, I have suggested (Bortolan 2020b) that a phenomenological investigation supports the claim that self-esteem is a unitary phenomenon: feeling worthy or worthless to different degrees is a particular kind of experience with a distinct qualitative character. This is however compatible with the recognition that there may be different aspects or components to self-esteem, a feature which, I argued, can be accounted for by appealing to Peter Goldie's account of affective phenomena as having a "narrative structure" (Goldie 2000; 2012).

6 Low Self-Esteem and Evaluation of Self and Other in Social Anxiety Disorder

As discussed in the previous sections of this study, in addition to alterations of interpersonal experience, social anxiety involves significant disruptions of self-experience and self-conception. We saw, for example, how people who suffer from social phobia tend to see themselves from the perspective of others, and to attribute to the self so perceived a set of negative features. More broadly, a low sense of self-worth seems to be central to the phenomenology of the disorder. Negative self-evaluations (Moscovitch *et al.* 2009) and reduced levels of confidence in one's self-assessments (Wilson and Rapee 2006) are common among social anxiety sufferers and lack of self-confidence is central to these painful experiences. For example, discussing the case of a particular patient, Tyrer and Emmanuel claim that:

> When asked what she regarded as the most important problem, she did not, as the doctor expected, say that the blushing was the most important, but that she lacked self-confidence. She used to have a series of thoughts (she called them fantasies) of how she would behave if she had more self-confidence. She also used to rehearse these repeatedly on occasions when she believed she would be exposed to formal situations and risk making a fool of herself again. (Tyrer and Emmanuel 1999, pp. 15–16)

People affected by social phobia, I have shown, exhibit distinct alterations of reflective self-consciousness, as this is both heightened and permeated with negativity. I had hypothesised that, similarly to what is the case in some instances of schizophrenia, such disturbances of reflectivity could be rooted in disruptions of pre-reflective experience, and it is now possible to see how these disruptions concern specifically the person's sense of self-worth. What is disrupted in social anxiety is also the person's implicit confidence in her ability and achievements, which can be radically and painfully low.

I illustrated in Section 5 how, from a phenomenological perspective, experiences of ability and achievement – which I jointly referred to through the notion of "self-esteem" – are best understood as a particular kind of background affective orientation, namely as a specific type of existential feeling. This, I suggested, generally operates at the pre-reflective level, while constraining the range of mental states one can entertain. In social anxiety self-esteem – as a form of experience of the self that works below the level of reflection – is significantly impoverished, and this is where some of the disturbances of reflectivity previously highlighted are rooted.

Due its nature as a background affective orientation, it is arguable that low self-esteem shapes the experience of socially anxious subjects in radical ways, and, in particular, it impacts on the manner in which the subjects evaluate both themselves and others. This is what is at the core of the negative self-bias which is common among people diagnosed with social anxiety disorder. A low sense of one's ability and worth may indeed lead to the expectation that one will perform badly in certain situations and domains (i.e. those which are considered by the person to be relevant to the determination of her value). If the sense of being unworthy is one of the factors which shape one's way of being in the world, then also the way in which the person expects her own future to unfold will be influenced by this. Furthermore, low self-esteem will impact not only on expectations concerning future performance, but also on one's evaluation of that performance. If one's experience is shaped by a radical sense of inadequacy and unworthiness, thus making it difficult for the subject to entertain thoughts and feelings which are in contrast with these self-evaluations, then it will also be hard to appraise one's actions and achievements in positive ways. On the contrary, the subject may be inclined to explain these away, for example by diminishing their significance, or by linking them to external factors like luck – so that a perspective on the world coherent with one's own low self-esteem is maintained (cf. Bortolan 2018).

As an existential feeling, low self-esteem may also have an influence on which criteria are seen by the person as relevant to the determination of their worth. A low sense of one's value may indeed be at the origin of an over-reliance on external – objective and intersubjective – evaluation measures, and the tendency to discount the validity of one's own appraisals. The lack of trust in one's own capacities may reflect on the degree to which one thinks of oneself as able to discriminate between what is good or bad, valuable or worthless. Low self-esteem may thus entail a lack of confidence in one's own capacity to determine what is worthy or not in the first place, and, if one cannot trust one's own judgment in this regard, external and social criteria are all is left to appeal to. This dynamic is outlined also by Trudy Govier in her description of the effects of low self-trust (which she considers to be intimately related to self-esteem):

> To lack general confidence in one's own ability to observe and interpret events, to remember and recount, to deliberate and act generally, is a handicap so serious as to threaten one's status as an individual moral agent. [...] With the self in default, something else

would take over. Perhaps one would be governed by others—a parent, husband, or charismatic leader. Or The Party. [...] Perhaps one would conform blindly to convention. Perhaps one would swerve with every external suggestion and bend to every passing fad. (Govier 1993, p. 108)

The necessity to rely on the perspective and values of others when it comes to the criteria against which one's worth should be measured plays a central role in the heightening of the subject's self-consciousness. If the measures of one's worthiness are determined primarily by others, then it is their perspective on the self which takes centre stage in one's experience. If it is first and foremost from an external, intersubjective point of view that one is to be appraised, then monitoring how one is seen from that point of view becomes a central preoccupation.

These dynamics may also be related to the tendency towards perfectionism associated with the experience of pathological social anxiety (cf. Flett and Hewitt 2014). If the self is perceived as deeply unworthy and one's self-evaluations are distorted by the presence of negative biases, then only the complete absence of flaws may be seen as a reliable sign that something of value has been achieved. What emerges in these cases is the sense that one is good only in so far as her performance is near on perfect. Worthiness and excellence are identified, and anything short of a flawless achievement is not enough to make sure that one has done something of value. This is illustrated, for example, by the following excerpt from Ford's memoir:

> Though I desperately wanted to be on top of everything, perfection proved impossible. I simply couldn't be the top student academically, athletically, musically, aesthetically, and socially. I was crushed to realize that many of my girlfriends were more fashionable, more athletic, better artists, better spellers, faster in math, and preferred by the boys in our class. [...]
>
> Instead of dusting myself off and gracefully accepting second, third, or eighth place, I dropped out of many activities. Unless I knew I was going to be very good at something, I didn't do it at all. (Ford 2007, pp. 22–23)

7 Social Interactions

In virtue of its pre-intentional structure, self-esteem thus radically impacts not only on the way in which one relates to oneself, but also, in various ways, on interpersonal dynamics. So far, I have highlighted how this is the case for self- and other-focused appraisals: for the person whose self-esteem is radically low, the views of others become of cardinal importance, and they provide the criteria against which one's own value is measured.

Self-esteem, however, is central to the social world also in virtue of how it may influence one's capacity to act in it. It has been shown, for example, that the sense of ability provides the grounds for agency, at both the personal and interpersonal level (Schmid 2011). The willingness to engage in intentional actions, in other terms, depends on the possibility to feel that one, as an individual and as a group, is capable of succeeding at it.

I have argued that, usually, self-esteem involves a form of awareness of the self that has a pre-reflective structure, and pre-reflectivity has been shown to enable smooth and spontaneous action and interaction (cf. Gallagher and Zahavi 2012, pp. 163–167). It is because we can focus our attention on others or the external world – while being only peripherally aware of ourselves – that we can perform complex activities, and sophisticated affective and communicative exchanges. An increased level of reflective self-consciousness, on the contrary, can interfere with personal and social agency. Having oneself at the forefront of one's own attention can hinder the ability to act and interact promptly, spontaneously, and effortlessly.

As such, if reflectivity is heightened, and self-esteem is anchored primarily to interpersonal forms of self-experience and self-evaluation, there can be negative effects concerning agency, in particular in the social domain, and this is indeed the case for social anxiety sufferers. For example, people who are affected by social phobia may experience marked levels of self-absorption and a reduced ability to appropriately and timely respond to other peoples' inputs in interaction (e.g. Beidel and Turner 2007, p. 30). Relatedly, interactions with others are no longer spontaneous, but are rather "planned" or "calculated", something that needs to be carefully anticipated and managed.

These disruptions of the flow of interpersonal experience are exemplified, for instance, by the following first-person reports from Grazia's memoir:

> My actions didn't come naturally to me and my conversations became "forced". I laughed when I thought I should laugh. I went out of my way to please others thinking that was the only way I could get them to like me. (Grazia 2010, p. 3)

> I went through the motions of acting as I thought I should just to feel part of my surroundings but inside I didn't feel that way. (Grazia 2010, p. 30)

In addition, it seems that when positive feelings accompany social interaction, this involves a retained or recovered ability to experience things pre-reflectively, namely without focusing on oneself, but by just "being" oneself:

> It is amazing how different I feel when I can be "myself" around certain people. [...] It is so freeing. I feel like my whole body just loosens up. I am able to express what I am truly feel-

ing inside rather than what I think I should be. When I laugh, it feels so good and real – not forced. My actions, words, and emotions come naturally. (Grazia 2010, p. 31)

8 Conclusions

In this paper I have suggested that, similarly to what is the case in certain instances of schizophrenia, social phobia sufferers experience a heightening of reflective self-consciousness, as they tend in particular to see themselves from the perspective of a judging other. I have argued that this transformation originates at the pre-reflective level of self-experience, and, in particular, that it is rooted in low levels of self-esteem. Conceiving of it as a specific type of existential feeling, I have highlighted that self-esteem has the power to constrain the range of intentional states we can entertain, profoundly shaping our mental and practical life. Drawing on this characterisation, I have then shown how low self-esteem leads to a particular way of relating to oneself and others, engendering the transformations of self- and other-consciousness identified as central to social phobia.

Acknowledgements

Earlier versions of this chapter were presented at academic events at Heidelberg University, Alpen-Adria University Klagenfurt, Technische Universität Berlin, and University College Cork. I am very grateful to the audiences at these events for helpful questions and feedback as well as to James Miller and Elisa Magrì for their comments and suggestions. To Elisa Magrì also go my deepest thanks for her collaboration, enthusiasm, and support throughout the preparation of this volume.

References

American Psychiatric Association (2013): *Diagnostic and Statistical Manual of Mental Disorders*. Fifth Edition. *DSM-5*. Arlington: American Psychiatric Association.
Beidel, Deborah C./Turner, Samuel M. (2007): *Shy Children, Phobic Adults: Nature and Treatment of Social Anxiety Disorder*. 2nd ed. Washington, D.C.: American Psychological Association.
Blankenburg, Wolfgang (2001): "First Steps Toward a Psychopathology of 'Common Sense'". Trans. Aaron L. Mishara. In: *Philosophy, Psychiatry, & Psychology* 8(4), pp. 303–315.
Bortolan, Anna (2018): "Self-Esteem and Ethics: A Phenomenological View". In: *Hypatia* 33(1), pp. 56–72.

Bortolan, Anna (2020a): "Self-Esteem, Pride, Embarrassment and Shyness". In: Szanto, Thomas/Landweer, Hilge (Eds.): *The Routledge Handbook of Phenomenology of Emotion*. London, New York: Routledge, pp. 358–368.

Bortolan, Anna (2020b): "Affectivity and the Distinction Between Minimal and Narrative Self". In: *Continental Philosophy Review* 53, pp. 67–84.

Clark, David. M./Wells, Adrian (1995): "A Cognitive Model of Social Phobia". In: Heimberg, Richard G./Liebowitz, Michael R./Hope, Debra A./Schneier, Franklin R. (Eds.): *Social Phobia: Diagnosis, Assessment and Treatment*. New York: Guilford Press, pp. 69–93.

Danto, Arthur C. (1975): *Sartre*. London: Fontana.

Flett, Gordon, L./Hewitt, Paul, L. (2014): "Perfectionism and Perfectionistic Self-Presentation in Social Anxiety: Implications for Assessment and Treatment". In: Hofman, Stefan G./DiBartolo, Patricia M. (Eds.): *Social Anxiety: Clinical, Developmental, and Social Perspectives*. 3rd ed. London: Academic Press, pp. 159–187.

Ford, Emily (2007): *What You Must Think of Me: A Firsthand Account of One Teenager's Experience with Social Anxiety Disorder*. Oxford: Oxford University Press.

Fuchs, Thomas (2005): "Corporealized and Disembodied Minds: A Phenomenological View of the Body in Melancholia and Schizophrenia". In: *Philosophy, Psychiatry, & Psychology* 12(2), pp. 95–107.

Gallagher, Shaun (2000): "Philosophical Conceptions of the Self: Implications for Cognitive Science". In: *Trends in Cognitive Sciences* 4(1), pp. 14–21.

Gallagher, Shaun / Zahavi, Dan. (2012): *The Phenomenological Mind*. 2nd ed. London, New York: Routledge.

Goldie, Peter (2000): *The Emotions: A Philosophical Exploration*. Oxford: Clarendon Press.

Goldie, Peter (2012): *The Mess Inside. Narrative, Emotion, and the Mind*. Oxford: Oxford University Press.

Govier, Trudy (1993): "Self-Trust, Autonomy, and Self-Esteem". In: *Hypatia* 8(1), pp. 99–120.

Grazia, Daniela (2010): *On the Outside Looking In: My Life with Social Anxiety Disorder*. USA: Booklocker.com.

Grünbaum, Thor/Zahavi, Dan (2013): "Varieties of Self-Awareness". In: Fulford, K.W.M./Davies, Martin/Gipps, Richard G.T./Graham, George/Sadler, John, Z./Stanghellini, Giovanni/Thornton, Tim (Eds.): *The Oxford Handbook of Philosophy and Psychiatry*. Oxford: Oxford University Press, pp. 221–239.

Hackmann, Ann/Surawy, Christina/Clark, David M. (1998): "Seeing Yourself Through Others' Eyes: A Study of Spontaneously Occurring Images in Social Phobia". In: *Behavioural and Cognitive Psychotherapy* 26(1), pp. 3–12.

Heidegger, Martin (1962): *Being and Time*. Trans. John Macquarrie/Edward Robinson. New York: Harper & Row.

Husserl, Edmund (1989): *Ideas Pertaining to a Pure Phenomenology and to a Phenomenological Philosophy. Second Book. Studies in the Phenomenology of Constitution*. Trans. Richard Rojcewicz/André Schuwer. Dordrecht: Kluwer.

Merleau-Ponty, Maurice (2012): *Phenomenology of Perception*. Trans. Donald A. Landes. London, New York: Routledge.

Minkowski, Eugène (1997): *Au-delà du rationalisme morbide*. Paris: Éditions L'Harmattan.

Moscovitch, David A./Orr, Elizabeth/Rowa, Karen/Gehring Reimer, Susanna/Antony, Martin M. (2009): "In the absence of rose-colored glasses: Ratings of self-attributes and their

differential certainty and importance across multiple dimensions in social phobia". In: *Behaviour Research and Therapy* 47(1), pp. 66–70.
Parnas, Josef (2003): "Self and Schizophrenia: A Phenomenological Perspective." In: Kircher, Tilo/David, Anthony (Eds.): *The Self in Neuroscience and Psychiatry*. Cambridge: Cambridge University Press, pp. 217–241.
Parnas, Josef/Sass, Louis A. (2001): "Self, Solipsism, and Schizophrenic Delusions". In: *Philosophy, Psychiatry, & Psychology* 8(2–3), pp. 101–120.
Rapee, Ronald M./Heimberg. Richard G. (1997): "A cognitive-behavioral model of anxiety in social phobia". In: *Behaviour Research and Therapy* 35(8), pp. 741–756.
Ratcliffe, Matthew (2005): "The Feeling of Being". In: *Journal of Consciousness Studies* 12 (8–10), pp. 43–60.
Ratcliffe, Matthew (2008): *Feelings of Being: Phenomenology, Psychiatry and the Sense of Reality*. Oxford: Oxford University Press.
Ratcliffe, Matthew (2010): "Depression, Guilt and Emotional Depth". In: *Inquiry: An Interdisciplinary Journal of Philosophy* 53(6), pp. 602–626.
Saks, Elyn R. (2011): *The Centre Cannot Hold: A Memoir of My Schizophrenia*. London: Virago Press.
Sartre, Jean-Paul. (1989): *Being and Nothingness*. Trans. Hazel E. Barnes. London, New York: Routledge.
Sass, Louis A. (2000): "Schizophrenia, Self-Experience, and the So-Called 'Negative Symptoms'". In: Zahavi, Dan (Ed.): *Exploring the Self: Philosophical and Psychopathological Perspectives on Self-Experience*. Amsterdam: John Benjamins Publishing Company, pp. 149–182.
Sass, Louis A./Parnas, Josef (2003): "Schizophrenia, Consciousness, and the Self". In: *Schizophrenia Bulletin* 29(3), pp: 427–444.
Schmid, Hans Bernhard (2011): "Feeling Up to It – The Sense of Ability in the Phenomenology of Action". In: Konzelmann Ziv, Anita/Lehrer, Keith/Schmid, Hans Bernhard (Eds.): *Self-Evaluation. Affective and Social Grounds of Intentionality*. Dordrecht: Springer, pp. 215–236.
Slaby, Jan (2008): "Affective Intentionality and the Feeling Body". In: *Phenomenology and the Cognitive Sciences* 7(4), pp. 429–444.
Slaby, Jan (2012): "Affective Self-Construal and the Sense of Ability". In: *Emotion Review* 4(2), pp. 151–156.
Stanghellini, Giovanni (2004): *Disembodied Spirits and Deanimated Bodies: The Psychopathology of Common Sense*. Oxford: Oxford University Press.
Stein, Edith. (1989): *On the Problem of Empathy*. In: *The Collected Works of Edith Stein*. Vol. 3. Trans. Waltraut Stein. Washington, D.C.: ICS Publications.
Tanaka, Shogo (2021): "Body-as-Object in Social Situations. Toward a Phenomenology of Social Anxiety". In: Tewes, Christian/Stanghellini, Giovanni (Eds.): *Time and Body: Phenomenological and Psychopathological Approaches*. Cambridge: Cambridge University Press, pp. 150–169.
Tyrer, Peter J./Emmanuel J. S. (1999): "Social anxiety disorder from the perspectives of ICD-10 and DSM-IV: clinical picture and classification." In: Westenberg, H.G.M./den Boer, J.A. (Eds.): *Focus on psychiatry: social anxiety disorder*. Amsterdam: Syn-thesis, pp. 11–27.

Wells, Adrian/Clark, David M./Ahmad, Sameena (1998): "How do I look with my mind's eye: perspective taking in social phobic imagery". In: *Behaviour Research and Therapy* 36(6), pp. 631–634.

Wilson, Judith K./Rapee, Ronald M. (2006): "Self-concept certainty in social phobia". In: *Behaviour Research and Therapy* 44(1), pp. 113–136.

World Health Organization (1992): *The ICD-10 Classification of Mental and Behavioural Disorders. Clinical Descriptions and Diagnostic Guidelines.* Geneva: World Health Organization.

World Health Organization (2021): ICD-11. *International Classification of Diseases.* 11th Revision. https://icd.who.int/en, last accessed on 14 September 2021.

Zahavi, Dan (1999): *Self-Awareness and Alterity: A Phenomenological Investigation.* Evanston: Northwestern University Press.

Zahavi, Dan (2008): *Subjectivity and Selfhood: Investigating the First-Person Perspective.* Cambridge, MA: A Bradford Book, The MIT Press.

Matthew Ratcliffe
Trauma, Language, and Trust

Abstract: In times of emotional upheaval, one's own words and/or those of others can seem strangely hollow, somehow off the mark. In extreme cases of individual- and group-level trauma, it is sometimes said that language fails us completely or that some experiences defy articulation. This chapter considers why certain experiences might pose particular linguistic challenges and what the experience of linguistic inadequacy consists of. I sketch a phenomenological approach that emphasizes (a) how words can be experienced *as* estranged from habitual contexts of use; and (b) how non-localized breakdowns of trust further impact on the experience of communication. This aids us in understanding experiences of trauma, while also providing broader insights into the phenomenology of language and how it relates to the habitually experienced world.

Introduction

Extreme forms of traumatic experience are sometimes said to resist articulation, to be difficult or even impossible to convey to others.[1] In particular, this theme has been noted in the testimonies of Holocaust survivors, some of whom remark that what they witnessed and lived through cannot be put into words. However, first-person accounts of other harrowing events suggest that the experience of language-failure is more widespread, encompassing events that may affect a whole culture, a group, or just a single individual. For example, reflecting on her own traumatic experience, the philosopher Susan Brison (2002, p. xi) wonders how we can "speak about the unspeakable without attempting to render it intelligible and sayable". Even where the experienced shortcomings of language are not quite so profound, a person may still struggle to convey experien-

---

[1] I use the term "traumatic experience" to refer to how certain events, sequences of events, or temporally extended situations, which almost anyone would regard as exceptional, disruptive, and distressing, are experienced. I take traumatic experience to encompass not only how those events were experienced at the time of their occurrence, but also their enduring effects on how a person experiences and relates to the world.

https://doi.org/10.1515/9783110698787-017

ces, feel that she has not been and never will be understood, or even resign herself to the impossibility of understanding on the part of others.²

At the same time, it is widely acknowledged that there are therapeutic benefits associated with being able to articulate what one has endured (Herman 1992/1997). Hence the nature of language-failure in trauma is not merely of theoretical interest, but also of potential practical importance. Amongst other things, a better understanding of difficulties involved in articulating experience has the potential to inform clinical empathy and, with this, therapeutic practices that emphasize the importance of helping someone put what has happened into words.

In what follows, I will offer an account of what experiences of *words failing* consist of. To do so, I will focus on two interdependent factors that feature in many cases, although perhaps not all. The first of these involves the disruption of projects and pastimes with which utterances are habitually associated. The second consists in a non-localized loss of what we might call "trust", "confidence", or "certainty". Together, they can comprise an experience of one's words as inadequate and of certain kinds of communicative acts as impossible.³ My account is not intended to be exhaustive. A range of other factors may interfere with articulation in any given case and what I describe will not be central to all of them. Even so, it will be present, to varying degrees, in all those instances where there is (a) profound disruption of life-structure, and (b) a non-localized erosion of interpersonal trust. It is consistent with a diagnosis of post-traumatic stress disorder (e.g. American Psychiatric Association 2013) and, in more extreme cases, with the increasingly recognized diagnostic category "complex PTSD" (as characterized by Herman 1992/1997). However, it is also diagnostically nonspecific. Loss of trust and disengagement from contexts of habitual practice are also central to forms of experience that can be associated with diagnoses including major depressive disorder, schizophrenia, and some variants of grief

---

2 As the difference between struggle and resignation might suggest, such experiences need not be associated with silence or reduced speech. Trying, but failing, to articulate and communicate one's experience could involve continually attempting to put things into words.

3 Where the experience of words failing is so pronounced that it involves a sense of "impossibility", this need not take exactly the same form in all cases. For instance, it might seem that no linguistic description could ever convey the relevant experience. Alternatively, failure might be taken to originate in the contingent limitations of one's own linguistic abilities or the shortcomings of other people. There is also a distinction to be drawn between "nobody can ever understand x" and "nobody who has not experienced x can understand x".

(Ratcliffe 2015; 2017). Wherever disruption of practice and loss of trust occur together, one will face the kinds of linguistic challenges identified here.[4]

Articulating Trauma

The themes of silence and the unsayable have been associated specifically with the testimonies of Holocaust survivors. In addressing the relevant literature, Martin Kusch (2017) introduces the term "linguistic despair" to capture the way in which language's failure is taken to be unavoidable and insurmountable. The phenomenon he refers to is mentioned explicitly in several well-known autobiographical accounts. For instance, here is how Elie Wiesel describes the linguistic challenge that one faces:

> Convinced that this period in history would be judged one day, I knew that I must bear witness. I also knew that, while I had many things to say, I did not have the words to say them. Painfully aware of my limitations, I watched helplessly as language became an obstacle. It became clear that it would be necessary to invent a new language. But how was one to rehabilitate and transform words betrayed and perverted by the enemy? Hunger – thirst – fear – transport – selection – fire – chimney: these words all have intrinsic meaning, but in those times, they meant something else. (Wiesel 2006, pp. viii-ix)

Charlotte Delbo (1985/1990, p. 3) describes the limitations of language in a complementary way, emphasizing a kind of *splitting* that encompasses language, self, and reality. There is the consensus world that one currently inhabits and there is also the world of the concentration camp.[5] As pointed out by Wiesel, words such as "hunger" and "chimney" had quite different connotations in that world, in a place where all that one once took for granted and that one's interpreters now take for granted was extinguished. To describe Context A to those residing in Context B, one relies upon words such as x, y, and z, which are familiar to interpreters situated in B. However, those words have importantly different connotations in A, which are obscured by their employment in B.

---

[4] See Sass and Pienkos (2015) for a discussion of linguistic experience in schizophrenia, melancholic depression, and mania, which documents phenomena that are similar to the kinds of experience discussed here. Although I emphasize forms of experience that arise in response to exceptional events that impact upon one's life, experiences of meaning-loss and diminished trust can be brought about in other ways too. For instance, serious illness, injury, and substance abuse can all result in phenomenological disturbances that are consistent with what I describe.
[5] See also Lawrence Langer's (1991) discussion of Holocaust testimonies for descriptions of this phenomenon.

Hence, in order to describe something, one must use words that someone else understands, but that same understanding eclipses the phenomenon in question. As Kusch (2017, p. 142) writes, "the struggle for words is essentially the struggle to communicate the destruction of much of what in 'ordinary life' we take for granted". There is a loss of ordinarily implicit, pre-reflective certainties that the workings of language more usually presuppose.

If this is what the phenomenon consists in, then it is also something that can arise at the level of the individual, something that can happen to "me" rather than to "us", where "us" might be a family, a larger group, or even a whole culture. Of course, there remain important differences. Nevertheless, a particular person can similarly experience the destruction of a habitual world that others presuppose, such that words cannot be successfully exported from one context to the other. For example, Annie Rogers (2007, p. 4) describes what she calls the "unsayable" in a way that seems to involve this (although it is not the explicit focus of her account): "I realized that whatever I might say could be misconstrued and used to create a version of 'reality' that would be unrecognizable, a kind of voice-over of my truths I could not bear". Later in her account, she writes, "here is the unsayable, where words are spoken, yet fall into disconnection with what they point toward" (Rogers 2007, p. 88).[6]

It should be added that the distinction between group-level and individual-level trauma is not straightforward. That something happened to "us" does not imply a sense of shared understanding among those who endured it. Where the *phenomenology* of trauma is concerned, what happened to "us" might still be experienced principally as "mine" rather than "ours". For instance, Shay (1994, pp. 205–6) reports that some Vietnam veterans did not feel solidarity with fellow traumatized soldiers, but instead construed their disclosures in terms of an adversarial "pissing contest". The trauma is experienced as something that happened to "me" -- something to be endured alone, which cannot be understood by or shared with others.

It is important to distinguish the following: (a) a struggle to find the right words oneself; (b) a failure on the part of others to understand those words. One might have the experience of conveying something in an entirely adequate way, associated with an experience of others failing to comprehend what is said due to lack of ability or motivation on their part. Conversely, one might feel that,

---

[6] In cases of childhood trauma, the linguistic challenge described here may be especially pronounced and perhaps also qualitatively different, given more limited abilities to comprehend and express various experiences, the difficulties involved in eliciting understanding from adults, and the possibility that phenomenological contexts for utterances do not take quite the same forms as in adulthood.

although words fail, certain empathic individuals still manage to understand. However, where language-failure is attributable to the movement of words between contexts, (a) and (b) have a common origin and are, in practice, thoroughly entwined. One struggles to find words because something is lost when those words move between contexts, and others fail to understand because a familiar context eclipses an unfamiliar one. The communicative task of the trauma survivor is therefore doubly difficult: the profound gulf between what she endured (and perhaps continued to endure) and what an interlocutor takes as given impedes both linguistic expression and linguistic comprehension.

Importantly, the problem does not consist merely in recognizing *that* words fall short; there is also an *experience* of those words *as* falling short. Even as they are being uttered, there is a sense or feeling of their inadequacy. With this, there is also a more pervasive experience of lack or absence. Something that once seemed integral to the world, like bedrock, is experienced as missing, perhaps altogether lost. My task in the remainder of this chapter is to clarify the relevant phenomenology. Two broad types of scenarios are to be distinguished: (i) one shares context B with another person and seeks to communicate the nature of context A to that person, while experiencing the gulf between where one once was (A) and where both parties are now (B); (ii) one inhabits A in an enduring way, thus experiencing a gulf between where one is now (A) and where the other person is now (B). I will focus principally on (ii), on those cases that involve an enduring experience of loss, rather than something that also seems alien to oneself much of the time. However, I also concede that the distinction between A- and B-type scenarios is not clear-cut.

Disturbances of World

Traumatic experiences can involve the disturbance of something that our utterances more usually presuppose, and this "something" has a phenomenology. Indeed, it is a central and pervasive aspect of human experience. When it is disrupted, one experiences *upheaval*, something that – in more extreme cases – involves a sense of enduring and irreversible loss. To better appreciate what is involved, I find it helpful to draw on the phenomenological tradition of philosophy and, more specifically, the theme of *having a world*. As conceived of by philosophers such as the later Husserl (e.g. Husserl 1954/1970) and also Merleau-Ponty (1945/2012), the "world" is not, first and foremost, an object of experience. Our most basic sense that the world "is" cannot be extricated from our sense of belonging to it. And our sense of belonging consists in a habitual, practical, affective immersion in our surroundings. When we have experiences and thoughts with specific contents, we already find ourselves in the world in this fashion.

Ordinarily, we experience our surroundings as imbued with a cohesive web of significant, practically engaging possibilities. For the most part, these take the more specific form of happenings that are *anticipated* with varying degrees of confidence and determinacy. The sense of belonging to a world consists in an all-pervasive "style" of practically engaged perceptual experience, involving the confident anticipation and fulfilment of cohesively organized, significant possibilities (Ratcliffe 2017, Chapter 5). To illustrate this, consider a concrete example of engaging in a habitual pattern of activity: getting off the bus, entering an academic department, walking up to one's office, unlocking the door, and switching on the computer to check one's email. As one goes about one's business in the absence of surprises, things show up in the usual manner: they *matter* in a range of mundane ways, which reflect how they actually or potentially impact upon one's projects, commitments, cares, and concerns. For instance, the arrival of the bus matters insofar as it relates to subsequently reaching one's office, where the computer and other items of equipment are then experienced as mattering relative to current and anticipated tasks, which themselves presuppose a wider backdrop of projects and concerns. It is against this backdrop that the emails one glances through are experienced as important or unimportant, urgent or nonurgent, surprising or unsurprising, welcome or unwelcome, and so forth.

Similarly, the conception of being immersed in a world that I draw from the phenomenological tradition takes a structured human life to involve various interlocking projects and wider concerns. In the majority of cases, these are etched into the experienced world as patterns of significant possibilities that relate, in one or another way, to potential activities. Belonging to the world in a pre-reflective, unproblematic way consists in experiencing the holistic, confident unfolding of significant possibilities.

If something along these lines is right, then the structure of world-experience is vulnerable to different sources of disruption. The factors that together specify the experienced significance of an entity, event, or situation fall into four broad categories: (a) bodily capacities that determine what we are able and unable to do; (b) projects and wider concerns, relative to which things can matter in one or another way; (c) relations with other people, which sustain projects and may even underlie the intelligibility of projects (as when I do something "for you" or when something only makes sense in relation to an "us"); and (d) shared norms of various kinds that constrain, enable, and/or render intelligible patterns of activity. These factors together specify whether and how something appears (and should appear) significant to us in a given context. Hence, interference with one or more of them will alter what we experience as significant and the kinds of significance that things have (at least insofar as our experience takes account of what has changed). The effect could be fairly specific or more diffuse. Where an event profoundly affects capacities, projects, interpersonal relations, and/or entrenched norms, its impact will be all-pervasive. Consider, for instance, the effects of serious illness or injury, of losing a job that was central to one's life projects, of losing the spouse with whom one shared a life, or of living through the unravelling of a culture. The experiences associated with these diverse forms of upheaval may well differ in important ways. Nevertheless, there remains a structural similarity: one experiences the loss of patterns of significant possibilities that were once taken for granted, patterns that were presupposed by one's experiences, thoughts, activities, and words.

This type of loss is integral to (although not exhaustive of) traumatic experience. And it is also one reason why traumatic experiences can be very difficult to communicate. They involve disturbance of something that is more usually pre-reflectively given, something that one's interlocutors may continue to presuppose. Given this, a struggle for words is inevitable. However, there is more to it than this. Disruption of one's world also incorporates a more specific disruption of language. Like patterns of purposive activities, our utterances ordinarily presuppose certain things. When world-experience is disturbed, that disturbance can also envelop what we might call an *experience of meaning*. The point applies to life-upheavals in general and is not exclusive to those life-events that are associated with clinically significant trauma. Nevertheless, it is an important contributor to the linguistic phenomenology of trauma.

To illustrate what the experience consists of and to further clarify *how* words relate to the habitual world, I will focus on one type of case in detail, that of bereavement and -more specifically- losing a partner. A prominent theme in first-person accounts of grief and bereavement is the erosion of practical meaning: things that were once taken as given cease to be intelligible. Almost all of one's projects, commitments, cares, concerns, and habitual activities may have come to depend on a particular individual in one or another way. In the case of a partner, it could be that "I cook meals for us"; "we enjoy walking in the park together"; "we are saving money for a house in which to spend our lives together"; "we are concerned about climate change": "when I finish work, I go home to her"; "I work to support our life together"; and so forth. Sometimes, cares, commitments, and projects are attributed to a "we" and may only be sustainable given that "we". However, even where "I" do something, it may similarly draw some or all of its practical meaning from how it relates to someone else, even if one merely anticipates telling that person about it afterwards or coming home to her when it is finished.

This loss of practical meanings is sometimes referred to in terms of engrained assumptions: "When somebody dies a whole set of assumptions about the world that relied upon the other person for their validity are suddenly invalidated" (Parkes 1996, p. 90). However, it is important to distinguish these "assumptions" from propositions that were once endorsed without question and are no longer endorsed. Following C's death, one might explicitly assent to propositions such as "C is no longer alive"; "I will never see C again"; and "I will never walk in the park with C again". However, despite recognizing the truth of these propositions, one retains – to varying degrees – a conflicting set of habitual expectations that permeate experience, thought, and activity. For instance, one might anticipate seeing C when one arrives home, even though one at the same time "knows" that one will not, and various things continue to appear significant insofar as they point to C's potential presence or involvement. It is not simply that conceptual thought gets updated while unthinking bodily dispositions lag behind. Recalcitrant "assumptions" include habitual ways of talking and thinking. So, however we might draw the distinction between what is explicitly recognized and what runs counter to it, language does not feature only on one side of the divide; our utterances can be just as habitual as our "thoughtless" activities.

One of the ways in which this disturbance is experienced is that, although habitual patterns of experience, thought, and activity may endure, they are at the same time associated with a pervasive feeling of incongruity and tension. For instance, a sofa in one's lounge might continue to offer certain possibilities that imply the potential presence of one's spouse, as in "we could snuggle up here and watch a film tonight". Yet, at the same time, those possibilities present themselves *as* unrealizable. Such experiences of conflict are not merely occasional and localized. Bereavement can also involve a more diffuse experience of things as no longer offering what they used to offer, as strangely unfamiliar and bereft of meaning: "The act of living is different all through. Her absence is like the sky, spread over everything" (Lewis 1966, p. 12).

For current purposes, the important thing to note is that disturbance of the habitual world also impacts more specifically on language and linguistic thought. Upheavals such as bereavement make salient a subtle kind of *self-referentiality* that is integral to much of our everyday talk. Take the thought "I am going home now". Home could be conceived of in a generic way, as something that possesses the properties *x*, *y*, and *z*. Whatever those properties might be (and regardless of whether or not they amount to necessary or sufficient conditions for home-hood), they can be stated in a way that applies to homes in general. However, when I refer to *my home*, those properties take a more particular, concrete form. In saying "I am going home", the most salient aspect of doing so might be going back to a particular person and immersing myself in activities that imply this person's actual or potential presence.

When habitually thinking or uttering "time to go home now", the bereaved person may be struck by the recognition that this is impossible, in much the same way that she embarks on a pattern of habitual activity and then recognizes that it is no longer intelligible. It need not be that she first thinks or utters p and only *then* remembers that p is no longer possible. A feeling of alienation from the utterance may arise even as it occurs. In some respects, going home still makes sense: I can still return to my private residence. In thinking "I am going home", that thought points both to this and to other possibilities that no longer apply. Hence, there is an experience of tension, conflict, even contradiction. In a way, one is going home. In another way, one cannot go home anymore. Thoughts of "home" that once harmoniously integrated these ways of going home are now oddly decoupled from the world, pointing to possibilities that no longer have a place.

We can account for the experience of linguistic meaning-erosion, then, by acknowledging that, when words relate to patterns of significant activities, they can be *experienced as* pointing to certain possibilities. In much the same way that a cup or a computer may be experienced as mattering, as harbouring significant possibilities, spoken and written words can similarly point to variably specific contexts of practice. We can also elaborate on the earlier observation that there is a gulf between two contexts, A and B, in which words are employed. As illustrated by the example of grief, an experience of disruption and meaning-loss is not constituted merely by the experienced gulf between those contexts but also by the tension-riddled interplay between them. As one utters the words, one is struck by their failure to apply.

An author who conveys this aspect of experience especially well is Joyce Carol Oates, in her memoir *A Widow's Story*. At one point, Oates reflects on the sense of impossibility attached to thoughts of collecting her husband's "belongings" from the hospital where he has just died and taking them "home":

> Someone must have instructed me to undertake this task. I am not certain that I would have thought of it myself. The word *belongings* is not my word, I think it is a curious word that sticks to me like a burr.
> *Belongings. To take home.*
> And *home*, too – this is a curious word. (Oates 2011, p. 64)

> These toiletry things – that they were *his*, but are now no longer *his*, seems to me very strange.
> Now they are *belongings.*
> *Your husband's belongings.*

> One of the reasons I am moving slowly – perhaps it has nothing to do with being struck on the head by a sledgehammer – is that, with these *belongings*, I have nowhere to go except *home*. This *home* without my husband – is not possible for me to consider. (Oates 2011, p. 65)

Importantly, this kind of *self-referentiality* is not exclusive to explicitly indexical words such as "home". In principal, it can extend to almost any utterance. Take the example of going to the cinema. In contrast to thinking "it is possible for an unspecified person to go to the cinema", when one thinks "I could go to the cinema", the prospect of doing so may also point to that of going with C, of sharing popcorn, of laughing together. Similarly, as one thinks about "the cinema", affirms that one will go, or responds to an invitation to go, such possibilities may be experienced *as* absent; the thought or utterance is seemingly negated as it arises. Yes, one can still go to the cinema; the proposition makes sense and also happens to be true. But doing so no longer relates to one's life in the manner it once did; a certain *way* of going to the cinema is no longer possible.[7] There is, we might say, a *clash of worlds*. The full meaning of the sentence, as uttered by a particular individual is pragmatically oriented. And words like "cinema" have self-referential connotations; they point to a specific, concrete, habitual relationship with the world. This comes into tension with other aspects of experience, thought, and activity that accommodate the bereavement. The gulf between the two worlds, past and present, is experienced, and so too is the inapplicability of words and utterances to a current situation.

Such experiences comprise only one aspect of grief and they are not specific to grief. The example is intended to illustrate a more general way in which words can be experienced as somehow lacking, at odds with a situation in a way that does not amount to straightforward falsehood.[8] This, I suggest, is often one of the reasons why a traumatic experience is difficult to put into words. Utterances are imbued with significant possibilities that relate to one "world" and not another. This, in turn, is compounded by others' failure to recognize that traumatic experience can amount to a profound disturbance of world, as opposed to a sa-

---

[7] I think this is what Rupert Read (2018, p. 181) has in mind in an interesting paper on grief, where he makes the following claim: "What 'denial' really means is the profound difficulty of marrying one's beliefs with the facts *even as one assents to them*". A kind of "denial", he adds, is integral to a longer-term process of acceptance, of adjusting to the new circumstances.
[8] For example, see Kirmayer (2007) for an account of how traumatized refugees are faced with something structurally similar, a gulf between "disparate worlds" that the imagination is tasked with bridging and also conveying to others.

lient and unpleasant sequence of events that are experienced as arising within an intact, shared world.

In the remainder of this chapter, I will show how this kind of linguistic experience can be exacerbated by an additional factor, one that operates alongside and also intensifies the experience of meaning-loss: a pervasive loss of trust. Where the two occur together, there is a more profound erosion of the ability and also the inclination to convey one's experiences to others. While "emotional upheaval" is not exclusive to trauma and not always clinically significant, the two factors combined (comprising, as they do, a profound disturbance of one's relationship with the social world) are consistent with a diagnosis of severe psychiatric illness. Again, however, I do not wish to suggest that they are exhaustive of traumatic experiences or, more specifically, of the linguistic challenges that such experiences might pose.[9]

Loss of Trust

Disturbances of the habitual world also impact, in various ways, on relations with other people. A traumatic event can be inextricable from one's relationship with a specific person: that person's death might render certain practices unintelligible, or something the person did might be responsible for the disruption of one's world. Concrete relations with others are also influenced by their responses to what has happened. However, changing relations with particular individuals, whatever form these might take, need to be distinguished from a shift in the overarching "style" of one's relations with other people in general, something that might occur during or after the events in which traumatic experiences originate.

Traumatic events, of the kinds that people often struggle to articulate, tend to involve suffering inflicted by other people, often deliberately and with the intention to cause harm. The most extreme scenario involves the deliberate, comprehensive, institutionalized destruction of a world. Primo Levi describes this vividly in his memoir of Auschwitz, and I will quote him at length:

> Then for the first time we became aware that our language lacks words to express this offence, the demolition of a man. In a moment, with almost prophetic intuition, the reality

---

[9] For instance, another important consideration in some cases is cultural and linguistic difference. In fleeing a country, undertaking a hazardous journey, and seeking refugee status in an unfamiliar place, one faces the further challenges of negotiating a new language, an alien culture, and responses from interlocutors that may appear strange and unpredictable.

> was revealed to us: we had reached the bottom. It is not possible to sink lower than this; no human condition is more miserable than this, nor could it conceivably be so. Nothing belongs to us any more; they have taken away our clothes, our shoes, even our hair; if we speak, they will not listen to us, and if they listen, they will not understand. They will even take away our name: and if we want to keep it, we will have to find ourselves the strength to do so, to manage somehow so that behind the name something of us, of us as we were, still remains.
>
> We know that we will have difficulty in being understood, and this is as it should be. But consider what value, what meaning is enclosed even in the smallest of our daily habits, in the hundred possessions which even the poorest beggar owns: a handkerchief, an old letter, the photo of a cherished person. These things are part of us, almost like limbs of our body; nor is it conceivable that we can be deprived of them in our world, for we immediately find others to substitute the old ones, other objects which are ours in their personification and evocation of our memories.
>
> Imagine now a man who is deprived of everyone he loves, and at the same time of his house, his habits, his clothes, in short, of everything he possesses: he will be a hollow man, reduced to suffering and needs, forgetful of dignity and restraint, for he who loses all often easily loses himself. (Levi 1987, pp. 32–3)

As well as involving the loss of a context within which words more usually operate, having one's world systematically and comprehensively dismantled in such a way amounts to a subversion of habitual expectations concerning other people.[10] It challenges a pre-reflective orientation towards others in general, which we might refer to as a form of "trust", "confidence", or practical "certainty".[11] Although we do not always anticipate the actions of others to exactly the same degree of precision and in exactly the same way, for many of us, much of the time, the default expectation is that others – in their various different roles and in most settings – will be fairly benevolent and dependable: they won't beat you up for no reason; they won't give you false directions for fun; they will offer at least some support in times of great need, and so forth. Granted, there are plenty of instances where we do not trust a particular person and we are often right not to, but these involve suspending a style of anticipation in a specific situation that continues to apply more generally. This "style" is a glue that is required to hold together any configuration of cares, concerns, commitments, projects, and pastimes – any kind of world. Without the prospect of certain types of relations with others, one's own capacities to act are significantly diminished,

---

[10] Elaine Scarry (1985) offers a complementary account of the structure of torture, which similarly emphasizes the way in which familiar items, of kinds that are ordinarily integrated into habitual patterns of activity, are subverted, turned against the person.

[11] For philosophical discussions that support the notion of a basic, non-localized form of trust, see Baier (1986), Jones (2004), Bernstein (2011), and Ratcliffe, Ruddell and Smith (2014).

many of one's projects become unintelligible, and other projects appear futile or doomed from the outset, given that nobody can be relied upon to help see them through. There is thus a loss of habitual "certainty" that is not reducible to the collapse of however many specific pastimes. The shift in what one anticipates from other people shapes all experience, thought, and activity. Herman describes this loss of non-localized, "basic trust" as follows:

> Traumatic events call into question basic human relationships. They breach the attachments of family, friendship, love, and community. They shatter the construction of the self that is formed and sustained in relation to others. They undermine the belief systems that give meaning to human experience. They violate the victim's faith in a natural or divine order and cast the victim into a state of existential crisis. (Herman 1992/1997, p. 51)

This theme arises frequently in studies of trauma, and also in autobiographical accounts. For instance, Jean Améry (1999) describes how a non-localized feeling of trust, of being safe in the world, is extinguished by the first blow of the torturer, never to return. In his study of combat trauma, Shay (1994) describes the experiences of Vietnam veterans, whose relationship with the army was akin to that between parent and child. A consistent theme in their accounts is that of being betrayed and abandoned by superiors. With this, Shay remarks, combat trauma destroys not only trust in however many individuals but, with this, a "*capacity* for social trust" (Shay 1994, p. 33).[12] Here is another example, this time concerning the predicament of traumatized refugees:

> Before being forced to flee, refugees may experience imprisonment, torture, loss of property, malnutrition, physical assault, extreme fear, rape and loss of livelihood. The flight process can last days or years. During flight, refugees are frequently separated from family members, robbed, forced to inflict pain or kill, witness torture or killing, and/or lose close family members or friends and endure extremely harsh environmental conditions. Perhaps the most significant effect from all of the experiences refugees endure is having been betrayed, either by their own people, by enemy forces, or by the politics of their world in general. Having misanthropic actions of others become a major factor controlling the lives of refugees has significant implications for health and for their ability to develop

---

12 Elsewhere, I have argued that this aspect of experience, which we might refer to as "trust", "confidence", or "certainty" is something that Husserl, Merleau-Ponty, and Wittgenstein all seek to describe, albeit in different ways. Ultimately, I suggest, their conceptions of it are largely consistent. In all cases, our most fundamental sense of certainty amounts to the non-localized, confident anticipation and fulfilment of an integrated system of significant possibilities (Ratcliffe 2007, Chapters 5 and 6). See also Kusch (2017) for the claim that the linguistic difficulties of Holocaust survivors can be construed in terms of losing what Wittgenstein, in *On Certainty*, calls "hinges".

trusting interpersonal relationships, which are critical to resettlement and healing. (Refugee Health Technical Assistance Center in Boston, 2021)

The common theme is an enduring, non-localized loss of ordinarily pre-reflective trust, a sense of betrayal and unfathomability that overturns engrained patterns of expectation. If one cannot depend on others, then one cannot depend on anything, as almost all of our expectations concerning the world in general depend in one or another way on our expectations concerning other people. Loss of trust is therefore inextricable from a wider loss of confidence or certainty. Because one cannot depend on anything, one can no longer assemble meaningful life projects, in terms of which past events are deemed significant in ways that are malleable, open to re-contextualization and reappraisal. Consequently, one cannot move on. Loss of trust thus consolidates practical disengagement by interfering with the ability to retain, repair, or replace any kind of meaningful life-structure. But how, one might ask, does it also contribute more specifically to the experience of language?

Communication and Trust

Loss of trust adds to the experience of linguistic inadequacy in two ways. First of all, it contributes to a pervasive sense of impossibility and futility, of a future devoid of any potential for positive development. The world appears bereft of all those possibilities associated with trusting relations with others, which include sustaining, repairing, and revising projects, and relating to people in ways that open up new possibilities. With no prospect of such relations, the future lacks openness, spontaneity, the potential for meaningful and positive alternatives to one's current predicament – for growth (Ratcliffe, Ruddell, and Smith 2014). With this, the more specific potential of language is also curtailed. It is not just that words currently fall short. As the future will not deviate in meaningful ways from the present, linguistic shortcomings are inescapable; there is no prospect of overcoming them or of opening up new communicative possibilities. In its most extreme form, loss of trust freeze-frames the linguistic predicament I have described; words are not just hollow; they are irrevocably hollow.

However, there is a further way in which loss of trust contributes to an experience of linguistic failure. As well as exacerbating the experience of meaning-loss, it undermines the conditions under which utterances are more usually produced, understood, and recognized as successful. In *How to do Things with Words*, J. L. Austin (1962) addresses how utterances can "misfire", fail to have their intended effects. The experience of meaning-loss already described constitutes a sense of words as somehow missing their targets, veering off course even as they are uttered.[13] In its most extreme form, this "misfiring" can amount to a seemingly inescapable form of *silencing:* you can say whatever you like, but you will still be unable to say what you strive to say.[14] However, also important for current purposes is Austin's discussion of "illocutionary acts", where we do something by saying something. Examples include the likes of announcing, pronouncing, questioning, answering, advising, suggesting, ordering, promising, warning, and informing. Like all acts, these can be successfully or unsuccessfully performed: "unless a certain effect is achieved, the illocutionary act will not have been happily, successfully performed" (Austin 1962, p. 15). Various factors contribute to whether or not an illocutionary act is successful, and it is not just a matter of what the speaker does. Success also requires "uptake" on the part of others (Austin 1962, p. 116).[15]

We have seen that, where words seek to convey one context but remain, for the interpreter, anchored in another, there is lack of uptake. However, Austin's discussion of illocutionary acts also points to a further impediment. The sense of one's words being taken up by others depends not just on how one experiences one's own speech, but also on how one experiences and interprets their responses to it. Consider the impact of a pervasive loss of trust on the extent to which one is able to anticipate and experience understanding on the part of others. Where there is distrust, one does not anticipate empathy, support, concern, or guidance but, rather, the likes of threat, condemnation, misunderstanding, derision, and indifference. This shapes the experience of communication.

It is not uncommon for philosophers to assume that the practice of interpreting others depends principally on ascribing two classes of mental states to them: beliefs (which are informational) and desires (which are motivational).[16] However, when we are interpreting one another's behaviour and, more specifically, linguistic behaviour in the context of interpersonal interaction, Austin rightly observes that our utterances do not take the form of bare statements of fact or

---

13 See also Brison (2002) for application of themes in Austin's work to the topic of trauma. She makes the point that words can "do" things, which include somehow altering traumatic memories: "*saying* something about the memory *does* something to it" (Brison 2002, pp. x–xi).
14 See also Langton (1993) for discussion of something similar: a form of silencing that does not depend on actively preventing someone from saying certain things or punishing them for doing so.
15 Thanks to Nancy Potter (personal correspondence) for drawing my attention to Austin's relevance here and, in particular, to the importance of "uptake". For an interesting discussion of uptake in psychiatry, see her *The Virtue of Defiance and Psychiatric Engagement* (2016).
16 See Ratcliffe (2007) for a detailed critique of this tendency.

expressions of desire. The task of mutual understanding involves recognizing a vast array of subtly different illocutionary acts, such as appealing, encouraging, dismissing, inquiring, and challenging. Austin (1962, Lecture XII) classifies these into five broad types:
- verdictives: giving a verdict
- exercitives: exercising powers
- commissives: committing oneself to doing something
- behabitives: a more heterogeneous group that concern social behaviour (e.g. congratulating, apologizing, cursing)
- expositives: specifying how utterances fit into arguments (e.g. I argue, I concede, I assume)

Once this complexity is acknowledged, it becomes clearer how loss of trust can interfere with the sense of being understood by another person, and equally with the *anticipation* of being understood. To anticipate and experience other people as taking up one's utterances in certain ways requires trust. Where trust is absent, a respondent's words and deeds will be taken to involve only certain kinds of illocutionary acts. The prospects of that person's sincerely promising, encouraging, advising out of concern, or questioning out of well-meaning curiosity do not arise; the interpersonal world is bereft of such possibilities. An experience of communicative failure or even futility may be further exacerbated by an interlocutor's genuine failure to recognize one's predicament, to recognize illocutionary acts such as pleading for understanding and respond accordingly. Hence, the *feeling of being understood* will be lacking and gestures on the part of others that might express understanding and concern will not be experienced as such. As Shay remarks of traumatized Vietnam veterans:

> The moral dimension of severe trauma, the betrayal of "what's right", obliterates the capacity for trust. The customary meanings of words are exchanged for new ones; fair offers from opponents are scrutinized for traps; every smile conceals a dagger. (Shay 1994, p. 181)

One inhabits a damaged world, which, in the absence of trust, no longer incorporates the prospect of rebuilding. And integral to this is a way of anticipating and experiencing other people that renders many kinds of illocutionary acts seemingly futile, destined from the outset to fail.

An understanding of first-person linguistic experience in trauma can thus feed into empathy, where "empathy" is construed in a fairly broad way as *understanding experiences had by a particular individual*. The point applies specifically to "clinical empathy", in those cases where phenomenological disturbances are sufficiently pronounced for clinical intervention to be deemed appropriate. However, it also applies to empathy more widely, given that experiences of emotional upheaval and associated experiences of language-failure are not always so profound and need not involve clinically significant levels of distress.

In seeking to comprehend the relevant aspects of experience, we come to see that the first step in an empathic process is not developing a positive understanding of what someone else experiences but, rather, recognizing the nature and extent of the potential gulf between one's own world and hers (Ratcliffe 2015; 2018). What is disrupted is something ordinarily taken for granted as shared by interpreter and interpreted, in the guise of a world that "we" inhabit and in which our differing experiences and thoughts arise. So, understanding the phenomenology of language in trauma involves appreciating how someone might be uprooted from a world that is more usually presupposed as "ours". Failures of empathy will occur when that person's experiences are interpreted against the backdrop of an intact, shared world, as those experiences are actually symptomatic of its disturbance. Such failures have the potential to exacerbate a sense of distrust, estrangement, and misunderstanding. Hence, in addition to being of philosophical interest, an appreciation of how language can be experienced as inadequate to the realities of trauma has the potential to inform therapeutic practice.

Acknowledgements

Thanks to Anna Bortolan, Craig French, Ian Kidd, Martin Kusch, Elisa Magri, and audiences at the University of York and UCLA for helpful comments and suggestions. This chapter was completed as part of the AHRC-funded project "Grief: A Study of Human Emotional Experience" (Grant Ref: AH/T000066/1).

References

American Psychiatric Association. (2013): *Diagnostic and Statistical Manual of Mental Disorders*. 5th ed. Arlington: American Psychiatric Association.
Améry, Jean (1999): *At the Mind's Limits: Contemplations by a Survivor on Auschwitz and its Realities*. Trans. Sidney Rosenfeld/Stella P. Rosenfeld. London: Granta Books.
Austin, J. L. (1962): *How to do Things with Words*. Oxford: Oxford University Press.
Baier, Annette (1986): "Trust and Antitrust". In: *Ethics* 96, pp. 231–260.
Bernstein, J. M. (2011): "Trust: On the Real but Almost Always Unnoticed, Ever-changing Foundation of Ethical Life". In: *Metaphilosophy* 42, pp. 395–416.
Brison, Susan (2002): *Aftermath: Violence and the Remaking of a Self*. Princeton: Princeton University Press.

Delbo, Charlotte (1985/1990): *Days and Memory*. Trans. R. Lamont. Evanston: Northwestern University Press.

Herman, Judith (1992/1997): *Trauma and Recovery*. 2nd ed. New York: Basic Books.

Husserl, Edmund (1954/1970): *The Crisis of European Sciences and Transcendental Phenomenology*. Trans. David Carr. Evanston: Northwestern University Press.

Jones, Karen (2004): "Trust and Terror". In: Des Autels, Peggy/Urban Walker, Margaret (Eds): *Moral Psychology: Feminist Ethics and Social Theory*. Lanham: Rowman & Littlefield, pp. 3–18.

Kirmayer, Laurence J. (2007): "Failures of Imagination: The Refugee's Predicament". In: Kirmayer, Laurence J./Lemelson, Robert/Barad, Mark (Eds.): *Understanding Trauma: Integrating Biological, Clinical, and Cultural Perspectives*. Cambridge: Cambridge University Press, pp. 363–381.

Kusch, Martin (2017): "Analysing Holocaust Survivor Testimony: Certainties, Scepticism, Relativism". In: Krämer, Sybille/Weigel, Sigrid (Eds): *Testimony/Bearing Witness: Epistemology, Ethics, History and Culture*. London: Rowman & Littlefield International, pp. 137–166.

Langer, Lawrence (1991): *Holocaust Testimonies: The Ruins of Memory*. New Haven: Yale University Press.

Langton, Rae (1993): "Speech Acts and Unspeakable Acts". In: *Philosophy and Public Affairs* 22, pp. 293–330.

Lewis, C. S. (1966): *A Grief Observed*. London: Faber & Faber.

Levi, Primo (1987): *If This is a Man* and *The Truce*. Trans. Stuart Woolf. London: Abacus Books.

Merleau-Ponty, Maurice (1945/2012): *Phenomenology of Perception*. Trans. Donald A. Landes. London, New York: Routledge.

Oates, Joyce Carol (2011): *A Widow's Story*. London: Fourth Estate.

Potter, Nancy Nyquist (2016): *The Virtue of Defiance and Psychiatric Engagement*. Oxford: Oxford University Press.

Ratcliffe, Matthew (2007): *Rethinking Commonsense Psychology: A Critique of Folk Psychology, Theory of Mind, and Simulation*. Basingstoke: Palgrave Macmillan.

Ratcliffe, Matthew (2015): *Experiences of Depression: A Study in Phenomenology*. Oxford: Oxford University Press.

Ratcliffe, Matthew (2017): *Real Hallucinations: Psychiatric Illness, Intentionality, and the Interpersonal World*. Cambridge, MA: The MIT Press.

Ratcliffe, Matthew (2018): "Empathy without Simulation". In: Summa, Michela/Fuchs, Thomas/Vanzago, Luca (Eds): *Imagination and Social Perspectives*. London, New York: Routledge, pp. 199–220.

Ratcliffe, Matthew/Ruddell, Mark/Smith, Benedict (2014): "What is a Sense of Foreshortened Future? A Phenomenological Study of Trauma, Trust and Time". In: *Frontiers in Psychology* 5, Article 1026, pp. 1–11.

Read, Rupert (2018): "Can There Be a Logic of Grief? Why Wittgenstein and Merleau-Ponty Say 'Yes'". In: Kuusela, Oskari/Ometiță, Mihai/Uçan, Timur (Eds.): *Wittgenstein and Phenomenology*. London, New York: Routledge, pp. 176–196.

Refugee Health Technical Assistance Centre in Boston, Massachusetts (2021): http://refugee healthta.org/physical-mental-health/mental-health/adult-mental-health/traumatic-experi ences-of-refugees/, last accessed on 10 January 2021.

Rogers, Annie G. (2007): *The Unsayable: The Hidden Language of Trauma*. New York: Ballantine Books.
Sass, Louis A./Pienkos, Elizabeth (2015): "Beyond Words: Linguistic Experience in Melancholia, Mania, and Schizophrenia" In: *Phenomenology and the Cognitive Sciences* 14, pp. 475–495.
Scarry, Elaine (1985): *The Body in Pain: The Making and Unmaking of the World*. Oxford: Oxford University Press.
Shay, Jonathan (1994): *Achilles in Vietnam: Combat Trauma and the Undoing of Character*. New York: Scribner.
Wiesel, Elie (2006): *Night*. Trans. Marion Wiesel. London: Penguin.
Wittgenstein, Ludwig (1975): *On Certainty*. Trans. Denis Paul/G.E.M. Anscombe. Oxford: Blackwell.

The social world: empathy, morality, and metapolitics

John J. Drummond
Empathy, Sympathetic Respect, and the Foundations of Morality

Abstract: This contribution summarizes a well-known phenomenological view of empathy and argues that it underlies both the respect and the sympathy that are central to and required by well-ordered interpersonal and moral relationships. I summarize an amalgam of the views of several phenomenologists, including Edmund Husserl, Edith Stein, Max Scheler, and Dan Zahavi, an amalgam that I shall refer to simply as *the* phenomenological understanding, even though it is undoubtedly *a* phenomenological understanding. I then outline the way in which empathy underlies both respect and sympathy and give brief accounts of each. I shall further sketch ways in which respect and sympathy are the two affective attitudes that in their unity jointly ground our ethical lives.

This chapter summarizes a well-known phenomenological view of empathy and argues that it underlies both the respect and the sympathy that are central to and required by well-ordered interpersonal and moral relationships. In what follows, I shall summarize an amalgam of the views of several phenomenologists, including Edmund Husserl, Edith Stein, Max Scheler, and Dan Zahavi, an amalgam that I shall refer to simply as *the* phenomenological understanding, even though it is undoubtedly *a* phenomenological understanding.[1] I shall then outline the

---

[1] There are, no doubt, higher, non-human animals having the biological complexity that supports conscious agency by serving as its material condition. They exhibit practical rationality; that is, they perceive things, pursue goods, and act in ways that realize those goods. There is, to my mind, a transcendental dimension—a meaning-disclosing dimension—to this experience. Empathy encompasses the recognition of such animals as conscious agents. In this paper, however, I shall focus my discussion on the empathetic recognition of human animals, that is, persons, who are embodied, practical, social, historical, and reflection-capable animals. Persons are distinctive in the manner in which they relate to truth and moral agency. Higher non-human animals make a non-linguistic distinction between truth and falsity that is similar to the pre-linguistic distinction humans make when, in a continuing perceptual experience, they correct their sense of an object. They do not, however, have the conceptual capacities to fix their original or adjusted beliefs with a degree of conceptual determination that gives rise to language and critical reflection. Persons, by contrast, are related to truth in an additional way; they are *concerned* with that truth. They are concerned with the *difference* between the true and the false, the good and the apparent good, and the right and the wrong (MacIntyre 1999, p. 37). The reflection-capable agent acts not merely to realize an end proper to its constitutively relevant

way in which empathy underlies both respect and sympathy and give brief accounts of each. I shall further sketch ways in which respect and sympathy are the two affective attitudes that in their unity jointly ground our ethical lives.

Empathy

Phenomenological accounts of intersubjectivity are frequently somewhat abstract discussions of our awareness of another subject. They are concerned to account for our experience of other subjects from, as it were, the ground up rather than to account for our everyday encounters of other persons in our joint dealings with one another and the surrounding world. Those everyday encounters include experiences such as the following: Janet sees someone she does not recognize across the room; Steve sees Walter approaching; Joe loves Ellen but, experiencing jealousy, sees Matt as a rival and fears losing Ellen's affection; Martha forms a business partnership with Janice; Beatrice joins a book group; Donald understands that Vladimir is a friend, but John sees a foe in Vladimir; and so forth. Nevertheless, the more abstract discussions are instructive, for they disclose a fundamental structure universally present in the concrete experiences of other persons. This structure is sameness-in-irreducible-difference. It underlies all interpersonal encounters, whether they be friendship, a business partnership, membership (in, say, a union or professional organization), citizenship, and so on.

Although our everyday, ordinary, and original encounter of others as friends or foes, acquaintances or strangers, co-workers, partners, fellow citizens, and so on are varied, complex, and multi-dimensional, they can be stripped down, as it were, to the basic and fundamental recognition of the other simply as a person. Just as mere perception is an abstraction from our everyday, ordinary, and original experiences with their affective and practical dimensions, this basic recognition—what phenomenologists call "empathy"—is an abstraction from our everyday, ordinary, and original encounter with others. In the mutual recognition of another subject as a person, we respond affectively to one another in a variety of ways that constitute fuller and richer levels of empathetic recognition. But the fundamental structure—the sense of sameness as persons in the irreducible difference among persons—underlies those affective responses as their cognitive basis.

---

animality but *from* a reflectively *chosen* end explicitly recognized as a (apparently) choiceworthy end.

We see this structure at work in Husserl's discussion of what he calls "analogical apperception" (Husserl 1970, p. 108).[2] The other person, in brief, is experienced as like me insofar as the other is embodied and capable of initiating voluntary actions in the way that I can, but the other person is also experienced as irreducibly different from me, insofar as I experience the other's bodily motility as expressive of conscious experiences and actions that I cannot experience in the way I experience my own. This pattern of the simultaneous "pairing" (Husserl 1970, pp. 112–113) and irreducible differentiation of persons is what is most important in Husserl's notion of analogical apperception and is operative in varied ways in all our encounters of other persons.

Let us examine this in greater detail. In order to understand what is unique in this account, however, we must first note a linguistic difficulty. In folk psychology and in the psychological literature, the English term "empathy" generally refers to the activity of or capacity for imaginatively understanding, identifying with, vicariously experiencing, or sharing the feelings of another from the other's perspective. The German terms used by the early phenomenologists (*Einfühlung* [by, for example, Husserl and Stein] and *Nachfühlen* [by Scheler]) similarly evoke the sense of entering into and vicariously sharing the same feeling as another. But this is not what the early phenomenologists mean by the term; indeed, Husserl, for one, gravitated toward the view that *Fremderfahrung* is the better term to denote the encounter of a "foreign" subject or to describe an "other-experience" (see Zahavi 2014, p. 114). Even this term, however, is not by itself fit to capture the special kind of other—another "subject" as the center and source of an experiencing life—that is the "object" of the encounter.

Empathy, on the phenomenological account and unlike the psychological account, is a cognitive rather than an affective experience. At the risk of oversimplifying, we can say that the basic face-to-face empathetic experience of another includes (1) the *perceptive recognition* of the other's bodily states, changes, and activities and (2) the *apperceptive recognition* of another center and source of conscious experience as expressed in those bodily states, changes, and activities. The bodily states, changes, and activities might be of various sorts. I might rec-

---

2 Husserl insists—as do other phenomenologists—that "analogy" and its cognates should not be understood in the sense of an argument by analogy. There is no inference at work here. Instead, the term "analogy" recalls medieval uses of the term. A word is used analogously when the term attributes the same property to different things, but the things possess that property in different ways. The most famous example of this, of course, is the attribution of properties to God. So too here: the term "self" is used in one sense to refer to the self of which I am pre-reflectively aware in experiencing objects, and it is used in another sense when referring to another self of which I am not and cannot be pre-reflectively aware.

ognize the other's adjusting her position and squinting her eyes so as to perceive better some object in the world, or I might recognize certain physiological changes, facial configurations, and gestures as expressions of emotions, or certain bodily actions expressive of choices, or I might hear the other's speech as expressive, say, of judgments or alarm. In experiencing another body in these ways, I do not experience a merely material thing, such as a stone, a tree, or a building, undergoing a change caused by some other material thing or physical event. I experience these bodily states, changes, and activities as expressive of a conscious being freely in control of the body I now encounter. I do not, for example, see mere changes in facial musculature; I see a smile. Empathy, then, is the perceptual recognition of an embodied, expressive center of conscious agency.

Four aspects of empathy reveal its uniqueness as a type of perception. First, in perceiving, say, a building from the front, I directly perceive the facade of the building and apperceive its other sides. Although only the facade is directly presented, the object of my perception is the building as a whole. I anticipate that undertaking certain bodily movements will bring other sides or aspects of the building to direct perception, and these bodily movements thereby contribute to the disclosure of the object. I can, at least theoretically, bring any of these apperceptive moments to direct perception through bodily movements. This is not, however, the case in empathy. I can bring apperceived dimensions of the other's body to direct perception, but I cannot bring the other's lived conscious experiences as expressed in her bodily activities to direct perception. The other as a center of conscious agency radically transcends my perceptual capacity in a way that the other sides of the building do not.

It is important to stress that I do not *infer* the presence of another conscious agency; I *apperceive* it (Husserl 1970, p. 108). I experience the other person *in* (and not *through*) the perceptual presentation of the other's bodily changes and activities; I encounter the other's anger *in* her facial expressions, her bodily motions, the volume of her voice, and so on. Nor, despite the connotations of the German terms *Einfühlung* and *Nachfühlen*, do I "feel myself into" the experience of the other or vicariously share her experience or stand in her shoes.[3] I do not, for example, need to experience anger in order to recognize another person as angry (Zahavi 2014, p. 113).

The basic idea is this: my pre-reflective self-awareness has both proprioceptive and exteroceptive aspects. I am proprioceptively aware of my body in somaesthetic and kinaesthetic sensations that not only contribute to the disclosure

---

[3] This modifies my earlier view; cf. Drummond 2006, p. 15.

of the object but underlie my sense of self as an interiority that, in experiencing objects in the world, expresses itself in bodily states and movements (Husserl 1973b, p. 491). My body is, however, also available to me (at least in part) for exteroception. I am exteroceptively aware of my bodily functioning as visually and tactually perceptible movements occurring in the world. This fusion or interplay between *interiority* and *exteriority* is a condition for the possibility of empathy (Husserl 1959, p. 62; 1973b, p. 457; Zahavi 2014, p. 137), and is a function of my living body's both performing a constitutive function in the disclosure of the world and expressing my experiential life.

The analogical base of my apperception of the other as a center of experience is, properly speaking, the fusion of my interiority and exteriority in my experiencing the world and expressing my mental states and experiences. Insofar as I experience [*erfahre*] certain bodily states, changes, and activities of another body as similar to the kinds of bodily states, changes, and activities that I proprioceptively experience [*erlebe*] and exteroceptively experience [*erfahre*] in the course of my disclosing the world, I take the similar bodily states, changes, and activities of the other as the externalization and expression of another interiority that I cannot directly experience and that the other conscious agent does proprioceptively experience [*erlebe*]. I encounter the other as a transcendent center of expressed conscious experience.

Given, however, that the empathetic recognition of an other can extend to non-human animals, the similarity between subject-objects cannot be found merely in the similarity of physical states, changes, and movements alone. The notion of the body is insufficient to ground the similarity since the physical movements of, say, a dog fleeing from danger are different from the movements of a person fleeing the same danger, yet we recognize the dog as a conscious being whose consciousness is expressed in its actions (Stein 1989, p. 59). Crucial, then, to understanding the similarity between the living and lived-through body of the one experiencing empathy and the perceived animate, but not lived through, body of the other is the notion of the body's movements and states as *expressive* of the subject's mental states. The dog's fleeing on four legs and the person's fleeing on two are similar insofar as they have the same purpose, one posited in a mental state, namely, the fear that recognizes the danger from which the dog and the person flee. The similarity is not a similarity between merely physical movements, but one that is purposive and expressive.

It is bodily expression, therefore, and not merely a similarity of bodily composition or modes of movement, that grounds the similarity central to empathetic experience. Bodily expression is a unified notion that can underwrite the similarity despite the asymmetry between experiencing my own body and that of another (Walsh 2014, pp. 221–225). In Walsh's view, we recognize a movement as expressive, rather than as externally caused, by virtue of the facts (1) that "the horizon of expectations associated with appearance of expressive movement is necessarily more vast than that associated with non-expressive movement" and (2) "the spatiotemporally extended parts of an instance of the appearance of expressive movement are uniquely interdependent such that an alteration of any of them would result in an alteration of the meaning or significance of the movement" (Walsh 2014, p. 224). So, empathy demands a certain understanding of the similarity-relation between my experienced (*erlebt*) body and expressive movement, on the one hand, and the other's experienced (*erfahren*) body and expressive movement, even as I experience the two bodies in different ways.

Whereas in the perception of a material thing I recognize the various appearances of the different sides and aspects of the object as manifestations of an identical object and achieve what Husserl calls a "synthesis of identification" (Husserl 1970, pp. 41–42), in the empathetic recognition of a person I recognize the *similarity* between my proprioceptively and exteroceptively perceived expressive bodily activities and the exteroceptively perceived expressive bodily activities of another animate organism. But I do not bring these into a synthesis of identification. Because the center of consciousness and source of the other's expressive movement is not my own, I cannot recognize that movement as belonging to the identical self that is myself. Instead, I recognize another self—like me, but not me—as "analogously" a self. My self and the other self are, to use Husserl's expression, brought into a synthesis of "pairing" (Husserl 1970, pp. 112–113). They form a unified pair but not an identical object; they are two.

From this it follows, second, that empathy is a unique kind of perceptual recognition, one that grasps not merely a material thing but a "subject-object" (Husserl 1973b, p. 457), that is, an object who is, like me, a subject. Since the fundamental element in my self-awareness is the sense of myself as an experiencing subject expressing itself in words and actions, my fundamental sense of the other "subject-object" is of another subject. I encounter this other subject as a co-subject sharing a world with me (Husserl 1973a, p. 427). In this most fundamental form of empathy, my attention is directed in the first instance to the object—the world—that the other and I share. When, for example, a student comes to my office to discuss a paper, both my student and I empathetically, but nonthematically, recognize the other as a subject, but our joint thematic attention is turned to the paper.

Third, this view entails that empathy involves a mutual recognition. In apperceiving another experiencing agent, I recognize that the other subject's disclosure of the world includes the disclosure of myself as another "subject-object" in the world for the other. I become a part of the world that the other intends. To put the matter another way, when I experience others I experience them as subjects who experience worldly objects, including myself (Husserl 1973a, pp. 4–5). In such encounters, I attain an enriched understanding of myself as a subject-object in the world (see Zahavi 2019). I now take on as part of my self-understanding the views that others have of me and the categories in terms of which they understand me. And this empathetic experience is duplicated by the other subject I encounter. Just as I empathetically and non-thematically recognize my student as a subject, my student empathetically and non-thematically recognizes me as a subject and also comes to an enhanced self-understanding in recognizing that she has become a part of my world.

Fourth, the mutual encounters of subject-objects disclosing a shared world establish a community of cognizers capable of achieving an objective understanding of the world and a set of practices that allow that community to realize shared goals. My student and I together work through her paper, discussing its merits and demerits, determining what further work needs to be done, and so on. Throughout such an encounter we find that empathy recognizes a subject-object who is like me but who, at the very same time, radically transcends me and my perceptive capacities and that this relation is reciprocal. I cannot experience [*erlebe*] my student's experiences from the first-person perspective in the way that I experience my own, and she cannot experience [*erlebt*] mine. I cannot experience her concern about the grade she might receive on the paper, and she cannot experience my frustration about my inability to make clearer to her what properly organizing a paper involves. But I might gain a sense of myself as being intimidating or being seen as concerned about the student and nurturing her abilities. Intersubjective relations, including, most fundamentally, empathetic perceivings, involve simultaneous identification and communalization (as persons) and irreducible differentiation, otherness, and individuation (Drummond 2002).

I turn now to two kinds of experience involving affective complements to empathy.

Respect and Sympathy

We experience a conscious agent in (1) empathetically and concretely experiencing the body of the other as expressive of cognitions, feelings or emotions, general moods (cf. Stein 1989, p. 50), and choices, and in (2) empathetically and concretely experiencing the other's actions as ordered toward realizing (apparent) goods contributing to her (apparent) well-being. We move beyond the recognition of a non-human agent to the recognition of a person and to the definitive features of respect when we encounter these beings as also capable of (i) articulating the goods they pursue and the choices they make, (ii) expressing their moral judgments and reasoning in words as well as actions, and (iii) reflecting on the choiceworthiness of the ends they pursue and on the choices they make in their pursuit.

To understand in greater detail what triggers our respectful affective response to the other I return our attention for a moment to the "analogical" base of empathy—ourselves. Our evaluative experiences (intentional feelings and emotions) possess a teleological dimension. In valuing and judging things as good, we tend toward an evidenced experience of them as good. Thinking they are truly good motivates desires to realize them, and we choose and act so as to do so, thereby fulfilling both our valuations and our practical intentions. This teleological dimension is present throughout our intentional life. As rational agents, we are teleologically ordered to the full exercise of reason in all its spheres. The task of reason, in other words, is always to ensure in fulfilling experiences—that is, direct and intuitive experiences—the "truthfulness" of our judgments about what is the case, about what is valuable, and about what is right to do. The *telos*—the good—of reason, and by extension of the person who minds the world, is in the broadest sense (i) to apprehend truthfully things and states of affairs, (ii) to have appropriate affective and evaluative attitudes towards those things and states of affairs, and (iii) to act rightly in response to and on the basis of our truthful cognitions and attitudes. As Husserl puts it, "Be a true human being; lead a life that you can continuously justify insightfully, a life of practical reason" (Husserl 1989, p. 36; see also Drummond 2010).

This good, however, is purely formal. It is not pursued directly but is instead a second-order good realized in the evidenced pursuit of first-order goods in our everyday experience. The variety of first-order goods available for our pursuit means that we must subordinate one good to another, and the agent whose life and striving are rationally well ordered must choose superordinate goods central to her well-being and flourishing as a rational agent. Identical in each of these material, substantive, first-order goods that are the direct objects of our pursuits is the formal, second-order good of evidential fulfillment that is realized indirectly and superveniently in the pursuit of them. Husserl speaks of this second-order good as "authenticity" (*Eigentlichkeit*), but I believe we might better think of it as "truthful self-responsibility." It is a matter of (i) grasping truthfully the way things are, (ii) having appropriate affective responses and evaluations of things, and (iii) acting rightly in the light of these evaluations. It is being able to give reasons and to take responsibility for our judgments, our identification and ordering of goods, and the actions we undertake in their pursuit. The person in the fullest sense, then, is the self-responsible agent of truth (Sokolowski 2008, p. 1). I take this understanding of the *telos* of the rational agent to be the eudaimonistic moment in terms of which we must understand the notion of the virtuous person, the one who is disposed to those activities that conduce to the realization of this *telos*.

What I propose regarding respect is that when we encounter another in whose actions we can note a firm and habitual commitment to overarching first-order goods that give meaning to that person's life and order it to the greatest degree possible as a morally coherent whole, our affective response is appraisal respect for the self-responsible rational agency intimated in that person's actions. What is empathetically and respectfully encountered in the first instance is the other's chosen actions as expressing beliefs about the good and about the actions conducive to that good. We do not—even in the encounter of the stranger—originally encounter persons in the abstract, as merely possessing the capacities to act self-responsibly; we originally encounter persons with particular characteristics and acting in particular ways on the basis of particular conceptions of the good. The recognition of another person as appraisal-respectable is impossible apart from the empathy-derived sense of the other as a radically transcendent subject, a subject who is irreducibly other and responsible for her attitudes, choices, and actions. The empathetic sense of the other as a self-responsible conscious agent, in other words, underlies and grounds appraisal respect for meritorious persons who pursue evidently true goods.

Recognition respect, by contrast, is more formal than appraisal respect, but, like everything abstract, it is rooted in particulars.[4] On the basis of our encounter with self-responsible moral agents eliciting appraisal respect from us, we recognize that the common ground of our respect for them is that their lives realize insightfully chosen goods to the greatest degree possible given the circumstances in which those lives are lived. At the same time, however, we recognize that such lives presuppose the rational, emotional, and volitional capacities whose exercise is the realization of those lives. The possession of these rational capacities is recognized as a necessary condition for and conducive to the self-responsible life.

We cannot recognize the capacities as worthy of recognition respect apart from experiencing their exercise in lives authentically committed to superordinating goods. Hence, appraisal respect is *phenomenologically* prior to recognition respect. However, recognition respect—as directed to the necessary conditions for the possibility of meritorious actions— is *morally* prior to appraisal respect. It is the possession of these capacities that constitutes the dignity of rational

---

[4] For the distinction between appraisal respect and recognition respect, cf. Darwall 1977.

agents, that makes them worthy of and demanding recognition respect. Recognition respect grasps beings possessing these capacities, whether or not they are well exercised, as having a certain dignity. Dignity, in Anthony Kenny's terms, is the "formal object" of recognition respect (Kenny 1963, p. 132; cf. Kriegel 2017, p. 124).

I have claimed that intersubjectivity involves both similarity and communalization in irreducible difference. The apprehension of the other as a conscious, free, rational agent underlies respect in both its forms. The two forms of respect presuppose and are affective complements of empathy, however, as apprehending the *irreducible difference* of the empathetically perceived subject. Respect, whether appraisal respect or recognition respect, apprehends the other as a self-responsible center of conscious experiences that are beyond my direct grasp. By contrast, sympathy, while also an affective complement of empathy, is grounded in the *similarity* and *communalization* of the empathetically perceived subject. In empathetically experiencing another as, say, grief-stricken, I am aware of the intentional object of the other's grief, namely, a loss, say, the death of a spouse. Empathy grasps the other as experiencing grief over this loss, a loss to which I, along with the empathized subject, primarily direct my attention. In sympathizing with the other, however, I do not merely recognize the other's grief; I have an affective reaction to that recognition. In sympathy I direct my attention not merely to the loss but to the grieving subject as someone about whose well-being I care. Sympathy, in other words, even while building itself upon empathy, distinguishes itself therefrom by virtue of involving a care for the well-being of the other subject that empathy on its own does not (cf. Husserl 2004, p. 194; Scheler 1954, p. 8; Darwall 1998, p. 261; Zahavi 2008, p. 516). Moreover, while we tend to think of sympathy as coming into play in cases where the other's well-being has been threatened or harmed, we should not collapse it into pity or commiseration (cf. Darwall 1998, p. 261). In empathetically perceiving another's joy, for example, I can sympathetically savor, relish, or rejoice in her joy.

Sympathy must also be distinguished from emotional contagion and emotional sharing. Emotional contagion involves "catching" or "infection by" the emotion empathetically perceived (Scheler 1954, p. 15). But this differs from sympathy in an important way. In sympathy, it is *your* emotion that *I* experience; *my* sympathizing is directed at *your* grief, *your* joy. We experience different emotions: sympathy, on the one hand, grief or joy, on the other. In emotional contagion, my emotion—the same as yours—is directed to what distresses you. I too, for example, grieve the loss, and I easily lose sight of your grief in my own grieving the loss.

In emotional sharing, by contrast, the empathetic perception of the other's state and my emotional experience are so intertwined that they are not even experienced as distinct (Scheler 1954, p. 1). This too transforms the notion of sympathy. Emotional sharing also remains focused on the loss, but it differs from contagion in that there is no danger of losing sight of your emotion. This is because emotional sharing is a relation that is no longer a relation that has two subjects experiencing two tokens of the same emotion type. Emotional sharing involves experiencing the emotion as *ours*, as *one* token. The subjects sharing the emotion are co-subjects, and what they feel is constitutively interdependent, i.e., dependent upon the relation in which they stand to one another. Scheler's famous example of emotional sharing is two parents grieving the loss of their young child. The relation of the parents one to another, just insofar as they are parents of the child, overcomes their separateness and they share a single experience of grieving. Emotional sharing, if a real possibility (which I doubt, at least in Scheler's strong sense), is not sympathy.

There is a tension in the claims I am making. I have said that recognition respect of the other as having the dignity that belongs to rational, free beings brings to the fore the irreducible difference between myself and the other, while sympathy directed to the other brings out the sameness and communalization between myself and the other. But I have also just said that sympathy, as opposed to emotional contagion and emotional sharing, thematically preserves the difference between myself as sympathizing with you in your grief and you as feeling grief. I can sympathize with a grieving person and feel grief at the same time, but I can also sympathize with a grieving person without feeling grief directed at whatever distresses that person. For example, say Joe loses his job because his application for tenure is denied. He is distressed by this development, potentially experiencing a range of emotions such as anger and something approximating grief about the loss of his job, something that he considers an important aspect of his identity. I can sympathize with Joe, i.e., feel sadness that he is distressed, without feeling distressed about him losing his job. I might think the decision to deny him tenure is correct, a thought that might be accompanied by regret that things did not work out well for him.

So, what is involved in the claim that sympathy discloses the other under the aspect of sameness-with-me? The idea is something like this: in recognition respect I am focused on the other precisely and exclusively as an alternate center of rational, conscious agency, as a person having dignity. The particular characteristics of that person's experiences are irrelevant to the nature of recognition respect. However, the persons I experience have particular experiences that I empathetically recognize. Insofar as empathy is a cognitive basis for affective responses to others, then in order to encounter others as the same in irreducible difference, it is necessarily the case that, along with respect, what Nancy Sherman (Sherman 1997, p. 175; 1998, pp. 175–81) calls "attractive" attitudes also arise.[5] Recognition respect is exercised in our efforts to cultivate a person's reason and emotions, to cultivate their ability to judge and to understand reasoned goods, all the while refraining from imposing judgments and decisions on them. To do this is to maintain the tension between sameness and difference. To do this involves attractive attitudes—we might better call them "cooperative" attitudes—that oppose the "repulsive" character of respect. Cooperative attitudes manifest themselves in care for the other, a care that first arises in sympathy and that motivates us to help the other to realize her chosen goods and, as in Joe's case, to sympathize with him when things do not work out well. A cultivated sympathy establishes a relationship with others; it inclines us toward caring for and aiding the other person that recognition respect discloses as a moral agent worthy of and demanding our own moral attention.

However, sympathy also runs the risk of motivating paternalistic or even oppressive actions. This is why, just as we need sympathy in relation to recognition respect, we need recognition respect in relation to sympathy. The irreducible difference between self and other cannot be lost from view as it might be were sympathy to morph into a paternalistic attitude. Each person in the community must "decide," that is, decide in the light of the best available evidence, for herself what is true, good, and right. The other is always irreducibly other, and recognition-respect of the irreducibility of the other—a conscious, free being in her own right—creates the moral space in which sympathy can work. Sympathy, conversely, fills the moral space bounded by respect. Respect and properly cultivated sympathy jointly motivate desires and actions that preserve the "sameness and communalization in irreducible difference" characteristic of the empathy grounding them.

---

[5] Sherman's use of the term "attractive" is an allusion to Kant's well-known analogy: "[W]e consider ourselves in a moral (intelligible) world where, by analogy with the physical world, attraction and repulsion bind together rational beings (on earth). The principle of mutual love admonishes them constantly to come closer to one another; that of the respect they owe one another, to keep themselves at a distance from one another…"; cf. Kant 1996, 6:407. The reference uses the pagination, reproduced in the margins of Gregor's translation, of the Königliche Preussische Akademie der Wissenschaften edition of *Kants gesammelte Schriften*.

The Foundations of Morality

We have seen that empathy is a perceptual recognition of another that is inseparable from our awareness of ourselves as rational beings whose bodies are both involved in the disclosure of the world and expressive of our mental states. Our embodiment entails that we have a limited perspective on the world. Empathy's recognition that the experienced other and I share an object, although from different perspectives or under different aspects, entails a recognition that the objectivity of understanding is fundamentally intersubjective. In other words, the mutuality in empathy introduces a communalization that is essential to objective knowledge (Husserl 1970, p. 120, Mertens 2000, pp. 10–14). Moreover, insofar as respect and sympathy are two affective responses to the empathetically perceived other, they complement our understanding of others and of the world by introducing value and motivations into our shared experience. I experience —or should experience—the other as having dignity and as a person with whose well-being and flourishing I am—or should be—concerned. I recognize —or should recognize—that, like all understanding, my understanding of emotion-concepts, value-concepts, and moral concepts is an intersubjectively achieved understanding that responds both to the way things are and to the histories, concerns, and commitments of both individuals and communities.

The respect-sympathy structure at the base of morality has further implications for ethics. The recognition of (1) the communalizing nature of empathetically grounded respect and sympathy and (2) the inherent limitations of one's own perspective as requiring supplementation with and completion by the perspectives of others entails that the flourishing of free, rational beings who seek to realize the *telos* of evidenced achievements in all the spheres of reason depends on other subjects. This recognition encourages the development of a—perhaps *the*— central virtue of intellectual humility. Intellectual humility is the disposition to recognize and accept the limitations of perspective inherent in one's intellectual capacities and to be welcoming of the complements and corrections to one's beliefs from others (see Whitcomb et al. 2017, p. 529).

This view has two important consequences. First, the intellectually humble person is unconcerned about—and therefore inattentive to—her intellectual status. It is not that one falsely underestimates that status; it is just that it is not a major issue for the humble person who recognizes that the inadequacy of her intellectual capacities requires that she not overestimate those capacities.[6]

---

[6] Robert Roberts and W. Jay Wood (2003, p. 271) define intellectual humility as this unconcern

Second, intellectual humility is by its very nature connected to other intellectual virtues. In particular, intellectual humility involves a balance between the seemingly opposed virtues of firmness and open-mindedness. The intellectually humble person is likely to be disposed to consider carefully the other's viewpoint, to consider convictions that conflict with her own, and, when appropriate, to revise her opinions. Such open-mindedness should not, however, be understood to suggest that we should simply and graciously accept or yield to any view offered for our consideration. That would be a form of intellectual servitude and is not a virtue. While it is not a part of intellectual humility, the person who is intellectually humble without being submissive will be firm-minded even as she is open-minded.[7] Intellectual firmness disposes us to hold on to our own convictions and not to yield at the first sign of counter-evidence without a further examination of the evidence and the arguments pro and con.

Intellectual firmness is especially important in the light of the phenomenological notion of evidence. The degree of tenacity involved in intellectual firmness varies with the convictions in question. We hold on to central beliefs more firmly than peripheral ones, and we hold on to convictions that have been consistently and continuously evidenced in prior experience more firmly than those that have not. We have more confidence in more fully evidenced convictions, and it is only in the face of a direct evidence sufficient to override such confidence that we should yield our view. Intellectual firmness holds us fast to this rule. But insisting on the role of evidence and the possibility of counterevidence accounts for the possibility of distinguishing firmness from rigid dogmatism and intellectual arrogance.

Intellectual humility is also intertwined with both intellectual charity and intellectual generosity, in whose conjunction we can again see the respect-sympathy structure at work. Charity as an intellectual virtue is the love of others as it operates in our intellectual life. It is directed to others insofar as they are our interlocutors and the authors of texts that we read. Intellectual charity is the disposition to exercise goodwill in listening to others and in reading a text so that we can faithfully understand the views of those who already command from us recognition respect as rational agents. Intellectual charity minimizes the tendency to misstate or caricaturize another's position, to focus one's attention on straw men, and to miss the important issues at stake. Lacking intellectual charity, the

---

with intellectual status, but I think this is instead a characteristic outcome of intellectual humility rather than its defining property.

7 Ian Church (2016) seems to incorporate firm-mindedness and open-mindedness into the definition of intellectual humility. Again, however, I think these are intertwined with intellectual humility without being definitive of it.

agent can recognize neither the ways in which his or her own convictions are supported or challenged by the other's views nor the ways in which the other's positions are supported or challenged by his or her own. The intellectually charitable agent attributes as much validity and intelligence to the other as is possible consistent with a careful, and therefore critical, understanding. Intellectual charity extends beyond recognitional respect insofar as the intellectually charitable agent treats the other as autonomously rational and with sympathy and goodwill, valuing the other precisely as a speaker or author. This notion of charity arises out of humility and contributes to the well-being of the intellectually humble and charitable person herself. The humble and charitable person welcomes the views of others for their broadening of her perspective, and she is joyful in gaining a better understanding of things.

The intellectually charitable agent also seeks to bring it about that the other receives some genuine intellectual goods in the exchange. This leads us to the virtue of intellectual generosity. Generosity in its ordinary sense is an agent's disposition to give freely to others without expectation of return and for the benefit of the recipients what is valuable to the agent herself, e.g., material goods, time, or attention. Generosity in the intellectual sphere, then, is the disposition to give freely of one's own ideas, attention, praise, recognition, and encouragement for the benefit of the recipient. The generous thinker expends time and energy in collaborative activities with the result that others gain from her efforts. The generous teacher guides students in ways that fully develop their capacity to determine and develop their own positions, and she rejoices in their success without concern to measure the degree of her influence upon them.[8] Being charitable in our reading and listening allows us to benefit from the insights of others; being generous benefits the other. In the exchanges between charitable and generous agents, the respect-sympathy structure is again instanced.

These accounts of selected intellectual virtues are not meant to be comprehensive accounts; they are meant only to exemplify how the flourishing rational agent is a social being who acts, when acting rightly, in a manner that exhibits both recognition respect of the other and the sympathetic care for the other's well-being. Nor do these accounts entail that the view of a phenomenological eudaimonism I have outlined with its foundations in empathy and the respect-sympathy structure is too heavily weighted toward intellectual virtues. For rational agents self-responsibility must be realized in rational activities. Anything else would be the eudaimonia of a non-rational being. Moreover, the forms of reason

---

[8] In addition to the previously cited articles, these brief sketches of some intellectual virtues are indebted to Roberts and Wood (2007) and Baehr (2011).

are not merely—and not even primarily—theoretical. A pure theoretical reason is an abstraction from our straightforward experience of and practical engagement with the world, and indeed, it is an abstraction that cannot fully leave behind the practical since theorizing is itself a special kind of praxis. The phenomenological notion of reason encompasses theoretical, axiological, and practical reason, each with its proper form of truthfulness.

More important, this account of *eudaimonia* and virtue points to an account of virtue in the sphere of action just as much as it does in the sphere of reason. Given that the intellectual virtues operate in all the spheres of reason, it follows that having the right attitudes—that is, emotions and desires—and performing the right actions belong essentially to the eudaimonism here sketched. Indeed, since the most encompassing of the three forms of reason is practical (because it presupposes both cognition and evaluative feelings and emotions), and since practical reason is concerned not merely with knowing what is good and right but in doing the right in all the spheres of human activity, these intellectual virtues underlie our grasp and exercise of the virtues of character as well. It is only when we apprehend truly the way things are, only when we truthfully discern what goods are worthwhile ends of action and around what loves and commitments we will order our lives, and only when we rightly choose those actions that are good in themselves and best conduce to these ends that we can exercise the virtues of character.

Finally, recall from our original discussion of empathy that minds—our own and those we encounter—are embodied. From this it follows that eudaimonia requires respect and care for the bodies of others. This requirement again points in the direction of the virtues that care not simply for the mind or intellect in the way that intellectual virtues do; it point towards virtues of character such as justice, material generosity, compassion, and so forth that care for the person, that care for embodied minds.

There are, of course, many other virtues that require identification and careful description. My aim has been only to sketch the view that our ethical lives are co-grounded in respect and sympathy, and, beyond them, in the empathetic apprehension of other subject-objects in the world, subjects both like the experiencing agent and irreducibly different from it.

References

Baehr, Jason S. (2011): *The Inquiring Mind: On Intellectual Virtues and Virtue Epistemology*. Oxford: Oxford University Press.

Church, Ian M. (2016): "The Doxastic Account of Intellectual Humility". In: *Logos and Episteme* 7(4), pp. 413–33.
Darwall, Stephen (1977): "Two Kinds of Respect". In: *Ethics* 88(1), pp. 36–49.
Darwall, Stephen (1998): "Empathy, Sympathy, Care". In: *Philosophical Studies* 89(2–3), pp. 261–82.
Drummond, John J. (2002): "Forms of Social Unity: Partnership, Membership, and Citizenship". In: *Husserl Studies* 18(2), pp. 141–56.
Drummond, John J. (2006): "Respect as a Moral Emotion: A Phenomenological Approach". In: *Husserl Studies* 22(1), pp. 1–27.
Drummond, John J. (2010). "Self-Responsibility and Eudaimonia". In: Ierna, Carlo/Jacobs, Hanne/Mattens, Filip (Eds.): *Philosophy Phenomenology Sciences*. Dordrecht: Springer, pp. 441–60.
Husserl, Edmund (1959): *Erste Philosophie (1923/24): Zweiter Teil: Theorie der phänomenologischen Reduktion*. Rudolf Boehm (Ed.). Husserliana VIII. Dordrecht: Springer.
Husserl, Edmund (1970): *Cartesian Meditations: An Introduction to Phenomenology*. Trans. Dorion Cairns. The Hague: Martinus Nijhoff.
Husserl, Edmund (1973a): *Zur Phänomenologie der Intersubjektivität: Texte aus dem Nachlaß. Dritter Teil: 1929–1935*. Iso Kern (Ed.). Husserliana XV. The Hague: Martinus Nijhoff.
Husserl, Edmund (1973b): *Zur Phänomenologie der Intersubjektivität: Texte aus dem Nachlaß. Zweiter Teil: 1921–1928*. Iso Kern (Ed.). Husserliana XIV. Dordrecht: Kluwer.
Husserl, Edmund (1989): *Ideas Pertaining to a Pure Phenomenology and to a Phenomenological Philosophy. Second Book: Studies in the Phenomenology of Constitution*. Trans. Richard Rojcewicz/André Schuwer. Dordrecht: Kluwer.
Husserl, Edmund (2004): *Einleitung in die Ethik: Vorlesungen Sommersemester 1920/1924*. Henning Peucker (Ed.). Husserliana XXXVII. Dordrecht: Kluwer.
Kant, Immanuel (1996): "The Metaphysics of Morals". In: *Practical Philosophy*. Trans. Mary J. Gregor. *The Cambridge Edition of the Works of Immanuel Kant*. Cambridge: Cambridge University Press, pp. 353–604.
Kenny, Anthony (1963): *Action, Emotion, and Will*. London: Routledge.
Kriegel, Uriah (2017): "Dignity and the Phenomenology of Recognition-Respect". In: Drummond, John J./Rinofner-Kreidl, Sonja (Eds.): *Emotional Experiences: Ethical and Social Significance*. London: Rowman & Littlefield International, pp. 121–36.
MacIntyre, Alasdair C. (1999): *Dependent Rational Animals: Why Human Beings Need the Virtues*. Chicago: Open Court.
Mertens, Karl (2000): "Husserls Phänomenologie der Monade. Bemerkungen zu Husserls Auseinandersetzung mit Leibniz". In: *Husserl Studies* 17(1), pp. 1–20.
Roberts, Robert C./Wood, W. Jay (2003): "Intellectual Humility and Epistemic Goods". In: Zagzebski, Linda/DePaul, Michael R. (Eds.): *Intellectual Virtue: Perspectives From Ethics and Epistemology*. Oxford: Oxford University Press, pp. 257–79.
Roberts, Robert C./Wood, W. Jay (2007): *Intellectual Virtues: An Essay in Regulative Epistemology*. Oxford: Oxford University Press.
Scheler, Max (1954): *The Nature of Sympathy*. Trans. Peter Heath. London: Routledge & Kegan Paul.
Sherman, Nancy (1997): *Making a Necessity of Virtue: Aristotle and Kant on Virtue*. Cambridge: Cambridge University Press.

Sherman, Nancy (1998): "Concrete Kantian Respect". In: *Social Philosophy and Policy* 15(1), pp. 119–48.
Sokolowski, Robert (2008): *Phenomenology of the Human Person*. Cambridge: Cambridge University Press.
Stein, Edith (1989): *On the Problem of Empathy*. Trans. Waltraut Stein. 3rd rev. ed. Washington, D.C.: ICS Publications.
Walsh, Philip J. (2014). "Empathy, Embodiment, and the Unity of Expression". In: *Topoi* 33(1), pp. 215–26.
Whitcomb, Dennis/Battaly, Heather/Baehr, Jason/Howard-Snyder, Daniel (2017): "Intellectual Humility: Owning Our Limitations". In: *Philosophy and Phenomenological Research* 94(3), pp. 509–39.
Zahavi, Dan (2008): "Simulation, Projection and Empathy". In: *Consciousness and Cognition* 17(2), pp. 514–22.
Zahavi, Dan (2014): *Self and Other: Exploring Subjectivity, Empathy, and Shame*. Oxford: Oxford University Press.
Zahavi, Dan (2019): "Second-Person Engagement, Self-Alienation, and Group-Identification". In: *Topoi* 38(1), pp. 251–60.

Andrea Staiti
Tolerance: A Phenomenological Approach

Abstract: In this chapter I present and criticize the dominant Two-Component View (TCV) of tolerance and propose to replace it with a One-Component View (OCV) based on Husserlian phenomenology. In the first part of the chapter I present the TCV as the view that tolerance consists of the conjunction of a positive and a negative component, and I discuss four specifications of the TCV by Preston King, Rainer Forst, Achim Lohmar, and Lester Embree. I argue that the paradox involved in the conjunction of two opposite components is not plausibly solved by any of these views. In the second part of the chapter I proceed to outline a Husserlian OCV, according to which tolerance is a moral attitude that neutralizes a positing of value in the context of empathy in order to avoid a value-conflict with another subject. When we tolerate another person we refrain from rebuking or otherwise sanctioning them because we care about their autonomous moral progress more than we care about being axiologically right about our value-positings.

Introduction

'Tolerance' is a highly contested concept. On the one hand, tolerance is celebrated as an essential ingredient for liberal-democracies, to the point that in 1995 UNESCO instituted a yearly International Day for Tolerance (November, 16th) and had all member states sign a Declaration of Principles on Tolerance to orient future legislation. On the other, tolerance is criticized for being a fundamentally asymmetric and paternalistic principle, involving a superior tolerating sovereign and an inferior tolerated subject. As Goethe effectively puts the point in a famous aphorism: "Tolerance should be a temporary attitude only: it must lead to recognition. To tolerate means to insult." (Goethe 2017, p. 30; translation modified). Critics of tolerance in the past century, such as Herbert Marcuse, have gone even further than Goethe and denounced tolerance as an attitude that promotes social acquiescence to abusive powers and silent acceptance of the *status quo* (Marcuse 1969).

Enthusiasm and criticism aside, what's puzzling about tolerance is that it is even unclear how to define the concept in a way that doesn't dissolve its intrinsic ambivalence, let alone identify standard examples that are unanimously recognized as involving tolerance[1]. Consider the UNESCO Declaration definition of tolerance as "respect, acceptance and appreciation of the rich diversity of our world's cultures, our forms of expression and ways of being human" (UNESCO 1995). If we 'respect', 'accept' and even 'appreciate' practices and beliefs other than our own, then, it seems, we are *no longer* merely tolerating them. Tolerance must retain within itself a measure of negativity, otherwise it ceases to constitute a self-standing moral attitude in its own right and simply dissolves into thoroughly positive attitudes such as the ones mentioned in the UNESCO definition. As one recent commentator writes: "UNESCO's definition […] distorts the concept of tolerance on the experiential level" (Skalski 2017, p. 63).

A variety of philosophical tasks emerges in light of these remarks. First, it is necessary to clarify how tolerance relates to other moral attitudes and how it differs from cognate stances such as acquiescence, forbearance, patience, endurance, indifference, etc. This is important in order to propose a definition that preserves tolerance as an attitude in its own right. Second, it is imperative to provide unambiguous examples of tolerance and interpret them in a way that fits the proposed definition. Third, moral philosophers are expected to produce some sort of justification of tolerance, both at the level of individual cases (when should we tolerate?) and in general (why should we be tolerant?). The present chapter aims to contribute to the contemporary debate on tolerance from a phenomenological perspective. This is meant to provide a faithful description of tolerance at the experiential level. In fact, there is little to no work devoted to the experience of tolerance. Philosophers who write about tolerance usually discuss it at a very abstract and conceptual level. With the following considerations I thus hope to start filling what seems like a huge gap in the existing literature on tolerance. I will argue that if we focus on the *experience* of tolerance we have to drop the main assumption that underlies virtually all philosophical contributions on this topic in the past few decades, namely, the view that tolerance necessarily involves two neatly distinct components, one negative and one positive, which I will henceforth refer to as the Two-Component View (TCV). I will set out to articulate a One-Component View (OCV) of tolerance using Husserlian resources and arguing that the kind of attitude involved in the experience of tolerance

---

[1] As David Heyd writes in his introduction to one of the few volumes specifically devoted to the philosophy of tolerance: "Perhaps the best indication of the shaky grounds on which the philosophical discussion of tolerance rests is the intriguing lack of agreement on paradigm cases. In the theory of rights, virtue, and duty, people who radically disagree about the analysis and justification of these concepts can still appeal to a commonly shared repertory of examples. But with tolerance, it seems that we can find hardly a single concrete case that would be universally agreed to be a typical object of discussion" (1996, p. 3).

is a form of modified valuing in the context of empathy. More specifically, I will suggest that tolerance is one of the ways in which the neutrality modification plays out in the sphere of valuing and willing when such valuing and willing is accomplished through the lens of empathy, as it were. I will then address the temporary nature of tolerance evoked by Goethe and describe it as provisional neutralizing consciousness in the sphere of empathetic valuing.

Before I conclude this introduction with a brief outline of the next sections, let me mention a fundamental distinction that should disambiguate the aim of this paper. Tolerance can be discussed as either an issue in political philosophy, i.e., roughly in the way that famous thinkers such as Locke, Voltaire or, more recently, Rawls discussed it, or as an issue in moral psychology and phenomenology. The discussion of tolerance in political philosophy focuses on legislation. It started in early modernity with passionate writings that urged monarchs to end the oppression of religious minorities and it continued all the way into the present as a reflection on the principles that should inform legislation in democratic states, as the UNESCO declaration testifies. The discussion of tolerance in moral psychology and, in this paper, phenomenology, focuses on the attitude of individual persons who tolerate. It asks what is distinctive about that attitude and what concepts and beliefs are necessarily involved in it. In what follows I will be concerned exclusively with the moral psychology and phenomenology of tolerance. As for the political dimension, it seems that the issue is easily resolved: tolerance was a commendable ideal in a world of absolute monarchs who could legislate by whim. In liberal democracies, where legislators are held accountable by the people for their decisions, tolerance cannot and should not be a principle informing legislation, *pace* the UNESCO declaration. It would be odd, at best, if legislators in a liberal democracy declared that a certain practice or minority should be *tolerated*. From the point of view of law, a practice is either permissible or impermissible and if it is permissible, then it is a citizen's right to engage in it. The right attitude toward a citizen who is engaging in a practice that is her right to engage in is certainly not tolerance! In a liberal democracy tolerance finds its legitimate place in the *enforcement*, rather than the *formulation* of law. This is why the moral-psychological and phenomenological dimension is so crucial. In liberal democracies where laws determine what is permissible and impermissible, rather than what is tolerable and what is intolerable, it is up to law enforcement officers, judges, and private citizens to handle problematic actions, practices, beliefs, etc. and determine when they should be sanctioned and when they shouldn't, i.e., when tolerance is called for and when it isn't. This leads us straight to the question of attitudes and the moral psychology and phenomenology of tolerance.

In the first section of the present chapter I will outline the TCV and the paradox it implies. In the second section I will offer a brief description of how theorists of tolerance have specified the TCV and tried to solve the paradox. Subsequently, in the third section, I will show that there is no way out of the paradox if we adopt the TCV and I will outline the OCV that should replace it. In section four I will turn to Husserl's conception of modalities and modalizations in the sphere of belief and, most importantly, in the sphere of valuing and willing. Section five will integrate the notions of modalized valuing and willing into the phenomenon of empathy, which can itself be described as a kind of modification of experience. The final section will offer a phenomenological description of tolerance in the context of a theory of modalizations and present it as a distinctively practical form of neutralized consciousness. In the conclusion I will return to Goethe's insightful remark about tolerance as temporary and reconsider it from a phenomenological point of view.

1 The Two-Component View (TCV) and its paradoxical nature

I have spoken above about a characteristic ambivalence of tolerance. Those who tolerate must have, so to speak, mixed feelings about the things they tolerate, otherwise their attitude turns into something else, be it esteem, outright contempt, or sheer indifference. The philosophy of tolerance of the past few decades has interpreted this ambivalence in terms of *two components* that constitute tolerance. The original formulation of the TCV is found in Preston King's seminal book *Toleration* (1976), which can be considered the standard text for all subsequent discussions of tolerance in the Anglophone world and beyond. King talks about an *objection* component and an *acceptance* component (King 1976, pp. 44–51) toward a given item as the characteristic ingredients of tolerance. We can state the TCV inaugurated by King in even more general terms as the view that tolerance necessarily involves a *negative* and a *positive* component. It is no exaggeration to say that *all* philosophers who have written on tolerance in the past fifty years agree on the TCV in these general terms. Disagreement is not on the TCV itself but on (1) how to specify the two components, (2) the *item or items* toward which the two components are directed, and, consequently, (3) how the two components relate to each other.

The TCV generates disagreement because, despite its wide acceptance, it is also perceived as deeply paradoxical: how can a *negative* and a *positive* component coexist in one and the same attitude without thereby undermining its coherence? Is it psychologically and conceptually possible to *simultaneously* hold a negative and positive stance toward the same item? Does tolerance exist as an integral and self-standing attitude or is talk of tolerance just shorthand for two different and even opposite attitudes, one negative and one positive, that merely coexist? Or do we need to split the object of tolerance and speak of a plurality of items, toward which its opposite components are directed, in order to salvage its coherence? These are the main questions that theorists of tolerance struggle with. In sum: everyone agrees on the TCV and everyone agrees that it implies a paradox. For this reason, there is disagreement on how to construe the TCV in such a way as to dispel the paradox and present tolerance as a coherent attitude in its own right. In the next section I will provide a few examples of how the TCV has been construed in order to address these difficulties.

2 Different approaches to the TCV: King, Forst, Lohmar, Embree

2.1 Preston King

Not only is Preston King the first proponent of the TCV. He also presents a particular *version* of the TCV that construes the negative component of tolerance as an *objection* to a certain item and the positive component as the ultimate *acceptance* of that item. Thus, tolerance involves a "conjunction of objection and acceptance" (King 1976, p. 44). How can one and the same item be simultaneously objected to and accepted? King recognizes that there is an apparent paradox here and he proposes an ingenious way to dissolve it: "in the tolerantial conjuncture [...] what we are discussing is a situation in which one's objection to an item is inferior to one's objection to some other item, *which might serve as a means to acting out the first objection* – as perhaps when one objects to theft less that to hanging thieves, to Catholics less than to hanging Catholics, [...] (and so on)" (King 1976, p. 28). In King's construal, thus, tolerance is an essentially "comparative concern" where at stake is always the ranking of a given objection "within a hierarchy of objections" (King 1976, p. 28). The reason why, in King's example, one ultimately accepts thieves or Catholics is because one has a certain set of priorities where the objection to thieves or Catholics does not rank as high as, say, the objection to death penalty. Accepting these groups of people thus means refusing to act out one's objection to them in order to preserve other values that rank higher on one's list. King's position is noteworthy in at least three respects: (1) tolerance is presented as a kind of rational choice procedure where the costs and benefits of a certain action are measured against the value-ranking of the tolerating individual; (2) the two components of tolerance are construed as objection and acceptance, such that the former determines the mindset, and the latter the behavior of the tolerating individual: "When we speak of an objection what we are basically concerned with is a disposition or assessment. When we speak of acceptance, what we are basically concerned with, by contrast, are those consequential acts that are assumed to flow from the disposition or assessment" (King 1976, p. 52); (3) tolerance is always directed to one single item, which can be just about anything: a person, a worldview, an action, an ethnic group, etc. The tolerated item is first assessed from an intellectual stance and found objectionable, and subsequently considered from a practical stance and found acceptable (i.e., not to be acted against) in light of the verdict of another intellectual stance toward something else that is deemed even more objectionable than the item itself (e.g. hanging people vs. Catholics). There is thus a clear priority of the intellectual dimension of tolerance, with the practical dimension of not acting out the initial objection presented as a mere appendix of the comparative consideration of one's objections.

2.2 Rainer Forst

In his monumental work *Toleration in Conflict* (Forst 2013) Rainer Forst follows King in distinguishing an objection and an acceptance component, but construes the tolerantial conjuncture, to echo King's phrase, in a significantly different way. In Forst's view, the acceptance component of tolerance bears directly on the assessment of the item under scrutiny, not merely on the consequential act that flows from the comparative consideration of one's priorities and value-rankings. This is how Forst describes the acceptance component in a passage worth quoting in full:

> In addition to the objection component, toleration [...] also has an acceptance component which specifies that the tolerated convictions and practices are condemned as false or bad, yet not so false or bad that other, positive reasons do not speak for tolerating them. The important point here is that the positive reasons do not cancel out the negative reasons but are set against them in such a way that, although they trump the negative reasons (in the respect relevant in the corresponding context), and in this sense are higher-order reasons, the objection nevertheless retains its force. (Forst 2013, pp. 20–21)

The difference with King is significant and Forst's careful wording is key in this regard. The acceptance component is not merely a practical appendix to an intellectual process that is exclusively concerned with comparing objections.

Rather, the acceptance component of tolerance is described as involving *positive reasons* that pertain directly to the tolerated item as such and make it appear as not being thoroughly false or bad, to the point that it is ultimately the acceptance component that wins out and *trumps* the objection component, although this latter somehow *retains its force*. If we go back to King's example, on Forst's account we do not first consider Catholics and find them objectionable, then turn to consider the means to eliminate Catholics (e.g. hanging), find those means even more objectionable than Catholics and therefore refrain from acting on our initial objection. Rather, after finding Catholics objectionable in a first-order negative stance (objection component) we reconsider them in a different light and find some *aspects in the Catholics themselves* that provide us with positive reasons not to oppress or eliminate them, thereby engaging in a second-order positive stance (acceptance component). The acceptance component does not determine merely our behavior toward a tolerated item. It is actually the predominant component in our very *disposition* toward the item, the one that ultimately trumps the negative reasons underlying our initial objection. This is why Forst describes tolerance as a "balancing of reasons" (Forst 2013, p. 21): the positive and negative components of the TCV are re-interpreted as *reasons* and the final configuration of tolerance is one where it is the positive, rather than the negative component that takes center stage. On this point, Forst's view is similar to King's: in tolerance, it is only the acceptance component that determines behavior, but, unlike King, the acceptance component *qua* positive reasons is part of the assessment of the item that is tolerated.

2.3 Achim Lohmar

Achim Lohmar has responded to both King and Forst in an essay titled *Was ist eigentlich Toleranz?* (Lohmar 2010). Lohmar finds fault with the idea that in tolerance the negative and the positive component form a mere conjunction, where it is only the acceptance component that ultimately determines behavior. By contrast, Lohmar argues that we need a theory of tolerance that clarifies how both components of tolerance work together to determine behavior. Commenting directly on Forst's quote above, Lohmar contends that when we are pondering what we should do about a problematic practice, such as the sacrificial killing of animals, there are certainly reasons that speak for and reasons that speak against its toleration; "however that doesn't entail that we simultaneously accept and reject" (Lohmar 2010, p. 19) that practice. As long as we are undecided, there can be no legitimate talk of acceptance and rejection, but "if the positive reasons outweigh the negative reasons or even *trump* them, as Forst says, then we obviously come to an unambiguously positive verdict" (ibid.). If the acceptance component wins out, then there is no longer any rejection or objection to the practice under scrutiny and the outcome is that we find the practice acceptable, rather than tolerate it. According to Lohmar, the TCV must be redefined without reference to objection and acceptance, whose combination in the same attitude and toward the same item is logically flawed. Lohmar proposes that we redefine the negative component of tolerance as an "aversion" (Lohmar 2010, p. 20), in order to underscore its conative, rather than intellectual nature. Moreover, such aversion must be *moral*, i.e., it has to be motivated by one's moral beliefs. I might have a strong gut-level dislike for religious people, but firmly believe that they should be allowed to practice their faith. If I started bullying religious people for what they do, it would be inappropriate to urge me to be tolerant. Rather, I should be reproached for letting an irrational, gut-level aversion take hold of me. I should be reminded that I actually believe in religious freedom. Irrational, gut-level aversions do not require tolerance, but rationality as a remedy. If my aversion is genuinely *moral* in nature, i.e., when it amounts to indignation for an action that is morally bad, then, on Lohmar's account, we can speak of tolerance when *despite* this unambiguously negative verdict I do not want to see the action sanctioned and the person punished. This happens through the intervention of a "second-order moral judgment" (Lohmar 2010, p. 25) about the emotional or cognitive situation of the person who acted in that particular way. If I saw a person stealing from a grocery store, my first-level aversion toward the immoral action of stealing might be connected to a second-level judgment on that person's economic situation, for instance, if I knew that she just lost her job and has nothing to feed her children. On the basis of this judgment, even if my moral aversion toward her action remains, I would not want to see this person sanctioned for what she did, because I believe that her broader personal and emotional situation exculpates her. Note that Lohmar attempts to solve the paradox of the TCV, which he accepts, by redefining the negative component in terms of moral aversion, and the positive component in terms of a second-order moral judgment and arguing that the two components are actually directed toward two different items: the action per se and the person who engaged in it with her emotional and cognitive situation. Thus, on Lohmar's account the way out of the TCV's paradox involves three steps: (1) differentiating between the conative nature of the negative component and the cognitive, viz. intellectual, nature of the positive component, such that no internal contradiction arises; (2) denying that tolerance involves opposite stances toward the same item: the negative component is directed toward an action, while the positive component is directed toward a person and her situation; (3) clarifying that tolerance is, strictly speaking, always directed toward a person and never toward an action, which, by contrast, is always either morally permissible or impermissible. If an action is permissible, then it should be accepted without further qualification, if an action is impermissible, then it should be rejected without further qualification: it is only when we view an action as carried out by a particular person in a particular situation that the conditions for tolerance are fulfilled, namely, when we don't want to see that particular person sanctioned in light of her overall situation.

2.4 Lester Embree

The last view on tolerance that is worth mentioning before we move on has been put forward by Lester Embree in a short but solid essay titled *Tolerance Reflectively Analyzed* (Embree 2007). Embree defines tolerance phenomenologically as an "attitude" (Embree 2007, p. 164) that, as such, has a subjective and an objective dimension, i.e., a dimension of encountering and a thing encountered: "the things encountered in tolerance are the beliefs, values, and practices of others" (Embree 2007, p. 165). Embree adopts, albeit implicitly, the TCV, but, unlike the authors discussed so far, he fleshes it out in terms of "valuings". The negative component of the TCV is described as first-level valuing that is "comparative or, more specifically, contrastive" (Embree 2007, p. 167). The two parties involved compare their respective attitudes toward a certain item and each of the parties finds her own attitude good and the other's attitude bad. Despite the result of the first-level comparative valuing (the negative component), "the tolerant person refrains from opposing the attitudes that she disvalues", because she is also invested in "the valuing of something else" (Embree 2007, p. 168). The positive component for Embree thus takes the form of an "overriding valuing that motivates the neutral willing in the practical respecting found in tolerance" (Embree 2007, p. 169). Embree gives the example of a vegetarian and a meat-eater sharing a meal. While the first-order valuing of the vegetarian finds the attitude of the meat-eater wrong, the vegetarian might refrain from killing the meat-eater because she values human life even more than abstinence from meat, or simply because the value of a pleasant meal overrides the value of striking a blow against meat-eaters. Embree's conclusion thus resembles very closely King's, even if it is formulated in positive, rather than negative terms. In tolerance "something is valued more highly than either the aggressive advancement of one's own attitude or the impeding of the opposite attitude and this valuing is the stronger when it comes to motivating action" (Embree 2007, p. 169). Despite the close similarity to King, Embree's analysis is worth considering on its own terms, not only because of its explicit adherence to phenomenology. Embree has the merit of bringing to the fore the "practical-volitional" (Embree 2007, p. 168) nature of tolerance and to describe it as involving *valuing* as a distinctive form of experience, particularly, as a kind of valuing that involves an intersubjective dimension, i.e., the recognition of the other's opposite valuing.

3 No way out: from the TCV to the One-Component View (OCV)

After this overview of four distinguished formulations of the TCV it is now time to ask whether any of them succeeds in providing a satisfactory description of tolerance and, most importantly, in solving its characteristic paradox. In order to do so we need to be explicit about the requirements of a satisfactory theory of tolerance and introduce a couple of notions and distinctions that will facilitate the transition to the phenomenological analysis of tolerance provided in the next sections.

As we anticipated above, a theory of tolerance should account for it as a distinguishable and coherent attitude in its own right, if at all possible. Part of its success is, then, to distinguish tolerance from cognate attitudes. Moreover, a theory of tolerance should present this attitude as common and viable enough to deserve the amount of attention it has enjoyed throughout the past centuries. If a theory presented tolerance as an attitude that we can assume only when highly improbable conditions are fulfilled, that theory should better be replaced. Finally, a theory of tolerance should present it as a *moral* attitude, that is, as an attitude that is both motivated by moral concerns and carried out in moral acts.

Let us now evaluate the four variants of the TCV. First, Preston King's theory fails to present tolerance as a distinctive attitude in its own right. Tolerance is described as an attitude whereby we refrain from acting out an objection to a certain item due to an even stronger objection to another item. On this account, tolerance doesn't seem like a distinctive attitude: King provides just a generic description of a basic axiological law, which Husserl and other phenomenologists dubbed 'law of absorption'. Compare King's tolerantial conjunction with the following situation: I look at today's menu in the faculty dining room and it turns out that the two options are sautéed broccoli and Cajun catfish. I really don't like Cajun catfish, but there is nothing I loathe more than broccoli, therefore I end up ordering catfish. I refrain from acting out my initial gastronomic objection to catfish by ordering it (or, better, by not not-ordering it), because I have an even stronger gastronomic objection to broccoli. Would we describe such situation as one involving tolerance? We might if we wanted to joke about the disgusting menu options with a friend. But didn't we simply act on the basis of a general principle that applies to just about everything and that is well captured by the famous saying "the better is the enemy of the good" or, in this case, "the worse is the enemy of the bad"? These phrases encapsulate the so-called law of absorption: When a greater value appears, a lesser value looks like a disvalue, i.e., something of negative value, (or an *adiaphoron* i.e., something practically indifferent and value-less) and, conversely, when a greater disvalue appears, a lesser disvalue looks like a value (or an *adiaphoron*). The same consideration applies to Embree's vegetarian valuing a pleasant meal more than striking a blow to meat-eaters. There is nothing distinctively 'tolerantial' about these situations, unless we want to stipulate that tolerance just *means* applying the law of absorption. But since we apply the law of absorption ubiquitously when we carry out evaluations, tolerance would stop being a distinctive attitude, thus violating the first requirement for a satisfactory theory of tolerance.

There's more. King's theory also violates the second requirement. Recall that, on his account, we tolerate an objectionable item when we object even more to another item, "*which might serve as a means to acting out the first objection*" (King 1976, p. 28). But if this were the case, then tolerance would be warranted only in those cases where *all possible means* to acting out an initial objection are even more objectionable that the item initially objected to. On King's account, if I object to Catholics tolerance would be warranted only if acting out my objection necessarily involved hanging them (supposing my objection to hanging is stronger than my objection to Catholics). But one should be rather unimaginative to believe that hanging Catholics is the only way to act out one's objection to them. What about funding a campaign to convince them that their beliefs are wrong? Or excluding them from participation in certain key segments of public life, such as education? Or offering them rewards if they abjure? Following King, the conditions for tolerating Catholics would only be fulfilled in the highly unlikely event that *all possible means* to acting out my objection to Catholics where judged even more objectionable than Catholics themselves. The case is even clearer with King's other example: thieves. I object to hanging thieves more than I object to thieves, but there are dozens of other ways that I could act out my objection to thieves without therefore having to hang them. It is plausible that for whatever initial objection to a given item there will be at least one way of acting out the objection that doesn't involve practices to which we object even more. But if that is the case, then tolerance is an attitude that almost never happens, and it is unclear why philosophers and common people in the past few centuries spent so much time thinking about it.

One thing is clear: if tolerance is possible as an attitude in its own right, it must be specifically distinguishable from generic comparative evaluation. It needs to be an attitude that doesn't involve looking away from the object that is tolerated and thinking about something else that we love or hate more, such as pleasant meals or hangings. Tolerance must be an attitude that is and remains intentionally directed toward Catholics, thieves, or carnivores and relates to *them* and *their* valuings in a distinctive way, rather than constituting a mere shift of intentional focus away from the item initially objected to and toward something even more objectionable.

Forst's position, by contrast is not vulnerable to these critical remarks. As we mentioned above, Forst construes the acceptance component in terms of positive reasons speaking in favor of an item that we initially objected to. However, as we saw, Achim Lohmar has a rather powerful objection to that construal. Pondering positive and negative reasons is not the same as objecting to and accepting an item at the same time, which would be contradictory. If, at the end of the day, the positive reasons trump the negative reasons, as Forst puts it, then there is no tolerance, but simply a positive verdict about a practice that initially struck us as problematic. The advantage of Lohmar's approach is that it construes tolerance as a genuinely moral attitude, i.e., an attitude that is intentionally directed toward persons, thus fulfilling the third requirement of a successful theory of tolerance mentioned above. However, Lohmar's construal of tolerance, too, involves a shift of focus away from the person's action and toward the person's emotional and cognitive situation. What Lohmar seems to have in mind is that we tend to be accommodating or to close an eye on a person's morally bad action (we do not proceed to sanction it and do not want to see it sanctioned) when we believe that the person was motivated to act a certain way given her broader circumstances. But is tolerance the same as being accommodating or closing an eye? Aren't these cognate attitudes that resemble tolerance in some respects but do not coincide with it? Doesn't sensitivity to circumstances characterize all sound moral attitudes, rather than specifically tolerance? Christian forbearance or sheer patience seem to be describable in much the same way Lohmar describes tolerance. When I decide to endure something unpleasant or annoying it is usually precisely due to a consideration of the circumstances in which it occurs. If this is the case, then Lohmar's description, despite its indubitable merits vis-à-vis the other theories, ultimately does not fare much better. Finally, how do we know about the other's cognitive and emotional circumstances and how are we related to them when we tolerate? Lohmar's account lacks a description of our awareness of others and their circumstances through empathy and it mistakes the co-living of other people's experience characterizing empathy with a second-order judgment about a set of facts, whose accessibility is not accounted for.

I believe that the problem ultimately rests on the TCV as such. If we describe tolerance as the conjunction of two components, one negative and one positive, there seems to be no way out of the paradox. Either we construe the two components as directed toward one and the same item, but then we end up with some form of logical contradiction or psychological impossibility, or else we construe the two components as directed toward two different objects, but then tolerance seems to lose integrity as an attitude in its own right and simply morph into some form of merely comparative evaluation: we endure a despised object either because we have ulterior motives, such as avoiding other things we despise even more, or we simply close an eye due to mitigating circumstances.

My proposal here is to drop the TCV altogether. The consistency, coherence, and psychological possibility of tolerance can only be preserved if we view it as a *straightforward* attitude, i.e., an attitude that has only one 'component' and that is intentionally directed toward one single item, the one that is tolerated. Is it possible, however, to articulate a One Component View (OCV) of tolerance without dissolving its characteristic ambivalence? In the next sections I will endeavor to do so with the aid of Husserlian concepts.

4 The Modalities of Willing and Valuing

Let us briefly retrieve four important phenomenological ideas that will be critical in the development of a Husserlian approach to tolerance:
(1) Intentionality: the basic principle of phenomenology is that consciousness is always consciousness of something, i.e., intentionality. Accordingly, in examining tolerance as an attitude it is crucial to bring to light its intentionality. This means, first, specifying the proper object of acts of toleration and, second, clarifying whether such acts are, as Husserl puts it in *Logical Investigations*, monothetic (i.e., single-rayed, like perceptions) or polythetic (i.e., multi-rayed, like judgments). It is also critical to bear in mind the distinction between empty and fulfilled intentions, i.e., intentions whose object is also given in an intuitive act as present 'in the flesh' (fulfilled), and intentions whose object remains absent, either provisionally or intrinsically (empty). Fulfilled intentions are the radical sources of justification of any claims.
(2) Valuing and Willing: in Husserlian phenomenology the attribution of value to an object and the act of striving toward that object are intimately related. We only will things that we anticipate as valuable. Both valuing and willing, however, are modes of intentionality and as such they, too, can be empty or fulfilled. When I anticipate a value in a certain object I anticipate that the attainment of that object will bring with it a direct, intuitive experience of the value that was emptily intended. If the intuitive experience of the value occurs, then my act of valuing receives the mark of legitimacy, if it

doesn't, my act of valuing turns out to be illegitimate, i.e., wrong in a distinctively axiological sense. The same goes with willing. The legitimation of an act of willing occurs when the action to which it gives rise actually achieves the (authentic) goal that it was meant to achieve. If that doesn't happen, the corresponding willing is illegitimate.

(3) Axiological attitudes and moral attitudes: in his lectures on ethics Husserl points out that there is a significant difference between a merely axiological attitude, i.e., one in which I assess actions, people, goods, etc. merely in terms of their respective values, and a genuinely moral attitude, i.e., one in which the intentional object is either myself or another self (Husserl 2004, pp. 244–247). Moral attitudes are intrinsically reflexive. In a moral attitude we are actively concerned with self-determination, that is, we are to ourselves a theme of explicit scrutiny and we engage in acts of self-positing, whereby we posit ourselves as the bearers of certain moral property ("I will henceforth stop behaving this way", "I will henceforth try to be the best possible father to my children", etc.). Others can be the target of moral attitudes, too, for instance, when we engage in the project of educating a child or when we do the best that we can, through advice and support, to foster moral self-determination in a friend.

(4) Empathy: the possibility of other-directed moral attitudes is guaranteed by empathy, i.e., conscious acts in which we directly experience the concrete subjectivity of others on the basis of our experience of their living bodies. Genuine empathy only occurs when others are physically present (see Staiti 2010) and it does not amount to a mere registering that another subject is there. Empathy opens our eyes and our heart (Husserl 2004, p. 228) for the other's feelings, valuings, willings, etc. Through empathy we can endeavor to put ourselves into someone else's shoes and feel, value, will 'through' them, as it were. In so doing we do not become lost in the other's subjectivity. Rather, we maintain our alterity, while our experience receives a distinctive kind of *modification*. As the next sections will show, the empathetic modification is crucial to understand tolerance correctly.

In order to articulate the OCV with Husserl we need to start with his doctrine of modalizations. In *Ideas I* Husserl points out that the basic mode of our perceptual experience and the judgments built upon it is 'certainty of being' (Husserl 2014, p. 207). When we perceive or judge, we usually *posit* an object or state of affairs as being and being such and such. Positing acts such as simple perceptions and judgments are confirmed when they receive intuitive fulfillment: I posit a bottle of water in the fridge and when I open it I see intuitively that the bottle is actually there. I posit the cat as being on the mat in a simple judgment and I see it intuitively fulfilled in all its components when I turn my head and see the cat lying there. Acts of positing that are carried out on the basis of intuitive fulfillment receive the legitimacy of being 'true' or 'authentic' [*wahrhaft*] and the corresponding objects and states of affairs are experienced as 'existing' or 'obtaining' [*bestehend*].

This, however, is not *always* the case. The being of an object or state of affairs can become doubtful, probable, and finally be canceled out as merely illusory. Husserl's remarkable point here is that being and non-being are not the only two qualifications that apply to objects. There is a whole spectrum of intermediate *modalities* in between: some of them are captured by phrases like 'probable', 'doubtful', 'unlikely', etc. (Husserl 2014, p. 206). The initial mark of certainty that accompanies positing acts can become *modalized*. When that happens, it is not just that on the subjective side of things something goes awry, while the object remains unaffected; rather, the object itself appears in a different light. It is *the object itself* that appears doubtful when I doubt and being-doubtful is a modality of the object standing between being and non-being, which implies the retrospective cancelation of a foregoing act of belief. In the sphere of belief, or, as Husserl calls it, in the *doxic* sphere there is always an intrinsic tendency to restore simple, unmodified certainty. We cannot live with doubt and mere appearance: whenever an object or state of affairs becomes doubtful, we experience a subjective striving to come to a conclusion that either restores the foregoing certainty or replaces it with a new one.

In addition to these doxic modalities, Husserl famously talks about a completely different form of modification, which he calls the *neutrality modification* (Husserl 2014, p. 213). Unlike doxic modalities that fall somewhere on the spectrum between being and non-being, the neutrality modification is a peculiar operation that discontinues all positing and non-positing. When we neutralize a given positing act, the object or state of affairs intended in it is still present, but we are completely disengaged with regard to its being or non-being. We become thoroughly non-committal about it and transform the foregoing positing act in a kind of semblance that is thoroughly immune to confirmation or disconfirmation. Husserl's examples include the neutralized perception that is involved in the contemplation of an image and the transition from an act of recollection to an act of imagination (Husserl 2014, p. 216). There is nothing structurally different between an act of recollection and an act of imagination involving the same objects, except for the fact that in pure imagination we are not bound by any kind of constraint regarding what actually happened. At any time, the neutrality modification can be lifted and the positionality of the act can be restored: what started as a recollection of a certain event can undergo a neutrality modification and turn into an unbridled fantasy, until I decide to restore the positionality of the initial act and reintroduce the binding distinction between what actually happened and didn't happen.

These descriptions are developed most extensively with regard to simple perceptual acts in the doxic sphere and then extended to the sphere of judgment. In section 116 of *Ideen I*, however, Husserl points out that the practical sphere of valuing and willing, too, includes positing acts, namely, acts that posit, respectively, values and goals (Husserl 2014, p. 229). Accordingly, we need to recognize and describe the characteristic modalities and modalizations that pertain to the practical sphere as modalized valuings and willings (Husserl 2014, p. 230). Husserl argues for a thoroughgoing parallelism between the theoretical and the practical sphere: one-rayed or monothetical perceptions in the theoretical sphere correspond to one-rayed valuings, or value-ceptions (*Wertnehmungen*) in the practical sphere, and multi-rayed or polythetical judgments in the theoretical sphere correspond to multi-rayed or polythetical willings in the practical sphere.

It's important to notice that the modalities of the practical sphere are *not* just the modalities of the theoretical sphere applied to practical objects. The unmodified consciousness 'certainty of being' is the basic mode of perceptual and judgmental experience in the doxic sphere. At the other end of the modal spectrum we find 'negation of being', i.e., a positing of non-being, and a variety of modalities in between. In the practical sphere we have a simple positing of value and *two* fixed-points in which its potential modalization can terminate, rather than just one. Something can be initially given as valuable, but then discordant motives can arise and put pressure on our commitment to the thing's value. The thing's value now appears as doubtful in a distinctively practical sense of 'doubt' for which we probably lack a name. That process of modalization can end in *three ways*, rather than two: the certainty of value can be restored, the thing can turn out to be an *adiaphoron*, or it can turn out to be a *disvalue*. By contrast, there are no such things as *adiaphora* in the doxic sphere.

In addition, there is also a distinctive form of *neutralized valuing*, which, as we will see in a moment, is key to understanding tolerance. Neutralized valuing is, by analogy with neutralized doxic belief, a form of non-committal value-consciousness (Husserl 2014, p. 231). The act of valuing is still present, but if I neutralize it, I disengage at once my commitment to things having such and such values, disvalues or *adiaphora*-like characteristics. Like doxic consciousness, the modalization of value-consciousness brings with it a form of striving toward stabilization. If the value of academic prestige starts becoming doubtful, I will strive to either turn this modalized value-consciousness into restoration of value, or to posit legitimately one of its two opposites: *adiaphoron* or disvalue. As a positing consciousness, value-consciousness, too, receives its legitimacy from *intuitive* experience, such as the revealing or epiphanic moments when academic prestige appears in its intrinsic vanity or even as a disvalue *vis-à-vis* the humble and honest pursuit of truth. None of this happens in neutralized valuings. The commitment to things having such and such values is suspended.

A full analysis of modalizations in the practical sphere far exceeds the scope of this chapter. Suffice to say that Husserl provides a detailed account of modalizations in the sphere of *willing*, as the *analogon* of judging, in his 1914 lectures on ethics (Husserl 1988, pp. 126–136), while his remarks on the modalizations of *valuing*, as the *analogon* of perceiving, remain rather sparse. As we anticipated above, for Husserl willing is entirely built upon valuing, since the positing of something as a goal presupposes its positing as valuable. Willing is more complex than valuing because it involves, for instance, the selection of the means to a certain end, which implies a variety of possible configurations, and the experience of conditional valuing of the means themselves as conducive to the desired end. For our present purposes it is important to keep in mind that practical consciousness, too, has its own modalities and its own version of the neutrality modification.

5 Willing and Valuing in the context of Empathy

As we anticipated in section four, empathy is the direct experience of another subject. The other subject is experienced as being like me, i.e., an embodied person who is in principle capable of all the subjective experiences that I myself am capable of. This is not the place to expand on the basics of Husserl's theory of empathy, which is widely known. Two aspects are nonetheless worth highlighting. First, empathy is not *just* the registering of the fact that there is another subject out there, who is like me, but not me. This is a first, fundamental dimension of empathy that enables us to distinguish intuitively between inanimate things and embodied subjects. This first fundamental dimension of empathy, however, inaugurates a second dimension, that is, the possibility to penetrate and share in the inner life of others, without thereby losing ourselves or 'fusing' ourselves with them[2]. This is the reason why Husserl talks about intuitive empathy as the experience that "opens up our mind's eye and our heart for the inner life of others" (Husserl 2004, p. 228). Penetrating the inner life of others through empathy, however, is unlike encountering perceptually a physical thing in space or

---

[2] An excellent analysis of the first dimension of empathy is offered in Costa 2006. I am much indebted to a helpful paper by Matias Graffigna (unpublished) presented at a conference in Graz on October, 4th 2019 for the clear distinction of these two dimensions of empathy. I had proposed a similar distinction in Staiti 2014, pp. 191–194.

focusing on our own mental states in reflection. It is also unlike simulating what others are thinking or feeling and then projecting our inner simulation onto them, as some contemporary theorists of mind would have it[3]. In order to grasp what is distinctive of the empathetic participation in the inner life of others, we need to consider the fact that empathy itself can be described as a kind of *modification of experience*, as it befits the general class of experiences to which it belongs: presentifications [*Vergegenwärtigungen*]. Husserl interprets empathy "as a modification of memory" (Husserl 1973, p. 185). This means that memories are, in a certain sense, the blueprint to understand empathy, since both experiences share the same structure (Husserl 1973, p. 260).

If we take our departure from our present experience, carrying out an act of memory amounts to an *extension* of the scope of our experience that stretches back into our past. In memory we don't just re-live a past episode, rather we re-live reproductively *ourselves* as the ones who lived that episode. In this process, our *ego* undergoes a distinctive kind of splitting (Husserl 2019, pp. 290 – 293): our present ego who carries out the act of recollection is distinct from our past ego who had the experience we are now recollecting. Our present *ego* experiences the past *ego* as identical with itself, but it also experiences a distinctive kind of distance, which creates the possibility to not share in the past ego's beliefs, value-positings, decisions, etc. Empathy works in much the same way, but the ego that appears in it is not identified with myself (Husserl 2019, p. 336). When I see another person perceive a tree and I carry out an empathetic act that is intuitively directed toward the other person and her perception, my experience is *expanded* in a peculiar way. What happens is a kind of empathetically modified act of perceiving: I am directed toward the tree through the other's act of perception, as it were. This situation is different from when I am perceiving the tree, you are perceiving the tree, and we both know that the other is perceiving the tree. In this case, there is no empathetic modification going on. I have an intuitive and actual intentional act directed toward the tree and my awareness of you perceiving the tree is just an inactual experience occurring in the background of my consciousness. If my act of empathy is intuitive and it penetrates your actual inner life, then *your* perception of the tree is part of the horizon of *my* experience as perception. Perceiving through another ego is still a form of perceiving, albeit one that has undergone the peculiar form of empathetic modification. Unlike memorative modification, empathetic modification does not include a splitting of the ego, because the egos involved are, from the very beginning,

---

[3] To my knowledge, the most thorough and convincing critique of simulation theories of empathy from a phenomenological viewpoint is offered in Costa 2010.

two; however, empathetic modification, too, creates a kind of distance that enables the ego not to automatically go along with or co-effectuate [*mitvollziehen*] the other's experience.

As an extension of the horizon of one's own experience, empathy *qua* modification can encompass all sorts of experiences, including valuings and willings: "All intentional contents which I could, perhaps, make explicit with respect to myself, could present themselves to me in the same manner in this modification of the *alter*, hence characterized as intentional contents in acts of the other" (Husserl 2019, p. 337). In this regard, Husserl talks about a "feeling-through [*nachfühlen*] and a valuing-through [*nachwerten*] that occurs in empathy" (Husserl 2004, p. 194). Such feeling and valuing is not first-hand: "our feeling and willing is not involved as actual, since we have only empathetic modifications of feelings and willings" (Husserl 2004, p. 191). Nonetheless, in feeling, valuing, and willing *through* the other I have a mediated access to the other's values, goals, and desires *as if they were my own*. I am not merely judging extrinsically and indirectly what the other values and wills, rather, if the act of empathy is intuitive and if I actively live in it, I can carry out acts of position-taking toward the other's values, goals, and desires *through* the lens of empathy. All the modalizations of valuing and willing discussed in the foregoing section can thus happen in the context of empathy, too. I can be intentionally directed toward a value through the other's act of valuing, and in my empathetically modified act of valuing I can either go along with the other's valuing, or withhold my positing, as the value becomes doubtful to me. My valuing still happens through the other's experience, i.e., it is empathetically modified, but I no longer partake of the other's axiological position-taking. Moreover, an act of "valuing through the other" can be neutralized: if I do so, I continue to be intentionally directed toward the value through the other's valuing, but I neutralize my position-taking and I henceforth comport myself neutrally toward the value that the other is positing.

6 Tolerance as Neutralized Practical Consciousness

We now have all the methodological and conceptual resources to outline an OCV of tolerance from a Husserlian standpoint. First of all, tolerance is, as we pointed out, a moral attitude, i.e., one in which we are intentionally directed toward the other's ego and her experiences and we are driven by the ideal of self-determination. The moral nature of tolerance distinguishes it from cognate attitudes that are merely axiological, i.e., attitudes that are exclusively interested in evaluating and ranking objects and actions considered in their own right. When we tolerate, however, we are turned empathetically toward the other in such a way as to stretch into her own lived experience. We co-live her own feelings, valuings and willings through the lens of intuitive empathy. To co-live another subject's experiences includes partaking of the motivations and associative processes that underlie her own position-takings *as if* they were my own. I am not merely judging from an external standpoint her supposed cognitive and emotional situation, as Lohmar would have it. Rather, I co-live that emotional and cognitive situation and I am aware of the fact that it could be my own situation.

However, the intuitive co-living of the other's motivations underlying her valuings and willings does not exhaust the horizon of experience that can occur in the context of empathy. As we anticipated above, valuings and willings are forms of positional consciousness and as such they can be evaluated normatively, i.e., in terms of their legitimacy. Legitimacy in the context of positing consciousness rests on intuitive fulfillment. A value that is posited on the basis of an intuitively fulfilled value-consciousness is valued legitimately, i.e., rationally. The same goes for willings. Through empathy I can co-effectuate the positing of value in the other's valuings, but I can also withhold that positing. For instance, I can realize that the values that she posits and the actions based upon them are not radically justified by intuitive fulfillment and even that the other is plainly *wrong* (in the axiological connotation of being wrong) about her valuings and willings. When conflicts arise in positional consciousness a decision is called for. Either my assessment of the other's valuing is mistaken, and further experience would reveal the lack of intuitive fulfillment in my own act of empathetic valuing-through, or it isn't, and then her valuing is mistaken and lacks intuitive fulfillment. This is the crucial juncture for the possibility of tolerance. If I remain in a positional attitude, where fulfillment and emptiness of the valuing consciousness are at stake, a clash is inevitable. Since willings and actions are based on valuing, if my empathetically modified valuing consciousness conflicts with the other's valuings, the idea that for some reason I would nonetheless abstain from acting out my objection is impossible to make sense of, hence the allegedly paradoxical nature of tolerance. But this is precisely the point where phenomenology offers a clear solution and a way out of the paradox: what happens is not that I refrain from acting; rather, I carry out a *neutralization* of my hitherto positional act of empathetic valuing-through, thereby removing in the most radical and effective way the conditions for conflict. There is no 'acceptance component' that follows and is conjoined with an 'objection component'. Rather, *the tolerantial conjuncture occurs when I neutralize a valuing-consciousness in the context of empathy and I do that for the sake of the other.* The intentionality of tolerance is monothetic: it is directed, through empathy, towards the value that the other intends and posits. There are no two components, but only one. When I tolerate, instead of getting involved in a conflict about the authentic fulfillment of the other's value-consciousness, which I evidently see lacking, I neutralize my co-valuing in order to prevent the conflict from flaring up. The fact that I don't intervene or do not want to see the other sanctioned are mere consequences of the neutralized value-consciousness that informs my behavior. If that weren't the case, then not acting out the 'negative component' of my attitude, as the TCV interprets the situation, would be simply irrational and it would cast doubt on the genuineness of my 'objection', i.e., in phenomenological terms, the refusal to co-effectuate the act of positing inherent in the other's value consciousness. The question that remains to be clarified is: why would I do so?

In order to answer, and conclude our analysis, let us consider a couple of examples of tolerance.

(1) The people I grew up with in my neighborhood start embracing ideologies that I *know* are fundamentally dangerous and ill-fated. I understand their motivations: unemployment, lack of political representation, etc. However, in my concrete exchanges with them I do not confront them directly about their political ideas and continue to interact with them peacefully for their own sake.

(2) During a global pandemic I find out that Catholics in my neighborhood are celebrating mass together despite lockdown rules. I understand that for them this is an important rite. Even though I know that what they are doing is wrong and rightfully sanctionable because it puts lives in danger, I do not reproach them and do not report them to public authorities.

(3) A single mother of three children in dire economic difficulties steals food from the grocery store. I understand her situation, but I also know that she could seek help with local charities and that she is eligible for child welfare services, but I do not denounce her theft, nor do I rebuke her about what she did.

First, all three situations might be externally indistinguishable from sheer indifference, but in order for them to be examples of tolerance I must *care*, i.e., I must be engaging in actual valuing. Second, all three situations must involve people that are concretely present, with whom I can actually and intuitively empathize. The actual valuing I engage in is empathetic valuing-through the other. Third, I must be *certain* that their acts of valuing lack intuitive fulfillment and are therefore illegitimate. If, in the first scenario, I am not sure about politics and my friends might actually be right about their extremist political views, then the reason why I do not confront them is the uncertainty about the intuitive fulfillment of the acts of valuing involved in our respective political positions. If we are uncertain about the values that are intuitively given, then we are just uncertain, rather than tolerant. Fourth, in all three cases I understand the motivations that led these people to value things the way they do and act accordingly, but these motivations are not sufficient to *justify* their valuings and actions. Suppose that, in the second scenario, I was already critical of lockdown measures and held that they illegitimately constrain religious freedom. In this case, the fact that celebrating mass is important to Catholics is already a *good reason* for me, and my attitude toward Catholics, even if I don't share their beliefs, is not one of tolerance. It is one of straightforward endorsement. The same goes for the third scenario. Suppose that I believe, as Husserl does (Husserl 1988, pp. 421–422), that a mother has absolute obligations toward her children that trump all other obligations and value-rankings. In this case, my attitude toward her is not one of tolerance, but perhaps even of admiration for doing something that is socially stigmatized in order to obey her absolute duties toward her children.

In order for the three situations to exemplify tolerance, I must be actively involved with the other: I must care and I must have an intuitive empathetic experience of her and her valuings. Moreover, I must be certain that her valuings and ensuing willings do not pass the test of intuitive fulfillment and are therefore illegitimate. Finally, I must understand her motivations but not find them sufficient to *justify* her valuings and willings. Despite all this, I must ultimately come to neutralize my co-effectuated valuings and willings in order to remove the conditions that would create a conflict. On this account, tolerance can only be a consistent and acceptable attitude if what drives my neutralization is genuine *care for the other's moral development through self-determination*, which is a necessary component of moral attitudes, as we pointed out in section four.

Why would I neutralize my empathetic valuing-through, which conflicts with the other's valuing, if I am absolutely certain that the other's positing of a value is illegitimate? If I am in a moral attitude, my overarching interest is in the other's self-determination and the enduring attributes that will define her personal character. I am motivated to neutralize my *legitimate* valuing-through in order to prevent a conflict with the other's *illegitimate* valuing, if I believe that such conflict, albeit justified, would be detrimental to her moral development. I realize that a rebuke, a critique, or a sanction, would only make the other defensive, harden her heart, and interrupt our relationship, thereby making it impossible for her to come to realize *by herself* the illusory and hence mistaken character of her value-positings. My ideological friends would likely stop being my friends and dig in their heels on their political views if I rebuked them, my Catholic neighbors would start considering themselves martyrs of sorts if I reported their illegal gathering, and the woman in the grocery store would feel even more estranged from and neglected by her community if I called the police about her shoplifting. If I *care* about the moral development of the people involved in the three scenarios presented above, I prefer to neutralize my legitimate act of valuing and let the others continue to value what they are valuing, even if I know it's wrong, because I hope that with time and interaction with different-minded persons they will come to modalize their valuing consciousness and eventually posit a disvalue where they now illusorily see a value. The potential paternalism in this attitude is dispelled because through empathy I co-live their motivations and I am aware of the fact that they could as well be my own. I do not regard them as 'inferior', but simply as people who are *de facto* wrong about their valuings, even if I can make sense of why they came to value things the way they do and believe that they have all the necessary resources to eventually realize that their positing of value is illegitimate.

This view of tolerance has the resources to answer the pressing question about when we should tolerate. If the motivation to neutralize our empathetic valuing-though is the good of the other, tolerance is unwarranted when the avoidance of a conflict on value is actually *detrimental* for her moral development. Sometimes a clear and honest statement (rebuke, sanction, etc.) is the best way for the other to realize the illegitimacy of her value-consciousness. In some other cases, we may want to lift our initial neutralization and let the conflict occur because we realize that the other would not by herself be able to find her way out of the illusory valuing in which she is engaged. Finally, we could realize that the other's valuings are so fundamentally wrong and dangerous that leaving her time to come to realize her mistake by herself and thereby grow as a moral person is simply not an option.

This finally brings us back to Goethe's quote from the opening paragraph, which is partly acceptable and partly unjustified. Goethe is right that tolerance must be a temporary attitude only: if it is grounded on the neutralization of empathetic valuing-through, such neutralization only remains in place until the other realizes her mistake in valuing, and then harmony is restored, or until it becomes clear that the neutralization should be lifted for the reasons just mentioned, and then a salutary conflict will flare up. Goethe, however, is wrong when he says that to tolerate is to insult. What he seems to have in mind is that if I know you are wrong and do not tell you, I don't consider you a rational peer and therefore believe that you are incapable to realize your own mistakes, which is insulting. This, however, is not the only possible scenario. There is nothing insulting about letting the other take the time she needs to realize her mistakes by herself and refusing to foist onto her convictions that, right as they may be, do not harmoniously fit her personal path of moral maturation. Our growth as moral persons is always a work in progress and there is nothing insulting about letting others come to grasp the illegitimacy of their valuings by themselves, no matter how long and hard we need to bite our tongue in the process, as they will likely have to bite theirs with us on some other occasion.

Conclusion

In this chapter I have sketched an OCV about tolerance, after criticizing the TCV that is found in virtually all existing literature on tolerance. I have argued that tolerance is an attitude intentionally directed toward a value *as* intended and posited by another subject. The conditions for tolerance obtain when we come to evidently realize that the other's positing of value is illegitimate, i.e., that the value-consciousness directed toward the value at stake does not receive genuine fulfillment, even though the other illusorily and hence mistakenly thinks it does. In tolerance, however, we neutralize our empathetic act of valuing-through and thereby remove the conditions for a conflict about our respective value-positings. We do so because we care about the other more than we care about being axiologically right. For this reason, we prefer to let the other realize by herself, i.e., following her own experience and respecting her personal journey, the wrongness in her valuing. This attitude is justified when, in fact, a direct conflict and the imposition of our (correct) valuing would be detrimental to the other's moral maturation; however, following Goethe, the neutrality modification should be revoked in due time, in order to return to a positional value-consciousness that either harmonizes or salutarily conflicts with the other's value-consciousness.

Let me conclude with one last remark. My analysis entails the potentially counterintuitive conclusion that disputes about intrinsically controversial and undecidable theological matters do not create the conditions for tolerance. Recall that, on my account, in order to tolerate I must be absolutely certain that the other's positing of value is illegitimate. This might sound counterintuitive because historically the reflection on tolerance has focused primarily on religious disagreement; however, if we come to realize that religious values ('what pleases God', 'what is conducive to salvation', etc.) are by necessity only partially fulfilled on earth ('*videmus nunc per speculum in aenigmate*', as Saint Paul puts it in the first letter to the Corinthians), then the attitude that is called for in the case of religious conflicts is not tolerance, but rather the healthy realization that none of our positings of religious values is truly as thoroughly fulfilled as to constitute fully intuitive consciousness. Therefore, nobody can be plainly wrong about 'what pleases God' and 'what is conducive to salvation' in the same way in which one can be plainly wrong about theft or violent political ideologies.

However, even extremely religious people who feel that their experiences of religious values are so richly fulfilled as to count as near certain, such that others may, in their eyes, be *wrong* about what pleases God or will save their soul, might resort to tolerance in order to let the others grow in their religious experience by themselves, rather than scaring them away from religion with conflictual interventions. Genuine care for the other as a moral and spiritual person may thus lead even the staunchest religious believer to implement a neutrality modification that may only be finally lifted in Heaven.

Acknowledgments

I would like to thank Dieter Lohmar and all the participants in the Phenomenology Workshop at the University of Cologne on May, 29th 2020 for their helpful feedback on an earlier version of this chapter.

References

Costa, Vincenzo (2006): "L'esperienza dell'altro: per una fenomenologia della separazione". In: Ferrarin, Alfredo (Ed.): *Passive Synthesis and Life-world – Sintesi passiva e mondo della vita*. Pisa: Edizioni ETS, pp. 109–125.
Costa, Vincenzo (2010): *Fenomenologia dell'intersoggettività: empatia, socialità, cultura*. Roma: Carocci.
Embree, Lester (2007): "Tolerance Reflectively Analyzed". In: *Environment, Technology, Justification*. Bucharest: Zeta Books, pp. 163–173.
Forst, Rainer (2013): *Toleration in Conflict: Past and Present*. Cambridge: Cambridge University Press.
Goethe, Johann Wolfgang von (2017): *Maxims and Reflections*. Los Angeles: Enhanced Publishing.
Graffigna, Matias (unpublished): "Phenomenology of Empathy. A Fundamental Distinction". Paper presented at the conference *Phenomenological Perspectives on Empathy and the Significance of Empirical Research. Women in Phenomenology: Edith Stein*. University of Graz, 4–5 October 2019.
Heyd, David (1996): "Introduction". In: Heyd, David (Ed.): *Toleration: An elusive virtue*. Princeton: Princeton University Press, pp. 3–17.
Husserl, Edmund (1973): *Zur Phänomenologie der Intersubjektivität. Texte aus dem Nachlass, Zweiter Teil: 1921–1928*. Iso Kern (Ed.) Husserliana XIV. The Hague: Martinus Nijhoff.
Husserl, Edmund (1988): *Vorlesungen über Ethik und Wertlehre 1908–1914*. Ullrich Melle (Ed.). Husserliana XXVIII. Dordrecht: Kluwer.
Husserl, Edmund (2004): *Einleitung in die Ethik. Vorlesungen Sommersemester 1920 und 1924*. Henning Peucker (Ed.). Husserliana XXXVII. Dordrecht: Kluwer.
Husserl, Edmund (2014): *Ideas I*. Indianapolis: Hackett.

Husserl, Edmund (2019): *First Philosophy: Lectures 1923/24 and Related Texts from the Manuscripts (1920–1925)*. Dordrecht: Springer.
King, Preston (1976): *Toleration*. London, Portland: Frank Cass.
Lohmar, Achim (2010): "Was ist eigentlich Toleranz?" In: *Zeitschrift für philosophische Forschung* 64(1), pp. 8–32.
Marcuse, Herbert (1969): "Repressive Tolerance". In: Wolff, Robert Paul/Moore, Barrington, Jr./Marcuse, Herbert: *A Critique of Pure Tolerance*. Boston: Beacon Press, pp. 95–137.
Skalski, Jonathan E. (2017): "The Historical Evolution of Tolerance, the Experience of Tolerating, and the Face of the Other". *The Humanistic Psychologist* 45(1), pp. 62–70.
Staiti, Andrea (2010): "The Primacy of the Present: Metaphysical Ballast or Phenomenological Finding?" *Research in Phenomenology* 40(1), pp. 34–54.
Staiti, Andrea (2014): *Husserl's Transcendental Phenomenology: Nature, Spirit, and Life*. Cambridge: Cambridge University Press.
United Nations Educational Scientific and Cultural Organization (UNESCO) (1995): Declaration of Principles on Tolerance: Adopted by the General Conference of UNESCO at its twenty-eight session in Paris. http://unesdoc.unesco.org/images/0015/001518/151830eo.pdf, last accessed on 9 March 2021.

Alessandra Fussi
Anger, Hatred, Prejudice. An Aristotelian Perspective

Abstract: Anger and hatred are examined in relation to contempt and prejudice. Aristotle's claim that anger responds to an *apparent* slight is interpreted to mean that a) the slight is apparent but not necessarily real; b) it is conspicuous; c) it is the enactment of the opinion that the offender despises the offended. Two points are made regarding contempt: a) someone may feel despised and loved at the same time, for example in paternalistic relationships, or when treated with benevolence in an environment dominated by prejudice; b) feeling belittled may have heuristic value and help discover injustice. The paper highlights the communicative aspects of anger, the hope embedded in it. In contrast, it addresses the thesis that hatred does not aim at the other *qua* agent, but *qua* representative of a negative property. Hate has a depersonalizing effect on the hater as well. It supposedly lacks communicative intent and is linked with feelings of powerlessness.

Introduction

In an influential book published in 1954 Allport observes that while in Latin the word *praeiudicium* referred essentially to judgments based on previous decisions, beliefs and experiences (or, in legal terms, to preliminary judicial inquiries), in modern times the word prejudice acquired mainly a negative connotation.

If we are prejudiced, we are emotionally resistant to change our minds even when new evidence contradicts our views. Thus, both cognitive and affective aspects are involved. Prejudice entails:

1) "A judgement formed without due examination and consideration of the facts – a premature or hasty judgment" (Allport 1954, p. 6).
2) "A favorable or unfavorable emotional attitude that accompanies such a prior and unsupported judgment" (Allport 1954, p. 6).
3) An inflexible attitude: "a prejudice, unlike a simple misconception, is actively resistant to all evidence that would unseat it. We tend to grow emotional when a prejudice is threatened by contradiction" (Allport 1954, p. 9).

When Allport refers to ancient times he considers only the Latin usage, but the frame of mind he describes (a mixture of hasty judgment and strong emotion) is well described by Aristotle when he addresses the lack of self-control caused by spiritedness (*akrasia tou thumou*). In contrast with someone overcome by hunger, the person who feels unjustified anger is not dominated by blind impulse: she can express what she feels and explain why she thinks she needs to act in a certain way. The problem is that she does not examine the facts carefully enough.[1]

In this chapter, I focus on Aristotle's discussion of anger and clarify his view of the difference between anger and hatred. His analysis, alert as it is to the social and political contexts in which anger and hatred originate, provides a useful basis for reflecting upon the relevance of stereotypes for these emotions. As I show, sometimes agents respond with anger to stereotypes that are not easily recognized as offensive because they are coated in affectionate behavior. In other cases, negative stereotypes contribute to the progressive transformation of anger into hatred.

In section 1, I analyze the metaphors of the servant and the dog, introduced by Aristotle to clarify the lack of self-control caused by spiritedness. In the example, the servant and the dog respond hastily and unreflectively to their environment, but, as I argue, their respective behavior expresses different cognitive and affective attitudes. The servant may remind us of someone who reacts with unjustified anger because he misunderstands the actions and words of others, while the dog can be more easily associated with someone who expresses animosity towards people he does not know because he is moved by prejudice.

---

[1] Rather than calling certain cases of anger and hatred unjustified, it would be arguably better to call them unfitting, as in D'Arms and Jacobson (2000): an emotion is unfitting when it does not correspond in shape or size to the evaluative property it purports to address. Being angry when there is no offense is unfitting: one does not grasp rightly the evaluative property to which the emotion is directed (i.e., what is offensive). Being very angry with respect to an irrelevant slight may be unfitting in the sense of disproportionate (the emotion is fitting in shape but not in size). Being angry at something offensive could be fitting but also imprudent or immoral, and these two characteristics, according to D'Arms and Jacobson, are independent of the emotion's fittingness. Aristotle does not formally distinguish between a fitting emotion, a justified emotion and a morally (or a prudentially) acceptable emotion, though he sometimes addresses emotions roughly along those lines. Furthermore, he links emotions not to perceptions, but rather to judgments. He views the incontinence caused by spiritedness as a form of irrationality, an incorrect cognitive and affective reaction. Fittingness is a problematic concept, since relevant properties are often linked to historical and cultural factors. Sometimes anger may be judged unfitting because the agent reacts to forms of disregard that are not yet commonly recognized as based on prejudice; or it may be judged fitting because the agent belongs to a privileged group.

In section 2 I focus on Aristotle's account of the cause of anger, i.e., feeling slighted. In particular, I concentrate on the claim that the slight to which anger responds is apparent (*phainomene oligoria*), and I propose three senses in which *phainomene* must be understood: in the first sense the slight is apparent but might not be real; in the second sense it is conspicuous, i.e., intersubjectively evident; in the third sense it is the enactment of an opinion, i.e., it brings to light and makes manifest to the person who feels slighted (or to both members of the relationship) what the offender really thinks of her. In section 3 I discuss the three forms of slight (contempt, spite and insult). My focus is on two questions: a) whether contempt is necessarily linked with hostility (my answer is no: certain forms of contempt based on prejudice are linked with warm feelings); b) whether one should distinguish being belittled from being unjustly treated (my answer is yes; however, I claim that sometimes behavior that seems to convey mere indifference or disregard may, on further reflection, be interpreted as unjust). In section 4, I highlight the communicative aspects of anger and the hope that underlies it. I focus on the desire that one's retaliation be conspicuous, and on the sense of power that makes anger a pleasurable experience. In section 5, I address Aristotle's thesis that hatred, differently from anger, does not aim at the other *qua* agent, but *qua* representative of a negative property. In this section, I discuss the depersonalizing nature of hatred and its link with a feeling of powerlessness.

1 Different ways to jump to the wrong conclusions: the servant and the dog

In the *Nicomachean Ethics* Aristotle claims that the incontinence caused by spirit derives from failed communication with reason. He offers two examples:

> Let us now consider the fact that incontinence in respect of spirit (*akrasia he tou thumou*) is less shameful than that in respect of appetites (*he ton epithumion*). For spirit seems to listen to reason to some extent, but to hear it incorrectly; it is like hasty servants who rush off before they have heard everything that is being asked of them and then fail to do it, and dogs that bark at a mere noise, before looking to see whether it is a friend. In the same way, spirit, because of its heated and hasty nature, does hear, but does not hear the command, and so rushes into taking revenge. For reason or mental imagery has shown that we have been wantonly insulted or slighted, and spirit, as though it had deduced that one should treat such a person as an enemy, loses its temper. (Arist., *NE*, 1149a)

I suggest that the examples offered in this passage illuminate two different attitudes: the servant who does not listen carefully enough may remind us of someone who flares up in anger before taking the time to check if what was done to him deserves immediate revenge[2]. The dog who barks at any unfamiliar noise resembles someone who identifies all members of a given outgroup as potential enemies. While the first example concerns hostility directed at specific actions and words, the second seems to identify an undiscriminating attitude, i.e., one that addresses the global self. As we will see, according to Aristotle this is typical of hatred.[3] One could say that unjustified anger and unjustified hatred are unified by the failure to pay attention to the whole context in a given situation. However, the failure is caused by different reasons. Unlike anger, unjustified hatred is not merely the misunderstanding of someone else's words or deeds, but a systematic mistake, caused by the wrong application of generalities to particulars.

The image of the dog is reminiscent of a passage in Plato's *Republic* (375b-c), in which the objection is raised that the warriors put in charge of the city's defense may be harsh to enemies but also dangerously aggressive towards one another and to fellow citizens. Is it possible to embody harshness and gentleness at the same time and in the proper way? The apparent solution is that the warriors should be similar to those pure-bred dogs who are "as gentle as possible to those they know and recognize, and the exact opposite to those they don't know" (*Rep.*, 375e; cf. 375c). Socrates calls the dog "philosophic," explaining that "when it sees someone it doesn't know a dog turns nasty, even though it hasn't been badly treated by him in the past. When it sees someone familiar, it welcomes him, even if it has never been at all well treated by him" (*Rep.*, 376a). This claim is puzzling: is someone a "true lover of wisdom" (376a) when she desires to discover what she does not know, or when she sticks to what she already knows and abhors the unknown? A careful reader of Plato's dialogues would call philosophic the first attitude, but Socrates chooses to call philosophic the latter.[4] At this stage in the *Republic* loyalty to what is known and fa-

---

[2] The text is not clear and interpretations abound. Is reason giving an order that *thumos* misunderstands, or is reason just stating a fact, which *thumos* mistakenly takes for an order? For a thorough discussion of this passage and of the interpretations and translations available, see Centrone (2020, pp. 26–38).
[3] Although both examples describe occurring emotions and Aristotle's overall analysis suggests that he has in mind anger, the dog loses its temper because of a deep-seated animosity towards strangers. Given that in the *Rhetoric* Aristotle's description of hatred seems to be of a disposition rather than of an emotion, one might conclude that hatred can be expressed through various negative emotions, such as anger, contempt, disgust, etc.
[4] Socrates's words in this passage are considered ironic by some scholars, while they have been taken literally by others. Those who view the analogy between the warriors and the noble dogs as ironic think that the warrior class is from the very beginning introduced with a view to its

miliar takes priority over impartiality. The paradigmatic principle (up to the revolution brought about in book V, when it becomes clear that not the warriors, but those who are genuinely curious about the unknown should rule the city) is allegiance to one's own.

While Plato allows his readers to wonder if the analogy between the noble dogs and the philosophers is ironic, Aristotle avoids all ambiguity and openly portrays the dog's barking at strangers as a model of unwarranted, preconceived hostility.

Such behavior of course has its merits, but it takes for granted that what is true sometimes —some strangers are enemies – must be true all the time. Some of the strangers approaching will have good intentions and deserve a friendly reception. However, dogs habituated to bark at all strangers will not consider this possibility. Nor will they question the categories under which they subsume particulars (why are certain people considered enemies? What is due to one's enemies and why?).[5] In sum, if we consider Aristotle's example as echoing Socrates's paradigmatic dogs in Book II of the *Republic*, we can conclude that for this particular kind of hostility the distinction between friends and enemies carries more weight than that between praiseworthy and blameworthy behavior.[6] What counts is not what someone did, but the out-group to which he belongs (notice that the well-bred dog barks even though it never received any injury from those outside the family). But because the category of friends and enemies defines who is to be hated and who is to be loved (and a group may be treated with hostility just because it happens to occupy a portion of neighboring territo-

---

shortcomings. On the problematic nature of the analogy, cf. Bloom (1968, p. 350); Benardete (1989, p. 57); Howland (1993, p. 95); Rosen (2005; pp. 83–86).

5 I am thinking here of two points Socrates makes with Polemarchus in the first book of Plato's *Republic:* 1. People sometimes mistakenly believe that their friends are good and their enemies bad, while the opposite may be the case (*Rep.*, 334bc). 2. "It is not just to treat anyone badly under any circumstances" (*Rep.*, 335e). These two points project a problematic light on the class of the warriors.

6 In the *Republic* (III, 414d-415c), Socrates introduces a "noble lie": the warriors, who were educated according to the models established by the founders of the city, have to believe that in fact they were born from the earth. This establishes an artificial distinction between those who live within the city and have to be treated as brothers and friends, and those who live outside and are to be considered potential enemies. What in present-day sociological jargon would be identified as the polarity between in-group and out-group is presented by Socrates as a political lie concerning the distinction between friends and enemies. On the Platonic distinction between friends and enemies as an ideological weapon, cf. Strauss (1964, p. 102); Fussi (2014, p. 159 ff.).

ry), the qualities that are considered hateful are suspiciously indefinite and shifting.[7]

Plato's and Aristotle's intuition corresponds to a point made by Kolnai, when he claims that there is no precise intentional object responding to the quality of "hateful":

> We fear a force that is capable of endangering the subject; one feels disgust in front of an object that has a 'disgusting' characteristic, a characteristic that has a defined content and is given in general types. Hatred, by contrast, does not address a quality of 'hateful', which does not exist. Kolnai (2007, p. 108; the translation from German is mine)[8]

The image of the dog exemplifies *akratic*, i.e., irrational behavior. This should not lead us to assume that for Aristotle all forms of enmity are necessarily unreasonable. If *misein* (hating) is the opposite of *philein* (feeling friendly) and if the best form of friendship has virtue as its intentional object, then, as Konstan (2006, p. 190) suggests, we can suppose that vice, the opposite of virtue, will be the proper object of hatred. However, this solution is problematic. From an Aristotelian standpoint, a virtuous person will hate vice, but she will also try to distinguish between people who happen to make mistakes and people who are utterly vicious. A person who commits a cowardly act is not necessarily a coward; even if he is a coward, he may still have some saving qualities. She will take into account the person's good qualities as well as his bad qualities before giving in to hostility. Furthermore, for Aristotle true friendship is a virtue, while hatred is not. It would be beyond the scope of this study to expand upon why this is the case. Suffice it to say that while friendship keeps cities together, hatred separates and destroys both cities and individuals.

There is also a conceptual problem in Konstan's suggestion, because it presupposes that love and hatred may be symmetric affective attitudes in all respects. This, however, is not the case. While we may love or hate people on the basis of their general characteristics (their virtues or vices), love and hate invite very different attitudes towards the qualities of others. When we love a person, we are interested in coming to know the minutest details of his life, we want to live close to him and we are interested in the reasons behind his actions and choices (as it is clear from Aristotle's description of true friendship in the *Nico*-

---

[7] Why do we hate certain groups? Do we hate them because they steal our jobs? Because they are atheists? Because they are religious fanatics? There does not seem to be any property to which our hatred can be predictably addressed.
[8] Szanto (2020) makes a similar point concerning the uninformative and "blurry" focus of intergroup hatred.

machean Ethics). When we hate someone, we cannot stand being near him. Our attention is fixed on the vice, which we tend to see instantiated in all he does. In hatred towards groups, the risk is overgeneralizing: we apply the same characteristic to all individuals ("they are all greedy"), and become unresponsive to diachronic changes and synchronic nuances. The hated group is identified with an immutable quality. The emotion is a globalizing response: it takes whole persons (or whole groups) as its objects.

The asymmetry between love and hatred is significant not just with respect to the desire to know the particulars of the other's life, but also with respect to the goals one may have. As Kolnai points out, the goal of hatred is relatively simple and univocal: we desire that the other may cease to exist. The goals of love, vice-versa, are as many as the ways in which we may wish to help someone realize his full potential.[9]

Anger is more similar to love than to hatred in this respect: we pay a lot of attention to the concrete other when we get angry. What agitates us is that he personally did or said things for which we blame him. And sometimes we get angry precisely because we care for someone. In the case of hatred, the other's actions and words are not nearly as important. The person we hate is, as it were, frozen in time. We identify him with a character trait that appears to us repulsive and irredeemably flawed. Hatred appears *inflexible*.

Let us develop this hypothesis by turning first to Aristotle's definition of anger and then to his comparison between anger and hatred in the *Rhetoric*.

2 The intersubjective nature of anger: feeling slighted

> Let anger be [defined as] desire, accompanied by [mental and physical] distress, for apparent retaliation (*timorias phainomenes*) because of an apparent slight (*dia phainomenen oligorian*) that was directed, without justification (*me prosekontos*), against oneself or those near to one. (Arist., *Rhet.* II, 1378a30 – 32)

Although anger may provide some pleasure if one can imagine a revenge (or a way to obtain redress), being angry is mainly painful. The distress is caused by the belief that someone committed *oligoria* directly against the agent, or against people and possessions with whom she identifies. Kennedy translates *oligoria* as "slight." The word derives from *oligon* (little, small), and we can literally envision an *oligoria* as a form of public belittling. In the quotation above,

---

9 Cf. Kolnai (2007, p. 116, ff.) and Kolnai (1998, p. 594).

phainomenen oligorian refers to an *apparent* slight. The role played by appearance in the experience of feeling slighted can be spelled out in three ways.

First, appearance is opposed to reality. The other's deeds and words appear as a slight to the agent, but the agent might be wrong, and discover later that she interpreted incorrectly the other's behavior – in which case anger evaporates.

Secondarily, the slight is apparent in the sense that it is visible to at least two participants: the offender and the offended.[10] Even if they are alone, they are actors in a public scene, because anger arises in connection with a concern for honor and regard. This makes sense in a social setting in which individuals occupy positions that are relative to each other and can be called into question by the lack of reciprocal recognition. Because honor is determined not only by objective factors (for example, by the power and the capacities one has), but also by fame (by the power and the capacities one is believed to have), a slight is a form of belittlement. The space a person occupies in the web of social relations all of a sudden appears to shrink: it is visibly diminished. Furthermore, Aristotle suggests that one may take offence also when under attack are the activities one finds worthy of being pursued. Someone proud of living a philosophical life may feel offended when others vilify philosophy (Arist., *Rhet.* II, 1379a35). She feels

---

10 Cf. Cope (2009, p. 10): "*phainomenes* and *phainomenen* are both emphatic; not merely 'apparent' and unreal, but 'manifest, conspicuous, evident'. *Phainomene timoria*: a punishment of which the effect can be perceived' [...] and *dia phainomenen oligorian*, 'due to a manifest slight'; a slight which is so manifest that it cannot escape observation; and therefore because it has been noticed by everybody, requires the more exemplary punishment in the way of compensation." See also Rabbås (2015, p. 633): "The person feeling anger does so on the ground that he takes himself to have been dishonored, or not shown proper respect, by the other, and his anger is a response to this: he finds it wrongful, is upset, and wants to seek rectification, i.e. to have his worth properly recognized." Cairns (2015), convincingly argues that *timoria* in legal Athenian contexts is neither "vengeance" (i.e., personal revenge), nor punishment (i.e., a purely legal way to solve disputes). *Timoria* is literally "restitution of *time*" (Cairns 2015, p. 653), and it can be sought not just through vengeance, but also through legal procedures (as when we say that a family seeks justice for its murdered son). Cairns translates the word as "redress." In the *Rhetoric*, the word *timoria* is translated by Kennedy as "retaliation. "Redress" might be preferable, since the restitution of *time* can be sought in different ways. I keep Kennedy's translation because Aristotle's examples mostly refer to personal retaliation (as in the case of Odysseus blinding Polyphemus at *Rhet.* II, 1380b20–27), but my view is close to that of Rabbås and Cairns. I understand Aristotle to claim that the offended feels pleasure when he can obtain revenge not because he finds pleasure in the other's pain, but because pain is related to awareness. Since revenge serves a communicative goal (recovering *time*), it can be replaced by other forms of communication. This would not be likely if the other's pain were sought without a communicative purpose. For the distinction between a sadist and the victim's vengeful desire to inflict pain, see Griswold (2013) and the literature he discusses.

offended because her hierarchy of values and her way of life are not given the weight they ought to have in the consideration of others.

One may object that sometimes people become angry simply because others do not respond to their needs (I said I was thirsty, but someone present in the room unthinkingly finished the only bottle of water available; the bus driver left exactly as I was arriving). The frustration of our desires is certainly relevant, but it is usually linked with the idea that others are inattentive and do not take us as seriously as they should (and if we are particularly self-centered, it is the world at large that irritatingly fails to comply). Interestingly, in this respect we become more easily angry with those we love than with people we do not know. This is because we do not expect to feel disregarded by those with whom we are intimate. It is particularly painful when this happens. That anger can be more frequent and more violent against people one loves is of course a significant difference from hatred.[11]

The third way in which appearance plays a role is in connection with interiority and exteriority, potentiality and actuality:

> Belittling [oligoria] is an actualization of opinion [energeia doxes] about what seems worthless [peri to medenos axion phainomenon] (we think both good and bad things worth serious attention, also things that contributed to them, but whatever amounts to little or nothing we suppose worthless) and there are three species of belittling: contempt [kataphronesis], spite [epereasmos], and insult [hybris]. (Arist., Rhet. II, 1378b11–15)

This somewhat cryptic passage offers an insight into what happens when someone feels slighted. We never really know what other people think of us, although we deeply care about it. In particular, we hope that those we would like to impress judge us worthy of their attention, and we often try to guess if they like us or appreciate what we do. Unfortunately, our hopes and guesses cannot reach into the most intimate thoughts of our acquaintances. We remain in the dark. Some of us feel anxious about this, others are more relaxed and self-confident. Given this strong interest, feeling slighted is a blow, a sudden and most unwelcome discovery. A slight painfully gives reality and shared visibility to the other's opinion. Being belittled strikes us not simply as an action we undergo and that we may judge as unjust, damaging, in bad taste, rude, etc. It is also

---

11 For the relationship between anger and the frustration of one's needs, cf. *Rhet.* II, 1379a11–29. For the claim that anger arises more easily with friends than with enemies or strangers, cf. 1379b2–6. Regarding the so-called "vending machine rage," Nussbaum (2016, pp. 17–18) rightly observes that we tend "to expect 'respect' and cooperation from the inanimate objects that serve our ends, and in the moment we react as if they were bad people, since they clearly are not doing 'their job' for us."

(and perhaps fundamentally) something of a revelation: "this is what you really think of me!"

Aristotle claims that "belittling [*oligoria*] is an actualization of opinion [*energeia doxes*] about what seems worthless." But what does it mean for an opinion to become actualized? One possible interpretation is that the other's opinion is not entirely real until it is expressed. It may be a fully formed view ("this person is worthless"), but it does not gain full reality while it remains just a thought, as suggested by Sokolowski (2014, pp. 234–235):

> What had been latent in *dynamis* now exists in *energeia*. Because it is an opinion that gravely concerns you, this enactment reverberates between you and me and everyone around us. This is what I have been thinking about you (or your skill as a painter) all this time. I activate my opinion that you (or your artistic product) are worthless; that is how you show up to me. I do something or I say something that shows actively what I think of you, and I display this for all to see. The metaphysics of *dynamis* and *energeia* reveals here its great power to explain things philosophically.

An alternative interpretation is that what is originally only a vague impression becomes a fully formed opinion only in the act of being expressed as a slight. Until they are communicated, our views remain indefinite, fleeting. They are often obscure, as episodic appearances in the flux of thought. Expressing them gives them definite shape. They acquire the solidity of facts. In this sense, the passage from potentiality to actuality may achieve something new for both members of the relationship: for the person who commits the slight (let's call her the offender) as well as for the person who feels slighted. Let us suppose that the offender's opinion was only vaguely present in her mind. It is in the moment she performs the contemptuous act that she and everybody else become aware of it.

Both interpretations are plausible, but they do not address directly the specific case Aristotle is discussing. They can be applied to the communication of any opinion, independently of the content. According to Aristotle the particular thought expressed in the slight is an evaluation: the offended belongs to those things that "seem worthless" (*to medenos axion*); his worth amounts to "little or nothing" (*meden ti e mikron*). If an offence actualizes the thought that I am worthless, the offender may have not yet formed a fully developed opinion about me *precisely because she despises me*. Her *doxa* about me was never fully formed until the slight happened, because she simply did not pay enough attention, as she certainly would have had she deemed me interesting enough to consider me good or bad ("we think both good and bad things worth serious attention"; Arist., *Rhet.* II, 1378b11–15). Her behavior proves that I have just not been on her radar screen at all. It is not surprising then that she may be made aware of her lack of consideration precisely by her act of disregard.

I prefer this interpretation precisely because the first form of *oligoria* Aristotle mentions is contempt (*kataphronesis*). A contemptuous person shows a lack of regard towards others mostly by his omissions: by not listening, by constantly interrupting, by standing in the way without apologizing, by not acknowledging the other on the street, etc. Basically, he behaves in such a way as to show at every step that the other's opinions and feelings have no relevance in his eyes, and he does so "*me prosekontos*," without justification. He has no business doing it, in two senses: first, I do not deserve such treatment; second, he has no reason to do it now and in this way. The act is arbitrary; thus it is all the more insulting.[12]

3 Disregard, aggression, affection. Social expectations and stereotypes

We should notice that *kataphronein* does not entail necessarily the active hostility associated with the word "contempt" today. What Aristotle has in mind is a form of disregard. We can find the same meaning in Hobbes's understanding of contempt as "being nothing else but an immobility, or contumacy of the heart" (Hobbes 1994; Book I, ch. 6, p. 28). It is because its objects are thought to be "vile and inconsiderable" that contempt arouses anger (and is listed by Hobbes among the causes of war in the state of nature). It is worth noting

---

[12] I agree with Sokolowski (2014, p. 235) on "*me prosekontos*." Konstan (2006, p. 55) understands it to refer exclusively to the social status of the offender: "Not every slight inspires anger [...], but only those 'on the part of people who are not fit to slight one or one's own'. [...] What counts as belittlement depends on status: if your position is inferior, it is no insult to be reminded of it." By contrast, I take "*me prosekontos*" to implicate both members of the relationship, the offended and the offender. The slight is inappropriate because it is perceived as undeserved by the offended, and because it is done by a person who, for various reasons (only one of which may be his status), has no business doing it. Cf. Honneth and Margalit (2001) on making someone feel invisible as an assertion of social non-existence, and as a way for the dominant to express their social superiority by not perceiving those they dominate. For a recent example, cf. director Bong Joon Ho's 2019 movie *Parasite*, which depicts the members of a destitute family being made invisible by the upper class family in which they insinuate themselves as domestic workers. The camera follows closely the facial expressions and the gestures by which the pampered rich express paternalism, contempt or indifference towards their newly acquired house-help. It is in response to grimaces of disgust at the way he smells that one of the characters explodes in anger and the movie culminates in an outburst of violence.

that, conceived in this sense, the contempt felt for someone's opinions may not exclude love. Elsewhere Aristotle observes that those who are ashamed of doing disgraceful things in the presence of people they respect, feel no shame before children or animals because they despise (*kataphronousin*) their capacity to arrive at the truth (*Rhet*. II, 1384b23). Someone who loves his children may consider them too immature to be able to form correct judgments. Consequently, he may take for granted that they have nothing significant to say on most matters. He despises their views not in the sense that he actively and passionately rejects them, but in the sense that he deems them of little account. At the same time, he enjoys his children's naïveté, and finds in it many welcome opportunities for playful exchanges and teasing.

Along the same lines, one may find it disturbing when a child expresses himself in ways that would be more fitting for an adult. In Plato's *Gorgias*, Callicles makes this point while raising his accusations against Socrates:

> [...] when I see a little child, to whom it is still natural to talk in that way, lisping or playing some trick, I enjoy it, and it strikes me as pretty and ingenuous and suitable to the infant's age; whereas if I hear a small child talk distinctly, I find it a disagreeable thing, and it offends my ears and seems to me more befitting a slave. But when one hears a grown man lisp, or sees him play tricks, it strikes one as something ridiculous and unmanly (*anandron*), that deserves a whipping. Just the same, then, is my feeling towards the followers of philosophy. (Plato, *Gorg.*, 485b–c)

On Callicles's interpretation, philosophy blurs the line between what is fitting for an adult and what is fitting for a child and, more fundamentally, it challenges his stereotypes about what a "real man" ought to do and what is fitting for a slave instead. Expressed differently, Callicles's attack on Socrates's philosophical enterprise is mainly based on prejudice. His aggressive stance can be explained by the worry that with his childish behavior Socrates may undermine the social *status quo* by challenging the fixed nature of certain roles. By contrast, Callicles does not need to be upset about those children who do not adequately embody his stereotype. A child speaking out of character can be annoying, but not as problematic as an adult who keeps away from politics and criticizes the Athenian way of life with young men at the corner of the streets.

If we extend these observations beyond the scope of Aristotle's (or Callicles's) intentions, we may consider that a similar mixture of affection and contempt can be detected in certain kinds of relationships between adults. In paternalistic relationships, for example, contempt goes hand in hand with love. From the beloved's point of view it is not easy to come to terms emotionally and intellectually with the confusing feeling of being despised and loved at the same time. On the other hand, a paternalistic attitude is even harder to acknowledge by the lover, since the beloved often inspires warm feelings precisely as long as he or she does not question the lover's need to assert his superiority. While Allport (1954) concentrated mostly on the hostility motivated by ethnic prejudice, more recent studies concentrated on forms of prejudice that are coated in favorable feelings. When members of a certain group aspire to social roles that are felt to be incongruent with the stereotype associated with the group, the pathbreakers meet with negative reactions and discrimination, while towards those members who accept their traditional social functions (for example women in domestic roles) prejudice takes the form of appreciation and affection.[13] Aristotle does not reflect on the role played by contempt in the relationship between genders, but he does acknowledge that a natural response to contempt is anger, and, as his observations about the lack of shame in the presence of children reveals, he clearly realizes that contempt is a form of disregard that can be associated with warm feelings. Aristotle perceives nothing wrong with this, but it is clearly a problem worth reflecting upon, not just from a moral or psychological point of view, but especially from a political and sociological perspective.

We have seen that according to Aristotle a slight can take three forms: contempt (*kataphronesis*), spite (*epereasmos*), and insult (*hybris*). If contempt is a form of slight concerning for the most part someone's judgment and activity, spite is addressed to the other's will. When one interferes with the realization of another's plans not because she desires to obtain the same things, but just so that the other does not get them, she belittles him. She would not act thus if she feared his reaction and took him seriously (once again, in this kind of behavior we can see actualized the opinion that the other is worth little or nothing). In turn, when one insults another just for the sake of feeling superior, one clearly commits *oligoria*, because he would not humiliate someone if he respected him.[14] In other words, a slight, in all its forms, is a public declaration that someone who occupies a certain role in the social fabric should in fact occupy a lower position, a position that is meant to be inferior to that of the person who commits the slight.

Whether the slight reveals a lack of regard for someone's judgment (contempt), for his intentions (spite), or for the person as a whole (insult), the con-

---

13 Cf. Dovidio, Glick, and Rudman (2005). On gender prejudice, cf. Glick and Fiske (1996); Eagly and Karau (2002).

14 On the relationship between *hybris* and particular injustice, see Cairns (1996, p. 6): "[...] in the paradigm case, in which *hybris* connotes vice and requires *prohairesis*, it requires a specific sort of motivation rooted deeply in a developed and settled state of character, a state of character which, in the sphere of honor, leads one to enjoy unfairly pressing one's own claims in the face of the legitimate claims of others."

sequence is that being slighted provokes shame: one feels diminished, unimportant. Shame in turn brings about a fear of social consequences: if one does not respond quickly and appropriately, one may worry that his opinions and wishes will stop carrying weight in the consideration and future deliberations of those who witnessed his impotent shame.[15]

Anger has an ethical weight that is stressed by Aristotle in the *Nicomachean Ethics*. There are things about which a virtuous person ought to get angry, and if someone remains emotionally indifferent when people close to him are unjustly treated, according to Aristotle one might suspect something is wrong with his character. Since anger offers the opportunity to show that one cares about justice, a lack of response on certain occasions betrays indifference and is therefore blameworthy.

We should not confuse being slighted with being unjustly treated, though. Being the object of unjust treatment entails disrespect, but not all cases of *oligoria* are also examples of injustice. The things one may find offensive are far more numerous than those most people would consider unjust. One can feel slighted when an acquaintance does not greet him on the street or forgets his name (*Rhet*. II, 1379b34), or when a friend does not seem to care that his desires be satisfied (*Rhet*. II, 1379b13). Yet, even the most self-centered among us would not consider such improprieties as examples of injustice.[16] Some people might get angry or indignant when struck by bad luck. They might rightly believe that they do not deserve to suffer. However, there is no injustice in bad luck (unless one considers oneself the target of a cosmic conspiracy).

While in Kantian terms failing to respect others as ends in themselves is the same as acting immorally, in Aristotelian terms disregarding others in the sense of committing *oligoria* does not mean failing to give them the respect they deserve *qua* rational agents. It means, rather, failing to give them the honor and consideration they deserve. Of course it is not easy to be good judges of the honor one deserves. A virtuous person has a fairly good idea of her own

---

[15] Strictly speaking, shame is concerned with the loss of reputation, independently of other consequences (*Rhet*., II, 1384a24). However, if shame is the fear of losing the respect of people who are important for me, it can easily lead me to worry that I might lose relevant goods linked with their respect: I might be deprived of their affection, of their trust, etc. On the fear of consequences in shame, cf. Fussi (2015, pp. 132–133).

[16] The fact that the range of things about which a person can become angry is so vast can give one pause about its moral significance. On anger as a vice linked to pride, cf. Taylor (2006, pp. 92–110); in a similar vein, Nussbaum (2016) finds status-anger narcissistic. I agree that on several occasions status-anger may have a narcissistic flavor, but the feeling of being belittled may also precede and make possible the awareness of being unjustly treated, especially when the contempt one experiences is rooted in social prejudice.

worth. Hence, she will not accept humiliating treatment, as she should not. However, she is not on the lookout for actions that she might find disrespectful: she reacts aggressively only on those occasions she finds appropriate, and maintains an even-tempered and forgiving attitude most of the time. By contrast, others fail to assess properly when certain behaviors are unacceptable and flare up in anger at the slightest provocation. They detect insulting words everywhere, explode too quickly and too often, but they have the good quality of calming down as rapidly as they explode. Aristotle calls them quick-tempered (*orgiloi; NE*, 1108a7; 1126a12), and contrasts their excessive animosity with the defective disposition of someone who seems incapable to take offence (the slow-tempered, *aorgetos; NE*, 1108a7; 1126a3). Clearly these two vices are related to other forms of imbalance: if someone cannot get angry when others insult him, should we not suspect that he lacks self-esteem? Should we not call him small-minded (*mikropsychos*)? And what about the person who gets angry all the time because he demands more honor than he really deserves? Would this not be the typical reaction of the vain (*chaunos*)?[17]

Oligoria is a matter of intersubjective recognition in a much more mundane (and sometimes frivolous or arbitrary) sense of the word than the lack of respect to which Kant refers, which is rooted in universally valid principles. *Oligoria* presupposes situated ethical life. By belonging to a particular social fabric, one develops attachments and expectations that contribute to defining her identity in the various groups to which she belongs. It is when such attachments and expectations are contradicted by the behavior of others that one may feel offended.

The virtuous person understands well what is offensive and why. However, as our reflections on Callicles's anger suggest, certain behaviors might be judged offensive only because they are at odds with practices that from a different and more critical point of view would appear affected by prejudice. Sometimes, one needs to understand not if anger is the fitting response, but if the behavior to which anger responds is considered fitting (or not fitting) on the basis of a social hierarchy that invites discrimination. Good habits and the well-balanced character that make one capable to grasping the fitting reaction at a given time are not sufficient if our shared habits are biased against certain groups. In this case a Socratic form of detachment from accepted conventions, and epistemic virtues such as curiosity and open-mindedness, will be most helpful.

---

17 Cf. Arist., *NE*, 1125a17–32.

4 The communicative nature of anger: the desire for redress

If someone treated with contempt does not react, he may be understood to accept his diminished standing. An offence is a form of communication: by insulting someone I affirm that his opinion and wishes are not as important as he thinks they are. Hence, according to Aristotle the perceived *oligoria* is not just a private feeling, but something that demands a form of public response. This is why anger is not simply the painful reaction to an act of disrespect, but the active desire for *apparent retaliation* (*timorias phainomenes*). We find here the fourth sense in which appearance plays an important role in anger: the desire to obtain redress with respect to honor belongs to the same communicative strategy as the offence. If others insult me with an apparent slight, they effectively diminish my social standing, until I make apparent by my words and actions that they should not belittle me.[18]

Anger cannot arise without an attribution of responsibility. The distinction famously drawn by Strawson in *Freedom and Resentment* between objective attitudes and participant reactive attitudes is useful in this context. While objective

---

[18] The idea that anger contains a desire to communicate is discussed by several philosophers who take up Strawson's (2008) distinction between reactive and objective attitudes. Some authors refer to Aristotle, while others concentrate on the most recent debate. Shoemaker (2015, pp. 105–106 ff.) embraces the Aristotelian perspective: "one simply does not count as being angry at someone without having some motivational impulse to communicate that feeling to the agent *qua* slighting party. [...] Agential anger with successful, but uncommunicated, revenge feels incomplete, whereas agential anger with successful, but non-vengeful, communication does not." Macnamara (2015) ignores Aristotle and takes up instead Strawson's distinction between personal reactive attitudes (such as resentment) and self-reactive attitudes associated with demands on others for oneself (such as guilt). Her thesis is that personal and vicarious reactive attitudes have the "interpersonal function of evoking uptake of their representational content in a recipient" (p. 562). More precisely, "emotional uptake of the representational content of resentment or indignation by the wrongdoer amounts to *guilt* [...] This is explained by the fact that the other and self-regarding attitudes have parallel representational contents. The former represent *another* as having done something morally significant and the latter represent *oneself* as having done something morally significant" (p. 559). Attention to the communicative impulse in anger is strong also among those who study intergroup conflicts. Interestingly, Halperin (2016, p. 50) proposes "the counterintuitive argument that although anger is felt very frequently and at high intensity among the majority of the citizens who are living in violent conflict zones, and although it may lead some of them to support or even take active part in aggressive actions, anger does not always yield such destructive consequences and under certain circumstances may even serve as a catalyst rather than as a barrier to peace."

attitudes deal with others as *objects* to be studied and modified, as 'things' to be handled or avoided, reactive attitudes involve others as participants in inter-personal human relationships. While it may be doubtful if hatred should be considered a reactive attitude, anger, as it is characterized by Aristotle, is *the* quintessential reactive attitude.[19]

In order to resent an offence, we have to think that it was intentional. Hence, as Aristotle affirms, we get angry with individuals, not with abstract categories, and the pain caused by the slight we received is accompanied by the pleasure derived from the hope that we will be able to restore our honor (Arist., *Rhet.* II, 1378a32-b10).

I cannot become angry if I have no hope of redress: anger presupposes a (justified or unjustified) feeling of power. Since redress is meant to restore my public image, when I plan it I feel empowered, and this is pleasant. But it is enjoyable also to daydream about the future, and to anticipate in the imagination the satisfaction I will get when the other will understand at his expenses that I should not be treated the way I was treated. I can see myself as someone whose voice can be heard. What I say and do has a bearing on what others say and do, and the hope that redress is possible assures me that I am not cut off from communication: the social fabric that was lacerated by the offence can be repaired.

This Aristotelian account is based, of course, on stereotypes regarding self-affirmation. Only certain kinds of people in this picture have a right to express their anger. Women and slaves are excluded. They cannot aspire to obtain redress autonomously, they do not have the power to make their voices heard. At most, they can hope that others, the citizens who are thought to be in charge of them (the slaves' masters, the women's husbands and fathers) can retaliate (or seek legal redress) in their place (cf. Bodei 2010, pp. 79–89).

In this light, it is significant that when in the *Nicomachean Ethics* Aristotle blames those who do not become angry when they should, he associates them with the slaves, who cannot protect themselves and are at the mercy of anyone who wishes to offend them: "and it is slavish to put up with being insulted oneself or to overlook insults to those close to one" (*NE*, 1126a6–8).

What is blameworthy and shameful for a citizen is the norm for a slave. Does this mean that people who feel powerless will be unable to experience anger?

---

19 In order to avoid confusion I will continue to call 'anger' a personal response to injury or disregard. Strawson (2008) calls this personal response 'resentment', while he stipulates to call 'indignation' the vicarious reaction to "the qualities of others' wills, not towards ourselves, but towards others" (p. 28). Whether hatred is a reactive or an objective attitude is a question discussed by Brudholm (2010).

Yes and No. They will be perfectly able to feel the pain of the slight but unable to feel the pleasure of seeking redress. The expression of their anger will be repressed. The pain of the offence and the feeling of powerlessness will be felt in their bodies as an oppressive weight. The lingering grudge will keep hurting them and slowly affect their character. They will become sulky and difficult to be with (Arist., *NE*, 1126a19–26).

Because anger entails the desire for redress, we cannot be angry in the full sense of the term if we deem reparation impossible to obtain. This is the case not only when we are hopeless about our power for retaliation, but also when we feel that the recipient is not in a position to receive our message. According to Aristotle, we cannot remain angry with people who are unable to appreciate that what they are undergoing is our revenge, for example if those who offended us die or become insane: in such cases we lose all interest in retaliation. Hence, it is preferable to provoke pain rather than cause serious but undetected evil:

> Also, [people are calm] when they think that [their victims] will not perceive who is the cause of their suffering and that it is retribution for what they have suffered; for anger is a personal thing, as is clear from the definition. Thus, the verse "Say it was Odysseus, sacker of cities," was rightly composed, since [Odysseus] would not have been avenged if [Polyphemus the Cyclops] had not realized both from whom and why revenge came. Thus, people do not vent their anger on others who are not aware of it nor continue it against the dead, since the latter have suffered the ultimate and will not suffer nor will they have perception, which is what angry people want. (Arist., *Rhet.* II, 1380b20–27)

An angry person wants the other to be in full possession of his mind: he must be capable to perceive and to suffer. In feeling pain there is awareness, while evil things are often accompanied by no pain and no awareness.

5 Hatred

Aristotle claims that while someone who is angry wishes that the other might feel pain, the person who hates wishes that the other suffer evil:

> Painful actions [inflicted by one person on another] are all perceived by the senses, but the greatest evils – injustice and thoughtlessness– are least perceived; for the presence of evil causes no pain. (Arist., *Rhet.* II, 1382a10–13)

This point reveals a fundamental difference between anger and hatred: *the communicative aspect of anger is mostly absent in hatred.* We saw that anger is always directed at individuals. Hatred, however, even when directed at individuals, is not concerned with them *qua* agents. Even though it may find its roots in past actions and responsibilities, what has been done and who exactly did it is not at the center of the hater's attention. Hate is directed first and foremost to categories of people, and only secondarily to individuals, who become relevant only insofar as they instantiate the negative properties associated with the groups to which they belong:

> Now anger comes from things that affect a person directly, but enmity also from what is not directed against himself; for if we suppose someone to be a certain kind of person, we hate him. And anger is always concerned with particulars, directed, for example, at Callias or Socrates, while hate is directed also at types (everyone hates the thief and the sycophant). (Arist., *Rhet.* II, 1382a2–7)

I can hate thieves without having ever met one. If someone tells me that a certain person is a thief, I do not need to know much about him to be able to hate him. It doesn't matter if his responsibilities are not clear. Insofar as he conforms to the stereotype associated with the out-group to which he belongs, there will be a strong resistance to admit that he might be an exception, and there will certainly be no inclination to question the validity of the stereotype itself.

Because anger is directed at agents while hatred is mainly directed at negative social categories, hatred can heavily rely on stereotypes. Hence, the logic of hatred moves in a direction that runs counter to the logic of anger.

Someone who is angry may come to think that a certain person is nasty because he repeatedly did nasty things. By contrast, the hater starts from the property (or the stereotype) and proceeds to infer nasty actions from it. Elster (1999, p. 67) makes this Aristotelian point quite aptly:

> The link to behavior is not 'because they do bad things, they are bad', but the converse, 'because they are bad, they do bad things'. Thus, evidence about their actual behavior will not affect the belief that they are bad, any more than evidence about the apparently mature behavior of a small child will affect our policy of assuming that he or she is likely to behave childishly. 'Their true nature will come out'.

But of course, if the target of hatred is perceived not as an agent but as the representative of a fixed category, it is natural to think that he will never change. As I pointed out earlier, anger presupposes hope and a sense of power: I feel my actions as effective and capable to produce conspicuous consequences. If, on the other hand, I cannot see the person I hate as someone with whom to engage in conversation, if it is impossible to imagine that he will respond, feel pain, apologize, or get upset, if I identify him only as the representative of an out-group, I cannot really hope that my behavior will influence his ways. I feel fundamentally powerless. He will continue to be what he is no matter what I do or say.[20] He acquires in my mind the persecutory force of a spiritual entity (evil incarnate) and I can easily lose track of the fact that, like me, he is human and vulnerable. Predictably, my strongest desire will be that he cease to exist.

The hater himself will be affected by the de-personalization projected onto his object of hatred. Qualities linked to responsibility will be downplayed: his own intentions, his own power, his effects on the world will be not nearly as relevant as they are when he is angry. If the object of hatred represents thieves, the agent represents honest people, if the other is a coward, the agent will identify himself with the noble group of the courageous. He will not care if his antagonist feels pain or simply suffers evil, if he dies or becomes mentally incapacitated. Above all, he is not interested in personally hurting him. It would be enough if others contributed effectively to the disappearance of his kind. The fight appears to be between polarized principles.

As Aristotle observes:

> Anger is also accompanied by pain [to the one who feels anger], but hate is not accompanied by pain; for the angry person is himself pained, the one who hates is not. One who is angry might feel pity when much has befallen [the person he is angry at], but one who hates under no circumstances; for the former wants the one he is angry at to suffer in his turn, the latter wants [the detested class of persons] not to exist. (Arist., *Rhet.* II, 1382a12–15)

The strange form of impersonality that characterizes hatred makes one wonder if it is really an emotion or, rather, a lasting disposition which progressively leads to a paralysis of feeling and thought. In hate I am not really an agent, but the member of a group set up against another group. I do not ask who the other is, what he did, if my category is correct, if he is an exception. More importantly, I cannot hope to affect him or other people like him by talking and listening.

6 Conclusions

As our analysis has shown, we can interpret both anger and hatred as affective responses rooted in spiritedness. In anger, however, the animosity and heat of *thumos* is in the foreground, while hatred entails a lack of feeling that suggests it might be best interpreted as a disposition rather than as an emotion properly.

---

[20] Still, according to Plutarch (1959; 538 c-d) hatred can be cured more easily than envy: if we discover that a person we hate is in fact virtuous we may forgo hostility, while envy increases with the other's virtue.

Our initial reflections on the dog barking at strangers in the *Nicomachean Ethics*' passage suggested that a hater is more likely than an angry person to address a stereotypical target rather than a concrete agent. Aristotle's discussion of hatred in the *Rhetoric* supports this view, because the target of hatred is not someone who did something wrong, but someone expected to do wrong in light of a negative quality (or a vice) with which he is identified. By contrast, we have seen that anger is a reaction to forms of belittlement, and we have discussed at some length the particular form of slight represented by contempt.

Although there are significant differences between anger and hatred, there is no reason to exclude the possibility that they might be affective stages in a continuous dynamic process. There may be several intermediate steps between my first reactions of anger to an offense and the lasting attitude of hatred I may acquire towards someone who repeatedly hurt me in despicable ways. One such intermediate step might be when I am no longer simply angry, but I am also not yet related to her in the cold, impersonal way described by Aristotle. I do not feel the need to express my distress, I do not cultivate the idea of a revenge, but, on the other hand, I do not see her yet as the mere instantiation of a negative property, or as belonging to a group of detestable people (as *a* thief, as *a* liar, as *a* traitor, etc.). What she did and how she did it have enough historical significance in my life to make me relate to her with deeply individualized hostility. I hate her because she is who she is. Yet, I have no wish to go out of my way to hurt her. If she is struck by lightning, ends up in prison, or moves to another country I am fine with it.[21]

Between the first stages of anger and the fully developed, cold disposition of hatred there are affective nuances that deserve further investigation. Still—and I believe this to be the most important Aristotelian insight—the development from anger to full-fledged hatred will involve my progressively losing hope that if I make myself heard she will change and I will obtain redress.[22]

We can see the importance of this insight also from the perspective of the person I hate. No matter what she has done, no matter how many times she did it, she may feel trapped in my stereotypical projection. She receives a lot of attention from me: she knows I wish her evil. Yet, she may rightly feel disregarded: there is nothing she can do to change my negative view. If people get angry when they are

---

[21] Salice (2020) objects to Szanto (2020), arguing that hatred is best understood as negatively targeting the other qua individual rather than, as it is traditionally conceived, as a negative affective reaction with a blurry focus and an overgeneralized target. Salice's paper deserves a longer discussion, but in my view the phenomenon he addresses as paradigmatic can be understood as an intermediate affective response in the process leading from anger to hatred.
[22] On the relationship between hope and agency, cf. Walker (2006).

made to feel invisible, one can feel disregarded when loved (as we have seen in the case of paternalistic relationships), as well as when hated. In both cases anger is understandable, insofar as it aims to retrieve a form of personal communication of which the hater and the hated risk losing track.[23]

References

Allport, Gordon W. (1954): *The nature of prejudice*. Cambridge, MA: Perseus Books.
Aristotle (2000): *Nicomachean Ethics*. Trans. Roger Crisp. Cambridge: Cambridge University Press. [*NE*]
Aristotle (2007): *On Rhetoric: A Theory of Civic Discourse*. Trans. George Kennedy. 2nd ed. Oxford: Oxford University Press. [*Rhet.*]
Benardete, Seth (1989): *Socrates' Second Sailing: On Plato's Republic*. Chicago: University of Chicago Press.
Bloom, Allan D. (1968): "Interpretive essay". In: Plato, *Republic*. Trans. Allan Bloom. New York: Basic Books.
Bodei, Remo (2010): *Ira. La passione furente*. Bologna: il Mulino.
Bong Joon-ho (Dir.) (2019): *Parasite*. South Korea. Distributed by CJ Entertainment.
Brudholm, Thomas (2010): "Hatred as an attitude". In: *Philosophical Papers* 39(3), pp. 289–313.
Cairns, Douglas (1996): "Hybris, Dishonour, and Thinking Big". In: *Journal of Hellenic Studies* 116, pp. 1–32.
Cairns, Douglas (2015): "Revenge, Punishment, and Justice in Athenian Homicide Law". In: *The Journal of Value Inquiry* 49, pp. 645–665.
Centrone, Bruno (Ed. and Trans.) (2020): *Problema XXVIII. Sulla temperanza e l'intemperanza, la continenza e l'incontinenza*. Pisa: Edizioni ETS.
Cope, Edward M. (2009): *The Rhetoric of Aristotle with a Commentary*. Vol. 2. Cambridge: Cambridge University Press.
D'Arms, Justin/Jacobson, Daniel (2000): "The Moralistic Fallacy: on the 'Appropriateness' of Emotions". In: *Philosophy and Phenomenological Research* 61(1), pp. 65–90.
Dovidio, John F./Glick, Peter/Rudman, Laurie A. (Eds.) (2005): *On the Nature of Prejudice: Fifty Years after Allport*. Malden: Blackwell Publishing.
Eagly, Alice H./Karau, Steven J. (2002): "Role Congruity of Prejudice toward Female Leaders". In: *Psychological Review* 109, pp. 573–598.
Elster, Jon (1999): *Alchemies of the Mind. Rationality and the Emotions*. Cambridge: Cambridge University Press.

---

[23] I am grateful for their generous interaction to philosophical audiences in Oslo, Genova, Pisa, who listened to different versions of this paper. My gratitude goes also to all the colleagues and friends who read it, submitted their criticisms and helped me clarify my arguments. In particular, I wish to thank Thomas Brudholm, Alfredo Ferrarin, Paola Gamberini, Danilo Manca, Leonardo Massantini, Øyvind Rabbås, David Roochnik, Alessandro Salice, Franco Trivigno. Special thanks go to Anna Bortolan and Elisa Magrì, who accepted my paper in this volume and took great care to publish it in its best possible form.

Fussi, Alessandra (2014): "Leo Strauss on Collingwood: Historicism and The Greeks". In: *Idealistic Studies* 44(2–3), pp. 149–162.
Fussi, Alessandra (2015): "Aristotle on Shame". In: *Ancient Philosophy* 35, pp. 113–135.
Glick, Peter/Fiske, Susan T. (1996): "The Ambivalent Sexism Inventory: Differentiating Hostile and Benevolent Sexism". In: *Journal of Personality and Social Psychology* 70, pp. 491–512.
Griswold, Charles L. (2013): "The Nature and Ethics of Vengeful Anger". In: Fleming, James E. (Ed.): *Passions and Emotions*. New York: New York University Press, pp. 77–124.
Halperin, Eran (2015): *Emotions in Conflict: Inhibitors and Facilitators of Peace Making*. London, New York: Routledge.
Hobbes, Thomas (1994): *Leviathan*. With selected variants from the Latin edition of 1668. Edwin Curley (Ed.). Indianapolis, Cambridge: Hackett Publishing Company.
Honneth, Axel/Margalit, Avishai (2001): "Recognition". In: *Proceedings of the Aristotelian Society, Supplementary Volumes* 75, pp. 111–139.
Howland, Jacob (1993): *The Republic: the Odyssey of Philosophy*. New York: Twayne Publishers.
Kolnai, Aurel (1998): "The Standard Modes of Aversion". In: *Mind* 107(427), pp. 581–596.
Kolnai, Aurel (2007): *Ekel Hochmut Hass. Zur Phänomenologie feindlicher Gefühle*. Frankfurt: Suhrkamp.
Konstan, David (2006): *The Emotions of the Ancient Greeks: studies in Aristotle and classical literature*. Toronto: University of Toronto Press.
Macnamara, Coleen (2015): "Reactive Attitudes as Communicative Entities". In: *Philosophy and Phenomenological Research* XC(3), pp. 546–569.
Nussbaum, Martha C. (2016): *Anger and Forgiveness. Resentment, Generosity, Justice*. Oxford: Oxford University Press.
Plato (1925): "Gorgias". In: *Lysis. Symposium. Gorgias*. Trans. W. R. M. Lamb. Loeb Classical Library 166. Cambridge, MA: Harvard University Press. [*Gorg.*]
Plato (2000). *The Republic*. G. R. F. Ferrari (Ed.). Tom Griffith (Trans.). Cambridge: Cambridge University Press. [*Rep.*]
Plutarch (1959): *Moralia. Volume VII*. Trans. Phillip H. De Lacy/Benedict Einarson. Loeb Classical Library 405. Cambridge, MA: Harvard University Press.
Rabbås, Øyvind (2015): "Virtue, Respect, and Morality in Aristotle". In: *Journal of Value Inquiry* 49(4), pp. 619–643.
Rosen, Stanley (2005): *Plato's Republic:A Study*. New Haven: Yale University Press.
Salice, Alessandro (2020): "I hate you. On hatred and its paradigmatic forms". In: *Phenomenology and the Cognitive Sciences*. https://doi.org/10.1007/s11097-020-09668-0, last accessed on 20 February 2021.
Shoemaker, David (2015): *Responsibility from the Margins*. Oxford: Oxford University Press.
Sokolowski, Robert (2014): "Honor, Anger, and Belittlement in Aristotle's Ethics". In: *Studia Gilsoniana: A Journal Of Classical Philosophy* 3, pp. 221–240.
Strauss, Leo (1964): *The City and Man*. Chicago: Rand Mc Nally.
Strawson, Peter F. (2008): *Freedom and Resentment and Other Essays*. London, New York: Routledge.
Szanto, Thomas (2020): "In hate we trust: The collectivization and habitualization of hatred". In: *Phenomenology and the Cognitive Sciences* 19, pp. 453–480.
Taylor, Gabriele (2006): *Deadly Vices*. Oxford: Oxford University Press.
Walker, Margaret U. (2007): *Moral Repair*. Cambridge: Cambridge University Press.

Danielle Petherbridge
Habit, Attention and Affection: Husserlian Inflections

Abstract: This chapter offers a consideration of the relation between affection, attention and perception in Edmund Husserl's genetic phenomenology with the aim of illuminating the account of affective attunement found in Axel Honneth's recognition theory. Specifically, it examines the role of affect and attention in understanding habitualized forms of perception in which other persons remain invisible or 'unseen', drawing on Charles Johnson's phenomenological descriptions. Johnson's account of frozen intentionality is brought together with Honneth's claim that such reifying forms of perception indicate a forgetfulness of primary forms of affective recognition. I argue that Honneth's claims can be understood more fully when brought into view through Husserl's genetic phenomenology in which we find reference to affection and attention, or to a form of affective-intentionality. Following Wehrle, then, intentionality is not understood as a cold, detached process but is attentive or affective. I conclude by considering the centrality of affection and attention not only in perceptual experience but also as fundamental to phenomenological reflection and how this might provide a means of modifying embedded habits of perception.

In his genetic analysis, Husserl offers a rich account of the role of affect and attention in the lower levels of perception. Although significant in its own right, here I wish to detail the manner in which Husserl's phenomenology might be employed to illuminate the account of affective-attunement found in Axel Honneth's recognition theory. More specifically, drawing on Charles Johnson's phenomenological descriptions, I examine the role of affect and attention in habitualized forms of perception, before moving to consider Honneth's claim that such forms of perception indicate a forgetfulness of primary forms of affective recognition. Of particular interest here are the questions that Honneth raises about the interrelation between perception, cognition and recognition as a means of understanding perceptual acts. Instead of considering that cognitive identification has genetic priority in the act of perception prior to recognition, Honneth claims we need to amend the status of cognitive acts vis-à-vis recognition. Furthermore, he considers reifying forms of perception to be a disavowal of an originary form of affective recognition that forms an antecedent identification of others and the world. I argue that Honneth's claims can be enriched and more

https://doi.org/10.1515/9783110698787-021

fully understood when brought into view through Husserl's genetic analysis. In the genetic elements of Husserl's work we find an account of perception that is underpinned by affection and attention, and a notion of affective-intentionality. In this manner, following Wehrle and Slaby, intentionality is not understood as a cold, detached process but is attentive or affective; objects and indeed other subjects do not appear in a neutral way, rather, they affect or interest us and such affective acts represent the expression of an evaluative perception. I argue for the significance of affection and attention not only in Husserl's account of perception, but also as fundamental to forms of critical reflection, and conclude by considering how a form of reflexive attention might provide a means of modifying embedded habits of racializing perception.

1 Recognition and Affective-Attunement: Johnson and Honneth on Evaluative Perception

Charles Johnson has written evocatively about what might be termed the phenomenology of recognition in a manner that elucidates the relation between invisibility, recognition and perception. In the following passage, Johnson describes what amounts to a failure of recognition in a moment of perception, one he experienced as a student in New York in the 1970s. He writes:

> Furthermore, I am black. I do not see what the white other sees in my skin, but I am aware of his intentionality, and – yes – aware that I often disclose something discomforting to him. My body gives me the world, but, as that world is given, it is one in which I can be unseen. I walk down the hallway at the university and pass a professor I know well. He glances up quickly, yet does not acknowledge that he knows me. He has seen a black, a body, that remains for him always in the background, seldom figured forth save as maid, taxi driver, or janitor. Passing, he sees me as he sees the fire extinguisher to my left, that chair outside the door. I have been seen, yet not seen... (Johnson 1993, p. 604)

Johnson's phenomenological account of racializing perception might be described as a process of dehumanization or social invisibilization in which the other has been deliberately ignored, or, as he describes it, seen yet unseen. Employing Husserl's phenomenology to describe the experience and perception of racialization, Johnson points to the body as central to the way in which the subject "reeves ... to a world" (Johnson 1993, p. 602), both individualizing her and anchoring her in history, operating as her reference on the universe and making perception possible. He describes the kind of sedimented habit that builds up over time and creates a history of perception, one that over time "exhibits ... a series of profiles or disclosures of being" (Johnson 1993, p. 612). He walks into a bar in New York patronized by 'whites' and conveys the way in which his world collapses "like a house of cards into the stained casement of [his] skin." In this scenario, he describes the manner in which his "subjectivity is turned inside out like a shirtcuff" and writes: "I must forever be on guard against my body betraying me in public; I must suppress the profile that their frozen intentionality brings forth…" (Johnson 1993, pp. 606; 607).

An important component of his analysis, then, is the way in which it pivots around the notion of intentionality, acknowledging it as the "structure which gives meaning to experience" and determining how we perceive the world (Johnson 1993, p. 602). As Johnson describes, though, to "'intend' an object or content of consciousness is to be 'in-formed' by it as well as to give form to it." But he also points to the way in which such intentionality is intertwined with motivations and associations, forms of affectivity and attention, when he writes: "that every act of intending involves to some extent, 'interest'." Johnson implies that such 'interest' motivates whether "I either bring an object forth for attention or let it remain undifferentiated in the 'ground'", an apt description of his professor's frozen intentionality as he passes in the hall (Johnson 1993, pp. 602–603). In this sense, as shall be discussed below, Johnson's recourse to the notion of 'frozen intentionality' is instructive, suggesting that in this case, affective and attentive levels of perception have ceased or become calcified.

In Honneth's terms, what Johnson points to is a form of evaluative intentionality that already indicates the worth or otherwise of persons in our basic perceptual awareness of them (cf. Jardine 2015). Honneth therefore draws our attention to the way in which perception of others is not merely understood as a form of primary identification but, at the same time, affirms the other's social existence. In this regard, Honneth seeks to highlight the way in which acts of recognition are affirmed through expressive and embodied gestures that indicate the perception of another human being. In the scenario that Johnson describes, his professor's invisibilizing glance would be transformed into an expressive act of acknowledgement through a nod or a smile as he passes Johnson in the hallway. Thus, rather than merely remaining undefined and dehumanized in the background along with chairs and fire extinguishers, Johnson would be brought forth and recognized as a subject, as a figure against a background in his own right.

When considered in this manner, following Honneth, it can be suggested that recognition involves 'an expression' of the perception of another that indicates or affirms his or her social validity. Honneth suggests that without such forms of expression, the other remains invisible in a social sense to his or her social counterpart. In this sense, Honneth's suggestion is that a direct connection can be made between perception, expressivity and affirmation. The lack of expressive acknowledgment demonstrated in Johnson's account indicates a pathologization or deformation of perception in the sense that an affirmative intersubjective perceptual act has failed to occur. Honneth therefore points to the way in which higher level judgments are already underpinned by lower levels of attentive and affective attunement. As we will see, in Honneth's work, this account of affectivity and expressivity in perception is underpinned by a reconceptualization of the relation between perception, cognition and recognition that has significant ramifications.[1]

To this end, Honneth attempts to reverse the relation between what might be termed literal and recognitive perception. The suggestion he makes, is that the visibility of the other must require more than an act of perception in the sense of perceivability understood as a form of elementary identification (Honneth 2001, p. 113). However, this is not to suggest that recognitive perception is secondary. Although it seems that for Johnson to be rendered 'invisible' as his professor passes him in the corridor he must have already been perceived within the professor's visual field, Honneth is making an alternative suggestion. The claim is not that the professor's invisibilization of Johnson is an active secondary element in the perceptual process that occurs after primary identification. Rather, to describe an act of perception as one of recognition points not to a cognitive act of identification followed by a secondary recognitive one, but instead to the *evaluative* nature of perception *per se*, in which as Honneth explains, "the worth of persons is 'directly' given" (Honneth 2001, p. 114; 125). The crux of Honneth's claim, then, is not that recognition is secondary to or builds upon primary identification or cognition in an act of perception. Rather, the suggestion here is that cognitive identification unfolds out of more basic affirmative and attentive acts of evaluative intentionality. As a consequence, instead of considering that cognitive identification of the individual has genetic priority in the act of perception, Honneth argues we need to reverse the status of cognitive and recognitive acts: affective recognition is understood to be prior to cognition and forms the basis of our perception of others. For Honneth, the lack of recognition that Johnson describes can therefore be understood as a "*deformation* of the human capacity for perception" or as an abstraction from a primary background form of recognition (Honneth 2001, p. 126).

The claim regarding the genetic priority of recognition in perception is also underpinned by Honneth's explication of an account of affective recognition as a

---

[1] Some of the material on Honneth and affective recognition discussed here is examined in an alternative manner in Petherbridge 2017; this work builds on that account. An earlier version of this material has also been published in Petherbridge 2021, pp. 67–90.

basic existential and emotional stance to others and the world (Honneth 2008). In this sense, Honneth assumes a primordial and affective perception of others that is prior to conceptualization, which is grounded in a primary form of intersubjectivity or relatedness. He argues that forms of reification, or what might be considered the deformation of perception, should therefore be understood to be a deviation from what he refers to as a 'genuine' mode of relating to others and the world (Honneth 2008, p. 90; 70 ff.). According to this formulation, for Honneth, objectification or reification of other subjects can be understood as the temporary loss, concealment, or 'forgetfulness' of an elementary form of recognition. In this sense, reifying or objectifying stances must already presuppose "a more primordial and genuine form of praxis, in which humans take up an empathetic and engaged relationship towards themselves and their surroundings" (Honneth 2008, p. 27). Honneth then seems to suggest that recognition is based in our direct perception of and interaction with others, and is akin to a pre-reflexive lived experience and form of practical engagement, rather than associated with a cognitive or contemplative stance (Honneth 2008, p. 27; 32; 38). Affective recognition then refers to a form of affective attunement or attentiveness to others and this primary form of 'affective engagement' is "prior to our acts of detached cognition" (Honneth 2008, p. 38).

Although Honneth does not elaborate further on this account, as we will see below, his work points to a form of affective-attunement and recognitive perception that is comparable to a notion of affective-intentionality found in Husserl's work. Honneth only offers a mere sketch of such an account in his work, but a gesture in this direction can be found in a clarificatory statement about affective recognition. In a reply to critics, Honneth articulates a primary form of recognition as affectedness or emotional receptivity when he writes that "[l]ove and hate, ambivalence and coldness, can all be expressions of this elementary recognition as long as they can be seen to be modes of existential affectedness" (Honneth 2008, pp. 151–152). In this sense, Honneth's account highlights: (1) a type of frozen intentionality or lack of affective responsiveness depicted by reified forms of perception through which others are perceived as 'thing-like'; (2) the connection between forms of affective responsiveness, recognition, and evaluative perception in a way that affirms the other's social validity. In this regard, affective and attentive forms of attunement form the precursor for all higher-level forms of identification or normative recognition stances, and this aspect of his work is suggestive of important parallels with the phenomenological account.

The account of Honneth's notion of affective recognition briefly outlined above has largely been overshadowed by his more normative and political account of the struggle for recognition, and where it has been given attention, it has often been problematized for introducing conceptual slippages and confusions (Petherbridge 2013; Varga 2015). However, I want to suggest that the kinds of claims Honneth is making can be understood more fully if we bring them into view through a phenomenological analysis found more explicitly in Husserl's later work. In his later work, Husserl offers an instructive phenomenological account of affection and attention that helps shed light on the complex of issues raised in Honneth's work, both enriching it and highlighting some of its omissions. In the following section, we turn to examine the detail of Husserl's genetic account, before in the final section considering how attention and affection also play an important role in higher levels of critical reflection.

2 Husserl's Genetic Account of Affection and Attention

In Husserl's genetic phenomenology, we find an account of affection that is conceptualized across several different levels and in which he explicates the role affection plays in attention. These levels range from passive modes that include what might be considered a form of affective attunement and basic forms of attention, to more active modes of cognition and conceptualization (Steinbock 2004, p. 38). In this sense, too, it is important to note the distinction Husserl makes in his genetic account between passivity and activity, or active and passive synthesis (Husserl 2001). For our purposes, the notion of passivity is significant as it refers to a kind of primordial constitution, or the way in which sense is constituted. At the passive level, as Steinbock suggests, the ego is not explicitly active, nor does it "actively orientate itself in the constitution of sense" (Steinbock 2004, p. 23). Rather, the passivity of which Husserl speaks can be understood as pre-reflexive and pre-linguistic perceptual experience, which forms the basis of more active levels of experience and makes them possible.

The meaning of the terms passivity and activity in Husserl's work vary across contexts, but as Corijn van Mazijk suggests, they can be taken to refer to the "degree of attention and participation of the 'pure ego' involved in experience" (van Mazijk 2016, p. 276). However, rather than merely speaking of 'perception' or 'sensibility', which would denote a focus on sensible capacities, Husserl instead understands perception as embodied and conceptualizes it in relation to his account of kinaesthesis (van Mazijk 2016, p. 276). As Dermot Moran suggests, Husserl refers to kinaesthetic sensations as "sensations of movement (*kinesis*) [that although] freely undertaken ... are not fully modes of will"; as Husserl clarifies, they are "'activities' in a certain sense, although not voluntary acts" (Moran 2002, p. 213; 215; Husserl 1973, § 19, p. 84). In this respect, what Husserl refers to is the way in which "[p]erception is not just the passive reception of sensory features of an object (its color, etc.); it also involves [movement toward and] the activities of the sense organs themselves" (Moran 2002, p. 213). For example, in order to see the play of the ball on a football field one must turn one's eyes and move one's head in the direction of play. Or, in order to feel a stone found on the beach, one stretches one's hand out to touch it and turns it over to inspect its profiles and feel its smoothness (Husserl 1973, § 19, p. 84). Husserl understands this as a kind of spontaneity that is part of bodily perception (Moran 2002, p. 213). Thus, in *Experience and Judgment* he writes: "We call these movements, which belong to the essence of perception and serve to bring the object of perception to givenness from all sides in so far as possible, *kinaestheses*" (Husserl 1973, § 19, p. 84, 89; Moran 2002, p. 214). Kinaesthetic gestures therefore indicate a turning away or turning toward something or somebody, and Husserl's claim is that without such movements and sensations, effectively without these motivations, the apprehension of a thing is unthinkable (Depraz 2004, p. 12). Moreover, it requires particular movements not only to be able to perceive an object but also to perceive it in a particular way and to have the possibility of perceiving it from different perspectives. In this manner, Husserl identifies the particular and complex relation between passivity and activity that is characteristic of perception. The important point is that perception initially might entail undergoing a particular experience, but it also requires an active attention or a turning toward (Moran 2002, p. 214).

As Husserl perceptively notes: "The coming-into-view of the images is 'in my power'; [but] I can also cause the series to break off, e. g. I can close my eyes. But what is not in my power, *if* I allow the kinaestheses to run their course, is having another image come into view" (Husserl 1973, § 19, p. 84, 89; Moran 2002, p. 214). Husserl's view of perception, then, always refers to both an element of 'interest' based in a series of sensations that elicit the motivational element, as well as bringing forth the properties of an object in the one act of perception. In other words, the sensings that motivate one to perceive an object in a sensory field (along with the modification of one's sensory organs) and the sensations elicited from the object (its texture, smell, colour, for example) contribute equally to the act of perception (Moran 2002, p. 214).

However, the passive or lowest levels of perceptual experience do not involve the attention of the ego in order for them to be brought forth. Rather, they occur in the background of our intentional awareness and Husserl refers to them in terms of a "broad lived experiential field" (van Mazijk 2016, p. 276). In this respect too, the fact that the subject's attention is inessential to these lower fields of passivity, suggests that they are not "intentionally constituted in the same way that the objects of the ordinary attentive perception conditions are" (van Mazijk

2016, p. 277). Rather, the lower levels of passivity are characterized by "a kind of felt or affective structure" and in this manner sensations are built into affective fields prior to the subject directing attention to them. According to this account, certain fields of sensations may emit an "affective allure [that] may penetrate the ego, thereby awakening it", and in turn, the allure may be such that the ego turns towards the object as the source of affection. This lower level of affective perception may then provide the basis for an intentional act of perception to occur (van Mazijk 2016, p. 278). As a consequence, for Husserl, affection refers to an originary "structure and affective meaning." As he writes: "By affection we understand the allure given to consciousness, the peculiar pull that an object given to consciousness exercises over the ego…" (Husserl 2001, § 32, p. 196). The crux of Husserl's view is that without the lower-level affective states intentionality could not take place, as it first requires "that the ego's attention is awakened and enticed to perform intentional acts" (van Mazijk 2016, p. 278).

Although such affectivity forms a kind of lower level of perception, it nonetheless plays a central role in more active levels of intentionality. Important here is the relation between attention on the subject-side and affective allure on the object-side, and the role that motivation plays in perception that is central to Husserl's account. Husserl explains that an object which "stands out from a homogenous background and comes to prominence [might be said to 'strike'] us and this means that it displays an affective tendency toward the ego" (Husserl 1973, § 17, p. 76; my insertion). In this sense, however, when Husserl speaks of affection on the side of the object he is not referring to "a causal stimulus" but as Steinbock describes it, rather to a motivational "solicitation or pull to attentiveness", which might lead to an active response on the part of the subject (Steinbock 2004, 21; p. 24). This also suggests that "[i]ntentionality is not a one-sided structure that stems from consciousness" but that "it is bilateral, as it were, an *'active-active' structure*", involving subject and object, what Steinbock refers to as "a *'constitutive duet'*" (Steinbock 2004, p. 24). In other words, the object and the horizon in which it is situated provide an orientation for the subject toward which it may be motivated to turn in order to consider something more closely or more attentively. The subject may hear, see or smell something that entices her toward the object, whether this is the smell of coffee wafting toward me, the azure blue of the water shimmering outside my window, or the waves crashing against the shore in the distance.

In the Husserlian account, then, when we speak of "something coming into relief, it is *always an affectively charged relief*" (Steinbock 2004, p. 24; Husserl 2001, § 34, p. 211; § 35, pp. 216–217; § 35, p. 221). For example, when walking through a forest, purple wildflowers are suddenly caught by the sunlight and emit an affective allure within the perceptual field. In this sense, within my horizon there may be competing objects that catch my attention simultaneously, or that in fact block one affective force from another (Husserl 2001, § 31–32, pp. 195–197). For example, I hear a bird warbling outside the window but as I turn toward it the phone rings and draws my attention away. In such a scenario, the allure of the bird call may fade into the background of the phone ringing and although the musicality of the warble continues to exercise an allure, it may be diminished. Although the bird call is still on the horizon of my perception and still emits an allure, the allure may not have the same effect (see Steinbock 2004, p. 25). As van Mazijk suggests, Husserl's idea seems to be that "[w]ithout something affectively rising to prominence from the background, there can be no motivation for the ego to attentively engage in a perceptual act" (van Mazijk 2016, p. 280).

However, this account of affection only accounts for one of the lower levels of Husserl's account of perception, one which remains at the level of passivity. Beyond those lowest passive levels, however, Husserl enriches this picture with a notion of attentive perception, where 'attention' refers to "a tending of the ego towards an intentional object" (Husserl 1973, § 18, p. 80). The lowest level of attentive perception refers to a form of 'simple apprehension', and such forms of apprehension may occur when a "particular affective content in the background starts to stand out and yields perceptual attention". In order for something to be apprehended in this manner, it must "yield an affective allure strong enough to awaken the ego's attention" (van Mazijk 2016, p. 282). One of the examples that Husserl mentions is of a melody playing in the background, one that initially does not exercise an affective allure but then emits "an especially mellifluous sound" to which the ego turns (Husserl 2001, § 33, p. 203). This turning toward does not have to be deliberate on the part of the ego, rather it may be a habitual response such that a particular chord or phrasing attracts the subject with a particularly strong allure given that it is a favourite piece of music (Husserl 2001, § 33, p. 203).

In other words, whereas the original sound was only part of a complex field of unfixed affections competing for attention, the favorite chords and the "particularity of the sound has made [the subject] attentive" and the music becomes the object of a single focus (Husserl 2001, § 33, p. 203). Yet, at this point the music has not become an object in the full sense of the term. Hearing the music and being able to identify that it is Beethoven's Fifth, for example, would require a higher level of activity which is not characteristic of the passive field we have been discussing. However, these more active or higher-level forms of activity are not characteristic of the level of attention or attentive turning toward that are our focus here. For Husserl, the forms of attention being referred to here are part of the individual's temporal stream of experience and are not shareable with others nor do they involve higher-level judgements at this point (van Mazijk 2016, p. 283). Moreover, at this level of perception, Husserl also refers to a sense of developing perceptual interest that takes into account not merely the unity of the object perceived but may focus on one or more of its parts. For example, instead of only apprehending the wildflowers on the forest floor, their purple colour may become the focus of the subject's attention (cf. van Mazijk 2016, p. 283; Husserl 1973, § 112).

Notably, at this level, when it comes to the perception of objects, Husserl does not take into account the way in which intersubjective aspects are factored into our perceptual experience, in the sense that the object of perception is also there for others. At these lower levels of perceptual experience, Husserl seems to suggest that the intersubjective context is not a "necessary condition for having perceptual experiences", for at this point, we are only referring to an individual's own temporal stream of experience, one that is not directly shareable with others (van Mazijk 2016, p. 284; 283). This is a point we shall return to below.

However, at this stage, the analysis of the lower levels of perception is aimed at a reflection on the field of 'pure perception'. This is not to deny or ignore the higher levels of ego-activity that are required to form judgments about perceptual objects, but instead to ascertain the phases of perceptual experience in their own right in order to reflect upon the affective basis of both cognition and judgement. In this sense, to be clear, I am not eliminating these aspects from a broader consideration of perception, but my intention here is to reflect upon the affective and attentive dimensions of Husserl's approach. More specifically, I am interested in examining these affective dimensions in order to try to make sense of Honneth's notion of affective recognition and his claim that 'recognition' is prior to cognition, as well as Johnson's account of 'frozen intentionality' and 'interest'. This requires a consideration of the ways in which forms of intentionality and higher forms of activity (including cognition and judgement), in fact, presuppose a form of receptivity or an affective openness to the world, or, an ego that opens itself to the affective field.[2] In this sense, as Steinbock suggests, if we follow Husserl's insight, "affection is fundamental for anything becoming prominent in the perceptual field" and "'precedes' ...the givenness of the object" (Steinbock 2004, p. 27). It is "only afterward", Husserl writes, "that the object awakens "the interest in cognition" or "accedes to 'contemplative interest'" (Husserl 1973, § 14, p. 64).

---

[2] In doing so, I leave to one side the more complete account offered by Husserl. It is beyond the scope of this paper to investigate all aspects of the higher active levels of perception including cognition and judgment.

We could say, then, that the lower passive phases of affection move to a proto-active turning toward an object and eventually to a cognitive interest (Steinbock 2004, p. 31). The turning of the subject toward the object represents a move from passivity to activity and indicates an openness and receptivity towards the affective field. The activity of turning toward is then the first step towards an object-like formation, however, as Husserl makes clear it is still not a form of judgment or a cognitive interest "but it can motivate such an interest" (Steinbock 2004, p. 32). As Husserl conceives of it, receptivity is then essential for the move from passivity to activity and such receptivity motivates a turning toward (2001, § 49, p. 276).[3] However, for Husserl cognitive interest would require more than receptivity and would include not only thematization but also the explication of the object as object (Steinbock 2004, p. 35). At this point, closer scrutiny of the relation between interest, affect and intention in Husserl's account is instructive, alongside an understanding of habit and the genetic history of perception.

Affection and Attention as Interest

Maren Wehrle has articulated these forms of affectivity and attention in terms of a notion of 'interest' or what she terms 'attention as interest' (Wehrle 2015). Her reading suggests that interest can be understood as contributing not only to the constitution of the intentional object but also the continual opening of perceptual horizons that in turn motivate new perceptions and actions. In *Experience and Judgement*, Husserl describes this concept of interest in broad terms, writing: "Among such acts [of interest] are to be understood not only those in which I am turned thematically toward an object, perceiving it ... but in general every act of turning-toward of the ego, whether transitory or continuous, every act of the ego's being-with (*inter-esse*)" (Husserl 1973, § 20, p. 86). Wehrle suggests that we can interpret this in a Merleau-Pontian style as an involvement or engagement with the world; a being with or towards the world (Wehrle 2015, p. 55). In this sense, the turning toward that signals a move beyond affectivity can "be defined as a *bodily form of interest*" that has been "awakened by affection." As we have seen, such bodily turning toward might involve movement such as one's eyes moving or a hand reaching out to touch an object. However, as Wehrle

---

3 As Husserl puts it: "[t]he affections proceed to the ego from out of the passivity of the background; they are what are presupposed [for the ego] to turn toward. Carrying out this turning toward, the ego complies with the affection; it directs itself toward what is exercising affection" (Husserl 2001, § 14, p. 276).

suggests this may also indicate that such movements may be shaped or formed by embodied habits or memories (Wehrle 2015, pp. 55–56).

In fact, Wehrle argues that the explanation for one stimulus attracting the attention of the ego more than another can be attributed to "a habitual dimension of interest [that influences] every subjective experience" and orders the field of perception into more or less significant parts (Wehrle 2015, p. 57). Thus, she suggests that we also need to understand Husserl's notions of affection and attention by considering the relation between habit and interest as a factor that creates particular sensitivities or creates particular patterns of interaction between the subject and the world, and this insight also accords with Johnson's intuition about interest and frozen intentionality (Wehrle 2015, pp. 57–58). As Wehrle suggests, such sensitivities or patterns of interaction are shaped by a particular perceptual style, and this includes individual embodied skills and habits as well as the temporality of experience (Wehrle 2016, p. 61) Moreover, this individual embodied style is also one that develops within a cultural context and is embedded in a social and historical milieu. Thus, cultural norms shape what we see or fail to see, indicating that perception is never neutral. As Wehrle notes, then, norms already operate at the "lowest levels of experience where embodied experience leaves its traces in sedimentation and habitualization", therefore shaping how the subject is 'affected' (Wehrle 2016, pp. 61–62).

In this sense, in more general terms in relation to both passive and active levels, we can understand the notion of habituation to refer to a kind of historicity of sense-perception. In Husserl's genetic analysis, the notions of habitualization and sedimentation, refer to the temporal relations between acts.[4] Husserl describes 'habit' in relation to associations and the manner in which a relation is "established between an earlier and later segment of consciousness within one Ego-consciousness", which may be "'sediments' of earlier acts" (Husserl 1989, pp. 233–234). Moreover, as Sara Heinämaa (2015, p. 125) suggests, we can also suggest that "perception is pre-personal in the sense that is has a history and a prehistory." In other words, "perception includes sedimented accomplishments of earlier acts, some of which are not our own acts but of others unknown and preceding us in time" (Heinämaa 2015, p. 125). It also "includes the idea of a communal history of perceivers and a generative relation between them" such that "the person who perceives takes up a perceptual tradition..." (Heinämaa 2015, p. 137). But, in this sense, perception can also be viewed as a re-modifica-

---

[4] As Husserl writes: "Every perception, as a consciousness intending an actual objectivity, has its horizon of before and after. It refers back to what was perceived before, which can be presentified in memories, even when these are not immediately connected with the respective perception..." (Husserl 1973, § 38, p. 162).

tion and it is possible to produce various modifications or new versions of earlier perceptions (Heinämaa 2015, p. 133). In other words, it is important to note that habitual forms of perception can also be changed or modified.[5]

Wehrle articulates these habits in terms of 'habitual feelings', which she argues are the motor of concrete perception. As she understands it, feelings such as love can characterize a motivational aspect of perception, in this sense, feelings toward an object or another subject may not only motivate a current interest in performing an intentional act but may also become temporally extended habitualized feelings that shape further perceptions. For example, "to love someone" in this analysis "cannot be reduced to an actual act of value-perception of a loveable object but must be characterized as an attitude or habitualized feeling." Such habitualized feelings can then develop into the particular perceptual style of the subject in general, in the sense that the subject may be drawn to or notice things because of a similar stirring of the love feeling (Wehrle 2015, p. 60). In this sense, objects might be affectively perceived as 'enticing, beautiful, ugly, disgusting', and, so on, and this may mean the object is turned toward with "uncertainty, hope, fear, surprise" (Wehrle 2015, pp. 45–64). In Wehrle's terms, this also suggests that everything that is perceived is filtered through a particular interest even if such interest might lie at a relatively passive level. The notion of interest, then, refers to forms of habit that influence what in a given moment is able to affect me, or awaken my attention, because it stands out from the background of my former experience. In this sense too, we can say that already in sensation and receptive perception there is an implicit valuing and a structuring of the experiential field, and in this respect, it is possible to suggest that Husserl's account has affinities with but also enables us to enrich the account found in Honneth's work in regard to affective and evaluative perception. In *Ideas II*, Husserl acknowledges the manner in which "value ... can also arise in the manner of non-originary pleasure" and suggests that an evaluation can be made by the subject "without the feelings being moved originally" or in a genuine way (Husserl 1989, pp. 196–197). Here, Husserl points not only to the use-value of certain objects, but importantly to the way others apprehend objects in the same way as me and therefore the manner in which certain forms of perception acquire an intersubjective value.

Wehrle extends the analysis of Husserl by suggesting that we might speak of a notion of affective-intentionality to indicate that objects do not appear in a

---

[5] As shall be discussed below, this involves a feedback loop between higher level forms of judgement and reflection that also challenge established values and beliefs, as well as the modification of embodied habits.

neutral way but that intentional acts involve a certain motivation and intensity. In order to take notice of something or of someone (whether that motivation is positive or negative), they have to *interest* me or *affect* me. In this sense, the way that we affectively relate to things or are affected by them influences how we experience them. As a primary form, what Wehrle (following Slaby) terms affective-intentionality, suggests that intentionality is not a cold, detached, purely cognitive affair but is affective and feelings-involving (Wehrle 2015; Slaby 2008).

In general terms, Wehrle's argument is that perception and intentionality are not neutral or detached cognitive processes but are embodied and can be understood as "an affective way of relating to the world" (Wehrle 2015, p. 62; Slaby 2008). As Wehrle suggests, to have interest in something therefore refers to an affective involvement with the lifeworld and can vary according to felt intensity and the amount of engagement or feelings at any given time. However, this also suggests that interests are not static and pre-determined but can be remodified and changed over time due to both, the subject's own experience but also the interactions between subjects in the intersubjective lifeworld context. As Wehrle explains, this suggests that "the experiencing subject is therefore always embedded in an affective horizon" and that "[t]he perceived and experienced lifeworld displays itself not as something objective but as a subjective and moreover an intersubjective phenomenon of relevance" (Wehrle 2015, pp. 62–63).

These final remarks are particularly instructive for understanding forms of habitualization and sedimentation inherent to perception such as those described by Johnson, and the importance of lower levels of affectivity and attention in perception that Honneth also seeks to identify. The Husserlian account is important for providing the detail and phenomenological richness of such an account of affective attunement and attentive acknowledgement. Husserl's work also points to the way in which a remodification or rupture of such habitualized forms of perception requires intervention at the affective and attentive levels and the importance of the intersubjective background context for such perceptual modifications that are impacted by historical and cultural elements.

3 Reflexive Attention and Modifying Habits of Perception: Between Husserl and Honneth

This explication of Husserl's account of attention and affection goes someway to explaining Honneth's claim that affective recognition is prior to cognition, as well as the manner in which affection is related to habits of perception. It is important to note, however, that in the phenomenological account, habits are conceived in a positive manner in the sense that they "enable normality" and provide the subject with a stable, familiar and coherent way of experiencing the world. This is not only the case at the level of individual experience, which develops into a subject's habitual style, but as Moran suggests, habit is also associated with habitus and "the sedimentation of culture as tradition" (Wehrle 2016, p. 57; Moran 2011, p. 68). In *Ideas II*, Husserl points to the way in which affects, feelings and thoughts can be "motivated by [a subject's] milieu" and influenced by others, "whether [by] way of understanding or tradition" (Husserl 1989, p. 358).[6] Following Wehrle, it is possible to suggest that even forms of "bodily habituation" and "passive layers of experience are permeable to historical discourses." In this sense, as Wehrle argues, cultural and social norms are "literally embodied" such that norms "not only influence the way we ... think about the world, but also how we perceive it and are affected by it" (Wehrle 2016, p. 62; 57). The implication here, as outlined above, is that norms already operate at the lowest levels of passive experience in affection and attention.

However, Husserl also explicitly describes the way in which habits are not merely formed "with regard to originally instinctive behaviour" but also "with regard to free behaviour." Moreover, he points out that one can "yield" to drives and instincts "habitually" or one can "resist" them, arguing that "habit and free motivation intertwine" (Husserl 1989, p. 267). As Moran rightly argues, then, habit "is not to be understood as something merely, mechanical or automatic, a matter of sheer mindless reflex or repetition" (Moran 2011, pp. 56–57). These arguments are important not only in their own right, but also because they indicate that in the phenomenological account, habit is not immune from critical reflexivity and modification. Nonetheless, as Steinbock has suggested, even "attentive postures" remain at the level of 'mundane' experience and operate with certain taken-for-granted preconceptions of the world (Steinbock 2004). In this sense, as mentioned above, we are orientated by the normalcy of the natural attitude that orientates not only lived experience and the familiarity of passive habituality but also cognition. The question then becomes, how do we modify our affective, attentive and habitual forms of perception?

---

6 Husserl also describes habit or habitus in *Experience and Judgement* where he writes: "No apprehension is merely momentary or ephemeral ... The lived experience itself, and the objective moment constituted in it may become 'forgotten'; but for all this, it in no way disappears without a trace; it has merely become latent. With regard to what has been constituted in it, it is a possession in the form of a habitus, ready at any time to be awakened by association" (Husserl 1973, p. 122).

In this final section, I want to suggest that affectivity and attention, in one way or another, are not only fundamental to perception but are also central to both Husserl's and Honneth's accounts of critical reflexivity. In Husserl's work this is disclosed as a particular kind of reflexive attitude and 'forgetfulness of self', such that the subject is receptive to the givenness of the other and open to being summoned by them. In Honneth's work, affective-attunement is the basis of a primary account of intersubjectivity from which a secondary normative account emanates and against which critique is then articulated.

In this sense, it is important to note that by employing the notion of affective recognition, Honneth means to articulate something more than the different affective levels or phases of perception as articulated in Husserl's account. As we saw above, Honneth also claims that reification indicates a 'forgetfulness of recognition', that a contemplative and detached form of cognition has disrupted basic affective and non-reifying forms of perception. However, in Honneth's account, this also refers to a normative intersubjective claim. A forgetfulness of recognition implies we can identify a 'pure' non-reified form of intersubjectivity and return to what Honneth refers to as primordial affective recognition state, an apprehension of the other that, in certain respects, can be compared to Husserl's account of empathy, which also discloses intersubjectivity as a form of 'comprehending experiencing' in an affective and non-reified manner.[7]

However, there is a second important implication of Honneth's account. Honneth assumes that some form of higher-level reflexivity is required to be able to identify and critique certain forms of perception as objectifying or reifying. The implications of Honneth's account are that we need a certain reflexive and normative awareness and perhaps discursive articulation to identify those

---

[7] It is important to point out that throughout his work Husserl also employs the notion of 'empathy' to explain the kind of attention or recognition that is specific to the perception of other human beings. There are different levels and accounts of empathy in Husserl's work, but the most fundamental form is that which allows us to apprehend the perceived body of the other as a sensing body like my own and this occurs passively (see, for example, Husserl 1999; 1989). Husserl's notion of empathy is equivalent to a 'comprehending experiencing' and is often taken to refer to "a unique kind of experiential understanding of others" or a basic form of intentionality directed toward the experience of others (see Zahavi, 2019, pp. 251–260). Although the account of empathy is important to consider in relation to Honneth's account of recognition, I do not have the scope to provide an extensive discussion here. Suffice to say that my claim is that, despite their differences, Husserl's account of empathy discloses fundamental intersubjectivity in a manner akin to Honneth's account of recognition, which through expressive gestures reveals underlying recognitive relations. My suggestion is that, as with Honneth's account of affective recognition, Husserl's account of empathy is a primary and non-reifying form of perception. For a full account of this discussion see Petherbridge Forthcoming.

instances where affectivity and attentiveness have failed, and where an active turning toward does not occur, as in Johnson's experience with which we began. The implications of Honneth's account, or the critical impetus behind it, suggest that reifying and objectifying habits of perception can also be modified or ruptured, and thereby redirected so that they can resume their affective flow (see Petherbridge 2017; Al-Saji 2014, pp. 142–143).

In Honneth's account the ability to modify or change reifying forms of perception, even at an affective level, is addressed through his two-level account of recognition, whereby affective forms of attunement form the basis of a primary level upon which a second explicitly normative level of recognition is built. To this end, Honneth's account relies on the critical and normative influence of social-historical struggles for recognition that subsequently feedback normative claims and modifications into the affective and attentive levels of perception. The impetus for remodification, then, and the ability to be able to redirect affectivity and awaken attentiveness, assumes some kind of reflexive practice that raises an awareness of habitual forms of perception and motivates the interruption and modification of habits, movements and bodily style. This is underpinned by a normative claim built into the intersubjective fabric of recognition that orientates Honneth's approach, and to this end, it is possible to argue that primary affective-attunement forms the basis for a critical reflexivity that underpins Honneth's two-level account of recognition.

Although working from within an alternative orbit of orientation, it is possible to argue that affectivity and attentiveness also describe the method of reflexivity that is offered by Husserl in his account of the phenomenological reduction. Importantly, as Steinbock suggests, "the phenomenological attitude" can in fact be considered "a particular kind of reflective attentiveness" (Steinbock 2004, p. 41). In this sense, the phenomenological attitude requires that we bracket our mundane or habitual attitude to the world and by describing phenomena and reflecting upon our perceptual experience, "we open ourselves implicitly to the direct experience of them, and in so doing, open ourselves to being 'struck' by them, instigating a perceptual, an epistemic, [or even] a moral ... insight and relation" (Steinbock 2004, p. 41). In fact, Natalie Depraz (2004, p. 5; 8), has suggested that focusing on 'attention' offers an alternative way of understanding the phenomenological method, pointing to Husserl's early references to a 'phenomenology of attention' in works such as *Ideas I*. In this respect, attention can be understood in relation to 'modulation' or changeability in acts of consciousness, whereby forms of variation and adaptation are associated with acts of intentionality. As Depraz writes: "Whereas intentionality is a formal model of the structure of consciousness, whose openness lies in a linear directedness toward the object, attentionality as modulation furnishes every act of our consciousness with a material fluctuating density due to its inner variations and its concrete changeablity" (Depraz 2004, p. 14). As we have seen, the importance of attention and the various modes of affective and attentive experience become central in Husserl's genetic phenomenology. Depraz argues that 'attention', then, offers the possibility for a different reading of Husserl's method, describing in far more concrete terms not only "genetic constitution" but also "the real praxis of intentionality" and "the reduction" (Depraz 2004, p. 7).

In this vein, as Steinbock writes, if we understand the phenomenological attitude as a form of reflective attention in which we distance ourselves from the natural attitude, we gain insight into the way meaning is constituted as well as the potential for a shift of attitude. However, this does not mean that one can be completely removed from experiencing an object. Instead, experience of the object is described *at the same time* as experiencing it, such that in the same moment we can view it as if from a distance, as a disinterested observer. In this regard, Steinbock suggests, that out of all the "attentive attitudes" phenomenology is "most receptive to affection" (Steinbock 2004, p. 40). In this manner: "To describe modes of attentiveness in relation to affective forces is precisely to be *reflectively attentive to attention* in a unique way, not merely as a meta-reflection on what something is, but as an inquiry into how or the way in which things are given in our openness to them" (Steinbock 2004, p. 39, my emphasis). The crux of Husserl's insights about attentiveness in regard to critical reflection, then, is that we open ourselves to phenomena and allow ourselves to be struck by them in any way they might appear to us. Notably, Steinbock refers to this process, as a *"forgetfulness of the self as the openness to the allure."* Accordingly, this might be described as a kind of submission to the givenness of the object or the other at the most basic level of passive attentiveness (Steinbock 2004, pp. 40–41). Thus, where Honneth speaks of a 'forgetfulness' of intersubjectivity or recognition, as the basis for a lack of attentiveness and the inability of the subject to open itself reflexively to the other or to objects in the world, Husserl points to the way in which an openness and receptivity to the allure of the other requires a suspension of self, or the capacity to put the self to one side. In essence, both positions point to the intersubjective ramifications of such critical reflection, in the sense, that if we follow the Husserlian insight, the affective openness of self enables one to be attentive to the givenness of the other and to be receptive to them. In Honneth's terms, another way of speaking about giving oneself over to receptivity and 'being true to how the phenomena give themselves' in relation to other subjects, would be to open oneself to pre-reified stances that reveal the other prior to abstraction and to allow oneself to be affected by the other at a primary level of experience.

It is possible to suggest, then, that affectivity and attentiveness are not only basic to primary forms of recognition in Honneth's work, and to primary forms of perception in Husserl's account, but also to the very practice of the phenomenological attitude. Husserl, then, implicitly shines the spotlight on the very basis of critical reflection by illuminating not a forgetfulness of recognition, but the force of the allure of the other as well as openness or receptivity towards the other in affectedness and attentiveness. In this sense, receptivity and responsivity require not only an external excitation from others but also that we are motivated by such stimulation arising from others and turn to them with interest (cf. Waldenfels 2006). In the case of racializing perception, for such interest to be fostered, we first need to be made aware of our habitual actions and movements, and then motivated to take up new habits and styles of perception that express a positive evaluation of the other in our basic perceptual awareness of them. Alternatively, when such acknowledgement does not occur, for example, in forms of racializing perception, it may motivate the subject who has been ignored or looked through to actively seek some kind of attentiveness or responsivity from the other. Importantly, then, there is a feedback loop between higher levels of reflexivity, cognition and judgement, and affective and attentive habits or forms of interest in basic perception. The claim for affective responsivity and attentiveness therefore requires an interplay between these different dimensions. It also means that reifying and objectifying forms of perception must be modified and changed not only at cultural, normative and intersubjective levels but also at embodied and affective ones. In this sense, an account of affective-intentionality and reflexive attentiveness is central to such an analysis and provides the basis for a more comprehensive analysis of the distorting 'affects' of habitualized and distorted forms perception.

References

Al-Saji, Alia (2014): "A Phenomenology of Hesitation: Interrupting Racializing Habits of Seeing." In: Lee, Emily S. (Ed.): *Living Alterities: Phenomenology, Embodiment, and Race*. Albany: SUNY Press, pp. 133–172.
Depraz, Natalie (2004): "Where is the Phenomenology of Attention that Husserl Intended to Perform? A Transcendental Pragmatic-Oriented Description of Attention". In: *Continental Philosophy Review* 37, pp. 5–20.
Gallagher, Shaun (2008): "Direct Perception in the Intersubjective Context". In: *Consciousness and Cognition* 17, pp. 535–543.
Heinämaa, Sara (2015): "Anonymity and Personhood: Merleau-Ponty's Account of the Subject of Perception". In: *Continental Philosophy Review* 48, pp. 123–142.

Honneth, Axel (1995): *The Struggle for Recognition: The Moral Grammar of Social Conflicts*. Trans. Joel Anderson. Cambridge: Polity Press.
Honneth, Axel (2001): "Invisibility: On the Epistemology of 'Recognition'". In: *Recognition, Supplement of the Aristotelian Society* 75, pp. 127–139.
Honneth, Axel (2008): *Reification: A New Look at an Old Idea*. Martin Jay (Ed.). Oxford: Oxford University Press.
Husserl, Edmund (1973): *Experience and Judgement*. Trans. James Churchill/Karl Ameriks. Evanston: Northwestern University Press.
Husserl, Edmund (1989): *Ideas Pertaining to a Pure Phenomenology and to a Phenomenological Philosophy, Second Book. Studies in the Phenomenology of Constitution*. Trans. Richard Rojcewicz/André Schuwer. Dordrecht: Kluwer.
Husserl, Edmund (1999): *Cartesian Meditations: An Introduction to Phenomenology*. Trans. Dorion Cairns. Dordrecht: Kluwer.
Husserl, Edmund (2001): *Analyses Concerning Passive and Active Synthesis: Lectures on Transcendental Logic*. Trans. Anthony J. Steinbock. Dordrecht: Kluwer.
Jardine, James (2015): "Stein and Honneth on Empathy and Emotional Recognition". In: *Human Studies* 38(4), pp. 567–589.
Jardine, James (2020): "Social Invisibility and Emotional Blindness". In: Daly, Anya/Cummins, Fred/Jardine, James/Moran, Dermot (Eds): *Perception and the Inhuman Gaze: Perspectives from Philosophy, Phenomenology, and the Sciences*. London, New York: Routledge.
Johnson, Charles (1993): "A Phenomenology of the Black Body". In: *Michigan Quarterly Review* 32(4), pp. 599–615.
van Mazijk, Corijn (2016): "Kant and Husserl on the Contents of Perception". In: *The Southern Journal of Philosophy* 54(2), pp. 267–287.
Moran, Dermot (2011): "Edmund Husserl's Phenomenology of Habituality and Habitus". In: *Journal of the British Society of Phenomenology* 42(1), pp. 53–77.
Moran, Dermot (2016): *Edmund Husserl: Founder of Phenomenology*. Cambridge: Polity Press.
Petherbridge, Danielle (2013): *The Critical Theory of Axel Honneth*. Lanham: Lexington Books.
Petherbridge, Danielle (2017): "Racializing Perception and the Phenomenology of Invisibility". In: Dolezal, Luna/Petherbridge, Danielle (Eds.): *Body/Self/Other: The Phenomenology of Social Encounters*. Albany: SUNY Press.
Petherbridge, Danielle (2021): "Habit, Attention and The Phenomenology of Recognition". In *Convivium* 33, pp. 67–90.
Petherbridge, Danielle (forthcoming): "Empathy or Recognition? Husserl and Honneth on Intersubjectivity".
Ratcliffe, Matthew (2012): "Phenomenology as a Form of Empathy". In: *Inquiry: An Interdisciplinary Journal of Philosophy* 55(5), pp. 473–495.
Slaby, Jan (2008): "Affective Intentionality and the Feeling Body". In: *Phenomenology and the Cognitive Sciences* 7, pp. 429–444.
Steinbock, Anthony J. (2004): "Affection and Attention: On the Phenomenology of Becoming Aware". In: *Continental Philosophy Review* 37, pp. 21–43.
Varga, Somogy. (2010): "Critical Theory and the Two-Level Account of Recognition -Towards a New Foundation?". In: *Critical Horizons* 11(1), pp. 19–33.
Waldenfels, Bernhard (2006): "Responsivity of the Body: Traces of the Other in Merleau-Ponty's Theory of Body and Flesh". In: Hatley, James/McLane, Janice/Diehm,

Christian. (Eds.): *Interrogating Ethics: Embodying the Good in Merleau-Ponty*. Pittsburgh: Duquesne University Press, pp. 91–106.

Wehrle, Maren (2015): "'Feelings as the Motor of Perception'? The Essential Role of Interest for Intentionality". In: *Husserl Studies* 31, pp. 45–64.

Wehrle, Maren (2016): "Normative Embodiment. The Role of the Body in Foucault's Genealogy. A Phenomenological Re-reading". In: *Journal of the British Society for Phenomenology* 47(1), pp. 56–71.

Zahavi, Dan (2019): "Second-Person Engagement, Self-Alienation and Group Identification". In: *Topoi* 38(1), pp. 251–260.

Nicolas de Warren
Die äusserste Feindschaft: Heidegger, Anti-Judaism, and the War to End All Wars

Abstract: The aim of this paper is three-fold. First: to outline the characteristic features of a dynamic that works itself through and shapes the philosophical landscape in Germany during the 1920s and 1930s, and which Heidegger, in his own manner, channels and re-configures. Second: to explore the sense in which the "great war" for Heidegger as a spiritual conflict did not end in 1918. My argument here is that Heidegger internalizes this continuation of the war by other, philosophical means into his own thinking such that his own search for another beginning for thinking during the 1930s understands itself as the pursuit of the great war by other means, namely, through the means of a thinking of being. Third: to demonstrate that it is in this dual context, the first internalized within the second, and the second the externalization of the first, that Heidegger's confrontation with Judaism and his anti-Semitism must be situated. Heidegger's thinking repeats in his own way of historical repetition the confrontation between Judentum and Deutschtum during the First World War, and that this repetition structures Heidegger's Davos Disputation with Cassirer. The confrontation at Davos, as the failure to confront explicitly the question of Judentum and Deutschtum, represents an after-effect of the First World War: the dynamic of a violent confrontation without genuine encounter.

The Obstinate Puzzle

Philosophical thought has always sought to understand itself in opposition to prejudice. This opposition would appear straightforward even if the struggle against prejudice would appear to be unending. In its critical function, philosophical thought defines itself in confrontation with prejudice, as an unmasking of prejudice *as* prejudice and as an attempt to either dissolve or transform prejudice through such a revelation. In its self-critical function, philosophical thought understands itself as a confrontation with its own prejudices, as striving to expose itself to its own critical regard. In both instances, with the critical relation of philosophy towards non-philosophy as well as the self-critical relation of philosophy towards itself, philosophical thought aspires to a stance without prejudices left unchallenged or unclaimed. The more philosophy opposes the prejudices of non-philosophy, the more philosophy challenges itself. The more philosophy opposes its own prejudices, the more philosophy challenges the prejudices of non-philosophy. And even when the question of whether prejudices can in fact be surmounted remains inconclusive, philosophical thought, in some form or another, nonetheless aspires to a vigilance without prejudice.

This philosophical struggle against prejudice is equally a struggle against cliché. Prejudice often trades in the currency of cliché, for a telltale characteristic of prejudice is unthinking repetition and self-proliferation, where the mindlessness that necessarily accompanies prejudice glides along with the effortlessness in the trafficking of cliché. The transcendental apperception of prejudice is the *impossibility* of an "I think" that always accompanies speaking in cliché. This affinity between prejudice and cliché is held together by a third element. Banality is the bonding agent that allows prejudice and cliché to adhere to each other. The effective element of banality is superficiality, as a flattening of the space of reason and the time of thinking that renders seamless and unbreakable the lives of those caught and preserved in the amber of prejudice and cliché. A world thus flattened resembles Edwin Abbot's *Flatland* in which the square cannot convince his fellow two-dimensional forms of the existence of the other dimensions. On this picture, the *greatness* of philosophical thought could be seen as the effort to surmount flatlands of all kinds in a movement towards height or profundity.

This inverse relation between philosophical thought and the trinity of prejudice, cliché, and banality is ideally the more pronounced, the more a philosophical thinker is recognized as "great." Of course, philosophical thought is liable to fall into prejudices of its own kind, but even with such errancy, the greatness of a philosophical thought remains in keeping with the greatness of its prejudice. The insistence on a demarcation between depth and surface still obtains within the domain of philosophical prejudices. For it requires an uncommon depth of philosophical insight to uncover the great prejudices of philosophical thought as opposed to those banal prejudices that are immediately identifiable through clichés. Philosophical prejudices worn on the sleeves, as it were, do not require any special philosophical insight for their discovery. Such flat-out prejudices do not amount to "blindness in insight," but on the contrary to blindness plain and simple. There is thus a difference to be made between the *unthought* of philosophical thought and the *unthought* of philosophical non-thinking. Whereas the former is philosophically productive, the latter is philosophically unforgivable, since it would seem to represent a blasphemy against the genuineness of philosophy itself.

From consternation to distress to outrage, the range of responses to the publication of the first three volumes (as of the time of the writing of this essay) of Heidegger's *Schwarze Hefte* have each in their own manner confirmed the impatience of justice or the ruse of special pleading in the face of Anti-Semitism. The name itself, *Schwarze Hefte*, both amplifies and deflects the problems posed, and has undoubtedly cast an invisible spell over their reception from which it would seem impossible to escape cleanly. Whereas the adjective "black" is charged with menacing anonymity and sinister concreteness, the term "notebook" deflects the weight of impending darkness. Straightforwardly neither private diary, philosophical sketches, phenomenological laboratory, or visionary tracings, the hermeneutical ambiguity of just what kind of writing one is dealing with renders all the more complex the question of approach, and hence the kind of encounter, or confrontation, thought to be pursued.

Of the many challenges posed to philosophy by Heidegger's philosophical thought, the publication of the *Schwarze Hefte* gives added sharpness and urgency to the question of how to understand the relationship between philosophy and prejudice. The reception of the *Schwarze Hefte* and their amplifying force for the already complex debates and interpretations surrounding Heidegger's thinking reveals how confusing it becomes to think philosophically once a great philosopher has violated most flagrantly the inviolable opposition between philosophy and prejudice, between depth and superficiality, between sophistication and crassness, between originality and banality. At issue is not the unthought of philosophical thought, the philosopher and his shadow, but the unthought of philosophical non-thinking, the philosopher without a shadow. In one stroke, the constitutive opposition for the self-understanding and self-investment of philosophy becomes neutralized. We are left in a space without philosophical orientation. Not surprisingly, the spectrum of reaction has been predictable: the battening down of hatches, the jumping ship of opportunists, the inflated sense of triumph and self-vindication of those who always knew better, the denial of anything there by those who know best, etc.

The trafficking in prejudices, clichés, and banalities in Heidegger's *Schwarze Hefte*, and more specifically, the *philosophical* status of Anti-Judaism in Heidegger's thinking, challenges directly an entrenched image of philosophy as well as a certain fixed idea of who we expect and demand the philosopher to be. This trafficking in philosophical contraband within an endeavor to produce the genuine article of philosophical thought produces an effect that is essentially uncontrollable (and hence the range of response stretches from extreme damage control to the extreme optimization of damage). We are faced with an hermeneutical disorder that challenges the principle of hermeneutical charity. Either one accepts hermeneutical charity and orchestrate some kind of hermeneutical separation between "thinker" and "thought" or some kind of hermeneutical compartmentalization between the true "depth" of Heidegger's thinking and its regrettable moments of "superficiality," or else one rejects any hermeneutical charity and regard Heidegger's thinking unforgivingly as fundamentally contaminated and non-philosophical. We face what George Steiner in his discussion of T. S. Eliot's anti-Semitism has insightfully called an "obstinate puzzle." As he remarks with regard to Eliot's anti-Semitism: "The obstinate puzzle is that Eliot's uglier touches tend to occur at the heart of very *good* poetry (which is *not* the case of Pound)" (letter to the *Listener* cited in Ricks 1988, p. 28). Whereas for Steiner, one would not necessarily lose the great poetry of Pound by jettisoning or disconnecting his undeniably shrill anti-Semitism, the "uglier touches" of anti-Semitism "are not only continuous with Eliot's greatness as a poet but are sometimes intimate with it" (Ricks 1988, p. 29). It is arguably this *intimacy* of prejudice and clichés to the greatness of Heidegger as a thinker that challenges to the point of blasphemy the self-understanding of philosophy that has endured since its first aspiration to surmount the flatland of unthinking banality and blinded animus.

The Approach

In order to approach this nest of problems, one would do well to begin with the historical situation of Heidegger's thinking—an historical situation that is not our own. As I shall explore here, this historical situation is decisively marked by the First World War and, to advance my thesis more explicitly, and for what most immediately concerns us, the *Schwarze Hefte*, and the emerging horizon during the Weimar Republic of a Second Thirty Years War. Although this notion is not without controversy among historians of the 20th-century, and was fashioned in an explicitly controversial manner by Ernst Nolte, a *sense* for this notion operates tacitly in Heidegger's philosophical thought during the 1930s in terms of which, as I shall argue, Heidegger's relation to Judaism and his anti-Semitism needs to be understood, that is, confronted and engaged.

In a lecture to students at his former Gymnasium in Konstanz on May 26 (or 27), 1934, in a speech called "Twenty-Five Years after Our Graduation," Heidegger reflects on the meaning of remembrance and mourning in light of the First World War that affected profoundly and irrevocably his generation. Rather than considering the War as an event of the past, as an event "already some twenty years distant from us," Heidegger encourages, in asking his audience to "please rise and think of them (*fallen comrades*)" to consider in a different light. As he proclaims, it is an "illusion" to think of the war as of the past, "for the Great War comes over us *now* for the *first* time." The grand illusion of the war is that the war has been lost. The war is yet to begin. As he warns: "The Great War must now be *spiritually* won by us, i.e., battle will become the *innermost law* of our existence." This coming and continuing "battle" (*Kampf*) is spiritual in its essence; it calls for the awakening of a new form of thinking and another beginning. As Heidegger remarks: "Our awakening (*der Aufbruch unserer*) to the two millions dead in all those endless graves—which the borders of the Reich and German Austria wear like some mysterious crown—only now begins (*beginnt erst*)" (Heidegger 2000, pp. 279–284).

Heidegger's 1934 Reunion Speech crystallizes a perception and mentality that was not uncommon during the years spanning 1918 and 1939. In Heidegger's speech we witness first hand the continuation of the "great war" after the ostensible cessation of hostilities in 1918, and this continuation occurred essentially on a spiritual (*geistig*) front of struggle. This spiritual continuation of the First World War reflects in part the profound cultural consequence of the German Revolution of 1918–1919 which effectively represented the continuation of the First World War through its *internalization* or *inwardization* within German culture. The dynamic and hostility released and mobilized during the war *against* external enemies became re-channeled *internally*, with an even more intense search for enemies and hardening of fronts. As the historian Sebastian Haffner argues, the German Civil War in January – May 1919 "laid down the shunts, or switches, for the disastrous history of the Weimar Republic that was both from it (the Civil War) and the emergence of the Third Reich, which was produced by it (the Civil War)" (Haffner 2008, p. 28). The irrevocable political and cultural parting of ways that became shunted along the tracks of violence and resentment established during this passage from World War to Civil War means that the war did not end in 1918 but was continued by other means. Indeed, it is arguably the Civil War of 1918 that marks the veritable center of gravity for Heidegger's conception of the "great war" as "still before us." And it is in this sense that the great war is still to begin and that this new beginning is in turn a repetition of the "first" world war into a "second" in which the "great test of all being" will be decided. As Heidegger revealingly observes in a note on Ernst Jünger in a lecture from 1939–1940: "His poetry, thought, and message (*Sagen*) is determined through the First World War. Now that surely goes for everything that realized itself as human-historical activity and thought in the period after the war (*Nachkriegszeit*) or we now say more accurately, in the period between the wars (*Zwischenkriegszeit*)" (Altman 2012, p. 5).

I want to proceed in three steps. First: I want to outline the characteristic features of a *dynamic* that works itself through and shapes the philosophical landscape in Germany during the 1920s and 1930s, and which Heidegger, in his own manner and style, both channels and re-configures. Second: I want to explore in greater detail the sense in which the "great war" for Heidegger as a *spiritual conflict* did not end in 1918 and was still about to begin. My argument here is that Heidegger internalizes this continuation of the war by other, philosophical means into his own thinking such that his own search for another beginning for thinking during the 1930s understands itself as the pursuit of the great war by other means, namely, through the means of a thinking of being. Third: I want to demonstrate that it is in this dual context, the first internalized within the second, and the second the externalization of the first, namely, that Heidegger's confrontation with Judaism and his anti-Semitism must be situated. Specifically, I shall argue that Heidegger's thinking *repeats* in his own sense of historical repetition the confrontation between *Judentum and Deutschtum* during the First World War, and that this repetition structures Heidegger's Davos Disputation with Ernst Cassirer—a debate that did not take place in the form in which it was to have taken place. In this respect, the confrontation at Davos, as the failure to confront explicitly the question of *Judentum and Deutschtum* reflects in turn a lasting after-effect of the First World War: the dynamic of a violent confrontation without genuine encounter, or, in other words, *der Fronterlebnis*.

Kriegsphilosophie

With the outbreak of hostilities in 1914, the war to end all wars became widely perceived as the "original catastrophe" of the 20[th]century. In the words of Henry James, writing to a friend: "The plunge of civilization into this abyss of blood and darkness by the wanton feat of those two infamous autocrats is a thing that so gives away the whole long age during which we have supposed the world to be, with whatever abatement, gradually bettering, that to have to take it all now for what the treacherous years were all the while really making for and *meaning* is too tragic for any words" (Letter of August 4, 1914; James 1920, p. 384). Even if too tragic for any words, the war nonetheless provoked an historically unprecedented "spiritual mobilization" (to adopt Kurt Flasch's felicitous expression; 2000) of philosophical and literary discourse, and in no other belligerent nation was this mobilization of the intellect in the cause of war as pervasive and committed as in Germany.

The sociological and cultural reasons for this exceptional German mobilization of spirit are to be sure complex. The cultural investment of philosophy within German universities entrusted philosophy with a critical function for German national self-consolidation. Exemplified in the iconic status of Fichte on the eve of the First World War, the idea of the German nation was inseparable from the Idea of German philosophy itself. From the heady days of August, 1914, as argued by Modris Eksteins, "most Germans regarded the armed conflict they were entering in spiritual terms. The war was above all an idea, not a conspiracy aimed at German territorial aggrandizement" (Eksteins 1989, p. 90). Indeed, this spiritual or metaphysical conception of the war, in which philosophy became primary theatre of contestation, is both echoed and amplified directly in Heidegger's 1934 Reunion Speech. As he declares: "the *actuality* of this gigantic event that we call the First World War is even now gradually entering a realm beyond the question of guilt or innocence of its origins, beyond all questions of imperialism or pacifism." Explicit in Heidegger's pronouncement is the belief that the war's genuine spiritual significance can only be discovered after the war has been, in one sense, declared "over" such that, in another sense, indeed, its genuine sense, the war can first truly begin. It is in this philosophical sense that Heidegger can speak in 1934 of the Great War as "coming over us *now* for the *first* time," and if such words are spoken at a class reunion, and not in an academic setting, one can infer with certainty that Heidegger's message spoke to audience for whom such a sentiment was neither unfamiliar nor unexpected.

Aside from this reciprocal cultural investment of philosophy and war, the exceptional mobilization of philosophical discourse in search of the war's meaning during the immediate war years of 1914–1919 reflected the absence of any unified and/or compelling rationale for the war within the public sphere (Münkler 2014, p. 215 ff.). The strategic-geographic position of Germany between two hostile fronts further exacerbated the confusion of war-aims. Who was the genuine enemy—France, England, or Russia? This absence of political clarity and open public debate, coupled with the cultural prestige of philosophy, invited divergent interpretations regarding the "meaning" of the war. As Thomas Mann observed, within this political vacuum, reflection on the war's meaning remained "unpolitical," entirely detached, in other words, from actual political considerations and influence. Rather than "war-philosophy" as the pursuit of politics by other means, in the absence of any clarity regarding the political aims of the war, the war discourse of German philosophy can be seen as the pursuit of an absent politics by other means, namely, through "extra-political" or "un-political" means. Philosophical discourse sustained the "de-politization" of the war by elevating the war's meaning to metaphysical significance at the expense of any clear-sighted political meaning and debate—a debate foreclosed by the military dictatorship that effectively governed Germany until the revolution of 1918/1919. Intellectual and political critique of the war was impossible and dissenting voices were immediately suppressed as with the imprisonments of Karl Liebknecht and Rosa Luxemburg.

Within this context, a particular dynamic took shape and form, and arguably transformed the landscape of German philosophical thought. Philosophical discourse became transformed—"weaponized"—into the pursuit of the war by other means. At the same time, the war itself became understood in metaphysical terms, and hence as itself the realization of philosophy by other means. Philosophy opened another front, indeed, the true "front" of the war, given the widely ascribed and *expected* spiritual, or philosophical, significance of the war. The function of philosophical discourse in its mobilization as *Kriegsphilosophie* thus consisted in *both* the illumination and legitimation of the war's spiritual dimension *and* the pursuit of the war within the realm of spirit itself. In this respect, the war was seen as a "philosophical war," as both an existential struggle for existence *and* as an existential struggle, or moment of decision, for fundamental values—spiritual values. Within this philosophical crucible—philosophy as the pursuit of war by other means and the war as the pursuit of philosophy by other means—became even more complex in Germany after the November Armistice of 1918. For even if 1918 brought a cessation of hostilities between Germany and the Entente Powers, it did not bring about a cessation to hostilities to Germany. Indeed, the dynamic of the war became internalized into a Civil War along with an increasing internalization of the war within philosophical thought. In this latter regard, philosophical discourse after the Armistice of 1918 in many respects can be understood as a continuation of the war by other means—its prolongation in spiritual terms even as the war had, in one sense, ended. Did the war in fact end in 1918? As exemplified in Heidegger's philosophical thought, it is arguably the case that the mobilization of philosophy in pursuit of the war's genuine significance *intensified* after the cessation of hostilities and "defeat" of Germany in November 1918. A volatile culture of philosophy was thus produced (in parallel to the volatile culture of the Weimar Republic): even though the war had been lost "materially" and "empirically," the war continued nonetheless within spiritual life, and indeed, as the spiritual life, of philosophical thought. In this manner, philosophy represented sublimation of the defeat of November 1918 into an expectation for a spiritual victory yet to come.

This cultural and spiritual reversal of Germany's defeat in 1918 through spiritual sublimation and renewal engaged another facet of the complex war-dynamic that structures philosophical thought during and after the war. During the conflict, German philosophers were fixated on the question "who is the enemy?" This obsession for the identity of the true enemy reflected on the geo-political plane Germany's strategic situation of occupying a middle-position between the Western and Eastern Fronts (and eventually a Southern Front, with the entry of Italy into the war). On a philosophical plane, the question of the enemy was configured in spiritual terms through an instable relationship between, on the one hand, an absence of clarity as to the truth of the veritable enemy and, on the other hand, a spiritualization of the enemy. The figure of enemy was no longer understood as a purely economic or even political configuration, but as a "metaphysical" and "existential" configuration; the enemy was not just a nation or civilization, but a philosophical idea embodied in a nation and culture. As the painter Franz Marc observed in his essay written shortly before his death on the front in *Das geheime Europa* (1914/1978): "Denn in diesem Krieg kämpfen wir nicht, wie es in Zeitungen steht und wie die Herrn Politiker sagen, die Zentralmächte gegen einen äusseren Feind, auch nicht eine Rasse gegen die andere, sonder dieser Grosskrieg ist in europäischer Bürgerkrieg, ein Krieg gegen den inneren, unsichtbaren Feind des europäischer Geistes."

This battle against "the invisible enemy" animated the discourse of *Kriegsphilosophie* and transformed philosophical thought itself into a form of *Fronterlebnis*. Philosophical *theoria*, as the theatre for philosophical insight, became transformed into a theatre of operations; it opened another front in the multiple fronts of the war and it is perhaps in this sense that we can truly speak of the war as "global," namely, not merely in the sense in which the war was fought in different military theatres of operation around the world (in Africa, in the Pacific Ocean, etc.), but that the war became fought within the theatre of philosophical theory itself. The transformation of philosophical discourses into itself a spiritual front, and hence its own form of *Fronterlebnis*, produced two paradoxical dynamics. The first was the configuration of philosophical discourse along Manichean oppositions without the possibility of *reciprocal* reconciliation. Framed within oppositions of extremes (e.g., French decadence vs. German *Spirit*), the meaning of triumph, or victory, took on the form of a transcendence or surmounting of the very terms of opposition in the name of purity or genuineness of an enduring set of values. Notions such as "purity" (*Reinheit*), "authenticity" (*Eigenlichkeit*), and "sacred" (*heilig*) took on a superlative and surcharged meaning: such meanings both framed the terms of extreme oppositions (e.g., spirit vs. materiality) *and* exceeded, or transcended, the dialectic of opposition such that the triumph of "spirit" could only have the form of an unconditional triumph over the opposition itself. And yet, this configuration of philosophical discourse along the frontlines of Manichean oppositions resulted in what is unquestionably the most distinctive dynamic of *Kriegsphilosophie* as what I shall call an existential investment in conflict without encounter. The intensity of confrontation inhibited any genuine encounter, and hence recognition, with "the enemy," and in this paradoxical sense, the enemy remained perpetually invisible, misrecognized, or "dis-recognized," as it were, precisely to the degree that the confrontation with the "enemy" became more intense and Manichean. *Polemos* is henceforth no longer understood within a dialectical logic of recognition and possible reconciliation or "higher synthesis."

This dynamic of confrontation without encounter results in the fashioning and circulation of the *figural presence* of the enemy in the form of caricatures, clichés, stereotypes, etc.—different modes of representation in which the figure of the enemy is *conjured* in a medium of non-thinking that gives such figures the opacity of the real and hence the sharpness of a real threat. The fashioning of such "figurations" of the enemy attests to the proliferation in the form of *Kriegsphilosophie* of what Sartre, in another context of analysis, has usefully termed "Idea-exis," or, in other words, the manner in which an idea becomes a collective "non-thought," as with the exemplary instance of racism. As Sartre observes in *The Critique of Dialectical Reason*: "The essence of racism, in effect, is that it is not a system of thoughts which might be false or pernicious [...] *It is not a thought at all* [...] The Idea as a product of the common object has the materiality of a fact because no one thinks it. Therefore it has the opaque indubitability of a thing" (Sartre 2004, p. 300). As a further consequence, any clear and stable separation between "pure" philosophy and ideology, between concept and cliché, collapses within this crucible of transformation, as structured by what I have called "extreme confrontation without encounter," or the confrontations whose aim is to miss any veritable encounter. The composition of philosophical discourse during the war and into the troubled years of the Weimar Republic resembles a sort of *collage* in which concept and cliché appear together and in conjunction within the same plane of discourse.

Eine Grossen Feind

Heidegger's reflections in the first *Schwarze Hefte* (*Winke X Überlegungen (II) und Anweisungen*) from October 1931 begin innocently enough with a question whose meaning *for us* today, in light of the publication of the *Schwarze Hefte*, has become even more complex and pressing than Heidegger himself could have then imagined: "Was sollen wir tun?" (GA 94, p. 1). Scattered among a set of opening reflections, or more accurately represented, questions concerning the task of philosophy, the being of human existence (*der Mensch*) and "nothing" (*das Nichts*), we find a number of reflections on Heidegger's own magnum opus *Sein und Zeit* that clearly express frustration and disappointment with its reception as well as its conception. It is during these years and also in these pages that Heidegger's philosophical thought comes to search for "another beginning" and "another thinking," thus moving away and beyond the horizon of thinking that defined the compass of *Sein und Zeit*. Within this mix of thoughts in answer to Heidegger's question—was sollen wir tun?—a question arguably as much *to himself*, one finds a revealing entry that allows for an insight into a nascent dynamic that would come increasingly to animate and shape the reflections in the *Schwarze Hefte*. In reference to *Sein und Zeit*, Heidegger remarks: "Einwand gegen das Buch: ich habe auch heute noch nicht genug Feinde – es hat mir nicht einen Grossen Feind gebracht" (GA 94, p. 9). The sentiment expressed here is obviously complex as it entangles within itself a marked sense of solitude (indeed, the *Schwarze Hefte* are characterized by the intimacy of a thought with itself), a profound disappointment with the failure of a great philosophical work's all too mundane and ontic, as it were, reception, and the search for a great struggle in which to measure and define oneself philosophically. Above all, this conglomeration of sentiments centers on the need for a "great enemy" and thus reveals the depth to which the polemical dimension of Heidegger's thinking turns on a confrontation with "great enemies," without which the "decision" between being and beings cannot be attained. As Heidegger reflects in another notebook (*Überlegungen IX*) from 1939:

> Der Gegensatz zum *polemos* (als dem Wesensgrund des Ab-wesens Krieg (Schlacht)) is nicht der lahme Friede und die blosse fortschrittliche Kulturförderung und 'sittliche' Hebung der 'Gesellschaft', sondern das ursprünglich ganz Andere zum *polemos* ist die Entscheidung zwischen Seyn und dem 'Seienden' (GA 94, p. 188)

An implicit distinction is drawn in this reflection between "mundane" and "great" enemy, and such a distinction mirrors the distinction between the opposition between war and peace, on the one hand, and the decision for and revelation of – in a word: thinking – the truth of being. As Heidegger spells out in the following reflection:

> Wer die Entscheidungen nicht weiss, kann auch nie wissen, was der Krieg ist, auch wenn er ihn 'mitgemacht' hat. Er kennt nur das Grauenvolle und Bittere der Schrecknisse dessen, was sich begibt, er kennt auch die Aufschwünge zu Opfer und Haltung innerhalb der abrollenden Begegnisse, er weiss aber niemals vom Wahrheitsgrund und Ungrund, davon, dass Krieg und Frieden immer noch auf der *einen* Seite – des Seienden – liegen und niemals die Kraft der Wesung einer Wahrheit *des* Seyns in sich tragen. (GA 95, p. 189)

Heidegger here echoes himself from his earlier 1934 Reunion Speech: "For the bourgeois, battle is always only argument, quarrelsome wrangling, and a disruption.—For essential men, battle is a *great test* of all being [...]." One can extrapolate from these statements that for the "essential philosopher" the struggle of philosophy is not a matter of "argument" or "quarrelsome wrangling," but an existential question of a "great test" and "great decision" for the truth of being, and that such greatness can only be achieved through a confrontation with a *great enemy*, and precisely not an enemy who appears and becomes confronted in an argument or a quarrelsome wrangling. The great enemy must remain, in one sense, *invisible* from the point of view of any oppositional dialectic of argument and wrangling and yet, in another sense, the great enemy remains invisible because, as of 1931, Heidegger's own thinking in the form of *Being and*

Time has not brought it forth, this great enemy without which thinking itself cannot endeavor upon its great struggle. Indeed, as I would like to suggest, the development of the *Schwarze Hefte* can be understood as Heidegger's increasing search *for great enemies* with which to orient his search for another beginning and another thinking. Such great enemies must be *metaphysical*, and such metaphysical enemies, by virtue of inhibiting a decision for being and beings—the truth of being—are not enemies with which understanding, communication, and argument are possible. On the contrary, as Heidegger remarks in *Überlegungen XIV* from 1940/41:

> Auch der Gedanke einer Verständigung mit England im Sinne einer Verteilung der 'Gerechtsamen' der Imperialismen trifft nicht ins Wesen des geschichtlichen Vorgangs, den England jetzt innerhalb des Amerikanismus und des Bolshewismus und d. h. zugleich der Rolle des Weltjudentums zu Ende spielt. Die Frage nach der Rolle des *Weltjudentums* ist keine rassische, sondern die metaphysische Frage nach der Art von Menschentümlichkeit, die *schlechthin ungebunden* die Entwurzelung alles Seienden aus dem Sein als weltgeschichtliche 'Aufgabe' übernehmen kann. (GA 96, p. 243)

A great enemy with whom no understanding (*Verständigung*) is possible or desirable is an enemy with which a veritable confrontation demands a logic of *non-contact and non-encounter*. It is an enemy whom must always remain invisible and yet whose invisibility must in turn carry the full presence of ontological threat or force against which a great struggle for the truth of being can be orchestrated. The enemy must take the form of figural presence, or, in other words, a metaphysical form of cliché.

1936

In an essay that deserves more attention than it has yet received, *Mal et modernité: Le travail de l'histoire*, first presented at a conference on Marc-Bloch in 1990, Jorge Semprún observes:

> Le plus scandaleux, donc, n'est pas que Heidegger ait appartenu au parti nazi. Le plus scandaleux est qu'une pensée originale et profonde, dont l'influence d'une manière ou d'une autre s'est étendu au monde entier, ait pu considérer le nazisme comme un contre-mouvement spirituel historiquement capable de s'opposer du déclin présumé d'une sociéte mercantile et massifiée. Il faut, en somme, affronter et assumer le scandale dans sa radicalité: ce n'ext pas parce que qu'il est l'un des plus considérables philosophes de ce siècle qu'il faut occulter, nier ou minimiser l'appartenance de Heidegger au nazisme. Ce n'est pas parce qu'il fut nazi qu'on peut refuser de questionner jusqu'au bout le fond et la raison de son questionnement. (Semprún 2012, p. 706)

It is a passage that would require an extended meditation. With the publication of the *Schwarze Hefte*, two significant *précisions* can be introduced with regard to Semprún underlying intuition in this set of reflections. The first is both a confirmation and complexification of Heidegger's search for another beginning through an alignment with National Socialism. In a reflection from *Überlegungen XI* in 1939, Heidegger corrects his own philosophical assessment of his earlier perception of National Socialism. As he notes:

> Rein 'metaphysisch' (d.h. seynsgeschichtlich) denkend habe ich in den Jahren 1930–1934 den Nationalsozialismus für die Möglichkeit eine Übergangs in einen anderen Anfang gehalten und in ihm diese Deutung gegeben. [...] Aus der vollen Einsicht in die frühere Täuschung über das Wesen und die geschichtliche Wesenskraft des Nationalsozialismus ergibt sich erst die Notwendigkeit seiner Bejahung und zwar aus *denkerischen* Gründen. Damit ist zugleich gesagt, dass diese 'Bewegung' unabhängig bleibt von der je zeitgenössenischen Gestalt und der Dauer dieser gerade sichtbaren Formen. (GA 95, p. 408)

Heidegger's own self-correction distinguishes between the contemporary and "empirical," as it were, movement of National Socialism—with its blind obedience, its racial conception of Judaism, its embrace of *Machenschaft*, etc.—and an envisioned *spiritual* form which would both be the horizon for his thinking as well as for the "other beginning" of philosophical thought. The second offers a clue for the *philosophical* form in which this alignment between a metaphysical, or spiritual, form of National Socialism, clearly distinguished by Heidegger from what he also calls vulgar National Socialism, and Heidegger's own thinking will be realized. In a reflection from *Überlegungen XII* (1939), Heidegger reflects: "'Der deutsche Idealismus' – ist ein sehr ungefährer Titel, in dem wir die damit genannte Metaphysik noch nicht in ihrer Deutschheit begreifen." In a sharpened echo of this reflection, Heidegger further remarks: "Der deutsche Idealismus ist für die Deutschen und damit für die Geschichte des Abendlandes *eine noch ungeschehene Geschichte*, in deren Bereich historische Gelehrsamkeit nichts zu suchen, weil nie etwas zu finden hat" (GA 96, p. 7; 11).

German Idealism is a German metaphysics in which the "Germanness" (*Deutschheit*) is thought and realized, and this metaphysical significance is not only for Germans but also for Western history as such. German Idealism has yet to begin, and hence the search for another beginning, when thought within the narrative of a *seynsgeschichtlich* manner of thinking, converges with the search *through or from thinking* (i.e., *aus denkerischen Gründen*) for a "spiritual" form of National Socialism. Semprún's underlying intuition leads directly, through these two parallel *précisions*, to Heidegger's conception of German Idealism as the philosophical form in which his confrontation with and search for "great enemies" will be orchestrated. As with the First World War, German Idealism becomes *die Träger* of Germanness (*Deutschheit*), German Spirit, and Germanic struggle, and as with the First World War, it is by way of a return to German Idealism that another beginning for Germany thinking is pursued, where this other beginning will be formed in the crucible of confrontation, albeit a confrontation without encounter.

Heidegger's 1936 lectures on Schelling's *Treatise on Human Freedom* is in this respect exemplary. 1936, as Semprún reminds us in his essay, is itself a momentous year in the crisis of the European spirit: the Spanish civil war has just begun, Stalin begins his show-trials in Moscow, Husserl delivers the first sections of his text *The Crisis of the European Sciences* to Cercle philosophique de Prague, Walter Benjamin writes his essay *The Work of Art in the Age of Mechanical Reproduction*. For a philosopher who is famed for having once started a lecture course on Aristotle in 1924 with the terse statement, "regarding the personality of a philosopher, our only interest is that he was born at a certain time, that he worked, and that he died," it is surprising indeed that Heidegger begins his lectures on Schelling with an extended discussion of the historical situation of Schelling's 1809 treatise.

The date is itself significant for as Heidegger remarks: "1809: Napoleon beherrschte, d.h. hier: bedrückte und schmähte Deutschland" (Heidegger 1995, p. 1). As Heidegger stresses in no uncertain terms, *das Reich* and hence Germany does not even exist in name (*bestand nicht einmal mehr den Namen nach*) after the defeat of Prussia at the battles of Jena and Auerstadt in 1806. With Napoleon's first defeat in 1809 at the battle of Aspern (meted by the Austrians) and Fichte's *Reden an die Deutsche Nation* in 1808, Prussia has begun a process of re-awakening, renewal of spirit and another, new beginning. Heidegger briefly lists a number of critical figures in this re-constitution of German *Geist:* Schiller, Goethe, Wilhelm von Humboldt, and, with a special emphasis, the *soldier*, Scharnhorst. As Heidegger comments: "Alle die neuen Männer aber – ganz verschieden und eigenwillig in ihrer Art – waren einig in dem, was sie wollten. Was sie wollten, kommt in jenem Mahnwort zum Ausdruck, das unter ihnen umging. Sie nannten unter sich den werdenden preussischen Staat den '*Staat der Intelligenz*', d.h., des Geistes" (Heidegger 1995, p. 2). As Heidegger rounds-out this cursory evocation of the renewal of German spirit from its humiliation, defeat, and destruction at the hands of the French, it is not, as he argues, and against Napoleon's statement to Goethe at their meeting in Erfurt in 1808, that "die Politik ist das Schicksal," but that, on the contrary, that "der Geist ist das Schicksal und Schicksal ist Geist," where moreover "das Wesen des Geistes aber ist die Freiheit." Schelling's treatise, in which this thesis is developed, is thus the more profound work of German Idealism, and along with Hegel, whose *Phenomenology of Spirit* appeared in 1806 (and was famously completed as Hegel heard the cannon fire from the battle of Jena), Schelling and Hegel "vollbrachten [...], jeder nach seinem Gesetz, eine Gestaltung des deutschen Geistes, deren Verwandlung in eine geschichtliche Kraft noch nicht vollzogen ist [...]" (Heidegger 1995, p. 3).

Notable is that it is for Heidegger Schelling and Hegel, and explicitly *not* Fichte, who represent the genuine form for a German Idealism yet to be fully realized (GA 96, p. 9). This displacement of the center of gravity within the constellation of German Idealism marks a substantial displacement of the form in which German Idealism functioned within the *Kriegsphilosophie* during the First World War in which Fichte served as the *Kriegsphilosophe par excellence*. In the war-writings of Eucken, but also in Husserl's lectures on Fichte's Idea of Humanity in 1917, the spiritual center of German Idealism, as both the original philosophy of the Nation and the original Nation of philosophy, resides with Fichte. Yet this displacement of the form in which German Idealism is evoked as the genuine philosophy, or metaphysics, of Germanness nonetheless *repeats*, albeit in this displacement, the form of *confrontation* in which and for which German Idealism stands. And this form of confrontation, this significance of German Idealism as marking a struggle and a front, is characteristically visible, or apparent, only to the extent that the *enemy* remains invisible, or partly visible, that is, appears only as a *spectral figure* or figural presence. In the passages just quoted from Heidegger's Schelling lectures, the single marker for this opposition is, of course, the figure of *Napoleon*, and hence, France. For in 1809 Napoleon "dominates" Prussia, and this means, according to Heidegger: *oppresses and shames*—an indirect allusion, I suggest, to the Treaty of Versailles. In fact, 1936 marked a crucial year in the emancipation of Germany from the Versailles Treaty under the leadership of Hitler: in 1936, Hitler decides to re-occupy the Rhineland, thus forcing the French garrisons to abandon their positions. As Hitler proclaims in a speech (March 22) with regard to this bold provocation: "We and all nations have a sense that we have come to the turning point of an age" (Fest 1973, p. 486).

It is the *unspoken elision*, however, that reveals the genuine sense and significance of the *repetition* of German Idealism as the form for a metaphysical orchestration and pursuit of *war* by other means set into motion in Heidegger's thought. For as Semprún has astutely remarked, in his evocation of the Spirit of 1809, as it were, "Heidegger trouve le moyen de passer sous silence l'événement historique qui cimenta cette amitié [*between Hegel and Schelling*], qui provoqua leur enthousiasme et leur réflexion: la Revolution française. Mais comment peut-on situer l'oeuvre de Schelling – ou de Kant, ou de Fichte, ou de Hegel, ou de Heine, ou de Herder, pour n'en citer que certains parmi les plus importants – en occultant les relations de l'Allemagne de l'époque avec la France révolutionnaire?" (Semprún 2012, p. 701). Heidegger's elision of any reference to the French Revolution is part and parcel of his emphasis on the original German conception of *freedom* and its metaphysical thinking in German Idealism *in conflict with* the historical consequence of the conception of freedom born of the French Revolution: Napoleon and the French "oppression" and "shaming" of Germany. Heidegger thus *repeats*, albeit in a displaced and transformed form, indeed, transplanted and reconfigured within the terrain of his *seynsgeschichtliches Denken*, the confrontation between the so-called "Ideas of 1914" and "Ideas of 1789" during the First World War. A thesis first advanced in Johann Plenge's *1789 und 1914: Die symbolischen Jahre in der Geschichte des politischen Geistes*, Ernst Troeltsch's "Die Ideen von 1914," and (the Swede) Johan Rudolf Kjellén *Die Ideen von 1914. Eine weltgeschichtliche Perspektive*, the First World War was understood in revolutionary terms, indeed, as revolution in historical force and significance akin to the French Revolution of 1789, yet fundamentally opposed with the idea of Freedom propagated by the French Revolution—individual freedom, atomic, self-interested democracy, etc. The point is *not* that Heidegger tacitly repeats and thus adopts the original notion of the Ideas of 1914, which he in fact does not. Rather, the point is that Heidegger's conception of German Idealism repeats the same logic of opposition to the French Revolution and the Idea of 1789, which, however, Heidegger transforms and invigorates within this *seynsgeschichtliches Denken* into the *Machenschaft, Bodenlosigkeit, and Weltlosigkeit* of Western Civilization. The First World War is thus *repeated* in the very sense in which Heidegger understands historical repetition, in the very sense, in other words, in which he spoke in his Reunion Speech in 1934, namely: "For the Great War comes over us *now* for the *first* time" such that "the Great War becomes today for us Germans—for us first and foremost among all peoples—the *historical* actuality of our existence for the first time." The awakening to the Great War in its historical repetition and actualization *for the first time* goes hand in hand with an awakening to German Idealism in its historical repetition and actualization *for the first time*. As Heidegger notes (already quoted above): "Der deutsche Idealismus ist [...] *eine noch ungeschehene Geschichte*." The Revolution of 1914 must become repeated in a Revolution of 1933, as the repetition of the First World War *philosophically speaking*, and hence, as the undoing of the French Revolution, and through this undoing, the *Machenschaft* that dominates the West. German Idealism is the *name and aspiration for* the philosophical revolution to come, this other beginning, for thinking and Germanness. And in fact, the dismantling of the the Parliamentary and legal institutions, unions, and impartial police forces during the year 1933 after the ascension of Hitler to power was intended as a social and political Revolution within which to undo the French Revolution. As the historian of Nazi Germany Johann Chapoutot points out: "Les nazis accomplissent donc bel et bien [*in 1933*] ce que Goebbels considérait comme leur mission historique: 'effacer 1789 de l'histoire'" (Chapoutot 2010, p. 98).

In a substantial reflection on German Idealism in *Überlegungen XII* (1939), Heidegger proposes that " wir die damit genannte Metaphysik [*German Idealism*] noch nicht in ihrer Deutschheit begreifen," and thus, by implication, that we still have yet to grasp essentially what *Deutschheit* itself *names* and calls into being. Crucially, however, Heidegger qualifies that the *Deutschheit* of German Idealism must not be vulgarized into "eine volkskundliche Rückführung dieser Philosophie auf ein bestimmtes Volkstum [...]"—a rejection of the National Socialist employment and meaning of *Deutschheit* even if in the same gesture Heidegger affirms a more emphatic "spiritualization" or "metaphysization" of *Deutschheit*. As Heidegger continues, "das Wesen des Deutschen bestimmt sich von da erst als das ureigene Vermögen" for a genuine metaphysical experience of thinking: an original experience of "beginning essence of being (*Seyns*) as *phusis*" (GA 96, p. 9). This essential thinking necessarily is an engagement in struggle, or battle (*Kampf*), and this struggle for *Deutschheit*, the truth of being, and genuine metaphysical experience of thinking stands before us as a future for which there is both risk and exposure, or, in other words, no shelter. As Heidegger ruminates: "Kampf der Besinnung ist das freie Wagen einer Wesensverwandlung, durch die alle bequem und üblich gewordenen Stützen und Krücken zerbrechen und die Not des Grundes ihre Gründer fordert [...]." We are once again returned to Heidegger's statement in his Reunion Speech—"for the bourgeois, battle is always only argument, quarrelsome wrangling, and a disruption. For the essential men, battle is the *great test* of all being"—and thereby returned to the return of another war, the genuine war, as the repetition of the first.

The Enemy Within

During the First World War, the "great test of all being"—the greatest battle of the war—was explicitly orchestrated as an issue of greatest bleeding. The infamous intention of General Erich von Falkenhayn's attack on the fortified French positions at Verdun was to inflict such a traumatic "ausbluten" of French forces so as to break the will of the French commitment to the war. The Battle of Verdun (from 21 February 1916 until 19 December 1916) caused over 700,000 casualties on both sides, and yet proved strategically inconclusive. This military inconclusiveness was, however, decisive on the spiritual plane (along with the German losses at the Battle of the Somme in 1916) for a marked transformation in the perception and expectation of the war. As the war progressed into 1917, prospects for any form of German triumph had irrevocably faded away with a corresponding and dramatic shift in the tone and dynamic of the war-discourse. Two transformations are here notable. The increase of pessimism regarding German victory translated into an increased concern with the question of who is genuinely German. Indeed, the more the war became hopeless, the more the question of who is authentically German became important. Along with this internalization of the confrontation with an enemy the war became increasingly compared with the scale and historical importance of the Thirty-Years War (Sieg 2013, p. 125).Both of these factors were part and parcel of a radicalization of war-discourse and hardening of the fronts, and with the latter, most significantly, the opening of another front, namely, an inner front against the enemy within.

The debate concerning the question of who was authentically German was inseparable from the question of what is authentically German. Both questions were framed through the Ideas of 1914 and the argument for a unique conception and tradition of German Freedom (*deutscher Freiheit*) in terms of which the existential struggle of the war was understood. Central to the Ideas of 1914 is a vision of a unified community of Germans made possible, in part, through the existential struggle of war. This ontological premium on inner unity directly implied an exclusion and hence hostility against any figure identified as an *inner enemy* (Sieg 2013, p. 125). This identification of the enemy within received an explicitly philosophical expression with Bruno Bauch's 1916 article "Vom Begriff der Nation," published in *Kant-Studien* (Bauch was the editor of the journal), and was specifically directed against the so-called "Jewification" (*Verjudung*) of German philosophy at the hands of Marburg Neo-Kantianism. In an earlier letter published in the populist monthly journal *Der Panther*, Bauch specifically challenged that Hermann Cohen, as a Jew, could not genuinely understand Kant's German philosophical thought. Jews, as he states, are merely "guests" in a German home but themselves not at home within Germany (Bauch 1916a). Bauch's attack responded to Cohen's patriotic attempt to align Judaism and the German Nation in his essay "Deutschtum und Judentum," published earlier in 1916 in a collection of essays with the revealing title: *Vom inneren Frieden des deutschen Volkes. Ein Buch gegenseitigen Verstehens und Vertrauens* (Thimme 1916). As a categorical rejection of Cohen's vision of a "harmonization" and "trust" between Germans and Jews, Bauch aggressively defined the Nation as the community of those who are born into it (*Gemeinschaft der 'Mitgeborenen'*) and thus as defined in terms of a community of blood (Bauch 1916b).[1] However,

---

[1] In the final paragraph of "Deutschtum und Judentum," Cohen prophesied: "Vielleicht – wer kann dem Lauf der Weltgeschichte ermessen – wird es einmal nicht zu den geringsten Kronen des deutschen Wesens gezählt werden, dass es seinen Juden nicht nur Schutzrechte und Bürgerrechte verliehen, sondern dass es ihnen auch Anteil am deutschen Geiste, an der deutschen Wis-

despite this ontological definition of the Nation and the German in terms of blood and earth (the emphasis on land is equally present in his thinking), Bauch targeted specifically German-Jews. As he claims that even if German-Jews have assimilated into German culture and achieved a command of German language and culture, it still stands to question, as he writes: "Der völkische Fremdling mag durch Generationen unter uns leben und keine andere Sprache mehr sprechen vermögen. Dennoch ist seine Sprache nicht die unsere." Indeed, as Bauch states: there always remains "ein Fremdes zwischen ihm und uns."[2]

Although Bauch's article took aim against Hermann Cohen, it was Cassirer who responded in an article, which, however, was never published, but remains instructive nonetheless for its incisive diagnosis of the dynamic of "confrontation without encounter" that structured Bauch's position. In fact, Bauch's attack on Judaism and the opening, as it were, of another, inner front against the enemy within—an enemy *within* German thought—can be placed within a broader spectrum of an increasing quotient for the abstraction of "the Jew" or "Judaism" from any concrete form of Jewishness or Judaism. As the historian Dirk Rupnow has argued, the traction of racial and biological anti-Semitism at the beginning of the 20th-century did not displace or supplant the historically more entrenched religious enmity against Judaism. On the contrary, cultural as well as biological elements of enmity against Judaism and anti-Semitism entangled and mixed together, thus rendered inseparable from each other (Rupnow 2011, p. 288). It is, arguably, however Cassirer in his unpublished response to Bauch who most acutely analysized this process in Bauch's thinking of "abstraction" as a function of intensity of confrontation, or, in other words, the necessary figurative presence of the 'Jew' as *cliché, prejudice, and banality* within a logic of confrontation without encounter.

Bauch's thinking is inherently constructed around a confrontation that admits of no encounter. It is also constructed around a difference that by default can neither be reconciled nor over-come, namely, between Jewish thinking and German thinking. Can "Jewish" or "German" at all function as a philosophical predicate of thinking? Would the allowance for a so-called "Jewish" thinking in contrast and conflict with a so-called "German thinking" lead logically to the characterization of "Jewish" or "German" logic, or, indeed, "Jewish" or "German" Freedom—as was in fact the case with the "German Freedom" celebrated by the

---

senschaft und Kunst, am deutschen Schaffen auf allen Gebieten, dass es ihnen für ihre Religion selbst, und zwar zum Heil der ganzen Welt, innerlichste Förderung erteilt [...]" (Cohen 2002, p. 132).

2 For more detailed presentation of the controversy provoked by Bauch's article, see Hoeres (2004, pp. 232–237).

advocates of the Ideas of 1914? As Cassirer remarks: "Wir alle sprechen vom 'griechischen Geist'," or, indeed, we all speak of 'German' Spirit—but can Spirit objectively be either Greek or German? Does the admittance of such a characterization not reveal a "purely dogmatic naturalism?" (Cassirer 2008, p. 42) As Cassirer argues against Bauch's hijacking of Fichte and Kant for his *völkisch* notion of Nation (based on blood and earth), the concept of freedom as autonomy, which marks the height of German Idealism, is not a "specifically German concept," but a concept that transcends national borders and limits because it expresses an Idea and a task (*Aufgabe*). It is at this point in his discussion that Cassirer, as he writes, "breaks off" from his argument to make a more general point. For as he writes:

> Im Grunde liegt freilich hier für Bauch keine Schwierigkeit und kein ernsthaftes Problem vor: denn die Beziehung zwischen Deutschen und Juden bestimmt sich für ihn sehr einfach nach einem allgemeinen Schema. Der Jude ist 'Gast im deutschen Haus': und so ist ihm seine Stellung ein für alle Mal durch das Verhältnis vorgeschrieben, das überhaupt zwischen 'Gastvölkern' und 'Wirtsvölkern' anzunehmen ist. *Es giebt sich hier ein äusseres Nebeneinanderleben, das aber niemals zu einer wahrhaft innerlichen, zu einer geistig-nationalen Beziehung führen kann. Denn alles, was eine solche Beziehung begründen könnte, ist dem Juden versagt* (Cassirer 2008, p. 47; my emphasis)

Cassirer's insight is here astute and prescient of Sartre's own trenchant—if in its own manner controversial—analysis of anti-Semitism in *Anti-Semite and Jew*. But it also formulates in precise terms the constitutive relationship between prejudice and *cliché* as bonded through the binding agent of banality. For on the one hand, as Cassirer remarks, Bauch construes the "problem" between German and Jew as in fact a non-problem, that is, not a serious problem: a serious problem that would require a serious encounter with both German and Jew. Yet, it is precisely to the degree that what is staged is here a "non-problem" that there can be no genuine encounter, and that instead, there is only confrontation—a confrontation from the outside. The problem becomes a confrontation within a serious problem *to be solved, or resolved*, when the confrontation is structured around "general schemas," or abstractions, or, in other words, prejudices without the possibility of an attending or corresponding thought. Framed according to such general schemas, the Jew is damned to eternity to a conflict that can neither be escaped nor, paradoxically, *entered*. It is conflict since eternity inscribed within positions that admit of no movement. The "external" relation or confrontation between German and Jew thus forms a frontline that cannot be over-come. Indeed, the confrontation is structured in such a manner that it cannot lead to an *inner and true* relation, or encounter. The Jew is figuratively and literally *framed*: he cannot be admitted into genuine Germanness for any evidence that he could proffer—mastery of language, contribution to culture, born on German soil, etc.—is refused (*versagt*) on account of *being Jewish* even as he is suspected of not-being-German by virtue of not possessing a genuinness of speaking, acculturation, etc. In other words, as Sartre formulated this having it both ways, anti-Semitism is a "truth" placed beyond the reach of evidence: the Jew must constantly prove his Germanness even as no proof could ever invalidate the truth of the ontological judgment already made against the Jew.

A final point in Cassirer's remark brings forth the connection between the constitutive function of prejudice as "non-thought"—as a thinking that does encounter true difficulty and hence, a genuine problem—and *cliché* as cemented through the flatlands of banality. As Cassirer further observes: "Der Schwierigkeit, der Zartheit und Komplikation der konkreten Lebensverhältnisse wird diese Theorie nirgends gerecht; ihr liegt nur daran, den Gegensatz zwischen dem 'Einheimischen' und 'Fremdvölkischen' in nüchterner, gleichsam bureaukratischer Genauigkeit durchzuführen" (Cassirer 2008, p. 49). Cassirer in this manner anticipates a critical insight in Sartre's diagnosis of "racism," including anti-Semitism as a form of "non-thought" (in contrast to the hidden profundity of the "unthought"). The clue is here Cassirer's characterization of the confrontation between *Einheimischen* und *Fremdvölkischen* as an expression of a "bureaucratization" of thinking, or, in this sense, a banality of thinking such that, to quote here Sartre, we are not dealing with "a system of thought which might be false or pernicious"; rather, in truth, such anti-Semitism is "not a thought at all" and cannot be formulated *as a thought*. As Sartre further examines: "the Idea [...] has the materiality of a fact because no one thinks it. Therefore, it has the opaque indubitability of a thing" (Sartre 2004, p. 301). A *cliché* is the idea that becomes thing in order to *not be thought* and to be a non-thought that nonetheless structures a clarity of confrontation without the veritable opacity of an encounter. In philosophical thought, the trafficking in *cliché and prejudice of non-thought* becomes constitutive when philosophical thought becomes mobilized in the name of a great confrontation for the exclusivity of greatness.

Nichtverstehen und Nichtverstehen und Nichtverstehen

In seeking to define itself in opposition to prejudice, philosophical thought has always sought to find another beginning. Whether in the form of an aspiration to height or depth, the emancipation of philosophical thought from the flatlands of non-thinking is a narrative of beginnings and endings, of what comes to begin through the awakening of genuine philosophical thought and of what comes to end through its transformative force. The war to end all wars was equally a war to begin the beginning of all beginnings. Reflection on what came to an end became inseparable from a search for another beginning, other than the beginning that came to a cataclysmic end with the war. The cessation of hostilities in 1918 did not mark, however, an end to the war nor an end to the quest for its philosophical meaning as another beginning. Already with the cultural and intellectual foreboding with regard to the loss of the war in 1916 and 1917, concentrated in a philosophical anxiety as to who and what is truly German, the war without spiritual end became increasingly polarized into a war in the name of another beginning. This spiritual struggle for another beginning became structured, on the one hand, in terms of a confrontation without genuine encounter and, on the other hand, in terms of a redemptive emancipation from the terms of such confrontation. The decisiveness of the confrontation rested in a movement of transcendence that demanded the holocaust of confrontation, or, in the sense this term carried prior to the Second World War, a *purification* of confrontation through its *non-dialectical* over-coming. In Henri Barbusse's 1917 preface to his war novel *Le feu*, he writes: "I will prevent the forgetting of the light of moral beauty and the perfect holocaust which burned in you during the monstrous and disgusting horror of the war." As the cultural historian Jay Winter observes: "Before the Nazis, the word [*holocaust*] meant what Barbusse intended it to mean: a purification by fire, a preparation through voluntary sacrifice of a better life to come" (Winter 1995, p. 183). The meaning in this usage within and immediately after the First World War is indexed to the redemption of another beginning that would transcend the very opposition or confrontation from which this new beginning itself started.

The dynamic of this breaking of a new dawn, or other beginning, is aptly described in a reflection in Heidegger's *Beiträge zur Philosophie:* "Der andere Anfang ist nicht die Gegenrichtung zum ersten, sondern steht *als anderes* ausserhalb des Gegen und der unmittelbaren Vergleichbarkeit" (GA 65, p. 187). The future "decision" and "decisiveness" of this other beginning forms an orthogonal transcendence, as it were: it has the form of the creative struggle, or battle (*schöpferischer Kampf*), of a genuine philosophical thought that is neither "propaganda" nor "apologetic," and thus that transcends the oppositional logic of cultures or worldviews, and by the same token, transcends a dialectical notion of confrontation, namely, a confrontation in which opposing positions could be reconciled and indeed measured with and against each other. As Heidegger stresses time and again in the *Beiträge zur Philosophie* as well as the *Schwarze Hefte* (and indeed, elsewhere in his writings during the 1930s), the genuine meaning of *die Auseinandersetzung des anderen Anfangs* is not to be thought in terms of *Gege-*

nerschaft who could be reconciled, understand, or even speak or see another in terms of mutual recognition. The struggle for being must be a struggle against shadows, or figurations, that nonetheless are imbued with the weight and presence of an unrelenting and irreconcilable enemy, or *Feind*. The *Feind* must therefore be pervasive, omni-present, and "total," and yet nowhere, *weltlos* and *bodenlos*.

Heidegger's rejection of any conflation of philosophical thought with a "worldview," a "total form of knowledge," or a form of culture—all of which he identifies with a modern metaphysics of *Machenschaft* and *Herrschaft*—equally distinguishes the philosopher as a singularity bereft of community and culture. The thinker is alone, or rather, his community remains unseen from the perspective of the flatlands of dialectical opposition, reciprocal recognition, and possible communication. Indeed, the *greatness* of philosophy and the *greatness of a philosopher* is compared by Heidegger to a *ragende Berge, unbestiegen und unbesteigbar*. As Heidegger elaborates this image: "Die Aus-einander-setzung mit den grossen Philosophien—als metaphysischen Grundstellungen innerhalb der Geschichte der Leitfrage—muss so angelegt werden, dass jede Philosophie als wesentliche als Berg zwischen Berg zu stehen kommt und so ihr Wesentlichstes zum Stand bringt" (GA 65, p. 187). The greatness of philosophical thought consists in an *Aus-einander-Setzung*—with the exclusivity of greatness, and such exclusively situates the philosopher in a confrontation with, on the one hand, those who have nothing to be understood, those of the flatlands, and those who cannot be understood, those other "mountains" whose shadow remains productively unfathomable. As Heidegger expresses this notion in his Schelling lectures: "dass dir grössten Denker im Grunde einander nie verstehen, eben weil sie jeweils in der Gestalt ihrer einzigen Grösse *dasselbe* wollen. Wollten sie Verschiedenes, dann wäre die Verständigung, d. h., hier das Gewährenlassen, nicht so schwer" (Heidegger 1995, p. 15). The insight is in its own manner profound: philosophers *must* misunderstand each other in order to come to terms with each other's greatness while those who come to understand each other never truly come to terms with any greatness. That great philosophical thought is not about *Verständigung* cuts both ways, however: it is both a principle for the introduction of depth into philosophical thought—for there is something absolutely compelling about this insight—*as well as* a principle for the injection of non-thinking into philosophical thought—for there is something absolutely presumptive about this thought. For if great thinkers never understand each other because their greatness consists in "wanting the same"—the "same" that remains the "unthought" or "shadow" of great philosophical thought—then it is equally true that great philosophers—at least in this particular case—can never understand what is putatively perceived as contesting greatness, or the same.

This non-understanding is not the non-understanding of *questioning*, or what Heidegger himself identifies as "das Fragen [als] ein Nichtverstehen aus der Leidenschaft des Ahnenden Wissens, das vermag im Bezug zum Wesenhaften auszuharren, selbst wenn es in der Irre verweilen muss." It is equally not what Heidegger in turn calls "die Verständnislosigkeit [als] der Unverstand als Unvermögen zum wesentlichen Denken" (GA 96, p. 129).For this form of *die Verständnislosigkeit* still requires the horizon of possible *Verständigung* and hence, according to the logic of dialectical opposition, a conversion from "Unvermögen" to "Vermögen zum wesentlichen Denken." Heidegger's remark that "Nichtverstehen und Nichtverstehen ist daher nicht das Selbe," as the difference between *die Verständnislosigkeit* and *das fragende Nichtverstehen*, re-inscribes the classical opposition between lack of thinking and thinking, where the latter, however, becomes re-cast as an essential "unthought" of greatness. And yet, there operates in the constitution of Heidegger's own philosophical thinking another darkness, not the shadow of the great "unthought" nor the shadow of lack of thinking (*die Verständnislosigkeit*), but the obtuse clarity of a cliché formed in "non-thinking" through which great philosophical thought confronts the enemy within of greatness and "the same," (what Heidegger calls "die äusserste Feindschaft"), *and thinks itself vindicated in thinking*. In his own words:

> Une vielleicht 'siegt' in diesem 'Kampf', in dem um die Ziellosigkeit schlechthin gekämpft wird und daher nur das Zerrbild des 'Kampfes' sein kann, die an nichts gebunden, alles sich dienstbar macht (das Judentum). Aber der eigentliche Sieg, der Sieg der Geschichte über das Geschichtslose, wird nur dort errungen, wo das Bodenlose sich selbst ausschliesst, weil es das Seyn nicht wagt, sondern immer nur mit dem Seienden rechnet und seine Berechnungen als das Wirkliche setzt (GA 95, p. 97).[3]

References

Altman, William H. F. (2012): *Martin Heidegger and the First World War. Being and Time as Funeral Oration*. Maryland: Lexington Books.
Bauch, Bruno (1916a): "Leserbrief". In: *Der Panther. Deutsche Monatsschrift für Politik und Volkstum*, 4(6), pp. 148–154.
Bauch, Bruno (1916b): "Vom Begriff der Nation". In: *Kant-Studien* 21, pp. 139–162.
Cassirer, Ernst (2008): "Zum Begriff der Nation. Eine Erwiderung auf den Aufsatz von Bruno Bauch". In: *Nachgelassene Manuskripte und Texte*. Vol. IX. Hamburg: Felix Meiner, pp. 29–60.

---

3 And also in the following reflection: "Eine der verstecktesten Gestalten des *Riesigen* und vielleicht die älteste ist die zähe Geschicklichkeit des Rechnens und Schiebens und Durcheinandermischens, wodurch die Weltlosigkeit des Judentums gegründet wird."

Chapoutot, Johann (2010): *Le meurtre de Weimar*. Paris: Presses Universitaires de France.
Cohen, Hermann (2002): *Kleinere Schriften VI 1916–1918*. Hildesheim: Georg Olms.
Eksteins, Modris (1989): *Rites of Spring. The Great War and the Birth of the Modern Age*. Boston: Houghton Mifflin.
Flasch, Kurt (2000): *Die geistige Mobilmachung. Die deutschen Intellektuellen und der Erste Weltkrieg*. Berlin: Alexander Fest Verlag.
Fest, Joachim (1973): *Hitler*. New York: Harcourt.
Haffner, Sebastian (2008): *Die deutsche Revolution 1918/1919*. Cologne: Anaconda.
Heidegger, Martin (2014a): *Überlegungen II–VI (Schwarze Hefte 1931–1938)*. Peter Trawny (Ed.). Gesamtausgabe 94. Tübingen: Niemeyer. [GA 94]
Heidegger, Martin (2014b): *Überlegungen VII–XI (Schwarze Hefte 1938–39)*. Peter Trawny (Ed.). Gesamtausgabe 95. Tübingen: Niemeyer. [GA 95]
Heidegger, Martin (2014c): *Überlegungen XII–XV (Schwarze Hefte 1939–1941)*. Peter Trawny (Ed.). Gesamtausgabe 96. Tübingen: Niemeyer. [GA 96]
Heidegger, Martin (2000): *Reden Und Andere Zeugnisse Eines Lebensweges*. Gesamtausgabe 16. Frankfurt: Vittorio Klostermann.
Heidegger, Martin (1995): *Schellings Abhandlung über das Wesen der menschlichen Freiheit (1809)*. Berlin: De Gruyter.
Hoeres, Peter (2004): *Krieg der Philosophen: Die deutsche und britische Philosophie im Ersten Weltkrieg*. Paderborn: Ferdinand Schöningh Verlag.
James, Henry (1920): *The Letters of Henry James*. Percy Lubbock (Ed.). Vol. II. New York: Charles Scribner's Sons.
Marc, Franz (1914): "Das geheime Europa". In: *Schriften*. Köln: DuMont, 1978. http://www.zeno.org/Kunst/M/Marc,+Franz/Schriften/Aus+der+Kriegszeit/32.+Das+geheime+Europa, last accessed on 14 April 2021.
Münkler, Herfried (2014): *Der grosse Krieg. Die Welt 1914–1918*. Berlin: Rowohlt.
Ricks, Christopher (1988): *T. S. Eliot and Prejudice*. Berkeley: University of California Press.
Rupnow, Dirk (2011): *Judenforschung im Dritten Reich. Wissenschaft zwischen Politik, Propaganda und Ideologie*. Baden-Baden: Nomos.
Sartre, Jean-Paul (2004): *Critique of Dialectical Reason*. London: Verso.
Semprún, Jorge (2012): *Le feu rouge de la mémoire*. Paris: Gallimard.
Sieg, Ulrich (2013): *Geist und Gewalt*. Munich: Carl Hanser.
Thimme, Friedrich (1916) (Ed.):*Vom inneren Frieden des deutschen Volkes. Ein Buch gegenseitigen Verstehens und Vetrauens*. Leipzig: Hirze.
Winter, Jay (1995): *Sites of Memory, Sites of Mourning. The Great War in European Cultural History*. Cambridge: Cambridge University Press.

Steven Crowell
Heidegger's Metapolitics: Phenomenology, Metaphysics, and the *Volk*

Abstract: For a long time now, a dispute has raged over whether Heidegger's involvement with National Socialism is somehow a necessary consequence of the analysis of Dasein he offers in *Being and Time*. While this paper does not address this question directly, it does make a distinction that, I believe, is necessary for approaching an answer – a distinction between the *transcendental* approach to Dasein in *Being and Time* and the *metaphysical* approach to the human being Heidegger takes up between 1927 and 1935. Heidegger called this latter approach "metontology." I argue that it is the attempt to bridge the gap between the transcendental and the metaphysical – between inquiry into the disclosure of the *meaning* of being and an *ontic* inquiry into "beings as a whole" – that leads Heidegger *necessarily* to political philosophy, which he calls "metapolitics." The key to this attempt is Heidegger's appropriation of Leibniz's idea of the monad, which serves Heidegger first as a way of clarifying the distinction between Dasein and animal life, and then as a way of determining the metaphysical character of a *Volk*. The failure of this metaphysical project – which Heidegger himself soon came to recognize – leaves the validity of the transcendental phenomenology in *Being and Time* untouched.

1 Introduction

In recent writings[1] I have been looking into what I call Heidegger's "metaphysical decade" – roughly between 1927 and 1935[2] – in which Heidegger tries to leverage the transcendental phenomenology of *Being and Time* into a phenomenological metaphysics. I am interested both in the general question of the relation between phenomenology and metaphysics, and in the particular question of what Heidegger's conception of metaphysics is and why he came to see the need to "overcome" it. In this paper I present some thoughts on these issues,

---

1 Parts of this paper have been drawn from Steven Crowell, "The Middle Heidegger's Phenomenological Metaphysics," *The Oxford Handbook of the History of Phenomenology* © the several contributors 2018, and are reproduced with permission of the Licensor through PLSclear.
2 Technically, of course, this is not quite a decade. For a more restrictive periodization of Heidegger's "metaphysisches Denken," see Stefan Schmidt (2016, p. 1).

https://doi.org/10.1515/9783110698787-023

with the caveat that I will make a number of argumentative leaps – somewhat filled in through shameless self-reference – for the sake of getting the bigger picture into view.

It is no accident, I think, that the beginning of Heidegger's turn away from metaphysics coincides with the collapse of his Rectorship and his political-pedagogical attempt to steer the National Socialist movement toward his own philosophical views. I will try to suggest the reason for this by showing that Heidegger's phenomenological metaphysics culminates in what in the *Black Notebooks* he calls the "metapolitics" of the *Volk* (Heidegger 2014, p. 116).[3] The argument can be summarized briefly: Husserl negotiated the paradox of human subjectivity – namely, that the human being *in* the world is also the locus of the constitution *of* the world – by appeal to a telos of reason extending from instinctual animal life through historical humanity to an infinite ethical community grounded in the idea of the Absolute Person. Heidegger, encountering the same paradox but with a very different conception of reason, could appeal only to a *particular* historical community, the German *Volk*, whose "vocation" it was to embody metaphysics in the state by "liberating the Da-sein in the human being." Filling in this argument, however, will require some preliminary work.

I begin with some general reflections on the relation between transcendental phenomenology and metaphysics in Husserl and Heidegger, leading up to Heidegger's idea of "metontology" (§ 2). This is followed by a some remarks on how the two phenomenologists approach the metaphysics of "world" (§ 3), which calls for a look at some differences between their views on intersubjectivity, interpersonal understanding, and collective intentionality (§ 4). Since Heidegger's concept of the *Volk* is intimately connected to his reflections on the species-being of animals, this will be the theme of § 5. We will then be in a position to understand how the *Volk* is supposed to function as the metapolitical crux of the relation between transcendental phenomenology and metaphysics (§ 6). Since I find neither Heidegger's nor Husserl's solution to the paradox of human subjectivity fully satisfactory, the relation between phenomenology and metaphysics remains, for me, an open question.

2 Phenomenological neutrality and metaphysics

Husserl originally conceived phenomenology as metaphysically neutral. By way of the *epoché*, phenomenological method is to be "presuppositionless" in the

---

[3] See Crowell (2016) for further contextualization of this notion.

sense that it does not begin with appeals to scientific findings or metaphysical constructions. This neutrality can be expressed in Kantian terms: phenomenology does not investigate the properties of entities but is a "transcendental" inquiry into the constitution of the meaning (*Sinn*) through which entities and their properties are given in experience. Though Heidegger's relation to the *epoché* is complicated, at the most general level there is a good deal of overlap with Husserl. When Heidegger says that "only as phenomenology is ontology possible" (Heidegger 1962, p. 60), he means, in part, that ontology must eschew all "free-floating constructions and accidental findings" in order to investigate the "being" (the "meaning and ground") of beings (1962, p. 50). To do so, phenomenology must begin with our own experience as questioners, as beings who are able to raise the question of what it means to be and so must already understand "being" in a "pre-ontological" way (1962, p. 32).

This amounts to a commitment to transcendental neutrality in the analytic of Dasein. Husserl defined transcendental subjectivity as the locus of meaning-constitution and so as neutral with respect to its instantiation in some "worldly" entity such as *homo sapiens*. There is no *necessary* connection between transcendental subjectivity and the natural kind, human being. Heidegger, in turn, designates Dasein as "the entity which each of us is him/herself" (1962, p. 27), without identifying that entity through any sortal predicate.

In a lecture course from 1928 Heidegger makes this neutrality explicit: "the peculiar *neutrality* of the term 'Dasein' is essential, because the interpretation of this being must be carried out prior to every factual concretion" (Heidegger 1984, p. 136). Thus "Dasein" refers essentially only to those features that show themselves to be necessary for an understanding of being: Dasein is care (*Sorge*), that being in whose "very being that being is an *issue* for it" (Heidegger 1962, p. 32). The categories constitutive of such a being include affectedness (*Befindlichkeit*), understanding (*Verstehen*), and discourse (*Rede*). Heidegger rejects Husserl's own categorial approach to the transcendental subject because he thinks that Husserl's focus on the intentionality of consciousness is insufficient for explicating the transcendental conditions for the constitution of meaning (Heidegger 1985, pp. 102–114). "Dasein" is neutrally defined as whatever it is that meets those conditions.

This transcendental neutrality entails methodological anti-naturalism, but Heidegger's move into metaphysics, like Husserl's, cannot avoid the question of "nature" altogether, since he recognizes that we discover these transcendental conditions in *ourselves*. As Heidegger puts it, "neutral Dasein is never what exists; Dasein exists in each case only in its factical concretion" (Heidegger 1984, p. 137), i.e., *contingently*, in "human beings" (*Menschen*). Transcendental phenomenology, *Sinnkritik*, may not start with the question "What is the human being?" but it leads to it, and it is this relation between transcendental inquiry and its concretion in a particular worldly entity that seems to require metaphysical treatment.

Metaphysics in this sense is occasionally mentioned in *Being and Time*, where it refers to a set of questions that cannot be properly formulated prior to the transcendental account of Dasein. For instance, after presenting his ontological concept of death, Heidegger remarks that a "metaphysic of death" lies outside its scope, dealing as it does with issues like "what 'meaning' [death] can have and is to have as an evil and affliction in the totality of entities [*All des Seienden*]" (Heidegger 1962, p. 292). In 1928 Heidegger explicitly takes up such metaphysics, labelling it "metontology." Here the neutral phenomenology of Dasein "turns back" (*Umschlag, metabole*) to the "metaphysical ontic in which it implicitly always remains" (Heidegger 1984, p. 158). Metontology is *ontic* – concerned with entities rather than with the *being* of entities – a "metaphysics of existence" (1984, p. 157).

The idea of metontology is deeply puzzling. On the one hand, inquiry into "beings as a whole" (*das Seiende im Ganzen*)[4] is neither a positive science nor an "inductive metaphysics" that gathers scientific results into an overall picture or "guide for life" (Heidegger 1984, p. 157). On the other hand, it is supposed to furnish the context in which "the question of an ethics may be properly raised" (1984, p. 157), where concepts connected to Dasein's "dispersal" into "nature," into "bodiliness and so thus into sexuality," are to be determined (1984, p. 138). In contrast to the regional concerns of the positive sciences, a *metaphysical* ontic inquiry situates Dasein within beings as a *whole*. But how? Some clarity on these matters can be gained by looking at how metontology is supposedly entailed by the phenomenological point of departure.

3 The phenomenological problem of world

In *Being and Time* Heidegger argued that the "roots of the existential analytic" are ultimately "*ontical*" (Heidegger 1962, p. 34). This seems to entail that ontology itself "requires an *ontic* grounding" (1962, p. 487), but what sort of ground is that?[5] In 1928 Heidegger describes it this way: "being is there only when Dasein

---

[4] In "What is Metaphysics?" Heidegger draws an important distinction between "the whole of beings [*das Ganze des Seienden*]" and "beings as a whole [*Seienden im Ganzen*]" (1998b, p. 87). Since this distinction does not impact the argument of the present paper, however, I will not pursue its details here.

[5] I address this question in more detail in Crowell (2000).

understands being. In other words, the possibility that being is there in the understanding presupposes the factical existence of Dasein, and this in turn presupposes the factual extantness of nature," i.e., presupposes that "a possible totality of beings is already there" (Heidegger 1984, pp. 156–157). The question is, what sort of presupposition (i.e., dependence) is meant here? What sort of "ontic grounding" is metontology supposed to thematize? It is neither the *causal* dependence studied by natural science nor the kind of essence-dependence that, for both Husserl and Heidegger, is the theme of "regional ontology."[6] Rather, it pertains to Dasein's facticity or thrownness (*Geworfenheit*), the ground of its "finite projection" of world (Heidegger 1984, p. 139). The kind of grounding at issue thus concerns Dasein's abandonment to the "overpowering" (*das Übermächtige*), which Heidegger associates with Aristotle's *theologike* (1984, p. 11). Heidegger calls this the "world-problem" (1996, p. 394) and argues that "the being-problem and the world-problem in their unity determine the genuine concept of metaphysics" (1996, p. 324). Fundamental onology (transcendental inquiry into the meaning of being) tackles the first, while metontology takes up the second (1984, p. 158). What, then, is the world-problem?

Husserl too held that transcendental phenomenology rests on a kind of ontic ground. Neutral inquiry into meaning yields essential insights, but it must begin anew with each thinker. It is "the philosopher's own quite personal affair" (Husserl 1969, p. 2), a matter of ultimate epistemic self-responsibility which involves a contingent commitment by the individual to live his or her life in the "transcendental attitude" (Husserl 1970, pp. 208–210).[7] This requires a kind of double vision. On the one hand, *Sinnkritik* discloses an asymmetry between consciousness and world: since the ontic meaning and ontic validity (*Seinssinn und Seinsgeltung*) of things depends on – i.e., is constituted by – the conscious acts in which such things are given, the world is transcendentally grounded in consciousness in a sense in which consciousness is not grounded in the world. Ontologically, however, there is no asymmetry. The being of the world is no less certain than the being of consciousness, though neither posseses "absolute" necessity (Husserl 2008, pp. 243–58). Rather, they have the "necessity of a

---

[6] For both Husserl (1983, pp. 18–23) and Heidegger (1962, pp. 28–31) regional ontologies thematize "essences," i.e., the eidetic features that define the particular ontic "regions" of being investigated by various positive sciences. But a metaphysical *ontic* inquiry does not concern essences in this sense.

[7] For illuminating treatments of the implications of this commitment, see Jacobs (2013) and Staiti (2010).

fact," an *Urfaktum*.⁸ Husserl's late understanding of metaphysics concerns precisely this sort of necessity – the factual, ontic symmetry between consciousness and world – and it allows him to treat transcendental meaning-constitution as a "depth dimension" of the embodied, historical, and social human being, i.e., as the *person's* "transcendental life" in the world.⁹

Husserl calls this metaphysical crossing of the transcendental and the empirical – the human being's mode of existing – the "paradox of human subjectivity" (Husserl 1970, p. 178), and the air of paradox is dispelled only by phenomenological reflection, which reveals "world" to be the one and unique *horizon* of all theoretical, evaluative, and practical life, the terminus of a rational teleology immanent to the movement of life itself.¹⁰ Because the world's necessity is factual, no ultimate reason for its being can be given; however, reason is not imposed on the world but is immanent to it as an individual and collective infinite task.

Heidegger's concept of metontology involves a similar crossing or double grounding. Though the transcendental phenomenology of neutral Dasein has methodological priority in accounting for our understanding of being, metaphysically there is no such priority. Dasein, as "human being," presupposes that a totality of entities is already there. But because Heidegger insists on the *finitude* of reason, his metaphysical world-concept cannot avail itself of a rational teleology. Instead, he combines elements of the phenomenological world-analysis found in *Being and Time* with the Leibnizian concept of *vis* (force, *Drang*) to propose an *ontic* concept of world as the "play of life" (*Spiel des Lebens*) – a crossing that provides the transcendental categories of *Being and Time* with a metaphysical interpretation.

The first of these is the category of affectedness (*Befindlichkeit*). In *Being and Time*, the "primary discovery" of the world is not cognitive but belongs to "bare mood" (Heidegger 1962, p. 177). The world does have an horizonal structure, but that horizon, the way things as a whole matter to us, is categorially tied to the "enigma" of Dasein's thrownness and so is not, even in principle, rationally determined (1962, p. 175). This phenomenological characterization of world continues to inform Heidegger's approach to *das Seiende im Ganzen* when, in a lecture course from 1928/29, he describes thrownness as "abandonment" in the midst of beings, registered in a mood of "floundering" (*Haltlosigkeit*), a sense of groundlessness within the "overpowering" whole (Heidegger 1996, pp. 328, 337). Our "having" of world (*Welt-haben*) is grounded in this mood, uptake of which can

---

8 Important discussions of the factical character of Husserl's metaphysics can be found in Tengelyi (2014), Schmidt (2016), Bernet (2004), Loidolt (2015), and De Palma (2019).
9 For some criticisms of this idea, see Crowell (2014).
10 On Husserl's notion of the one and unique world as "horizon" see Crowell (2019).

take two fundamental forms: "sheltering" (*Bergen*) and "self-control" (*Haltung*) (1996, p. 357).[11] The former yields the world-forming project of myth, which Heidegger understands as a distinct way in which Dasein secures a "hold" (*Halt*) in the overpowering whole through submission, supplication, and ritual (1996, p, 360). Against Ernst Cassirer (1996, p. 370),[12] who held that the symbolic form of myth prefigures scientific explanation, Heidegger understands myth not as incipient reason but as a manner of world-forming that is eventually replaced by an entirely different one, "self-control," without which there could be no science or philosophy. Self-control reverses the normative orientation of myth from the world to the self: instead of submission, stand-taking; instead of ritual, method; instead of supplication, self-responsibility or self-assertion (1996, pp. 366–370).[13] To appreciate the implications of this reversal, a second transcendental-phenomenological category that Heidegger imports into metontology must be brought into play, namely, understanding (*Verstehen*) as "projection of possibilities" (Heidegger 1962, pp. 182–85).

If for Husserl "world" is a horizonal whole normatively structured by a telos of reason, for Heidegger the normative moment derives from Dasein's understanding – not a cognitive achievement but a pre-reflective form of self-awareness: comporting oneself (*sich verhalten*) "for the sake of" (*Umwillen*) some specific "ability to be" (*Seinkönnen*) (Heidegger 1962, p. 119). Only because I can act for the sake of being a teacher, for instance – that is, *try* to be one by letting the norms of succeeding or failing at it ("what it means to be") matter to me – can I "have" the "world" of teaching, i.e., disclose a "totality of significance" in which entities like students, pencils, or chalkboards show up as what they in truth are (1962, pp. 119, 101).[14] Of course, I can *recognize* such entities without trying to be something in which they become relevant, but such nominal recognition does not *disclose* them in their being. That is possible only if I "bind" myself to them by commiting myself to being a teacher, i.e., by letting the meaning of teaching (what it is to be a teacher) be at issue for me, normatively *matter*.

---

11 Though *Haltung* might be translated in many ways (e.g., "stance"), I choose "self-control" here to emphasize its contrast with *Bergen*, or "sheltering," as an attitude, and also to suggest its connection with Dasein's "comportment" (*Verhalten*), which plays a central role in Heidegger's metontology.
12 For an alternative reading of Cassirer's view on the relation among "symbolic forms" see Truwant (2018).
13 Later, of course, these features of the "metaphysical" way of world-having motivate Heidegger's call to "overcome" metaphysics and cultivate an attitude of *Gelassenheit*: releasement or letting-be.
14 I explain these matters in more detail in Crowell (2013, Part III).

In his metaphysical decade, Heidegger interprets this normative aspect of comportment in terms of Plato's Idea of the Good (*idea tou agathou*): what binds me in my commitment, the good in the matter of teaching, is beyond beings (*epekeina tes ousias*) and so enables a distinction between what a teacher *is* (the social normative status) and what a teacher *ought* to be. The world of teaching is thus "had" through understanding, Dasein's freedom to pass beyond *das Seiende im Ganzen* toward what is best in the matter of teaching. This sort of "transcendence," or finite freedom, is not cognition of meaning; meaning is ever only at issue, "in play," in the choices we make. For this reason, Dasein's fundamental comportment – its "ownmost possibility" (*eigentlichste Seinkönnen*) – is its *answerability* (*Verantwortlichkeit*) for its understanding of what it means to be, its responsibility for being the ground of its way of going on in whatever it is trying to be (Heidegger 1962, pp. 330 – 34).

On this view of world as the normative horizon of that for the sake of which I act, there is a plurality of worlds (teaching, parenting, public service, you name it). What then becomes of *the* world, Husserl's one and unique world? In contrast to the transcendental phenomenology of *Being and Time,* Heidegger's metaphysics of world must confront this question, since metontology treats Dasein as human being, one worldly entity among others. The "world" at issue, then, must be the normative context in which I act for the sake of being human as such. Elsewhere (Crowell 2007) I have argued that this project makes no sense, but Heidegger's metaphysics tries to provide an account of what such acting is by situating the human being within the totality of "life" or nature, his synechdoche for *das Seiende im Ganzen*. This brings with it a version of the paradox of human subjectivity: the metaphysical relation between the human animal and the "Da-sein in us."

Husserl's genetic phenomenology disarmed the paradox by attributing the telos of reason, characteristic of transcendental subjectivity, to life as such, and Heidegger makes a similar move: the essential feature of transcendental subjectivity – Dasein's being at issue in what it does – becomes the metaphysical essence of life. World is the "*Spiel des Lebens*" (Heidegger 1996, p. 309). The concept of play is supposed to capture the sense in which acting for the sake of something, unlike making something, does not aim at a particular outcome but continually adjusts to circumstances in light of a measure of success, the meaning of which is continually at issue in acting. If life as a whole has this character, then it becomes conceivable that, in the human being's life, an *explicit* "having" of world as a whole (metaphysics) might be possible as the "forming" of world through the human being's own kind of play. The ontic ground of ontology would thus lie in the human being's capacity for world-forming (*Welt-bildung*), and the paradox of human subjectivity would be resolved by recognizing that one manner of world-having – namely, self-control (*Haltung*) – contains the transcendental condition for disclosing its own ground *as* world-forming. However, this schema leaves a key question open.

Because playing is normatively promiscuous – becoming normatively determinate only when I act for the sake of some *specific* way to be – no explanation has been given of how the human being passes from the normative promiscuity of life to neutral Dasein's ontological or transcendental capacity to disclose truth (what things in truth are). In *Being and Time*, this capacity is termed Dasein's "disclosedness" (*Erschlossenheit*), "the most primordial phenomenon of truth" (1962, p. 263). But world-*formation*, as a metaphysical notion, belongs to *both* forms of world-having (or world-view) – sheltering and self-control – and so does *not* have an intrinsic relation to truth. Thus, the capacity for world-disclosure remains only externally connected to the world-forming power of the human being. If Husserl could unite transcendental with empirical subjectivity by means of a telos of reason, Heidegger will have to find another way to explain the connection between play and truth upon which his whole metaphysics depends.

This way is mediated by the concept of the *Volk*, which already played a passing role in *Being and Time* but takes on enormous significance in Heidegger's metaphysics.[15] In place of a telos of reason, the transcendental and the empirical are united only in a particular *Volk*, the Germans, and a particular "generation," those of the present. In order to understand this shift, we need to clarify Heidegger's transcendental approach to intersubjectivity and interpersonal relations – his neutral concept of Dasein as "being-with" (*Mitsein*) – which subsequently receives a metaphysical interpretation in terms of the two fundamental "powers" (*Grundmächte des Seins*): nature and history.

4 Being-with and selfhood

In the transcendental neutrality of *Being and Time*, Dasein is always *Mitsein:* whenever Dasein is, it is "with others" in the sense that acting for the sake of

---

[15] The concept appears in the section on historicality (1962, p. 436). But as Carl-Friedrich Gethmann argued – correctly, in my view – this section "adds nothing new" to the to the systematic argument of *Being and Time* but is a kind of "excursus" or "concrete application" of it (Gethmann 1974, p. 314). This would make it an early example of Heidegger's metontology. Karl Löwith mentions a conversation with Heidegger in which the latter remarked that "his concept of 'historicality' was the basis of his political 'engagement'" (Löwith 1986, p. 56), thus suggesting his transformation of metontology into metapolitics. See § 6 below.

some possibility of being already involves reference to others in various ways. Dasein understands itself in terms of what "one" does, and even the extreme *solus ipse* of authenticity retains this reference to others (Heidegger 1962, pp. 156, 233).[16] Because this leaves no methodological room for asking how a relation to the other is originally constituted, Heidegger rejects an ontological role for "empathy" (*Einfühlung*), understood in Husserlian terms as the original experience of the alter ego as alter (Husserl 1969, p. 92). This does not mean that Heidegger denies empathy any role at all, but it is the *ontic* or empirical one of "interpreting" the other who appears, in one way or another, as the stranger (Heidegger 1962, p. 163). Empathy does not provide access to the other's "inner life" but is required whenever what someone is doing or saying becomes questionable, and it targets the other's "behavior" (*Benehmen*) in relation to things that the other and I already "share" as being in the world "together" (Heidegger 1996, pp. 131–2, 146). All interpersonal understanding, then, however fraught with potential misunderstanding, rests upon a primordial *familiarity*.

For Husserl, this begs the question. If neutral phenomenology is a phenomenology of *consciousness*, the question of how another consciousness is originally given becomes inescapable. Less abstractly, interpersonal understanding always rests on recognition of a radical (i.e., irreducible) *alterity*. Though for the Heidegger of *Being and Time* there is no such radical alterity, his metontology is forced to acknowledge one. Since neutral Dasein "is never what exists" – i.e., since Dasein is *necessarily* dispersed, and *contingently* dispersed in the human being – the category of *Mitsein* requires a metaphysical-ontic interpretation of the human animal, thus complicating *Being and Time*'s neutral account of selfhood.

For methodological reasons, as Heidegger notes, *Being and Time* focused on an "extreme possibility" of Dasein's being a self – namely, Dasein's radical individuation, acting for the sake of one's ownmost possibility, i.e., being answerable (Heidegger 1984, p. 186). In contrast to "existentiell ethical egoism," this extreme possibility has the phenomenological function of revealing the "I-ness" – the first-person *singular*, I-myself – achieved in Dasein's freeing itself from the anonymity of *das Man*. But this "metaphysically neutral egoicity" does not encapsulate Dasein in an isolated ego; rather, it grounds the possibility of "an I-Thou relation": only if the other appears as "you-yourself" – i.e., in *its* egoicity – can it be a thou (1984, p. 187). Put otherwise, because Dasein is always *Miteinandersein*, it is never an "ego" in the solipsistic sense; its "selfhood" is a kind of

---

[16] The canonical "Wittgensteinian" reading of Heidegger's *Mitsein* is found in Dreyfus (1991). Important contrasting readings are offered by Olafson (1998), Vogel (1994), and McMullin (2019).

"mineness" that pertains equally, if asymmetrically, to the other: we can say "'I-myself' and 'you-yourself' but not 'thou-I'" (1984, p. 188). Thus neither the I nor the Thou is an *instance* of ontological egoicity; rather, the I, thou, we, us – all the various forms of interpersonal understanding – are ontologically *grounded* in egoicity, and their various differences are constituted factically as distinct modes of behavior mediated by "being alongside" (*sein bei*) things in the world (1984, pp. 187–88).[17]

Why does Heidegger specify the ontological notion of *Mitsein* as "egoicity" in his metaphysical period? The answer, I think, is that it prepares the way for understanding the ontic ground of ontology as a "radicalization" of Lebniz's concept of the monad, which Heidegger calls "one of the cleverest ideas in philosophy since Plato" (Heidegger 1996, pp. 145, 143). It answers to his complaint that while human sociality has always been recognized as fundamental – as in Aristotle's characterization of human being as *zoon politikon* – the issues surrounding it have most often been dealt with in "ethics" but never as a matter for first philosophy, that is, from the perspective of a "metaphysics of Dasein" (1996, p. 142). Leibniz alone, despite his embrace of the Cartesian idea of subject as substance, makes metaphysical room for something like *Mitsein*. For Leibniz, *Miteinandersein* is basic: individual monads include each other from the start. As "ensouled," each monad, a "metaphysical point" – or *vis* (*Drang*), a unity of *appetitus* and *representatio* – represents the universe (*das Seiende im Ganzen*), including itself (*apperceptio*), from a particular "point of view." Against Husserl's own contemporaneous appropriation of Leibniz's monadology,[18] Heidegger argues that the monad's lack of "windows" – its lack of "receptivity" – does not require that a window to (radical) alterity be produced through empathy. Monads "don't need any windows" if understood as neutral egoicity, since Dasein is already "outside," even if talk of "outside" is misleading (1996, pp. 144–45).

If this appropriation of Leibniz provides the background for Heidegger's move from a phenomenological ontology of Dasein to a metaphysics in which Dasein's neutrality has been "broken" and "ontic" determinations (e.g., "male" and "female") become significant (Heidegger 1996, p. 146), then it should be evident in the way he characterizes Dasein's dispersal in the human being, one natural kind among others. One question, in particular, looms large here: can the monad's (neutral) "openness" to beings as a whole – its "windowless-

---

17 For a keen phenomenological criticism of this approach, see Römer (2018, pp. 254–306).
18 On the role of Leibniz in Husserl's metaphysical thinking, see Mertens (2000) and De Santis (2018).

ness" – be maintained at the metaphysical level of Dasein's dispersal into the human, into bodiliness, sexuality, cultural sociality, and so on?

Before exploring Heidegger's answer it will be helpful to return to Husserl, who also takes up interpersonal relations in his own attempt to move from transcendental phenomenology to metaphyiscs. To begin, we must recall that Husserl's argument in *Cartesian Meditations*, which moves from the "sphere of ownness" to the first emergence of "another ego" in my "world," is based on a methodological abstraction (Husserl 1969, p. 93). In this respect it mirrors Heidegger's appeal to "neutral Dasein," which is "never what exists." However, the vast majority of Husserl's investigations into social reality and interpersonal understanding take place at the "personalistic" level, which is social from the start.[19] As Anthony Steinbock (1995) has shown, these analyses culminate in the concepts of Homeworld and Alienworld, which address issues in what Heidegger called a "hermeneutic of empathy" (1962, p. 163): encounters between more or less differently structured normative orders. Steinbock argues that this is *basic* for Husserl, and that therefore his talk of the "one" world of "humanity" is out of place, even though this is clearly contradicted by Husserl's own writings (Steinbock 1995, pp. 237–247). This textual situation can best be explained, I think, if we consider Husserl's treatment in light of Heidegger's idea of metontology.

Even if the sphere of ownness is a methodological abstraction at the level of static phenomenology, it seems to have a real counterpart at the level of genetic phenomenology: the development of the child and its emergence into sociality. The infant is certainly a conscious being, and it eventually possesses a distinction between self and other. This suggests a genetic-phenomenological account of the conscious experiences that enable such a distinction and give rise to the forms of sociality that are founded on it. Thus Husserl can disarm the paradox of human subjectivity by grounding the "one world" of rational humanity in the genesis of human being from conscious life itself. Heidegger, however, denies that this developmental story belongs to *transcendental* phenomenology. Reflections on childhood are part of a phenomenologically informed, but distinct, metaphysics of the human animal.

Heidegger argues that *if* neutral Dasein is understood as the human being (an animal, a natural kind), it has a childhood (Heidegger 1996, pp. 123–26). But this is accessible only "privatively," i.e., in the absence of direct phenomenological evidence. The human child is not Dasein; it is an animal, and like all an-

---

[19] See, for instance, Husserl (1993, pp. 181–293), but volumes XIII-XV of *Husserliana* contain much more.

imals it is conscious. However, such consciousness "lacks a certain luminosity [*Helligkeit*]"; the infant does not "discover" (*entdecken*) entities as entities but, as belonging to the *Spiel des Lebens*, tacks toward and away from things in a manner that lacks a "goal" (1996, p. 125).[20] However, because the phenomenology of infant experience is privative rather than constitutive, Heidegger denies the "Feuerbachian" thesis that the luminosity the infant will eventually acquire is a *developmental consequence* of the animal's species being (1996, p. 146). For example, animal sexual differentiation cannot explain the "world" of gender. The latter belongs to Dasein, grounded in transcendence (*epekeina tes ousias*) toward the good (*ta agathon*). Further, considered neutrally (i.e., as belonging to the category of thrownness), Dasein's bodiliness can take many forms; once it is sortally specified as the human *animal*'s body, however, it cannot, since body then belongs to a metaphysically contingent species-being. The implication for genetic phenomenology is that the capacities of transcendental subjectivity will always appear to involve an existential leap in which the animal is "transformed into Da-sein." The difference between a child playing at being something and Dasein trying to be it, or between babbling and speaking, is not a continuum.

Obviously this raises its own problems, but whether these problems are more or less objectionable than the ones raised by Husserl's genetic phenomenology cannot be pursued here. The point is that for both Husserl and Heidegger the transcendental subject is essentially social, and if, for both, metaphysics concerns the relation of this subject to a particular worldly entity, the human being, then metaphysics must provide an account of the latter, a "metaphysical ontic" of the human animal. Husserl tells a developmental story in which transcendental subjectivity emerges from nature, while Heidegger denies such a continuum. But how then does he characterize the relation? Here we return to the question of whether Heidegger's "Leibnizian" approach to metaphysics can make sense of the radical openness to what is that belongs to Dasein (considered ontologically) while starting from its dispersal into the "fundamental power" of *nature* – animal life, the species-being of the human being.

---

20 Here "goal" is meant in the sense of a technical "end" or *ergon*. As we shall see in the next section, talk of "goals" in relation to animal life has its place, but such talk remains, from a phenomenological point of view, "privative."

5 "The animal is world-poor": Heidegger's Leibnizian metaphysics

Heidegger's lecture course, *Fundamental Concepts of Metaphysics* (1929/30), is as close as he comes to an account of "the essential nature of life" (Heidegger 1995, p. 192), and it tells us much about his approach to metaphysics: "We cannot separate metaphysics and positive research"; indeed, "the inner unity of science and metaphysics is a matter of *fate*" (1995, p. 189). The bridge between science and metaphysics is provided by "phenomenology" (1995, p. 232). Specifically, Heidegger draws upon Jacob von Uexküll's ecology for a description of life that can help "transpose" his students into animal experience, a "going along with what it is and how it is" that uncovers "what it is like to be this being" (1995, p. 202). Crucially, such transposition is never complete; there is a radical alterity to animal being that can never be overcome.[21]

Mirroring the debate about empathy in Husserl, Edith Stein, Theodor Lipps, and others, Heidegger insists that "self-transposition" does not mean abandoning oneself; rather, it is that whereby we "are able to go along with the other being while remaining *other* with respect to it" (1995, p. 203). In regard to physical things, the idea of transposing oneself into them makes no sense; in regard to human beings, we always find ourselves already transposed, already "with" the other in some way.[22] Though the various modes of interpersonal understanding can range from merely "going alongside" one another to being "for" or "against" one another, there are also forms of collective intentionality in which we "*share* one and the same comportment *with one another*, without this shared experience being fragmented in the process" (1995, pp. 205–206). In regard to our being with animals, however, things are quite different. The fact that the human being is an animal does not guarantee that it is transposed "into animals […], into living beings generally" (1995, p. 209). Domestic animals, for example, "live" with us, but despite the fact that we too are living beings, such animals are not really "with" us; they "feed" (*fressen*), for instance, but do not "eat" (*essen*) with us (1995, p. 210). As Heidegger puts it, animal being "*invites* human transposedness into it, even while refusing the human being the possibility of going along with" it (1995, p. 210). Thus, in a *certain* manner the human being finds itself transposed into the animal, but only against the

---

[21] A fuller treatment of these issues is found in Crowell (2017). See also Engelland (2015) and McNeill (1999).

[22] Here Heidegger *presupposes* the "neutral egoicity" discussed in the previous section; however, as we shall see, attributing it to the "human being" proves to be highly problematic.

background of a radical alterity: "The animal displays a sphere of transposability or, more precisely, the animal itself *is* this sphere, one which nonetheless refuses any going along with" – i.e., any genuine *understanding* of what it is like to be this being (1995, p. 211).

Approaching what animal being is like thus requires a two-step method. Heidegger first adopts a *privative* approach: starting with the phenomenological "essence of the human being" (i.e., Dasein), the alienness of the animal is determined by identifying something it lacks when measured against what can be phenomenologically demonstrated in our own being (1995, p. 211). Phenomenology reveals human being to be world-forming,[23] so Heidegger characterizes animal life as "world-poor" while admitting that this serves a merely methodological purpose: in its own terms, animal life is "a domain which possesses a wealth of openness with which the human world may have nothing to compare" (1995, p. 255). This openness is a kind of intentionality: unlike the stone, animal behavior displays an "openness for..." (1995, p. 248), where the ellipsis indicates the impossibility of characterizing the noetic and noematic correlates in a genuinely first-personal way. The animal encounters beings, but not from out of the "world" in the phenomenological sense – that is, it cannot encounter beings *as* beings because it lacks transcendence, the world-forming capacity to act for the sake of some ability-to-be by binding itself to a measure of success or failure that lets beings be *as* such. But how do we know what animal intentionality is like? Here the privative method gives way to an "ontic" phenomenology scientifically informed by von Uexküll's ecology.

Heidegger's reflections on ecology are informed by his interpretation of Leibniz's monadology.[24] The animal has something "self-like" about it (Heidegger 1995, p. 237): whereas lifeless things conform to external law, the animal's "drive" (*Trieb*) is a kind of internal "prescription" (*Vorschrift*) – not a "purpose" but a "point of view" by which it "is intrinsically regulative and regulates itself" (1995, pp. 238–239). The animal's "capacities" (*Fähigkeiten*), evident in its "behavior" (*Benehmen*), are governed by this prescription or autopoietic code, such that it remains "proper [*eigen*] to itself" without any "self-consciousness" or "reflection" (1995, p. 233). Animal capacities govern the functioning of organs, which in turn delimit the scope of the animal's specific kind of openness to beings. Borrowing terms from Max Scheler, Heidegger defines the self-like character of the animal as a "captivation" (*Benommenheit*) that can be "disinhibited"

---

[23] Here we should recall the caveat that "world-forming" is not the same as "world-disclosing."
[24] In this, of course, he stands in a long line of German anthropological and biological thought that stretches from Leibniz through Herder and Schelling, and in which von Uexküll also belongs. This tradition has been extensively researched in Zammito (2002) and Zammito (2018).

(*ent-hemmt*) by certain things according to the capacities granted to its organs. For instance, the bee has a "proper" (*eigen*) "openness to..." the flower and its nectar thanks to the capacities enabled by its drive (1995, pp. 241–43).

For Heidegger, the metaphysical point lies in the Leibnizian grounding relation between an animal's organs and its instinctual capacities. The animal does not have a capacity because it possesses an organ that serves a function; rather, *because* its instinctual drive codes for a certain capacity, it can develop an organ that serves a function. As Heidegger puts it, it is not the *organ* that has a capacity, but the *organism* (1995, p. 221). What, then, is an organism? Heidegger denies that it is "the morphological unity of the body"; rather, "the unity of the animal's body is grounded [...] precisely in the *unity of captivation*" (1995, p. 258). The unity of captivation – which von Uexküll called the *Umwelt* – is not an environment of occurrent entities accessible to any animal at all, but a space of disinhibition cleared by the animal's prescriptive code. To distinguish it privatively from "world" in the ontological sense, Heidegger refers to this space as the animal's "encircling ring" (*Umring*). Animal life is "precisely the struggle [*Ringen*] to maintain [its] encircling ring" (1995, p. 255).

Two points of particular importance for grasping Heidegger's metaphysics follow from this. First, an animal's *Umring* is *species-specific*; no two species occupy the same *Umring*, and they interact only to the extent that their code allows for such disinhibition. Between species, then, *radical alterity* obtains. There is no room here for imagining the various animal prescriptions as incipient forms of reason embedded in life itself. Second, if the organism that possesses specific capacities is not the individual animal body but the species-*Umring*, then the individual animal body is an *organ* of the species, the executor of certain prescribed capacities. This holds also for human being, in which Dasein is dispersed: it is an animal species with its own *Umring*. But the human being is also Dasein, finite freedom. It does not "behave" but "comports itself" (*verhält sich*); that is, it does not act according to a code but for the sake of a measure to which it binds itself and so is a self in the proper sense. In doing so, it is "world-forming": oriented not to this or that disinhibited thing within a species-specific *Umring* but to "beings as a whole" (1995, p. 283).

The goal of Heidegger's phenomenology of life is the metontological one of grasping Dasein as the human being, i.e., as situated in nature, the "totality of beings" that "is already there" (Heidegger 1984, p. 157). Hence metontology must operate simultaneously in a transcendental and in an ontic register. Transcendentally (*sinnkritisch*), Heidegger rejects von Uexküll's view that the human being is an animal species wholly embedded in nature. Ontically (metaphysically), however, he also rejects Scheler's (and Husserl's) view that "nature is to be regarded as the plank or lowest rung of the ladder which the human being would ascend" to the Absolute. Rather, "living nature holds us ourselves *captive* as human beings" (Heidegger 1995, p. 278). The metaphysical question thus concerns how this captivation (or dispersal) belongs to our essence. If the human being is captivated by nature, then Dasein (care, finite freedom) constitutes a *rupture* in the human being, an ontological difference between animal life and Dasein that is not a version of the "coded" difference that obtains between various animal species (1995, p. 264).

Thus a form of Husserl's paradox of human subjectivity reappears here. Metaphysically, the individual human animal is an organ of the species-specific capacity or organism; but transcendentally, Dasein's freedom – its answerability for what it is trying to be – precludes conceiving the individual as an organ of some higher metaphysical unity. Where Husserl addressed this problem by arguing that the meaning-constituting capacities of the transcendental subject are teleologically prefigured in the animal's behavior, Heidegger insists on an "abyss" between Dasein and the human animal (1995, p. 264). And so, in place of Husserl's genetic phenomenology Heidegger offers a metontological *pedagogy* whose aim is to "liberate the Da-sein *in* the human being" (1995, p. 172).

On the face of it, such an approach seems only to transform the paradox into a "gnostic" dualism where *no* grounding relation between human being and Dasein obtains, but only the presupposition of a fall or dispersal into an alien medium. However, Heidegger's Leibnizian metaphysics suggests a different way of specifying the ontic ground of ontology, namely, by appeal to *history* as one of the two "powers," along with nature, into which Dasein is dispersed. For human being is not only an animal species; it belongs as well to an historical *Volk* – a concept that also has a monadological structure. If conceiving the individual human being as an organ of its animal species cannot do justice to Dasein's transcendence, then perhaps the abyss separating the human animal from Dasein can be bridged if the individual is seen as the executor of capacities that belong to its *Volk*, since it is *conceivable* that the *Vorschrift* of one such *Volk* might *be* to liberate the Da-sein in the human being.

6 Metapolitics: *Volk*, history, and state

In the *Black Notebooks* from the early 1930s, the term "metontology" is replaced by "metapolitics." Behind this terminological shift is a philosophical shift from concern with the phenomenology of radical individuation in *Being and Time* to concern with the phenomenology of collective intentionality ("we-intentions"). Of course, this was not altogether absent from *Being and Time*. There, all forms of collective intentionality take place against the background of the anonymously "public" normative order in which our being-with one another finds itself. However, in Heidegger's metaphysical period, this metaphysically neutral approach is superceded by the the search for the *ontic* ground of ontology, which requires that neutral *Mitsein* be thematized as the particular "we" into which the human being is already dispersed – a *Volk*.

This move from a phenomenology of *Mitsein* to a metaphysics of collective intentionality is already suggested in *Being and Time*. Authentic Dasein is neutrally defined as "resoluteness" (*Entschlossenheit*), i.e., being answerable for its uptake of the norms of the ability-to-be for the sake of which it acts. Such abilities-to-be are not invented by me but are given as a *heritage* which I resolutely take over. In doing so, I embrace my *fate*, a way to be "which [I] have inherited and yet have chosen" (Heidegger 1962, p. 435). Heidegger calls this choice-structure "historizing."

Since Dasein is always *Mitsein*, "its historizing is a co-historizing and is determinative for it as *destiny*" (1962, p. 436). The concept of co-historizing raises difficult phenomenological questions about collective intentionality and decision. Of course, when I resolutely pursue being a teacher, I exemplify an idea of what teaching ought to be, and this may or may not conform to what others take teaching to be. In this sense, my historizing is a co-historizing, since my uptake of any possibility is an *Auseinandersetzung* with the heritage in which we – the others among whom I am – are involved. But who are those others, and how is the heritage that belongs to them to be described? Heidegger continues: co-historizing is "how we designate the historizing of the community, of a *Volk*" (1962, p. 436).

To identify others with "the community" leaves much open – a community of teachers or baseball fans, a community of partisans, a community of parents, a religious community – and this comports well with the phenomenological analysis of the variety of possible identities that come down to me. "Heritage" will mean something different depending on what identity is at issue. To designate the community as a *Volk*, however, is far more specific. If individual Dasein can have a fate, what sort of entity can have a "destiny"? *Being and Time* does not answer this question, but Heidegger's metapolitics attempts to do just that.

We saw that in 1928 Heidegger described neutral *Mitsein*, in Leibnizian fashion, as "egoicity," a form of selfhood that is "prior to all I, thou, we, you" (Heidegger 1998a, p. 43). If, in the transcendental phenomenology of *Being and Time*, the "extreme existentiell possibility" of radical individuation was privileged in order to reveal the authentic "I-myself," the metaphysical search for the *ontic* ground of ontology requires a different emphasis, namely, on the "we" into which I-myself am already dispersed. Because the capacities of selfhood belong not only to me and to you but to "us," the socio-historical whole is not a mere collection; it is genuine selfhood, and indeed a selfhood in which the individual's choice is subordinated to a criterion of collective adequacy. Saying "I" is ever only authentic in the context of saying "we." Metontology is thus, essentially, *metapolitics*.

What this means can be understood by starting with the phenomenological example of collective intentionality Heidegger offers his students, the pedagogical situation: We are students and teacher, those who have "subordinated themselves to the [normative] demands of education," which means to the institution of the university (1998a, pp. 56–57). As Heidegger sees it, this *institutional* involvement means that we are also "willing the will of a state [*Staates*]," and the state "wills nothing else than to be the ruling will and the ruling form of a *Volk*" (1998a, p. 57). Thus, in trying to be students and teachers we are always already "*this Volk* itself"; indeed, "our selfhood is the *Volk*" (1998a, p. 57). Is this equation between the *Volk* and the "we" at issue in collective intentional projects phenomenologically justified? What is a *Volk*?

After canvassing various possible answers – in terms of "body" (life, blood, race), "soul" (customs, mores), and "spirit" (distinguishing between the "riff-raff [*Pöbel*]" and the "better sort"), Heidegger dismisses all anthropological approaches (1998a, pp. 65–67). Yet his own view entails that the *Volk* still has one foot in nature, as it were: our metaphysical dispersal into human being is such that "belonging to a *Volk*" can "never" be chosen (1998a, p. 60). Nevertheless, the question "Who is *this Volk*, that we ourselves are?" remains amenable to a kind of choice: unlike animals, who "cannot deviate from their essence," we can "wander from our essence and become untrue to it" (1998a, p. 69). For this reason, the *being* of a *Volk* is "historical" in the form of a state, and the state is something whose meaning and structure *can* be at issue in our collective decision-making (Heidegger 2015, pp. 38–39).[25]

Since Heidegger here ascribes the ontological characteristics of neutral Dasein to the first-person plural of the *Volk*, he (fatally) applies the whole analysis of decision found in *Being and Time* to the "we" (1998a, pp. 70–77). Just as individuals are concerned with their own being, so the *Volk*, the "being that actualizes the state in its being," is a self who "knows the state, cares about it, and wills it" (2015, p. 48). Heidegger never explains the nature of this collective willing, saying only that "the will of the people is a complicated structure that is

---

[25] Material cited from Heidegger (2015) stems from student transcripts of a seminar Heidegger delivered between November 1933 and February 1934. Thus, particular wording cannot be confidently attributed to Heidegger. Nevertheless, the movement of thought is clearly consistent with the ideas we have been developing here.

hard to grasp" (2015, p. 60). I have argued elsewhere (Crowell 2004) that the transcendental structure of first-person *singular* responsibility is not phenomenologically applicable to the first-person plural, but it is clear that, for Heidegger, in addition to being answerable for what I take teaching, fatherhood, or friendship to mean, I am simultaneously answerable *to* the *Volk* that we ourselves are.

The state is not the social institution studied by the human, as opposed to the natural, sciences; it is "a way of being in which humans are," and "the *Volk* is the being that *is* in the manner of a state" (Heidegger 2015, p. 38). Thus Heidegger does not view the state as grounded in individuals who collectively pursue decisions through discourse and *praxis*; nor is it an "organism"; it is an ontological order of "mastery, rank, leadership and following" (2015, p. 38).[26] The state is at issue such that we, the *Volk*, must "decide for" it – bring it "to power" – so that "the state may form our essence" (2015, p. 39). Thus the concept of *Volk* belongs to the metaphysical dispersal of Dasein. If Dasein metontologically presupposes that a totality of beings is already there, then this totality now includes not only a natural plurality of radically alien animal species but also an *historical* plurality of radically alien *Völker*. And just as the human being is captivated in the species-specific capacities of the human animal, so it is captivated in its *Volk*-specific history. The *Volk*, as the "substance" and "supporting ground" of the state, is not merely "race and the community of the same stock" – though it is that *too* – but "a kind of being that has grown under a common fate and taken distinctive shape within a *single* state" (2015, p. 43).

For the individual, whose relation to the state is "voluntary" rather than "organic," the order of the state depends on "binding" oneself together with others to "*one* fate" and to the actualization of "*one* idea" (2015, p. 49). But this one idea is not arbitrary; rather, it belongs to the *Volk* itself, like the instinctual code that governs the animal species. Thus the historical *Volk* is a monad constituted by a principle that belongs to it and no other.

In Heidegger's reflections on the *Volk* as an historical monad, the categories of neutral Dasein are once more given a metaphysical interpretation. Our openness to beings as a whole is accomplished in "mood," which is not an inner "bodily" phenomenon, but *Bodenständigkeit* – that which roots the body in the ground, the soil (*Boden*), where it is "supported, sheltered, and threatened by nature" (1998a, p. 152). The "present," then, is the "work" we do in coming to terms with this rootedness, but work can carry us "away into the manifestness of what is and its structure" only because it is supported by past (*Gewesenheit*)

---

[26] Here we cannot explore the echoes of Plato's *Republic* found in Heidegger's texts from this period, including the *Rektoratsrede*, but see the discussion in Fried (2000, pp. 136–185).

and future (*Zukunft*) (1998a, p. 154). These neutral ek-stases of Dasein's temporality, conceived in a metaphysically ontic way, become the "consignment" (*Sendung*) and the "assignment" (*Auftrag*). The *Volk* is thus not a "collective" constituted by "agreements" (*Abmachungen*) but gains its unity from a "vocation" that has been consigned to it as a heritage and assigned to it as a task or destiny (1998a, p. 158).

From the point of view of the individual, the assignment is always at issue. As resolute, the individual must always be normatively guided by the assignment, and thus is "continually exposed to the possibility of death [*Untergang*] and sacrifice" (1998a, p. 160). No matter what else an individual tries to be, it is authentically itself only if it measures its comportment against "empowering the power of the state" (1998a, p. 164).[27] Authenticity is no longer neutrally defined as answerability for the measures or norms in light of which one acts; rather, it is metaphysically defined as answerability to a specific measure that one *necessarily* possesses as a birthright.

Thus, while the state is not an organism, it is the being of an entity, the *Volk*, that looks very much like one, a metaphysically "originating unity" – the "law of historical being" – to which individual human beings belong as organs of its capacity. This capacity, or vocation, is *normatively prescribed* by a *Volk*'s consignment and assignment. If animal life is the struggle to preserve its species-specific *Umring*, a *Volk*, understood metaphysically, is an entity whose "drive" or historical vocation is "the preservation of its consignment and the fight for its assignment." Socialism, then, means *national* socialism: the collective intentionality of a *Volk* as "care for the measures and the essential constellation of [its] historical being" in a state (1998a, p. 165).

As an educator, Heidegger understood his primary task to be to awaken his students to their rootedness in the specific assignment of the German *Volk*. Only if the individual body (a mere "citizen") recognizes what it truly is by embracing its status as an organ of the *Volk* can its (objectionably liberal) "free" will "bind itself" in the *right way* to the collective law of its being. Metaphysically, Dasein exists as a plurality of historical monads, *Völker*, each of which is world-forming on the basis of its unique vocation. And because Heidegger holds that the vocation the German *Volk* is "metaphysics" itself (Heidegger 2010, pp. 62–63), his students are uniquely positioned within beings as a whole to mediate between the human animal and the "Da-sein in the human being," thereby fulfilling

---

[27] Thus, as Marion Heinz (2015, p. 73) notes, the world as the correlate of care is "narrowed down to care for Being within the community of the *Volk*" and "Dasein is now conceived as directed teleologically in advance to a particular possibility: existing in the political community."

the promise of a genuinely *philosophical* world-view that emerged when the attitude of self-control (*Haltung*) replaced that of sheltering (*Bergen*).

But this metaphysics – the metaphysical ontic that is to provide the ontic ground of ontology – also claims to be phenomenologically grounded, and in this it is an abject failure. Heidegger's ambition for metaphysics was *nominally* the same as Husserl's: to accomplish an other beginning (Husserl: *Endstiftung*) of the "first beginning" (*Urstiftung*) of the philosophy that arose in Greece. But if Husserl's version is phenomenologically unconvincing in its *ground* – i.e., its attribution of a rational teleology to life itself – the absence of phenomenological warrant in Heidegger's version yields unconvincing (to say the least) *implications*. While Husserl preserved at least the *idea* of "one world" in which otherness did not signify radical alienness, Heidegger's metapolitics turns the paradox of human subjectivity into a justification for domination. With its "complete disempowerment of reason" (Heinz 2015, p. 84), Heidegger's monadology of historical *Völker* leaves us only one option: a world "led" by the "metaphysical people." Since other *Völker* remain radically alien in their vocation, they can only be subordinated to the German *Volk* as other animal species are subordinated to the one animal species that is not world-poor but world-having. As Heidegger would soon learn, however, the empirical and the transcendental do not belong together in this way. The inference from phenomenology to metaphysics, from *Sinnkritik* to metapolitics, merely papers over the abyss that separates them and leads to what Kant presciently labeled "fanaticism" (Kant 1929, p. 32).

References

Bernet, Rudolf (2004): "Husserl's Transcendental Idealism Revisited". In: *The New Yearbook for Phenomenology and Phenomenological Philosophy* 4, pp. 1–20.

Crowell, Steven (2000): "Metaphysics, Metontology, and the End of *Being and Time*". In: *Philosophy and Phenomenological Research* LX(2), pp. 307–333.

Crowell, Steven (2004): "Authentic Historicality". In: Carr, David/Cheung, Chan-Fai (Eds.): *Space, Time, and Culture*. Dordrecht: Kluwer, pp. 57–71.

Crowell, Steven (2007): "*Sorge* or *Selbstbewußtsein?* Heidegger and Korsgaard on the Sources of Normativity". In: *European Journal of Philosophy* 15(3), pp. 315–333.

Crowell, Steven (2013): *Normativity and Phenomenology in Husserl and Heidegger*. Cambridge: Cambridge University Press.

Crowell, Steven (2014): "Transcendental Life". In: Heinämaa, Sara/Hartimo, Miria/Miettinen, Timo (Eds.): *Phenomenology and the Transcendental*. London, New York: Routledge, pp. 21–48.

Crowell, Steven (2016): "Reading Heidegger's *Black Notebooks*". In: Farin, Ingo/Malpas, Jeff (Eds.): *Reading Heidegger's Black Notebooks 1931–1941*. Cambridge, MA: The MIT Press, pp. 29–44.

Crowell, Steven (2017): "We Have Never Been Animals. Heidegger's Posthumanism". In: *Études phénoménologiques / Phenomenological Studies* I, pp. 217–240.
Crowell, Steven (2018): "The Middle Heidegger's Phenomenological Metaphysics". In: Zahavi, Dan (Ed.): *The Oxford Handbook of the History of Phenomenology*. Oxford: Oxford University Press, pp. 229–250.
Crowell, Steven (2019): "Determinable Indeterminacy: A Note on the Phenomenology of Horizons". In: Scott, Robert H./Moss, Gregory, S. (Eds.): *The Significance of Indeterminacy: Perspectives from Asian and Continental Philosophy*. London, New York: Routledge, pp. 127–147.
De Palma, Vittorio (2019): "Deskription oder Konstruktion? Husserl und die Grenzen der Phänomenologie". In: *Husserl Studies* 35, pp. 185–202.
De Santis, Daniele (2018): "'Metaphysische Ergebnisse': Phenomenology and Metaphysics in Edmund Husserl's *Cartesianische Meditationen* (§ 60). Attempt at Commentary". In: *Husserl Studies* 34, pp. 63–83.
Dreyfus, Hubert (1991): *Being-in-the-World: A Commentary on Heidegger's Being and Time, Division I*. Cambridge, MA: The MIT Press.
Engelland, Chad (2015): "Heidegger and the Human Difference". In: *Journal of the American Philosophical Association* 1(1), pp. 175–193.
Fried, Gregory (2000): *Heidegger's Polemos: From Being to Politics*. New Haven: Yale University Press.
Gethmann, Carl-Friedrich (1974): *Verstehen und Auslegung: Das Methodenproblem in der Philosophie Martin Heideggers*. Bonn: Bouvier Verlag.
Heidegger, Martin (1962): *Being and Time*. Trans. John Macquarrie/Edward Robinson. New York: Harper & Row.
Heidegger, Martin (1984): *The Metaphysical Foundations of Logic*. Trans. Michael Heim. Bloomington: Indiana University Press.
Heidegger, Martin (1985): *History of the Concept of Time: Prolegomena*. Trans. Theodore Kisiel. Bloomington: Indiana University Press.
Heidegger, Martin (1995): *The Fundamental Concepts of Metaphysics: World, Finitude, Solitude*. Trans. Will McNeill/Nicholas Walker. Bloomington: Indiana University Press.
Heidegger, Martin (1996): *Einleitung in die Philosophie*. Otto Saame/Ina Saame-Speidel (Eds.). Frankfurt: Vittorio Klostermann.
Heidegger, Martin (1998a): *Logik als die Frage nach dem Wesen der Sprache*. Gesamtausgabe 38. Günter Seubold (Ed.). Frankfurt: Vittorio Klostermann.
Heidegger, Martin (1998b): "What is Metaphysics?". In: *Pathmarks*. William McNeill (Ed.). Cambridge: Cambridge University Press.
Heidegger, Martin (2010): *Being and Truth*. Trans. Gregory Fried/Richard Polt. Bloomington: Indiana University Press.
Heidegger, Martin (2014): *Überlegungen II-VI (Schwarze Hefte 1931–1938)*. Peter Trawney (Ed.). Frankfurt: Vittorio Klostermann.
Heidegger, Martin (2015): *Nature, History, State 1933–1934*. Gregory Fried/Richard Polt (Eds. and Trans.). London: Bloomsbury.
Heinz, Marion (2015): "*Volk* and *Führer*." In: *Nature, History, State 1933–1934*. Gregory Fried/Richard Polt (Eds. and Trans.). London: Bloomsbury.
Husserl, Edmund (1969): *Cartesian Meditations: An Introduction to Phenomenology*. Trans. Dorion Cairns. The Hague: Martinus Nihjoff.

Husserl, Edmund (1970): *The Crisis of European Sciences and Transcendental Phenomenology*. Trans. David Carr. Evanston: Northwestern University Press.

Husserl, Edmund (1983): *Ideas Pertaining to a Pure Phenomenology and to a Phenomenological Philosophy, First Book: General Introduction to a Pure Phenomenology*. Trans. F. Kersten. The Hague: Martinus Nijhoff.

Husserl, Edmund (1993): *Ideas Pertaining to a Pure Phenomenology and to a Phenomenological Philosophy, Second Book: Studies in the Phenomenology of Constitution*. Trans. Richard Rojcewicz/André Schuwer. Dordrecht: Kluwer.

Husserl, Edmund (2008): *Die Lebenswelt. Auslegung der Vorgegebenen Welt und ihrer Konstitution. Texte aus dem Nachlass (1916–1937)*. Rochus Sowa (Ed.). Husserliana XXXIX. Dordrecht: Springer.

Jacobs, Hanne (2013): "Phenomenology as a Way of Life? Husserl on Phenomenological Reflection and Self-Transformation". In: *Continental Philosophy Review* 46, pp. 349–69.

Kant, Immanuel (1929): *Critique of Pure Reason*. Trans. Norman Kemp Smith. London: Macmillan.

Loidolt, Sophie (2015): "Transzendentalphilosophie und Idealismus in der Phänomenologie. Überlegungen zur phänomenologischen 'Gretchenfrage'". In: *Metodo* Special Issue I, pp. 103–135.

Löwith, Karl (1986): *Mein Leben in Deutschland vor und nach 1933*. Stuttgart: J. B. Metzler.

McMullin, Irene (2019): *Existential Flourishing: A Phenomenology of the Virtues*. Cambridge: Cambridge University Press.

McNeill, William (1999): "Life Beyond the Organism: Animal Being in Heidegger's Freiburg Lectures 1929–30". In: Steeves, H. Peter/Regan, Tom (Eds.): *Animal Others: On Ethics, Ontology, and Animal Life*. Albany: SUNY Press, pp. 197–248.

Mertens, Karl (2000): "Husserls Phänomenologie der Monade. Bemerkungen zu Husserls Auseinandersetzung mit Leibniz". In: *Husserl Studies* 17, pp. 1–20.

Olafson, Frederick (1998): *Heidegger and the Ground of Ethics: A Study of Mitsein*. Cambridge: Cambridge University Press.

Römer, Inga (2018): *Das Begehren der reinen praktischen Vernunft: Kants Ethik in phänomenologischer Sicht*. Hamburg: Felix Meiner.

Schmidt, Stefan (2016): *Grund und Freiheit: Eine phänomenologische Untersuchung des Freiheitsbegriffs Heideggers*. Dordrecht: Springer.

Staiti, Andrea (2010): *Geistigkeit, Leben und geschichtliche Welt in der Transzendentalphänomenologie Husserls*. Würzburg: Ergon Verlag.

Tengelyi, László (2014): *Welt und Unendlichkeit. Zum Problem phänomenologischer Metaphysik*. Freiburg: Verlag Karl Alber.

Truwant, Simon (2018): "The Hierarchy Among the Symbolic Forms: Cassirer's Enlightened View of Human Culture". In: *Cassirer Studies* VII-VIII, pp. 119–139.

Vogel, Lawrence (1994): *The Fragile "We". Ethical Implications of Heidegger's "Being and Time"*. Evanston: Northwestern University Press.

Zammito, John (2002): *Kant, Herder, and the Birth of Anthropology*. Chicago: University of Chicago Press.

Zammito, John (2018): *The Gestation of German Biology: Philosophy and Physiology from Stahl to Schelling*. Chicago: University of Chicago Press.

Index

Absolute 7, 37, 48, 83f., 86–90, 94f., 100, 102, 104, 106, 112, 118, 128f., 132, 141, 157, 202, 206f., 214, 221, 227f., 232, 234, 265, 295, 297, 299, 365, 384, 462, 465, 477
– Absolute attitude 8, 86, 105f.
– Absolute givenness 93–95
Abstract movement 142–144, 148
Acceptance component 366, 368–370, 374, 382
Affection 18, 176, 182, 226, 229, 236, 298, 307, 346, 399–402, 413f., 418, 420–424, 426f., 430
Affective intentionality 18, 311, 413f., 417, 425f., 431
Affectivity 13, 18, 188, 236, 254, 257, 265, 310f., 313, 415f., 420, 423, 426, 428f., 431
Alienation 10, 13, 182, 220–222, 261, 263, 331
Allport, Gordon W. 17, 389f., 401
Al-Saji, Alia 261, 429
Alteration 13–15, 125, 166f., 182, 264, 266f., 273, 303f., 306f., 309f., 314, 350
Alterity 5f., 8, 11f., 100, 105, 166, 168, 201, 203, 205, 216f., 221f., 225f., 230–234, 237, 376, 470f., 474–476
Altman, William H.F. 439
American Psychiatric Association 303f., 324
Analogy 170, 204, 208, 211f., 218, 233, 347, 356, 378, 392f.
Anger 16f., 176, 283–285, 348, 355, 389–392, 395–397, 399, 401–410
Anonymity 8, 91, 94f., 184, 203, 216, 437, 470
Answerability 468, 477, 481
Anti-Semitism 435f., 438, 440, 453–455
Apodictic 6, 8f., 57, 61, 68, 74, 117f., 122, 132f.
Apperception 25, 34, 69, 75f., 78, 80, 172, 182, 262, 269f., 273, 347, 349, 436

– Apperceptive transference 34, 233
– Appresentation 12, 78f., 100f., 129, 169, 233f.
Aristotle 17, 389–396, 398–409, 448, 465, 471
Association 65–67, 78, 168, 210, 225, 232, 269, 271, 415, 424, 427
Attention 5f., 10, 13f., 18, 30, 73, 117, 130, 132, 137, 226f., 253f., 256, 261, 266, 268, 273, 281, 297–299, 304–307, 309f., 312, 317, 337, 350, 352, 354, 356, 358f., 372, 392, 395, 397f., 404, 407, 409, 413–415, 417–430, 446
Austin J.L. 336–338
Authenticity 352, 443, 470, 481
Axiology 16, 158f., 189f., 192, 197, 261, 265, 360, 372, 376, 381f.

Bachelard, Gaston 139, 257
Baehr, Jason S. 359
Baldwin, James 262–264
Baron-Cohen, Simon 23, 27
Bassler, O. Bradley 230
Bauch, Bruno 19, 452–454
Bazalgette, Peter 23
Beidel, Deborah C. 317
Being-in 8, 32, 83, 89, 99, 103f., 209
– Being-in-another 84, 95, 104
– Being-in-the-world 24, 38, 89, 93, 208, 243, 315, 462, 470
Being-with 5, 24, 37f., 40, 84, 423, 469, 478
– Being with one another (*Miteinandersein*) 5, 37f., 470f., 478
– Shared existence (*Mitdasein*) 38
Benardete, Seth 393
Benveniste, Émile 39
Bernet, Rudolf 85, 166, 173, 190, 222, 466
Blankenburg, Wolfgang 306f.
Bloom, Paul 23
Bodei, Remo 405
Bortolan, Anna 14f., 274, 290, 303, 305, 311–313, 315, 339, 410

Brentano, Franz   49, 55
Breyer, Thiemo   261, 280
Brison, Susan   323, 337
Brudholm, Thomas   405, 410

Cairns, Douglas   110, 396, 401
Canguilhem, Georges   9f., 137–141, 153–161
Captivation (*Benommenheit*)   475–477
Cassirer, Ernst   19, 435, 440, 453–455, 467
Categorial attitude   9, 146–148
Centrone, Bruno   392
Chapoutot, Johann   450f.
Charity   358f., 437
Church, Ian M.   358
Clark, David M.   308
Clinical empathy   324, 338
Coexistence   76f., 80, 99–101, 105f., 202, 237
Cogito   63f., 75, 90f., 94, 132, 139, 188, 204, 206f., 213
– Certainty of the cogito   8, 83, 88, 92
Cohen, Hermann   3, 265, 452f.
Collective intentionality   83, 181, 462, 474, 477–479, 481
Commitment   17, 165, 279, 328f., 334, 353, 357, 360, 378f., 451, 463, 465, 468
Communication   17, 30, 39, 114, 188, 193, 196, 212f., 218, 262f., 323, 336f., 391, 396, 398, 404f., 410, 446, 457
Community   11, 30, 33, 39, 63, 73, 76, 78, 81, 86, 178, 180f., 193–195, 197, 235f., 262f., 335, 351, 356, 385, 452, 457, 462, 478, 480f.
Comportment   202, 207, 209–215, 217, 467f., 474, 481
Concrete attitude   9, 146–148
Concrete movement   9, 142–145, 148
Conflict   17, 220, 267, 272f., 330f., 358, 363, 368, 382–386, 404, 435, 439f., 442f., 450, 453f.
Constitutive negativity   138f., 152f., 159
Cooke, Deryck   245, 252f.
Cope, Edward M   281, 292, 396
Coplan, Amy   23
Co-presence (*Kompräsenz*)   36, 40

Costa, Vincenzo   379f.
Courtine, Jean   230
Crowell, Steven   19, 83, 85f., 461f., 464, 466–468, 474, 480

Danto, Arthur C.   306
D'Arms, Justin   390
Darwall, Stephen   16, 353f.
Dasein   38, 141, 157, 461, 463–473, 475–481
Davos   435, 440
Decision   191, 193, 203, 215, 355f., 365, 380, 382, 389, 442, 445f., 456, 478–480
De Monticelli, Roberta   266
De Palma, Vittorio   466
Depew, David   25
Depraz, Natalie   419, 429f.
De Santis, Daniele   471
Descartes, René   10, 54f., 75, 90, 188
– Cartesianism   188, 204, 208f., 211, 229
Destiny   296, 478, 481
Dilthey, Wilhelm   23, 28f., 32
Disclosedness   469
Disease   153, 156–159
Dispersal (*Zerstreuung*)   464, 471–473, 477, 479f.
Dissonance   13, 267, 271–274
Dovidio, John F.   401
Dreyfus, Hubert   470
Drummond, John J.   16, 265, 345, 348, 351f.
Dynamic approach   154

Eagly, Alice H.   401
Egoic   11, 25, 33, 37, 39, 96, 182, 189–192, 197
– Concrete ego   64, 71, 79f.
– Egoicity   470f., 474, 478
– Egoic subjectivity   39
– Egology   8, 86, 109, 113–115, 130f.
– Eidos Ego   68, 74
– Empirical Ego   67
– Transcendental ego   7, 63, 65–79, 81, 97, 101, 103, 194, 232f.
Eidetic intuition   6f., 56f., 60f., 68

Einfühlung 23, 25, 28 f., 31, 33, 38, 40, 100, 115, 117, 120, 123, 169, 347 f., 470
Eksteins, Modris 440
Eliot, T.S. 438
Ellison, Ralph 261–264
Elster, Jon 286, 292, 407
Embodiment 4, 100 f., 104, 150, 175, 255, 357
Embree, Lester 16, 363, 367, 371, 373
Emmanuel, J.S. 314
Emotional 24–27, 30–32, 39, 245, 252 f., 280, 312, 323, 333, 339, 353–355, 370, 374, 382, 389, 404, 417
– Emotional contagion 27, 30 f., 354 f.
– Emotional response 24, 245, 253
– Genuine emotional sharing 30
Encircling ring (*Umring*) 476, 481
Enemy, the 18 f., 325, 373, 442–444, 446, 449, 451–453, 458
Engelland, Chad 474
Envy 12–14, 279–300, 408
– Existential envy 14, 279 f., 290–300
Epistemology 139, 160
Epoché 116, 124 f., 132, 150, 182, 462 f.
Eudaimonia 359 f.
Ewert, Otto 28
Exceedance 12, 225–229, 236–238
Existential Feeling 15, 310–315, 318
Experience of the other (*Fremderfahrung*) 4, 24, 33, 80, 121, 165 f., 169, 173–175, 177, 179 f., 204 f., 208 f., 213, 219, 231, 237, 347 f.

Facticity 85, 99, 106, 142, 148, 194, 238, 465
Fainstein Lamuedra, Graciela 236
Fanon, Frantz 262–264
Feelings, of 17, 23, 26, 30–32, 60, 89, 91 f., 174 f., 183, 189, 191, 251–253, 279–284, 287–290, 292, 300, 311, 313, 315, 317, 347, 351 f., 360, 366, 376, 381 f., 391, 399, 401, 425–427
– Feelings of inferiority 282, 284, 287
– Feelings of powerlessness 284, 287 f., 389
– Feelings of self-worth 280, 289

Fernández de la Mora, Gonzalo 295–297, 299
Fest, Joachim 449
Fidalgo, António 29
Fink, Eugen 228
First-person 4, 10, 26, 32, 39, 47, 50, 98 f., 165, 169, 171, 173–176, 182 f., 203, 207 f., 214, 261, 273, 308 f., 317, 323, 329, 338, 470, 475, 479 f.
– First-person awareness 50
– First-person perspective 33, 52, 54, 98, 169, 179, 202, 351
Fiske, Susan T. 401
Flasch, Kurt 440
Flesh of the world 87, 95
Flett, Gordon, L. 316
Ford, Emily 308 f., 316
Forst, Rainer 16, 363, 367–369, 374
Foucault, Michel 9, 137–139, 141, 159 f.
Freud, Sigmund 39
Fricker, Miranda 261
Fried, Gregory 445, 452, 480
Fuchs, Thomas 306, 308
Füreinandersein 182
Fussi, Alessandra 17, 284–287, 294, 389, 393, 402

Gadamer, Hans-Georg 29, 255
Gallagher, Shaun 14, 304 f., 317
Gasché, Rodolphe 229
Gehring, Petra 87
Generativity 12, 83, 193, 195, 226–228, 230, 235, 237
Generosity 16, 358–360
Genetic phenomenology 11, 18, 133 f., 227, 268, 271, 413, 418, 430, 468, 472 f., 477
Geniusas, Saulius 226, 229
Georgiades, Thrasyboulos 248
Gethmann, Carl-Friedrich 469
Glick, Peter 401
Goethe, Johann, Wolfgang von 363, 365 f., 385 f., 448
Goldie, Peter 23, 314
Goldman, Alvin I. 23, 25, 170
Gomes Barbosa, William 228
Gomes de Castro, Thiago 228

Gould, Stephan Jay   52
Govier, Trudy   315f.
Graffigna, Matias   379
Gratier, Maya   39
Grazia, Daniela   309, 317f.
Grief   30f., 252, 281f., 284f., 287, 290, 293, 324, 329, 331f., 339, 354f.
Griswold, Charles L.   396
Grünbaum, Thor   303

Habit   11, 18, 119, 190, 296, 334, 403, 413f., 423–427, 429, 431
– Habituality   11, 190, 269, 427
Hackmann, Ann   308
Haffner, Sebastian   439
Halperin, Eran   404
Hamilton, Andy   256
Hanslick, Eduard   252
Harold, James   25
Hatred   17, 189, 251, 254, 292f., 295, 297–299, 374, 389–392, 394f., 397, 405–410, 417
Hauptmann, Moritz   257
Heidegger, Martin   4f., 16, 18f., 23, 29, 35–39, 83, 85, 93, 141, 157, 229f., 244f., 248, 254, 311, 435–442, 444–451, 456–458, 461–482
Heimberg, Richard G.   308–310
Heinämaa, Sara   10f., 187, 192, 195, 272, 424f.
Heinz, Marion   481f.
Held, Klaus   98, 128f., 134, 191, 252, 254, 262, 365, 384, 436, 465, 467
Henry, Michel   11f., 225f., 230–238, 244f.
Herman, Judith   324, 335
Hermeneutics   10, 23, 149, 168
– Hermeneutics of the normal and the pathological   9, 137, 140f., 149, 152
Hewitt, Paul L.   316
Heyd, David   364
History   4, 18, 23, 28, 30, 65f., 138f., 181, 183, 190, 196, 203, 227–229, 245, 248, 252, 268, 325, 414, 423f., 439, 447, 461, 469, 477, 480
– Historicality   469
– Historizing   478
Hobbes, Thomas   399

Hoeres, Peter   453
Honneth, Axel   18, 261, 399, 413–418, 422, 425f., 428–431
Howland, Jacob   393
Hume, David   23, 26, 30, 271
Humility   16, 357–359
Husserl, Edmund   3–13, 16, 18f., 23–26, 28f., 31–40, 47–61, 63–81, 83–106, 109–120, 123–128, 130–134, 141f., 145, 152f., 165–171, 174–184, 187–197, 201–203, 225f., 228–237, 244, 246f., 251, 261–274, 303, 305, 327, 335, 345, 347–352, 354, 357, 366, 372, 375–381, 384, 413f., 417–431, 448f., 462f., 465–474, 476f., 482
Hyle   8, 83, 88, 91f., 104

Idealism   19, 73, 75–77, 81, 84–87, 89, 96f., 148, 202, 206, 447–451, 454
Illocutionary acts   15, 337f.
Image   30, 147, 176, 219f., 246, 377, 392, 394, 405, 419, 437, 457
– Aural image   250
– Imaginary   139, 142–145, 220, 246f., 250f., 253
– Imagination   148, 150, 332, 377, 405
– Imaginative identification   30f.
– Mirror image   219–222
Intellectualism   89, 143, 146, 149, 187, 197, 206f., 220
Interpersonal experience   4f., 12, 14–16, 23, 181, 303f., 306, 314, 317
Inverso, Hernán   11f., 225–227, 230, 238
I-thou relation   175, 470

Jacobs, Hanne   191, 265, 465
Jacobson, Daniel   390
James, Henry   318, 440
Janicaud, Dominique   238
Jardine, James   261, 415
Johnson, Charles   18, 413–416, 422, 424, 426, 429
Jones, Henry Stuart   28, 334
Judaism   18f., 435, 437f., 440, 447, 452f.

Kant, Immanuel   10, 85f., 105, 143, 150,
    187f., 193f., 197, 206f., 214, 222, 268,
    356, 402f., 449, 452, 454, 463, 482
Karau, Steven J.   401
Kenny, Anthony   20, 354
Kerman, Peter   252
Kern, Iso   100, 133, 190, 230
King, Preston   16, 363, 366–369, 371–373
Kivy, Peter   245
Kolnai, Aurel   394f.
Konstan, David   394, 399
Kriegel, Uriah   354
Kusch, Martin   325f., 335, 339

Lacan, Jacques   218, 220, 222
Landgrebe, Ludwig   229
Lauer, Quentin   47
Laurand, Valéry   28
Lefebvre, Henri   256f.
Leibniz, Gottfried Wilhelm   7, 19, 63,
    73–76, 81, 103, 189, 194, 461, 466,
    471, 473–478
Levi, Primo   333f.
Levinas, Emmanuel   34, 36, 87, 166
Lhermitte, Jean   210
Liddell, Henry George   28
Life-world (*Lebenswelt*)   32, 35f., 39f., 84,
    88, 93, 151, 228, 426
Lipps, Theodor   23, 28f., 31, 474
Lived body   40, 89, 169–173, 175, 257, 312
– Body image   220, 222
– Body schema   137, 140, 142, 147, 160,
    210, 212–214, 218
– Body-subject   137, 140–148, 150, 157
Lived experience   3, 7, 10, 32, 89, 92, 95f.,
    98, 103, 128, 156, 169, 172–174, 183,
    207, 234, 382, 417, 427
Lohmar, Achim   16, 363, 367, 369f., 374,
    382
Lohmar, Dieter   126, 134, 269, 271, 387
Loidolt, Sophie   7f., 83, 94, 192, 466
Lotze, Hermann   28
Love   11, 27, 33, 35, 92, 176, 189, 192,
    251f., 254, 291, 297, 334f., 346, 356,
    358, 360, 374, 392, 394f., 397, 400f.,
    425

Löwith, Karl   469
Luft, Sebastian   230

MacIntyre, Alasdair C.   345
Macnamara, Coleen   404
Magrì, Elisa   13, 248, 261, 264, 266, 273,
    300, 318, 410
Makkreel, Rudolf A.   29
Marc, Franz   443, 446
Marcuse, Herbert   363
Marder, Michael   25
Margalit, Avishai   399
McMullin, Irene   470
McNeill, William   474
Melody   247, 250, 253f., 257, 421
Mendelssohn, Felix   252, 257
Mental events   48, 52–55, 57f., 60
Mental states   6, 24, 47, 50, 52, 54–60,
    168, 176, 310, 315, 337, 349, 357, 380
Merleau-Ponty, Maurice   6–11, 39, 83,
    87–95, 99, 104f., 137, 139–150, 152f.,
    157, 159–161, 169, 176, 183f., 187f.,
    190, 195–197, 201–222, 244–246,
    268, 270, 304f., 327, 335
Mertens, Karl   194, 357, 471
Metaphysics   5, 19, 75, 84–86, 95, 106,
    398, 447, 449, 457, 461–469, 471–
    474, 476–478, 481f.
Metapolitics   19, 461f., 469, 477–479, 482
Method   6–9, 12, 19, 47–49, 56f., 61, 68,
    96, 109f., 114–116, 118f., 121f., 126,
    131, 133f., 159, 161, 226, 228–230, 237,
    429f., 462, 467, 475
Metontology   19, 461f., 464–470, 472,
    476f., 479
Mills, Charles   261, 264
Minkowski, Eugène   306
Mirroring   101, 103, 296, 474
Monad   8, 52, 67, 71, 73–79, 81, 84–87,
    95f., 99–104, 106, 119f., 184, 189, 194,
    197, 227, 461, 471, 480f.
– Intermonadic time   101
– Monadic causality   101, 103
– Monadology   7, 19, 63, 75f., 83, 86, 95,
    105, 194, 471, 475, 482

Moran, Dermot   3–5, 23 f., 27, 49, 83, 178, 190 f., 195, 222, 229, 262, 265, 418 f., 427
Moscovitch, David A.   304, 314
Multiplicity   63, 66–70, 73, 75, 81, 119, 246
Münkler, Herfried   441
Murray, Charles   51
Music   12, 28, 243–256, 421
– Musical Meaning   12, 251

Nancy, Jean-Luc   251, 253, 256, 337
Natural attitude   7, 9, 35, 38, 67, 69, 86, 97, 99 f., 102, 104, 106, 115, 120, 126, 130, 132, 228 f., 262, 272, 427, 430
Naturalism   6, 47–49, 52, 57, 65, 99, 138, 150 f., 266, 272, 454, 463
Nature   48–50, 56 f., 59 f., 67, 72 f., 77, 80 f., 86, 93, 95, 97, 103 f., 130, 141, 155, 187, 228, 244, 255, 399, 463–465, 468 f., 473, 476 f., 479 f.
Nenon, Charles   6 f., 47, 56, 58, 262
Neo-Kantianism   202, 206, 452
Neutrality   17, 365, 377, 379, 386 f., 462 f., 469, 471
Noema   8 f., 11 f., 59, 75, 91 f., 117, 120, 127, 129, 206, 225 f., 231, 234, 236 f., 475
Noesis   8, 59, 117–120, 127–129, 236, 475
Noetic-noematic   75, 120, 236
Non-positivistic conception of pathology   137, 140, 153
Non-quantitative approach   155
Normal subject   143–145, 148–150
Norms   6, 16, 18 f., 48, 59 f., 151, 153–157, 180, 206, 261, 265, 273, 328 f., 417, 424, 427–429, 431, 467–469, 472, 478 f., 481
Nussbaum, Martha C.   397, 402

Objection component   366, 368 f., 382
Objectivity   7, 10, 24, 50, 54, 59, 72–74, 77, 79, 81, 101, 165 f., 174, 179, 357, 424
Offense   390, 409
Olafson, Frederick   470
Oneness   72
Ontic   19, 75, 195, 445, 461, 464–466, 468, 470 f., 473, 475–478, 481 f.

Ontology   6 f., 11, 19, 38, 83 f., 86 f., 89–91, 93, 95, 105, 140, 148 f., 181, 183, 187, 201, 208 f., 228, 292, 446, 452 f., 455, 463–465, 468–471, 476–480, 482
Organism   19, 161, 233, 350, 476 f., 480 f.
Otherness   7, 33, 63, 73, 75, 94 f., 145, 170, 172, 202, 205, 213–217, 221, 236, 351, 482

Pairing   66 f., 78 f., 168, 232–234, 347, 350
Paradox of human subjectivity   462, 466, 468, 472, 477, 482
Parnas, Josef   306–308
Passive synthesis   65, 272, 418
Pathology   9, 158 f.
– Pathological behavior   137, 140, 142, 145–152, 157, 160
– Pathological phenomena   137 f., 140, 142, 145 f., 150 f., 158, 160 f.
– Pathological subject   144 f., 149, 151
– Psychopathology   5, 142, 306, 310
Patočka, Jan   91, 181
Perceptual experience   10, 166, 169, 171, 179, 202, 209, 218, 269, 273, 304, 328, 345, 376, 413, 418 f., 422, 429
– Evaluative perception   18, 414, 417, 425
– Social perception   13, 261–264, 271
Person   5, 10 f., 13 f., 16 f., 19, 24–28, 30, 33, 35, 40, 47, 51–56, 58, 60 f., 63, 68, 70, 95, 99–101, 103, 123, 142, 145 f., 150, 156, 176 f., 181, 183 f., 189–191, 197, 203 f., 206, 211 f., 243, 247, 252, 255, 261 f., 266, 269–272, 279–285, 287 f., 291–299, 306, 308 f., 312, 314–316, 323, 326 f., 329–334, 338 f., 345–353, 355–360, 363, 365, 368, 370 f., 374, 379 f., 385, 387, 390 f., 394–396, 398 f., 401–403, 406–409, 413, 415 f., 424, 462, 466
Personal character   55, 384
Personalistic attitude   32, 35, 40, 263, 266
Petherbridge, Danielle   18, 261, 413, 416, 418, 428 f.
Phenomena   9, 13, 23, 47–49, 51–54, 56–59, 65 f., 88, 90, 138, 153, 161, 201,

208, 218, 225–229, 234, 237, 243 f., 268, 307, 311, 314, 429 f.
Phenomenological ontology 210, 217, 471
Phenomenology of intersubjectivity 8, 109 f., 113–115, 168, 226
Phenomenology of language 323, 339
Phenomenology of perception 9, 11, 87–89, 137, 140, 142, 146, 152 f., 201, 208, 217, 220, 244
Plato 246, 392–394, 400, 468, 471, 480
Plurality 7, 74, 77, 81, 85, 87, 94, 100, 115, 120, 171, 178 f., 182, 194, 209, 246, 252, 255, 262, 272, 367, 468, 480 f.
Plutarch 408
Positing 16 f., 65, 190, 271, 363, 376–386
Prejudice 17–19, 51, 151, 389–391, 400–403, 435–438, 453–455
Pre-reflective 14 f., 19, 91, 142 f., 145, 147, 151, 160, 204, 303–308, 310–312, 314, 317 f., 326, 328, 334, 336, 348, 467
Primal facticity (*Urfaktum*) 84, 96, 466
– Primal facticity of "coordination" 101
Primordial sphere 8, 80, 116–120, 127–129, 132, 232 f.
Psychologism 49

Rabbås, Øyvind 396, 410
Race 479 f.
– Racialization 414
Rapee, Ronald M. 304, 308–310, 314
Ratcliffe, Matthew 15, 262, 311 f., 323, 325, 328, 334–337, 339
Reactive attitudes 404 f.
Recognition 4, 16, 18, 24, 33, 35, 175, 261, 269 f., 273, 291, 294, 298, 345–351, 353–359, 363, 372, 396, 403, 413–417, 422, 426, 428–431, 443, 457, 467, 470
Reduction 6, 8 f., 11 f., 67, 69, 77, 88 f., 98 f., 109–113, 116, 119 f., 122, 124–133, 137, 140, 150, 206, 229–231, 245 f., 248 f., 253, 430
– Apodictic reduction 9, 113, 131–133
– Egological reduction 8, 109–117, 119, 122–127, 130–134
– Eidetic reduction 10, 68, 150
– Epistemological reduction 113, 131–133

– Intersubjective reduction 8 f., 109–115, 119–126, 133 f.
– Musical reduction 244, 247
– Pathological reduction 9 f., 137, 140, 145, 148, 150–152, 159 f.
– Phenomenological Reduction 8 f., 12, 55, 67 f., 88, 99 f., 109–113, 119, 123, 125–128, 130–133, 137, 140, 145 f., 150–152, 159, 230, 244–246, 249, 256, 429
– Primordial Reduction 7–9, 109, 112, 116, 127–130, 132 f.
– Psychological reduction 111, 113, 115, 119, 123, 126, 130, 133
– Transcendental Reduction 8, 68, 76, 83, 88, 96–98, 101, 111–113, 115, 119 f., 123–127, 130–133, 231 f.
– Universal transcendental reduction 8 f., 109 f., 115 f., 124, 126, 130–132
Reflective 14 f., 57, 70, 75 f., 145, 148, 150, 215 f., 287, 303–310, 312, 314 f., 317 f., 429 f.
Reflexive attentiveness 431
Resoluteness (*Entschlossenheit*) 478
Respect 16, 31, 174 f., 257, 313, 345 f., 351–360, 364, 396 f., 400–404
Restrepo, Carlos 238
Revenge 283 f., 391 f., 395 f., 404, 406, 409
Rhythm 12 f., 190, 243–250, 254–258
Ricks, Christopher 438
Roberts, Robert C. 357, 359
Roesner, Martina 230
Römer, Inga 471
Rosen, Stanley 393
Rudman, Laurie A 401
Rupnow, Dirk 453
Russon, John 257

Saks, Elyn R. 307
Salice, Alessandro 3, 284, 286 f., 289 f., 409 f.
Sandmayer, Bob 229
Sartre, Jean Paul 91 f., 100, 104, 139, 249, 303, 306, 444, 454 f.
Sass, Louis A. 306 f., 325
Scheier, Claus 230

Scheler, Max   4, 23f., 27f., 30–33, 36, 38f., 211, 283f., 291, 295–297, 299, 345, 347, 354f., 475f.
Schizophrenia   5, 14, 303, 306–308, 310, 314, 318, 324f.
Schmid, Hans Bernhard   313, 317
Schmidt, Stefan   461, 466
Schrijvers, Joeri   238
Science   4–6, 23, 28, 47–51, 53, 55–57, 59–62, 68, 87, 97, 137–139, 141, 153, 157–160, 187, 193f., 228f., 266, 269, 448, 464f., 467, 474, 480
– fallible science   6, 47
– rigorous science   6f., 47f., 56, 60–62, 265
Scruton, Roger   247, 256f.
Seebohm, Thomas   227f.
Self   4, 6, 10–15, 18, 27f., 31f., 36f., 39f., 48, 60, 62, 64, 67–70, 73, 76, 78–80, 88, 91, 94, 96, 98f., 101, 104, 145, 165–167, 169, 171, 173–175, 177, 179–183, 187–195, 197, 201–211, 213–222, 225, 227, 229, 232, 234, 236f., 243f., 251, 254, 258, 261, 264, 279–281, 283–290, 293f., 297, 299f., 303–318, 325, 330, 332, 335, 347, 349–354, 356, 359, 364, 367, 376, 381, 384, 390, 392, 397, 402, 404f., 428, 430, 435–438, 440, 447, 450, 462, 465, 467, 469f., 472, 474–476, 478f., 482
Self-awareness   40, 50, 55, 58, 60, 174, 177, 182, 202–204, 210, 213f., 222, 307, 310, 348, 350, 467
Self-consciousness   14f., 53f., 58, 60, 177, 184, 204f., 207f., 213, 215–218, 220f., 303–306, 308–312, 314, 316–318, 475
Self-esteem   15, 286, 289f., 293, 297, 303, 310–318, 403
Self-experience   12, 14f., 40, 78, 96, 168, 174, 178, 203, 303f., 307f., 310, 314, 317f.
Self-identity   207, 214, 216f., 219
Self-other relation   10, 40, 165–167, 175f., 178
Self-worth   14, 279f., 288–290, 293f., 297, 300, 303, 311–314
Semprún, Jorge   446–449

Shay, Jonathan   326, 335, 338
Sherman, Nancy   356
Shoemaker, David   404
Sieg, Ulrich   452, 458
Skalski, Jonathan E.   364
Slaby, Jan   311, 313, 414, 426
Social anxiety   14f., 303f., 308–310, 314–318
Sokolowski, Robert   353, 398f.
Sound   12f., 84, 94, 99, 160, 243–247, 249–251, 253–257, 268, 308, 374, 386, 421
Spectatorial subject   89, 98
Sphere of ownness   5, 8, 10, 73, 78, 109, 116, 166f., 171, 173, 177, 472
Spiritedness   17, 390, 408
Staiti, Andrea   16f., 230, 363, 376, 379, 465
Stanghellini, Giovanni   5, 303, 306, 308
State, the   363, 365, 448, 462, 477, 479–481
Stein, Edith   4, 23–26, 28–33, 35f., 39, 303, 345, 347, 349, 351, 438, 474
Steinbock, Anthony J.   83, 179, 189f., 194f., 227f., 237, 266, 273, 418, 420–423, 427, 429f., 472
Strauss, Leo   393
Strawson, Peter F.   404f.
Subjectivity   4f., 8f., 11, 23, 26, 37–39, 54f., 63, 70–72, 84, 87, 89, 93–95, 99f., 102, 113f., 116f., 119f., 123, 144, 158f., 194f., 201, 203, 205, 208–211, 213–215, 218, 220–222, 227, 232, 234, 376, 415, 462, 466, 468f., 472, 477, 482
Sympathy   16, 23, 25, 27–31, 255f., 345f., 351, 354–360
Szanto, Thomas   3, 5, 24, 394, 409

Tanaka, Shogo   309
Taylor, Gabriele   285f., 291f., 294, 402
Temporality   10, 12, 36, 67, 80, 173, 178, 187, 191, 226, 243, 424, 481
Tengelyi, László   84, 168, 466
Thimme, Friedrich   452
Tolerance   16f., 363–376, 378, 381–387

Tone   12f., 25, 57, 98f., 143, 244, 246f., 249–251, 253–258, 452
Transcendence   7, 10f., 34, 63f., 71–73, 78f., 81, 86, 95, 101, 105, 118, 148f., 174, 195, 201–208, 211, 213, 215, 234, 246, 443, 456, 468, 473, 475, 477
Transcendental empathy   9, 120–122
Transcendental experience   72, 76f., 116, 118, 121f.
Transcendental intersubjectivity   73, 78, 83f., 100, 125, 166, 179, 193f., 197
Transcendental reflection   118f., 121
Transcendental subjectivity   7, 9f., 65, 70, 88, 98, 116f., 119–122, 125, 127, 129, 132, 193–195, 201, 204–208, 213–218, 221, 463, 468, 473
Transformation   10, 19, 156, 167, 180, 264, 310, 318, 390, 443f., 451f., 469
Transposition   28, 167, 474
Trauma   12, 15, 261f., 264, 323–327, 329, 333, 335, 337–339
Trust   12, 15, 315, 323–325, 333–338, 402, 452
Truthfulness   352, 360
Truwant, Simon   467
Turner, Samuel M.   317
Tyrer, Peter J.   314

Uexküll, Jacob von   474–476
Unamuno, Miguel de   291f., 298
UNESCO   363–365
Unity   7f., 52–54, 63f., 66, 69–72, 74–76, 78–81, 96, 101, 115, 127, 129, 131, 149, 167–169, 171, 174, 176, 178, 181, 195f., 202, 204f., 209–212, 214, 216, 218, 221, 248, 250, 271, 273, 345f., 422, 452, 465, 471, 474, 476f., 481
Universal transcendental sphere   112, 116, 124, 131f.
Uptake   15, 337, 404, 466, 478

Value   14, 16f., 24, 31, 33, 37, 48, 51, 55, 60f., 154f., 158–160, 180, 191f., 262f., 265, 279f., 282, 287–290, 293f., 315f., 334, 357, 363, 367f., 371, 373, 375f., 378–387, 389, 397, 425, 442f.
Van Mazijk, Corijn   418–422
Varga, Somogy   418
Vocation   11, 192f., 462, 481f.
Vogel, Lawrence   470
Voigtländer, Else   14, 280, 288–290
Volk   19, 452, 461f., 469, 477–482

Waldenfels, Bernhard   166, 261, 431
Walker, Margaret U.   30, 409
Wallon, Henri   218–220, 222
Walsh, Philip J.   349f.
Walton, Roberto   227, 229, 235
War   18, 391, 399, 401, 435, 438–445, 448f., 451f., 456
– First World War   18, 435, 438–441, 447–451, 456
– Second World War   139, 456
Warren, James   18f., 169, 231, 435
Wehrle, Maren   18, 266, 413f., 423–427
Wells, Adrian   308
Welton, Donn   228
Whitcomb, Dennis   357
Wiesel, Elie   325
Wilson, Judith K.   304, 314
Winter, Jay   456
Wiskus, Jessica   250
Wolff, Francis   246, 250, 252f.
Wood, W. Jay   357, 359
World constitution   23, 73, 195, 245, 462
World Health Organization   303f.

Zahavi, Dan   5, 11, 14, 30, 55, 83, 85, 101, 106, 110, 174–177, 179f., 182, 194, 201–205, 207f., 214, 221, 269, 303–305, 307, 317, 345, 347–349, 351, 354, 428
Zammito, John   475
Zukerkandl, Victor   249–251, 255

Erratum

published in: Anna Bortolan and Elisa Magrì,
Empathy, Intersubjectivity, and the Social World,
ISBN: 978-3-11-069863-3

The following correction was made to the bibliography on page 410:
Cairns, Douglas (2015): "Revenge, Punishment, and Justice in Athenian Homicide Law". In: *The Journal of Value Inquiry* 49, pp. 645–665. We apologize for the accidental omission of the reference in the original chapter.

www.ingramcontent.com/pod-product-compliance
Lightning Source LLC
Chambersburg PA
CBHW031720230426
43669CB00007B/194